CW01020629

THE ASHGATE RESEARCH COMPANION TO BORDER STUDIES

ASHGATE
RESEARCH
COMPANION

The *Ashgate Research Companions* are designed to offer scholars and graduate students a comprehensive and authoritative state-of-the-art review of current research in a particular area. The companions' editors bring together a team of respected and experienced experts to write chapters on the key issues in their speciality, providing a comprehensive reference to the field.

The Ashgate Research Companion to Border Studies

Edited by

DORIS WASTL-WALTER
University of Bern, Switzerland

ASHGATE

Published by
Ashgate Publishing Limited
Wey Court East
Union Road
Farnham
Surrey GU9 7PT
England

Ashgate Publishing Company
Suite 420
101 Cherry Street
Burlington,
VT 05401-4405
USA

www.ashgate.com

British Library Cataloguing in Publication Data
The Ashgate research companion to border studies.
  1. Boundaries.
  I. Research companion to border studies II. Wastl-Walter,
  Doris, 1953-
  320.1'2-dc22

Library of Congress Cataloging-in-Publication Data
Wastl-Walter, Doris, 1953-
  The Ashgate research companion to border studies / Doris Wastl-Walter.
     p. cm.
  Includes index.
  ISBN 978-0-7546-7406-1 (hardback) -- ISBN 978-0-7546-9047-4
(ebook) 1. Boundaries. 2. Borderlands. 3. Political geography. 4. Human geography. 5. Ethnicity. I. Title.

  JC323.W37 2010
  320.1'2--dc22
                                                                2010047875

ISBN 9780754674061 (hbk)
ISBN 9780754690474 (ebk)

MIX
Paper from
responsible sources
FSC
www.fsc.org   FSC® C018575

Printed and bound in Great Britain by the
MPG Books Group, UK

Contents

PART IV: BORDERS AND TERRITORIAL IDENTITIES: THE MECHANISMS OF EXCLUSION AND INCLUSION

PART V: THE ROLE OF BORDERS IN A SEEMINGLY BORDERLESS WORLD

PART VI: CROSSING BORDERS

List of Figures and Maps

List of Tables

Notes on Contributors

Jason Ackleson is Associate Professor in the Department of Government at New Mexico State University in Las Cruces, New Mexico, USA. As a Truman and British Marshall Scholar, he earned his PhD in International Relations at the London School of Economics and Political Science. At the LSE, he also served as the senior editor of *Millennium: Journal of International Studies*. Working and publishing on questions of security, borders, and globalization, Dr Ackleson is active in the U.S. Department of Homeland Security's National Center for Border Security and Immigration, a national university consortium led by the University of Arizona. Within the Center, he is working on major multi-year research grants that are examining border security and international governance.

Elisabeth Bäschlin is a geographer. She has been a lecturer for human geography at the University of Berne (Switzerland) from 1983 to 2010. Her special topics are urban history, planning, development and developing countries, and feminist geography. In 1974-1975, she worked as an urban planer in Algeria. In 1977, she became a member of the Swiss Support Committee for the Sahrawis (SUKS) and has been its president since 1992. She has written many articles and contributed to several conferences on the political problem of Western Sahara and the Sahrawi society in transition. She is the co-editor of the journal of the Swiss Society on Middle East and Islamic Cultures.

Tim Bunnell is an Associate Professor jointly appointed by the Department of Geography and Asia Research Institute at the National University of Singapore. He holds a Bachelor and a Doctorate in geography from the University of Nottingham, England. The main focus of his research has been the politics of urban landscape change in and around Kuala Lumpur, Malaysia. Various strands of Dr Bunnell's more recent research concern cross-border geographies of Southeast Asia, including the transnational lives of Malay communities in the UK, cross-Straits linkages between Aceh and Malaysia as well as Singapore's trans-border hinterland.

Eunyoung Christina Choi is a postdoctoral research fellow at the University of British Columbia's Liu Institute for Global Issues. Her main fields of research interest include gender, migration and geopolitics of Northeast Asia. She worked as an assistant for refugees and displaced persons in Yanbian, China, and in Syracuse, USA.

Karin Dean is a senior researcher at the Estonian Institute of Humanities, Tallinn University. Her research interests include the issues of territoriality and bordering, especially de- and reterritorialization of spaces and power in academia and/or the postmodern world, focusing on the borderlands in mainland Southeast Asia. She has researched the Sino-Myanmar border since 2000, while in 2002-2006, she was also working with the ethnic ceasefire and non-ceasefire groups at the Thai-Myanmar border. Her current research focuses on local practices and places as important nodes of networking in the wider struggle for control of various socio-technical networks.

Alexander C. Diener is Assistant Professor of Geography at the University of Kansas. He is the author of *One Homeland or Two?: Nationalization and Transnationalization of Mongolia's Kazakhs* (Stanford University Press and Woodrow Wilson Center Press 2009) and Homeland Conceptions and Ethnic Integration among Kazakhstan's Germans and Koreans (Mellen Press 2004). He is the co-author of *Borders: A Very Short Introduction* (Oxford University Press forthcoming) and the co-editor of *Borderlines and Borderlands: Political Oddities at the Edge of the Nation State* (Rowman and Littlefield Publishers 2010). His regional specialty is Central Eurasia and his research interests include migration, transnationalism, mobilities, post-socialist urban change, and the socio-political consequences of territorialization.

Heikki Eskelinen is Professor of Regional Studies at the Karelian Institute, University of Eastern Finland. He studied at the universities of Helsinki, Oulu, Reading, and Joensuu. His main research areas are regional and spatial development, border regions and cross-border co-operation. He is in charge of the Finnish Contact Point of the ESPON 2013 (European Spatial Planning Observation Network) research programme, and led the project 'Reconstitution of Northwest Russia as an Economic, Social and Political Space: the role of cross-border interaction' funded by the Academy of Finland.

Juliet J. Fall is a political geographer who has studied at the University of Geneva and the University of Oxford. She has held research fellowships at the universities of Durham (UK), British Columbia (Canada) and UCLA (USA), as well as a RCUK Fellowship at The Open University (UK). She is now an Associate Professor at the University of Geneva, in Switzerland, in the Faculty of Social and Economic Sciences. Her current work is on the instrumentalization of nature in discourses of identity, in particular on 'natural boundaries' and invasive species.

Sanette L.A. Ferreira is Associate Professor at the Department of Geography at Stellenbosch University in South Africa. She holds a PhD from the University of South Africa, where she started lecturing in Geography in 1986. In 2000, her family relocated and she commenced her career at Stellenbosch University. Currently, she is responsible for a third-year module in Geography of Tourism, tourism analysis and synthesis at honours level and supervises masters and doctoral students in the following research areas: tourism and regional development, tourism and small towns, sustainable tourism development, tourism and crime, tourism and transfrontier parks.

Valérie Gelézeau is Associate Professor at the Ecole des Hautes Etudes en Sciences Sociales (Paris) and Fellow of the Institut Universitaire de France. Gelézeau, who was awarded a Bronze Medal of the French Centre for National Scientific Research in 2005, is the author of *Séoul, ville géante, cités radieuses* (*Seoul, Giant City, Radiant Cities*, CNRS Editions 2003) and *Ap'at'ŭ konghwaguk* (*The Republic of Apartments, Seoul*, Humanitas 2007), which focuses on the extraordinary rise of apartments in South Korea. Since 2004, she has been studying the transformation of the inter-Korean border region.

Lassi Heininen is University Lecturer and Docent at the Faculty of Social Sciences, University of Lapland, Finland. Among his other academic positions are Adjunct Professor at Frost Center for Canadian Studies, Trent University, Canada; Docent at the Faculty of Geography, University of Oulu, Finland; Visiting Professor at University of Akureyri, Iceland; and Director of the International Summer School in Karelia, Russia. Dr Heininen is also the chairman of the Northern Research Forum (NRF). His research fields include international relations, geopolitics, security studies, environmental politics, political history, and northern/Arctic Studies. His publications include 27 peer review scientific articles, approximately 50 other scientific articles in international scientific journals and edited volumes, approximately 75 scientific articles in Finnish scientific journals and conference proceedings, and 13 scientific monographs.

Alan K. Henrikson is Director of Diplomatic Studies at The Fletcher School of Law and Diplomacy, Tufts University, where he teaches American diplomatic history, contemporary U.S.-European relations, political geography, and the history, theory, and practice of diplomacy. During the year 2010-2011 he was Fulbright Schuman Chair of U.S.-EU Relations at the College of Europe in Bruges. He also has been Fulbright/Diplomatic Academy Visiting Professor of International Relations at the Diplomatische Akademie in Vienna. He has previously taught at the National Institute of Defense Studies in Tokyo, at the China Foreign Affairs University in Beijing, and as Lloyd I. Miller Visiting Professor of Diplomatic History at the U.S. Department of State in Washington.

Károly Kocsis is Member of the Hungarian Academy of Sciences (HAS), the Director of the Geographical Research Institute of the HAS (Budapest) and Professor-Director of the Institute of Geography at the University of Miskolc in Hungary. His research is mostly focussed on the geographic study of ethnic, religious and political patterns of Central and Southeastern Europe. The majority of his 310 publications deal with the Hungarian and Roma minorities, the border issues in the Carpatho-Pannonian area and the geographic background of the ethnic conflicts in the Balkans.

Vladimir Kolossov (PhD 1979, Moscow University; habilitation 1992 Institute of Geography of the Russian Academy of Sciences) is the head of the Center of Geopolitical Studies at the Institute of Geography and a Professor at the Moscow

Institute of International Relations. He was nominated as Professor at the Universities of Toulouse-Le Mirail (2001-2003) and has been a visiting professor at the universities of Paris-Sorbonne IV, Paris-I Panthéon-Sorbonne, Le Havre and Tampere. His research interests lie in the fields of political geography and geopolitics, social geography and large metropolitan areas. He is the author of more than 350 publications, including the most popular textbook on political geography in Russia. He chaired the International Geographical Union Commission on Political Geography (1996-2004) and is now the first vice-president of the IGU.

Stefanie Kron, PhD in sociology, is currently Assistant Professor for research and teaching at the Department of Sociology at the Institute for Latin American Studies, Freie Universität Berlin. Her regional focus includes North America, Mexico, and Central America. Her research interests are postcolonial, gender, border, and refugee/migration studies. She has conducted fieldwork in Guatemala, Costa Rica, Nicaragua, Bolivia, Venezuela, and Ecuador. Her current research project deals with the regionalization of migration and border policies in North and Central America.

Edgardo Manero holds an MA in Social Sciences from the Latin American Faculty of Social Sciences (FLASCO) and a PhD in Sociology from the Ecole des Hautes Etudes en Sciences Sociales (EHESS). He was a researcher at CONICET in Argentina and Professor for International Relations at the National University of Rosario and he taught at the University of Paris XII and Toulouse II. Currently, he is a researcher at CNRS (France) and teaching at the universities of Paris II and Ecole des Hautes Etudes en Sciences Sociales. Manero is the author of *L'Autre, le Même et le Bestiaire. Les Représentations Stratégiques du Nationalisme Argentin: Ruptures et Continuités dans le Désordre Global* (Harmattan 2002) and *Mondialisation et 'Nationalisme des Indes'. Contestation de l'Ordre Social, Identités et Nation en Amérique Latine* (Méridiennes 2007). While interested in the evolution of strategic thinking, his research has focussed on security issues in Latin America.

Jan D. Markusse studied Human Geography in Utrecht and Amsterdam. He is a lecturer in the Department of Geography, Planning and International Development Studies at the University of Amsterdam. His specialization is political-cultural geography. He has published on regions with national minorities, among others on the Italian province of South Tyrol. He has co-edited a book on Nationalizing and Denationalizing European Border Regions.

John C. Mavris is Director of Communications at the University of Nicosia, and a Member of the Cyprus Sociological Association. He has an MA in Cultural History (Distinction) from the University of Manchester, and a CIPR Diploma in Public Relations (Distinction) awarded by the Chartered Institute of Public Relations (CIPR), UK. He acted as Project Administrator/Research Fellow for Cyprus (Partner in the Research Consortium) of the FP6 European Commission Project 'Searching for Neighbours: Dynamics of Physical and Mental Borders in the New Europe'. His research interests include border studies, ethnic conflict, and identity formation.

Pirouz Mojtahed-Zadeh lectures on Political Geography and Geopolitics mainly at Tarbiat Modares post-graduate University of Tehran. He is known for his contribution to the studies of the issues of the Middle East and its two adjacent regions: The Persian Gulf and The Caspian Sea. He completed his PhD in Political Geography at Oxford (1979) and London (1993) Universities and has published extensively in Persian and English with translations in Arabic and French. He has also lectured widely in Europe, North America, the Middle East and the Far East. In 2011 he retired from his post as chairman of Urosevic Research Foundation of London.

Hamzah Muzaini is currently a Visiting Fellow at the Department of Geography, National University of Singapore. He holds a Bachelor's and a Master's degree from the National University of Singapore and has recently earned his Doctorate in Geography from Durham University, England. His research interests include the material practices and politics of war memory and commemoration in Southeast Asia, backpacking tourism and aspects of Singapore's transborder histories and geographies. The focus of his doctoral research has been on the ways in which the Second World War is commemorated in Malaysia, particularly through the conceptual lens of postcolonial landscapes and heritage, everyday objects and bodily acts of remembrance.

David Newman is Professor of Geopolitics and Political Geography in the Department of Politics and Government at the Ben Gurion University in Israel. He is currently the co-editor of the journal *Geopolitics*. His work has focussed on the territorial and spatial dimensions of ethnic conflict, with a particular focus on the changing role of borders in conflict and conflict resolution. He has published widely on the territorial dimensions of the Israel-Palestine conflict and has been involved in the discussions concerning the nature of the borders in a two-state solution to this conflict.

Heather Nicol is an Associate Professor at Trent University in Canada. She is a political geographer whose research interests focus upon Canadian issues. She has written extensively about the Canada-US border and borderlands, the circumpolar North, and Canada-Cuba relations in context of their geopolitical content. Her most current research explores the structure and operation of the Canada-US border, with special emphasis on the impacts of security. She is also interested in the Canadian North as a geopolitical and geo-economic space, and the relationship between the interests of Arctic nation-states in the circumpolar the north.

Anssi Paasi has been a Professor of Geography at the University of Oulu in Northern Finland since 1989. He currently serves as an Academy Professor at the Academy of Finland (2008-2012). His theoretical and empirical research themes include for example, political boundaries, territoriality, regionalism, region-building processes, and spatial identities. He has published extensively in international journals and edited collections. His books include *Territories, Boundaries and Consciousness* (J. Wiley & Sons 1996). He was the editor of the political geography section in the *International Encyclopedia of Human Geography* (2009) and is co-editor of *Progress in Human Geography*.

Vera Pavlakovich-Kochi is Senior Regional Scientist at the Eller College's Business Research Center and Associate Professor in the School of Geography and Development at the University of Arizona (UA). She is also a Fulbright scholar (Austria 1997). Educated as a geographer, she holds BA and MA degrees from the University of Zagreb, Croatia, and a PhD degree from Kent State University (USA). Her research interest is focussed on border regional development with an emphasis on the U.S.-Mexico border and Southeast Europe. Prior to her current position, she was Director of Regional Development in the UA Office of Economic Development.

Nicos Peristianis is President of the Council of the University of Nicosia and, until recently, President of the Cyprus Sociological Association. He holds a doctorate in Sociology from Middlesex University, UK. He is Managing Editor of *The Cyprus Review*, a biannual refereed journal which focusses on social, economic and political issues pertinent to Cyprus. He recently co-edited the books *Divided Cyprus: Modernity, History, and an Island in Conflict* (Indiana University Press 2006) and *Britain in Cyprus: Colonialism and Post-Colonialism* (Bibliopolis 2006). His research interests include nationalism, ethnic conflict, and identity formation.

Roos Pijpers is an Assistant Professor at the Department of Human Geography and Spatial Planning at Radboud University Nijmegen, the Netherlands. Her primary research interests centre on the geography of work and employment, with an emphasis on labour migration. More generally, she draws on various mainstream and alternative approaches to economic geography to understand the quantitative and qualitative changes in the global economy and the localized consequences for working people. The latter include people's strategies to incorporate and resist these changes.

Nicola Piper is Senior Research Fellow at the Arnold Bergstraesser Institute at Freiburg University in Germany. Her research and numerous publications revolve around international economic migration, gender, global governance, non-governmental organizations and transnational political activism, and the rights of migrants, with empirical focus on Southeast and East Asia, Latin America, and Europe.

Gabriel Popescu is an Assistant Professor of political geography at Indiana University South Bend. His major research interests include critical geopolitics, border studies, reterritorialization and diaspora politics. His recent work has appeared in *Geopolitics*, *Political Geography* and in several edited volumes. He is also the author of a book entitled *Bordering and Ordering the Twenty-First Century: Understanding Border Spaces* (Rowman & Littlefield 2011).

Parvati Raghuram is Lecturer in Geography at the Open University. In a series of papers she has been exploring the intersection between family, labour markets and immigration regulations, especially as they relate to gender and skilled migration. She has co-authored *The Practice of Cultural Studies* (Sage 2004), *Gender and International Migration in Europe* (Routledge 2000) and co-edited *South Asian Women in the Diaspora* (Berg 2003) and *Tracing Indian Diaspora: Contexts, Memories, and Representations* (Sage 2008).

Clive Schofield is Director of Research at the Australian Centre for Ocean Resource and Security (ANCORS), University of Wollongong, Australia. Professor Schofield is the recipient of an Australian Research Council Future Fellowship (FT100100990). Prior to this appointment he served as Director of Research at the International Boundaries Research Unit (IBRU), University of Durham, UK. His research interests encompass the delimitation of international maritime boundaries, technical aspects and the law of the sea, maritime boundary disputes, transboundary resource management, and dispute settlement.

James Wesley Scott is Professor of Geography at the Karelian Institute at the University of Eastern Finland and Research Fellow at the Leibniz Institute for Regional Development and Structural Planning in Erkner (Germany). Scott studied Geography and Political Science at the Free University of Berlin and the University of California Berkeley. Among his research interests are: urban and regional development policy, geopolitics, border studies, transboundary regionalism in Europe and North America, changes and the spatial implications of Eastern and Central European transformation processes. Recently, he has coordinated European research projects on cross-border cooperation within the EU's Fifth and Sixth Framework Programmes.

Mohamed Sidati (Ould Sidati Ma el-Ainin), diplomat and poet was born in Western Sahara; the family moved to Tarfaya, then Tan Tan (South Morocco), escaping from Spanish authorities. He was admitted to Mohamed V University in Rabat, where he became active in a Sahrawi students' circle 'for the liberation of the Sahara'. In 1972-1973, he obtained his *licence* in economics at Rabat University and in 1975 he was awarded his doctorate 3rd cycle/PhD at Grenoble University (France). Since 1975, he has assumed several diplomatic and political positions for the Sahrawi Arab Democratic Republic (SADR), such as Ambassador, Foreign Minister, Minister of Communication, and currently as Minister-Delegate in Brussels for contacts with the European Union.

James D. Sidaway holds a BA (with a major in Geography and Development Studies) from Bulmershe College, England, an MA in International Studies from the University of Reading, England and a PhD in Geography from Royal

Holloway, University of London. He is currently Professor of Political and Cultural Geography at the University of Amsterdam. His research is mostly focussed on the intersections of development, geopolitics and urbanization. Professor Sidaway has worked on these themes (and attendant cross-border dynamics) in Southeast Asia, Southern Africa, the Persian Gulf and Western Europe. His other scholarly focus is on the history and philosophy of geographical thought.

Henk van Houtum is head of the Nijmegen Centre for Border Research, Department of Geography, Radboud University of Nijmegen, The Netherlands and Research Professor at the University of Bergamo, Italy. Van Houtum has written numerous articles on the geopolitics and (im)morality of b/ordering, ordering and othering. In addition, he (co-)edited various books on borders, among which *B/Ordering Space* (Ashgate 2005). He is editor of the *Journal of Borderlands Studies*.

Monika Mária Váradi, CSc is a sociologist and senior research fellow at the Centre for Regional Studies of the Hungarian Academy of Sciences. Her research focusses on the post-socialist economic and social transformation of rural Hungary, including issues of poverty and exclusion as well as problems of ethnic and national minorities. She is also interested in the problems of border areas and has participated in several comparative border research projects.

Doris Wastl-Walter is Professor for Human Geography at the University of Bern and Director of the university's Interdisciplinary Center for Gender Studies. She was a Fulbright Research Scholar at the University of Arizona and from 2000 to 2008, Chair of the International Geographical Union's Commission for Geography and Public Policy. She worked as a team leader in border research projects within the EU's Fifth and Sixth Framework Programmes and has published widely on border issues. She is also the editor of the Border Regions Series at Ashgate Publishing. Teaching and supporting young scholars has also been a main focus. She has headed three graduate schools and her previous teaching experience includes the Universities of Klagenfurt, Trier, Bern, Lausanne, and Chandigarh, indicating her additional interest in cross-cultural academic exchange.

Alison J. Williams is Lecturer in Human Geography in the School of Geography, Politics and Sociology at Newcastle University, UK. Her research interests coalesce around issues of critical geopolitics, the geographies of airspaces and air power, and international boundary matters. She has published on maritime boundary disputes in the East China Sea, the legacy of Stephen B. Jones 'Boundary-Making' handbook, the use of unmanned aircraft to secure borders, and the violation of state sovereignty from above.

Chun Yang is Assistant Professor and Associate Director of Urban and Regional Development in the Asia-Pacific Program at the Hong Kong Institute of Asia Pacific Studies, the Chinese University of Hong Kong, Hong Kong. Dr Yang's research areas and interests focus on urban and regional development in China, particularly the Hong Kong-Pearl River Delta region, foreign investment, especially overseas Chinese investment and cross-border production networks and industrial clusters, and indigenous innovation and regional innovation systems in China. Her research has been extensively published in leading internationally refereed journals, such as *Environment and Planning A, Economic Geography, Political Geography, Regional Studies, Urban Studies, Habitat International, Eurasian Geography and Economics, Tijdschrift voor Economische en sociale Geografie, International Development Planning Review* and *The Annals of Regional Science*.

Michele Zebich-Knos, PhD, is Professor of Political Science and Director of the International Policy Management Program at Kennesaw State University (USA). Her research focusses on environmental policy issues and foreign policy related to Latin America. She co-edited, with Heather Nicol, *Foreign Policy toward Cuba: Isolation or Engagement?* (Lexington Books 2005), and is the author of 'Ecotourism, Park Systems and Environmental Justice in Latin America' in David Carruthers (ed.) (2008): *Environmental Justice in Latin America* (Cambridge: MIT Press); and 'Conflict Avoidance and Environmental Protection: The Antarctic Paradigm' in Saleem Ali (ed.) (2007): *Peace Parks: Conservation and Conflict Resolution* (Cambridge: MIT Press). She also serves on the External Advisory Board of the Institute for Environmental Diplomacy and Security (IEDS) at the University of Vermont.

Tatiana Zhurzhenko studied political economy and social philosophy and is an Associate Professor at V.N. Karazin Kharkiv National University (Ukraine). From 2002-2004, she did research on the Ukrainian-Russian border as a Lise Meitner Fellow at the Institute for East European History, University of Vienna. Since 2007, Tatiana Zhurzhenko has been Elise Richter Research Fellow at the Department of Political Science at the same university. Her new project deals with politics of memory and national identity in the Ukrainian-Russian and the Ukrainian-Polish border regions. Her latest book *Borderlands into Bordered Lands: Geopolitics of Identity in Post-Soviet Ukraine* (Stuttgart: ibidem, 2010) was awarded the 2010 Best Book Prize of the American Association for Ukrainian Studies.

To Ladis D. Kristof

(1918-2010)

Introduction

Doris Wastl-Walter

The purpose of this collection is to provide an authoritative, state-of-the-art review of current research in the multidisciplinary and global field of border studies. An array of highly respected and experienced scholars in border studies has been gathered to write chapters on their particular areas of interest to furnish a comprehensive reference for the field. The volume is intended to be global in scope both as to the range of its entries and the affiliation of its contributors. The contributors have been chosen on the basis of their ongoing significant publications as well as their recognized international standing; we have also attempted to achieve a gender-balanced selection of contributors. In addition to the most eminent and well-known experts on border issues, promising younger scholars who have already distinguished themselves through their publications have been given a platform to offer readers recent perspectives and fresh interpretations of the field. In addition to the most recent perspectives on well-known cases and border disputes, some lesser-known examples that either offer interesting solutions or that are potential global conflicts are included. The *Companion* is intended to become an important complementary textbook for students and scholars in related disciplines, for example political geography, international relations, political science, environmental studies, conflict studies, and history across the world. Additionally, planners and practitioners, especially regional planners and experts who are establishing and institutionalizing cross-border contacts and cooperation, should also be able to benefit from the concepts and case studies presented here.

Rationale of the volume

Over the course of history, the functions and roles of borders have continuously changed and can only be understood in their context; they are shaped by history, politics, and power as well as by cultural and social issues. Borders have been actively contested and negotiated throughout the past, appearing and disappearing (Paasi 2003). Borders are therefore complex spatial and social phenomena which are not static or invariable but which must be understood as highly dynamic; this is similar to the field of border studies itself, which has undergone major transformations during the past century and has been experiencing a flourishing renaissance over the course of the past fifteen years (Grundy-Warr and Schofield 2005; Kolossov 2005; Newman 2006; Paasi 2005, 2009).

In the 1980s, a new, multidisciplinary generation of border scholars emerged, composed of, for instance, political geographers, historians, anthropologists, political scientists, economists, sociologists, and lawyers, giving the field an increasingly interdisciplinary character. Starting in the early 1990s, an exponential growth of border studies predominantly in Europe and North America has occurred. In many places, border research institutes were established and a great range of articles and books have been published. This revitalization of border studies has been substantially driven by the collapse of the East-West Cold War configuration and the multiplication of country boundaries as a consequence. However, border scholars conceptualize borders not only as spatial or geographic phenomena that demarcate the sovereign territories of states but also as social, political or economic expressions either of belonging or of exclusion within state territories, for example, nations, religions, groups and individuals (Paasi 2003).

Today, in an era characterized by globalization, regional integration, the formation and consolidation of blocs including the European Union (EU), the North American Free Trade Agreement (NAFTA), the Southern Common Market (MERCOSUR) and Asia-Pacific Economic Cooperation (APEC) and by the triumphal procession of cyberspace, the world political map has undergone significant changes (Paasi 2005). Many boundaries have become more permeable for people, goods, capital, and information; as a consequence of these trends, notions of a *'borderless world'* and political *'deterritorialization'* have recently been taken up by some scholars, especially by economists and information scientists. However, Newman (2006) argues that despite these trends, human activities continue to take place within well defined territories. He furthermore points out that the notion of a *'borderless world'* has been coined by the West, specifically by a Western European perspective in which the permeability of borders is currently being actively promoted. Nevertheless, this trend has not gained ground around the globe. For example, in the post-9/11 era, borders have been re-erected or reinforced in many places. Hence, the current world-wide political situation which is distinguished by the prevalence of fear of terrorism and security concerns can be interpreted as a sign for a *'reterritorialization'* rather than a *'deterritorialization'* of the world.

In summary, borders are still ubiquitous, are manifested in diverse ways, and have various functions and roles. They can be material or non-material and may appear in the form of a barbed-wire fence, a brick wall, a door, a heavily-armed border guard or as symbolic boundaries, that is, conceptual distinctions created by actors to categorize components of belonging and exclusion. Such manifestations of borders affect people in their freedom of action and are perceived differently by different actors and groups. For example, while a brick wall may represent security for some, for others, it may be a symbol of suppression of and limitation to their freedom. Over the past fifteen years, besides a renewed interest in concrete territorial lines, such new approaches to borders have grown in importance. There has been an increasing interest in the process of bounding and 'the way in which people and groups are enclosed within a variety of social and spatial compartments' (Newman 2003, 128) as well as in best practices as to how to overcome borders. However, so far, there has been no comprehensive volume in the field of border studies including these emerging tendencies and case studies and experiences from across the world. Hence, there is a need for a major collection of readings which not only cover the traditional strands of the field but also take into consideration these latest developments. It is hoped that this *Research Companion to Border Studies* will therefore close a major gap and provide a valuable reference work to the illustrious research community working in the field of border studies around the world and to graduate students in various disciplines.

Synopsis of the volume

Since the field of border studies is quite broad and set in a multidisciplinary framework, the eight sections of the volume reflect the current main strands of the field ranging over political, social, economic and environmental aspects of the concept of borders.

Part I – Theorizing Borders: Conceptual Aspects of Border Studies

Even though there is no commonly acknowledged theoretical basis of border studies as such, there are common terms and concepts on which border scholars from different disciplines base their work. The six chapters within this section provide an overview of the conceptual aspects of the multidisciplinary field of border studies, starting with Anssi Paasi and David Newman, who give an overview of various approaches in border studies and contemporary research agendas. Henk van Houtum then argues that 'a border is a verb', and later 'a territorial border is a belief' and finally 'the border is a mask'. Whereas he questions the whole concept of borders, Tatiana Zhurzhenko shows the historical reasoning for and legitimating of borders through collective memory. The chapter by Alan K. Henrikson introduces the concept of good neighbourhood, which he developed to overcome the social and political division that borders often represent for neighbouring peoples. In the last chapter of this section, Stefanie Kron presents the concept of intersectionality as a methodological tool to better understand the combination of some axes of difference in borderlands.

Part II – Geopolitics: State, Nation and Power Relations

In the first chapter of this section, James Wesley Scott traces the historical development of borders and Border Studies in Europe and shows how borders have been shifted as a result of the fall of the former 'Iron Curtain' in 1989 and the EU enlargement in 2004. The subsequent four chapters provide a series of case studies on some of the world's most disputed borderlands, including the island of Cyprus by Nicos Peristianis and John C. Mavris. They consider the different

3

meanings of the dividing line, as well as the attitudes and actions meant to sustain or undermine the 'border', by both Greek- and Turkish-Cypriots, and how these have fluctuated in recent years in relation to new steps toward closure along national(ist) lines. Vladimir Kolossov presents the post-soviet boundaries influenced by recent geopolitical changes and new power relations between neighbouring countries as well as by the growing discussion about securitization. Both factors have brought about new border regimes in the post-soviet area. Lassi Heininen and Michele Zebich-Knos compare the situation at the two Polar Regions, indicating similarities and substantial differences, especially given the recent climate change and the melting of circumpolar ice, which makes new raw materials exploitable. Karin Dean reports on the special situation at the borders of Myanmar and the complexity of the lived spaces challenged by the international boundaries. She uses ethnographic methods to more deeply understand local practices and specialities.

Part III – Border Enforcement in the 21st Century

Despite all the academic and political discourses of improving cross-border relations, notions of a *'borderless world'* and more permeable boundaries, in the aftermath of 9/11, in many places borders have been re-erected or reinforced. The five chapters of this section go further into the question as to how borders around the world are being enforced and managed in the post-9/11 era. Beginning with the chapter by Jason Ackleson, in which he explores some of the general political dynamics of contemporary border management from a comparative perspective, this section's main focus is on the issue of *securitization* of borders and mobility, both at states' frontiers and within them. Heather Nicol critically assesses the changes at the United States (US)-Canadian border, where the power relations between the US and their neighbors come into play. She shows that despite trilateral treaties and repeated discourse about friendly relations, the US attempt to impose their concept of security and homeland protection on other sovereign states. Alison J. Williams goes a step further and emphasizes the militarization of the US borders to secure international borders. The chapter's aim is to investigate the extent to which the deployment of ever-more militarized forms of border-securitization technologies, such as unmanned aerial vehicles (UAVs), are having a two-fold impact, serving not only to blur the boundaries between military and civilian law enforcement agencies, but also conversely to sharpen the borders which they patrol, making them ever more impenetrable to a host of perceived threats. Edgardo Manero then gives an overview of border regimes in Latin America, focussing also on the main conflicts and the most important actors there. In the final chapter, Valérie Gelézeau discusses one of the most closed and tightly controlled borders of the world, that between North and South Korea in the so-called 'demilitarized zone' (DMZ) along the cease-fire line.

Part IV – Borders and Territorial Identities: The Mechanisms of Exclusion and Inclusion

Border scholars conceptualize borders as socially constructed phenomena in order to distinguish between the internal and the external border - the *'us'* and the *'them'*. People living inside bounded territories are consistently spatially socialized as members of the territorial entity they live in. The three chapters in this section examine the mechanisms by which territorial identities and belonging or exclusion is being constructed. The section includes case studies from Europe, Mongolia and Iran. In the first chapter, Jan D. Markusse discusses in general the case of national minorities in Europe, where most states have autochthonous minorities, many of them living in border regions. He then elaborates on three specific examples of multiple boundary-making in border regions with interface minorities. These are the Basque Country, the autonomous Province of Bozen-Alto Adige and the Slovak-Hungarian border region. Alexander C. Diener investigates one single minority, the Kazakhs in Mongolia and their struggle for territorial belonging. Finishing the section, Pirouz Mojtahed-Zadeh discusses the entire concept of borders and territorial identities from the unconventional and intriguing perspective of Persian history and mythology.

Part V – The Role of Borders in a Seemingly Borderless World

This section's four chapters focus on the consequences of cross-border economic regimes on border regions and the people living in borderlands. The section, including case studies from Europe, Asia and the US-Mexican border region, describes the roles borders play in times of an increasingly global economy. Roos Pijpers gives the example of how people use border management practices in the EU to (re)direct labour migration in order to maximize their profit in industries at the Dutch-German border. The two Asian examples turn attention to the institutional frameworks and disputes or difficulties resulting from economic developments reaching across (national) borders. In the first, Chun Yang closely examines the Greater Pearl River Delta, one of the most prosperous and fastest developing zones in China and at the specific situation of neighbouring Hong Kong. James D. Sidaway, Tim Bunnell, and Hamzah Muzaini then look at another Asian global city, Singapore, and demonstrate how this city-state economically, socially and politically extends beyond its borders by establishing industrial and recreational areas in the borderlands of a neighbouring state. Lastly, Vera Pavlakovich-Kochi discusses the economic cross-border cooperation at the US-Mexican border in the frame of NAFTA. In some respects, mainly economic, she adds a perspective that complements the discussions of North American border situation in the chapters of Heather Nicol and Alison J. Williams.

Part VI – Crossing Borders

Migration of any kind always involves crossing borders, be they international or domestic. Whereas globalization seems to have made international borders more porous for capital and goods, the crossing of international borders for migrants was made more difficult in many places by expanding boundary enforcement and militarization (see Part III). In this section, the phenomenon of primarily international migration is addressed using case studies from Asia and Africa. First, Eunyoung Christina Choi presents the geopolitical frame, its changes along the North-Korean/ Chinese border, and the various ways of bordering local people there. She describes how they deal with changes in the border regimes and try to make a living by everyday practices around the border and what happens if they fail. Second, Parvati Raghuram and Nicola Piper discuss the various meanings of borders to different people, focusing on the ways in which female migrants deal with borders and presenting the social and economic differences of gendered border geographies in Asia. In the third and final chapter, Elisabeth Bäschlin and Mohamed Sidati discuss the case of a state without (internationally recognized) national borders: The Sahrawi in Western Sahara, still living in a kind of preliminary situation as a state without territory and national boundaries. To the Sahrawi, a former nomadic people, national borders did not make much sense, although of course they had boundaries for their living space. The authors investigate the Sahrawi's various and changing boundary conceptions and their border realities today.

Part VII – Creating Neighbourhoods

Since the 1990s, the European Union has funded projects in different programs to assist regions on the inner and outer borders of the Union to form partnerships so they can work together on common projects designed to strengthen economic and social cohesion throughout the EU and also beyond. The chapters in this section describe examples of such support for border regions in the European context and give examples of best practices on how to transcend national borders. Heikki Eskelinen details the case of the Finnish borders with very different historical backgrounds, indicating how interethnic relationships and neighbourhoods can be developed across national borders. Károly Kocsis and Monika Mária Váradi consider the situation in the Carpatho-Pannonian Area where history still has a very strong influence on everyday neighbourhood relationships and national minorities exist along all state borders. Gabriel Popescu then closely examines the Lower Danube Euroregion. Euroregions have been built to initiate, facilitate and institutionalize cross-border cooperation in different fields and to create neighbourhoods where they have never existed or, more often, have been cut by geopolitical changes. Gabriel Popescu's contribution discusses the difficulties and opportunities of such an endeavour at the limits of the European Union.

Part VIII – Nature and Environment

With global environmental change and a rising consciousness of endangered species and limited resources, cross-border bilateral, trilateral or international cooperation has become increasingly important. Issues like the delimitation of borders, even in areas that were previously without economic value, or of maritime borders continue to grow in importance as a way of avoiding violent conflicts. In the chapters of this section, peaceful but also disputed transboundary management of natural resources is described. Juliet J. Fall's and Sanette L.A. Ferreira's chapters discuss the situation in which there is a basic agreement to cooperate and protect the environment, but the concepts of 'nature' and 'natural resources' as well as protection methods vary between the states involved. Juliet J. Fall provides a more theoretical introduction to the transnational governance of transboundary protected areas, struggling with the fact that nature (fauna and flora) are dynamic and cross national boundaries. Sanette Ferreira presents the difficulties and future perspectives of the situation in South Africa, where institutional and political structures as well as financial limits hinder the realization of already agreed upon Transfrontier Conservation Areas and Peace Parks. The final chapter of the book opens the topic of maritime borders. Clive Schofield describes the global situation of maritime borders and argues for the delimitation of borders and international treaties to avoid conflicts or to at least find productive ways to save living natural resources and to use all natural resources in a peaceful and sustainable way.

Acknowledgements

This book could not have been published without the substantial contribution of many people. I received invaluable support from my colleague Béla Filep, a competent border scholar in his own right and a first-rate manager as well. He generously invested all the time that I myself could not find in editing the contributions to weave them into a whole. Without him, the book could not have been published in a reasonable time and not to this quality. Here I would like to explicitly acknowledge Béla Filep's commitment and to publicly express my warmest gratitude to him. I would also like to sincerely thank my friend and colleague Jeannette Regan for her sensitive language editing. She made every attempt to transmit the specific cultural experiences of our contributors in their own words in English, their acquired language, while still assuring clear expression in highly standardized academic English. My thanks also go to Mirjam Macchi, who worked with me when we started with the project. She supported its beginnings in a most competent and professional way. My junior assistants Cornelia Jost and Germaine Spoerri worked admirably to keep track of the progress of the volume and to produce the final version of all the papers. Urezza Caviezel and Dina Spoerri worked with great care on the indices and proofreading. When it came to managing the entire editing process in its final stage, Michael Regli worked most conscientiously, shouldering the responsibility readily and reliably. Without his exceptional commitment, we would not have finished. I thank them all as well as my husband, Rudolf Wastl, for his help with many of the maps. Each of them and the others on my outstanding team have supported the long process of producing the volume. I would also like to extend my thanks to my friends and experts for their anonymous reviewing. I deeply appreciate the time and thought they invested in the various chapters. My gratitude also goes to the Editors Valerie Rose, Gemma Hayman and Katy Crossan at Ashgate Publishing for their patience and their comments as the *Companion* took form.

Last and most sincerely, I would like to thank the authors. The book is based on the contributions of distinguished authors from various disciplines and different parts of the world and I want to express my appreciation to them for their stimulating texts, their readiness for any questions and revisions, and their patience. Each contributed greatly to the achievement of the book.

This book is dedicated to Ladis D. Kristof (1918-2010), the founder and admirable doyen of the discipline, who not only transcended so many borders in his personal life, but also set the path for Border Studies worldwide. He was profoundly human and very wise and all of us who had the great good fortune of working with him have been deeply enriched by our encounter with this *grand homme*.

References

Grundy-Warr, C. and Schofield, C. (2005), 'Reflections on the Relevance of Classic Approaches and Contemporary Priorities in Boundary Studies', *Geopolitics* 10:4, 650-62.

Kolossov, V. (2005), 'Border Studies: Changing Perspectives and Theoretical Approaches', *Geopolitics* 10:4, 1-27.

Newman, D. (2006), 'The Lines That Continue To Separate Us: Borders In Our "Borderless" World', *Progress in Human Geography* 30:2, 143-61.

Newman, D. (2003), 'Boundaries', in Agnew, J., Mitchell, K. and Toal, G. (eds.), *A Companion to Political Geography* (Oxford: Blackwell Publishing), 123-37.

Paasi, A. (2009), 'Political boundaries', in Kitchin, R. and Thrift, N. (eds.), *International Encyclopaedia of Human Geography* (Oxford: Elsevier), 217-27.

Paasi, A. (2005), 'Generations and the "Development" of Border Studies', *Geopolitics* 10:4, 663-71.

Paasi, A. (2003), 'Territory', in Agnew, J., Mitchell, K. and Toal, G. (eds.), *A Companion to Political Geography* (Oxford: Blackwell Publishing), 109-22.

PART I
THEORIZING BORDERS:
CONCEPTUAL ASPECTS OF
BORDER STUDIES

A *Border Theory*: An Unattainable Dream or a Realistic Aim for Border Scholars?

Anssi Paasi

Introduction

After a relative silence during the post-World War II decades, political borders have become highly salient objects in research during the last two decades. This has not been merely a coincidental change in academic winds but has been related to major transformations in the international geopolitical landscape. The collapse of the rigid Cold War divide between West and East at the turn of the 1990s and the accelerating globalization – related to economics, culture, and consciousness – were the principal macro-level backgrounds (Paasi 2003). The rise of the politico-economic importance of *regions* as part of the re-scaling of new state spaces in global capitalism (Brenner 2004) has provided another background. This has triggered off new keywords such as cross-border regions (Kramsch and Hooper 2004; Perkmann and Sum 2002), regional states (Ohmae 1995), or city regions (Scott 2001). The development of information technology – partly generating globalization and partly illustrating it – was also a significant context.

The politico-territorial and scalar consequences of the 9/11 terrorist attack in the USA in 2001 and the transforming hegemony of the USA on the global geopolitical (Agnew 2005) and regional scene (Katzenstein 2005) have also forced politicians and the prevailing statecraft to consider the lines dividing societies, nations, states and even *cultural realms*. New fears, images of friends and enemies, dividing lines between us and them, and insides and outsides have emerged, perhaps mocking the optimism of the early post-Cold War period and challenging the seeds of cosmopolitanism that emerged after the collapse of the dividing lines which characterized that period. This has not, however, discouraged the representatives of critical, socially situated cosmopolitanism from searching for a new basis for their thinking, which seems to have become more differentiated spatially in the current world (Delanty 2006). This challenges us to recognize such emerging asymmetries related to borders as the gendered and generation-based features of de-bordering and re-bordering.

The expansion and the ongoing integration of the European Union have rapidly transformed Europe as the major context and laboratory for border studies (another major laboratory being the US-Mexico border). European integration was set in motion originally in order to maintain peace between the enemies of the World Wars, and the EU has invested a lot in promoting cross-border cooperation, regional economies and the development of infrastructures. There are currently over 100 new regions within the EU, varying greatly in their areal scope and economic functions (Deas and Lord 2006). The borders of the EU are nowadays often seen rather stereotypically as simply becoming lower inside the Union and stronger around its outside. The Union's area is more complex, however, and such features as the Schengen zone make a major difference. The situation of the EU and its internal and external borders serve to characterize more broadly the key issue related to borders: their *selective openness*.

This is the complex setting that border scholars have faced from the 1990s onwards. It is no wonder, then, that contrary to much of the social science dominated by Anglophone scholars, border studies are today more international than many other fields of social science. Much of the current research and conceptual ideas come from scholars working outside the Anglophone linguistic realms. But in spite of this fact, the accelerating flow of new book titles and journal articles published in the English language implies that one more new dimension behind the mushrooming of border studies is *academic capitalism*. This phenomenon, which is related to the globalization of knowledge production and international competition between states, becomes apparent in the first instance in the increasing numbers of researchers in various countries (several border research institutes, for instance, have been established since the 1990s) and secondly in the demands expressed for scholars to operate internationally. The simultaneous establishment of academic merit systems around the world, based on competition and publications, also brings the corporate interests of international publishing businesses into play (Paasi 2005). The relative numbers of researchers and published scientific articles have become indicators of the *international competitiveness* of a state. Paradoxically, it may then be argued that such a tendency towards internationalization and *border crossings* is based on *academic nationalism*.

This chapter will scrutinize the current state of *border studies* and reflect particularly on the role of theory in a situation where borders and border studies are becoming more diverse, more integrated – and more *international*. The major motive for looking at such a theme is the fact that claims have recently been made regarding the need for a theory in border studies (Newman 2003). The key aim here is to reflect the rhetorical question put forward in the title: is *border theory* a realistic aim, an unattainable ideal or perhaps something that is not needed at all, as the empiricist tradition of political geography has implied? Or is this a question that is, as I suggest, crucially related to our concept of *theory* and the need to see this as a verb, that is *theorization*? This chapter will not only look at how the need for *theory* has been expounded and justified in border studies but will also illustrate how our understanding of borders is itself perpetually transforming and that this continual striving to re-define them has been a crucial part of theorization, whether the aim has been to work towards *universalistic certitude* or to recognize historical-geographical contingency (Agnew 2006).

The chapter is organized as follows. It will first discuss the complexity of political borders as research objects and then go on to investigate the purported shaping of the interdisciplinary field of border studies. This will be followed by a discussion on how various concepts of theory could inform border studies, after which it will scrutinize some recent debates in which the concept of border has been challenged, re-interpreted and expanded. This discussion aims at showing how there can be gaps not only between various *camps* in academic debates but also between such debates and the concrete world, and that such gaps may ultimately be unfortunate and prevent the development of new theoretical approaches in border studies. Finally some conclusions will be set out.

The complexity of borders as research objects

Political borders are currently attractive but simultaneously complex objects of research. The first background to this complexity is the perpetually increasing number of state borders, their changing roles and functions in the globalizing world and the international pressure existing in each border area. They are all factors that make a difference. The current world harbours some 200 states and more than 300 land borders between them, and in addition there are scores of sea boundaries. This *corpus* has been perpetually expanding along with the rise of new states, especially after major upheavals such as wars. This is exemplified by the fact that there are some 600-800 cultural groupings or purported nations in the world (according to some opinions as many as 4,000, based on diverging languages), many of which are struggling to establish a state of their own. These efforts are balanced and managed by international law and other agreements and by certain regional systems of rules such as the Organization for Security and Cooperation in Europe (OSCE). Such systems often draw on the principle of collective security, placing states into an alliance of shared responsibilities, as it were. One of the EU's key requirements for new members, for example, is that they should not have unresolved border conflicts with their neighbours. One further variable that complicates this constellation arises from the perpetually changing meanings of sovereignty (Murphy 1996; Krasner 2001).

Political borders are processes and institutions that emerge and exist in boundary-producing practices and discourses, and they may be materialized and symbolized to greater or lesser extents (Paasi 1996). Ó Tuathail and Dalby (1998) have pointed out that approaches looking at boundary-producing practices should investigate both the material borders at the edges of states and the conceptual borders that designate material boundaries between an apparently secure interior and 'an anarchic exterior'. It will also be argued below that such conceptual/

symbolic borders may be located outside the border areas proper. The meanings of borders are not constant, as the case of the EU shows, and political transformations may cause some borders become lower or *softer* fairly rapidly, while some others become *harder*. This is also illustrated by the situation of *failing states* with corroding and porous borders (Juss 2008), most of which are currently to be found in Africa, with Somalia, Sudan and Zimbabwe as the most recent examples.

While conflicts rarely occur nowadays between states, for example, across their borders, internal conflicts are still common, often displaying the perpetual power of ethnicity. The year 2007 was the fourth consecutive year in which no interstate conflict existed in the world. According to statistics compiled by Stockholm's Peace Research Institute (SIPRI), 14 major armed conflicts were actively going on in 13 locations around the world in 2007, implying that the number of active conflicts of this kind has declined globally over the past decade or so. The decline has been uneven, however, and has varied on a yearly basis, with major drops occurring in 2002 and 2004 and an increase in 2005 (SIPRI 2008).

Even though the number of border-related conflicts has been decreasing, we have been recently reminded of the power of military-strategic interests by the events in Ossetia, where citizens suffered severely from the conflict between Russia and Georgia. For some observers this represented a return to both power politics and the sphere-of-interest way of thinking that characterized the geopolitical order during the Cold War. Of course, the activities of the US-led coalition in Iraq were much wider examples of this thinking, and Georgia's aspirations towards the NATO and its close relations with the US may be regarded as one more example of sphere-of-interest thinking.

Secondly, the complexity of state borders as research objects is based on the fact that the meanings attributed to such borders are *inward-oriented*: They are closely related to the ideological state apparatus, ideological practices such as nationalism (and related national identity narratives) and the material basis of such practices, which manifests itself in territoriality. Territoriality is an ideological practice and discourse that transforms national spaces and histories, cultures, economic success and resources into bounded spaces (Sack 1986; Paasi 1996). The most significant and widely exploited territorial form of ideology is nationalism, the proponents of which often gain some of their ideological power from discourses and practices that make a contrast between a community *(We)* and *The Other*. This phenomenon has been recognized by border scholars in various contexts since the 1990s and has been seen to manifest itself in foreign policy discourses, educational practices and popular culture. The processes of *Othering* and the means by which such processes become part of a banal or mundane nationalism, a theme invented in cultural and postcolonial studies (Said 1978), have been scrutinized in many International Relations (IR) and geographical studies (Campbell 1992; Dalby 1990; Paasi 1996).

It is, indeed, difficult to find any book on nationalism and nationhood that does not somehow recognize the historical importance of territory and boundaries in the practice of state territoriality and in the making of a *homeland* (Sack 1986; Kaiser 2002). Everywhere, the legislation generated by the state and its instruments of socialization aim at constructing the limits of nationality, citizenship and identity by defining the borders of inclusion and exclusion. And this again raises complicated questions regarding the power and operation of social institutions, symbols and national iconographies. Identification with a territory may occur in various more or less *material* practices, for example in economic or political spheres, and not purely at the level of mental acts and discourses as identity is often understood.

Thirdly, the spatial scale also makes a difference with respect to the complexity of borders. While state borders are often regarded as both local and national phenomena, some borders are also global and their meanings fluctuate in the sense that so many economic and symbolic practices, discourses or emphasis on difference can be associated with them. Think, for example, the changing meanings of the US-Mexico border or the EU's external boundaries. Besides state borders, which are relatively *hard* in terms of purported territorial control and nationalist ideologies and practices, each state also harbours a number of *soft* internal political boundaries that are perpetually being produced and reproduced (some of these sub-state borders in all states are concomitantly state borders, which fuses their spatial meanings with those associated with such borders). Sub-state borders (and territories) are produced and institutionalized by the state in various forms of territorial governance or through processes of devolution. Such changes and the corresponding new regionalizations may also be expressions of efforts to manage and control the activities of ethno-nationalist or regionalist groupings (Paasi 2009a). In spite of globalization and the apparent opening of borders, states still have a great interest in maintaining their relative power in the governance of space economy, the minds and well-being of citizens, and thereby social order and cohesion. The key administrative vehicle in this process is the resilient modification of the structures of regional governance and policy. The multi-scalar importance of borders is accentuated by the fact that while the number of states has quadrupled since World War II, the number of sub-national units of governance has multiplied even more (Lovering 2007).

A reappraisal of state spaces towards higher scales has occurred simultaneously with this, and an increasing number of supra-state boundaries have been drawn, some of which are crucial to the organization of international economic and strategic relations and the control of flows of various kinds, for example in the context of blocks such as the EU, NAFTA, Mercado Común del Sur (Mercosur), Association of Southeast Asian Nations (ASEAN) and so on (Paasi 2009a). The importance of such units is increasing, and some scholars have suggested that normative regionalism and cosmopolitanism are currently significant factors, for example in Asia and Europe, and that they could serve as alternatives to nationalism and narrowly defined globalism (Delanty and He 2008).

Fourthly, there are several methodological approaches to border studies that draw on diverging theoretical principles. Such approaches often operate at different levels of abstraction and can be used in relation to different conceptual apparatus (for example state, nationalism or identity theory), and at the same time are available on different spatial scales. For some political economists, for instance, it is the macro-level mobility of capital across borders and the possible control of such flows that is at stake and which normally forces researchers to reflect the changing faces of capitalism and the changing global conditions and strategies of capital accumulation (Sparke 2006). For those interested in the power of statecraft and foreign policy elites in shaping images of threat and associated fears in international relations it has been the analysis of foreign policy texts, media space texts and various popular texts (written, pictorial, cinematic) that has attracted the attention of scholars. Such textual approaches originally drew on the poststructuralist thinking promoted by dissident IR scholars and representatives of critical geopolitics, who strived to deconstruct the self-evident traits associated with bounded territories and the meanings of mobile identities and shifting boundaries (Campbell 1992; Shapiro and Alker 1996; Ó Tuathail 1996). Accordingly, attention has been paid to the state and governmental boundary-drawing practices and performances that characterize the everyday life of states and their relations to each other.

For researchers interested in the local narratives that people associate with borders and border crossings in their everyday lives, it is often ethnographic approaches, participant observation, depth interviews and narrative analysis that draw their attention (Paasi 1996; Vila 2003). Such approaches may draw on normal neutral *mapping* of border life and experiences, but they may equally well be based on participatory action research, where researchers may actively struggle to lower boundaries between social groups living in separate territories. Such cross-border work can be based on approaches where scholars together with border citizens make a critical examination of national or regional stereotypes, for example, consider the content of national or regional identity narratives and their impact on interaction, and correspondingly try actively to transform existing inclusive and exclusive practices and discourses (Paasi and Prokkola 2008).

The complexity of borders and the need to conceptualize various dimensions of them has been summarized by Anderson (1996). For him, as for many political geographers today, borders are not merely lines on maps or between states but elements that are inseparable from the emergence of the states that they enclose. Some scholars have labelled this emergence as the institutionalization of territories, which brings together such processes as the shaping of borders, symbols and institutions (Paasi 1996). Also Anderson (1996) regards borders as institutions and processes. As institutions they are established by political decisions and regulated by legal texts. Indeed, borders are basic political institutions in the sense that no rule-bound economic, social or political life in complex societies could be organized without them. We can also add here the cultural and symbolic meanings of the regions that become institutionalized along with the territory.

From separate academic fields to the shaping of an interdisciplinary field of border studies

International political borders were regarded for a long time as unique research objects, which they certainly are to some extent. Researchers in different academic fields have by tradition studied borders largely from their own disciplinary perspectives and premises. Prescott (1965) condensed the tradition of political geography by suggesting that borders are concrete, empirical phenomena that have to be studied using empirical material, and that generalizations about them are very difficult. The development of geography towards positivist thinking led also political geographers to attach more weight to models and generalizations, and to make generalizations about borders, too (Minghi 1963). They gradually recognized the psychological/perceptual meanings attached to borders and border landscapes, again following more general academic trends and the rise of behavioural approaches in the field (Rumley and Minghi 1991). It was only during the 1990s that new approaches drawing on post-structuralism and ethnographic standpoints emerged (Newman and Paasi 1998), and it was at this stage that geographers took steps towards the emerging interdisciplinary field of border studies and began to look at approaches developed for instance in anthropology.

The functional roles of borders, their meanings as barriers and questions of how to cross them have been crucial for economists. The ongoing process of economic integration, for instance, has led economists to develop new approaches to the transformation of border regions from barriers into active spaces. This tendency has been especially significant in the EU, where the key motive of spatial politics has been to lower the boundaries between states. Anthropologists, ethnologists and sociologists, for their part, have often looked at the cultural and social boundaries affecting communities and the identities of border citizens (Cohen 1986; Donnan and Wilson 1999). Although sociologists like Simmel discussed the roles of boundaries in social life, sociologists in general have been relatively silent on borders, but this situation is changing (O'Dowd 2007). Meanwhile political scientists have often regarded boundaries as lines separating and stabilizing the system of states as sovereign power containers in a supposedly anarchic world, a view that was questioned during the 1990s by *dissident* IR scholars, whose ideas were followed by critical geopoliticians (Shapiro and Alker 1996, Ó Tuathail and Dalby 1998).

Some common keywords have also emerged among border scholars. Identity, for instance, is one of watchwords in current interdisciplinary border studies, often associated with others such as difference and inclusion/exclusion or inside/outside. These ideas are shared by political geographers (Newman and Paasi 1998), IR scholars (Walker 1993; Albert et al. 2001), anthropologists (Donnan and Wilson 1999) and linguists (Benwell and Stokoe 2006), so that they are clearly not a monopoly of any field.

The same holds good with general categories such as de-territorialization and re-territorialization that many border scholars have readily used since the 1990s. These categories were originally coined in somewhat cryptic ways by Deleuze and Guattari (1987) when depicting the impact of capitalism on the fragmentation and reorganization of the social world. In cultural studies, de-territorialization has referred to loss of the *naturalized* relation between culture and geographical and social territory – a theme discussed by border scholars as well (Paasi 2003) – and this has also been taken to include the relocation of old and new forms of symbolic production (Lull 1995, 151). Correspondingly, re-territorialization embraced two coactive phenomena, in that while the foundations of cultural territory (ways of life, artifacts, symbols and contexts) were seen to be open to new interpretations and understandings, this idea implied that culture is perpetually reconstituted through social interaction (Lull 1995, 159). Lull points out that cultural re-territorialization is *not* something done to people, over which they do not have any control.

Most border scholars have been much more straightforward when using these ideas, so that de-territorialization has simply referred to the purported situation characterized by the disappearance of borders in the globalizing world, or at times to the need to deconstruct their fixed or apparent meanings. Re-territorialization, for its part, normally refers in border studies to the situation where new borders are created or emerge. Both de- and re-territorialization occur in various institutional practices and discourses and display economic, cultural and political power relations. Since both processes are taking place continually, they are overlapping and intermittent, and they inevitably result in differentiation of the already complex spatialities of borders. Furthermore, it may be argued that these two expressions are often used in a metaphoric sense in border studies, not referring to specific, concrete borders. In many of the recent debates concerning the *re-location of borders* (or to be more exact, debates on new forms of surveillance of border crossings) inside states, for example access to airports, streets or shopping centres, or on the future of global borders in the globalizing, post-national world, borders in general have been used as metaphors referring to *processes* of establishing 'borders'.

It may be argued that now, following the first wave of the broadening interest in borders that initially emerged in separate academic fields, the terrain of border research is now fusing and it is becoming increasingly difficult to distinguish separate academic realms with their own objects, concepts or methods of border research. Correspondingly, some scholars have called for anti-disciplinarity or rather transdisciplinarity (Lugo 1997). This is evident in current research. Thus political and other human geographers may now well be interested in border-related personal, collective and literary identity narratives, as traditionally studied by anthropologists. The multifarious roles of the state in the production and reproduction of borders are nowadays being studied not only by political geographers and IR scholars but also by anthropologists, historians and literary theorists. Scholars concerned with literary or cultural theory, for example, have looked at both real *hard* borders and *soft* borders and also considered border crossings in multicultural locations, through concepts such as benevolent nationalism, cultural essentialism or multiculturalism and the social boundaries of bodies and human subjectivity (Michaelsen and Johnson 1997). It is also typical nowadays for border scholars to cross the *borders* of academic fields in edited collections and even to engage in cooperation.

But what would a *theory* of such a complicated constellation of borders and related social institutions and ideologies actually deal with? Is it a theory of *borders* or should it rather be a theory of *bounding* and boundary producing practices – that see borders as specific forms of practice, symbols and institutions – as has been suggested by political geographers? (See Ó Tuathail and Dalby 1998; Paasi 1996, 2003; Newman 2003.) It is obvious that the challenge for border studies lies in the perpetual theorization of borders and boundary producing practices rather than in a solid border theory of some kind. This means that, rather than fixed ideas, our theorizations on boundaries should be tractable heuristic tools that could be used and re-conceptualized further in various empirical settings (Paasi 2009b). To follow Sayer (1992), the role of theory for the organization of facts and empirical observations should be a secondary one and the key aim of theorization should be to conceptualize the directly and indirectly observable elements of the research object(s). This is often the case with objects of research in the social sciences when studying abstract economic relations, social cohesion, values or emotions, for instance. The major task is to recognize conceptually dimensions and relations of the research object that are significant for its production, reproduction and functioning. This approach lays stress on the fact that observations are theory-laden, but it also identifies the significance of empirical observations. Correspondingly, theory is not a separate realm that should be freely *circulated* as such, but it should inform concrete research practice, which should in turn help to shape the theory. On the other hand, while such conceptualization should be contextual, it should not be bound only to a specific local context but should be related to broader social and cultural theory.

Bounded spaces – a mobile world: borders and the changing contexts of politics

To show how complicated, and at times contrasting, the views expressed on the roles of boundaries may be (and this complexity doubtless has its impact on the way they are theorized), this section will discuss some alternative paths for conceptualizing borders that have been proposed in recent debates. The first challenges the existence and dominance of borders in current political-territorial grammars and the second strives to make the current complex roles of borders visible by expanding our understanding of what borders mean and where they are actually *located*. The third example discusses a traditional border-related theme, nature, but does this in the context of ecopolitics and biopolitics.

Relational Challenge

At the same time as new theoretical viewpoints and empirical border studies have been mushrooming, there has been a parallel discussion on the roles of boundaries, a discussion that simply seems to be progressing, superficially at least, in the opposite direction. Contrary to the ongoing lively debates on borders, this discussion has been more normative and 'academic' in the sense that it is not related to any specific political border. New ideas have been represented by *relational thinkers*. Amin (2003), for example, argues against the conceptualization of territories as bounded and suggests that they should be regarded as spaces of relation in which 'all kinds of unlike things can knock up against each other in all kinds of ways' (Amin et al. 2003, 6).

It is interesting that, in spite of making claims regarding the meanings of borders, relationalists such as Amin are *not* border scholars, that is, they have not studied concrete political borders. Rather, they are interested in borders as hindrances to progressive politics, and therefore regard boundaries *generally* as regressive and, in a way, as optical illusions associated with the cartographic legacy of measuring location on the basis of geographical distance and territorial jurisdiction. This legacy is not unfamiliar for political geographers and political scientists, who have reflected on it for a long time and have used such expressions as 'embedded statism' (Taylor 1996), 'territorial trap' (Agnew 1994) or 'cartographic anxiety' (Krishna 1994) or 'spatial socialization' (Paasi 1996) to characterize this phenomenon. But while often being consistent with the normative arguments of relationalists, these scholars have related their arguments to the operation and power of the state.

The discussion on the need to erase borders has not arisen of the blue but echoes voices raised earlier in critical anthropology (Gupta and Ferguson 1992). The representatives of the *mobility paradigm* have also questioned the naturalized relations between bounded spaces and certain groups of people. Correspondingly, 'the emerging mobility paradigm thus argues against the ontology of distinct places and "people". Rather there is a complex relationality of places and persons connected through both performances and performativities' (Hannam et al. 2006, 13).

Postnationalism and transnationalism similarly suggest that *sovereignty* is diffusing away from the nation-state, which would weaken the link between political identities, participation and the territorial state. Especially for transnational theorists identities and political activities are now multilocal and loyalties are no longer seen to correspond to the nation-state, that is, territory and politics are not in a one-to-one relation (Nagel 2004). Such thinking forces us to consider especially the role of citizenship, a status that is quite dramatically related to borders and border crossings.

Similar, a rather normative approach is taken at times by scholars who make claims regarding cosmopolitanism and imply that attachment to a nation's territory should ideally be replaced by an attachment to the whole planet. For Guibernau (2007, 168-9) cosmopolitan identity is the privilege of an elite and she does not see its expansion among the masses in the near future. Critical cosmopolitanism, however, is a new line of thought that differs from such a stereotypic *world polity* cosmopolitanism. This viewpoint is not reducible to concrete identities (national or global) but rather is a form of cultural contestation (Delanty 2006).

It is clear that such a principled challenging of borders must be a crucial issue for any border scholar who is interested in the moral and ethical issues involved in the definitions, practices and discourses of border crossings, the right to cross borders, to change one's place and to seek opportunities for a better life elsewhere. Such concerns are not merely academic, of course. Networks of activists operating across borders are becoming increasingly significant in challenging the politics of borders that takes them for granted. Such activism has by tradition included diverse groupings such as anti-slavery and women's suffrage campaigners and more recently the environmental and anti-globalization movements. Keck and Sikkink (1998) have noted how such movements can be significant as sources of identity, values, norms and new ideas, and refer to them as 'transnational advocacy networks'. Such social movements often develop common interpretations of the world to nurture solidarity and identifications.

Without leaning uncritically on realist accounts of the importance of states and of the 'anarchy' rampaging outside them, it is still useful to remember that only three per cent of the world's population are currently living outside the state where they were born (O'Dowd 2007). Of course it is mostly the people belonging to this three per cent – for example asylum seekers and refugees – that will face the most serious impacts of borders and the construction of global lines of exclusion and inclusion. Academic guest workers and high-flying international business people are part of this minority, but may be subject to different rules. Sparke (2006), for instance, in analysing the new biopolitical production of citizenship and control mechanisms in the post-9/11 neoliberal USA, speaks about new forms of citizenship that are divided between business-class civil citizenship that extends across transnational spaces concomitantly with economic liberalization and new forms of national security that have curtailed the citizenship of others and led to various forms of exclusion.

Such new divisions force us to ask what is the lesson to be learned by a border scholar from the fact that 97 per cent of people still live in their country of origin and are normally effectively wrapped and subjugated under the national ideological apparatus and national practice designed to take individuals politically into the possession of the state. Rather than closing our eyes to such practices and downplaying their importance, we still need to scrutinize how and in what practices and discourses such border-producing identity narratives are produced and reproduced. Is it so that nationalism is just a more aggressive label for an apparently harmless idea of national identity, a label that can actually be rapidly mobilized into a political and discriminatory practice which gives concrete shape to such apparently neutral identity narratives? We still know very little of such nation-building processes and the roles of borders in them. The key reason for this is that border scholars more often than not seem to be interested in the present situation prevailing in border areas rather than tracing borders as historically contingent processes (Paasi 1996).

These are serious questions for border scholars. Even though national boundaries are becoming lower in some areas of the world and are losing their at times dramatic roles as obstacles to mobility, each international border normally has a specific place in the history of nation-building processes and national identity narratives that may sometimes be highly conflict-ridden and sometime be based on long periods of peaceful development. Such memories and related performances are often unscrupulously exploited in nationalist ideologies, which hide them in the rhetoric of national identities and heritage. It is also known that, historically, people originating from border areas have been strongly represented in many nationalist movements (Hutchinson 2005).

The above discussion does not mean that relational claims or claims regarding the need for cosmopolitanism are not highly important politically and most laudable in terms of human values – on the contrary. It is simply intended to remind us that making relational claims without studying concrete border practices and ideologies does not help us very much in understanding how these practices of producing and reproducing borders work generally and contextually.

Borders are everywhere

Another strand in recent debates on boundaries has been the suggestion that borders have not disappeared but have rather become so diffuse that they have transformed whole states into borderlands (Balibar 1998). Their meanings are thus changing. As Rumford (2006, 2008) suggests, surveillance technologies associated with increasing border control – to prevent terrorism, for example – may exist everywhere, even beyond the borders proper: at airports, in shopping precincts, in streets, and so on. This may in fact strengthen bordering in a society (Rumford 2006) and be constitutive of social, cultural and political distinctions.

It is possible to argue that this *borders are everywhere* thesis exists in two historically and spatially contingent forms (Paasi 2009b). If borders are understood as marking the spread of societal and political control into society (and even outside of existing state borders), there must also be other ways in which borders are present more widely. Borders are – as expressions of territoriality – normally crucial to what can be called the discursive landscape of social power. This is a construct that has become institutionalized in a society in the long term and manifests itself in material landscapes, military commemorations, ideologies and nationalist performances all over that society's territory (Paasi 1996). That these things often draw on banal forms of nationalism (Billig 1995) makes them even more persistent in daily life. It is not difficult to understand how much emotional bordering is loaded into national celebrations, flag days, independence days, military parades, selective national landscapes and other elements of national iconographies. Given that the current mechanisms of surveillance and societal control are expanding deep into society, it may similarly be argued that the key *location* of a national(ist) border does not lie at the concrete line but in the manifestations of the perpetual nation-building process and nationalist practices, and the roots of these manifestations have to be traced to the histories of these practices and iconographies.

It may be suggested that the *boundaries are everywhere* thesis has correspondingly two societal contexts that may actually operate in the same direction, to strengthen the national community as a bounded unit (Paasi 2009b). The fact that borders are part of the discursive landscape of social power, which is related to symbolic (for example education) and physical violence (for example army, police), simply means that we have to be sensitive to the meanings associated with national borders. Children and young people already learn through their education at school and in the family, and especially through the printed and electronic media, that such borders (often defined on historical grounds), *are* the justified (and at times when we are being taught that they are wrong, *'non-natural'*) territorial borders of *'our'* *community or 'us'*. We are also forced or persuaded to learn what are the legitimate and hegemonic national meanings attached to these borders and what are the pools of emotions, fears and memories that we have to draw on in this connection (such meanings can, of course, always be challenged and can even change as a consequence of revolutions, occupations and the like). These pools of meanings can be labelled as *emotional landscapes of control*.

The power of borders for nationalism and national identity narratives is not a homogeneous phenomenon; rather it is crucially context dependent, and even the power and salience of the individual borders of a state can vary dramatically. To take one example, for instance, the role of the relatively open border of Finland with Sweden and Norway has been quite different from that of the Finnish-Soviet/ Russian border, which has been perpetually exploited *as a border that divides*. It still has deep symbolic meanings even though its ideological role between east and west has largely disappeared as a consequence of the collapse of the Soviet Union and of the division between East and West. And while this border has become much more open since the collapse of the Soviet Union, it is still a cultural, political and economic dividing line that exists deep in the national memory and even in the national iconography. A fitting example of the meaning of this border *outside* of the border area is the memorial to Olli Tiainen, a peasant leader named *the border captain* (see Figure 1.1). He has a heroic reputation (part of which has been fabricated by the authorities later) for his activities during the war between Sweden-Finland and Russia (1808-09), after which the Finnish areas of Sweden-Finland became an autonomous part of Tsarist Russia for more than 100 years before Finland gained independence in 1917 (Paasi 1996). The statue was erected in 1932 in Joensuu and reflects the nationalist overtones of the 1930s, as it carries the coat of arms of Karelia, which represents the perpetual opposition between the East (a scimitar) and the West (a sword), and the inscription 'Freedom germinates from blood and iron'.

On the other hand, the long period of openness on the Finnish-Swedish border and the close cultural and linguistic relations between the people living in the adjacent border areas does not mean that this has automatically led to a diminishing of the border in the national imagination or socialization. Even the current active EU-based cross-border projects have not caused such meanings and horizons to disappear (Paasi and Prokkola 2008).

Figure 1.1 Memorial to the 'Border Captain Olli Tiainen' (1932)
Source: A. Paasi.

Figure 1.2 'Freedom Germinates from Blood and Iron': A detail in the
memorial to 'the Border Captain Olli Tiainen'

Source: A. Paasi.

Now, to return to the thesis of Balibar, borders have become elements of control and surveillance infrastructures in the current dynamic world characterized by flows of people, ideas, ideologies and goods and by a fluctuating fear of terrorism, even though they are often apparently *invisible* and diffuse, no longer existing as mere concrete border landscapes (although such landscapes can still be significant in some contexts). If the landscapes related to nationalist ideas and national identities can be labelled as 'emotional landscapes of control', such 'technical landscapes of control and surveillance' are also gaining importance (Paasi 2009b), and although emotional landscapes of control exist in all national states, such technical landscapes of control are also gaining in strength. The manner in which these exist in various societies is a context-bound feature, however. We certainly have cases where emotional landscapes and symbolic violence do not work, while effective use is made of technical landscapes and physical violence. Fitting examples would be weak, conflict-ridden states run by dictators who do not care about local, regional or national legitimacy. While the number of major armed conflicts has declined globally and there have been no interstate conflicts for several years, this has not reduced the struggles over democracy, justice and power inside states. In many states the borders created in media spaces and education, are controlled very effectively. The life of dissident journalists, for example, can be very risky and even murders are common.

Borders, ecopolitics and biopolitics

Reflections on the relations between borders and nature have led to the development of the idea of ecopolitics (Kuehls 1996), referring to the fact that while – due mostly to human aspects associated with control – borders may be crucial obstacles to social life and the movement of citizens, goods and ideas, they can at times have a very limited role in relation to nature, which seems to imply a need to *reject* borders. Think of major natural catastrophes (floods, earthquakes) or environmental accidents caused by human agency, like the Tshernobyl nuclear power accident or the oil catastrophes in the coastal areas of Europe or the US. These are harsh reminders that the state borders drawn on maps do not stop the effects of such catastrophes, but as institutions, such borders can effectively complicate measures taken to alleviate the effects of such catastrophes or simply to obtain information on them. In the face of large-scale transborder environmental problems individual sovereign states simply have to pool their resources. The EU, for example, has attempted to promote renewable energy resources, conserve fisheries, manage agriculture in more sustainable ways, address sulphur dioxide emissions and regulate chemical waste disposal. Smith and Pangsapa (2008, 175) argue that such events and processes also challenge traditional state-bound ideas of citizenship and show how environmental activism has become important around the world. As one example of the new importance of nature in border studies, the management of border areas in relation to the environment has also become an interesting theme (Ramutsindela 2004; Fall 2005).

Borders are crucial elements of biopolitical practices that are exploited to produce and reproduce state territoriality. Such practices are often related to health and disease issues, and these phenomena are crucially related to mobility, which challenge the fixity of borders in many ways although states still try to maintain control over such risky and potentially uncontrollable flows. The collection edited by Bashford (2006) demonstrates that control over the movements of people for health reasons is certainly not a recent thing but actually emerged in parallel with the need to define the modern nation-state and when developing its administrative structures and forms of governance. A 'civilized state' was seen to be able to protect its borders and its citizens against health risks. Health and control over space were thus crucial elements of nationalism. This biopolitical control was often taken into national narratives in the form of images of an enemy and *the other*, seen as a transmitter of diseases and vermin. Diseases also motivate the creation of structures of political control, as in the recent cases of mad cow disease, Severe Acute Respiratory Syndrome (SARS) and *bird flu* (H5N1 virus). Health issues have been a neglected theme in border studies, but they will certainly become more important in the increasingly mobile world.

Discussion

One of the most striking features of the post-Cold War period has been expansion of border studies into a broad interdisciplinary field. Researchers have co-operated and published in edited collections, but this new interdisciplinarity has manifested itself also in the flow of ideas across disciplinary borders. Think, for example, of how the ideas of difference and the *other* – originally developed within cultural studies – soon became significant in many fields. Scholars have scrutinized the ways in which difference has been constructed historically and reproduced in various geographical contexts and how such ideas have been used on various spatial scales. This led to analyses of the images of threat that have been exploited in many contexts for hundreds of years. One major issue is how scholars can work constructively with borders and difference and contribute to the development of respect towards those living *on the other side of the border*. This must be based on a historically sensitive understanding of border cases.

One of the recent claims in border studies has been to develop a *border theory*. This chapter suggests that a general *border theory* would seem in many ways unattainable, and perhaps even undesirable. Why would such a theory be undesirable? There are two main reasons. Firstly, since individual state borders are deeply characterized by contextual features and societal power relations and their meanings change in the course of time along with broader, typically state-related societal relations and conditions, there can hardly be one general theory that would be valid everywhere. On the other hand, since borders are context-bound phenomena and are deeply rooted in social, cultural, political and economic practices and discourses, a general theory of borders would suggest that they are more or less separate objects of social

27

research that can be universalized in the form of a theory that would obviously then be, contrary to the variegated nature of contexts, more or less fixed. A general theory of borders is hence problematic not because the borders between states are unique – although each of them indeed is – but rather because borders can be theorized reasonably only as part of a broader effort towards social-cultural theory (Paasi 2009b).

Borders are a very complex set of social institutions that exist on and through various spatial scales and are related to a number of social practices and discourses in which they are produced and made meaningful. Such institutions are linked to a variety of social realities that often go beyond the border – and might be labelled as representing the *relational aspect* of borders. This also provides some clues regarding how a *theory* of borders should perhaps be understood. Instead of a fixed, all-encompassing theory, it is perhaps the idea of theorizing or conceptualization that could provide more tools for border scholars.

Yet there is an obvious need to theorize both boundary producing and reproducing practices in context. Any valid contextual theorization of boundaries should combine at least such processes, practices and discourses such as the production and reproduction – or institutionalization – of territoriality/territory, state power, human agency and human experience. These practices are normally institutionalized, involve both formal and informal institutions, and may be deeply symbolized. They are rarely only local, but may have their origin and constitutive power at a distance, on various *scales* (which are not fixed), from local to global. This simply means that the strands of power that constitute the spatialities of complicated boundary-producing practices make it increasingly difficult to think of certain borders as local and of others as global. But the context makes a difference, and it remains a challenge for the imagination of the researcher to conceptualize and study empirically contextually manifested practices that may have their origins on diverging spatial scales and bring together events and processes from these.

References

Agnew, J. (2006), 'Open to surprise?', *Progress in Human Geography* 30:1, 1-4.
Agnew, J. (2005), *Hegemony: The New Shape of Global Power* (Philadelphia: Temple University Press).
Agnew, J. (1994), 'The territorial trap: The geographical assumptions in international relations theory', *Review of International Political Economy* 1:1, 53-80.
Albert, M., Jacobson, D. and Lapid, Y. (eds.)(2001), *Identities, Borders, Orders* (Minneapolis: University of Minnesota Press).
Amin, A., Massey, D. and Thrift, N. (2003), *Decentering the National: A Radical Approach to Regional Inequality* (London: Catalyst).
Anderson, M. (1996), *Frontiers: Territory and State Formation in the Modern World* (Oxford: Polity).

Balibar, E. (1998), 'The borders of Europe', in Cheah, P. and Robbins, B. (eds.), *Cosmopolitics* (Minneapolis: University of Minnesota Press).

Bashford, A. (ed.) (2006), *Medicine at the Border: Disease, Globalization and Security* (Basingstoke: Palgrave Macmillan).

Benwell, B. and Stokoe, E. (2006), *Discourse and Identity* (Edinburgh: Edinburgh University Press).

Billig, M. (1995), *Banal Nationalism* (London: Sage Publications).

Brenner, N. (2004), *New State Spaces* (Oxford: Oxford University Press).

Campbell, D. (1992), *Writing Security* (Minneapolis: University of Minnesota Press).

Cohen, A.P. (1986), *Symbolizing Boundaries* (Manchester: Manchester University Press).

Dalby, S. (1990), *Creating the Second Cold War* (London: Pinter).

Deas, I. and Lord, A. (2006), 'From a new regionalism to an unusual regionalism? The emergence of non-standard regional spaces and lessons for the territorial reorganization of the state', *Urban Studies* 43:10, 1847-77.

Delanty, G. (2006), 'The cosmopolitan imagination: Critical cosmopolitanism and social theory', *British Journal of Sociology* 57:1, 25-27.

Delanty, G. and He, B. (2008), 'Cosmopolitan perspectives on European and Asian transnationalism', *International Sociology* 23:3, 323-44.

Deleuze, G. and Guattari, F. (1987), *Anti-Oedipus: Capitalism and Schizophrenia* (Minneapolis: University of Minnesota Press).

Donnan, H. and Wilson, T.M. (1999), *Borders: Frontiers of Identity, Nation and State* (Oxford: Berg).

Fall, J. (2005), *Drawing the Line: Nature, Hybridity and Politics in Transboundary Spaces* (Aldershot: Ashgate).

Guibernau, M. (2007), *The Identity of Nations* (Cambridge: Polity Press).

Gupta, A. and Ferguson, J. (1992), 'Beyond "culture": space, identity, and the politics of difference', *Cultural Anthropology* 7:1, 6-23.

Hannam, K., Sheller, M. and Urry, J. (2006), 'Editorial: mobilities, immobilities and moorings', *Mobilities* 1:1, 1-22.

Hutchinson, J. (2005), *Nations as Zones of Conflict* (London: Sage Publications).

Juss, S.S. (2008), *International Migration and Global Justice* (Aldershot: Ashgate).

Kaiser, R.J. (2002), 'Homeland making and the territorialization of national identity', in Conversi, D. (ed.), *Ethnonationalism in the Contemporary World* (London: Routledge).

Katzenstein, P.J. (2005), *A World of Regions: Asia and Europe in the American Imperium* (Ithaca: Cornell University Press).

Keck, M.E. and Sikkink, K. (1998), *Activists beyond Borders* (Ithaca and London: Cornell University Press).

Kramsch, O. and Hooper, B. (eds.)(2004), *Cross-Border Governance in the European Union* (London: Routledge).

Krasner, S.D. (2001), *Problematic Sovereignty* (Cambridge: Cambridge University Press).

Krishna, S. (1994), 'Cartographic anxiety: Mapping the body politic in India', *Alternatives* 19:4, 507-521.

Kuehls, T. (1996), *Ecopolitics* (Minneapolis: University of Minnesota Press).

Lovering, J. (2007), 'The new imperial geography', in Bagchi-Sen, S. and Lawton Smith, H. (eds.), *Economic Geography: Then, now and the future* (London: Routledge).

Lugo, A. (1997), 'Reflections on border theory, culture, and the nation', in Michaelsen, S. and Johnson, D.E. (eds.), *Border Theory* (Minneapolis: University of Minnesota Press).

Lull, J. (1995), *Media, Communication, Culture* (Cambridge: Polity Press).

Michaelsen, S. and Johnson, D.E. (eds.) (1997), *Border Theory* (Minneapolis: University of Minnesota Press).

Minghi, J. (1963), 'Boundary studies in political geography', *Annals of the Association of American Geographers* 53, 407-28.

Murphy, A. (1996), 'The sovereign state system as political-territorial ideal: Historical and contemporary considerations', in Bierstaker, T.J. and Weber, C. (eds.), *State Sovereignty as Social Construct* (Cambridge: Cambridge University Press).

Nagel, C. (2004), 'Questioning citizenship in an "age of migration"', in O'Loughlin, J., Staeheli, L. and Greenberg, E. (eds.), *Globalization and its Outcomes* (New York: Guilford Press).

Newman, D. (2003), 'Boundaries', in Agnew, J., Mitchell, K. and Toal, G. (eds.), *A Companion to Political Geography* (Oxford: Blackwell).

Newman, D. and Paasi, A. (1998), 'Fences and neighbours in the postmodern world: Boundary narratives in political geography', *Progress in Human Geography* 22:2, 186-207.

Ó Tuathail, G. (1996), *Critical Geopolitics* (London: Routledge).

Ó Tuathail, G. and Dalby, S. (1998), 'Introduction: Rethinking geopolitics', in Ó Tuathail, G. and Dalby, S. (eds.), *Rethinking Geopolitics* (London: Routledge).

O'Dowd, L. (2007), 'Sociology, States and Borders: Some Critical Reflections', *Norface seminar on Globalization and borders, 18-19 September 2007* (London: Royal Holloway).

Ohmae, K. (1995), *The End of the Nation State* (New York: Free Press).

Paasi, A. (2009a), 'The resurgence of the "region" and "regional identity": Theoretical perspectives and empirical observations on regional dynamics in Europe', *Review of International Studies* 35, 121-46.

Paasi, A. (2009b), 'Bounded spaces in a "borderless world": border studies, power and the anatomy of territory', *Journal of Power* 2:2, 213-234.

Paasi, A. (2005), 'Globalisation, academic capitalism and the uneven geographies of international journal publishing spaces', *Environment and Planning A* 37:5, 769-90.

Paasi, A. (2003), 'Boundaries in a globalizing world', in Anderson, K., Domosh, M., Pile, S. and Thrift, N. (eds.), *Handbook of Cultural Geography* (London: Sage).

Paasi, A. (1996), *Territories, Boundaries and Consciousness* (Chichester: John Wiley).

Paasi, A. and Prokkola, E.-K. (2008), 'Territorial dynamics, cross-border work and everyday life in the Finnish-Swedish border', *Space and Polity* 12:1, 13-29.

Perkmann, M. and Sum, N.L. (eds.)(2002), *Globalization, Regionalization and Cross-Border Regions* (London: Palgrave Macmillan).

Prescott, J.R.V. (1965), *The Geography of Frontiers and Boundaries* (Chicago: Aldine).

Ramutsindela, M. (2004), 'Glocalisation and nature conservation strategies in 21st-century Southern Africa', *Tijdschrift voor Economische en Sociale Geografie* 95, 161-72.

Rumford, C. (ed.)(2008), 'Citizens and borderwork in Europe', Special Issue of *Space and Polity* 12:1.

Rumford, C. (2006), 'Theorizing borders', *European Journal of Social Theory* 9:2, 155-69.

Rumley, D. and Minghi, J. (1991), *The Geography of Border Landscapes* (London: Routledge).

Sack, R.D. (1986), *Human Territoriality* (Cambridge: Cambridge University Press).

Said, E.W. (1978), *Orientalism* (London: Routledge).

Sayer, A. (1992), *Method in Social Science: A Realist Approach* (London: Routledge).

Scott, A.J. (ed.) (2001), *Global City-Regions* (Oxford: Oxford University Press).

Shapiro, M.J. and Alker, H.R. (eds.)(1996), *Challenging Boundaries* (Minneapolis: University of Minnesota Press).

Stockholm International Peace Research Institute (SIPRI) (2008), *SIPRI Yearbook 2008*.

Smith, M.J. and Pangsapa, P. (2008), *Environment and Citizenship* (London and New York: Zed Books).

Sparke, M. (2006), 'A neoliberal nexus: Economy, security and the biopolitics of citizenship on the border', *Political Geography* 25:2, 151-80.

Taylor, P.J. (1996), 'Embedded statism and the social sciences: Opening up to new spaces', *Environment and Planning A* 28:11, 1917-1928.

Vila, P. (ed.) (2003), *Ethnography at the Border* (Minneapolis: University of Minnesota Press).

Walker, R.B.J. (1993), *Inside/Outside: International Relations as Political Theory* (Cambridge: Cambridge University Press).

Contemporary Research Agendas in Border Studies: An Overview

David Newman

The study of borders has undergone a renaissance during the past two decades. From a descriptive analysis of the course and location of the lines separating states in the international system, to the study of the dynamics of the bordering process as it impacts society and space, borders have taken on a multi-dimensional meaning. No longer the exclusive domain of the geographer, cartographer or diplomat, the study of borders is discussed by sociologists, anthropologists and border practitioners, focusing on the functional significance of the bordering process as a dynamic in its own right at different social and spatial scales. Borders may signify the point or line of separation between distinct entities, separating one category from another, in some cases institutionalizing existing differences, while in other cases creating the difference where none existed previously. Contingent upon social and political conditions, borders experience processes of opening or closing, reflecting the degree to which cross-border separation or contact takes place. As borders open, so trans-border frontier regions, or borderlands, evolve, areas within which borders are crossed, the meeting of the differences takes place and, in some cases, hybridity is created. This is as true of territorial spaces in close proximity to the physical borders of the state or urban neighbourhoods, as it is of the social and cultural borderlands which interface between religious and ethnic groups, or economic categories.

This chapter seeks to identify the common themes of the bordering process, themes which are common to all border scholars and practitioners. The way in which the diverse border functions are expressed on the ground, between countries, groups or social categories, may be vastly different (one) from the other, but they reflect a common concern with the way in which borders are created (demarcated and delimited) subsequently institutionalized and perpetuated (managed) and eventually crossed, opened or even removed altogether, in a world of changing social, economic and political conditions.

There is no single border situation. Borders are opening and closing throughout the world at one and the same time. Borders are differentiated through society and space, such that while they are becoming more porous and amenable to crossing in one place, they are becoming more restrictive and sealed to movement in other places (Anderson and O'Dowd 1999; Berg and Ehin 2006; Blake 2000a). During the 1990s, border research in North America focused on the ways in which borders became more flexible and easier to cross within the context of globalization and the opening of economic markets spurred on by NAFTA and the widening trade links between neighbouring countries. Since the events of 9/11, the focus has shifted back to the ways in which borders can be closed and sealed in the face of perceived global terror threats, as part of the renewed securitization discourse. Equally, borders may be opening to certain social, cyber and economic functions while, at one and the same time, they can be closing to other political and security functions. This causes tensions between different institutional interests, ranging from the government, the military, the welfare and health, the economic, the human rights and the Non-Governmental Organizations (NGOs). Thus, power relations, reflecting the different interests of the social and economic gatekeepers, are a major determinant in the way that borders are demarcated and managed through space and time.

Although much of this book is focused on the geographical borders which separate states from each other in the changing global and international system, this discussion of border research agendas does not limit itself to the physical and the geographical. It moves beyond the disciplinary boundaries to examine the nature of borders as delimiters of social, economic and cultural categories no less than the geographical. Moreover, the chapter discusses the dynamics of the bordering process as it is relevant to all types of border – geographical and non-geographical – drawing some of its terminologies and categorizations from the former for an understanding of the latter.

Boundary Demarcation and Delimitation as Agents of Inclusion and Exclusion

The demarcation of boundaries has been one of the main areas of traditional research into borders. Boundaries have been classified into diverse categories and typologies, relating to their genetic or time phases (Hartshorne 1936; Jones 1943, 1959; Minghi 1963; Prescott 1987). The temporal categorization of borders reflected existing ethnic and linguistic differences, or was the catalyst which brought about the evolution of ethnically different groups on both sides of the border. Other demarcation classifications have related to the legal status of the border, the extent to which they resulted from warfare or from bilateral agreement and, to a lesser extent, some simple functional classifications reflecting the extent to which international boundaries were open to trans-boundary movement.

Much of the boundary demarcation categorization is seen as descriptive in nature, but with little reference to the functional and political significances of the bordering process as a dynamic process in its own right. It focuses on borders as a static outcome of the political process, rather than a factor which is as much an input as it is output. Moreover, the traditional categories, such as demarcation, delimitation, superimposition, antecedent and subsequent (terms borrowed by early boundary scholars from the realm of physical geography and fluvial geomorphology) have contemporary significance if transformed to the realms of social, cultural and political behaviour.

Demarcation is not only about the lines on the map which are then transformed into physical fences and walls on the ground. It is as much about the way that the societal mangers determine the nature of inclusion and exclusion from various social categories and groups. The inclusion of one person in a religious category may, for instance, depend on a particular interpretation of religious law and the extent to which any particular sect within the religion enjoys greater influence than others in determining the demarcation procedures. Classifying populations into various social and economic categories, as a result of which an individual may be eligible for government assistance and benefits, or may have to pay taxation at a certain higher or lower rate, is also an arbitrary demarcation of borders which determine who is included and who is excluded from any particular category. The demarcation of fixed borders creates the ecological fallacy, where some who should be included are left out, while others who should be excluded find themselves inside. This social construction of compartments and their borders is necessary for the ordering of society, but will always be contested, because there can rarely be a single border which is totally congruous with the absolute category. In some cases, the incongruity between boundary demarcation and the spatial or social category is due to a lack of accurate information and data, while in other cases it is because categories change over time through social and economic dynamics while the borders, once created and imposed upon the social or spatial landscape, remain inert and unchanging. In other cases still it is because of the power relations and the imposition of systems of control over spaces and groups which are subservient to their political or economic power.

Power Relations and the Management of Borders

Borders are social and political constructions. Someone creates them and, once created, manages them in such a way as to serve the interests of those same power elites (Newman 2003). Borders are always initially created as a means of separation, the construction of a barrier between two sides, normally as a means of perceived defence from outside influences, be it the invasions by foreign troops, the unhindered movement of migrants, or the flow of cheap goods which would undercut the local producers. Thus, borders are often created by those who see themselves as acting in the interests of the collective whom they represent, be it the state, the religious faith or the private country club. Borders are created by those who have the power to *keep out* those people and influences which are perceived, at any point in time, as being undesirable or detrimental to the home territory or group.

Equally, the opening of borders is also undertaken by power elites. These may be different power elites than those who constructed them in the first place, resulting from a change in government, changing social mores and/or the defeat of a group or country by an external power elite who have overcome the barrier function of the existing border. Where social or economic mores have changed, it may be the same power elites who, previously having created and closed the border in the first place, now decide that it in their political or economic interests to open the borders to movement and trans-boundary circulation. This would be particularly true with respect to the economic elites who create the borders of customs tariffs when it is in their interest, but equally open up the borders to the free movement of goods and global capital when it serves their interests in a changing economic and global environment.

Once created, borders become transformed into a reality, a default situation which impacts upon daily life patterns and social mores, determine the parameters of exclusion and inclusion, and creates the categories through which social and spatial compartmentalization is perpetuated. As such, borders are transformed into institutions which have their own set of rules, part of which are implemented for the sake of self perpetuation, as in all institutional structures. The institutions which are borders are managed in such a way as to control the movement of people, goods and ideas from one side of the border to the other. This is the single most important function of border management, controlling the means of border crossing. But this involves much more than technical aspects of institutional management. By controlling the crossing function, border management fulfils the role determined by the power elites, for whom the border is an agent of control in defining societal parameters.

Contextually, the demarcation and management of borders can be bilaterally negotiated by two power elites, one on each side of the border, or they can be imposed by the powerful upon the weak. Bilateral borders are always better than the unilaterally imposed borders, but it does not necessarily make them any more or less effective. Only when the existence, or specific parameters, of the border can be challenged by the *other* side, do they experience change or potential removal. Conflict over the existence of borders exist, sometimes because of dissatisfaction with the way in which the borders were created in the first place, or because of changes in the political, economic and global conditions which make the existing boundaries increasingly out of synchronization with changing territorial or social realities (Newman 2004). This is perhaps less the case with the territorial and physical borders separating states in the international system, than it is with a diverse range of social, economic and cultural boundaries which, for long periods of time, delimited the categories of a hierarchical and class based society and which, in a classless meritocracy, have become relict – to be replaced by a new set of socio-economic borders.

Borderlands, Frontiers and Zones of Transition/Hybridity

Borders are lines. They constitute the sharp point at which categories, spaces and territories interface. One category ends, the adjoining category begins. Historically, this has been of greatest importance in terms of the territorial boundaries separating states, determining the territorial extent of sovereignty and exclusive state control. This is true of any type of border where the demarcation process is rigidly defined in absolute locational terms. It is less the case where borders are defined in general terms, allowing for a degree of movement within the border zone, within which the absolute notions of inclusion or exclusion are fuzzy and undefined.

These fuzzy definitions of borders give rise to the concept of borderlands, areas in proximity to the border which constitute a transition zone between two distinct categories, rather than a clear cut-off line (Blake 2000b; Martinez 1994; Minghi 1991; Pavlakovich et al. 2004). It is an area within which people residing in the same territorial or cultural space may feel a sense of belonging to either one of the two sides, to each of the two sides, or even to a form of hybrid space in which they adopt parts of each culture and/or speak both languages.

Borderlands exist on both sides of borders. Where the border has been imposed upon a previously single cultural landscape, this is easy to understand. Ethnic groups continue to have a natural affinity with the people living on the other side of the border, rather than with the majority population of their own country of residence but with whom they have no common religious, cultural or linguistic past. In these cases, such as in the Balkans, the Kurdish regions of Iran, Iraq and Turkey, the former line of separation between East and West Germany, or in Israel/ Palestine, it is the context of ethnic conflict which has brought about the imposition of borders and, as such, states attempt to seal the border and to prevent contact between the two sides – for fear of secessionist demands and boundary redrawing. Notwithstanding, there exists in these regions a natural ethno-cultural borderland straddling both sides of the border, even if the rigidity of the border prevents it from becoming transformed into a functional region. States have often attempted to dilute minority ethnic population who live on close proximity to this type of border, in some cases through the forced out-movement of ethnic groups from the border region, or through land settlement policies which encourage other population groups to reside in these areas, populations whose orientations are towards the state core and the interior, rather than external and beyond the border.

Borderland regions are an important part of the process through which borders are opened. Prior to the removal of borders in the expanding European Union (EU), the EU created a series of trans-boundary regions, within which people from both sides who did not share ethnic characteristics, came into contact with each other through common economic and cultural cooperation (Anderson et al. 2002; Blatter et al. 2001; Perkmann 1999; Perkmann and Sum 2002). Through meeting and interaction, people become less fearful of the other, acknowledging the common concerns of daily life practices in the fields of commerce, education and recreational pursuits, rather than the distant considerations of statecraft and international diplomacy.

There is no set limit for the existence, or extent, of any particular borderland. They can exist on one side of the border but not on the other. They may extend for large distance (spatial or cultural) on one side but are much more limited on the other. Their existence is contingent upon the extent to which development, social or economic interaction which takes place in these spaces is influenced by their location in proximity to the border. The existence of the border impacts the activities which take place in these spaces, partially explaining why development in these regions is different from the expected patterns of urban and regional planning. In areas where borders are contested, governments may decide to invest development resources into the region as a means of influencing the local resident population to stay in what may be a potentially volatile environment, or because they want to make a point to the government on the other side that they are rooted in the area and have no intention of withdrawing from the region. Equally, the government on the other side of the border may decide that it is too dangerous for human habitation and will transform the region from a civilian ecumene to a fortified and military zone. In each case we have a borderland, within which development is a function of the proximity to a contested border, but the characteristics of which are significantly different on each side of the border.

Conversely, borderlands can become transformed into zones of transition in regions of stability and cross-border cooperation. Where borders are opened after long periods of being closed, the borderland becomes a space in which contact takes place and in which the threat of difference is gradually removed. Transition zones may result in cross-border hybridity in which local populations take on characteristics of both sides of the border, enabling a continuum from the absolute characteristics of one group to the absolute characteristics of the other. But meeting particularly after periods of length conflict and cross-border tensions does not always result in spatial hybridity. The meeting may serve to strengthen national or group uniqueness, as each side seeks to cultivate its own feelings of difference and cultural superiority. As Oskar Martinez has pointed out, there is a borderland continuum stretching from a situation of full cross-border integration in which the existence of the border is hardly felt, to a situation of borderland alienation in which there is no contact at all between the peoples on either side of the line of separation (Martinez 1994).

Cultural and social borders are also characterized by borderland spaces and zones of transition, even if these cannot be defined in spatial or territorial terms. Belonging to a religious group is varied. There are those who are included within the border by virtue of their adherence to the dogma in its totality, while there are others for whom a less dogmatic and less segregated form of religious affiliation is combined with the characteristics of the wider environment. Moving from one religious category into another often requires a process of conversion, through which the crossing of the border means leaving one form of social behaviour behind, while taking on another.

Equally, someone whose economic status has moved from one category to another by virtue of becoming wealthy, may not necessarily share the social attributes of his/her new economic status and, as such, may find themselves in a transition zone between highly stratified socio-economic class distinctions. The list is endless. There is always movement beyond the border, as people try to move from one social or spatial category to the other. Some succeed in crossing the territorial or the cultural border, others do not. Some succeed in crossing the territorial border but find themselves unable to cross the cultural border and are transformed from a member of an ethnic majority in their place of origin into an ethnic minority in their new destination, finding that the cultural borders of integration are much more difficult to cross than were the land borders between the states. The crossing of the cultural borders, the movement out of the ethnic ghetto may never take place, or it may wait for the second and third generation descendants of the original border crossers to undertake the necessary cultural and socio-economic adjustments.

Globalization, Securitization and the Porosity of Borders

Are borders opening or are they closing? During the 1990s, almost all border related research focused on the perceived impacts of globalization on the opening of borders and, in some cases, their total erasure. Globalization posited the notions of deterritorialized and borderless worlds (Dittgen 2000; Hudson 1998; Kolossov and O'Loughlin 1998; Newman 2006a; Newman and Paasi 1998; Ohmae 1990; Paasi 1998; Shapiro and Alker 1996; Toal 1999; Yeung 1998). In a world of unimpeded global flows, especially flows of capital and information, borders were considered as being redundant. No amount of government attempts to erect barriers in the form of walls, fences and stringent boundary management, could stop the force of cyber flows which no longer took account of the existence of borders. The relative political stability of the 1980s and 1990s, coupled with the collapse of the Iron Curtain, resulted in the easing of border restrictions, making it easier for more people throughout the world to cross borders than in the past. In the extreme case of the European Union, borders between states, which only fifty years previously had been embroiled in one of history's bitterest acts of warfare, were removed altogether, such that the only border relics were those chosen by the government to remain in situ for purpose of tourism and historical memory.

The opening and crossing of borders was reflected in the research and publications on border related issues of the 1980s and 1990s. Although the absolutist notion of a totally borderless world was seen as being a step too far, the impact of globalization on the functions of borders could not be ignored, as they became easier to negotiate and to cross. Even where the boundaries were not removed altogether, many governments cooperated with each other in the creation of trans-boundary regions, in which peoples on both sides of previously closed and sealed boundaries came together for reasons of commerce, culture, tourism and even education.

Just as the globalization discourse had a significant impact on the opening of borders, so too did the events of 9/11 and the subsequent securitization discourse have a major impact on the re-closing of many borders (Andreas and Biersteker 2003; Andreas and Snyder 2000; Laitinen 2003). The threat of global terror resulted in governments reimposing stringent management procedures aimed at preventing *undesirable* elements from crossing the border, all in the name of a potential *security threat*. Nowhere has this been more marked than in the case of the USA borders, with Mexico in the south and, more surprisingly, with Canada in the north (Andreas 2000, 2003; Ackleson 2004; Brunet-Jailly 2004a; Coleman 2004; Nevins 2002: Nicol 2005; Olmedo and Soden 2005; Purcell and Nevins 2004). It has become more difficult for people to cross the border, even for the legitimate purposes of employment and/or tourism. For the Department of Homeland Security, every one of the million Mexicans who cross in and out of the USA on a daily basis, are a potential security threat until proven otherwise. This has been accompanied by the construction of walls and fences along previously unfenced sections of the USA-Mexico border, as well as the formation of localized private militias, known as minutemen, who patrol the unpatrolled parts of the border for illegal migrants. Thus the securitization discourse is being used as a means of addressing another issue altogether, the flow of *illegal* migrants from Mexico seeking nothing more than employment and a better life in the territory of the world's economic superpower. Equally, the outer border of the expanding European Union, the Schengen border, has become transformed into the point at which entry is denied to economic migrants, while in some cases the transit camps where potential migrants are checked are located in neighbouring countries outside the territorial domain of the EU itself.

Contextually, scholars of borders in North America note the fact that during the 1980s, the main funders for border related research came from North American Free Trade Association (NAFTA) and related economic organizations, interested in making the borders easier to cross for capital, goods and people, strengthening the economic relations between the countries. But since 9/11, most of this funding has fallen away and has been replaced by agencies such as the Department of Homeland Security who are interested in the opposite question, namely how borders can be made more difficult to cross, how they can be re-closed and re-sealed as a means of preventing the movement of people and suspect goods. Thus the respective economic and securitization discourses fight it out with each other over their contrasting visions of the border as agents of national policies, one seeking to ease restrictions to strengthen American economic prosperity, the other seeking to impose more stringent restrictions as a means of strengthening American security and safety.

Both discourses serve the interests of the state but in different spheres. Although they have changed the ways in which borders are perceived by national governments, they are not absolute in the sense that borders are neither totally opening (in the 1990s) or closing (in the post 9/11 period). The opening of borders remains highly geographically differentiated, opening in some places, remaining closed and even being constructed for the first time in other places. The extent to which borders undergo functional change is contingent upon political and geographical conditions, which in turn, is mediated by the securitization turn of the past decade. It is somewhat ironic that the European colonial superimposition of borders in regions such as Africa and Asia, in which the past territorial orders were very different to European notions of territorial fixation, is now perceived by those same powers as being largely irrelevant. In the name of their superimposed borders, tribal warfare, refugee displacement and even genocide has taken place almost continuously during the past 70 years. But just as many of these states begin to come to terms with the recently imposed state territorial orders, along comes Europe and tells them that in an era of globalization and post-nationalism [*sic*] these borders are no longer relevant. In reality, contemporary Africa and Asia live with a duality of territorial orders – territorial fixation imposed by the physical borders, with tribal and nomadic movement continuing to take place within many of these countries, albeit far less across the state borders which now constitute a barrier (often a ruthless barrier) to their unhindered seasonal movement and search for pasture and economic livelihood.

Daily Life Practices: Localized Border Narratives

As some borders are removed, it does not necessarily follow that the border no longer has an impact on the daily life practices of the people residing in close proximity to the border, or that the representations of the border and its influence disappear from individual and collective memories. Even when borders exist, but their physical attributes (walls, fences, guard posts) are removed, they impact the life practices of the local inhabitants. Our understanding of this localized impact is gleaned from localized border narratives, grass roots empiricism creating the border stories and representations even where governments may argue the border has been removed and is no longer of relevance (Sidaway 2005; Wastl-Walter et al. 2002).

Until July 2007, residents of villages straddling the non-existent physical border between Northern Ireland and the independent Republic of Ireland, continued to frequent pubs and night clubs *beyond* the border where smoking was still allowed in public places until, that is, the United Kingdom (UK) also adopted the no smoking laws which had gone into effect in the Republic some years earlier. Prior to the extension of drinking hours in the UK some years earlier, residents of the North had equally walked down the road and crossed the non-existent border into the South when they desired to continue their drinking beyond the limited hours which were permitted in the UK.

Following the Six Day War in Israel/Palestine, the Israeli government announced that the Green Line boundary separating Israel from the West Bank had been removed. But for the ensuing 40 years, it continued to be an important administrative boundary, determining the citizenship of people residing on both sides of the *non-existent* line and, when necessary, constituting the point where barricades and curfews were implemented following terrorist incidents. Israeli civilian law was applicable on one side of the line, the military administration on the other. Until, that is, the line was re-established with the construction of the Separation Barrier (Fence/Wall) from 2003 onwards and the reincarnation of the Green Line boundary as the potential border for the new state of Palestine, if and when this is to occur (Newman 1993, 2009).

Travelling through and beyond the boundaries of Western Europe, travellers may be unaware that there ever was a border in these areas. But the rapid removal of all signs of the previous borders has made some governments step in and prevent the demolishing of the last border posts and fragments of fences, transforming them into attractions for American and Japanese tourists who can learn their European history through these last border relics and, at the same time, providing a commercial boost for local shops and stalls who sell souvenirs of previous borders. Dutch residents close to the border with Belgium send their children to schools beyond the *non-existent* border because, they argue, the education and the discipline is better on the *other side*. Many Danish residents of Copenhagen have now relocated their place of residence to the *other* side of the Denmark-Sweden border just across the newly constructed land bridge linking the two countries, because, they argue, taxes are lower and quality of life is higher on the *other* side of the *non-existent* boundary.

Clearly, boundaries impact daily life patterns and practices. For most people, far removed from the realms of international diplomacy and statesmanship, it is the small matters of schooling, food, taxation and drinking hours which affect them most. If the existence or formal removal of a boundary enables them to enjoy better conditions in any one of these, or many other parameters of daily life, then the border becomes an instrument through which life quality is improved. As such, the borders which may have originally been constructed as barriers between peoples and their separate spaces are now transformed into places which are manipulated for the common betterment of life, rather than disappearing altogether. The governments and local authorities on both sides of the *open* border exploit the border crossing to mutual benefit of populations on both sides, rather than remove them altogether.

Ethics and the Bordering Process

An important question on the contemporary border agenda concerns the ethics of the bordering process (Buchanan and Moore 2003; van Houtum and van Naerssen 2002). This relates back to the question of power relations, although the focus here does not concern those who create the boundaries but rather those who are impacted by the establishment of borders. The restriction of movement, the nature of the management and detention process at the border and the ways in which some are allowed to enter and others are prevented from crossing the border, raise significant questions of ethics and human rights. As border management becomes more stringent than in the past, due to the securitization imperatives, so too many potential border crossers are treated more harshly. Not only are their documents checked more thoroughly, but they are often subject to increased body searches, are held in holding rooms or cells for longer periods of time and may even be subject to various x-ray and/or dog sniffing mechanisms.

The question discussed above: 'In whose interests are borders created, and by whom?' does not deal with the question 'do we have the right to create borders which, by definition, make movement more difficult?' It runs counter to modern and post-modernist understandings of a free world, in which people have the basic right to move, to have freedom of employment and residence, as long as they do not threaten the physical well being of their new co-habitants and neighbours. The securitization discourse is an excuse for the closing of borders, but this does not mean that the resultant closing, even sealing, of the borders is morally right.

This is even more problematic in cases where borders constitute the barriers which prevent people from reaching health care facilities, or from visiting their families and loved ones. Using borders as means of entry prevention is bad enough, while using borders as a means of preventing exit from a place of origin is even worse. In such cases, borders constitute the equivalent of the walls of the prison, a situation which may be decreasing in a globalized world but has by no means disappeared altogether. There remain plenty of regimes which prevent their citizens from leaving their country, and this is separate from the question of whether these same people would be successful in crossing the borders into a new place of destination.

The most blatant examples of exit prevention are those places where physical fences and walls continue to be constructed. The Separation Barrier which has been constructed between Israel and the West Bank may serve a securitization objective (the prevention of suicide bombers) but it has caused much hardship for innocent civilians whose daily life patterns have suffered severe dislocation. Prior to the construction of this barrier, the walls and fences in Germany (finally removed in 1990), Cyprus, Korea and, more recently, along parts of the USA-Mexico border create a sense of invisibility and threat which go far beyond any legitimate political or security objectives, enabling states to manage these borders in such a way as to question the basic values and ethics of a supposedly more humane world. Achieving the right balance between the legitimate needs of the state in defending its population, and the extent to which this justifies the negation of the human rights of innocent civilians, has become increasingly complex in the post 9/11 era, where notions of securitization have become the keyword to justify actions on the part of the state, actions which were assumed to have disappeared from the Western World in the utopianized era of globalized and borderless [sic] worlds.

Concluding Comments: Is There a Single Model for the Study of Borders?

Is it possible to combine the notions of borders discussed in this chapter into a single model or theory of borders? Perhaps borders are too diverse and varied for a single model to be applied, not least given the vastly different empirical understandings of what constitutes a border as perceived by an anthropologist, a geographer or an expert in International Relations, respectively (Brunet-Jailly 2004b, 2005; Kolossov 2005; Newman 2003, 2006b; Paasi 2005; van Houtum 2005). Notwithstanding, this chapter has highlighted a number of common themes which would appear to be applicable to most, if not all, understandings of borders, especially when the focus is shifted from the physical dimension or location of the border to an analysis of the dynamics and functionality of the bordering process.

All borders either create or reflect difference, be they spatial categories or cultural affiliations and identities. All borders are initially constructed as a means through which groups – be they states, religions or social classes – can be ordered, hierarchized, managed and controlled by power elites. It is the latter who determine the demarcation and delimitation criteria for the construction and the perpetuation of the border as an institution which is strongly linked in with the agencies of power. There will always be groups and individuals who desire to cross the border, either as a means of escaping the category (social or spatial) in which he/she are located, and/or because he/she believes that the grass is always greener on the other side of the border. Transition zones, frontiers and borderland spaces exist in close proximity to all types of border, in some cases creating a trans-boundary zone of meeting, interaction and hybridity in and around open and porous borders, while in other cases emphasizing the differences which exist on either side of sealed or closed borders. This ties in with the fact that most borders, by their very definition, create binary distinctions between the *here* and *there*, the *us* and *them*, the *included* and the *excluded*.

In this sense, there are common themes which are relevant to all types of border, even if this does not constitute a single model or theory in its own right. Social scientists have much to contribute to our understanding of these border dynamics, taking them beyond the limited understandings which are limited to a single academic discipline, by virtue of their inability, or lack of willingness, to cross their own professional borders which separate one discipline form the other. An important step in this respect is the creation of a common language, or glossary of terms, which are recognizable by border scholars, regardless of their specific compartmentalized discipline. Some of this common language has been created during a decade of intensive border research and inter-disciplinary workshops, although it remains to be seen whether this has created any meaningful common discourse over and beyond the physical meeting in the transition or frontier zone between disciplines.

References

Ackleson, J. (2004), 'Constructing security on the U.S.-Mexico border', *Political Geography* 24:2, 165-84.

Anderson, J. and O'Dowd, L. (1999), 'Borders, border regions and territoriality: Contradictory meanings, changing significance', *Regional Studies* 33:7, 593-604.

Anderson, J., O'Dowd, L. and Wilson, T. (2002), 'Why study borders now? New borders for a changing Europe: Cross border cooperation and governance', *Regional and Federal Studies* 12:4, 1-13.

Andreas, P. (2003), 'Redrawing the line: Border security in the twenty-first century', *International Security* 28:2, 78-111.

Andreas, P. (2000), *Border games: Policing the U.S.-Mexico Divide* (New York: Cornell University Press).

Andreas, P. and Biersteker, T. (2003), *The rebordering of North America* (New York: Routledge).

Andreas, P. and Snyder, T. (eds.)(2000), *The Wall Around the West: State Borders and Immigration Controls in North America and Europe* (Oxford: Rowman & Littlefield).

Berg, E. and Ehin, P. (2006), 'What kind of border regime is in the making? Towards a differentiated and uneven border strategy', *Cooperation and Conflict* 41:1, 53-71.

Blake, G. (2000a), 'State limits in the early twenty-first century: observations on form and function', *Geopolitics* 5:1, 1-18.

Blake, G. (2000b), 'Borderlands under stress: some global perspectives', in Pratt, M. and Brown, J. (eds.), *Borderlands Under Stress* (London: Kluwer Law International), 1-16.

Blatter, J. and Norris, C. (eds.)(2001), 'Cross border cooperation in Europe', *Journal of Borderland Studies* 15:1, 13-15.

Brunet-Jailly, E. (2005), 'Theorizing borders: An Interdisciplinary perspective', *Geopolitics* 10:4, 633-49.

Brunet-Jailly, E. (2004a), 'NAFTA, economic integration and the Canadian-American security regime in the post-September 11 era', *Journal of Borderland Studies* 19:1, 71-93.

Brunet-Jailly, E. (2004b), 'Toward a model of border studies', *Journal of Borderland Studies* 19:1, 1-18.

Buchanan, A. and Moore, M. (2003), *States, Nations and Borders: The Ethics of Making Boundaries* (Cambridge: Cambridge University Press).

Coleman, M. (2004), 'U.S. statecraft and the U.S.-Mexico border as security/economy nexus', *Political Geography* 24:2, 185-209.

Dittgen, H. (2000), 'The end of the nation state? Borders in an age of globalization', in Pratt, M. and Brown, J. (eds.), *Borderlands Under Stress* (London: Kluwer Law International), 49-68.

Hartshorne, R. (1936), 'Suggestions on the terminology of political boundaries', *Annals of the Association of American Geographers* 26:1, 56-7.

Hudson, A. (1998), 'Beyond the borders: Globalization, sovereignty and extra-territoriality', *Geopolitics* 3:1, 89-105.

Jones, S. (1959), 'Boundary concepts in setting time and space', *Annals of the Association of American Geographers* 49, 241-55.

Jones, S. (1943), 'The description of international boundaries', *Annals of the Association of American Geographers* 33, 99-117.

Kolossov, V. (2005), 'Border studies: changing perspectives and theoretical approaches', *Geopolitics* 10:4, 606-32.

Kolossov, V. and O'Loughlin, J. (1998), 'New borders for new world orders: territorialities at the fin de siecle', *Geojournal* 44:3, 259-73.

Laitinen, K. (2003), 'Post-Cold War security borders: A conceptual approach', in Berg, E. and van Houtum, H. (eds.), *Routing Borders Between Territories, Discourse and Practices* (Aldershot: Ashgate), 13-34.

Martinez, O. (1994), 'The dynamics of border interaction: new approaches to border analysis', in Schofield, C. (ed.), *Global Boundaries: World Boundaries 1* (London and New York: Routledge), 1-15.

Minghi, J.V. (1991), 'From conflict to harmony in border landscapes', in Rumley, D. and Minghi, J.V. (eds.), *The geography of border landscapes* (London: Routledge), 15-30.

Minghi, J.V. (1963), 'Boundary studies in political geography', *Annals of the Association of American Geographers* 53, 407-28.

Nevins, J. (2002), *Operation Gatekeeper: The Rise of the 'Illegal Alien' and the Making of the U.S.-Mexico Boundary* (London: Routledge).

Newman, D. (2009), 'The Green Line and the Separation Fence: Oddly shaped boundaries for Israel/Palestine', in Diener, A. and Hagen, J. (eds.), *Border Lines: Stories of Odd Borders and Contemporary Dilemmas in World Politics* (New York: Rowman & Littlefield).

Newman, D. (2006a), 'The lines that continue to separate us: Borders in our borderless world', *Progress in Human Geography* 30:2, 1-19.

Newman, D. (2006b), 'Borders and bordering: towards an interdisciplinary dialogue', *European Journal of Social Theory* 9:2, 171-86.

Newman, D. (2004), 'Conflict at the interface: the impact of boundaries and borders on contemporary ethno-national conflict', in Flint, C. (ed.), *Geographies of War and Conflict* (Oxford: Oxford University Press), 321-45.

Newman, D. (2003), 'On Borders and Power: A Theoretical Framework', *Journal of Borderland Studies* 18:1, 13-24.

Newman, D. (1993), 'The functional presence of an "erased" boundary: the re-emergence of the "green line"', in Schofield, C.H. and Schofield, R.N. (eds.), *World Boundaries: The Middle East and North Africa* (London: Routledge), 71-98.

Newman, D. and Paasi, A. (1998), 'Fences and neighbours in the post-modern world: boundary narratives in political geography', *Progress in Human Geography* 22:2, 186-207.

Nicol, H. (2005), 'Resiliency or change? The contemporary Canada-US border', *Geopolitics* 10:4, 767-90.

Ohmae, K. (1990), *The Borderless World* (New York: Harper Collins).

Olmedo, C. and Soden, D. (2005), 'Terrorism's role in re-shaping border crossings: September eleventh and the U.S. borders', *Geopolitics* 10:4, 741-66.

Paasi, A. (2005), 'Generations and the development of border studies', *Geopolitics* 10:4, 297-325.

Paasi, A. (1998), 'Boundaries as social processes: territoriality in the world of flows', *Geopolitics* 3:1, 69-88.

Pavlakovich-Kochi, V., Morehouse, B., and Wastl-Walter, D. (eds.)(2004), *Challenged Borderlands: Transcending Political and Cultural Boundaries* (Aldershot: Ashgate).

Perkmann, M. (1999), 'Building governance institutions across European borders', *Regional Studies* 33:7, 657-67.

Perkmann, M. and Sum, N.-L. (eds.)(2002), *Globalization, Regionalization and Cross-border Regions* (Houndmills: Palgrave).

Prescott, V. (1987), *Political Frontiers and Boundaries* (Chicago: Aldine).

Purcell, M. and Nevins, J. (2004), 'Pushing the boundary: State restructuring, state theory, and the case of U.S. – Mexico border enforcement in the 1990s', *Political Geography* 24:2, 211-35.

Shapiro, M.J. and Alker, H.R. (eds.)(1996), *Challenging Boundaries: Global Flows, Territorial Identities* (Minneapolis: University of Minnesota Press).

Sidaway, J. (2005), 'The poetry of boundaries: reflections from the Spanish-Portugese borderlands', in van Houtum, H., Kramsch, O. and Zierhoffer, W. (eds.), *B/ordering Space* (Aldershot: Ashgate), 189-206.

Toal, G. (1999), 'Borderless worlds: Problematising discourses of deterritorialization in global finance and digital culture', *Geopolitics* 4:2, 139-54.

van Houtum, H. (2005), 'The changing geopolitics of borders and boundaries', *Geopolitics* 10:4, 672-9.

van Houtum, H. and van Naerssen, T. (2002), 'Bordering, ordering and othering', *Tijdschrift voor Economische en Sociale Geografie* 93:2, 125-36.

Wastl-Walter, D., Varadi, M. and Veider, F. (2002), 'Bordering silence: Border narratives from the Austro-Hungarian border', in Meinhof, U. (ed.), *Living (with) border: Identity discourses on East-West borders in Europe* (Aldershot: Ashgate), 75-94.

Yeung, H. (1998), 'Capital, state and space: Contesting the borderless world', *Transactions of the Institute of British Geographers* 23:3, 291-310.

The Mask of the Border

Henk van Houtum

Introduction

Infinity is the original fact. What has to be explained is the source of the finite.
(Nietzsche, my translation)

From my home in Nijmegen it is about a quarter of an hour by bike to Germany. The perception of that time travel in this borderland is very special, because I not only leave Nijmegen, I leave the Netherlands. It is hence a bicycle tour 'abroad', to a foreign country. In perception however, Germany lies much further away than a quarter of an hour. The one day trip feels like the beginning of a holiday. Physically, the border is not obviously present. A sign with *'Willkommen in Deutschland'*, an old, expired customs office, an artistic border monument and an occasional police van, these are the physical remnants of the political border. What dominates in this inner borderland of the European Union is the void, the disappearance. The vagueness of the morphological border may be striking, yet this is not to say that the border actually disappeared. The border is not present, yet it is not absent. Maybe imperceptible to the untrained eye, but vividly present and mentally powerful, there is still a border between the Netherlands and Germany. Once one has crossed the border, one does *de jure* and *de facto* enter another country. Crossing a border makes one from a human from the interior into a human from the exterior, a foreigner, someone from them over there. The opening-not-disappearance of borders in the European Union after 1993, it is clear that the border in the European Union, is still filled with meaning, and internalized in everyday practices, institutions, conventions, acts and mentalities. It is clear that this certainly holds for borders that are not as open as is the case of the European Union. Hence, it is safe to say that despite a strong rhetoric of global world, as we saw in the '90s, borders continue to play a persistent part of the daily lives of human beings. This contribution deals with the question why and how in general borders are socially produced and/or reproduced Why do we border ourselves and at with what gains and at what price for ourselves and others? And if we do accept that borders are indeed human constructs, does that mean that it is possible to reconstruct the border, to give it another meaning? I will argue that the void of the border in terms of its morphological absence should not be interpreted as a symbolic void. The borderland may be emptied of the border proper; the head of the borderlander is not emptied. Although indeed the heads may be full, and some may be more full (of themselves) than others, this does not mean that the function and mentality that we still implicitly attach to borders, even if these have been opened as is the case in the European Union, could not be deconstructed and reconsidered ontologically. It is that deconstruction which opens the way for a new dynamism in this time and age, in order to make it possible to ontologically reinterpret this persistent phenomenon called the border.

A border is a verb

Let no one who cannot think geometrically enter.
(Inscription at the door of the Platonic Academy)

When people talk about territorial boundaries, often first attention is given to their physical appearances. That which is most visible is given the most attention. Admittedly, heavy armed border guards or a high stone wall does catch one's eye. But there is no ur-border in terms of its morphological appearance. A barbed wire, a wall, a gate, a door, a barrier, a line on the map, a river, a line in the sand, it can all be borders. A border has no original model, it is a simulation of a model. It is as the French philosopher Baudrillard would argue, a simulacrum, a manifestation of a copy, but with its own reality. That reality of the border then is created by the meaning that is attached to it. A line in the sand is not always a limit, as well as a border is not always a line in the sand. A line is geometry, a border is interpretation. The objective form of the border does not necessarily equal the influence of the border. Obviously, the Berlin Wall was more difficult to cross by foot, car or bike than an average linguistic border, but the influence of the material reality of the border is independent of the force and interpretation of the border. A door may be a border for some and a passage for others. And a wall may be a 'protection' against the pernicious influence of others behind that wall for some and to others mostly a place to spray graffiti on. A border can spatially be drawn everywhere. It is the symbolic meaning attributed to the appearance of the line which must be seen as constructor of the normative form. A border should thus be more broadly interpreted than as an object alone. A limited perspective of the border as a line or object, often leads to the often heard, but unfounded claim that we live in a global village, borderless or flat world in which borders no longer matter. What is important to the study of the ontology of borders is hence not the item of the border per se, but the objectification process of the border, the socially constituent power practices attached to a border that construct a spatial effect and which give a demarcation in space its meaning and influence.

A border is not a military defence alone. To create a border is essentially the creation of an Innerspace of reflection, a narcissian centripetal orientation, a truth in which one can find pleasure and ease. Drawing borders, the making of a nation, is as philosopher Sloterdijk has recently argued in his book Spheres, the making of a national self-portrait. This act of mirroring is a continual space-fixing process which according to philosopher Zygmunt Bauman gives the *impression* as if it is a physically identifiable entity with objective and unchangeable borders. No border is built for a short term, a border is built for eternity. Knowing at the same time that there is no border in history that has not disappeared, the creation of a border is hence, as philosopher Peter Sloterdijk argues in Spheres, precisely this, a big NO against the death of the nation. It is a testament of the desired eternal life. The border gate as a gate to heaven on earth. The Law of the territorial border is a faith, a belief. A border is an ideology that is believed in, with the walls acting as the fundament of the own temple. It is a belief in the presence and continuity of a spatial binding power, which is objectified in our everyday social practices. The spatial separation that a border represents is goal and means at the same time. The power of this belief is determined by the interpretations and consequential (violent) power practices of those who construct and help to reproduce the border. The border makes and is made. Hence, a border is a verb. As argued together in an article with Ton van Naerssen in 2002, we should speak of border*ing* (van Houtum and van Naerssen 2002). This active and vigorous understanding of the ontology of a border leads to an ambiguous picture of the supposedly limitless world. It could be argued that the stronger ideologically is believed in the utility and importance of the protection of what is seen as own, the greater the difference is made by the border.

A border is a fabricated truth

> *I have kept in mind the idea that the earth is in effect one world, in which empty, uninhabited spaces virtually do not exist. Just as none of us is outside geography, none of us is completely free from the struggle over geography. That struggle is complex and interesting because it is not only about soldiers and cannons but also about ideas, about forms, about images and imaginings.*
> (Said 1993, 7)

A border can serve the interests of a territorial power, a gang, a democratically elected political representation, an academic discipline, a self. The list of border makers is endless. Common to the border makers is that the practice of the border making, of *bordering*, confirms and maintains a space, a locus and focus of control. The world outside the domain-making border will be instrumentalized by representing it symbolically as a foreign country, the competitor, the enemy, the other, or chaos, against which the unique consistent and uniform cultural identity and tradition of the own unity will be mirrored. In so doing, a window on the world is represented, an invented reality, an appealing truth. For many, what they see as their border, however defined and wherever drawn, is the start as well as consequential culmination of the image we have of the world. In mirroring the world, most classically, maps are used that depict and aim to represent the power division. We have travelled a long way since the first maps of the world and the first borders were drawn and published. Yet, still, an average map is used and seen as cartographically ordered power-logic with lines and colours and points that delineate the borders of territorial-differential sovereignties. Rather than a process of discovering truth, a border as well the map that represents it, is making truth. A map not only re-presents the world, it also is productive, it fabricates an image, a lens on the world. It serves the geo-political goal that a state is imagined and believed to be different and distinct from other cities. Using a map for political purposes is what could be called carto-politics, drawing-table politics. A map of a border is therefore *active*: it represents space which facilitates its domination and control, it communicates a truth, it actively *constructs* knowledge, it silences the unrepresented, it exercises power and a map can be a powerful means of promoting social change. As Harley (1989) argues, it is no wonder that in modern Western society maps quickly became crucial to the maintenance of state power – to its boundaries, to its commerce, or its internal administration, to control of populations, and to its military strength. Mapping soon became the business of the State. Yet, the making or adjusting of borderlines and dots on a map, how good its intentions may be, border and orders not only spaces but also people. And where borderlines and dots become dominant, people are erased. Hence, carto-politics in its core is cartographic cleansing. It consciously silences what is not represented and it dehumanizes the landscape. The signifier of the map is not the world as we know it, the signified, as philosopher Foucault already argued discussing the work of the surrealist painter René Magritte (ceci n'est pas une pipe). The map of a border is *sur-real, it is not a border*. What a map of a border creates is a gap, a difference. Representing is making a difference. It is a image of reality, a truth outside truth itself. The border represented on a map colonizes the free and constantly ontologically reinterpreted space that truth necessarily is. The border demarcates, represents and communicates truth, but it is thereby not truth itself. The consequence is that a border, just like the map of it, is inescapably a fabricated truth. Borders are the construction of a reality and truth in a certain context, and in certain spatial entity. What is seen as truth in one domain can be a lie in the space and/or eyes of an other. And what conventional reality is in the own domain can be a doomed image or fantasy in the domains and/or eyes of the other.

To illustrate the above, the Netherlands exists because the highly engineered and constantly redefined and reinvented truth is believed that a private domain called the Netherlands exists, that is uniquely different and can be rightfully disentangled and separated from other countries. The space with the name the Netherlands is seen as jointly owned. Foreigners are seen as guests, aliens, strangers, visitors, tourists, migrants, or foreigners, in any case as people originally not from here. What original means and to which imagined unity in the past it refers to, nobody precisely knows in this context, but it is clear that they are not Dutch. These non-Dutch must ask for permission to enter this domain called the Netherlands, as if a country was a house in which one united family would live. In the case they wish to stay longer than we had originally allowed for, they must ask for our permission to do so, as if this imaginatively separated country was a club with membership cards and privileges. The Netherlands thus makes a difference in space. It marks and demarcates a threshold, a gated house, and membership in space. It politicizes space. Famously, Benedict Anderson speaks not in terms of family or a club but of an imagined community (Anderson 1991). The idea here is that we can not all know our fellow citizens, but we believe and narrate to each other that we have something in common.

In the attempt to give meaning to the national identity, nations often define themselves in comparison with the immediate neighbour-landers but also increasingly with people from abroad. To illustrate, in the narration, reinvention and redemarcation of Dutch symbols, maps and citizenship rights, it is typically imagined that fellow Dutchmen are different and better than the non-Dutch. One of the most favourite others for the Dutchman was until recently the big neighbour, the Germans, the post-World War II followers of the Belgians, who were the big other before during and after the Belgian-Dutch war. Today, after the terrorist attacks in the US and the consequent War on Terror that was launched in 2001, and the consequent advent of right-wing populist politicians like Pim Fortuyn and Geert Wilders, increasingly, the *allochtoon* (he/she who comes from another (*allos*) ground (*chtonos*) has taken over the role of the other. The *allochtoon* is thereby often reduced to the Muslim. The Dutchman does not want to be German, nor Belgian, nor *allochtoon*, but what the 'Dutchman' then is remains unclear. Precisely because national identity is not something that one can hold in one's hands, imagined as it is, the Dutchman is being reinvented everyday. The national political rhetoric and strongly nationally oriented focus of the printed media help to ordering and anchoring a belief in the Netherlands as *our* own historical land and *our* own destiny. Through the use of both symbolic unifiers (flags, hymn, number plates, signs) and educational unifiers (language, geography and history education) the Dutch border is daily reproduced in space. Especially, national politicians, elected to represent the own nation, do not seldom consciously invoke the national pride and identification. The promotion of national identification is mostly done from the perspective of social bonding and cohesion. In international perspective usually the desired image and international aspiration to be an important country plays an important motivation. In doing so, national politicians explicitly stress the vision of the Netherlands as one community, as a 'we' and 'here'. As such, national borders are being reproduced and reconstructed on a daily basis.

One of the most striking forms of the manifestations of the Dutch bordering and ordering of a place and identity in space is the admission policy with regard to foreigners. The Netherlands admits immigrants for a period longer than three months (the time period of the tourist via) only if their presence serves an essential Dutch interest, if they are entitled to live here under an international agreement (such as Family Reunion), or if there are compelling humanitarian reasons for admitting them (asylum). In practice this means that foreigners who do not belong to the highly welcome group who are of direct Dutch essential interest (such as investors, entrepreneurs and high-skilled labour) and are entering the Netherlands only get a residence permission to stay for longer than three months after they have been 'appropriated' by the state of the Netherlands. That is, after they have learned basic Dutch and have accepted the norms and values of Dutch society. All this is tested preferably before they are allowed to come, in a civic integration examination. If a foreigner wishes to acquire more than just a residence permit and also wants to become 'truly' Dutch, he/she will have to go a 'naturalization' process (*nomen est omen*). To be naturalized means that one gets the same status as a person who is born 'naturally' in the Netherlands. The nation therefore is in its wording still seen in terms of blood and soil. To be born in the nation (nation comes from naissance, birth), is still seen as *natural*. All this is at a price obviously, which is an extra effectual border. The exam, a visa, or a residence permit, or the naturalization process will soon already cost a foreigner a few hundred euros, or more depending on what precisely he/she wants/needs. Foreigners who wish to become 'naturally' Dutch often first have to strip off, have to lose, their old 'natural' nationality, they have to become naked again as it were, like with a real birth. After this, if he/she complies to the criteria that are set out to become a natural Dutch, such as he/she is already legally in the Netherlands for five years, is well integrated in Dutch society and has a residence permit, he/she will be appropriated by the Dutch state and will be given the status in a naturalization ceremony. The foreigner is then 'born again' as a Dutch citizen.

The national mask

From a totally different perspective also international football is an important as well as beloved signifier and producer of national borders and national identities. In a time in which the football industry is heavily determined by commercial and media interests that do not respect national borders, and the international labour market for football players is increasingly becoming a normal labour market without exploitation and slavery, a competition based on national representation is a strikingly archaic phenomenon. It is still seen, by many, as an honour to represent the nation on an international championship. Sports, and especially football, that battle between players from two nations on a green field, has become a simulation of the heroic symbolism that used to be attributed to fights on that ur-battlefield, the war field. The fight for the national honour, the taste of the sweet sensation of a victory and the bitter drama of a lost match all have become more important in football over the last decades, not less. The symbolism and semiotics, although usually fortunately with a carnivalesque intention, gives the individual supporter a feeling of togetherness, of solidarity, of a common and just cause and community. The Dutch are by no means an exception to the rule of the growing patriotic circus that international football games have become (van Houtum and van Dam 2002). Yet, largely due to the missing of the feeling of a historical shame when it comes to nationalism, such as in Germany, Austria or Belgium, and probably because of the possibility to be proud of and be internationally recognized as a small country in a sports that is so widely played, the Dutch nationalism, the 'Orange feeling', is remarkably strong and vivid. Be that as it may be, the extravagant and ecstatic enthusiasm with which people dress up as the stereotypical national icons and colour their hairs and paint their faces with the national colours, this seemingly unquestioned moral conformism to represent and perform the nation, never stops to amaze me every time a new international football match, let alone championship, is beginning.

In a sense, the metaphorical carnivalesque Orange mask that Dutch people put on during international football games and championships on a massive scale, is not an exception, but a magnification. We increasingly live in the time of the mask. Quite literarily, cities, regions and nations nowadays mask and brand themselves with slogans and fitting flags and emblems that mean to showcase the city as unique and attractive. In the imagined rat race between cities, regions and nations it is apparently more important how the own territorial domain is marketed and showcased than what the actual contents is behind the slogan and the branding. The exterior, the shape is becoming more important: the mask of the own identity. The Dutch Orange mask that Dutch people metaphorically put on during every international championship, fits in this trend of wishing to outcompete the other and showing the branded, stereotypical image of ourselves to each others. It is striking that we play along with this national masked ball so obediently. The Dutch philosopher Erasmus wrote in his joyful and mockery 'Lof der Zotheid' (In Praise of Folly) that foolishness works as a fantasy that softens the pain of the everyday life. The mask covers the emptiness, the void, the eternal shortage in us, the Nothingness. The mask gives a sense of belonging, a sense of rootedness; it gives one a face in the crowd. In this context it is illustrative perhaps that today's word 'person' is derived from the Latin persona, which means mask.

If masks become dominant, then a city or a nation becomes a theatre, a spectacle that is exploited politically and commercially and which is full of nothing. To use the words of a play of Shakespeare, it becomes Much Ado about Nothing.

In the international football arena of today, the players are well paid club actors and the coaches their temporary 'entertrainers'. When playing for the national team, they perform, they act nationality. The nation itself is increasingly becoming a dated one-dimensional mask of a multi-layered multiplicity of identities and club interests. Increasingly, players and coaches are born somewhere else than the nation they represent. At the last European Championships in Austria/Switzerland there were 16 national teams playing to each other, but the players were of in total 33 nationalities. A coach like Guus Hiddink, a hero and example for many, has become a national marionette as no other coach. He has coached teams of the Netherlands, Australia, South-Korea, Russia and currently Turkey. He wears the national mask of the team and plays the patriot of the team that hires him, no matter what flag he has to plea allegiance to and what national hymn he has to sing. Also the spectators of the international championships increasingly play multiple roles. Instead of being only spectators, they have become actors themselves as well. As argued above, they dress up in the national colours and put on the mask of the nation and in doing so, they are also co-producing the national theatre as mercenaries of the nation. But this spectacle of the national theatre cannot disguise that the desire will last. Because the desire of he/she who puts on the mask of the collective is never fulfilled. Wishing to reach that imagined and utopian ecstatic endpoint, at which we all would be proud collectively of the boys on the field, is addictive and endless. There will always be a next match. The void cannot be filled forever.

Self-repression

The examples of the immigration policies and national football games explained above exemplify that a national border is a symbolic demarcation of an appropriated space, an imagined Truth, that carries its own name and that is being reproduced symbolically, semiotically and formally every day in time and space. The question that becomes pertinent then is the following. If the national border is intrinsically and inescapably an imagined or fabricated truth, why do we believe in this fantasy? Because demarcating and symbolic reproduction of the border can only be successful if those who are subject of these strategic border (re)productions also have an interest (see also Foucault 2007). So the border must be believed as a truth. But why would people who live in a certain land on the globe, where the political borders of that land are neither natural nor self-evident and where the political borders have been established by unpredictable historical coincidences, believe in the self-evident truth of these borders (see also Fromm 1942)? Especially because as I have shown above, social construction of a national identity is also social self-repression. Why do people tend to be self-repressive? Identification with a social environment and a community, and to call that our own, apparently gives an important sense of value of oneself. Even though it is often realized that the nation is an imagined community, a fantasy of the collective, it is still seen as a necessary one. The self gains a collective value, the personal identity becomes part of a national identity. One becomes part of a powerful and meaningful national narrative; one gains a national belonging, a membership in the socios. Through the nation, the self gets a roof above its head, the roof of the national house that is constructed and maintained by a community of which the self is one. The fact that this national identity that is constructed is of a collective makership, for many it is only furthering the importance of the self, since he/she is a co-constructor, a co-maker, which is seen as a meaningful function. In addition to the feeling of being part of meaningful collective and having co-makership in the collective outcome and direction of the common narrative, constructing and demarcating a spatial unity feeds into the desire to have spatial beacons and priorities in daily life. To demarcate a border is in fact saying: keep your distance. A border is a distance. A national border creates a distance with the world outside. It creates a national home, a refuge with doors that can be closed. To take refuge, to take shelter behind a collectively constructed window on the world that produces a collective frame and view on the world, a distance is created to what is outside the shelter, that which is exterior, foreign. The other that is herewith constructed is constitutive for the own identity. One recognizes oneself best in the reflection of the eyes of the other. This b/ordering of worldview and identity potentially gives one ease, comfort and security. This may help to explain why in this age of globalization, shifting borders and migration, there is so much longing to nostalgia for the imagined loss of shared values and norms, and why there is so much emphasis on the control and protection of borders. To many, the openness feels as an intruder. It clouds and troubles the comfortable mental b/ordering of the world and with the imagined purity of the own (com)unity. Helping to uphold the borders of the nation – be it in active terms such as the reporting of co-arresting of unwanted border crossers by some American civilian groupings in the borderland of Mexico-United States, the fanatical cheering of the national football team – or in more passive terms such as the accepting of restrictive border controls or the accepting of civic integration examinations for immigrants – maintains the national ordering and purification. By definition, borders are partial, selective and opportunistic, in their representation as well as in the interests that they wish to serve. Borders close in some areas and some people and exclude other areas and people. The ordering and purification of the own space and own identity works as a drug. The constitution of a shared space, with a shared narrative, and fantasy, a shared truth create an immediate satisfaction, it masks and covers the void, the emptiness in us for a short time, but the consequence is a long-term desire for new appropriation and control of the own truth when this truth is perceived to be threatened. The desire, the wish for the (comm)unity of tomorrow, the dream of the national utopia is never-ending.

The price of the fabricated truth

What are your lines? What map are you in the process of making or rearranging? What abstract line will you draw, and at what price, for yourself and for others? (Deleuze and Guattari 1988, 203)

The drug that is the nation has a price. Addiction to the own unity can be threatening to others. At this moment, the EU is very active in intercepting those people who wish to get to the continent without papers. Non-EU travellers without a residence permit or those who stay here without the proper papers will be expelled or deported. Over the last decade or so, many migrants have died on their way to the EU. It has become abundantly clear even in the case of the often praised so called soft power and benevolent union that the price of exclusion can be extremely high. What makes this even more macabre is that the selfishness of the collective that is the EU is legitimized by the capitalistic logic that has been implemented politically. Serving the private interest has become a public task. Controlling the borders is thus largely serving a commercial interest: comfort. Borders therefore are not only relative in the sense that they reflect and constitute the other, but they are also moral. The maintenance of borders can uphold comfort, preserve a self-productive ease and maintain the narrative of certainty and the just order, but a national border can also be immoral against those who are excluded. Making a domain exclusive, brilliant, a brandable shining precious diamante for the included, also implies an exclusion of those who are believed or narrated to make the own order dirty, filthy or less valuable. Who this other is, who is defined to be a 'barbarian' to the civilized world is decided and narrated by every b/ordered 'civilization' differently. As explained above, an important group of non-natives in the Netherlands are the Germans. But these non-native inhabitants of the Netherlands, these *allochtonen*, are almost totally neglected in the debate on immigrants in the Netherlands. The Germans are still seen as a 'favourite enemy' that the Dutch like to beat especially in football or economic competition, but the politicization of enmity and fear is now focused on the Muslim. Here not the spirit of a sportive battle is politicized, but a kind of *'Unheimlichkeit'*, a fear to lose the own identity, and to lose the control over the own space and undividedness. This is a fear that touches upon the existence itself, a fear for the void in oneself, for the missing of the difference, a fear for open space, a space without a refuge, a borderless world. This existential fear for some migrants reaffirms old or produces new borders. Some even incline to close the borders totally for these new 'barbarians'. But borders are not like eyes that can be shut. The other, however defined and targeted, is necessary for the constitution of the own order and identity. The reflection in the eyes of the other through which one can identify oneself, can only be done with open eyes. By closing the borders, closing the eyes, the fear for the other will not be shut off. The uncertainty will only be greater. With eyes closed, the other will become a fantasy, a ghost, a monster, an invader, an illusion reigned by distrust. Not the forest outside is fearful, but the stories that is told about it. It is the border of the forest that as an entrance to another world – a world of the darkness, the chaos, the wild, the barbaric – is cultivated and reproduced by the stories about it. Hence, a border may be a necessary distance, but to distantiate the world outside does not only produce comfort and ease. The stronger the border is closed, the more imaginary and whimsical the stories and the larger the unease and uncertainty. A closed community with closed borders in the end does not trust a single strange element. Increasingly, this fear together with ongoing process of globalization has lead to a radical diffusion of borders. The border, once a territory's beginning and end, has crawled and crept itself into many spaces and has taken many forms, such as the borders of and in airports, detention centres, and camps. In addition, increasingly, our eyes and fingerprints are scanned and our bodily movements in public space traced and tracked (see also van Houtum, 2010a). Our bodies have become the passports and maps that we carry. So, as Freud already has argued, paradoxically, a severe border control and self-repression, goes together with heavy sacrifices in terms of personal freedom. Hence, the paradoxical result is that the strong border believers have become trapped in a spatial matrix of codes of their desire of and plea for more comfort, security and freedom for themselves.

The Janus face of the border

> *...everything was on the lines, between the lines, in the AND that made one and the other imperceptible, without disjunction or conjunction but only a line of flight forever in the process of being drawn, toward a new acceptance, the opposite of renunciation or resignation- a new happiness?* (Deleuze and Guattari 1988, 206-7)

A socially constructed border is a form and manifestation of self-repression. It suppresses the total potential of personal mobility and freedom by constructing a sphere of trust inside and a fear for what is out there, beyond the self-defined border. Yet, at the same, the world outside that is constructed by a border also expresses a desire, a wish, the longing to be somewhere else (see also van Houtum 2010b). It is the desire to experience and live the personal freedom despite or thanks to the fear for the unknown, the non-routine. That is the desire to turn to the other, the desire to cross the line. The unknown, the stories about the exotic and the mythical, the adventure, the wild or the culturally different, can work like the Siren song on our ears. A border therefore also reflects liberty, the desire to de-border oneself, to become stranger oneself. The desire to leave behind what is familiar, to close the door behind, to turn the key and to leave – into the world, or in the words of philosopher Rudi Visker – to become strange and to stay strange (Visker 2005).

A border is hence much more than a protection wall behind which one hides or takes refuge. It is also a threshold to an other world. The border is a Janus face, named after the Roman God Janus of the end and the beginning, of the passage, of the guard between upperworld and underworld. Janus has two faces, the centripetal, inward oriented and the centrifugal, the outward oriented face. The desire to escape from one's home, one's self, to de-appropriate one's home and one's self, is of all ages and has many shapes. The most well-known is of course holiday, vacation, that expresses a desire to stay and be home away from home in the land of the other for a few weeks, to be a stranger oneself for a few weeks. Some people wish to be a stranger longer and buy a second home in the land or the place of the other. Others decide to migrate for ever and to exchange one's own house and home for the house and home in the land of the other. Whether with that the desire to be a stranger sometimes, to long for the other side stops, remains dubious.

Border(e)scape

> *Are we certain enough to love without the right to possession? Need we always divorce when we turned our eyes? Would our trust allow us to be waves, rising and falling, rolling up the sand and seeping back, leaving moments of patterns...?* (Reichert 1992)

If the border is on the one hand indeed a fabricated truth, an art of self-repression and on the other hand a departing means to lose oneself, the art of self-denial, where do we position ourselves on this Janus-continuum (see also van Houtum 2010b)? Do we dare to de-border ourselves, do we dare to embrace the untamed freedom but with preservation of certainty, comfort and ease? Do we dare to cross the border of the imagined dark forest out there and enter the forest without fear, or does the forest precisely exist because of our stories about it? Is a road to a familiar openness thinkable, dreamable? Is there a space for an agora at the level of an inter-polis or even cosmo-polis? According to geographer David Harvey, more than ever before, we now live in a time to start the change, to formulate an alternative vision without lying anymore to ourselves:

> *There is a time and place in the ceaseless human endeavour to change the world, when alternative visions, no matter how fantastic, provide the grist for shaping powerful political forces for change. I believe we are precisely at such a moment. Utopian dreams in any case never entirely fade away. They are omnipresent as the hidden signifiers of our desires.* (Harvey 2000)

I started this chapter with my account of a cross-border bike trip in the borderlands of Germany and the Netherlands as an illustration of the persistence of borders. In the academic road trip that followed in the form of this chapter I have made clear that it is highly unlikely that the spatial b/ordering of our self-interest to increase our own comfort and to diminish the fear of loss of control will ever end. But that does not mean that we unwillingly and uncritically need to reproduce our own borders or that we are forced to close our eyes obediently. We are not only victims of the border, but also the producers of it. Making a border, demarcating a line in space is a collaborative act. And so is the interpretation of it. The interpretation and meaning of borders is always open for reforms and transforms. De-bordering, searching for ways for a cross-border dialogue and using the public in between-spaces of the Interpolis/Cosmopolis is therefore also in our own hands. The world of tomorrow will have a different we, different barbarians, different here and there's. In other words, a border is and can never be an answer. It is a question. The imperative geo-philosophical border question of our time is how and why we create a just border for ourselves and thereby for others. In this sense, we have all become borderlanders

Acknowledgements

I would like to thank Mark Eker en Martine van Kampen with whom I have had tremendous pleasure in working on a joint research Dutch report 'Grenslandschap' (Borderscape), in which I wrote a chapter that has been used as a base for this contribution in this edited volume.

References

Anderson, B. (1991), *Imagined Communities* (London: Verso).
Deleuze, G. and Guattari, F. (1988), *A Thousand Plateaus: Capitalism and Schizophrenia* (London: Athlone Press).
Eker, M., van Houtum, H. and van Kampen, M. (2007), *Grenslandschap* (Amsterdam: Eker en Schaap).
Foucault, M. (2007), *Security, Territory, Population, lectures at the collège de France 1977-1978*, edited by Senellart, M. (New York: Palgrave Macmillan).

Freud, S. (1915 [1987]), 'Het onbewuste', in Freud, S. (ed.), *Psycho-analytische theorie* 2 (Meppel/Amsterdam: Boom), 87-152.

Fromm, E. (1942), *Escape from freedom* (New York: Farrar and Rinehardt).

Harley, J.B., (1989), Deconstructing the map, *Cartographica* 26:2, 1-20.

Harvey, D. (2000), *Spaces of Hope* (Edinburgh: Edinburgh University Press).

Nietzsche, F. (1969), 'Nachgelassene Fragmente aus 1872/1873', in Nietzsche, F. (ed.), *Le livre du philosophe* (Paris: Aubier-Flammarion).

Reichert, D. (1992), 'On boundaries', *Society and Space* 10, 87-98.

Said, E. (1993), *Culture and Imperialism* (London: Chatto and Windus).

van Houtum, H. (2010a), 'Human blacklisting: the global apartheid of the EU's external border regime', *Environment and Planning D: Society and Space* 28(6), 957-976.

van Houtum, H. (2010b), 'Waiting before the Law; Kafka on the border', *Social Legal Studies* August 31, 2010 19(3), 285-297.

van Houtum, H. and van Dam, F. (2002), 'Topophilia or Topoporno? Patriotic Place Attachment in International Football Derbies', *HAGAR International Social Science Review* 3:2, 231-48.

van Houtum, H. and van Naerssen, T. (2002), 'Bordering, ordering and othering', *Tijdschrift voor Economische en Sociale Geografie (TESG)* 93:2, 125-36.

Visker, R. (2005), *Vreemd gaan en vreemd blijven* (Amsterdam: SUN).

Borders and Memory

Tatiana Zhurzhenko

Introduction: A tale of two cities

'Today Trieste seems a quiet Italian backwater, a city whose obsession with the past – both its glories and its traumas – mirrors its economic stagnation and political isolation, imparting a melancholy, almost oppressive, air' – writes the American anthropologist Pamela Ballinger in her book on memory and identity in Istria (Ballinger 2003a, 28). She cites Joseph Cary, a writer who had long known and loved Trieste in its literary evocations: when finally confronted with its reality he called it a 'ghost town'. There is another city on the Eastern margins of Europe which fits this metaphor. This is Lviv (Lvov, Lwów, Lemberg) once compared to a 'ghost-ship' by the famous Ukrainian writer, Yuri Andrukhovych. Lviv, like Trieste, is a border town, but even more important, in some sense they both find themselves in the past. There are many parallels in their historical destinies. Two aspects of this historical experience shared by Lviv and Triest – the rearrangement of political borders and the contestation of collective memories – will be addressed in this chapter.

Throughout the catastrophic twentieth century, dramatic transformations reshaped the political geographies of the former imperial peripheries and turned Lviv and Trieste, thriving centres of cosmopolitanism and multicultural diversity, into nationalist peripheries of modern states. The two World Wars and the new political boundaries, (re-)negotiated and (re-)drawn by the winners, but even more their local effects – expulsions, resettlements, ethnic cleansings – dramatically changed the urban culture of both cities. While Trieste was cut from most of its historical hinterlands, Lviv experienced dramatic demographic changes and was integrated in its Ukrainian surroundings. Intended to erase memories and to unify the cultural landscape, the politics of readjusting the populations to the (moving) political boundaries produced, instead, new victimized groups and 'communities of memory'. Fascism and communism often reinforced ethnic divisions as the competing nationalisms supported one or the other. Thus, the status of various social and ethnic groups as 'victims', 'heroes', or 'collaborators' was institutionalized not only on the national level, but also as a part of the Cold War architecture of Europe. This established hierarchy of collective memories and political statuses collapsed together with the Iron Curtain. While nationalists and populist politicians today try to mobilize the memory of victim groups, 'transnational' narratives and symbols – such as the Galician myth and 'Istrian identity' – become important sources of cross-border and regional cooperation (Bialasievicz and O'Loughlin 2002; Minghi and Bufon 2000).

Both Trieste and Lviv have their narratives of the *golden age*, the Habsburg era, a period of economic growth and cultural flourishing. At the heart of this narrative is the myth of a cosmopolitan place where various ethnic groups and religious confessions co-existed in peace and mutual tolerance. *Fin de siècle* Lviv was the home of Poles, Germans, Jews, Ruthenians (Ukrainians), and Armenians. Trieste's Jewish community enjoyed the most privileged status in the Habsburg Empire; the city population included Italians, Germans and Slavs (most notably Slovenes), Armenians, Greeks and so on. Today this multiculturalism is evoked as an important part of the city's self-image, and not only for purposes of tourism. Studying the nature and functions of this 'imperial nostalgia', particularly in the case of Trieste, Ballinger notices that the myth of the 'cosmopolitan past' reflects our own 'contemporary concern with multicultural societies and cosmopolitanism' (Ballinger 2003b, 89). The idealized cultural diversity of the Habsburg Empire becomes a synonym for a desired 'Europeanness', which is believed to be found rather on the periphery. The kind of 'Europe' which is evoked here is the world 'before' nationalisms and national boundaries, projected onto an utopian vision of the future – a multicultural Europe without borders. We are inclined to forget that 'imperial cosmopolitanism' was based on a power hierarchy of 'civilizers' and those to be civilized: German and Latin cultures versus Slavic 'barbarism', Austrians versus Poles, Poles versus Ukrainians. The European Union nowadays also presents itself as a civilizing force, but borders and hierarchies still remain. The Triestians who, in the last two decades, have seen Albanian, Yugoslav and, most recently, African asylum seekers, and the inhabitants of Lviv, who have to queue for days to get a Polish visa, can tell a lot about this side of Europe.

Today's Lviv and Trieste, once symbols of multiculturalism and cosmopolitanism, are products of brutal nationalization politics. Lviv (Lwów) was claimed by the Polish and Ukrainian nationalists and, following the military conflict of 1918-19, was under Polish rule. In 1939 the city was occupied by the Soviets and in 1941 by the Nazis, then liberated/re-occupied by the Red Army in 1944, and eventually incorporated into Soviet Ukraine. While the Jewish population perished in the Holocaust, the brutal Polish-Ukrainian ethnic conflict in 1943-44 took thousands of lives on both sides. The Ukrainian nationalists, being in many cases perpetrators, later became victims of Stalinist repressions themselves. The forced resettlements of Poles and Ukrainians in 1944-47 completed the arrangement of the new Polish-Soviet border. Lviv, predominantly a Polish city before the war, became overwhelmingly Ukrainian afterwards, but in the first place Soviet. Trieste, contested by Italians and (Yugo-)Slavs, became a site of aggressive nationalization under Mussolini, but the old hostilities re-emerged during World War II. If Slovenes can tell about the repression by the Italian fascists, many Italians remember the partisan terror and Istrian exodus. Like Lviv, Trieste has become a site of competing memories of victimhood. After some years of uncertainty, Trieste remained on the 'western' side of the Iron Curtain, while Lviv's fate was different. Consequently, if Trieste today is obsessed with memories and traumas, Lviv in many aspects still suffers from the amnesia imposed in Soviet times. Emancipated from its Soviet identity, it is re-shaping itself as a 'truly Ukrainian' city, evoking an exclusive ethnic version of collective memory. But the recent rediscovery of the city's multicultural past helps open public debates on guilt and historical responsibility.

Once located in the contact zones of different cultures and on the frontlines of political blocks, today Lviv and Trieste see the borders of Europe transforming and shifting once again. The collapse of Yugoslavia, the border dispute between Slovenia and Croatia, the accession of Slovenia to the EU, all this has changed the role of Trieste in the region once again. The Ukrainian-Polish border has also been going through dramatic changes: sealed in Soviet times, it was open for visa-free movement during the 1990's, but with the enlargement of the Schengen zone in 2007 the border regime has been tightened considerably. Lviv, branding itself as a 'gate to Europe', has to cope today with the institutionalization of the new external EU border.

In the first part of this chapter I try to answer two interrelated questions: why the issues of historical memory have become especially important in post-Cold War Europe and why borders and borderlands have become crucial sites for the recovery of memories, their contestation and re-negotiation. In the second part I introduce some concepts which are widely used in the multidisciplinary field of 'memory studies' and can be applied in border research. In the third part, the politics of memory in the borderlands is discussed and is then illustrated in the fourth part by some examples from Lviv and Trieste.

Nomadic borders and the geopolitics of memory

In the modern era the stability of political boundaries has been rather an exception than a rule. The rise of modern nationalism, the collapse of three continental empires – the Austro-Hungarian, the Russian and the Ottoman –, two World Wars, the Cold War, the end of the bi-polar world order and, most recently, EU enlargement have been constantly changing the political map of the European continent. German sociologists Mathias Bös and Kerstin Zimmer (2006) argue that we usually associate borders with the migration of people, but in fact it is often borders which 'migrate' and move over the populations. This 'migration of borders'[1] destroys old communities and shapes new ones, causes resettlements, deportations, and even ethnic cleansing, creates new minorities or homogenizes population inside the new borders. Especially on newly acquired territories, not only the political and legal system, but also education, official national symbols,

---

1   'Nomadic borders' is another metaphor, suggested by Russian sociologists Brednikova and Voronkov (1999).

dominant historical narratives, and even the official language can change (Bös and Zimmer 2006, 161). Territorial expansion, colonization, fusion of states, collapse of an empire, separatist and irredentist movements reshape not only political boundaries, but also the collective memories and identities of populations. A new nation state usually requires a new national history, it needs symbols and myths to be identified with. New minorities which suddenly find themselves on the other side of the border often indulge in nostalgia and resist change; those who were resettled or expelled shape their identity around this traumatic experience. While the 'winners' try to institutionalize the new national memory through education, media and the cultural landscape, 'the losers are unable to accept what happened and are condemned to brood over it, relive it, and reflect how different it might have been' (Burke 1989, 106). Since the era of nationalism, populations of borderland territories in particular have been living through 'symbolic and physical violence attendant to the ultimately impossible project of rendering state and nation congruent' (Ballinger 2003a, 11).

In their essay, Bös and Zimmer differentiate three phases of border changes in Europe. The first phase is the collapse of the classical empires and the rise of the USSR and of Nazi Germany, both striving for territorial expansion. The second phase starts with the end of World War II and ends with the disintegration of the Soviet Union and the 'Eastern Bloc'. The third phase extends from 1989 to EU enlargement in 2004. While the diplomatic solutions resulting from World War I failed to provide Europe with stable political boundaries, the outcome of World War II was rather different. During the decades of the Cold War, border changes were taboo for the key political actors both East and West – mainly because of the opposition between the two political systems and the threat of nuclear conflict (Bös and Zimmer 2006, 172). This 'hyper-stability of border structures' was, to some extent, also secured by means of memory politics. While in the East unwanted memories were repressed, or, in the words of Timothy Snyder, 'cleansed' (Snyder 2003, 202), in the West it was selective forgetting, 'an exclusion and a quarantine of the dead', which served to suppress traumas and 'pull all energies into reconstruction' (Müller 2002, 4). Such 'selective amnesia' was instrumental for building a liberal order and preventing the re-emergence of old hostilities as well as securing the stability of borders. Creating and celebrating myths of the resistance in the West, and of the antifascist Communist underground in the East, on the one hand, and being silent about expulsions, mass collaboration with the Nazis, Stalinist repressions, on the other, served to maintain the Cold War geopolitical order (Judt 2002).

According to Pierre Nora, at the end of 1970's 'a world-wide upsurge in memory' started in Europe and has taken a variety of forms:

> ... criticism of official versions of history and recovery of areas of history previously repressed; demands for signs of a past that had been confiscated or suppressed; growing interest in 'roots' and genealogical research; all kinds of commemorative events and new museums; renewed sensitivity to the holding and opening of archives for public consultation; and growing

attachment to what in the English-speaking world is called 'heritage' and in France patrimoine. (Nora 2002, 18)

While there were different reasons for this phenomenon in the various countries of Western Europe, it was certainly influenced by the political crisis of the Soviet bloc and its growing deficit of legitimacy due to the Prague events of 1968 and the activities of the dissidents. The fall of the Berlin Wall and the collapse of communism in the Soviet Union were followed by a 'recovery of memory' also in the Eastern part of the continent (Nora 2002). Not by accident, the break-up of 'Stalin's empire of memory' (Yekelchyk 2004) coincided with the third phase of border changes. 'After the collapse of communism, memories of the Second World War were "unfrozen" on both sides of the former Iron Curtain ... liberated from constraints imposed by the need for state legitimation and friend-enemy thinking associated with the Cold War' (Müller 2002, 6).

In most cases the 'recovery of memory' in Eastern Europe did not re-animate old border conflicts and did not stir up new territorial claims, mainly due to the fact that it was targeted against communism as a common enemy and pursued for the sake of a new project, the 'return to Europe'. Although old animosities re-emerged on the margins of post-communist societies, there was a broad consensus among the political elites that the traumatic side of history should be kept away from politics. Thus, the border between post-communist Poland and united Germany was re-legitimized at the beginning of 1990's and a series of cross-border cooperation projects was launched, including the new Viadrina University in Frankfurt (Oder). Influenced by the *émigré* magazine *Kultura* published in Paris by Jerzy Giedroyc, the Polish political elite gave up their dream of regaining the *kresy* (eastern borderlands) and supported Ukrainian independence in 1991. And President Havel apologized for the expulsion of the German minority after World War II. It is mainly due to the EU as a new stabilizing factor that the borders of the Cold War era could survive the 'thaw of memories' caused by the collapse of communism. The only exception in this region – the peaceful disintegration of Czechoslovakia – just confirms the rule.

However, this peaceful 're-unification of Europe' is only one side of the story. The other side is represented by the disintegration of the Soviet Union and the break-up of Yugoslavia. In the new 'nationalizing states' borders still are, to use a term of Friedrich Ratzel, 'power barometers' between neighbours. While in ex-Yugoslavia and in the post-Soviet space history is used as an argument for legitimizing national boundaries, conflicting collective memories often become a catalyst of new/old conflicts. Border disputes and territorial conflicts (such as the conflict between Armenia and Azerbaijan), and separatist regions (Abkhazia and South Ossetia in Georgia, Transnistria in Moldova) make it difficult to imagine the political map of Eurasia as finally settled. Competing geopolitical ambitions of NATO and EU on the one hand, and of Russia on the other, also encourages the instrumentalization of historical memory in interstate conflicts. For example, Sevastopol, a port town on the Crimean peninsula, which has been part of Ukrainian territory since 1954 and still hosts the Russian Black Sea Fleet, recently has become a site of 'memory wars'. Traditionally perceived as a 'city of Russian glory' (Plokhy 2000) it is a highly important place in Russian symbolic geography. Political conflicts around Sevastopol escalated particularly when the issue of Ukraine's NATO membership was discussed at the Bucharest summit in April 2008. While pro-Russian forces in Sevastopol initiated a monument to the Russian empress Catherine II (erected in 2008), some commemorative projects were launched in order to articulate the Ukrainian narrative of the city's history.

Post-Soviet Russia uses the symbolic capital of the 'great victory over fascism' in order to legitimize its regained status as a great power. Historical memory – not only symbols and narratives of the Russian Empire, but also carefully selected Soviet myths – is used in contemporary Russia to legitimize its geopolitical status, national territory, and sphere of influence. During Yeltsin's presidency, Russia pushed for 'open' and 'transparent' borders between the CIS countries and instrumentalized the East-Slavic unity narrative for the purpose of various post-Soviet integration projects (Zhurzhenko 2004), while Putin considered strictly controlled national borders an important attribute of state sovereignty. Not by accident, some cities on the new Western border of Russia have re-invented themselves as military fortresses, border outposts throughout centuries of Russian history.[2] The other interesting example is the revival of the Cossack movement in Russia, which strongly identifies itself with the historical task of protecting Russia's borders from external intrusion (Nikiforova 2005).

It seems that the European Union, as a 'post-modern polity', is quite unique in following the new logic of de-historicizing and de-memorizing national borders. The EU project is based on the general consensus that historical arguments and victimhood claims do not legitimize border changes. Instead, mechanisms of reconciliation and cross-border cooperation, protecting minority rights and regional development are promoted as instruments for healing former wounds and reconnecting divided communities. Internal EU borders change their political status, their functions, and also their attached symbolic meanings – they become places of encounter, communication, exchange, and learning from each other, seams where Europe, in the words of Karl Schlögel, 'grows together'. Does a Europe without borders need also a common 'European memory'? Or is it sufficient to have national narratives open for dialogue and understanding of the other's suffering? While some historians believe that the Holocaust constitutes a universal basis for European memory, others point to the incompatibility and inequality of West European and East European memories.[3]

However, the changing nature of borders in Europe – from conflict lines to sites of reconciliation and communication – does not mean their 'de-memorialization' but rather a re-narration of memory. Cross-border cooperation projects, euro-regions, and joint cultural events evoke symbols of former regional unity. Sometimes borders are also re-narrated as new sites of European solidarity, as happened in

---

2   For the example of Ivangorod on the border with Estonia, see Brednikova (2004).
3   See, for example, the discussion 'European histories: towards a grand narrative?', *Eurozine*, available at <http://www.eurozine.com/comp/focalpoints/eurohistories.html>.

Andau (Kovacs 2000). During the 1956 uprising, this small Austrian near-border village offered thousands of Hungarian refugees temporary shelter, food and clothes. On the occasion of the fortieth anniversary of 1956, the small bridge across which refugees had fled was reconstructed, in a common effort by the communities of Andau and its cross-border neighbour, Kapuvár, in order to commemorate the dramatic events. Fragments of the wired fence still bearing the warning inscriptions are kept as reminders of the past. Several information panels honour the helpfulness of the Austrian officials and population. On the initiative of the Andau community, the road to the bridge (called *Fluchtstraße*) was decorated with sculptures by Eastern European artists, most of them bearing an anti-totalitarian message.

Figure 4.1 Andau Bridge at the Austro-Hungarian Border
Source: T. Zhurzhenko.

Figure 4.2 Road to Freedom in Andau – Thomas Eller: 'Ein Weg' (1995)

Source: T. Zhurzhenko.

Even when promoting 'European' and 'transborder' narratives, the national elites invest borderlands with national symbols and commemorative sites. In the era of 'banal nationalism', European nation states still perform an important function as 'identity containers' and, if not politically, national borders remain culturally relevant. In this sense, European integration even generates a proliferation of borders, as is the case with Catalonia and Scotland. 'Borderland' identities, which are characteristic of so many border regions, are built on the local historical narratives and myths, stressing regional differences from the national heartland. Borderlands, sites of cruel territorial conflicts and wars in the past, become today attractive tourist destinations (for example the Anglo-Scottish border). European integration has radically changed the functions of national borders and the symbolic meanings attached to them, but borders and borderlands – for various reasons – still remain important sites of memorialization.

At the external borders of the European Union, history and memory are not less important. Although the EU designed its New Neighbourhood Policy to prevent new divisions on the European continent, the debates about the limits of EU enlargement and the 'proper borders of Europe' reinforce historical and cultural arguments à la Huntington. Following this logic, the Habsburg heritage, the remnants of baroque architecture and Catholic influences serve as proofs of 'Europeanness', while the legacy of Russification and Soviet modernization mark the 'Eurasian' space. According to Eder (2006, 256), 'hard', institutionalized borders rely on the symbolic power inherent in 'soft' borders, which includes narratives, memories, the production of meaning. This meaning production becomes more important, the more the institutional borders of Europe are not finalized and open to political struggles. Therefore, outside the European Union the remobilization of historical memory becomes an instrument of affirming European identity and striving for EU membership.

Nation, territory and collective memory

The concept of 'collective memory' was introduced by the French sociologist Maurice Halbwachs in 1925. He argued that personal memory is always constructed and located in the social environment. By belonging to social groups, individuals learn narratives about their world and engage in repetitive cultural performances which provide continuity between past and present. Halbwachs introduced the important distinction between autobiographical and historical memory. Building on this distinction, Jan Assmann differentiates between 'communicative memory' and 'cultural memory' (Assmann 1997). Communicative memory entails direct contact with people who have lived through a particular time and reaches back three generations at the most. Cultural memory is indirect and transmitted through cultural artefacts such as school books, films, photography, and museum exhibitions. In cultural memory the remembered becomes part of 'the culture' and thereby more and more codified, structured, and hierarchical.

The relationship between public and private remembrance is complicated since 'ordinary individuals rather selectively attend to the now growing and diversifying storehouse of public memories' (Irwin-Zarecka 1994, 47). 'Communities of memory' are formed 'by individuals with not only common experience but a shared sense of its meaning and relevance' – for example Holocaust survivors (ibid., 54). The 'reality of the past' created in such communities by active remembrance (narrations and rituals) provides the basis for public commemorations. On the other hand, private 'making sense of the past' is influenced by the powers inherent in public articulation of collective memory (ibid., 4).

'National memory' assumes a certain consensus on what should be remembered and how; at the same time, there is no modern nation that hasn't experienced internal conflicts and 'wars' over memory. National memory is therefore hierarchical; various social groups compete for access to the public sphere in order to establish the hegemony of their narrative. A nation is always founded on the common possession of a rich legacy of memories, while, at the same time, as Ernest Renan noted already in 1882, 'forgetting is a crucial factor in the creation of a nation' (Renan 1990, 11). 'National memory' is located not so much in the minds of the citizens, but rather in the institutions, resources and practices they share. In the

1980s French historian Pierre Nora introduced the concept of *lieux de mémoire* [sites of memory]. Such sites include geographical places, historical events, heroic figures, commemorative rituals, works of art, symbols, monuments and memorials, archives and museums, institutions (Nora 1997). A site of memory is a crystallization point, a narrative abbreviation of the 'collective memory', endowing a sense of identity. Although often controversial or invested with ambivalent meaning, (common) sites of memory are crucial attributes of a nation.

In the process of nation building, politics of memory often becomes a battlefield for competing interpretations and narratives of the past. Especially in new nation states, the 'nationalization of memory' is important for consolidating a heterogeneous population, integrating minorities and accommodating shifts of state borders. The integration of a (new) nation by means of memory politics includes changes in school curriculum, particularly in history teaching, the revision of the official calendar (new national holidays, jubilees and so on), creating a new pantheon of heroes and martyrs, and reshaping the commemorative landscape (new monuments, memorial sites, changes in urban toponymics). State-led politics of memory is an important part of domestic policy aimed at the cultural integration and construction of national identity; it also helps to legitimize foreign policy orientations. For example, the opening of the Museum of Soviet occupation in Tbilisi (Georgia) in 2007 was supposed to help move the country from the ambiguous Eurasian geopolitical space to the European or rather Euro-Atlantic one (Zhurzhenko 2007).

As a rule, collective memory is related to territory. Social groups 'represent the past through place in an attempt to claim territory, establish social boundaries and justify political actions' (Till 2003, 289). In the modern world the dominant form of territoriality is still the nation state, which has sovereign power on a particular territory. Political geographer Peter Taylor, using the description of a state as a 'power container' (a term coined by Anthony Giddens), suggests the notion 'cultural container'. As an 'imagined community' a modern nation is also 'indissolubly linked to the land in which it developed. This completely changed the nature of territory, especially the integrity of its borders. From being parcels of land transferable between states as the outcome of wars, all territory, including borderlands, became inviolate' (Taylor 1994, 155). Paasi (1996) demonstrated how Finnish national territory and particularly the Finnish-Russian border was constructed through the twentieth century by a variety of instruments (geography and history textbooks, maps, tourist brochures and images of everyday life). Focusing on the processes of geopolitical, and more specifically, 'territorial socialization', he also pays attention to collective memory embedded in the ideas and representations of national territory, borders and borderlands.

Some authors, however, point to the limitations of a constructivist and elite-centred approach. According to Serhy Yekelchyk, 'states and intellectuals do not have a free hand to invent or manipulate national traditions and memories because, as Arjuna Appadurai noted back in 1981, history is not "a limitless and plastic symbolic resource"' (Yekelchyk 2004, 7). Anthony Smith believes that it is the 'territorialization of memory' that turns particular territory into ancestral homeland. His approach helps to explain the 'fervent attachments of populations to particular stretches of territory, and their readiness, in certain circumstances, to defend them to the last inch' (Smith 2000, 150). Smith introduces the notion of *ethnoscapes* which

> ... *cover a wider extent of land, present a tradition of continuity and are held to constitute an ethnic unity, because the terrain invested with collective significance is felt to be integral to a particular historical culture, community or ethnie, and the ethnic community is seen as an intrinsic part of that poetic landscape.* (Smith 2000, 150)

The ethnoscapes emerge because certain terrains are believed to provide 'the unique and indispensable setting for the events that shaped the community': 'Across the landscape lie the "sites of memory"; the monuments to the fallen, the places of peace treaties, the temples of priests, the last resting places of saints and heroes, the sacred groves of spirits and gods who guard the land' (ibid., 151-52). The graves of the ancestors 'testify to the uniqueness and antiquity of particular landscapes' (ibid., 151). That is why, as Katherine Verdery demonstrated, the post-communist states after 1989 pay so much attention to the 'proper re-burial' of their national heroes, re-establishing in this way the link between the recovered nation and its territory (Verdery 2000). Some ethnoscapes are endowed with extraordinary quality and generate powerful feelings of reverence and belonging – according to Smith they become 'sacred territories' central for the ethnic identity. Smith's approach can be particularly applied to border conflicts, where 'two communities compete for possession of the selfsame homeland territories' (Smith 2000, 154).

Political geographer Robert Kaiser also investigated the 'construction of homelands' as a process in which the nationalist elites mobilize 'the myths and images of a primordial homeland to reinforce the depiction of the nation as an ancient community of belonging, an organic singularity "rooted" to a particular place' (Kaiser 2002, 230). In the context of a national revival, the linking together of history and territory is essential for the conceptualization of a land as a national homeland. The spacialization of historical myth and the mythologization of space in terms of history are two sides of the same cultural coin. 'The outcome is that space is invested with historical meanings and mythical associations, while history and memory are concretized as locations; memorial spaces and historical places make history visible and therefore tangible' (ibid., 235). Historian Serhii Plokhy demonstrated the spacialization of historical myth in the case of Ukrainian nation building (Plokhy 1994). Ukrainian Cossackdom was the foundational myth of the Ukrainian nation throughout the nineteenth and early twentieth centuries. Originally related to the limited territory of *Sich* on the lower Dnieper, the Cossack myth has successfully expanded to other Ukrainian ethnic lands. Paradoxically, 'it was preserved best of all in a historically non-Cossack territory, Galicia, and with the beginning of glasnost made its successful return to the Cossack historical lands – the Eastern territories of Ukraine on its current borderland with Russia' (ibid., 165). Until today Cossack mythology has been used to claim the integrity of the Ukrainian territory, united by the same glorious Cossack past. However, as Yekelchyk points out, the Ukrainian intellectuals of the nineteenth and twentieth centuries 'had limited cultural space for their social engineering: they were evoking narratives, objects and images that were already associated with certain inherited notions or emotions' (Yekelchyk 2004, 7). Thus, the 'invention of tradition' pursued by the elites builds on a long history of collective remembrance existing before the birth of the modern nation.

Politics of memory in the borderlands

As we have seen, borders and borderlands are important sites where the link between collective memory and territory, community and place, 'blood' and 'soil' is established. Borderland territories have often been exposed to changing powers, to military and political expansion of the neighbours and to ethnic and religious conflicts. Thus most borderlands in Europe are 'victim intensive' places, with their historical memories shaped by collective traumas, former hostilities, and shared guilt. Following Anthony Smith, borderland territories can become 'sacred lands' invested with a special symbolic meaning and contested by two (or more) different communities. At the same time, they have often been places where different cultures coexist and enrich each other, creating 'hybrid' or 'Creole' identities, sometimes seen as a challenge to the nation-building efforts of the political elites. Thus, borderlands are not marginal places but central sites of power where the meaning of national identity is created and contested. It is particularly in the borderlands that the memorial landscape can be seen as an arena 'for social actors and groups to debate and negotiate the right to decide what is commemorated and what version of the past will be made visible to the public' (Dwyer and Alderman 2008, 171).

National borders are not just demarcation lines between national 'cultures of remembrance' but an important factor directly involved in their reproduction and transformation. It is the borderlands where different national (and local) 'cultures of remembrance' come into contact and conflict, negotiate and borrow from each other. In his study of the US-Mexico border, Martinez (1994) suggests a useful classification of borderlands according to the criteria of intensity of cross-border contacts and the mode of relations between neighbouring countries: alienated, coexistent, interdependent and integrated borderlands. As these categories do not represent stable statuses but dynamic tendencies and open options we can apply this classification to the variety of memory politics in border regions. The transition from alienated to integrated borderlands is usually followed by reconciliation processes, common commemorative projects, and an intensive 'transfer of memory'. The *Memorial de l'Alsace Moselle* in Schirmeck (Alsace/Elsass, France), constructed in 2001, is an example of such a project re-narrating the history of the region in a new way. Alsace/Elsass is a borderland region between France and Germany claimed by both countries several times in modern history. The *Memorial de l'Alsace Moselle* uses unusual representation strategies to inform about the conflicting history of the region from the Franco-Prussian war of 1870-71 to the end of World War II. The visitor is confronted with a plurality of tongues commenting on the history of the region in French, German and Alsatian dialect. Passing through spaces devoted to Nazification, repression and resistance, the visitors enter a bright hall symbolizing German-French reconciliation and the idea of a united Europe. The memorial is part of the new project *'Alsace: Lieu de memoires - terre sans frontière'*,[4] which connects twenty memorial sites along one tourist route and offers visitors various commemorative and informational events.

If, however, the process of nationalization of collective memory aimed at the cultural integration of borderland inhabitants into the core nation prevails, interdependent borderlands change into coexistent or even alienated ones. A new international border encourages the nationalization of memories and generates differences in a formerly common 'culture of remembrance', as has been happening since 1991 in the post-Soviet borderlands. The 'twin cities' Narva and Ivangorod, situated on the Estonian-Russian border, can serve as an example of these tendencies. By the end of the 1980's Estonian Narva was a 'rather typical Soviet industrial town with a predominantly Russian population mostly formed by migrants and their descendants' (Nikiforova 2004, 150-1). The two cities constituted an integrated geographic and social space. After 1991, as the former administrative border became an international one, Narva has been marginalized due to its geographic location and 'problematic' ethnic composition. Ivangorod, the former satellite of Narva on the Russian side, has been cut from the common infrastructure and social network and turned into a Russian border town. Brednikova (2004) analyzed the changes in the commemorative landscapes of these two cities and compares the new narratives of place created by popular representations of history such as museums, monuments and souvenirs. While the historical narrative of Narva is pluralistic and fragmented, more entertaining than didactic, Ivangorod presents itself as a scene of heroic Russian history, a Russian border fortress. The new histories replacing the former common Soviet meta-narrative 'do not start a dialog, do not compete or solidarize in the interpretation of the same events' (ibid., 340). Although Narva presents itself as a 'European' rather than Estonian city, its Russian speaking majority is virtually uninvolved in the reinvention of the city's past.

Sometimes, the new border itself becomes the main factor of identity formation and re-memorialization, as has happened with the Setos, a small ethnic group traditionally living in the Estonian-Russian borderlands south of the Peipus (Pskov) lake. Known only to professional ethnographers before 1991, with the new international status of the Estonian-Russian border the Setos gained public attention as a 'divided people'. On the initiative of Seto activists, 'efforts have been made to nationalize the territory of Seto settlements, to stitch together the two parts of the whole by (re)narrating this place as an ethno-cultural Seto homeland, the transborder region of Setomaa' (Nikiforova 2005, 207). Maps and tourist brochures have been published, 'several Seto museums, monuments and important Seto heritage sites appeared on both sides of the border' (ibid.).

---

4   <http://www.alsace-lieudememoires.com/startseite.html>

At the same time old borders, which disappeared from the political map a long time ago, still continue to exist as symbolic boundaries dividing a nation along the lines of historical memory. Polish sociologist Tomasz Zarycki (2007) has shown that the legacy of the tripartite division of Poland in the nineteenth century is still relevant for today's regional development. On the one hand, regional differences in economic culture and political behaviour correspond with the borders of partitions, on the other hand, symbolic conflicts over identity politics and the interpretation of history affect debates on regional development and post-communist restructuring. Similarly, in Ukraine the former border between the Habsburg Empire and Russia (1772-1918) marks persisting differences in political preferences and 'cultures of remembrance'; this border is constantly reproduced in the political and cultural discourses as a boundary between the 'European' and the 'Sovietized' parts of the Ukrainian nation. But the most recent and telling example is the East-West German border. Having disappeared as a political border, it has persisted and indeed been reinvented as a cultural boundary between East and West Germany. Political anthropologist Daphne Berdahl (1999) demonstrates this with the example of the small Eastern German village, Kella, at the former border with Western Germany, in the first years after reunification. She shows that the same people who had welcomed the fall of the SED regime and celebrated the end of the village's isolation and the long desired freedom of movement at the same time actively and passively resisted what she calls the 'asymmetrical nature of remembering in united Germany' and 'organized forgetting', refusing to see their past as meaningless. Here, the boundary between the East and West is being reproduced through an ongoing renegotiation of identities and re-evaluation of the past, in oscillation between 'discourses of nostalgia and mourning' (ibid., 218). The 'Border Discourse' research project of Ulrike Meinhof, Doris Wastl-Walter et al. also analyzes how the vanishing borders once separating Eastern and Western Europe have been living on in collective memories after the fall of the Iron Curtain (Meinhof 2002).

That the 'work of memory' is a complex political process is particularly visible in borderlands. Although central governments use state-led politics of memory for the nationalization and integration of 'problematic' borderlands, regional political elites often make their own use of such political initiatives and involve local symbolic resources to boost regional identities and the feeling of local patriotism. Moreover, relations between the national centre and the periphery, the level of political centralization, the degree of consolidation of the regional elites, and the influence of regional lobbies in the capital set the frame of memory politics in border regions. Local elites, political parties and NGOs, churches, professional associations (historians, architects, and journalists), ethnic and cultural minorities play an important role in memory politics. Thus, (re-) shaping collective memory in democratic societies assumes a multiplicity of political actors and their interaction.

Back to Lviv and Trieste

Today both Lviv and Trieste can prove that 'as a place of memory, the city is a site for both symbolic control and symbolic resistance' (Rose-Redwood et al. 2008, 162). I will discuss here two cases which illustrate the politics of memory in borderlands as a complex, hierarchical, and multi-scalar process. The first example is the story of the Polish military cemetery in Lviv (also called Eaglets' cemetery), whose fate throughout the twentieth century reflects the turbulent history of Polish-Ukrainian relations and whose official reopening in 2005 revealed not only the legacy of 'difficult neighbourhood' but also internal contradictions and political conflicts within both transitional societies. The Eaglets' cemetery is a symbol of one of the bitter moments in Polish-Ukrainian history – the November 1918 fight for Lviv following the collapse of the Habsburg Empire. As Ukrainian military formations took control of Lviv, Polish volunteer groups were formed in response. Hundreds of young Poles and Ukrainians were killed in this conflict. As the Polish military came to the rescue from Cracow, Poland gained control of Lviv. The construction of the memorial to the 'Polish defenders of Lviv', which included a monumental cemetery complex and a Glory Monument, was started in the early 1920's. When Lviv became Soviet after World War II, the memorial was abandoned and partly destroyed as the Polish identity of Lviv had to be replaced by the image of a 'Soviet Ukrainian' city. The restoration of the memorial became possible only after 1991 when the authorities of independent Ukraine approved the Polish initiative. Good Polish-Ukrainian relations (Warsaw was the first to recognize the independent Ukrainian state) created a solid basis for historical reconciliation, and the official reopening of the memorial in Lviv under the supervision of the two presidents was supposed to crown this process. However, the official opening was postponed for years because some details of the memorial's design as well as the wording of the inscription could not be agreed. Characteristically, the main controversy emerged not between Kyiv and Warsaw, but between Kyiv and Lviv. The Lviv city council objected to the symbolics of the memorial and repeatedly said it would not permit the opening of a Polish cemetery which glorified the Polish Army.

However, the main motivation of the Lviv city council was not anti-Polish resentment. Rather, Lviv politicians used this opportunity to present themselves as true Ukrainian patriots and to sabotage the politics of President Leonid Kuchma, extremely unpopular in Western Ukraine. At the same time, the idea of Polish-Ukrainian reconciliation found support in Lviv's Ukrainian community – a joint mass celebrated at the Polish cemetery by the cardinals of both the Roman and the Greek Catholic church was attended by thousands of citizens. And many Lviv intellectuals, being sympathetic to Poland and aware of its role as Ukraine's advocate in the EU, were very critical of the rigidity of the city council as well as Kyiv's lack of sensitivity.

Figure 4.3 Polish Military Cemetery in Lviv
Source: T. Zhurzhenko.

The conflict around the Polish memorial revealed the burden of the old Polish-Ukrainian rivalry for Lviv and Eastern Poland/Western Ukraine. At the same time the memorial became a site of internal political struggle, first of all between the presidential administration, which tried to monopolize the symbolic capital of Polish-Ukrainian reconciliation, and its political opponents from Western Ukraine. Eventually the conflict was resolved and the official reopening of the memorial took place in July 2005 under the auspices of Aleksander Kwasniewski and the freshly elected Viktor Yushchenko. That a compromise between Kyiv and Lviv was reached was certainly due to the high support the new president enjoyed in Western Ukraine.

However, this memorial site of Polish-Ukrainian reconciliation is not without ambivalence. To counterbalance the impressive Polish memorial symbolically, the Ukrainian side has started a major reconstruction and expansion of the neighbouring Memorial to the Warriors of the Ukrainian Galician Army. Not only have the old graves been renovated, but the remains of other Ukrainian fighters for independence from 1918 to 1950, most remarkably Ukrainian Insurgent Army (UPA)[5] soldiers, have been reburied here, thus reconstructing the continuity and legitimacy of the Ukrainian armed struggle for liberation. With the reburial of some Ukrainian military and political leaders the graveyard has become a kind of regional

---

5   The Ukrainian Insurgent Army was formed in 1942 in Western Ukraine to fight for a Ukrainian independent state.

pantheon of national heroes, supporting the legitimacy of the Ukrainian claim for Lviv. This corresponds with one of President Yushchenko's main political projects – the rehabilitation and heroization of the UPA, which Soviet propaganda had accused of collaboration with the Nazis for decades. In addition, a new impressive monument to Stepan Bandera, the leader of the UPA who is considered in Poland to be responsible for the massacre of thousands of Polish civilians in 1943-44, was erected in Lviv in 2007. It seems the ghosts of the old nationalist rivalry are not dead. They can be easily evoked and politically instrumentalized again.

Figure 4.4 Memorial to the Warriors of the Ukrainian Galician Army in Lviv
Source: T. Zhurzhenko.

As in Lviv, in Trieste old traumas and tensions over the difficult past have been heavily politicized in the last two decades. The fiftieth anniversary of the end of World War II once again revealed deep fractures in the city's collective memory. While the Slovene community and the Italian left kept to the traditional narrative of the 'antifascist resistance', the Italian nationalists and the Istrian exiles organized alternative ceremonies commemorating the victims of the 'Foibe massacres'[6] and

---

6   In the local dialect the *foiba* is a deep *karst* sinkhole typical for the Istrian landscape.

denouncing the Italo-Yugoslav Peace Treaty of 1947 which gave most of Istria to Yugoslavia (Ballinger 2003a, 97-101). The massacres – revenge killings committed by the Yugoslav partisans, when they entered the region in 1945, and targeted against fascist collaborators, political enemies, and 'unwanted elements' – were not a subject of public debate for decades. During the Cold War Italian politicians were reluctant to raise this issue for fear of irritating Yugoslavia, seen as a buffer between the Soviet Bloc and Western Europe. In exchange, the nation could comfortably forget the war crimes committed by Italian fascists and military in the Balkans, in Libya and Ethiopia. The myth of antifascist resistance helped consolidate the nation and mobilize it for reconstruction while cleaning up the image of Italy from the earlier alliance with Hitler. Only in Trieste, which has always been a stronghold of radical right and nationalist forces, have the memories of the *foibe* been cultivated in the exile milieu.

Under the conservative government of Silvio Berlusconi, and on the initiative of Gianfranco Fini, leader of the far right *Alleanza Nazionale*, the Italian Parliament approved a law which declared February 10 the National Memorial Day of the Exiles and Foibe. Celebrated since 2005 throughout the country with exhibitions and commemorative ceremonies, this day has become a symbolic counterweight to the traditional Day of the Republic (April 25) associated with the 'liberation from Nazi occupation'. Recent shifts in Italian politics of memory are reflected in the contradictory landmarks of Trieste's commemorative landscape – the Foibe of Basovizza and the Risiera di san Sabba. Already in 1965 the Risiera di San Sabba, the only Nazi extermination camp on the territory of Italy, became a national memorial site and in 1975 was transformed into a museum. A Holocaust site also associated with Slovene suffering under Italian fascism, it has first of all been an anti-Nazi symbol and a site of official commemorative ceremonies. For the left, the Risiera has symbolized the link between Italian fascism, Nazism and the Holocaust. The memorial to the Foibe of Basovizza, which was erected in 1959 and had only local relevance for a long time, reflects an alternative memory of the war and a revisionist approach to its history. As a site of nationalist pilgrimage, it has symbolized for the far right the dangers of Slavic communism (Grainger). In 1992 Basovizza was also given the status of a national monument. The leaders of the left (for example Walter Veltroni) recently visited the Foibe of Basovizza and admitted the responsibility of the Communists for silencing the issue during the past decades. At the same time, left politicians see the discussion as being manipulated by the right wing parties and consider it an attempt to compromize Italian anti-fascism and resistance.

While reflecting basic shifts in Italian domestic politics, the issue of the *foibe* atrocities raised diplomatic tensions between Italy and Croatia. In February 2007, Italian President Giorgio Napolitano called the killings an 'ethnic cleansing', motivated by 'a wave of bloodthirsty hatred and fury' as well as by a 'Slavic annexation plan'. The Croatian president Stipe Mesić, in turn, talked about racism

---

Bodies of the victims were thrown into these pits. The number of victims is estimated from several hundred to several thousand. The Basovizza *foiba*, which became a symbol of this crime, was actually not a natural karst hole but a man-made mine.

and a desire for political revenge.[7] While Italy wants negotiations on Croatia's EU accession to include the issue of compensation for property Italians lost in Istria and Dalmatia during World War II, the Croatian side has suggested a mutual commission to investigate crimes committed by both sides at the time.

Conclusion

Collective memories, historical narratives, myths and symbols are usually attached to a particular territory making it unique and indispensable for a certain group. The construction of 'national homelands' in the modern era re-establishes this deep symbolic connection as a central axis of nation building. Not by accident, the attempts by elites to appropriate and control national history go hand in hand with claims for 'ethnic lands'. Borderlands are central in this process as they are often contested by neighbours, become an object of political and military expansion, or a site of ethnic conflicts. Border regions also might cultivate particular 'hybrid' identities, nurture separatist movements, or push central governments to reconciliation and cooperation with the neighbouring state. In any case, borderlands are not just peripheries but central sites of state power where national identities are created, challenged, and reinvented, reflecting local needs and external geopolitical pressures. Depending on interstate relations and the dynamics of cross-border contacts, politics of memory in the borderlands can support territorial claims, serve the symbolic demarcation of the national territory, or become an instrument of reconciliation and transnational cooperation. Politics of memory in the borderlands involves a multiplicity of actors on the national, regional and international levels, whose interests and identities depend on the (geo-)political context and are constructed through negotiations and conflicts.

European integration is built on the idea of overcoming former hostilities and coping with a difficult past. Therefore, the European Union supports *Vergangenheitsbewältigung* [coming to terms with the past] and reconciliation processes among its member states. Although a single 'shared' European memory might be a utopian idea, 'shareable narratives' (Luisa Passerini) of the common past seem to be a precondition of European solidarity. However, collective memory is still instrumentalized for political purposes and, outside the EU, 'memory wars' often go hand in hand with territorial conflicts.

---

7   'Italy-Croatia WWII massacre spat', by Cristian Fraser, BBC news, Rome, 14 February 2007, available at <http://news.bbc.co.uk/nolpda/ukfs_news/hi/newsid_6360000/6360429.stm>, accessed 4 November 2008.

References

Assmann, J. (1997), *Das kulturelle Gedächtnis, Schrift, Erinnerung und politische Identität in frühen Hochkulturen* (München: C.H.Beck).

Ballinger, P. (2003a), *History in Exile: Memory and Identity at the Borders of the Balkans* (Princeton University Press).

Ballinger, P. (2003b), 'Imperial nostalgia: mythologizing Habsburg Trieste', *Journal of Modern Italian Studies* 8:1, 84-101.

Berdahl, D. (1999), *Where the World Ended. Re-Unification and Identity in the German Borderland* (Berkeley: University of California Press).

Bialasiewicz, L. and O'Loughlin, J. (2002), 'Galician identities and political cartographies on the Polish-Ukrainian border', in Häkli, J. and Kaplan, D.H. (eds.), *Boundaries and Place: European Borderlands in Geographical Context* (Lanham: Rowman & Littlefield).

Brednikova, O. (2004), 'Historical text *ad marginem* or a divided memory of divided towns', *Ab Imperio* 4, 289-312. [in Russian]

Brednikova, O. and Voronkov, V. (eds.)(1999), *Nomadic Borders*, Proceedings of the Seminar held in Narva, 12-16 November 1998 (St. Petersburg: CISR, Working Paper 7).

Bös, M. and Zimmer, K. (2006), 'Wenn Grenzen wandern: Zur Dynamik von Grenzverschiebungen im Osten Europas', in Eigmüller, M. and Vobruba, G. (eds.), *Grenzsoziologie. Die Politische Strukturierung des Raumes* (Wiesbaden: Verlag für Sozialwissenschaften), 157-84.

Burke, P. (1989), 'History as social memory', in Butler, T. (ed.), *Memory: History, Culture and the Mind* (Oxford: Basil Blackwell), 97-113.

Dwyer, O.J. and Alderman, D.H. (2008), 'Memorial landscapes: analytic questions and metaphors', in *GeoJournal* 73, 165-78.

Eder, K. (2006), 'Europe's borders', *European Journal of Social Theory* 9:2, 255-71.

Grainger, I. (2004), 'Trieste and the Foibe: nation and memory', *Bulletin of the Society for Italian Studies* 37, <http://www.sis.ac.uk/Bulletin/bulletin2004.pdf>, accessed 4 November 2008.

Halbwachs, M. (1992), *On Collective Memory* (Chicago: University of Chicago Press).

Irwin-Zarecka, I. (1994), *Frames of Remembrance: the Dynamics of Collective Memory* (New Brunswick, New Jersey: Transaction Books).

Judt, T. (2002), 'The past is another country: myth and memory in post-war Europe', in Müller, J.W. (ed.), *Memory and Power in Post-War Europe: Studies in the Presence of the Past* (Cambridge University Press).

Kaiser, R. (2002), 'Homeland making and the territorialization of national identity', in Conversi, D. (ed.), *Ethnonationalism in the Contemporary World* (London and NY: Routledge), 229-47.

Kovacs, E. (2000), '"Grenzerzählungen", lokale Eigenmythen und "Rahmengeschichten" als identitätsformende Texte in Gemeinden an der österreichisch-ungarischen Grenze', in Haslinger, P. (ed.), *Regionale und nationale Identitäten. Wechselwirkungen und Spannungsfelder im Zeitalter moderner Staatlichkeit* (Würzburg: Ergon), 241-58.

Martinez, O. (1994), *Border People: Life and Society in the U.S.-Mexico Borderlands* (Arizona: University of Arizona Press).

Meinhof, U.H. (2002), *Living (with) Borders: Identity Discourses on East-West Borders in Europe* (Aldershot: Ashgate).

Minghi, J.V. and Bufon, M. (2000), 'The upper Adriatic borderland: from conflict to harmony', *GeoJournal* 52:2, 119-27.

Müller, J.W. (2002), 'Introduction: the power of memory, the memory of power and the power over memory', in Müller, J.W. (ed.), *Memory and Power in Post-War Europe: Studies in the Presence of the Past* (Cambridge University Press).

Nikiforova, E. (2005), 'Narrating "national" at the margins: Seto and Cossack identity in the Russian-Estonian borderlands', in Wilson, T.M. and Hastings, D. (eds.), *Culture and Power at the Edges of the State. National Support and Subversion in European Border Regions* (Münster: LIT Verlag), 191-228.

Nikiforova, E. (2004), 'The disruption of social and geographic space in Narva', in Alapuro, R., Liikanen, I. and Lonkila, M. (eds.), *Beyond Post-Soviet Transition: Micro Perspectives on Challenge and Survival in Russia and Estonia* (Saarijärvi: Kikimora Publications), 148-64.

Nora, P. (2002), 'Gedächtniskonjunktur', *Transit - Europäische Revue* 22, 18-31.

Nora, P. (1997), *Realms of Memory* (New York: Columbia University Press).

Paasi, A. (1996), *Territories, Boundaries and Consciousness: The Changing Geographies of the Finnish-Russian Border* (London: John Wiley and Sons).

Plokhy, S. (2000), 'The city of glory: Sevastopol in Russian historical mythology', in *Journal of Contemporary History* 35:3, 369-83.

Plokhy, S. (1994), 'Historical debates and territorial claims: Cossack mythology in the Russian-Ukrainian border dispute', in Starr, F.S. (ed.), *The Legacy of History in Russia and the New States of Eurasia* (Armonk, New York: M.E. Sharpe), 147-70.

Renan, E. (1990), 'What is a nation?', in Bhabha, H.K. (ed.), *Nation and Narration* (London and NewYork: Routledge), 8-22.

Rose-Redwood, R., Alderman, D. and Azaryahu, M. (2008), 'Collective memory and the politics of urban space: an introduction', in *GeoJournal* 73, 161-64.

Smith, A. (2000), *Myths and Memories of the Nation* (Oxford: Oxford University Press).

Snyder, T. (2003), *The Reconstruction of Nations: Poland, Ukraine, Lithuania, Belarus 1569 – 1999* (Yale: Yale University Press).

Taylor, P.J. (1994), 'The state as container: territoriality in the modern world-system', *Progress in Human Geography* 18:2, 151-62.

Till, K.E. (2003), 'Places of memory', in *A Companion to Political Geography* (London: Blackwell), 289-301.

Verdery, K. (2000), *The Political Lives of Dead Bodies* (New York: Columbia University Press).

Yekelchyk, S. (2004), *Stalin's Empire of Memory: Russian-Ukrainian Relations in the Soviet Historical Imagination* (Toronto: University of Toronto Press).

Zhurzhenko, T. (2007), 'Geopolitics of memory', *Eurozine* <http://www.eurozine.com/articles/2007-05-10-zhurzhenko-en.html>, accessed 4 November 2008.

Zhurzhenko, T. (2004), 'Cross-border cooperation and transformation of regional identities in the Ukrainian-Russian borderlands: towards a Euroregion "Slobozhanshchyna"?', *Nationalities Papers* 32:1, 207-32; 32:2, 497-514.

Zarycki, T. (2007), 'History and regional development: a controversy over the "right" interpretation of the role of history in the development of the Polish regions', *Geoforum* 38: 3, 485-93.

Border Regions as Neighbourhoods

Alan K. Henrikson

Introduction

Generally, boundaries – perhaps particularly borders between nations – have been thought of as *problems*. As the geographer Jean Gottmann observed, 'The record of history demonstrates that political limits in geographic space have been and remain a major source of tension and conflict' (Gottmann 1980b, 433). The emphasis of the present chapter shall be, instead, on the actual and potential role of political borders, especially the administrative regimes set up to control them, as solutions – as potential ameliorative factors in situations which might, otherwise, erupt in local recrimination or even wider violence. In short, 'border incidents', if imaginatively and skilfully managed, can lead to peace as well as war. What is required is thus a new way of looking at boundaries, theoretically as well as practically, as definers of 'neighbourhood', as generators of 'good neighbourly relations' between countries.

A diplomacy of *bon voisinage*, as I have characterized it, that might significantly contribute to peace between nations and in the world would depend on fulfilment of a number of major conditions. I shall seek in this chapter to identify what these are, and to explain their causal importance. Let me state them briefly at the outset. The first is that the nations in question must 'face', or consciously confront and also formally address, one another – the crucial issue here being whether the countries and their leaders are sufficiently oriented toward, and therefore attentive to, one another. Whether they thus emphasize and highlight their mutual relations may depend on the historically conditioned geopolitical orientations of the countries involved, that is, where the general population of each of the adjoining countries conceives the 'front' and the 'back' of that country to be. A 'front'-to-'front' relationship is more likely to have diplomatic significance than a 'back'-to-'back' one, or even a 'front'-to-'back' one or 'back'-to-'front' one.

A second requirement is that the two facing countries must be internally organized, constitutionally ordered, and socially connected in such a way as to allow the effects of positive transborder relations to flow throughout their respective national 'bodies'. At issue is not just whether the border area is transparent and permeable, but also whether the remainder of each of the national societies involved can efficiently process, and beneficially absorb, what is transmitted at the border – the goods and services that may pass through as well as the ideas and the images conveyed. The very 'picture', or visual landscape, of a border zone – natural features as well as border installations – helps to give content to a nation's view of its transborder and other relationships with a neighbouring country. It is a 'lens' through which the other is seen. The more positive (physically and socially attractive) the borderscape on both sides, the better. 'Positive'-'positive' imagery here is obviously to be preferred to 'negative'-'negative', or 'positive'-'negative' or 'negative'-'positive'. The border-area picture, whatever its character, must be socially communicated in order to be politically effective.

A third condition of successful bordering diplomacy, particularly to be emphasized in this chapter, is that the 'skins' of countries – reflecting the geographer Friedrich Ratzel's notion of the boundary as the 'peripheral organ' of a state (Ratzel 1892) – should somehow be bonded, legally and even institutionally, to the political epidermises or borders of the countries adjacent. The key issue here is whether the mutual chafing that can occur at borders from discrepancies that exist between countries can be avoided by joint management. The effectiveness of most bilateral transborder relationships around the world usually can be reinforced by systems, bilateral or multilateral, of transfrontier cooperation. Such 'internationalization' of border-area cooperation can create large common-border systems, like those now developing within the geographic area of the expanded European Union (EU). In most parts of the globe, however, this degree of amalgamation, with supranational controls, is not possible. Therefore, international diplomacy as opposed to supranational administration of border arrangements must be emphasized. Even in Europe, especially in the east and south, continued diplomatic attention to borders is warranted – as the EU has recognized with its European Neighbourhood Policy (ENP).

In most countries or regional groupings of countries there is an interplay between capital communities and border areas: between 'centres' and 'peripheries' (Gottmann 1980a). As is the case in Europe where there is wider international involvement – particularly big-power or supranational-organization interest – in the making of local boundary arrangements, there may be different levels of centre/ periphery forces at play. For convenience of future reference, those forces operating at the national level, within nations or directly between nations, will be noted as national-'central' (with a small c) and national-'peripheral' (with a small p), and those of a wider scope as international-'Central' (with a capital C) and international-'Peripheral' (with a capital P).

Increasingly today, in negotiations concerning borderlands and cross-border issues, there is a complex involvement of national-level centres and peripheries – in the immediately juxtaposed or neighbouring countries – and Centres and Peripheries – representing factors in the larger international community. An examination of *bon voisinage* or 'good neighbour' diplomacy must take account of these multi-level dynamics. Border-focused diplomacy, to be successful, must coordinate the interests of centres and peripheries within and across national lines, and also respond to Central and Peripheral concerns where they exist. At present, it is still usually the national-level relationships that are the dominant ones. Both of the central governments and also both of the peripheral communities that are involved must be able, in harmonizing their relations, to define a border-related dispute between them in terms of a common interest.

Two pairs of centres and peripheries are implicated under these circumstances, and these can interact, directly and indirectly, regardless of national lines. There can be 'inter-State' transactions between the neighbouring countries, that is, between central-government officials situated in their respective national capitals or perhaps meeting one another elsewhere. There can be 'core-periphery' transactions between the central areas and border regions within each of the two countries, and also 'frontier zone', or immediate cross-border, transactions. Finally, there can be 'core-periphery *adjacent* State' transactions, involving some, limited, contact between the centre of one country and the periphery of the other (House 1980, 466) (see Figure 5.1). A modification of this model makes a further distinction between 'capitals' and 'provincial centres', both of which can deal with 'border settlements' – as they do with each other, both internally and also internationally (Prescott 1987, 160) (see Figure 5.2). These diagrams, with the nearby 'provincial centres' added, exhibit in a simplified and effectively graphic way the networks – political, economic, and social – that can transform borderlands into neighbourhoods.

Even if the four actors – the centres and peripheries of both sides – actually do engage in active exchanges, they may vary in their attitudes, and their responses. In order for successful border-based diplomacy to occur, all four of the actors (c's and p's) must recognize that such interchange, possibly to result in an international agreement, is advantageous to them, individually as well as collectively. So, too, if the larger international community is involved, should the major powers or leading organizations therein (the C's), and also the weaker but nonetheless influential (P's), appreciate the advantage that a particular border agreement may bring. For an international border accord to be perceived as fair and just, and for it to be implemented effectively, all four parties must concur. This outcome can be achieved more readily if there is a guiding concept to inspire and direct the diplomacy of international border-making.

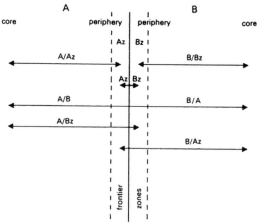

Figure 5.1 Frontier Transaction Model

Source: House 1980.

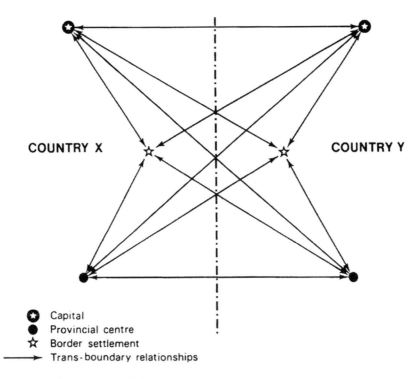

Figure 5.2 Border Relationships

Source: Prescott 1987.

The Concept of 'Good Neighbourhood'/*Bon Voisinage*

'In the field of world policy', declared Franklin D. Roosevelt in his first inaugural address as U.S. President in March 1933, 'I would dedicate this nation to the policy of the good neighbour – the neighbour who resolutely respects himself and, because he does so, respects the rights of others – the neighbour who respects his obligations and respects the sanctity of his agreements in and with a world of neighbours' (quoted in Guerrant 1950, 1).

Roosevelt's statement is echoed in the Preamble of the Charter of the United Nations, signed at San Francisco on 26 June 1945: 'We the Peoples of the United Nations' express determination 'to practice tolerance and live together in peace with one another as good neighbours' (United Nations 1990, 1). The French-language text, always a little different, replaces 'good neighbour' with *'esprit de bon voisinage'* [spirit of good neighbourliness] (Nations Unies 1997, 3). Article 74 of Chapter XI, concerning Non-Self-Governing Territories, commits members of the UN holding such territories to respect there on the colonial periphery no less than in metropolitan international areas, 'the general principle of good-neighbourliness, due account being taken of the interests and well-being of the rest of the world, in social, economic, and commercial matters' (United Nations 1990, 39). The French text, almost identical, affirms *'le principe général du bon voisinage dans le domaine social, économique et commercial, compte tenu des intérêts et de la prospérité du reste du monde'* (Nations Unies 1997, 48).

It is obvious from these historically celebrated and important international expressions of the good neighbourhood idea, that the 'policy' or 'principle' of good neighbourhood is not a strictly defined legal concept. Nonetheless, certain distinct elements of the neighbourly spirit-idea are clear, the most basic being the notion of mutuality or reciprocity and of the equivalency of station and interchange. Neighbours are to be accepted as being equal and thus deserving of respectful regard when an action that might adversely affect them is being contemplated, just as if the shoe were on the other foot. Moreover, there is an implied acceptance of a commitment to tolerance of difference. Force must not be used to change things. There is thus a specific implication of non-interference in the internal affairs of others. Noteworthy also is the possible generality of the concept, its being considered as an important element in the development of 'world' policy.

These were the meanings associated with the idea from the time of the Roosevelt administration's 'Good Neighbour Policy'. In practice, this policy was applied mainly to U.S. relations with Latin American and Caribbean countries, that is, the Western Hemisphere. At the Seventh Pan-American Conference in Montevideo, Uruguay, in December 1933 the American republics approved a Convention on the Rights and Duties of States prohibiting intervention by any state 'in the internal or external affairs of another'. This expressed an absolute commitment to non-intervention. This pledge had origins also in the dialectic of U.S.-Latin American relations during the preceding Republican administrations (Welles 1944, 185-241; Wood 1961). As far back as February 1848, with the signature of the Treaty of Guadalupe Hidalgo on 'Peace, Friendship, Limits, and Settlement' that ended the war between the United

States and Mexico, the 'good neighbourhood' phrase was used. Suggested by the Mexican delegation (Wood 1961, 124), this mention is considered the locus classicus of the modern concept (*Dictionnaire de la terminologie du droit international* 1960, 94).

The preamble to the Treaty of Guadalupe Hidalgo states that the United States and Mexico, as between themselves, would 'establish upon a solid basis relations of peace and friendship, which shall confer reciprocal benefits upon the citizens of both, and assure the concord, harmony and mutual confidence, wherein the two Peoples should live, as Good Neighbours'. Article 21 of the treaty provides specifically for what should and should not be done if 'disagreements' arose. It stated that there must be no resort by either country to reprisals, aggression, or hostility 'until the Government of that which deems itself aggrieved, shall have maturely considered, in the spirit of peace and good neighbourship, whether it would not be better that such difference should be settled by arbitration of Commissioners appointed on each side, or by that of a friendly nation' (Bevans 1972, 792, 803). The possibility, even then, of third-party or international involvement in the maintenance of bilateral U.S.-Mexican relations is worthy of particular note.

The broader meaning of Roosevelt's 1933 use of the 'good neighbour' expression, in its conceptual character and in its span of geographical application (into the realm of 'world' policy), 'has been lost', as Sumner Welles later commented (Welles 1944, 192-3). Moreover, events of the early twenty-first century suggest that 'good neighbour' diplomacy may become increasingly important under conditions of heightened insecurity along and across borders around the world. The present re-examination of the concept of 'good neighbourhood' is an effort to recover some of the lost content of the idea in an age of globalization.

In truth, *bon voisinage* is not a practice that has been unknown to other parts of the world. The antecedents are many, but they rarely have been seen to serve a larger political purpose. The historical geography of Europe, which happens to have more kilometres of political boundary per unit of land than any other continent, is replete with examples of boundary cooperation. Most of these have been very localized. John House, for example, describes Europe's designation of parallel frontier zones of varying widths on either side of a border within which local residents are granted special customs and other privileges. Such zones, promoting small-scale frontier exchanges, usually have been negotiated bilaterally, and are in the limited interest of the border residents (House 1980, 459).

An illustrative historical case is the boundary arrangement contained in a 1926 commercial treaty between Hungary and Yugoslavia (Boggs 1940, 237-45; League of Nations 1929-30, 117-29). Its purpose was 'to afford reciprocal traffic between the frontier zones the facilities required for daily needs', and, to that end, the text defined two 10 to 15 kilometre border zones on either side of the line. The agreement enumerated the foodstuffs (for example fresh vegetables and milk) and other necessary items (for example firewood and building materials) that could be transported across the border without payment of duties. For the benefit of local-area farmers, it provided that fields could be tilled and livestock pastured on the other side of the boundary line. 'Frontier permits' would be issued also to other persons who needed to cross the border regularly. Specific crossing places and times were designated. In urgent situations, 'frontier passes' could be given out summarily. During emergencies such as floods, forest fires, or other widespread calamities, frontier residents were authorized 'to cross the frontier by all routes by day or by night'.

The 1926 Hungarian-Yugoslav treaty provided as well for some bilateral cooperation of an institutional kind. With a view to 'ensuring mutual assistance' and to 'creating between the frontier authorities on both sides the atmosphere of good neighbourliness', the chief officers of the two nations' frontier authorities were to meet regularly. Those officers were to 'endeavour to remove any difficulties arising from incidents of slight importance and redress any grievances of the inhabitants of the frontier zones'. This suggests different levels at which border-related diplomacy can be conducted, although the full international potential of 'good neighbour' diplomacy is not yet recognized.

Three Levels of Transborder Diplomacy

A diplomacy of *bon voisinage* can occur at any or all of three levels. The first, and highest, level is 'summit' meetings between national political leaders that may include discussion of border-related matters. Not uncommonly, these take place at border locations. Such sites at or near the political boundaries between countries may be seen as symbolically located, even if they are not exactly situated geometrically, midway between the two nations' capitals, making it possible for their leaders 'to meet each other halfway'. These meetings remain essentially centre-to-centre encounters, though the border settings highlight the factor of the two countries' contiguity.

The 'halfway' sites chosen may not actually be at formal boundary lines but, rather, at the common edges of their respective spheres of control – geopolitical equilibrium points. Sometimes they are at military fronts, where armies meet, for example, the historic meeting spot in 1807 of Napoleon and Alexander I on a raft in the Neman River near Tilsit (now Sovetsk, on Russia's Kaliningrad Oblast border with Lithuania), where they divided European power between themselves. When leaders' meetings take place at settled borders of already recognized state domains, they can gain resonance. The border location enhances (as does the very boundary line) the concept of 'equal sovereignty'.

An example of a regular series of border-situated leaders' meetings, occurring in the North American context, are the encounters that, traditionally, have taken place at or near the border between the United States and Mexico when a new U.S. President is elected. The *encuentro* that occurred in January 1981 between the American President-elect, Ronald Reagan, and the President of Mexico at the time, José López Portillo, illustrates the pattern. For Americans, this border powerfully defines the U.S.-Mexican relationship. 'Our friends south of the border' was the way President Reagan referred to the leaders and officials of Mexico (and even of other, more distant Latin American nations). It is worth noting, too, that Reagan's actual 'first trip out of the country' following his inauguration was 'a get-acquainted meeting', as he termed it, with the Prime Minister of Canada, Pierre Elliott Trudeau (Reagan 1990, 240). This took place in Ottawa, the capital of Canada – a political centre, but also a location close to the northern border of the United States and thus, perhaps, from a Washington-centric perspective also a peripheral location.

President Reagan's first instinct, as the new American leader at the time, was to keep the fences of the United States mended with the nation's 'friends' to the south and to the north. There happened to be a larger, longer-term policy purpose in his diplomatic design as well: to lay a basis of neighbourly understanding at the leadership level for negotiation of what he had termed, in November 1979, a 'North American accord' – the germ of what became the North American Free Trade Agreement (NAFTA). As Reagan later recalled, he had long believed that 'the largest countries' of North America should 'forge a closer alliance and become more of a power in the world'. A grouping of the United States with Mexico and Canada would be 'to our mutual economic benefit', and the example of the three North American countries working together 'might be able to help the Latin American countries help themselves'. Reagan's notion of tripartite North American cooperation was deeply rooted in the concept of neighbourhood. His very term, 'accord', suggests direct, heart-to-heart contact between nations. Revealingly, when he initially proposed the North American accord idea in 1979, he said: 'It is time we stopped thinking of our nearest neighbours as foreigners' (Henrikson 1993, 77; Reagan 1990, 240).

Subsequent U.S. presidents have continued the practice, now diplomatically *de rigueur* within the North American neighbourhood, of early meetings with their Mexican and Canadian counterparts. This is now also done in a 'trilateral' context, partly to broaden the three-way economic cooperation that began with NAFTA but also to address serious new issues that have arisen, including cross-border terrorism and narco-trafficking. During the presidency of George W. Bush, at a meeting in Waco, Texas, in March 2005, the Security and Prosperity Partnership of North America (SPP) dialogue among the three countries was initiated. Part of its stated purpose was to develop 'Smart, Secure Borders', involving collaboration to establish 'risk-based screening standards' for goods and people but also to facilitate cross-border travel and trade throughout the continent by improving 'supply chain security'. There was also provision for the exchange of 'additional law enforcement liaison officers' to assist in criminal and security investigations (White House 2006). Some critics, fearful of a supranational 'North American Union' modeled on the EU was being contemplated, imagined that a 'NAFTA Super-Highway' was being planned. While these suspicions were unfounded, the three countries, and their component states and provinces, have made efforts to improve their road systems and traffic supervision for safer trucking. The SPP continues as does NAFTA. President Barack Obama, like his predecessors, met early with his southern and northern counterparts. He saw President Felipe Calderón in Washington in January 2009 while he himself was still president-elect and he went to Ottawa in February – it was his first foreign trip as president – to visit with Prime Minister Stephen Harper and to demonstrate his neighbourliness with Canada.

The second, or middle level, of the diplomacy of good neighbourhood is that which occurs through ministerial or subministerial contacts. These, too, are often regularized and, to an extent, are even institutionalized. Not only the ministries of foreign affairs, notably the U.S. State Department, but also other departments and agencies of governments have interests in border-related policy matters. Commerce and immigration authorities and also senior officials dealing with the environment and public health, as well as crime, increasingly are involved. In 1976, in order to coordinate the handling of U.S.-Mexican relations across a broad institutional front, President Jimmy Carter and President López Portillo established a new Consultative Mechanism. The following year a Border subgroup was set up (House 1982, 256). Even older are the treaty-based binational commissions that have been established for the management of borders, including possible adjustment of the borderline itself. In the context of U.S.-Mexican border relations, there is the International Boundary and Water Commission (IBWC), dating from the 1848 Treaty of Guadalupe Hidalgo, and also a boundary water treaty of 1889. In the U.S.-Canadian context, there is the International Joint Commission (IJC), created by the 1909 Boundary Waters Treaty. This has a somewhat broader purview, and has developed a strong environmental interest.

The third, and lowest, level is the subnational level. 'Diplomacy' at this level may be conceived to include consultations that take place directly across national lines between state (or provincial) and also municipal authorities (Duchacek 1986). Discussions that occur between nongovernmental or private-sector groups desirous of good-neighbourly relations also might be included. Examples are the U.S. SW Border Regional Commission and, on the Mexican side, a Co-ordinating Commission of the National Programme for the Borders and Free Zones, which were created in 1977 (House 1982, 256). A particularly innovative effort, based on the concept of the Rocky Mountain bioregion bisected by the U.S.-Canadian border is the citizen-initiated Yellowstone to Yukon Conservation Initiative (Y2Y) (Chester 2006). To the extent that such entities are established not just for the purpose of advancing interests of the resident communities in the border areas but also for the sake of a wider comity between neighbouring countries, they can be understood to have a 'political' purpose. This broader national-level and even international purpose may justify the non-strict use of the term, 'diplomatic', to describe the politically relevant portion of such inter-local representation and discourse. 'Citizen diplomacy' can genuinely exist, if it is structured and also if it is strategic.

As suggested above, 'border incidents' can be used to develop deeper international connections, at every 'diplomatic' level. For example, the violence that has been occurring in Mexico along its border with the United States, largely owing to the inter-cartel 'drug wars' that have been going on there, has commanded American attention, not least because U.S. citizens have been killed. The murder of three members of the 'official family' of the U.S. Consulate in Ciudad Juárez in March 2010 provoked a strong response, from the Mexican government as well as the American government. The previous March, Secretary of State Hillary Clinton had traveled to Mexico City, and then to Monterrey, where she declared: 'This situation is intolerable for honest, law-abiding citizens of Mexico, my country or of anywhere people of conscience live'. She also, however, frankly acknowledged during her trip that the United States carried some of the blame for the crisis because of its 'insatiable' appetite for illicit drugs and its role as a source of smuggled arms for the cartels. Although considered long overdue, her acknowledgement was well received by the news media and politicians in Mexico. It no doubt helped to gain the Calderón government's acceptance of an Obama administration plan to place more U.S. personnel along the border and inside Mexico itself – in 'fusion centres' where American intelligence agents would be embedded with Mexican analysts (Ellingwood 2009; *The Economist* 2010). Americans have considered Mexicans 'distant neighbors' (Riding 1986). But trouble has brought them closer.

Local and National 'Mending Walls': Consociative Diplomacy

Ideally, a political boundary between communities should be a 'Mending Wall', to use the title of Robert Frost's widely known poem about boundary-keeping in New England (Frost 1946). Frost posited that, in 'walking the line' between fields, physical neighbours could become, by virtue of their common effort of jointly maintaining a boundary line, neighbours in a further sense – together making a neighbourhood. The reciprocating process of boundary maintenance – fence mending – pulls the divided parties together – like a zipper. Boundaries are, as a chief cartographer of the U.S. State Department, Bradford Thomas, has written, the 'mortar' that holds together, as well as simply delineates, 'the giant mosaic' that is the global map (Thomas 1999, 69). To a degree, they are the 'mortar' that binds the political world itself.

Conventional thought suggests that there are two basic strategies for making peace between communities: those of an associative kind and those of a dissociative kind. The former are based on the premise that removing barriers between hostile or suspicious parties will help to reconcile them. The latter hold to the opposite assumption, that keeping antagonistic parties apart will reduce their antagonism and, in time, even placate them. Here a third strategy, the 'consociative', is proposed. More than just a combination of the first two strategies, it is based on the idea that the interaction, and even actual linking, of societies at and across boundaries in space, with the semi-permeable boundary zone working to form as well as to define a relationship, is a key to peacemaking.

There are 'schools' of belief concerning this subject. Those of an idealistic turn of mind have tended to favour the associative approach, preferring boundaries that are 'meeting places'. A few writers, such as the British geographer Lionel William Lyde, have argued that boundary lines should be drawn where they can have an 'assimilative' effect. He went so far as to propose during the First World War that boundaries should be 'anti-defensive'. He meant not only that boundaries should not be highly fortified. They should be 'identified with geographical features which are associated naturally with the meeting of peoples and persons in the ordinary routine of *peaceful* intercourse' (Lyde 1915, 2).

The dominant perspective on political boundaries, however, surely has been the realistically-minded assertion that boundaries are, by definition, dissociative – or 'dissimilative', in Lyde's lexicon. As a former geographer of the U.S. Department of State, Samuel Whittemore Boggs, pointed out in 1940, 'To at least some degree they restrict the movements of peoples and the exchange of goods, of money, even of ideas' (Boggs 1940, 11). Much the same basic outlook upon boundaries is adopted by Stephen B. Jones. Taking issue with Lyde's assimilationist argument, Jones declared: 'Almost inevitably an international boundary offers some impedance to the circulation of people and goods. Therefore there may be some advantage – other things being equal – in locating a boundary in a zone where circulation is relatively weak' (Jones 1945, 8). Earlier, Lyde's 'academic idealism' had been criticized also by the British boundary-maker, Colonel Sir Thomas H. Holdich, who asserted that 'the first and greatest object of a national frontier is to ensure peace and goodwill between contiguous peoples by putting a definite edge to the national political horizon, so as to limit unauthorized expansion and trespass' (Holdich 1916, x).

The trouble with both of these contending 'schools' is that they do not clearly recognize the essential relation between the associative and dissociative aspects of boundaries. A consociative border strategy integrally connects these. Its essence is structured cooperation – spatial and functional. Consociatively connected countries are confederated in contiguity, so to speak, through formal and informal transborder linkages. The human use of these joint structures, in day-to-day local dealings and in wider transactions as well, can stitch foreign and even alienated countries together. This style of politically conscious border-based exchange and communication between countries may be called 'consociative diplomacy'.

Confrontation, Communication, and Internationalization

There must be 'a better way' to make as well as represent boundaries between countries, so as to help resolve international tensions and engender peaceful and productive relations. As indicated earlier, there are three basic conditions that an effective peace-through-bordering, or 'good neighbour', diplomacy may need to fulfill. It is to these that we now turn.

The first premise of effective transborder diplomacy, as suggested at the outset of this chapter, is that for border relations to bring larger intercommunal or, if between sovereign parties, international peace, the political actors, seated in their respective territories, must think of themselves as 'facing', or geopolitically confronting and also directly addressing, one another. Indeed, the very word 'frontier', derives from the Latin word, *frons*, for 'forehead'. Thus an anthropomorphic factor is built into the very idea of international relations at and across frontiers.

The orientation of a country is a very complex matter, involving not only geography itself but also history and culture – as well as, more specifically, a country's foreign policy traditions and habitual style of diplomacy. The basic point is a deceptively simple one: in order to negotiate effectively with another country, a country must *face* that country. It is only thus that a vista of opportunity can be opened up, which an entire society as well as its leadership can and will 'see'. And, of course, the diplomatic confrontation should be mutual: the neighbouring country must 'see' these prospects, too. As suggested earlier, direct 'front'-'front' negotiations, though not the only ones possible, are the most likely to result in breakthroughs for peace.

Besides the requirement that countries must 'face' each other for an improvement of transborder relations to have a pervasive effect throughout their societies, there is a second condition that, as has been suggested, needs to be met: that the physically juxtaposed societies be organized internally in such a way as to enable relevant information and imagery from the border areas to be communicated to the centre, and around the rest of the country. The country must work cybernetically (Deutsch 1966). The national 'body' must be well articulated. It must have a solid skeleton – that is to say, a strong constitutional-political framework as well as a sound transportation infrastructure grid. It must have an efficient digestive, or economic, system, so that internal flows of goods and services occur without price discrimination or other distorting effects. It must have a responsive nervous system as well, so that impulses from the periphery are transmitted freely and throughout the whole society. The effectiveness of transfrontier diplomacy requires that border zones and their populations must be adequately represented at the centre, or at least have sufficient communication with it. The capital or, more broadly, the national government must have some presence in, or at least good correspondence with, the border areas. The importance of the internal 'structure' of a country in shaping its external geographical relationships, as Jean Gottmann noted, has not been well recognized (Gottmann 1973, 143-54).

The third condition for a successful 'peace through neighbourhood' strategy, as indicated, is the international one. There can be agreements across borders, including not only bilateral pacts but also, where relevant, multilateral ones affecting whole international regions, which advance and support transfrontier relationships. These agreements, because they join pairs or groups of countries formally, can enhance international stability and serve as a basis of confidence for transactions of economic and other kinds. They are often legal as well as political commitments. They are to be taken seriously because they can be binding. In particular, treaties which include good neighbourhood, or *bon voisinage*, provisions joining countries together via cooperative border arrangements are needed, not only to symbolize but also to actually secure 'close' relations between contiguous nations.

In the part of the world of the original good neighbour policy, there have been many occasions for the practice of transfrontier diplomacy, sometimes resulting in formal accords. The New World, born in intercolonial rivalry with a plurality of 'pre-modern' heritages as well, is notorious for its disputes over territory and boundaries. Some of the notable ones have been those between Bolivia and Paraguay, Peru and Colombia, Haiti and the Dominican Republic, Guatemala and British Honduras, and Peru and Ecuador, a recurrent conflict that in 1995 again broke out in open warfare. In every one of these cases, the peace machinery of the Inter-American System, a moral-political-legal framework, was used to help contain and resolve the controversy.

The Peru-Ecuador case is unusual in that a number of the hemisphere's great powers were directly involved, as guarantors of a settlement – functioning as a kind of 'Western Hemispheric Centre'. The effective instrument was the Peruvian-Ecuadorian Protocol of Peace, Friendship, and Boundaries signed in Rio de Janeiro in 1942 both by the disputants and by Argentina, Brazil, Chile, and the United States. Brazil has been the leader of the guarantors group. The controversy was not completely settled in 1942, in part because of specific alignment disagreements (termed *impases*) concerning several sectors of the Rio Protocol boundary line (Thomas 1999, 79-80). After further fighting in 1981, in 1984, and in 1995, the matter finally was resolved in an agreement – the Brasilia Presidential Act – signed by Peru's and Ecuador's presidents under Brazilian auspices on 26 October 1998. This new treaty was 'sealed' and put into effect not in Brazil but on the frontier itself on 13 May 1999, at the border town of Puesto Cahuide. Peru's President, Alberto K. Fujimori and Ecuador's President Jamil Mahuad met there, shook hands, and ceremoniously together dedicated an orange-painted boundary stone. This was the last of the settings marking the border and it completed the boundary gestalt, so to speak, spatially and temporally. 'Here is the final frontier [boundary] between two neighbouring peoples that managed to come together and reach agreement', declared President Fujimori. 'We are putting an end to disputes', said President Mahuad, 'closing wounds to start a new, healthy life' (*The New York Times* 1999). Photographs and other recordings publicized the event throughout Peru and Ecuador, Latin America, and the world.

In its substance, the Peru-Ecuador border agreement might not have been possible but for the two countries' acceptance of an arbitration decision rendered by the Brazil-chaired guarantors – the Centre. The agreement was a 'package deal'. It collectively settled all of the issues assigned to binational commissions dealing with commerce and navigation, with border integration, with confidence-building measures, and with on-site border demarcation. A vital element of the package was Ecuador's final acceptance in principle of the 1942 Rio Protocol's line of division, which had precluded it from being an 'Amazon' (and thus Atlantic) country, as well as a Pacific coastal country. This favoured Peru, though Ecuador did actually gain a square kilometre of private – not formally sovereign – territory on the Peruvian side of the border. This symbolic piece of real estate, at Tiwinza on top of the Cordillera del Condor, was the site of Ecuador's last military holdout against Peru in the 1995 war. The place was to be consecrated by a monument to the country's war dead. The other key element was Ecuador's gaining navigation rights, again without sovereign access, to the Amazon River and its tributaries in Peru, along with two trading centres thereupon. The treaty further provided for establishment, by both countries, of a transborder ecological park across which transit would be guaranteed and within which no military forces (only police) would be allowed (Simmons 1999, 15, 20). In separate understandings, the two countries planned also to link up their electrical grids; and Peru agreed that Ecuador, an oil producer, could have access to one of its underutilized pipelines (*The New York Times* 1998).

The 'incentives' for this border accord were both national and international. Each country would save in terms of defence expenses and the cost of human lives. It was clearer than ever before to both Peru and Ecuador that mending fences between themselves was a de facto precondition of their being accepted, by other hemispheric countries, in a broader neighbourhood of international cooperation. This included involvement with the trading group, MERCOSUR, as well as some USD 1.5 billion in international loans for future development of the two countries' poorer regions that was on offer from the Centre (The New York Times 1999). The internal and external attractions of the agreement were such that it could be observed from afar that 'South America may, for the foreseeable future, in 1995 have seen its last war over territorial claims' (*The Economist* 1998a).

Conclusion

How significant are these peace-via-borders international arrangements? Are they likely to prove to be effective in engendering further bilateral processes of reconciliation and, more generally, the spread of a spirit of regional good neighbourhood? Are they, in short, relevant today, given that they emphasize action at the level of the nation-state, or modernity, and may not take adequate account either of pre-modern ethnicity issues or the future prospect of post-modern, post-intergovernmental integration on a global plane? Maybe the very idea is anachronistic.

The common sense of the matter seems to be that borders, though their technical functions and policy contours are changing, are as important as they ever have been. To be sure, the processes of 'globalization' would seem to be indifferent, or even hostile, to borders. 'But it is almost as though international politics obeyed some strange principle of the conservation of finitude', The Economist speculatively observes. 'As some borders fall, so others rise' (*The Economist* 1998b). In Europe, in particular, one has seen that, as internal restrictions on the flow of goods, capital, and persons within the EU itself are being removed, pressures increase for greater controls at the outer margins of the Union as it has enlarged. Some relatively new EU members, such as the Austrians, that in the past had quiet border towns on their frontiers have found themselves, along their reopened borderlands, on the administrative front lines, for Europe generally. This has increased the need for the European Union 'to arrive at more coherent frontier region policies' (Anderson 1996, 126).

Transboundary diplomacy, whether based on treaties or not, may not produce enormous 'spillover' effects. This is true even though some boundary-focused international agreements, such as the 1996 Hungarian-Romanian treaty, reach well into the interiors of the countries involved, illustrating the 'core-periphery adjacent State' type of transaction that is described in House's model. Some of these contacts and exchanges may seem legal and technical. Moreover, functional integration across borders does not automatically lead to 'political and social integration', as Michael

Keating concludes from an extensive analysis of European regional cooperation policies (Keating 1998, 182). Nevertheless, international contacts across borders, which may be facilitated by programmes such as those sponsored by the Council of Europe or by the European Commission's INTERREG programme, do form networks that can have a definite cohesive force (Anderson 1996, 121; Keating 1998, 180-1).

Increasingly, there is developing, not only in Europe, a phenomenon that Keating describes as 'an interpenetration of territorial policy spaces' (Keating 1998, 183). This interpenetration can blur the distinctions between places and it can confuse identities, in what might otherwise be a beneficial post-modern fashion. Pre-modern patterns – that is, the relationships of ethnic or nationality groups to their homelands – may fade badly. Even modern, or nation-state, ties of belonging – the psychological level at which diplomacy traditionally is conducted – may loosen, pulled apart by a welter of competing juridisdictions, on different geographical scales, varying with the different policy purposes being served. Ways of holding social entities together are needed. 'Traditional diplomacy', as Keating rightly recognizes but does not stress positively enough, 'covers the whole range of state interests and seeks to present a united front to the world' (Keatin 1998, 178).

There is something to be said for keeping conventional political boundaries of nations at the fore. They are the sovereign 'interface' between countries. The entities which they define remain, still, the locus of loyalty, of patriotic feeling, for peoples in most parts of the world. The international system is yet, basically, an interstate system. Diplomacy, the method by which states address each other, retains a fundamental importance. This may even be increasing. Diplomatic contact is the only way by which countries can deal with each other as wholes. For diplomacy to work, nations must continue to have 'personalities'. *Persona*, by definition, is unitary (Strawson 1959, 87-116).

In this situation, the personification of international relations through meetings between nations' political leaders at borders can have a pivotal, even transformative role, for such encounters interconnect the 'bodies politic' of countries in ways that other kinds of communication, even summit meetings held elsewhere, may not. The national body 'gestures' made at border locations have a directness, spontaneity, and force that those made in capital cities rarely have. They actually touch another country; and its people, and those of the country doing the touching, can feel it.

Boundaries do make friends as well as foes. They function, at any level, in a way to stabilize social relationships. As John Brinckerhoff Jackson, philosopher of landscape, has written, 'They make residents out of the homeless, neighbours out of strangers, strangers of enemies' (Jackson 1972, 15). They can be transformative, and so can a diplomacy that imaginatively takes account of them.

It has been the fundamental purpose of this chapter to challenge the notion that international political boundaries are chiefly, as the Geopolitiker Karl Haushofer considered them, 'fighting places'. They are not, however, simply 'meeting places', either. Borders and border control systems are more complex phenomena: they both divide and unify. When synthesized across national lines they can be, in addition, 'joining places', capable of connecting wholly different countries, consociatively, in organized cooperation, across border regions, in good neighbourhood.

Acknowledgements

This chapter is based in part on the author's (2000, 2005) article, 'Facing Across Borders: The Diplomacy of *Bon Voisinage*', *International Political Science Review* 21:2, 121-47, and the chapter 'Good Neighbour Diplomacy Revisited', in Nicol, H.N. and Townsend-Gault, I. (eds.), *Holding the Line: Borders in a Global World* (Vancouver: UBC Press), 348-77.

References

Anderson, M. (1996), *Frontiers: Territory and State Formation in the Modern World* (Cambridge: Polity Press).

Bevans, C.I. (comp.) (1972), *Treaties and Other International Agreements of the United States of America, 1776-1949* (Washington, DC: United States Printing Office).

Boggs, S.W. (1940), *International Boundaries: A Study of Boundary Functions* (New York: Columbia University Press).

Chester, C.C. (2006), *Conservation across Borders: Biodiversity in an Interdependent World* (Washington DC: Island Press).

Deutsch, K.W. (1966), *The Nerves of Government: Models of Political Communication and Control* (New York: Free Press).

Dictionnaire de la terminologie du droit international (1960), (Paris: Librairie du Recueil Sirey).

Duchacek, I.D. (1986), 'International Competence of Subnational Governments: Borderlands and Beyond', in Martínez, O.J. (ed.), *Across Boundaries: Transborder Interaction in Comparative Perspective* (El Paso: Texas Western Press).

Ellingwood, K. (2009), 'Hillary Clinton wraps up Mexico visit, calls drug violence "intolerable"', *Los Angeles Times* 27 March 2009.

Frost, R. (1946), *The Poems of Robert Frost* (New York: The Modern Library).

Gottmann, J. (ed.)(1980a), *Centre and Periphery: Spatial Variation in Politics* (Beverly Hills: Sage Publications).

Gottmann, J. (1980b), 'Spatial Partitioning and the Politician's Wisdom', *International Political Science Review* 1:4, 432-55.

Gottmann, J. (1973), *The Significance of Territory* (Charlottesville: University Press of Virginia).

Guerrant, E.A. (1950), *Roosevelt's Good Neighbor Policy* (Albuquerque: University of New Mexico).

Henrikson, A.K. (1993), 'A North American Community: "From the Yukon to the Yucatan"', in Binnendijk, H. and Locke, M. (eds.), *The Diplomatic Record, 1991–1992* (Boulder: Westview Press).

Holdich, T.H. (1916), *Political Frontiers and Boundary Making* (London: Macmillan).

House, J.W. (1980), 'The Frontier Zone: A Conceptual Problem for Policy Makers', *International Political Science Review* 1:4, 456-77.

Jackson, J.B. (1972), *American Space: The Centennial Years, 1865-1876* (New York: Norton).

Jones, S.B. (1945), *Boundary-Making: A Handbook for Statesmen, Treaty Editors and Boundary Commissioners* (Washington DC: Carnegie Endowment for International Peace).

Kasperson, R.E. and Minghi, J.V. (1969), *The Structure of Political Geography* (Chicago: Aldine Publishing Company).

Keating, M. (1998), *The New Regionalism in Western Europe: Territorial Restructuring and Political Change* (Cheltenham: Edward Elgar).

League of Nations (1929-30), 'Treaty of Commerce Between Hungary and Yugoslavia, concluded 24 July 1926', *Treaty Series* 97(2222), 103-63.

Lyde, L.W. (1915), *Some Frontiers of Tomorrow: An Aspiration for Europe* (London: A. and C. Black).

Nations Unies (1997), *Charte des Nations Unies et Statut de la Cour internationale de justice* (New York: le Département de l'information des Nations Unies).

Prescott, J.R.V. (1987), *Political Frontiers and Boundaries* (London: Allen and Unwin).

Ratzel, F. (1892), 'The Laws of the Spatial Growth of States', in Kasperson, R.E. and Minghi, J.V. (eds), *The Structure of Political Geography* (Chicago: Aldine Publishing Company).

Reagan, R. (1990), *An American Life* (New York: Simon and Schuster).

Riding, A. (1986), *Distant Neighbors: A Portrait of the Mexicans* (New York: Vintage Books).

Simmons, B.A. (1999), 'Territorial Disputes and Their Resolution: The Case of Ecuador and Peru', *Peaceworks* 27 (Washington, DC: United States Institute of Peace).

Strawson, P.F. (1959), *Individuals: An Essay on Descriptive Metaphysics* (London: Methuen).

The Economist (2010), 'Turning to the Gringos for help', *The Economist* 27 March 2010, 41-2.

The Economist (1998a), 'Peace in the Andes', *The Economist* 31 October 1998, 35-36.

The Economist (1998b), 'Good Fences', *The Economist* 19 December 1998, 19-22.

The New York Times (1999), 'Peru and Ecuador Leaders Seal Border Treaty', *The New York Times* 14 May 1999.

The New York Times (1998), 'Peru and Ecuador Sign Treaty to End Longstanding Conflict', *The New York Times* 27 October 1998.

Thomas, B.L. (1993), 'International Boundaries: Lines in the Sand (and the Sea)', in Demko, G.J. and Wood, W.B. (eds.), *Reordering the World: Geopolitical Perspectives on the 21st Century* (Boulder: Westview Press).

United Nations (1990), *Charter of the United Nations and Statute of the International Court of Justice* (New York: Department of Public Information, United Nations).

Welles, S. (1944), *The Time of Decision* (New York: Harper and Brothers).

White House (2006), 'The Security and Prosperity Partnership of North America: Next Steps', *Office of the Press Secretary* 31 March 2006.

Wood, B. (1961), *The Making of the Good Neighbor Policy* (New York: Columbia University Press).

The Border as Method: Towards an Analysis of Political Subjectivities in Transmigrant Spaces[1]

Stefanie Kron

Introduction

The emergence and reproduction of transnational social networks, economic alliances, political ideologies, citizenship practices, and cultural identities created by cross-border migration are at the centre of current sociological research on international migration in the Americas. These studies are influenced by the so-called 'transnational turn' (Levitt and Sørensen 2004).[2] However, little systematic research has been carried out so far on the importance of borders and border crossings for the analysis of political subjectivities. This chapter aims to help fill this gap by theorizing borders and border crossings with the aid of postcolonial and feminist approaches in order to draft a methodological framework for the empirical analysis of political subjectivities in transmigrant spaces.

---

1   I thank William Hiscott for his assistance with the translation of the Spanish and German excerpts and the primary editing of this chapter. I would also like to thank Maria Lidola for her well-informed suggestions regarding the discussion on the intersectionality concept.

2   Since Linda Bash et al. started the discussion on the transnational turn in American migration studies with the publication of *Nations Unbound: Transnational Projects, Postcolonial Predicaments, and Deterritorialized Nation-States* (1993), an abundance of books and papers on diverse aspects of 'migrant transnationalism' has been published. A selection of more recent and influential publications includes for example Guarnizo et al. (2003), Khagram and Levitt (2008), Levitt and Schiller (2004), Mahler and Pessar (2001), Portes and DeWind (2007), Pries (2004, 2005), Smith (2006), Sørensen (2008) and Vertovec (2009).

The Empirical Background

Even though this chapter deals with methodological problems, it will be supported empirically by the findings of my own research on the return movement of Guatemalan war refugees. This movement, known as *el retorno*, can be considered as a paradigmatic case for the projected debate on borders, cross-border migration, and political subjectivities in the Latin American context (see, among others, Pessar 2001).

The vast majority of the approximately 23,000 returned refugees stem from indigenous peasant families who had been displaced to Mexico in the early 1980s. In particular, indigenous mothers were seen as a 'threat to the nation' and thus suffered from severe persecution by the Guatemalan army. In the 1990s, after an yearlong and ultimately successful process of political mobilization and negotiation with the Guatemalan government for their right to return in dignity, which included demands for self-organized and collective return, access to land, social security, physical integrity, demilitarization, and local cultural and political autonomy, the refugees returned to Guatemala and created new rural settlements influenced by the model of social organization of the indigenous community [*comunidad indígena*]. Afterwards, national and international scholars as well as professionals in peace and conflict studies considered the returned refugees [*retornados*] and, among them, especially the women returnees [*retornadas*] to be important pressure groups in the peace process (see Garbers 2002, 165). My own research on the *el retorno* movement was carried out in 2002 in several communities of returned refugees in Guatemala. It included ethnographic fieldwork as well as biographical interviews (see Kron 2005, 2007, 2008).

State of the Art and Hypothesis

In general, the few empirical surveys which deal with the effect of border crossings on political consciousness-building and subject constitution lack necessary complexity. The main reason for this is that social scientists tend to base their analyses on fixed categories of social inequality and identity. This can be clearly shown by a revision of the state of the art on *el retorno*. Almost all publications concerning the refugees' political mobilization for return consider it to be nourished by a sort of 'search for a place in the nation' even though the *el retorno* movement emerged in the transnational setting of the Mexican refugee camps. These camps were mainly managed by the United Nations High Commissioner for Refugees (UNHCR) and international NGOs.[3] Notwithstanding, three different patterns of interpretation can be distinguished: first, *el retorno* is analysed mainly as a process of the refugees' self-

---

3   An exception here is Patricia Pessar's article on *el retorno* (2001). Pessar argues that the politicization of refugee women included citizenship claims beyond the nation developed in line with the transnational human rights discourse of the international organizations which ran the Mexican refugee camps.

awareness as part of the discriminated indigenous Maya population of Guatemala (see for example Crosby 1999; Nolin Hanlon 1999; Stepputat 1994; Warren 1998). Second, it is interpreted as a process which primarily involved the formation of a class identity as peasants and day labourers (see for example Avancso 1992, Falla 1992; Manz 1988). A third pattern of interpretation, in turn, considers *el retorno* to be a process which, above all, formed a strong gender consciousness especially among the refugee women (see for example Arbour 1994; Maquín and CIAM 1994; and Pessar 2001). In sum, although the majority of the previous studies stress the importance of the refugees' border crossings – displacement to Mexico and return to Guatemala – to their political consciousness-building, next to the assumption of the formation of a national identity, in each study only one of the prevalent identity categories and axis' of social inequality, either race, class, or gender, is stipulated to be the 'motor' for the political articulation of the refugees.

Aided by the findings of my own research on *el retorno*, in contrast, I will bring forward the argument that transmigration contributes to the constitution of 'nomadic subjectivities' which are primarily performed both by the crossing of political borders and by transgressions of symbolic boundaries such as race, class, and gender.

Organization of this Analysis

The following section will be dedicated to the question regarding the manner in which the theoretical concepts of *intersectionality* and *border feminism* support or fail to support the argument outlined above. The third section will then discuss methodical problems concerning the empirical implementation of this theoretical framework. Subsequently, the fourth section includes a showcase analysis of the political subjectivities related to the *el retorno* movement by applying the theoretical and methodical considerations outlined in the previous two sections. The fifth, and last, section offers a conclusion of my findings.

Theoretical Remarks: Intersectionality and/or Border Feminism?

Intersectionality: A Contested Field?

According to Kimberlé Crenshaw, the 'pioneer' of the intersectionality approach, the main problem of identity politics is not 'that it fails to transcend difference, as some critics charge' but rather the opposite, namely 'that it frequently conflates or ignores intra-group differences' (Crenshaw 1991, 1242). In order to face this problem, Crenshaw introduced the term *intersectionality* in the mid-1980s as a concept to mediate 'the tension between assertions of multiple identities and the ongoing necessity of group politics' (ibid., 1296). Since then, the discussions mainly addressed two methodological problems to the intersectionality approach. These problems concern, first, which axis' of social inequality and which identity categories, such as race, class, gender, religion, region, and so on, should be included in the concept of intersectionality. Feminists such as Leslie McCall and Gudrun-Axeli Knapp, in contrast, strive to avoid the debate regarding the importance or non-importance of social categories. Whereas McCall (2005, 1771) defines intersectionality broadly as 'the relationships among multiple dimensions and modalities of social relations and subject formations', Knapp sums up the basics of intersectionality by focussing more on the experiences of discrimination: 'The predominant perspective has been looking at how different categories interact in shaping subjective experiences, often experiences of discrimination, how they determine access to resources and options, and how they are taken up in constructions of identity' (Knapp 2005, 259).

Second, the very basic analytical principle of intersectionality has also been questioned, that is the analytical category of social categories. Postcolonial or feminist theorists, for example Avtar Brah (1996) and Judith Butler (1993), express concern about the analytical category of social categories by stressing its effects on the production, structuring, and reproduction of power relations. Both Brah and Butler point out that social categories must be seen as contingent, that is that they are embedded in a specific history and in a particular social and cultural context. These concerns on social categories are summed up by the so-called 'anti-categorical complexity approach' which deconstructs analytical categories. Social life is considered too irreducibly complex – overflowing with multiple and fluid determinations of both subjects and structures – to make fixed categories anything but simplifying social fictions that produce inequalities in the process of producing differences (McCall 2005, 1773).

Border Feminism and its Critique

The 'anti-categorical complexity approach' comes very close to 'border feminism', also called '*mestiza* feminism'. As did the intersectionality concept, border feminism emerged in the 1980s. It was strongly influenced by the *Chicana* movement in the United States (see for example García 1989)[4] and was theoretically conceptualized by the *Chicana* activist and intellectual Gloria Anzaldúa. In her book *Borderlands/la Frontera: The New Mestiza* (1987), Anzaldúa defined the term 'borderland' in the following manner:

> *A borderland is a vague and undetermined place created by the emotional residue of unnatural boundary. It is a constant state of transition. The prohibited and forbidden are its inhabitants.* (Anzaldúa 1987, 3)

This conceptualization of the border as a transit zone also implies the potential for 'radical political subjectivity' which, according to Nancy Naples (2008, 7), can be considered the hallmark of the analysis of *Borderlands/la Frontera*:

---

4   *Chicano* is another term for Mexican Americans.

Anzaldúa and other scholars influenced by her work view borderlands as sites that can enable those dwelling there to be able to negotiate the contradictions and tensions found in diverse settings.

The borderland concept has been strongly criticized by Pablo Vila, who sees 'the tendency to construct the border crosser or the hybrid ... into a new *privileged subject of history*' (2003, 307). Furthermore, Vila expresses concern about what he describes as analytical homogenization of borders and border-crossing experiences. He states that current border theory runs the risk of considering a borderland to be

any physical or psychic space about which it is possible to address problems of boundaries: borders among different countries, borders among ethnicities ... , borders between genders, borders among disciplines, and the like. ... This approach not only homogenizes distinctive experiences but also homogenizes borders. (ibid., 308)

Vila's critical remarks on border theory reveal the need to specify the term borderland by defining the 'type' of border being conceptualized as the object of inquiry in each individual study. This also includes a visualization of the various researchers' aims and disciplinary backgrounds, even though the borderland concept implies an interdisciplinary methodology. Taking these considerations into account, in the case of this analysis, it should be mentioned that my disciplinary background is empirical political (micro-) sociology as well as social anthropology. My research focuses on Latin American studies with a special focus on transnational migration studies. I am especially interested in the importance of cross-border migration, migrants' encounters with national borders, and their experiences of border-crossings within the context of the processes of political consciousness-building and subject constitution.

Thus, I define borders as political borders which separate two nation-states by means of an imagined line. This line demarcates the formal territory of two different political, legal, cultural, and social orders. But, as the historian Walther L. Bernecker (2005) points out, since independency from colonial rule, political borders in Latin America have, de facto, always been culturally and socially permeable and politically undetermined because the subsequent postcolonial nation-state institutions were widely unwilling, uninterested, or incapable to establish complete territorial control in the border regions of their countries. Thus, the geographic regions surrounding the political borders can be considered as transit zones. To define these hybrid territories and socio-cultural spaces, I use the term borderlands, borrowed from Anzaldúa, as a methodological concept for empirical sociological research on transnational migration. In contrast to my definition of borders, I define 'boundaries' as what Vila calls 'borders among ethnicities' or 'borders between genders' (2003, 308). Accordingly, boundaries between members of various ethnicities, races, and genders, but also between members of different classes, religions, languages, and so on are symbolic and discursive borders of social constructions which form power relations, legitimize social inequality, and mould subjective experiences and personal and collective identities.

Coming to Vila's concern about the conception of political subjectivity in border theory, I would like to start with some considerations which I have deduced from my definitions of borders, boundaries, and borderlands. Border-crossing migrants not only must deal with the formal or legal aspects of border crossings (immigration regulations), which imply violent practices (for example persecution and deportation of irregular migrants), but they must also deal with the social and cultural boundaries linked to the presence of political borders. A borderland, therefore, is not only constituted by the incapacity of governments to establish effective control over their territories, but also by the history and presence of cross-border migration and transborder interactions, and by practices and strategies of negotiation and transgression of cultural and social boundaries on part of the border crossers. In this sense, I agree with Anzaldúa's idea of radical political subjectivity because it stresses the migrants' agencies which, according to Chéla Sandoval, may imply the appropriation of a diasporic strategy of consciousness and politics by means of 'a mobile crossing between races, genders, sexes, cultures, languages, and nations' (1998, 360). The inclusion of this 'subjective face of migration' (Karakayali and Tsianos 2007, 13) into the analytical framework of research on migration and borders also implies moving beyond 'methodological nationalism' (Schiller and Wimmer 2003). In doing so, the history and presence of the 'autonomy of migration' can be visualized and analysed as resisting and escaping forms of sociality to capitalism and nationalism. These forms of sociality have been hidden or marginalized by nationally-defined historiographies and social science (Papadopoulos et al. 2008, 202). Thus, the 'radicalness' of the borderland not only lies in the political subjectivity of border crossers but also in the methodology. However, taking into account Vila's critique that border theory tends to idealize the border crosser as a 'privileged subject of history' (2003, 307), the migrants' experiences of exclusion and violence at borders should be added to border theory because these experiences also form the border crossers' constitution as subjects (see Nayak and Suchland 2006, 480).

Border Feminism, Intersectionality, and Empirical Praxis

The principles of border feminism outlined above bring up the question regarding how to link this theoretical input with the praxis of empirical research. Here, the main problem is that the empirical implementation of a theory of borderlands and diasporic subjectivities seems to be difficult if not impossible without recourse to the analytical category of social categories. In order to face this problem, Brah distinguishes between the conceptual meaning of social categories as 'an object of social discourse, as an analytical category, and as a subject of political mobilization'. In doing so, she does not see categories as essential or fixed, but rather as markers of a 'field of contestation' formed 'within discursive and material processes and practices' (1996, 110).

As Brah points out, this implies that social categories may assume different meanings depending on the specific historical, economic, social, cultural, political, and academic contexts. Furthermore, the meaning of social categories may shift when different discourses access the same category. These considerations, in turn, pose even more questions in light of the praxis of empirical research. For example, which methodical instruments are appropriate to cover the concept that categories assume different meanings? Or, how does the meaning of these categories shift when the individual is placed into other categories? And, which social categories must be highlighted by the researcher, in other words, how can social categories relevant to the construction of political subjectivity be detected?

In order to cover these methodical concerns, I propose with Brah to utilize the following multi-level approach. Regarding the macro level, the context in which the respective social group of border crossing migrants is embedded should be reconstructed by applying 'multi-sited ethnography' (Marcus 1995) and the method of 'thick description' (Geertz 1973). The aim here is to identify what is called a 'system of cultural representation' by Stuart Hall (1997) or a 'narrative' by Homi K. Bhabha (1990). These terms are influenced by Benedict Anderson's (1983) idea of the nation as an 'imagined community' based and reproduced on a collective historical narrative. As Bhabha (ibid.), Hall (1990), and Gilroy (1993) point out, ethnic minorities and migrant or refugee groups create their own historical narratives as part of political consciousness-building. These are systems of cultural representation of political communities which are as imagined as the nation, but which transcend the borders of given nation-states by stressing marginalized experiences of (forced) displacement and exile. Thus, they are considered 'diaspora narratives' by Gilroy and 'counter-narratives' to the nation by Bhabha.

Coming to the micro level of political subjectivity in my multi-level approach, Brah interprets the 'narrating self and the rest' to be essential to it (1996, 138). Accordingly, I propose biographical methods (see Schütze 1983) in order to reconstruct what Hall calls 'self-narration' (1994, 183). According to Hall, a sense of personal identity is created through a biographical self-narration. As Marie-Françoise Chanfrault-Duchet points out, this self-narration contains several 'myths of self' that give meaning and coherence to the particular experiences of a person (1991, 81). In turn, the self-narration is embedded in a collective pattern of meaning, in a system of cultural representation which entails collective myths as well as gender-specific images, social constructions, and models. By doing so, it creates symbolic places for gender-specific subject positioning and for articulation of narrations of self. But, as Brah and Hall argue, this positioning of the subject is always momentary and elusive depending on the time, the place, and the counterpart of narrating the self.[5]

---

5   Brah's and Hall's considerations of the momentary character of subject constitution also highlight problems of cultural translation and power relations within biographical and ethnographical research methods (see also Behar 1993; Radcliffe and Westwood 1993).

El Retorno, Border Crossings and Political Subjectivities

In this section, I will draft a number of theses on the Guatemalan refugees' return movement *el retorno* in order to give a more vivid shape to the methodological framework outlined above.

Reconstructing the Context: Racism and Community-Building in Guatemala

The *el retorno* movement followed a counter-narrative to the nation which I call a 'predominant narrative of return'. This collective narrative, the self-narrations, and political subjectivities linked to *el retorno*, however, can only be understood before the backdrop of the specific history and form of the postcolonial nation-state in Guatemala. This is based on the construction and exclusion of the indigenous 'other'. The ethnically-determined fragmentation of space has long become the central ruling principle in Guatemala, a geography of power which Yvon Le Bot (1995, 309) characterizes as an 'apartheid regime'. This postcolonial concept of the so-called *ladino* Nation[6] marks as a discursive formation all modernization projects in Guatemala, from the implementation of the liberal, agricultural export state in the 1870s to the counter-insurgency and modernization programme 'National Plan for Security and Development' [*Plan Nacional de Seguridad y Desarollo* – PNSD] on part of the military governments in the beginning of the 1980s. The construction of ethnic difference functioned in the context of these projects as a dynamic mechanism of social demarcation. In this sense, the ethnic ascriptions such as *indio*, *ladino*, and *criollo* have shifted over time (Smith 1990, 3). Before this backdrop, the indigenous community [*comunidad indígena*] can be understood as a flexible concept of the (trans-) local communitarization, social membership, and cultural identification of indigenous groups in Guatemala. The political distribution of power accordingly, the *comunidad* opened itself more or less to the (nation-) state and its ruling society

---

In other words, the narrator, trying to fulfil assumed expectations of the interviewer or trying to be 'culturally understood' by the interviewing person, may highlight specific subject positions, whereas other positions which possibly would have been important for subject constitution in other moments of the life course are pushed to the background or ignored by the narrator.

6   In colonial times, *ladinos* were persons who lived neither in the *reducciones* and *pueblos de indios* [indian towns] founded and controlled by the Roman Catholic Church, nor in the urban settlements of Spanish colonial society. Over time, the term *ladino* shifted in definition to denote persons who had given up, according to descriptive criteria, the 'indigenous way of life' for a *mestizo* existence (see Le Bot 1995, 20). After the liberal reforms in 1871 in Guatemala, a further linguistic shift took place in that the *ladino* became to be defined in contrast to both the *criollo* (descendents of the Spanish conquistadors or European immigrants) and the *indio* as the imaginary national subject of the new nation-state. The term *ladino* marks therefore a differentiation from the European and the autochthonous groups in Guatemala (ibid., 88).

(Garbers 2002, 26-35). Nonetheless, the relationship between the 'world of the *comunidades*' and the national society in Guatemala was and still remains marked by an 'antagonistic relationship' (Smith 1990, 13).

The PNSD implemented under the military government of General Efraín Ríos Montt radicalized the national communitarization efforts in Guatemala. Ríos Montt aimed to destroy the *comunidad indígena* as a form of local social organization and cultural identification. The most significant element of his efforts was the murdering, division, and displacement of the indigenous groups whom he decried as a 'communist danger'. Another element was the consequential integration of the 'defeated' indigenous men into paramilitary structures (Stepputat 1999, 224). A third central element consisted in systematic sexual violence against indigenous women. Due to the perception of the indigenous women as biological and cultural reproducers of the *comunidad*, the indigenous 'mothers' and in particular the 'widows' of murdered dissidents were declared to be a 'national security danger' and therewith a military target (see CEH 1999).

Thus, the general context of *el retorno* can be described in the following manner. Central principles of rule bound to the concept of the nation-state in Guatemala, specifically the segregation and exclusion of indigenous groups, have led to plural social and cultural practices, to a divergence of geographic space and culture (nation versus *comunidad*) within the borders of the state and to a 'small-scope nation'. Flight and exile are manifestations of this divergence beyond the borders of the state and in the transnational space of Mexican refugee camps. For the Guatemalan refugees in Mexico, although 'exile' meant the destruction and loss of their homeland, it did not mean that they were homeless in the sense of that they were 'nationally uprooted'. *El retorno*, as a form of political articulation, made visible their social and cultural practices outside of the national culture.

The System of Representation: Return as a Counter-Narrative to the Nation

El retorno implied a specific system of cultural representation articulated through a predominant narrative of return based to a large degree upon the dissociation from the *ladino* nation and the Guatemalan nation-state.

In this manner, as Stepputat (1994) points out, the political representatives of the refugees in Mexico who used the term *el retorno* as the name of their project thus distanced themselves linguistically from the state-run repatriation campaigns carried out by the Guatemalan government in the refugee camps in Mexico which began in 1986/1987 under the term *repatriación* [repatriation]. Through its programme, the government envisioned the integration of returning migrants from Mexico into a militarized social order and the recruitment of the male refugees into paramilitary organizations. Because of this, the differentiation between *retorno* and *repatriación* became politically charged. The representatives of the refugees rejected paramilitarism and the concept of a national community of 'armed patriots'. Instead, they formulated their own political project of *retorno*.

At the same time, a normative concept of the social being of the refugee coalesced with the concept of *el retorno*. In contrast to the figure of the paramilitary combatant, the (male) subject of the 'real refugee' was constructed. This is a discursive figure that embodies the norms regulating social activities and moral standards within the refugee community. Belonging to this figure of the 'real refugee' are the experiences of migration and exile – for example violence, displacement, and dispossession – and, above all, the perception of exile as borderland, as transitory time-space. This is illustrated in the term *posada* [harbourage for passengers], a term with a strong religious connotation used by many refugees to denote their stay in Mexico. In this sense, the 'real refugee' saw his purpose in the struggle for return.

Furthermore, the refugee representative organizations established a collective narrative concerning the specific locations in which the concept of land ownership [*tierra*], the *comunidad indígena*, and poverty was conceptualized anew. They stressed the history of the struggle of the poor for economic progress, autonomy, dignity, and the resistance against the 'rich and their military' who were waging a war against the poor and who took possession of their land. Also, they envisioned a common future, during which the refugees return together, receive their land back, found autonomous *comunidades*, and live in safety.

Accordingly, the system of cultural representation of the *el retorno* movement was connected to the organization of a collective and community-oriented return to the *comunidades*. Above all, *tierra* is significant to this historical construct. Many refugees were influenced by the experiences of the internal migration in Guatemala in the 1960s and 1970s. During this time, these emigrated from the poverty-stricken highlands in western Guatemala to the Roman Catholic's colonization projects in the Ixcán lowlands. There, they obtained their own land for the first time. The reacquisition of this land, the *tierra*, in Ixcán sometimes even took on an obsessive character (see Le Bot 1995; Garbers 2002; Stepputat 1994). The myth was created of the Ixcán as 'promised', 'holy', or 'desecrated' land (see IGE 1987, 127, 144). Politically, this demand developed into the benchmark for mobilization for the whole return movement, although only around 13,000 of the approximately 45,000 recognized refugees in Mexico were from Ixcán (see CEH 1999, 259).

This historical construct of the refugees is clearly linked to groups and activists from the milieu of the *acción católica* [Catholic Action], an association oriented towards liberation theology and persecuted by the military governments. A group of activists from the *acción católica* founded in Mexico the *Iglesia Guatemalteca en el Exilio* [Guatemaltecan Church in Exile – IGE]. This church had close relations with displaced persons in the refugee camps, and it published and disseminated various publications regarding the fate of the refugees. It was, however, especially the work of Ricardo Falla, a cultural anthropologist and Jesuit who accompanied the refugees for many years, who aided in the construction of the *el retorno* narrative. In his time with the refugees, Falla recorded their experiences and life histories, 'translated' them into a coherent narrative, and published extensively on the topic (Falla 1992 and 1995).

Falla (1995) interprets forced displacement, exile, and return as a collective and personal rite of passage. He describes the movement in the time-space of flight and displacement as a *'tiempo de sueños'* [time of dreams], as a threshold experience, through which a human being is no longer that what he or she once was, but not yet that what he or she will become: '[w]e found ourselves in the beyond, in a nowhere, in the liminality' (ibid., 24). As he writes, Falla 'composed' the experiences of the refugees as a 'gospel', a 'religious epic', a 'trilogy' of displacement [exodus], exile [*posada*], and return [deliverance] (ibid., 33-8, 40, 56).

In a similar manner, the 'passage' is also central to the IGE's positions (1987). It is discussed in a number of variations: the male subject is transformed through its experience of flight and migration from displaced settler or wandering day labourer, previously without property and civil rights, into an autonomous peasant [*campesino*]. The community of refugees struggling for return is represented as a history-making 'brotherhood' of dispossessed *campesinos* against the representatives of the nation and the 'rich and their military'.

In the *el retorno* movement, this construction of history and community was raised to the level of a dominant narrative of return. As a narrative, it contains female images often in reference to the figure of the Roman Catholic Virgin Mary. In the aforementioned work by the IGE, for example, female representations are presented in connection with the image of the 'desecration of the holy land' (Ixcán) through the military, an image of death and loss. An important element of these representations is the 'mother' who is passive and who suffers (see IGE 1987, 134). Although it is constructed as passive and suffering, the female figure of the 'mother' in the dominant narrative of return offered female refugees, who, as indigenous women, especially were widely excluded from the national culture and exterritorialized as displaced persons, a symbolic place for the subject positioning and political articulation through self-narration. An example of this will be illustrated in the following section by an extract analysis of a biographical interview, conducted with the returned refugee Gabriela García.[7]

Self-Narration and Political Subjectivity: The 'Mother of Community'

Gabriela García was born in 1942 in a small *comunidad* in the Guatemalan western highlands closed to Mexican border. In 1982, she fled with her husband and three of their children to Mexico after the military had committed a number of massacres in the surrounding region. In the first weeks of her flight, Gabriela gave birth to her fifth child, a daughter. She lived the next 16 years in various refugee camps in Chiapas, the southernmost state of Mexico. In the beginning of the 1990s, she became politically active in the context of the return movement. In 1998, Gabriela and her family returned to Guatemala along with 150 other families.

Central to Gabriela García's text passage on her flight to Mexico is an account of the circumstances surrounding the birth of her daughter:

---

7   The original first name and surname of the interviewed person has been changed.

And I said to my husband, if we stay here [in a reception centre for refugees on the Mexican side of the border], I wouldn't be able to bear the suffering. I feared that something would happen to me. I proposed that we seek out another posada. So, he wandered with me deeper into Mexico. ... There, he looked for a posada. I became calmer and thought that I could stay there to bring my child into the world. But, this did not come to pass, because the migration police came by shortly afterwards and told us ... that [we] should gather on the other side of the country road farther away [from the border]. So, we left the area and went there where a group of comrades was already staying in a single house. There, I said to my husband – I was very close to delivery – I said to him: 'Perhaps I will set myself up here. You, I don't want to wander any farther with my burden'. But this did not come to pass, and we left and went to Guadalupe Victoria. ... But, we didn't stay there either. Instead, we went to a rancho [small farm or stable], it was called Coyugual. And, two weeks after we arrived, I gave birth to my daughter. The night was full of suffering for me, for we had no midwife. I sit alone with my back turned towards the fire, only my husband accompanies me, only the nocturnal animals come in and sing during the night. They come in and make their rounds, but do not stay long.

As Mary Louise Pratt (2004) points out, New Testament representations constitute common narrative patterns in order to give meaning to personal experiences of migration, flight, and displacement. Gabriela as well describes her experiences of displacement, constantly moving around and the impending birth of her daughter with the aid of a familiar narrative pattern, one which can also be found in the dominant narrative of return: Gabriela uses the image of a suffering mother, thus updating the rite of passage concept brought forth by Falla and the concept of the religious epic in order to arrange her experiences of displacement and continuous movement in her self-narration. She relates the impending birth of her child during her flight as a variation of the birth of Jesus. The term that she uses in her narrative – *posada* – has the same meaning and similar imagery to the religious narrative in the New Testament. She and her partner wander around, looking for a *posada* to bring her child into the world. They find it in an empty *rancho*, a type of stable.

The birth of her daughter constitutes her 'myth of self'. With her use of a passage that connotes a religious epos, the narrator Gabriela brings herself to the forefront as a new female subject of the emerging refugee collective. In the context of this subject positioning the following contextual symbolic and political meanings of motherhood play a central role.

As Enakshi Dua (1999, 12) writes concerning subaltern women in Canada, the indigenous woman cannot adopt the symbolic status of a reproducer of culture or 'mother of the nation'. She can, however, take on a symbolic positioning as 'mother' within an indigenous community. Dua interprets this subject position as a 'mother of community' (ibid., 13). In this sense, Gabriela constructs herself in her self-narration as a 'mother of an imagined returned community'.[8]

Furthermore, this 'myth of self' has a very concretely political meaning. For the Latin American context, Sarah Radcliffe and Sallie Westwood (1993) point to various strategies of appropriating, reinterpreting, and politicizing motherhood of marginalized women with reference to Roman Catholic imagery of the Virgin Mary. These compete with the image of the ethnically-privileged 'mother of the nation', from which indigenous women are excluded. In the context of the anti-insurgency programmes of the Guatemalan military governments, indigenous mothers were even declared to be a national danger and thus a military target (Radcliffe and Westwood 1993, 14). Gabriela's accentuation of her pregnancy and the birth of her child can therefore be interpreted as a statement for the indigenous woman's right to motherhood as well as for the integrity of her family and body.

The significance of Gabriela's 'myth of self' as 'mother of community' becomes even clearer when the previous passage of her narrative of her daughter's birth is linked to the following passage:

> Our lives continued and my daughter grew up and everything. We left Guadalupe, went to a refugee camp, our small home was built. We struggled for retorno. Then, the peace agreements were signed. It was as they told us, that we would have the opportunity to return to our homeland, that we would have the possibility of receiving a small plot of land. We fought for five years to be able to return. ... My daughter was already 17 when we returned to Guatemala. We were in Mexico for 17 years, as long as she had been alive. Two weeks before her birth, I went to Coyugual, and she was already a young woman when she returned ... and this is how the time passed.

Gabriela gives the birth and childhood of the youngest daughter an important function in the construction of time and space of exile. She rushes through her 17 years in Mexico and the struggle for return, using her daughter's growth as a benchmark. This illustrates that Gabriela interprets Mexico as a borderland, a liminal time-space of transit and in terms of transition to something new. This form of shaping of time and space in her narration not only helps to the self-positioning as a diasporic subject, but rather birth and growth are also metaphors for Gabriela's imagination of a collective future for refugees or returnees – on the other side of the border.

---

8   The term 'imagined returned community' was introduced by Stepputat (1994) to denote *el retorno*'s system of cultural representation.

Concluding Remarks

The analysis of the *el retorno* counter-narrative and the short interview extract is based on a combination of Anzaldúa's borderland conception and Brah's idea of contingent social categories and her arguments for a methodical approach. It could be shown that the predominant narrative of return, the returnees' self-narrations and political subjectivities linked to *el retorno*, are primarily performed by border crossings on diverse levels. Forced displacement to Mexico and return to Guatemala occurred on the material level. On the symbolic and discursive levels, the influence of religious narrative patterns of liberation theology stands out. Thus, through in a narrative manner, the returned refugees transformed their experiences of border-crossings into a personal rite of passage. Here, Mexico appears as a borderland, a time-space of transit, which is denominated by *posada*. The male returnees perform their subject positioning by accessing existing and active social models for men, for example the autonomous peasant. The returned refugee women like Gabriela, in contrast, cannot connect themselves to existing social models. Instead, they stress their motherhood in order to appropriate, transgress, and politicize Roman Catholic images such as the Virgin Mary or 'forbidden' subject positions as the indigenous mother. The political dimension of the subject positioning as indigenous women, however, remains invisible without a reconstruction of the context of the macro level, that is that the Guatemalan society is built on racism and allowed for the severe persecution of indigenous mothers during the war. Thus, motherhood constitutes a 'field of contestation'.

In the context of the *el retorno* movement, motherhood implies a radical political subjectivity. Through this subject position, on the one hand, subversion and resistance to the racist *ladino* nation-state and Guatemalan society as well as claims for the rights to physical integrity of the body and family were articulated. On the other hand, in the transitory *posada* setting, motherhood symbolized the creation and reproduction of a community of to-be returned refugees as well as a common future imagined on the other side of the border. However, emerged in a liminal borderland, motherhood also constituted a diasporic subjectivity in the sense that, as a political subject, can disappear as fast as it emerged – and that is what actually happened after returning to Guatemala. But this would be another story to tell.

References

Anderson, B. (1983), *Imagined Communities. Reflections on the Origin and Spread of Nationalism* (London and New York: Verso).

Anzaldúa, G. (1987), *The Border/La Frontera. The New Mestiza* (San Francisco: Aunt Lute Book).

Arbour, F. (1994), 'Voices of Women: A New Force Shaping the Guatemalan Return', *Refuge* 13:10, 16-7.

Arenas, C. (1992), ¿Dónde está el futuro?: Procesos de reintegración en comunidades de retornados (Guatemala City: Asociación para el Avance de las Ciencias Sociales en Guatemala (AVANCSO)).

Bash, L. et al. (1993), Nations Unbound: Transnational Projects, Postcolonial Predicaments, and Deterritorialized Nation-States (London and New York: Routledge).

Behar, R. (2003 [1993]), Translated Woman. Crossing the Border with Esperanza's Story (Boston: Beacon Press).

Bernecker, W.L. (2005), 'Staatliche Grenzen – Kontinentale Dynamik. Zur Relativität von Grenzen in Lateinamerika', in Braig, M. et al. (eds.), Grenzen der Macht – Macht der Grenzen. Lateinamerika im globalen Kontext (Frankfurt am Main: Biblioteca Ibero-Americana/Verfuert), 11-37.

Bhabha, H.K. (1990), Nation and Narration (London and New York: Routledge).

Brah, A. (1996), Cartographies of Diaspora. Contesting Identities (London and New York: Routledge).

Butler, J. (1993), Bodies that Matter: On the Discursive Limits of Sex (London and New York: Routledge).

Chanfrault-Duchet, M.-F. (1991), 'Narrative Structures, Social Models, and Symbolic Representation in the Life Story', in Berger Gluck, S. and Patai, D. (eds.), Women's Words. The Feminist Practice of Oral History (London and New York: Routledge), 77-92.

Comisión para el Esclarecimiento Histórico (CEH) (1999), Guatemala. Memoria del silencio. Tz'inil na'tab'al (Guatemala City: CEH).

Crenshaw, K. (1991), 'Mapping the Margins: Intersectionality, Identity Politics, and Violence against Women of Color', Stanford Law Review 43:6, 1241–99.

Crosby, A. (1999): 'To Whom Shall the Nation Belong? The Gender and Ethnic Dimension of Refugee Return and the Struggle for Peace in Guatemala', in North, L.L. and Simmons, A.B. (eds.), Journeys of Fear – Refugee Return and National Transformation in Guatemala (Montreal and London: McGill-Queen's University Press), 176-96.

Dua, E. (1999), 'Introduction. Canadian Anti-Racist Feminist Thought: Scratching the Surface of Racism', in Dua, E. and Robertson, A. (eds.), Scratching the Surface. Canadian Anti-Racist Feminist Thought (Toronto: Women's Press), 7-31.

Falla, R. (1995), Historia de un gran amor. Recuperación autobiográfica de la experiencia con las Comunidades de Población en Resistencia, Ixcán (Guatemala City: Universidad San Carlos).

Falla, R. (1992), Masacres de la selva: Ixcán, Guatemala (1975-1982) (Guatemala City: Editorial Universitaria).

García, A.A. (1989), 'The Development of Chicana Feminist Discourse 1970-1980', Gender & Society 3:2, 217-38.

Garbers, F. (2002), Geschichte, Identität und Gemeinschaft im Rückkehrprozess guatemaltekischer Kriegsflüchtlinge (Münster, Hamburg and London: LIT-Verlag).

Geertz, C. (1973), 'Thick Description: Toward an Interpretive Theory of Culture', in Geertz, C. (ed.), The Interpretation of Cultures: Selected Essays (New York: Basic Books), 3-30.

Guarnizo, E. et al. (2003), 'Assimilation and Transnationalism: Determinants of Transnational Political Action among Contemporary Migrants', *American Journal of Sociology* 108:6, 1211-48.

Gilroy, P. (1993), *The Black Atlantic: Modernity and Double Consciousness* (London and New York: Verso).

Hall, S. (1997), 'The Work of Representation', in Hall, S. (ed.), *Cultural Representation and Signifying Processes* (London: Sage Publications), 13-74.

Hall, S. (1994), *Rassismus und kulturelle Identität. Ausgewählte Schriften 2* (Hamburg: Argument-Verlag).

Hall, S. (1990), 'Cultural Identity and Diaspora', in Rutherford, J. (ed.), *Identity: Community, Culture, Difference* (London: Lawrence and Wishart), 222-37.

Iglesia Guatemalteca en el Exilio (IGE) (1987): *Nosotros conocemos nuestra historia* (Mexico: IGE), 1.

Karakayali, S. and Tsianos, V. (2007), 'Movements that Matter. Eine Einleitung', in Transit Migration Forschungsgruppe (eds.), *Turbulente Ränder. Neue Perspektiven auf Migration an den Grenzen Europas* (Bielefeld: transcript), 7-17.

Khagram, S. and Levitt, P. (eds.)(2008), *The Transnational Studies Reader. Intersections and Innovations* (London and New York: Routledge).

Knapp, G.-A. (2005), 'Race, Class, Gender: Reclaiming Baggage in Fast Travel-ling Theories', *European Journal of Women's Studies* 12:3, 249-65.

Kron, S. (2008), '"Am Rande erzählt" Geschichtspolitiken im Kontext von transnationaler Migration, Exil und Diaspora', in Molden, B. and Mayer, D. (eds.), *Vielstimmige Vergangenheiten. Geschichtspolitik in Lateinamerika* (Münster, Hamburg, Berlin, Vienna, London and Zürich: LIT-Verlag), 171-90.

Kron, S. (2007), 'Nach dem Exil. Guatemala: Politische Subjektivität in Erzählungen der Rückkehr', in Schütze, S. et al. (eds.), *Transkulturalität und Geschlechterverhältnisse* (Berlin: Tranvía), 66-90.

Kron, S. (2005), *'Las Retornadas' – Nach dem Exil: Dimensionen von Gemeinschaft und politischer Subjektivität in Erzählungen der Rückkehr. Eine Fallstudie über Guatemalas Kriegsflüchtlinge*, Dissertation (Berlin: Freie Universität Berlin), published online 13 December 2005 <http://www.diss.fu-berlin.de/2005/337>.

Le Bot, Y. (1995), *La guerra en tierras mayas – Comunidad, violencia y modernidad en Guatemala (1970-1992)* (Mexico City: Fondo de Cultura Económica).

Levitt, P. and Schiller, N.G. (2004): 'Conceptualizing Simultaneity: A Transnational Social Field Perspective on Society', *International Migration Review* 38:3, 1002-39.

Levitt, P. and Sørensen, N.N. (2004), 'The Transnational Turn in Migration Studies', *Global Migration Perspectives* 6, 1-13.

Mahler, S.J. and Pessar, P. (2001), 'Gendered Geographies of Power: Analyzing Gender across Transnational Spaces', *Identities: Global Studies in Culture and Power* 7, 441-59.

Manz, B. (1988), *Repatriation and Reintegration: An Arduous Process in Guatemala* (Washington: Georgetown University, Center for Emigration Policy and Refuge).

Maquín, Mama and Women's Centre for Research and Action (CIAM) (1994), *From Refugees to Refugees: A Chronicle of Women Refugees Experience in Chiapas* (Comitán, Mexico: CIAM).

Marcus, G. (1995), 'Ethnography in/of the world system: the emergence of multi-sited ethnography', *Annual Review of Anthropology* 24, 95-117.

McCall, L. (2005), 'The Complexity of Intersectionality', *Signs: Journal of Women in Culture and Society* 30:3, 1771-802.

Naples, N.A. (2008), *Crossing Borders: Feminism, Intersectionality and Globalisation* (Hawke Research Institute Working Paper Series 36).

Nayak, M. and Suchland, J. (2006), 'Gender Violence and Hegemonic Projects', *International Feminist Journal of Politics* 8:4, 467-85.

Nolin Hanlon, C. (1999), 'Guatemalan Refugees and Returnees. Place and Maya Identity', in North, L.L. and Simmons, A.B. (eds.), *Journeys of Fear – Refugee Return and National Transformation in Guatemala* (Montreal and London: McGill-Queen's University Press), 213-234.

Papadopoulos, D. et al. (2008), *Escape Routes. Control and Subversion in the 21st Century* (London: Pluto Press).

Pessar, P. (2001), 'Women's Political Consciousness and Empowerment in Local, National, and Transnational Contexts: Guatemalan Refugees and Returnees', *Identities: Global Studies in Culture and Power* 7, 461-500.

Portes, A. and DeWind, J. (2007), *Rethinking Migration: New Theoretical and Empirical Perspectives* (New York: Berghahn Books).

Pratt, M.L. (2004), 'Globalización, desmodernización y el retorno de los monstruos', in Pajuelo, R. and Sandoval, P. (eds.), *Globalización y diversidad cultural. Una mirada desde América Latina* (Lima: Instituto de Estudios Peruanos), 399-415.

Pries, L. (2004), 'Determining the Causes and Durability of Transnational Labour Migration between Mexico and the United States: Some Empirical Findings', *International Migration* 42:2, 3-39.

Pries, L. (2005), 'Configurations of Geographic and Societal Spaces: A Sociological Proposal between "Methodological Nationalism" and the "Spaces of Flows"', *Global Networks* 5:2, 167-90.

Radcliffe, S. and Westwood, S. (1993), 'Gender, Racism and the Politics of Identities in Latin America', in Radcliffe, S. and Westwood, S. (eds.), *Viva! Women and Popular Protest in Latin America* (London and New York: Routledge), 1-29.

Sandoval, C. (1997), 'Mestizaje as Method: Feminists-of-Color Challenge the Canon', in Trujillo, C. (ed.), *Living Chicana Theory. Series in Chicana/Latina Studies* (Berkeley: Third Woman Press), 352-70.

Schiller, N.G. and Wimmer, A. (2003), 'Methodological Nationalism, the Social Sciences, and the Study of Migration. An Essay in Historical Epistemology', *International Migration Review* 37, 576-610.

Schütze, F. (1983), 'Biographieforschung und narratives Interview', *Neue Praxis* 13:3, 283-94.

Smith, C. (1990), 'Introduction: Social Relations in Guatemala over Time and Space', in Smith, C. (ed.), *Guatemalan Indians and the State, 1540 to 1988* (Austin: University of Texas Press), 1-30.

Smith, R.C. (2006), *Mexican New York: Transnational Lives of New Immigrants* (Berkeley: University of California Press).

Sørensen, N.N. (2008), *Living across Worlds: Diaspora, Development and Transnational Engagement* (Geneva: International Organization on Migration).

Stepputat, F. (1999): 'Repatriation and Every day Forms of State Formation in Guatemala', in Black, R. and Khoser, K. (eds.), *The End of the Refugee Cycle? Repatriation and Reconstruction* (Oxford: Berghahn Books), 210-26.

Stepputat, F. (1994): 'Repatriation and the Politics of Space: the Case of the Mayan Diaspora and Return Movement', *Journal of Refugee Studies* 7:2-3, 175-85.

Vertovec, S. (2009), *Transnationalism. Routledge Series. Key Ideas* (London and New York: Routledge).

Vila, P. (2003) 'The Limits of American Border Theory', in Vila, P. (ed.), *Ethnography at the Border* (Minneapolis: University of Minnesota Press), 306-41.

Warren, K.B. (1998), *Indigenous Movements and their Critics: Pan Mayan Activism in Guatemala* (Princeton: Princeton University Press).

PART II
GEOPOLITICS:
STATE, NATION AND
POWER RELATIONS

Borders, Border Studies and EU Enlargement[1]

James Wesley Scott

Introduction

The study of state boundaries and their general societal significance has become a truly international phenomenon. Furthermore, the study of borders is developing both quantitatively in terms of the amount of research being undertaken and qualitatively in terms of new interdisciplinary approaches. However, it is in Europe that border studies appear to have expanded most rapidly. This is no coincidence as borders have posed a central problem to the emergence of a transnational political community within Europe. The state of the art in border studies can indeed be related to overlying geopolitical events, reflecting the concerns of the times. This, of course, also includes the ways in which Europe and its internal and external borders have been perceived.

Various geopolitical conceptualizations of *Europe* have been and remain greatly influential to the development to border theory. As I will argue, processes of EU integration and enlargement have affected perceptions of borders and boundaries – both in the social sciences and in more everyday realms of public life.[2] The state of the art in border studies is therefore about tracing different, often

---

1   This chapter is based on research carried out within the scope of the project EUDIMENSIONS (contract: CIT-CT-2005-028804), financed by the European Union's Sixth Framework Programme for Research (see <http://www.eudimensions.eu>) and EXLINEA: Lines of Exclusion as Arenas of Cooperation: Reconfiguring the External Boundaries of Europe – Policies, Practices, and Perceptions, (contract HPSE-CT-2002-00141), funded through the Community Research Fifth Framework Programme of the EU (see <http://www.exlinea.org>).

2   In terms of disciplinary contributions it also seems clear that human geography has been at the forefront of the social science disciplines contributing to a broader understanding of the significance of borders. Having developed from naturalistic and deterministic roots in the nineteenth century to an integrative and critical discipline, geography has contributed to the fact that borders are now largely perceived as multifaceted social institutions.

conflicting, understandings of state boundaries. A re-reading of classic border studies, for example, reminds us how embedded in wider academic discourses past and present *border paradigms* have been (and remain). At least three specific periods of European history can be highlighted in this respect: the advent of continental nation-states in the late nineteenth century, the post-Paris Peace Treaty Europe of newly created and recently fragmented states and the post-Maastricht European Union within the context of enlargement and the emergence of a new *pan*-European idea. These historical periods also correspond to overall scientific paradigms as they have shifted with time. The determinism that, among others, helped provide the *theoretical* foundation for imperialist geopolitics and national-socialist ideology would be replaced after World War II by a generally positivist drive for objective facts, scientific rigour and *value-free* studies of borders. The complexities of globalization and, finally, the post Cold War *disorder*, revealed in turn the deficiencies of empiricism, description and categorization. Furthermore, dissatisfaction with the apolitical and *objective* assumptions of empiricism have led to the application of a variety of critical approaches that characterize contemporary debate.

What does all this signify for the study of borders *per se*? Whereas until the early sixties the field was pre-dominantly focused on the study of the demarcation of boundaries (thus of lines and limes), the field of boundaries and border studies has arguably shifted from boundary studies to border studies (Newman 2001). Put differently, attention has moved away from the evolution and transformation of the territorial confines of the state to the more general social production of borders, complexly understood as sites at and through which socio-spatial differences are communicated.[3] However, this notion of *border* only really takes on meaning when understood as a product of *bordering* processes (van Houtum and Naerssen 2002).

European integration and the emergence of the EU as a geopolitical actor reflect the multifarious nature of bordering processes. This chapter will hence interpret changes in the research focus of border studies within a wider European context. The author makes absolutely no claim to exhaustive inclusiveness and will focus instead on a limited set of research perspectives that have characterized the development of border studies. The work of important scholars within the field will also be discussed. Presently, there is no single theory, concept or discourse on borders that enjoys predominance within the context of European integration and enlargement. On the contrary, many different strands of thought are contributing to the EU's policy-driven approach to borders that has emerged since 1989.

This chapter begins with a short historical overview of different scientific paradigms that have influenced border studies and the ways in which borders have been perceived in the European context. Discussion then focuses on more contemporary events: subsequent phases of EU integration, enlargement and post-

---

3   Confusingly, in anthropology, the definition can be quite the opposite, here a boundary generally means the socio-spatially constructed differences between cultures/categories and a border generally stands for a line demarcated in space (Barth 1969; Donnan and Wilson 1999).

enlargement – as well as the political rationales and discourses they have brought forth – have facilitated the emergence of at least two broad and often overlapping schools of thought, one pragmatic and the other *critical* in the poststructuralist sense. In addition, I suggest that a critical and pragmatic theoretical approach can help interpret the complex post-enlargement context of shifting border-related policies and discourses. The present situation provides, for example, a stark contrast to the situation before the 1995 enlargement when discourses of *border transcending* enjoyed substantial currency. While cooperation between the EU and non-EU neighbours is presently heralded as an important historical step towards the consolidation of a European political community, the EU's external borders have become formidable barriers that symbolize a civilizational gap between *East* and *West*.

European Perspectives on Borders 1: Determinism and Imperialist Geopolitics

Before World War I, Europe was largely characterized by competing empires and would-be nations struggling for autonomy. At heart was the notion of the absolute sovereignty of nation-states, fed by cultural particularisms that justified *special roles* for Europe's most powerful countries. Borders in Europe were seen to consolidate the nation-state and a sense of national identity. Among the scholars who can be discussed in this context are Friedrich Ratzel, Otto Maull and Karl Haushofer – German pioneers of political geography and border studies. Research questions that they saw as scientifically relevant dealt with the relationships between border morphology and nation-state development and the geographical development of national spheres of influence (geopolitics). As such, central concepts that informed this perspective included the belief that natural and deterministic laws formed a basic logic for the organization of human societies in space. Specifically, concepts emerged in this context that were informed by a decidedly geodeterminist ideas with often spurious analogies with the natural sciences (for example the State as *organism* and borders and frontiers as protective *organs* of the State). Ultimately, the belief that states were locked in a Darwinistic struggle for survival and that only strong states with *good* and/or *strong* borders could persevere provided a scientific rationale for the imperialist geopolitics of the late nineteenth and early twentieth centuries.

Friedrich Ratzel (1903, 1923) is regarded as the 'father' of human and political geography (he, in fact, coined the phrase *Anthropogeographie*). His primary goal was to establish geography as a holistic discipline that integrated physical and human elements (for example in terms of *Länderkunde*) and that was scientifically grounded in *Darwinian* laws of natural selection and evolution. The theoretical basis was one of geodeterminism, although interrelationships between human settlements and physical environments were also emphasized. As far as political geography is concerned, one of the main consequences of this scientific position is the notion of an objective evolutionary basis for the emergence, rise and fall of nation-states. As mentioned above Ratzel's most (in)famous analogies is that of the state as living organism, with internal organs, external protective boundaries and an inherent drive towards expansion. The drive for territorial expansion, understood as a strategy of survival would be subsequently developed by other scholars.

Otto Maul (1925) was a student of Ratzel. His contribution to political geography was a systematization of Ratzel's concepts and the application of biodeterminist and geodeterminist principles to the study of European state development. His goal was to advance Political Geography, not only as a subdiscipline of *Anthropogeographie* but also as a stand-alone science, by giving it a firm empirical and theoretical basis. For Maull, natural determination was the central element influencing the *Society-Environment-System* [*Mensch-Umwelt-System*], but he also emphasized the importance of the *willful political act* to establish states and boundaries. He elaborated on Ratzel's analogy of that state; it is not an *organism* in a biological sense but an *organization* created by human societies to secure the survival and viability of cultural groups [*Völker*]. He focused much attention, much more than Ratzel, on border morphologies and their relationships to political conditions of nation-states. In his scientific vocabulary we find words such as: frontier or border zone [*Grenzsaum*], borderlines [*Grenzlinien*], separating borders [*Trennungsgrenzen*], structural borders [*Strukturgrenzen*] and anti-structural borders [*strukturwidrige Grenzen*]. Maull was also interested in such things as relating total lengths of state borders to territorial area as a measure of *border-orientation* of European states.

Importantly for our discussion of border studies, Maull made a distinction between *good* and *bad* borders. This related to their defensive character and stability. He asked the questions: 'Do political borders coincide with natural barriers (mountains, rivers, waterways) and/or socio-ethnic borders (language areas, cultural areas)?'; 'do borders represent an abstraction of the frontier, in which a transition between state-cultural areas is possible, or are borders sharp dividing lines that truncate such areas?'[4] Maull unquestionably saw *anti-structural* borders as *bad* borders. In his view, these do not correspond to physical conditions of the earth's surface nor to the distribution patterns of socio-cultural areas. They do not have a true frontier where the state border can act both as a bridge and a filter, protecting the state organization at the same time that it allows interstate interaction and trade to flourish. Typical of such borders are those established after wars by victorious powers or by colonial powers outside Europe. Maull, writing after the Paris Peace decrees of 1919 and despairing over the loss of German territory and the disintegration of Austria-Hungary, saw many of Europe's new borders as bad

---

4   To quote Maull (1923, 143): 'Die geographische Frage bei allen Untersuchungen politischer Grenzen ist die: Hat der politische Willensakt des Staates zur Anlehnung an geographischen Grenzen (Strukturgrenzen) geführt? Ist die politische Grenze dank dieser Anlehnung gleichsam der Natur entlehnt? Ist dabei die beste Strukturgrenze gewählt worden? Welches sind die anderen Möglichkeiten? Oder aber: hat keinerlei Anpassung stattgefunden?'.

borders, where formerly internal areas without borderland experiences or histories of suddenly became peripheral organs of the states. These bad borders, having violated *natural laws* of border-formation, would, in Maull's opinion, be the source of instability and conflict between states.

Karl Haushofer (1928) developed political geography into an applied science. Inspired by work of Kjellen, Mackinder and others, Haushofer saw a validation of the Ratzel school of Anthropogeographie in the systematic study of geopolitics. More concretely, Haushofer was interested in borders as delimiters of territorial control and ideology. His basic assumption was that of a natural will of cultures and states toward expansion as a strategy of survival. Through the analysis of interrelationships between physical geography, border delimitations, conflicts, imperial expansion and so on, Haushofer attempted to assess the vulnerability of states within the world system. This knowledge could then be applied politically in order to avoid future conflict or prevent a subsequent loss of territory, influence and, as a consequence, state/cultural viability (that is that of Germany and its *Volk*).

The demoralizing effects of defeat and territorial losses (both of Germany's colonial empire and *traditional* cultural areas in Silesia, Posen, Pomerania, Elsass-Lorraine) after World War I were essential to the development of Haushofer's geopolitics. He argued that the neglect of the scientific basis for strategic thinking had cost Germany dear and must never be repeated. Unfortunately for Haushofer and geopolitics in general, National-Socialism appropriated many of these concepts in order to legitimize a cultural *struggle* for domination and subjugation of *inferior* and/or *dangerous* cultures. Nazi ideology and its interpretations of geopolitics went far beyond the military-strategic balance that Haushofer (naively!) was hoping to achieve.

Perspectives on Borders 2: *Systematics*, Functionalism and Empiricism

The determinism that, among others, helped provide the *theoretical* foundation for imperialist geopolitics and national-socialist ideology would be replaced after World War II by a positivist drive for objective facts and scientific rigour. As a result, the determinism of Ratzel and Haushofer would give way, both in Anglo-American and European geography, to attempts at *value-free* studies of borders. Hence, the scientific tradition (for example in political geography) that emerged between 1940 and (about) 1975 was largely characterized by a lack of a central *metatheory*. Instead, functionalism, positivism, and a focus on uniqueness and *Kantian* space prevailed. An important scientific issue in this context was the functional genesis of the nation-state. Border studies thus focused not only on the description, classification and morphologies of state borders but were concerned as well with the emergence of *core areas* of nation-state formation and the *centrifugal* and *centripetal* forces that influenced the growth and development of states.

Concrete examples of research questions pursued in this conjunction dealt with border functions in terms of state development (for example the role of frontiers, corridors, core areas and so on) the study of border landscapes, and the analysis of border formation as a political process.

Richard Hartshorne was for many years one of the most influential geographers in the Anglo-American tradition. In Hartshorne's view (1950, 128) 'Geography is the study of areal differentiation. Areal differentiation is both most marked and most important in respect to units of land at the level of state-areas'. Hartshorne understood that biodeterminism and the German tradition of Anthropogeographie established by Ratzel had, in fact, served to discredit Political Geography. Attacking this tradition as pseudo-scientific (allusions to the state as *organism* appeared particularly offensive after the excesses of World War II and the Nazi regime), Hartshorne argued that a systematic methodology based on objectively confirmable *fact* was necessary in order to put political geography back on track. One of Hartshorne's research approaches to borders was the (by then) well-established study of border landscapes; he suggested that the interaction between political borders and cultural landscapes were an important source of spatial differentiation. More importantly, however, Hartshorne suggested that the analysis of function and, more expressly, the functioning of the state, would provide a meaningful context for scientific rigour. In this functionalist perspective, relevant research questions related to the various elements that determine the integrity of the state: centrifugal (that is fragmenting) and centripetal (that is integrating) forces that over time have defined its physical contours, internal political organization and external connections. To quote Hartshorne (1950, 192): 'State areas are important, both in the practical and academic sense, primarily in terms of their functions; namely what the state-area as a whole means to its parts and its relations as a whole with outside areas'. Consequently, we conclude that the rational, scientifically reliable and realistic approach to the study of state-areas is to start with the phenomena with which we are most concerned, the functions of the state-area, to determine how these have been affected by the character of the area itself, its structure and contents, and to utilize historical facts of genesis insofar as these aid us in understanding structural features previously determined to be significant' (ibid., 193).

Three prominent scholars of the functionalist school whose works continue to have considerable bearing on border studies are Victor Prescott, Ladis Kristof and Julian Minghi. These authors focused research attention on the emergence of borders based on forms of social-political organization and processes of nation-building. Victor Prescott (1965), an Australian geographer, was mainly concerned with identifying spatial relationships between politics and geography and thus to focus political geography towards *relevant* areas of inquiry. He saw the exercise of political sovereignty, of which borders are the formal delimiters, as an important source of morphological and functional variation of space. Ladis Kristof, a follower of Hartshorne's ideas on political geography, similarly devoted himself to the systematic study of borders and boundaries as aspects of *Realpolitik* and as organizing elements of the state.

In a famous article published in 1959, Kristof used the functional approach to illustrate the differences between frontiers and borders. For Kristof, the primary function of boundaries as legal institutions is clear (1959, 220): '... in order to have some stability in the political structure, both on the national and international level, a clear distinction between the spheres of foreign and domestic politics is necessary. The boundary helps to maintain this distinction'. Kristof (ibid.) also states that while frontiers and boundaries are important elements of state formation, their relationship to the centres of state power are quite different:

> Both frontiers and boundaries are manifestations of socio-political forces and as such are subjective, not objective. But while the former are the result of rather spontaneous, or at least ad hoc solutions and movements, the latter are fixed and enforced through a more rational and centrally co-ordinated effort after a conscious choice is made among the several preferences and opportunities at hand.

In Kristof's conceptualization, borders are inwardly oriented to the state, they divide and separate, strengthening the territorial integrity of the state and are thus *centripetal* in their function. Frontiers in contrast, are outwardly oriented, integrate different ecumenes and challenge the control functions of the state. Frontiers, according to Kristof, are therefore *centrifugal* in character.

In terms of European perspectives on borders that coincided with functionalism we can detect a clear Cold-War era reification of the nation-state, despite the fact that attempts to create political and economic institutions in Europe began shortly after 1945. Almost sacrosanct was the principal of national sovereignty as a source of geopolitical stability; a stability that national borders could (and should) provide by serving as effective containers of state power. In all fairness, however, functionalist views on borders did imply a certain questioning of the assumptions of border *objectivity* by exploring the social-political contexts that influence border formation (Guichonnet and Raffestin 1974; Raffestin 1990). As such, with the functionalist perceptions of borders were also influenced by the notion of *permeability*. By no means a new concept, permeability re-emerged as an elementary border function in academic discussion due, in great part, to the increasing interdependence of border cities such as Geneva and Basel and the momentum of EU integration processes (see Guichonnet and Raffestin 1974). Differing degrees of permeability were thus seen to reflect the differential momentum of interstate cooperation and alliances – in other words, interstate cooperation (for example the European Economic Community, NATO, Benelux and so on) was seen to provide frameworks that allowed sovereignty to be shared with other countries in order to achieve strategic balance, militarily as well as economically. On the other hand, permeability implied a dual border function as *bridge* and *barrier* that exerted powerful structuring influences on the cultural landscape.

Perspectives on Borders 3: Critical European Studies on Borders and Identities

For much of the Cold War period, the notion of strategic balance and alliances held sway in political geography and in border studies. Of course, critical social sciences and scholars and international political economy actively criticized the *absolutization* of states and borders long before the end of the Cold War. Wallerstein's interpretations of the world system focused quite centrally on mechanisms of centre-periphery relationships and the exploitation of weak countries by powerful states. However, the momentous political events of 1989/1990 and their aftermath comprehensively challenged many of the comforting paradigmatic assumptions that had been held in relation to the importance of strategic balance, Western solidarity and political unity. The ideological confrontation that had sublimated more subtle but increasing fragmentation within the world system and national societies ended abruptly, forcing the field of border studies to go beyond more traditional state-centred approaches.

Border studies were thus not immune to the *cultural turn* in the humanities and social sciences that had already begun to take hold in North American and European universities. This was evidenced by a questioning of the *essence* and the assumed immutability of national identities as well as by challenges to the notion that nation-states might be – out of some civilizational necessity – a permanent feature of the world system. Furthermore, dissatisfaction with the apolitical and *objective* assumptions of empiricism, especially in the light of increasing international conflict and development inequalities, led to the application of critical political economy, anti-colonialist and anti-imperialist perspectives on borders and border-defining processes.

Presently, critical approaches to the study of borders are often associated with *postmodern* perspectives that analyse the social construction of borders in terms of discourses and agency (practices). European examples of authors working in this tradition include Anssi Paasi, Gerald Toal, John Agnew and others. Concepts central to the *critical* perspective are multiple interpretations of border significance, borders as socio-cultural constructs, deconstruction of border discourses, analysis of neo-liberalism and its effect on nation-states. Examples of research questions: border-related elements of identity-formation, socio-cultural and experiential basis for border-defining processes, power relations in society and geopolitical orders, critical analysis of geopolitical discourses.

The choice of Finnish geographer Anssi Paasi (1991, 1998, and 2001) as a representative of a socially critical school of Political Geography is not arbitrary. Indeed, he has pioneered work on borders and frontiers based on a rejection of positivism and a criticism of the concepts and empirical frameworks developed since the beginning of the twentieth century. While it would be unfair to label Paasi a *postmodernist* (the term itself is not a hard and fast *category* but rather a term that helps us comprehend paradigm shifts), he shares the notion that there is no central *essence* to borders, frontiers, regions and even nation-states, but that these are socio-cultural constructs constantly subject to change. Identity and ideas are central factors within Paasi's Society-Environment scheme. He develops the notion that regional spaces are created through a process of *Institutionalization* involving boundaries, symbols and the institutions that maintain them (1991). In many ways, this notion of region and boundary as a social construct is related to the idea of Imagined communities as postulated by Benedict Anderson (1991). In other words, according to Paasi (2001, 143): 'attention should be paid not only to how ideas on a territory and its boundaries shape society's spatial imaginations (...) but also to analysing how these ideas gain significance as far as the spatial identity of territorial entities and the people living in them is concerned'.

How then does Paasi define borders? They are symbols, discourses and institutions that interpenetrate all realms of society and that exist everywhere in society, not only at the formal boundary of national sovereignty. 'Boundaries can be understood as part of the process by which territories and their identities and meanings are formed and renewed' (2001, 135). Therefore it is not only the mere function of borders, but also their meanings that are relevant to social sciences:

> *The challenge for researchers (geographers) is to develop critical approaches to understand the changing meanings of boundaries in the current world. One should not try to focus attention simply on the economic, political or psychological processes occurring in border areas, but rather one should attempt to deconstruct the meanings of boundaries in connection with territorial symbolism and the creation of institutions.* (Paasi 2001, 141)

Furthermore, Paasi defines three primary elements of contemporary bordering processes as those involving: First, *political boundaries* where physical changes of boundaries as demarcation lines take place, second, *boundaries of politics* in which spatial scales of governance are redefined in response to globalization and third, *politics of boundaries* in which boundaries are produced and reproduced in response to shifting relations between nation, state, territory and identities.

European Perspectives on Borders 4: Borders and Dynamics of Cross-Border Cooperation

Finally, I argue that a critical yet realist strand of border research has emerged since 1990 that merits mention. This strand informs a border research perspective that is both pragmatic (problem-solving being the main objective) and critical (with social equity, cultural inclusion and the improvement of the quality of life being the basic values). Pragmatic approaches are not only about *borders* per se but, similar to the cultural criticism of so-called postmodernists, also engage questions of national identity and national borders in Europe. Furthermore, pragmatism offers an important philosophical insight into the social sciences, and one that is particularly suited to an interdisciplinary understanding of borders. Pragmatism emphasizes the centrality of *social practices* – rather than predefined *theory* – in addressing problems facing society. At the same time, social practice is not a question of insular, group-specific hermeneutics but conditioned by influences operating at all levels – inside the community, outside the community, within the region or state and in virtual space. Social practice is thereby subject to constraints and empowering forces that, in turn, social practice produces, modifies and mediates. Furthermore, a research perspective based on pragmatics situates values, power and knowledge at the centre of societal development (Flyvbjerg 2001).[5] This perspective can be seen to be as a synthesis of sorts of the preceding geographical perspectives on borders. The pragmatic view accepts that definitions of borders and identities are neither fixed nor permanent. Central organizing principals such as those proposed by conventional geography are viewed with scepticism. However, pragmatists believe in the possibility of positive social action within a perceived *working reality*.

Examples of research questions elaborated within this perspective are: How are borders changing in an enlarging Europe? What do these changes mean in terms of their societal impacts? In more concrete terms, this could, for example, involve the analysis of cross-border cooperation patterns, pragmatic interpretations of border-related discourses, contextual analysis of discourses and social practice in boundary formation, and the analysis of cross-border cooperation as a governance issue. Liam O'Dowd (2002), a sociologist at Queens University, Belfast, offers an excellent *pragmatic* and, at the same time, socially critical reading of the significance of borders within the context of European integration and enlargement. O'Dowd shares the *optimistic scepticism* of the pragmatic view. Among his research goals has been to illustrate how (2002, 29): 'one of the key lessons to be drawn from the history of state formation in Europe is that the structure, functions and meanings of state borders seldom remain fixed or stable for long periods.' In addition, states O'Dowd (2002, 32), 'the *European project* is reconfiguring borders as both barriers and bridges'.[6] However, O'Dowd also admits that the existence of territorial state

---

5   With pragmatism, experiences of cross-border cooperation become more than mere *empirical anecdotes* but a central element in bordering processes. Practical knowledge is thus comprehended both as a social resource and scientific key to understanding the workings of society. Epistemic knowledge (derived strictly through *scientific* method and theory) and technical knowledge (techme) are not given a privileged role. Similarly, structure and agency are seen as a unity. Dualisms are eschewed and disciplinary boundaries transcended: 'Actors and their practices are analyzed in relation to structures and structures in terms of agency, not so that the two stand in an external relations to each other, but so that structures are found as part of actors and actors as part of structures' (Flyvbjerg 2001, 137).

6   O'Dowd (2002, 32) corroborates the notion that perceptions of border significance are very much informed by our own past experiences: 'Those who grew up in strong welfare states will know that the State gained maximum control over borders between 1950 and 1980 when the state role in political, economic and social spheres was at its zenith. But this appears to have been a very special historical event and by no means the rule. State borders, at least in Europe, are now consolidating into a new relative

borders have been a sine qua non for the development of representative democracy. In his overview article quoted here, O'Dowd discusses the development of cross-border cooperation in Europe in terms of historical state formations and changing border regimes. Using a rather uncomplicated terminology, O'Dowd attempts to show how European borders are presently being reconfigured in terms of their (often conflicting) significance as Barriers, Bridges, Resources *and* Symbols of Identity and how these reconfigurations relate to the project of European integration and enlargement.

European integration is seen in this view as progress in the sense that a more *democratic regulation* of borders has emerged. The question that arises with globalization and the new permeability of borders is how borders in Europe can continue to be regulated democratically. O'Dowd is also concerned with whether political regionalization at the borders can contribute to their democratic regulation. Finally, O'Dowd acknowledges the multilevel contingency of cross-border interaction; heterogeneity is the rule and generalizations about cross-border practices are often difficult to justify.

Bordering and the Post-Enlargement Environment

Table 7.1 summarizes three general socio-spatial perspectives on borders as represented by the work of three authors discussed in this text. These different perspectives have emerged within the context of cooperation and conflict between European states and it is evident that border formation is a complex societal process that takes place in many settings, not just at the site of state borders. In this last section, I suggest that all three strands of border research contribute – in their own ways – to a critical interpretation of more recent events and their impacts on border-related discourses and practices. Within the setting of the last phase of EU Enlargement and the emergence of European *neighbourhood* policies, borders have become conditional and arbitrary – seen as necessary for the consolidation of a quasi neo-national space and a powerful resource with which to expediently structure relations with third countries.

---

permanence, but their barrier function has diminished remarkably due to a number of reasons'.

133

Table 7.1 State of the Art: Three Traditions of Border Studies

Authors	Maull	Paasi	O'Dowd
Ideological Basis	Determinism Geodeterminism Positivism	Relativism, Critical Analysis (deconstruction)	Pragmatism, Possibilism
Scientific Objectives	Systematization of Political Geography, uncovering objective laws behind Bordering processes	Questioning of Bordering categories, uncovering power relations and interests behind Bordering processes	Solution of societal problems through reflective learning processes
Definition of Borders	'peripheral organs' of the State	socio-cultural constructs	political and social institutions
Central Questions	Relation between state viability and border morphology	Relation between discourses and the creation of borders	Interrelationships between functional transformations of borders and societal transformation
The Border Problem	Tension between border zones and borderlines: the will to 'perfect' structural borders	Exclusion and conflict: the strengthening of power relationships	Barriers to cooperation, socio-economic discrimination
European Identity	Identity defined through the struggle of cultures and nations to create viable states, equi-librium obtainable via 'perfect' borders	European identity not predetermined but constantly redefined	European identity as a project of cooperation and the creation of democratic border regimes

Source: © J.W. Scott.

In order to relate such disparate epistemic positions to one another it is, however, necessary to elaborate on the notion of *bordering*. In contemporary debate, boundary-making or *bordering*, is about the everyday construction of borders through ideology, discourses, political institutions, attitudes and agency (van Houtum 2002; Scott and Matzeit 2006). Bordering is, by nature, a multilevel process of re-territorialization. It takes place at the level of high politics and is manifested by physical borders and visa regimes. Bordering is also reflected in media debates over national identity, legal and illegal immigration and language rights. Within this context, borders can be read in terms of one, a politics of identity (who is *in*, who is *out*), two, a regionalization of difference (defining who is a neighbour, a partner, a friend or rival) and three, a politics of *interests* (in which issues of economic self-interest, political stability and security play a prominent role).

The 2004 enlargement of the EU can be seen a high water mark in the political attempt to extend the 1980s and 1990s momentum of *de-bordering* beyond the territory of *Core Europe*. Since 2004, borders in Europe have re-emerged in practical and discursive terms as markers of sharp – to an extent civilizational – difference. European border studies have been quick to react to this change in perspective: its social, political and cultural contradictions are only too evident (see for example van Houtum and Pijpers 2006 and Popescu 2006). Scholars see, for example, an obvious discrepancy between discourses of security and selectivity that affect more general perceptions of borders. In this respect, it is often difficult to separate supranational EU policies from national policies; while the EU, for instance, has required new member states to introduce visas for citizens of neighbouring states, national governments are negotiating the particulars of new visa regimes. Conversely, national governments are establishing policies affecting the status of migrants (and thus border regimes) and subsequently appeal for EU support. In the meantime, local institutions in border regions, though generally less powerful, are anything but passive: they are part of *multiscalar politics* and are reacting to national and supranational policies affecting them. This multilevel interaction generates a complex political-territorial environment in which cross-border cooperation must operate.

Europeanization and Consolidation as Bordering Concepts

Contemporary European border studies focus much attention on the European Union and its attempts to create a coherent political, social and economic space within a clearly defined multinational community (see Aalto 2006; Moisio 2007; Scott 2005). A central aspect of this re-territorialization process is the definition of rules, norms and practices that aim to *Europeanize* national spaces; from this derive the objectives and values that create a *common* set of discourses in which various policy issues can be negotiated (Clark and Jones 2008). Europeanization is expressed, on the one hand, by core documents, such as treaties and agendas, which spell out the EU's various societal and political values. Furthermore, regional development and spatial planning policies as well as research funding schemes aim at the production of *new knowledges of Europe* that go beyond strictly national orientations (see Jensen and Richardson 2004). Europeanization is thus also evident in cross-border situations. Cross-border cooperation is seen to provide ideational foundations for a networked Europe through symbolic representations of European space and its future development perspectives. More importantly, the practice of establishing Euroregions has been understood in terms of an active re-constitution of borders. Euroregions, local and/or regional government associations devoted to cross-border cooperation, have spread throughout the EU, on its external borders and beyond. Consequently, the Euroregion concept has proved a powerful tool with which to transport European values and objectives (Perkmann 2002; Popescu 2006).

Paradoxically perhaps, Europeanization does not only imply *transcending* national spaces per se. It also serves to confirm state sovereignty. In effect, while the space within the EU is being gradually *integrated*, a border is being drawn around the EU-27 in order to consolidate it as a political community and thus manage regional heterogeneity, core-periphery contradictions and political-organizational flux. This also involves an attempt to structure EU-European space through, for example, central political agendas, structural policies, spatial planning strategies and research-funding programs. In effect, EU-European space is being differentiated from the rest of the world by a set of geopolitical discourses and practices that extol the EU's core values. Consolidation, and the border confirming practices it entails, is seen as a mode of establishing state-like territorial integrity for the EU and thereby also strengthening its (in part contested) image as a guarantor of internal security.

However, the enforcement of exclusionary borders is a challenge to the identity of the EU as a supranational *force for good in the world* that transcends national and socio-cultural divisions (see Barbé and Nogue 2008). Because of geographical proximity, long-standing (for example post-colonial) economic, social and political interrelationships and deepening mutual interdependencies, the EU is keen to assume a *stabilizing* role in Post-Soviet, Eurasian and Mediterranean regional contexts. The very norms, values and *acquis* that define EU-Europe (for example the virtues of cooperation, democratic *ownership*, social capital and general values such as sustainability, solidarity and cohesion) are thus being also projected upon the wider regional *Neighbourhood* in order to provide a sense of orientation and purpose to third states. This is a geopolitical vision of Europeanization – a de-bordering discourse based an ideational projection of power and the notion of *privileged partnership* – that is, of a special, multifaceted and mutually beneficial relationship with the EU, in some cases in place of concrete perspectives of EU membership.

The European Neighbourhood Policy Instrument (ENPI) is the most explicit form of geopolitical integration between the EU and its immediate region. It is a policy framework that aims to structure relations between the EU and its neighbours according to criteria ostensibly set by both the EU and its *partners*. The countries involved are: Algeria, Armenia, Azerbaijan, Belarus, Egypt, Georgia, Israel, Jordan, Lebanon, Libya, Moldova, Morocco, the Palestinian Authority, Syria, Tunisia and Ukraine.[7] As such, the geographical reach of the ENPI – and hence of the concept of neighbourhood – is considerable. Two major neighbouring countries, Russia and Turkey, are not included within the ENPI but have concluded special agreements with the EU; membership negotiations, although controversial and troubled, have been initiated in the case of Turkey. As has been documented elsewhere, the ENPI is a means by which to maintain the momentum of Europeanization and promulgate the values of the EU without actually offering direct membership to third states

---

7   While formally included in the ENPI, no agreements have been established with Belarus and Syria.

(Commission of the European Communities 2004a; Wallace 2003). Ultimately, the central objective of the ENPI is to create a wider security community in Europe; illegal immigration, human trafficking, terrorism and cross-border organized crime remain issues that will require an especially intensified co-ordination between the EU and its neighbours. However, the ENPI's scope is complex and multilayered (Scott 2005). This is primarily due to the EU's broad definition of security as being environmental, economic and social (and not only military) in nature as well as a realization (not always translated into practice) that security concerns must be shared rather than imposed externally.[8]

As a result, the EU suggests that cultural understanding and the recognition of mutual interdependence are means with which to establishing a common political dialogue. Furthermore, it is not only the enhancement of the EU's international influence that is at stake but also the strengthening of its identity as a stabilizing element in the world system with *exportable* (that is universal) democratic values. With its notion of partnership, the EU pursues the objective of achieving community through *shared* values (such as human and gender rights, commitment to an open market economy, democratic participation and so on), common goals and intensive cooperation on a broad range of EU internal policies.[9] In the words of the EU Commission (2003, 3):

> *Interdependence – political and economic – with the Union's neighbourhood is already a reality. The emergence of the euro as a significant international currency has created new opportunities for intensified economic relations. Closer geographical proximity means the enlarged EU and the new neighbourhood will have an equal stake in furthering efforts to promote trans-national flows of trade and investment as well as even more important shared interests in working together to tackle transboundary threats – from terrorism to air-borne pollution. The neighbouring countries are the EU's essential partners: to increase our mutual production, economic growth and external trade, to create an enlarged area of political stability and functioning rule of law, and to foster the mutual exchange of human capital, ideas, knowledge and culture.*

The central quandary of this geopolitical project lies in an attempt to reduce ambiguities associated with the EU and its future political, economic and social role. However, the EU's geopolitical bordering practices contribute to post-Cold War divisions by creating a spatial *other* (the Neighbourhood) where the *positive* and *shared* values of the EU are both measured and applied. With the demise of

---

8   The EU's security policies with regard to the Neighbourhood are targeted at enhancing public security through combating environmental hazards, terrorism, organized crime, smuggling and other illegal activities (Vitorino 2004). At the same time, peace and stability are to be achieved through closer economic cooperation and the avoidance of divisive gaps in living standards.

9   As defined in Commission of the European Communities (2004a, 11-12).

ideological bordering after the end of the Cold War, EU-Europe is engaged in a struggle for political and social recognition, often pitting the EU not only against its neighbours but also its own member states. Opposition to the EU's attempts at consolidation has resulted in slow progress towards establishing constitutional frameworks for a clearer political role of the EU in particular – as well as a persistent lack of unity in issues such as immigration, foreign policy, citizenship and minority rights point to the complexity of building a supranational political community. However, while the EU's geopolitical project of reordering Europe and its regional neighbourhood is – at best – incomplete, it remains highly influential and thus deserves critical investigation. Zaki Laidi (1998) has attempted to come to terms with the EU's fragmented and contradictory nature by focusing on its attempts to establish coherence within a complex global context. As Laidi maintains, one vital element in the post-Cold War reorganization of the world system is the construction of macroregional *spaces of meaning*, in which the *deepening* and *widening* of European Union has played a pivotal role. As a *space of meaning*, Europe is defining itself both externally (as a *regional and global player*) and internally (as a political community) in terms of a distinctive set of values and a sense of purpose (Scott 2005).[10]

Conclusions

Various geopolitical conceptualizations of *Europe* as well as important geopolitical events have been greatly influential to the development of border theory. These have also reflected the concerns of the times and the ways in which Europe and its internal and external borders have been perceived. The primary focus of this discussion has been on the post-Maastricht European Union within the context of enlargement and the re-emergence of *pan*-European ideas. It has been the author's intention to show that the various (that is political, economic, social and cultural) ramifications of Europe's consolidation and cooperation projects necessitate a multidisciplinary analysis of borders. At the same time, and on a critical note, it appears that notions of a post-Westphalian and postmodern *de-territorialization* of state borders overshoot the mark. Despite a tendency to downplay the societal significance of borders – either for political or ethical reasons – Ratzel's and Maull's determinism (and the fear of *bad borders* they have engendered) is still present in current day European geopolitics. The harsh reality of militarized and separating borders has disappeared from many parts of post-Cold War Europe. However, borders in Europe are also being reconfigured by geopolitical events, by local patterns of cross-border interaction, by a renewed European identity politics and ambiguous discourses of inclusion and exclusion. Borders at the EU's outer

10 Admittedly (perhaps somewhat ironically in this case) the geopolitical concept of Europe as a *pan-Idea* is not new, Karl Haushofer's (1928) depiction of a European geopolitics saw a continent unified by history and a colonial empire pitted against *Pan-Slavic, Pan-American* and British imperial spaces.

frontiers are again becoming formidable barriers and border regions risk becoming permanent peripheries.

For this reason, I argue that EU geopolitics can be interpreted in terms of contested projects of re-territorialization and bordering. This involves, on the one hand, the consolidation of an economic, social and political European space, partly through the flexible construction of Europe within a context of a composite polity. On the other hand, with its Neighbourhood policy the EU pursues a role of stabilizer and promoter of greater cooperation. This rather *messy* and contradictory panorama of bordering practices indicates a course of development informed by discourses of civilizational differentiation, core-periphery dynamics (both within the EU and with regard to the rest of Europe) and struggles over *core values* – but also by processes of gradual accommodation. What consequences might the emergence of messy EU geopolitics imply? Perhaps the main regional concern that emerges from this multilevel complexity (and from the ambiguities embedded in EU policies) is the possible exacerbation of *socio-economic inequalities and cultural difference through exclusionary practices.* On the one hand, the tightening of the border regime at the EU's eastern borders threatens to reinforce social inequalities in the borderlands and could lead to a widening of the development gap between the EU and its eastern neighbours. On the other hand, if one follows national debates about immigration policies, the integration of foreign-born citizens, a possible Turkish accession to the EU, or about perceptions of intractable cultural antagonisms, especially between Christianity and Islam, EU-Europe also seems to signify closure, with identity politics played out in both public and private arenas.

To conclude, borders are multifaceted social institutions. Borders exert an ideational power that not only helps individuals and societies form identities but also exerts a sense of security and comfort. Even within our so-called borderless Europe, national borders are still seen as central to the organization of economic activities and the protection of economic interests. At another level, borders continue to influence socio-spatial behaviours and attitudes. For example, border-related policies, perceptions of *neighbours* across borders and cooperation practices as central elements for the development of a sense of cross-border region. For us border *theorists*, the challenge lies, on the one hand, in understanding the multilevel contingency of bordering; that is the complex construction of borders from a political, economic, socio-cultural and psychological standpoint. As Liam O'Dowd (2002, 30) has argued:

> *Heterogeneity arises from different experiences of border formation, and formal and informal cross-border relationships, along with the relative economic and political power of contiguous states and the role, if any, played by external powers or regional ethnic and national questions. Moreover, the EU's stress on market integration and economic competitiveness impacts in differential ways on pre-existing border heterogeneity.*

On the other hand, there are no neat models of EU geopolitics and the EU's attempts to influence societal development within Europe and the wider

Neighbourhood are hard to map. It might well be that we need new approaches to not only track and critically evaluate *non-scripted* geopolitical discourses and representations of the EU but to also provide concrete alternatives to its border constructions, and thus its exclusionary representations.

References

Aalto, P. (2006), *European Union and the Making of a Wider Northern Europe* (London and New York: Routledge).

Anderson, J. and O'Dowd, L. (1999), 'Borders, Border Regions and Territoriality: Contradictory Meanings, Changing Significance', *Regional Studies* 33:7, 593-604.

Barbé, E. and Johansson-Nogués, E. (2008), 'The EU as a Modest "Force for Good": The European Neighbourhood Policy', *International Affairs* 84:1, 81-96.

Barth, F. (1969), 'Introduction', in Barth, F. (ed.), *Ethnic Groups and Boundaries: the Social Organization of Cultural Difference* (London: George Allen and Unwin), 9-38.

Clark, J. and Jones, A. (2008), 'The Spatialities of Europeanisation: Territory, Government and Power in "Europe"', *Transactions of the Institute of British Geographers* 33:3, 300-18.

Commission of the European Communities (2003), 'Communication from the Commission to the Council and the European Parliament: Wider Europe – Neighbourhood: A New Framework for Relations with our Eastern and Southern Neighbours', *COM (2003) 104 final* (Brussels: Commission of the European Communities).

Donnan, H. and Wilson, T. (1999), *Borders: Frontiers of Identity, Nation and State* (Oxford: Berg).

Flyvbjerg, B. (2001), *Making Social Science Matter. Why Social Inquiry Fails and How it Can Succeed Again* (Cambridge: Cambridge University Press).

Guichonnet, P. and Raffestin, C. (1974), *Géographie des frontières* (Paris: PUF).

Hartshorne, R. (1950), 'The Functional Approach in Political Geography', *Annals of the Association of American Geographers* 40:2, 95-130.

Haushofer, K. (1927, 1939), *Grenzen in ihrer geographischen und politischen Bedeutung* (Heidelberg, Berlin, Magdeburg: Kurt Vohwinckel).

Haushofer, K. (1928), 'Geopolitik der Pan-Ideen', *Weltpolitische Reihe* 21 (Berlin: Zentral-Verlag).

Houtum, H. van (2002), 'Borders of Comfort, Spatial Economic Bordering Processes in the European Union', *Regional and Federal Studies* 12:4, 37-58.

Houtum, H. van and Naerssen, T. van (2002), 'Bordering, Ordering, and Othering', *Journal of Economic and Social Geography* 93:2, 125-36.

Houtum, H. van and Pijpers, R. (2007), 'The European Union as a Gated Community: The Two-Faced Border and Immigration Regime of the EU', *Antipode* 39:2, 291-309.

Jensen, O. B. and Richardson, T. (2004), *Making European Space. Mobility, Power and Territorial Identity* (New York and London: Routledge).

Kristof, L. K. D. (1959), 'The Nature of Frontiers and Boundaries', *Annals of the Association of American Geographers* 49:3, 269-82.

Laidi, Z. (1998), *A World Without Meaning. The Crisis of Meaning in International Politics* (London and New York: Routledge).

Maull, O. (1925), *Politische Geographie* (Berlin: Gebrüder Borntraeger).

Moisio, S. (2007), 'In Search of the Emerging Territoriality of the EU', *Geopolitics* 12:3, 538-48.

Newman, D. (2001), 'Boundaries, Borders and Barriers: Changing Geographic Perspectives on Territorial Lines', in Albert M. et al. (eds), *Identities, Borders and Orders, Rethinking International Relations Theory* (Minneapolis: University of Minnesota Press), 137-50.

Ó Tuathail, G. (1996), *Critical Geopolitics: The Politics of Writing Global Space* (London and New York: Routledge).

Ó Tuathail, G. (1998), 'Thinking Critically About Geopolitics', in Ó Tuathail, G. (ed.), *The Geopolitics Reader* (London and New York: Routledge), 1-12.

O'Dowd, L. (2002), 'The Changing Significance of European Borders', *Regional and Federal Studies* 12:4, 13-36.

Paasi, A. (1991), 'Deconstructing Regions: Notes on the Scales of Spatial Life', *Environment and Planning A* 23, 239-56.

Paasi, A. (1998), 'Boundaries as Social Processes: Territoriality in the World of Flows', *Geopolitics* 3:1, 69-88.

Paasi, A. (1999), 'Boundaries as Social Practice and Discourse: The Finnish-Russian Border', *Regional Studies* 33:7, 669-80.

Paasi, A. (2001): '"A Borderless World"' Is it Only Rhetoric or will Boundaries Disappear in the Globalizing World?', in Reuber, P. and Wolkersdorfer, G. (eds.), *Politische Geographie. Handlungsorientierte Ansätze und Critical Geopolitics* (Heidelberg: Heidelberger Geographische Arbeiten), 133-45.

Perkmann, M. (2002), 'Euroregions: Institutional Entrepreneurship in the European Union', in Perkmann, M. and Sum, N.-L. (eds.), *Globalization, Regionalization and Cross-Border Regions* (Basingtoke: Palgrave Macmillan), 103-24.

Popescu, G. (2006), 'Geopolitics of Scale and Cross-Border Cooperation in Eastern Europe: The Case of the Romanian-Ukrainian-Moldovan Borderlands', in Scott, J. (ed.), *EU Enlargement, Region Building and Sifting Borders of Inclusion and Exclusion* (Aldershot: Ashgate), 35-51.

Raffestin, C. (1990), 'La frontière comme représentation: discontinuité géographique et discontinuité idéologique', *Relations Internationales* 63, 295-303.

Ratzel, F. (1903, 1923), *Politische Geographie* (München and Berlin: R. Oldenbourg), (see especially chapter 19: 'Die Grenze als peripherisches Organ', 428-45).

Scott, J. (ed.) (2006), *EU Enlargement, Region-building and Shifting Borders of Inclusion and Exclusion* (Aldershot: Ashgate).

Wallace, W. (2003), 'Looking after the Neighbourhood: Responsibilities for the EU-25', *Policy Papers of Notre Europe-Groupement des Etudes et de Recherches* 4, available at <http://www.notre-europe.eu/uploads/tx_publication/Policypaper4_02.pdf>.

Vitorino, A. (2004), 'The Future of the European Union Agenda on Asylum, Migration and Borders', Speech to the Conference of the European Policy Center and King Baudouin Foundation, Brussels, 4 October 2004.

The 'Green Line' of Cyprus:
A Contested Boundary in Flux

Nicos Peristianis and John C. Mavris

Introduction

In the years leading to Cyprus' accession into the European Union, hopes had been fostered that EU membership would have been accompanied by the solution of the 'Cyprus Problem', the re-unification of the country, and the eradication of the 'Green Line'[1] – the boundary cutting through the island from east to west, separating Greek-Cypriots from Turkish-Cypriots (see Figure 8.1). Indeed, the accession process did bring about the partial opening of the 'border'[2] in 2003, just a year prior to entry. Hopes for a solution were dashed, however, in April 2004, when, only weeks away from formal accession, a UN-sponsored plan aiming for re-unification was turned down after a referendum. Consequently, although in theory the whole of Cyprus entered the EU in May 2004, in practice the *aquis communitaire* is not applicable in the Turkish-Cypriot controlled northern part of the island. This has created an 'ambiguity' for EU borders, since until a solution to the conflict is reached, 'the UN Green Line Zone will act as a kind of frontier running across the island' (Neuwahl 2005, 25). The EU has thus inherited the unresolved 'Cyprus Problem', and will have to deal with a disputed internal boundary and part of its territory alienated from its control until the conflict is resolved.

But what lies behind the impasse in Cyprus and the resulting line of division? Samuel Huntington sees the conflict on the island as signalling 'a fracture between two civilizations, of Islam and [Christian] Orthodoxy'; hence, as justifying the 'cultural paradigm' which traces explanation to the *clash of civilizations*.[3] Others see the division as the inevitable outcome of deep ethno-national differences and

---

1   The name is attributed to British Major-General Peter Young, and is derived from the line he drew across a map of the capital in green-coloured pencil, following inter-communal disturbances in 1963, to bisect Nicosia into two zones (Greek and Turkish).
2   The term 'border' is highly contested in Cyprus – as will be described subsequently.
3   Huntington (1997) quoted in Blanc (2002, 15). For Huntington's general thesis, see Huntington (1993).

primordial hatreds. Others still, as the result of major power politics and strategic interests in the Eastern Mediterranean (Fouskas and Tackie 2009).

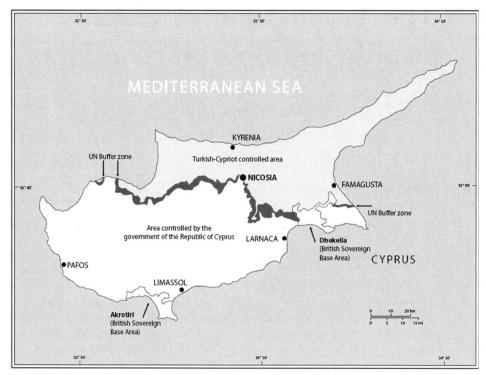

Figure 8.1 Map of Cyprus

Source: adapted from CIA World Factbook – available at <https://www.cia.gov/library/publications/the-world-factbook/maps/maptemplate_cy.html> (accessed 28 April 2011).

Without denying the importance of geopolitics as providing a useful context of analysis, the chapter utilizes Wimmer's neo-Weberian approach (2002, 32-3, 52-64), in attempting a complementary reading, which views a country's boundaries as linked to modern politics and, more specifically, to the national idea – modernity's 'central principle structuring inclusion and exclusion', along which different forms of closure (cultural, legal, political, military, social) are organized. The accumulation of these forms of differentiating the collective national 'self' from the corresponding 'other(s)' makes the 'nationalist representation of the world more and more plausible', so that social phenomena are made to appear to be natural realities (ibid., 57).

The first part of this chapter seeks to situate the construction of the 'Green Line' within relevant key historical processes. The remaining sections consider the differential meanings of the dividing line, as well as the attitudes and actions meant to sustain or undermine the 'border', by the Greek- and Turkish-Cypriots, and how these have fluctuated in recent years in relation to new steps of closure along national(ist) lines.

The establishment of the 'Green Line': from cultural to territorial boundaries

In his seminal work on *Ethnic Groups and Boundaries*, Barth reminds us that, in investigating issues of ethnicity, the critical focus should be the *boundary* that defines the group – with primary consideration being given to the 'social boundaries', though these may have 'territorial counterparts' (Barth 1998 [1969], 15).

From the Ottoman millet system to British ethno-communalism

In Cyprus, the roots of ethnic heterogeneity and of the 'social boundaries' date back to Ottoman rule, during which the Muslim community was constituted.[4] The newcomers lived side by side with the pre-existing Christian communities, the largest of which were the Orthodox *Romioi* (Romans).

As is well known, the multicultural Ottoman Empire was based on the universalistic principles of religion and viewed scriptural religions (Christianity and Judaism) as its ancestors. As such, the respective communities of faith (*millets*) were tolerated and granted autonomy in governing themselves, under their own ecclesiastical leaders (Grillo 1998). In Cyprus, the Orthodox community was granted special privileges, whereby it would enjoy 'preference and precedence' over all other Christian communities on the island. The Orthodox Church acquired increasing prominence, including tax collection rights and representing the local Orthodox subjects at the Porte, thereby assuming vital administrative and political roles and amassing great wealth (Theodoulou 2005).

Under these arrangements, ethnic differences were not significant in the public sphere. The ruling elite of the Ottoman Empire adhered to Islam, but was not comprised of a particular ethnic or linguistic group, since conversion was open to all; in fact, both the administration and armed forces utilized mostly converts, and not free-born Muslims, ensuring the non-ethnic character of the state (Braude and Lewis 1982). Ethnic differences did survive in the private realm, at the local community level in the villages and in town quarters. At this level, families and ethno-linguistic groups acquired primary importance in the transmission and reproduction of religious beliefs and practices, as well as of social customs and

---

4   Through the settling of the conquering forces, population transfers from Anatolia and, subsequently, through intermarriages of Muslims with local women, and conversions to Islam (Kyrris 1976).

of the mother language or dialect. These ethno-cultural communities tended to concentrate in separate neighbourhoods, had their own churches, schools and charitable institutions and, as already pointed out, were largely self-governed. Such life conditions fostered a rather unique sense of solidarity and attachment to the community, and of the primacy of the group over the individual; which was to lay the basis for the peculiar national consciousness and nationalism of the Balkans and the Middle East, underpinned by 'a distinctive communal characteristic' [sic] (Karpat 1973, 13). As a result, Ottoman subjects had a double identity – the religious identity, attaching them to their ethno-cultural community, and the other (much weaker) political identity, attaching them to the Ottoman state and the Sultan himself.

Despite the tolerance towards the non-Muslim religious communities, the latter had to suffer a number of handicaps which put them in a deliberate 'state of humiliation' (Armstrong 1982, 92); such as paying special levies to compensate for not having to join the army, having to wear different clothes to the Muslims, and not being able to testify in sharia courts against Muslims (Armstrong 1982; Grillo 1998). Often, this inferior position was the cause of religious conversions. Intermarriages, primarily of Orthodox women from poor families to richer Muslim males, and the practise of *devshirme*, whereby young Christians were taken into the Empire's military and administrative elite corps, accounted for further conversions.

The various possibilities of conversion to the ruling *millet* indicate that the social boundaries between the major religious communities were not impervious. In fact, a number of these converts maintained a hybrid identity, adopting Muslim practices in public, whereas maintaining the Christian faith in private; after Ottoman rule, many of these returned to their previous faith (Kyrris 1976).

Hence, social segregation of the communities was a fact, but the dividing line between them was not so solid. Many from both communities (but mostly the Muslims) spoke the others' language. Sometimes, they would worship the same saint. Many villages were mixed and, in such cases, it was difficult to distinguish the houses of Christians from those of Muslims. There was some territorial separation[5] but, as Jennings points out, this stemmed from tradition and preference rather than indicating an outcome of state or legal requirements (Jennings 1993). Moreover, most non-religious distinctions were of a socio-economic than of an ethnic nature. No wonder uprisings were commonly staged by the lower classes of both communities, in protest to the policies of the local Ottoman rulers and the Orthodox prelates (Attalides 2003 [1979]; Kyrris 1976).

In the latter years of 'Ottoman decline', religious Orthodox consciousness in the Balkans and the Eastern Mediterranean was to gradually evolve into ethnic consciousness (Stavrianos 2002 [1958]). The carriers of ethnic ideas, influenced by the French Revolution and the Enlightenment, were Greek and Graecophone Orthodox merchants and literati (*logioi*), closely connected to the Greek diaspora communities (*paroikies*). Modern political ideas about nations and states were to

---

5   In 1881, three years into British rule, there were 342 mixed, 342 Christian, and 114 Muslim villages (Attalides 2003 [1979], 89).

form the basis of liberation plans in Ottoman-controlled lands. To forestall these subversive new ideas, the Ottoman central authorities tried to introduce a number of reforms and to cultivate *Ottomanism* as a unifying identity, to link the religious communities comprising the multicultural empire into a new entity – namely, a multinational state. Such efforts, however, proved abortive mainly because the *millets* were already being transformed along ethnic lines. In Cyprus, the creation of the Greek state bolstered the spread of nationalist ideas, within the context of the Grand Idea (*Megali Idea*) irredentist ideology, aiming to unite all Greeks under the roof of a single state.[6]

By the time the British arrived in Cyprus (1878), ethnic feelings and ideas had already taken root, carried to the island from the *paroikies* and from Greece. These proto-national sentiments and ideas were to grow much faster under the more conducive liberal colonial regime. Viewing Cypriot society as already deeply divided along ethno-communal lines, the British proceeded to institutionalize communal representation in the various political bodies (such as the Legislative Council) and in the Boards of Education – despite fears by some that such policies would create a 'wall of demarcation' between the two communities (Demetriadou 1988, 133).

Ethno-national sentiments and the demand for union with Greece (*enosis*) continued to strengthen among the Greek-Cypriots throughout the colonial era. By the late 1920s, the British Governor, Sir Ronald Storrs, was complaining that Greek symbols were everywhere and that a 'flag spirit' prevailed throughout the island (Storrs 1945). Although schools were not yet anti-British, they were 'actively Hellenizing' the students. The curriculum used in class came from Greece and was adopted by the Board of Education; the textbooks had to be approved by the Greek government in Athens. This prompted Storrs to comment on the territorial imagination of Greek-Cypriots, noting that there were 'elaborate maps of modern Greece' in the classrooms, while that of Cyprus, 'if to be found at all was as a rule small, out of date, worn out, and frequently thrust behind the blackboard' (ibid., 467-8). This meant that students knew even minute details concerning Greece and the Greek nation, but had very little knowledge of Cyprus itself.

In the initial years of their rule, the British made little effort to foster an overarching Cypriot identity and, when they belatedly tried to do so, in the 1930s, the 'wall' separating the Cypriots was already too strong. In fact, the locals perceived this new policy as an attempt at undermining their national(ist) feelings, for the sake of cultivating loyalty to the British imperial empire (Persianis 1978).

---

6   The *Megali Idea* (or *Panhellenism*) refers to the vision of reconstituting the Byzantine Empire by extending the authority of the 'mother-state' to include any areas where there were Greeks (Pollis 1996).

Geo-strategic interests, the Republic of Cyprus and the first division

After World War II, the Greek nationalist movement gathered momentum. The contest between the traditional forces of the Right, led by the Church, and the newly emerged Left (AKEL), for hegemony over the Greek-Cypriot community; and the increasingly inflexible British attitude towards Greek-Cypriot demands for self-determination, particularly as their strategic interests over the island acquired greater significance, led to the 1955 anti-colonial guerilla struggle (Joseph 1997). Masterminded by the Right, the struggle deliberately excluded both the Left and the Turkish-Cypriots.

Meanwhile, Turkish-Cypriot ethnic consciousness had been developing separately and in opposition to Greek-Cypriot aspirations. Initially, close contacts were maintained with the Ottoman state and, subsequently, with Turkey, the emphasis shifting from *Ottomanism* to *Turkism* (which focused on the virtues of the Turkish nation, culture and history), and from an Islamic to an ethnic secular identity, according to Kemalist principles;[7] similarly, self-identifications shifted from the 'Muslims' to the 'Turks' of Cyprus. In 1955, when the Greek-Cypriots set up a guerilla organization (EOKA)[8] to push for *enosis* with an armed struggle, the Turkish-Cypriots responded by setting up their own military organization (Volkan, which in 1958 gave its place to the more violent TMT) to push for partition of the island (*taksim*).

To resist nationalist pressures, the British resorted to divide-and-rule tactics; in 1956, they waged the threat of double self-determination on the Greek-Cypriots, while prompting Turkey to become more actively involved with ensuing developments in Cyprus. To combat EOKA insurgents, they set up an 'auxiliary police force', staffed by Turkish-Cypriots: predictably, after the first deaths of their own by EOKA, the Turkish-Cypriot masses took to the streets. Inter-communal violence was to escalate in 1958; the same year featured increasing intra-communal violence, as EOKA and TMT both resorted to murdering leftists, presumably as collaborators with the 'enemy' (the British, in the case of EOKA; the Greek-Cypriot Left, in the case of TMT) but, primarily, as a move to consolidate the Right's hegemony, in view of an impending settlement. The clashes between the two communities caused the British to undertake the first physical division of Nicosia, separating Greek- from Turkish-Cypriot neighbourhoods with barbed wire (the 'Mason-Dixon Line').

The 1959 Zurich-London agreements attempted to balance the interests of Britain, Greece and Turkey, and of the two Cypriot communities, through setting up an independent state, at the permanent exclusion of both *enosis* and *taksim*. Prior attachments to these conflicting goals, however, had crystallized into ethno-national

---

7   The modern Turkish Republic was founded upon Mustafa Kemal Ataturk's principles (Kemalism), including a shift toward secularism and a focus on nationalism – reflecting the intention to emulate Europe, via a process of Westernization and modernization (see Kinross 2001).

8   National Organisation of Cypriot Fighters.

and political polarization, so that 'by the time of independence, the two groups had formed only a limited sense of being Cypriot' (Fisher 2001, 309). The Republic of Cyprus (1960) was a power-sharing regime between the two main communities of the island, based on consociational principles.[9] Almost none of the ingredients required for the success of such an arrangement were there, however, which meant the crucial first years of the fledgling Republic were marred by dissension and political deadlock. In 1963, after the proposals of the Greek-Cypriot President of the Republic, Archbishop Makarios, for changing the Constitution were turned down by Turkey and the Turkish-Cypriots, conflict erupted and the bi-communal state collapsed.

The main consequence of the inter-communal conflict, which began in December 1963 and continued intermittently until 1967, was the exodus of large numbers of Turkish-Cypriots from areas where they were in the minority, into a number of self-contained enclaves, where they set up their own separate administration.[10] This was the 'first partition' on an island-wide scale, leading to the extensive territorial separation of Greek- and Turkish-Cypriots (Drousiotis 2005). The resulting isolation of the latter brought upon them economic hardship, unemployment, migration, and increasing dependence on Turkey. The Greek-Cypriots, on the other hand, won a major political victory when the UN Security Council recognized the now Greek-Cypriot dominated government of the Republic of Cyprus as legitimate, and called for the creation of a 'United Nations Force in Cyprus' (UNFICYP), charged with preserving 'peace and security' and with assisting the government 'in restoring law and order'.[11]

The new state of affairs augmented tensions between Greece and Turkey. The USA, as the new western superpower in the region, keen to prevent a rift within NATO (of which both 'mother countries' were members), tried to promote a solution whereby Cyprus would be united with Greece and, in exchange, Turkey would be given a military base on the island.[12] Fearing this scheme would eventually lead to partition and/or 'double enosis' (union with the respective 'mother countries'), Makarios rejected it, along with other similar schemes, which brought him disfavour with the USA and successive Greek governments.

Relations with Greece worsened when a military junta seized power in 1967. Soon after, Makarios turned to the policy of the feasible (*efikton*), aimed at consolidating independence, while minimizing the powers of the Turkish-Cypriots.

---

9   The four main characteristics of consociational regimes are: elite grand coalition; proportionality in the allocation of powers and resources; mutual veto powers on matters of vital interest; and segmental autonomy (Lijphart 1977).

10 The enclaves covered 3-4 per cent of the land of Cyprus, a much smaller percentage than the Turkish-Cypriot population ratio (18 per cent) at the time.

11 UNFICYP was assigned to patrol the length of the Buffer Zone, between the two communities. Sent to the island under Security Council Resolution 186 (1964), it was to remain in Cyprus for three months, but is still on the island today! (see Republic of Cyprus 2003).

12 This became known as the 'Acheson Plan', having been masterminded by Dean Acheson, the former US Secretary of State.

The negotiations between the two communities for amending the Constitution came to a halt in 1974 when a Greek-junta-inspired coup (led by the National Guard and an extreme right-wing paramilitary group (EOKA B) insisting on *enosis*) overturned Makarios; a week later, Turkey intervened militarily – presumably to restore constitutional order and to protect the Turkish-Cypriots, but primarily aiming to promote its own strategic interests. The outcome of the violence was the effective partitioning of the island into two 'ethnically clean' territorial zones.

Differential accounts of division and of the dividing line

For the Greek-Cypriots, the 1974 developments amounted to complete catastrophe: about a fourth of their population was forcibly displaced from the north (where they had constituted 80 per cent of the population); almost 40 per cent of the island came under Turkish control; and the economy was in disarray. The dream of union with Greece (*enosis*) was buried for good and many were disillusioned with the motherland, holding it responsible for the coup and for not having protected the Greek-Cypriots from Turkey's onslaught.

The new ideal became that of the re-union (*epanenosis*) of Cyprus. There was thus a belated 'turn to Cyprus', to whatever was of Cyprus and could serve to re-unite the country. There was a new emphasis on the common traits, attitudes and interests of all the island's inhabitants – part of *Cypriotism*, a wider argument which stressed a distinctly Cypriot identity and mode of life, as against all outside encroachments (including those by the 'mother-countries').[13] Along with this, a novel interpretation of the past was born, emphasizing the traditional 'harmonious co-existence' of the two communities.

Henceforth, a policy of rapprochement (*epanaprosengisi*) was to be pursued, aimed at bringing the two communities together as in the 'good old times'. Independence Day began to be celebrated for the first time, while there was a parallel de-emphasis of the Greek national day, previously the focus of celebrations. Also, for the first time after independence, the Cypriot flag began to be hoisted widely on public buildings, next to the Greek flag, which up to that time was the one almost solely used. The state acquired increasing importance, as it became vital in the Greek-Cypriots' struggle for survival: in re-housing the thousands of refugees, rekindling the economy, and in holding together the devastated Greek-Cypriot community. Above all, the Republic managed to retain international recognition as the legitimate government, which was to prove an invaluable shield against Turkey's overwhelming military might, and a formidable weapon in the battles of the Greek-Cypriots against the 'realities' on the ground. Additionally, there was a new appreciation of how the state could act as an alternative basis of identity formation, forging 'unifying civic' rather than 'divisive ethnic' values.

---

13 On *Cypriotism* (or Cypriotness), see Attalides (2003 [1979], 73-7); Peristianis (2000); Stamatakis (1994).

Within the mainstream Greek-Cypriot perspective, division is anathema and the Green Line an aberration. Division is attributed mostly, even solely, to the expansionist designs of Turkey, which, aided by foreign powers (the US and Britain), came to spoil the pristine state of peace and harmonious co-existence on the island; the Turkish-Cypriots are equally seen to be the victims of these dire developments, since they too suffer from the consequences of division – the blame resting squarely with Turkey and the Turkish-Cypriot collaborating leadership. The dividing line is thus commonly called the 'Attila Line'[14] or 'Occupation Line', viewed as a symbol of aggression and violation, 'a reminder that they are still at war, and [under] an immanent threat' (Defereos 2005, 142). Officially, it is not recognized as a border, but is regarded as merely a ceasefire line, a 'frontier', marking the 'free' from the 'occupied' areas, beyond which the Republic temporarily exercises no territorial control (the defining characteristic of statehood).

The Turkish-Cypriots have different interpretations of past and present realities. Their official narrative attributes the source of the problems to the Greek-Cypriots' insistence on *enosis*, despite their own wishes and apprehensions. They emphasize that the 1960 Republic was a bi-communal partnership between two equal communities, which the Greek-Cypriots tried to undermine. For them, it is 1963 which acts as the watershed of modern history as, since then, they have been forced into isolation and marginalization.

Their own official re-interpretation of history, therefore, highlights past conflict and violence, and the difficulties of co-habitation with Greek-Cypriots. In this context, the 1974 'intervention' of Turkey is hailed as a 'Peace Operation', necessary for their rescue. Consequently, the border is a 'Peace Line', viewed as 'a non-negotiable symbol of security' (Defereos 2005, 142). The 'provisional administration' set up after the 1963 clashes has progressively hardened into the 'Turkish Republic of Northern Cyprus' (TRNC). Despite the fact that this self-proclaimed state has received no international recognition, save that of Turkey, it has tried hard to fulfill all the functions expected of a state, aiming to secure eventual legitimacy.

As we have seen, the two sides have been engaged in long-time discussions over resolving the 'Cyprus Problem'.[15] Yet, ever since a summit agreement in 1977, where it was agreed that a future solution will be some form of federal system, they have been unable to agree on the specifics, each pushing in different directions as to the desired federal regime. The Greek-Cypriots aim for the re-incorporation of Turkish-Cypriots into a federal state with a strong central government (which would be in a position to block secessionist moves); put differently, while their current ideal

---

14 'Attila' was the codename of the Turkish military operation in the island in 1974 – a reference to King Attila, ruler of the Hun Empire: considered a brave conqueror for the Turks, but regarded as primitive and savage by many in the Western world (including Greek-Cypriots). See also Kokkinos (2002, 3).

15 Negotiations began in 1968, after Makarios had adopted the policy of the feasible; they were briefly interrupted by the 1974 developments, recommencing however shortly afterwards.

solution would be a unitary state without internal borders, their compromise position is a federal solution with a rather permeable border between the two communities or component polities. The Turkish-Cypriots aim for a re-grouping of two equal partners into a confederal regime (whereby the constituent parts would have maximum autonomy, resembling sovereign states to the extent possible); put differently, while their current ideal solution would be two separate states with a strong border separating the two communities, their compromise position is a confederal solution with only a slightly permeable border (Peristianis 1999).

Overall, the present positions of the two parties relate to their ideal past aims, the concessions they have been forced to make so far, and the ultimate compromises they would be willing to make to come to a solution (see Figure 8.2):

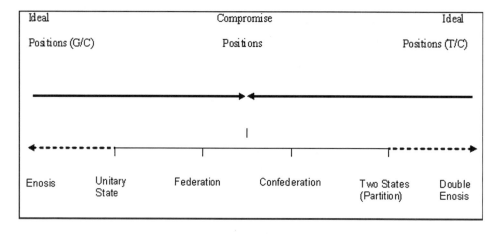

Figure 8.2 Ideal and Compromise Positions of Greek- and Turkish-Cypriots

The above obviously presents a simplification of the views of the two sides, since the two communities are not homogeneous entities but are internally diverse, within which a range of ideologies and discourses abound. The most important division is that between Right and Left: but whereas elsewhere the usual load of these terms relates to a differing stand on issues of political economy, in the case of Cyprus, and as a consequence of the historic trajectory already outlined, the primary distinction relates to their different stand on 'national' issues.[16]

The composition of both the 'Self' and the 'Other' is largely determined by the content and focus of the 'ethno-history' or national narrative espoused. The articulation of these narratives takes the differing forms of *Hellenism* and *Turkism* (identities borne of identification with the respective 'motherland') versus *Cypriotism*

---

16   For an assessment of the traditional Left / Right dichotomy in Greek-Cypriot politics, see Papadakis (1998, 153-6); Peristianis (1995, 123-56). For the corresponding Turkish-Cypriot political dichotomy, see Gutman Killoran (1994).

(a common Cypriot identity), exhibited in the political arena in both parts of the divide. Post 1974, the Right primarily adhered to the 'mother-country' narrative, wherein the island of Cyprus was viewed as an integral part of the wider Greek or Turkish world. The Left, on the other hand, promoted a narrative of shared community between Greek- and Turkish-Cypriots, wherein *Cypriotism* was advanced.[17]

While these distinctions remain on a broader level, intra-party divergences have become more pronounced, resulting in shifting intra-party cleavages and inter-party convergences. Indeed, most parties enfold both 'Hellenocentric' and 'Cyprocentric' factions, which often come into conflict with each other.[18]

Contesting the boundary and the politics of (non)-recognition

We have seen how over the years the Turkish-Cypriots have sought increasing autonomy or partition, culminating in their 1983 unilateral declaration of independence and the creation of the TRNC. The Greek-Cypriots have refused to acknowledge the legitimacy of the TRNC and its 'borders'. Since undoing the realities on the ground lies beyond their powers, however, they have been engaged in diverse forms of contestation and subversion instead.

A first type of contestation relates to Greek-Cypriots' attempts to prevent the international recognition of the Turkish-Cypriot self-proclaimed state (TRNC). This has involved persistent, strenuous efforts at various international political fora, starting with the UN General Assembly and the UN Security Council: given the strength of the norms protecting the sovereignty and territorial integrity of established states, and the fear of opening Pandora's box encouraging secessionist moves around the globe, recognition of the run-away Turkish-Cypriot state has not been forthcoming in such fora. On their part, the Turkish-Cypriots have persisted in their efforts to gain such recognition, using every available means to do so. The stakes in this contest have been so high that it has extended into a generalized (non-)recognition warfare, or 'game', involving a 'distributive, zero-sum or "us" versus "them" approach' (Hocknell 2001, 348); implicating not only diplomats and politicians, but also ordinary Cypriot citizens. The semiological battle rages fiercely on all fronts: Greek-Cypriots meticulously place references to the TRNC and its institutions in quotation marks, or (especially in oral speech) use the prefix 'pseudo' – as in pseudo-state, pseudo-president, pseudo-elections, and so on.

Next come activities which may imply some form of international recognition: foreign politicians and diplomats are expected not to meet with their TRNC

---

17   The limitations of using a one-dimensional left / right ideological axis have been well-noted, not least of which is its inability to fully explain such intra-party ideological nuances (Giddens 1994; Kitschelt and Hellemans 1990; for Cyprus, see Peristianis 2006).

18   For further details, see Peristianis (2006), who notes another axis of division on the terms and type of solution to the Cyprus Problem, between 'hardliners' and 'softliners'.

counterparts; Turkish-Cypriots are to be obstructed from participating in international meetings as official delegates of TRNC institutions; commercial or other organizations are to be prevented from opening branches, or appointing representatives in the north. In fact, as some analysts point out, efforts to block recognition have 'extended to almost any imaginable activity of an international nature', ranging from trading with companies in the north, to sporting events and academic conferences, many of which are 'devoid of any explicit political content' (Constantinou and Papadakis 2001, 129). In parallel, Turkish-Cypriots seem to pursue such types of 'recognition' with similar perseverance, aiming at a gradual acceptance of the TRNC and its institutions, and a normalization of its existence.

Hence, every activity or event which is seen to imply the danger or promise of any degree of recognition is turned into a battleground. For Greek-Cypriots, preventing the seceding state from acquiring legitimacy is tantamount to protecting the survival of their own state; hence, engaging in acts blocking such recognition amounts to one's patriotic duty – much like defending one's country in time of war. In contrast, Turkish-Cypriots' patriotic duty is to press for the recognition of the TRNC, arguing that this is in accord with the principle of political equality on which the 1960 partnership state was based: if a future common state is to be rebuilt, it can only be as a coming together of two equal partners.

Alongside the issue of international recognition for the TRNC and its external borders, a second type of contestation concerns the legitimacy of the TRNC's internal territorial 'border' – the Green Line. After the 1974 forced division of the island, Greek-Cypriots engaged in various individual and collective actions contesting this boundary. Prior to its partial opening, in 2003, individuals often attempted to violate the 'border' and to cross into the Turkish occupied north, in order to visit their homes or properties.[19] On the collective level, annual rituals of protest against the occupation and division, have tried to express the community's resolve 'not to forget'. To this end, there are two major 'Pancypriot'[20] protest rituals endorsed by the Republic of Cyprus: the first, on 20 July, commemorates the 'black' anniversary of the Turkish Invasion of 1974; the second, on 15 November, is a protest against the 1983 declaration of independence by the so-called TRNC.[21] On both occasions, Greek-Cypriots gather near the boundary, usually in the area of the Ledra Palace barricades.[22]

---

19   Stamatakis (1994, 334) points to repeated attempts by displaced Greek-Cypriots to cross the boundary in order to return to their homes – either to see it, or to bring items from the 'occupied' to the 'free' areas.

20   Pancypriot translates into 'for all-Cypriots', but is used widely by Greek-Cypriots to refer solely to all Greek-Cypriots.

21   Many other locally-based protest rituals are organized by regional refugee associations and performed annually on the name day of the regional patron saint.

22   Before and during 1974, Ledra Palace Hotel was the meeting place for the negotiations between the two communities; after 1974, the hotel, located within the UN-controlled neutral zone separating the two sectors of Nicosia, became the major checkpoint across the dividing line (mainly used by diplomats, some tourists, and by the enclaved Greek-

The rituals of protest include chanting slogans against the Turkish occupation and singing patriotic songs. The aim of all activities is to proclaim the Greek-Cypriots' determination not to accept the dividing line. Since forcefully breaking through the line is next to impossible, given the Turks' immensely stronger military capability, contesting the line remains a purely symbolic ritual. Yet, on certain occasions, prior to 2003, the demonstrators went beyond the standard rituals, and attempted to take the further step of crossing into the occupied lands; such climaxes entailed skirmishes with Greek-Cypriot policemen and UN soldiers who, in turn, tried to block demonstrators from crossing into the neutral zone and becoming embroiled with Turkish-Cypriot policemen (and/or Turkish soldiers). On several occasions, young Greek-Cypriots attempted to bring down the TRNC flag from flag poles in the neutral zone. In some cases, such actions led to arrests and imprisonments, while in worse cases, relating to the motorcyclist incidents in 1996 in the village of Dherynia, they led to two deaths: one young man was killed by a mob of Turkish-Cypriot extremists, because he transgressed the territorial border; another was shot dead by a Turkish military officer-cum-politician, because he transgressed against the TRNC's identity symbol (the flag), demarcating the border (Peristianis 2000, 193-4).

Although all Greek-Cypriots contest the Green Line, the way the 'border' is challenged varies according to ideological orientation. Typically, the more militant forms of activity have been undertaken by Hellenocentrists. A good example is the case of the 'Women's Walks' (or marches) – a protest ritual organized by groups of Greek-Cypriot women after 1974, contesting the occupation and the enforced division of the island. In 1975, the first such event, which gained significant international participation and publicity, ended with a peaceful demonstration which stopped at the checkpoint. Subsequent marches (in January and November 1987), however, revealed intense differences between participating women groups – rooted in ideological divergences; Cyprocentrists underlining the need for the walks to send messages of peace and to serve the cause of *rapprochement* with the Turkish-Cypriots, while Hellenocentrists arguing for the right to avow one's ethnicity and to more assertively condemn the occupation and the violation of Greek-Cypriots' human rights. After a split in the movement, mainly over these issues, the last Women's Walk (July 1989) ended up stressing ethnic symbols – for instance, the chosen protest site was a Greek school and a church in the Buffer Zone, where a priest commenced the Orthodox liturgy – prompting the violent attack of Turkish-Cypriot policemen and the arrest of many participants.

Despite such differences, in all these protest rituals '[t]he culmination and, at the same time, the defining moment of the "ritual of resistance", [...was] crossing the line', which demarcates the division of the island (Stamatakis 1994, 268).

Cypriots visiting relatives in the south) – and, thus, the major site for contestation rituals.

Box 8.1 Pyla: A liminal space with porous borders

Pyla is a typical Cypriot village in the south-east part of the island, near Larnaka Bay. It is, however, (in)famous as the sole village to have retained its bi-communal composition post-1974. Explanations for this continued cohabitation abound, dependent on one's political outlook on the Cyprus Problem. Pure pragmatic cooperation, unshakable harmonious coexistence, or the permanent presence of a UN contingency (UNFICYP), are some of the reasons put forward. In any case, this is a locale in which Greek- and Turkish-Cypriots must constantly negotiate the common space they share. Moreover, Pyla lies within the Buffer Zone (or *Dead Zone*), created in the wake of the island-long dividing line – a status which has accorded the village much public attention as 'a potent political symbol for all concerned sides' (Papadakis 1997, 360). The prevailing Greek-Cypriot (G/C) narrative of diachronic intercommunal cooperation is used to refer to Pyla as an example of continuing harmonious relations between the communities in the present – as an achievement of 'civic nationalism', wherein the 'ethnically' oppositional 'Greek' and 'Turk' are replaced by an inclusive 'Cypriot' label. Conversely, the prevailing Turkish-Cypriot (T/C) narrative of longstanding intercommunal antagonism is used when referring to the difficulties of joint administration in the village – as a problematic example of communal power sharing between 'Greeks' and 'Turks', which serves to reinforce the case for (physical/political) segregation and promotes, by extension, 'ethnic nationalism'.

The above is compounded by the various manipulations of space/landscape by each community. For example, a Greek flag was painted upon the G/C coffee shop's sign, in the same way that a Turkish flag was painted upon the T/C coffee shop's sign – despite UN restrictions concerning such displays, which have obviously not deterred 'ethno-nationalists' from employing the flag of their respective 'motherland' permanently. Moreover, the G/C coffee shop is named *Macedonia*; as an indication of support towards Greece's dispute with the Former Yugoslav Republic of Macedonia (FYROM).[1] Likewise, the T/C coffee shop is labelled *Turkish Coffee Shop of Pyla*, dispensing with the suffix 'Cypriot'; thereby, explicitly emphasizing the 'ethnic' Turkish character of its clientele. Situated in the main square, these coffee shops are the daily focal points of all (male) inhabitants. Hence, these clearly chauvinistic emblems apparently act as a 'constant visual reminder to locals from both ethnic groups of the [...] opposed identifications of Greece, Turkey, Greek Cypriots and Turkish Cypriots' (Papadakis 2004, 21) (see Figure 8.3). The names and affiliated flags of the respective coffee shops represent a wider (island-wide) undertaking of staking a claim in the *topos* (place) (Leontis 1995, 19) – evidenced by the existence of separate coffee shops for each community.[2] Defining *topos* as 'a site where the past makes its presence felt', Leontis underscores how attempts to secure such a site/*topos* have manifested in various constructions and symbols. More generally, on either side of the Green Line, a concerted attempt has been engaged in to transform the landscape into an expression of the post-1974 condition. In Pyla, a village both literally and figuratively in the middle of this struggle, it appears that the members of the two communities are striving to do the same.[3]

Notes

1. For an account of this dispute and its varying Cypriot viewpoints, see Papadakis (2004).

2. Many villages exhibit more than two coffee shops: for example G/C villages usually have a leftist (AKEL) and rightist (DISY) coffee shop, while some have a centrist (DIKO) and/or socialist (EDEK) one too.

3. For symbolisms evident in Pyla, see Papadakis (2000).

Figure 8.3 One Village Square, Two Coffee Shops:
    The two 'nationalist' coffee shops lie within Pyla's main square,
    literally and figuratively opposed

The fracturing of the Wall and the 'Great Reversal'

As already noted, contestations of the dividing line have mainly come from Greek-Cypriots. Turkish-Cypriots have been striving for greater autonomy or separation, and have thus been the defenders of the borderline. Yet things were to change with the dawn of the twenty-first century, and Turkish-Cypriots would be the ones to partially open up the checkpoints in April 2003. Only a year later, in April 2004, in a referendum which would have led to a solution to the 'Cyprus Problem' and to the removal of the boundary, the Greek-Cypriot 'No' vote inadvertently gave a new lease of life to the 'Green Line', the Wall that continues to separate Greek- from Turkish-Cypriots. What may explain this paradox, this 'Great Reversal'?

The Turkish-Cypriots' revolt against the Wall

Although the opening of the checkpoints in April 2003 appeared to be the action of just one man – namely, Raulf Denktash, 'President' of the TRNC, old-time nationalist, and strong advocate of separation – in reality, it was the result of a massive build up which threatened to sweep away the regime and its leadership, much as in the case of the Iron Curtain dividing Europe. What was the background to these developments?

Ever since their withdrawal into self-contained enclaves in 1963, Turkish-Cypriots have been isolated from the external world, and have had to increasingly rely on Turkey's help for their survival.

The hard-liners' policy of separation was vindicated in 1974, with Turkey's invasion, and the capture of the northern part of Cyprus, which became the Turkish-Cypriots more comfortable home. Yet, despite acquiring abundant land, factories, hotels and other wealth-generating resources, the Turkish-Cypriot economy did not manage to take-off. One set of factors explaining this failure relates to the historical patterns of division of labour, along broadly ethnic lines: the Turkish-Cypriots tended to concentrate in public administration posts and landownership, thus undervaluing the more dynamic entrepreneurial activities (where Greek-Cypriots tended to predominate). Another set of factors had to do with the success of the Republic of Cyprus, not only in depriving the TRNC of international recognition, but also in enforcing an international embargo against it, which severely curtailed any prospects for the development of its trade and tourism sectors. The insecurity of investors over the TRNC's future prospects, the overgrowth of the public sector (used as a means of creating jobs for the unemployed masses, but also as a pool of votes for the regime), and the inefficiencies and mismanagement of a largely unproductive economy, have increased the Turkish-Cypriots' reliance on Turkey.

The first opposition party, the Republican Turkish Party (CTP), founded in 1970, was to shift leftwards in the post-1974 period, when it strengthened its links with the Greek-Cypriot AKEL and the international communist camp – leading it to adopt a more vocal anti-imperialist discourse, as well as a critical stance against Denktash's policy of separation and increasing dependence on Turkey; arguing instead for a new partnership with Greek-Cypriots in a bi-communal federal state. In subsequent years, other opposition parties and organizations were to emerge, though they suffered from division and antagonisms among their leadership, as well as from a lack of a focused, common ideology. Until the 1990s, therefore, Denktash and the right-wing parties (often collectively referred to, by the opposition, as the 'Establishment', or the 'nationalists/chauvinists') managed to rule almost unhampered, despite criticism by a vocal, albeit inefficient, opposition.

At the end of the 90s, the resort to violence by extreme nationalists, and by the ruling regime itself,[23] galvanized opposition parties, unions and other organizations, to rally together into the *Platform of 41 Organizations*, under the slogan 'This Land is Ours';[24] which managed to incite the crowds to take to the streets, protesting the regime's oppressive policies and demanding the release of arrested opposition journalists.[25] Soon after, there was a collapse of a number of Turkish-Cypriot banks, leading hundreds to unemployment and thousands to bankruptcy. Turkey, which had to bear the brunt, pushed for unpopular economic recovery policies; one such measure, the devaluation of the Turkish lira in 2001, only worsened things.

Meanwhile, the economic wellbeing of the south, and the progress of the Greek-Cypriots' application for joining the European Union,[26] provided an unfavourable comparison reference and enhanced dissatisfaction with the TRNC's own performance. The final catalyst to developments was the submission of the UN peace plan (which came to be known as the Annan Plan, on account of then UN Secretary-General, Kofi Annan) in November 2002. The Plan provided for a bi-communal, power-sharing regime, which maintained many consociational principles from the 1960 agreements, but added important federal provisions (inspired by the Swiss and Belgian models of federation). It was hoped that, following a solution based on the Plan, a re-united Cyprus would enter the EU; special ties of friendship with Greece and Turkey would be encouraged; the new state would be committed to supporting Turkey's accession to the EU; and unique provisions would facilitate closing the economic gap between the two communities, while safeguarding their permanent cultural autonomy.

Although the Annan Plan was unwelcome by Denktash, it was received as a god-sent by the majority of Turkish-Cypriots, who held their leadership responsible for the TRNC's political isolation, economic regression, corruption, and complete dependence on Turkey. All these features had encouraged a steady stream of Turkish-Cypriot migration abroad, while thousands of destitute Turks were imported from Anatolia to provide cheap labour (and votes) for the regime: the cultural differentials between these immigrants and the locals created a great deal of friction and resentment. Both legal and illegal settlers (including migrants) kept flooding into the TRNC from all directions. A proliferation of night clubs, casinos, sex trafficking, drug-dealing and money laundering constituted other dimensions of the local economy. Increasingly, Denktash was deemed no longer fit

---

23 An expression of which was the murder of Kutlu Adali, a popular Turkish-Cypriot anti-establishment journalist, in 1996. His death brought together seventeen Turkish-Cypriot organizations (especially teachers and public servants) into the *Platform for the Trade Union Struggle*, constituting the first step in the process of uniting the opposition.

24 The union was later to grow in size, hosting another 45 organizations, and renamed the *Platform of Shared Vision*.

25 These protests were also precipitated by the closure of *Europa* newspaper – which was later reopened with the new name *Afrika*, to ridicule the 'primitiveness' of Denktash's regime.

26 For a discussion of the case of Cyprus' accession into the EU, see Christou (2004).

to understand and express Turkish-Cypriot interests, while many began pondering whether Turkey was turning from a liberator into an occupying force.

Shortly after the Annan Plan's submission, the mass rallies organized by the opposition began drawing unprecedented support. In March 2003, against the backdrop of steadily rising public pressure, the Hague negotiations for a solution collapsed and all parties blamed it on Denktash's intransigence. In April of that year, the Republic of Cyprus signed the accession agreement, according to which the Greek-Cypriots could still join the EU, even if the 'Cyprus Problem' was not solved. For the Turkish-Cypriots, this meant they were to remain in their prison state, and the Green Line would become a de facto 'border' with the EU, while their neighbours would enjoy all the benefits of EU citizenship.

To console the Turkish-Cypriots, the EU and the Greek-Cypriot government came out with a number of 'privileges' for the former – which, inevitably, would have led to the further erosion of Denktash's sovereignty. Meanwhile, feelings of frustration and dissatisfaction were gathering force with ordinary Turkish-Cypriots, ready to explode. Fearing the worst, and instead of standing in the way or using force, Denktash took the pre-emptive step of partially opening the border himself – in terms of allowing crossings, so far prohibited. Even though events had been steadily leading to this, it was a development few had expected.[27]

The fractured Wall and the Greek-Cypriots' dilemma

To some extent, the opening of the checkpoints was similar to the fall of the Berlin Wall: the majority of Turkish-Cypriots had been questioning an inefficient, corrupt and suppressive regime, pushing for the gates to open and for access to a perceived freer world.[28] There were, however, important differences between the two cases. In Cyprus, the Wall did not fall – it just fractured.[29] Moreover, while Denktash partially opened the gates, he insisted on maintaining the semblance of a state (hence, the insistence on the showing of passports), thereby affirming the existence of the boundary and the 'sovereignty' of the TRNC. More importantly, the people in the German case were not ethnically divided: once re-united within a single state, they had no need to preserve their separate identities and to press for a power-sharing formula. These considerations were to prove paramount in the way developments unfolded in Cyprus.

---

27   Demetriou (2007) argues that the checkpoint openings should not have been surprising, linking this with the announcement of a package of measures (denoting a plan of 'free movement') in the respective press of each side only a month earlier (see *Kibrish*; *Phileleftheros*; *Politis*; *Yeniduzen* 2003).

28   Faustmann (2004) recognises certain similarities with the German case: a) both divisions were the outcome of 'military invasions from outside powers'; b) sustained through a systematic 'process of alienation', where contact was prohibited and propaganda was employed.

29   On this, Hannay (2005, 226) remarked, 'It gradually dawned ... that the Green Line was not the Berlin Wall'.

The government of the Republic was caught unprepared for such a turn of events.[30] The dilemmas were grave and they became clearer in the days which followed. Since the Republic claimed jurisdiction over the whole of Cyprus and over all Cypriots, Turkish-Cypriots could obviously claim citizenship rights; which meant they could request passports of the Republic of Cyprus, which would automatically (following accession) make them citizens of the EU. They could, furthermore, lay claim to all the benefits citizens of the Republic enjoyed (such as free access to public hospitals, state schools and so on), whilst not being held accountable for any obligations to the Republic. The above is precisely what Turkish-Cypriots did *en masse*, immediately after the opening of the checkpoints.

At the same time, since the north was still under Turkish control, the Republic could have no jurisdiction over Turkish-Cypriots, or over Greek-Cypriots venturing into the northern part of their country! Even worse, to cross to the other side, Greek-Cypriots would have to show their passport, which was felt to carry the danger of acknowledging the TRNC's sovereignty. Indeed, the initial reactions of the Republic's government were to remind everyone that Denktash's actions only aimed at confirming the TRNC's legitimacy and the existence of a 'border'. It also questioned the wisdom of Greek-Cypriots' crossings after showing their passports. These cautious, if not negative, remarks made most Greek-Cypriots hesitant to cross. Meanwhile, Turkish-Cypriots were crossing, as were some daring Greek-Cypriots, taking advantage of the fact that their government had not explicitly asked them not to.

As time passed, and as the number of Greek-Cypriots crossing increased, the government of the Republic had to face a growing dilemma: if it maintained a sceptical attitude or officially adopted a negative stance on crossing (as the hardliners were asking it to do), it ran the risk of coming into conflict with at least some of its citizens who appeared determined to cross – or worse, it ran the risk of simply being disobeyed by these citizens – and then what? Once they did cross, the Republic would have no control over them: it could only punish them for their choice upon their return, but this could create further reactions and defiance by citizens who disagreed with such a stance. The issue was quickly turning into a nightmare, when an ex-Attorney General of the Republic took a public stand and opined that, according to international law, recognition of a state cannot result from the actions of individuals (such as showing a passport), but can only derive from the acts of other states. This statement gave the green light to masses of Greek-Cypriots to cross; it acted much like a pardon paper, assuring those who did commit the 'sin' of crossing that they were not trespassing on forbidden ground, and were not being disloyal to their country and nation.

Yet, the issue of crossing or not crossing was not to die so easily.[31] For several months after it was declared acceptable to cross, the hardliner nationalists kept questioning the wisdom of this 'laxity', which allowed citizens to return to the

---

30   Demetriou (2007) argues that this surprise was retrospectively constructed, as a means of dealing with an 'unimaginable' development.

31   On this, see Demetriou's (2007) aptly titled article 'To Cross or not to Cross'.

sacred, occupied lands, not as owners of their properties, but as mere visitors, who had to ask permission to enter from those who had 'stolen' them. Worse than that, some Greek-Cypriot 'visitors' appeared to act like tourists – they had meals and drinks in Turkish-Cypriot restaurants and even seemed to enjoy themselves. It was not long before journalists started reporting on cases of Greek-Cypriots spending exorbitantly in the 'occupied lands', in the Turkish-Cypriot casinos and cabarets.

In addition to giving money to the 'illegal' TRNC, which served to finance its existence, all such acts and the accompanying attitudes of disrespect towards what these lands stood for were to be condemned. The north was a wounded and enslaved part of the collective body, towards which the only 'proper' attitude was that of reverence for all the loss and pain suffered by the community. If one was to visit the occupied areas (something questionable to begin with), the appropriate way of viewing them would be as 'sacred' lands; and the visit itself as a 'pilgrimage',[32] undertaken with the respective devotion fit of a pilgrim, and not as a trip of amusement, undertaken with the frivolity of a tourist.

In practice, there were all kinds of attitudes and motives held by the thousands of Greek-Cypriots who did cross the border.[33] One thing common to all was that they crossed with excitement into the land they were barred access to for almost thirty years. Turkish-Cypriots did not share the same dilemmas as the Greek-Cypriots, but they also partook in the excitement of visiting the long forbidden lands across the divide. With time, however, the excitement was to wane: crossing became routine, the 'other side' lost much of its sacred mystique, ending up a mundane activity, while passions for re-uniting the island subsided (Dikomitis 2005). Another strong push in this direction was to come with the Annan Plan referendum, when Greek-Cypriots chose to say 'No' to the Plan: regardless of the underlying motives, the end result was that the Cypriot boundary received a new lease of life.

The referendum maintains the fractured Wall and the surrounding ambiguities

In February 2003, just before the checkpoints had partially opened, the Greek-Cypriots elected Tassos Papadopoulos as the new President of the Republic. Papadopoulos was the leader of DIKO,[34] a small centrist party, who came to power with the backing of the much larger 'communist' AKEL and the smaller socialist EDEK.[35] The three parties had joined forces to oust Glafkos Clerides, the founder and ex-leader of DISY,[36] who had been in office for two consecutive terms (1993-2003). Clerides had risen to power, and had subsequently kept his post, by

---

32   Dikomitis (2005) expounds upon three 'readings' of the Cypriot boundary as regards Greek-Cypriot (non-)crossings, one of which was defined as a 'pilgrimage'.

33   For a fuller account of this, see Webster and Dallen (2006).

34   The Democratic Party, representing rather conservative, centrist policies.

35   Movement for Social Democracy: poses as a centre-left party, pursuing socialist policies.

36   Democratic Rally: the leading right-wing party.

maintaining the image of a realist politician who could, however, pursue a hard line when circumstances demanded it.[37] Following the EU green light for accession, the pressures (from both Europe and the US) for maintaining a more moderate stance on the Cyprus Problem had increased. The new Greece of Prime Minister Costas Simitis, who had adopted a policy of reconciliation with Turkey, was also pushing in the same direction. But when Clerides did adopt a softer line, the opposition parties indicted him of not being in a position to continue negotiations involving the UN-sponsored Annan Plan, which they believed had to be considerably improved before it was accepted. Papadopoulos, an old-time hardliner was presented by the opposition as a more suitable candidate for pushing the necessary changes to the proposed solution plan.

Once in power, Papadopoulos appeared to be firm, yet certainly softer than 'intransigent' Denktash. As negotiations progressed, however, and the referendum on the Plan approached, Papadopoulos (along with DIKO, EDEK and other 'hardliners') adopted an increasingly tougher line. Towards the close of a tense campaign, in which the hardliners predominated, Papadopoulos, with only a few days to go for the vote, publicly and vehemently advised the Greek-Cypriots to opt for a 'resounding no' in the referendum. Bearing in mind the entirely different path of developments in the north, with hardliner Denktash completely overwhelmed by the opposition, the result was not surprising: 76 per cent of Greek-Cypriots voted 'No', whereas 65 per cent of the Turkish-Cypriots voted 'Yes'. The question remains as to why such a large majority of Greek-Cypriots voted against the Annan Plan, preventing a solution and maintaining the Wall of division, which they so much wanted to go.

Many explanatory accounts have stressed the strength of the 'No' campaign and the determining role of Papadopoulos' negative stance, which are seen to have 'brainwashed' the masses into the 'resounding no'. Yet, such explanations fail to reveal why polls much ahead of the referendum were already showing negativity towards the Plan; or why AKEL, the *rapprochement* party par excellence, ultimately turned to a 'No' vote, allegedly after immense pressures from its constituency. It rather seems that Papadopoulos expressed the 'common denominator' of what the Greek-Cypriots as a community felt or feared during that particular period – as indicated by Papadopoulos' soaring popularity at the time.[38]

Papadopoulos seems to have come to embody, to represent, and to express the Greek-Cypriots *qua* imaginary community. Despite ideological differences between them, a strong attachment to the independent state had gradually evolved post-1974. Unlike the Turkish-Cypriot 'state', which had proved inefficient, corrupt and suppressive, and had won neither external nor internal security, the Republic of Cyprus had played a key role in the restructuring of the country and had retained

---

37   Clerides had the support of a split constituency, the majority of which were moderates and a vocal minority of staunch nationalists – united through the espousal of traditional pro-Greece (Hellenocentric) values.

38   For a detailed account of the reasons which swayed the Greek-Cypriot vote, see Palley (2005, 221-37).

international recognition. The economy thrived and the standard of living came to approximate that of the most advanced states of the West. The political system was democratic, welfare provisions were improving and human rights were respected. Additionally, over time, the Republic had become less dependent on Greece. Overall, the state had become the 'sacred canopy', identified with the very survival of Greek-Cypriots, who proved highly sceptical of letting it go in favour of a federal regime whose future seemed uncertain and insecure. Furthermore, the imminent accession to the EU promised a future rid of insecurity and fear – and, surely, a future rid of 'walls' or 'borders'. Unfortunately, for Greek-Cypriots, EU membership was to lead to rather unexpected outcomes.

Conclusion

Prior to accession, Greek-Cypriots were perhaps the strongest supporters of the European Union. This rested mainly on the hope that joining this perceived 'security community'[39] would somehow lead to the solution of the 'Cyprus Problem', through the enforcement of European principles of justice – which, to them, meant EU pressures on Turkey to withdraw from Cyprus.[40] Following the 2004 referendum, however, the EU seemed to turn bitter towards the Greek-Cypriots for their negative vote, and more sympathetic towards the Turkish-Cypriots (and Turkey) for their more positive position on the Annan Plan.[41]

In the first post-accession presidential elections (February 2008), Papadopoulos lost to the more moderate leader of AKEL, Demetris Christofias, who appeared more willing to work with the Turkish-Cypriots in finalizing a new agreement; and to be more acceptable to the international community than his predecessor. Meanwhile, in the north, Denktash had given way to CTP's more moderate leader, Mehmet Ali Talat. With two ardently pro-solution leaders in power, and within the current EU context, the future certainly seemed to offer the possibility of a solution to the 'Cyprus Problem'. Indeed, the opening of Ledra Street by the two leaders, a central area of daily and extended interaction between the communities, was hailed as a symbolically significant gesture of goodwill, which promised to take things forward in days to come (see Figures 8.4 and 8.5).

---

39 Within the topical paradigm of *Liberal-Institutionalism*, the EU is valued for its 'potential for cooperation, both through multilateralism and institutional integration' (see Hyde-Price and Aggestan 2000, 234-43). See also Nugent (2003): the EU accords 'soft security protection' (as opposed to the 'hard security' offered by NATO), but is viewed as equally useful in promoting stability.

40 In line with the conception of the EU as a 'guardian of the people' (see Mitsilegas et al. 2003 on this 'guardianship' role).

41 See Coufoudakis (2007 [2004]), who outlines the international perspective in the wake of the Annan Plan referendum.

Figure 8.4 Ledra Street 'Tourist Bunker': A military outpost marked the artificial end of Ledra Street, with a frequent flow of visitors lining up to peer into the Dead Zone from the vantage point it offered

Indeed, it was hoped that as Cypriots on both sides of the divide became imbued with the values and norms fostered by the European Union; as they adopted a new over-arching identity, beyond existing ethno-national identities; and as trust grew on the basis of holding 'dependable expectations' that their differences could be resolved in amicable ways (within the context of the EU 'security community'): Cypriots would find it possible to move towards re-unification and, thus, to rid themselves of the 'Green Line'.

Such hopes have thus far not materialized, since the 'Green Line' has proven to be more than just a transient social phenomenon. As this chapter has tried to demonstrate, the process of division in Cyprus started long ago, and has continued unabated ever since. From early on, processes of closure followed ethnic lines, leading to the erection of boundaries around, and between, the two communities – and not inclusive of the totality of the people. The once porous social boundaries between the religious communities in Ottoman times, transformed, over time, into the more impervious identities of ethnicity – upon the impact of modernity and its attendant structuring principle of nationality. In British colonial times, political closure and the institutionalization of ethnicity resulted in the hardening of these

165

Figure 8.5 Ledra Street Crossing Point Today: the 're-opened' street now facilitates the steady flow of people to and from the 'other' side, though subject to the showing of identification (passport or ID card)

social boundaries, so that, by the end of the period, territorial boundaries had begun forming. During Independence, the 'first partition' became a reality, and the two communities took steps towards consolidating segregated modes of existence – creating separate militia, setting up separate governing structures, and so on.

Following the island-wide division of 1974, the territorial boundary became as firm as that between warring sovereign states. Ethno-national ideas were further entrenched, dominating the thinking on both sides: with Greek-Cypriots striving for the re-union of the regime, thus contesting the 'border' in all possible ways; and Turkish-Cypriots persistently defending the boundary and their communal autonomy.

Yet, the non-recognition of the Turkish-Cypriot 'state' prevented legal closure, maintaining the possibility that somehow the process of separation could be put on hold, or even reversed. Paradoxically, the successful completion of multiple forms of social closure by the Greek-Cypriot controlled Republic of Cyprus, rendered it much like a nation-state (homogeneous, sovereign, and bounded – having a legitimate territorial boundary), so that when the time came for Greek-Cypriots to decide whether they were prepared to risk letting go of the security and other benefits that having their own state entailed (irrespective of the contents of the offered solution), they chose not to venture into the unknown (under a new regime which seemed too complex and fragile) – thus, unintentionally, rescuing the 'border' they so much wished to see go.

Hence, overall, notwithstanding the new realities of EU membership (including the strong desire and activity of the EU to rid itself of this 'problem'); and in spite of the concerted hopes and efforts of many (including Cypriots) to push towards a solution; and even in the face of the recent 'softening' of the 'borders': the fact that the two communities have grown separately for so long, closing in on themselves, renders the 'Green Line' of Cyprus a highly resistant, even if contested, boundary, still very much in flux.

References

Armstrong, J. (1982), *Nations before Nationalism* (Chapel Hill: University of North Carolina Press).

Attalides, M.A. (2003 [1979]), *Cyprus: Nationalism and International Politics* (Mönhesee, Germany: Bibliopolis).

Barth, F. (1998 [1969]), 'Introduction', in Barth, F. (ed.), *Ethnic Groups and Boundaries: The Social Organisation of Culture Difference* (Illinois: Waveland Press), 9-38.

Braude, B. and Lewis, B. (eds.)(1982), *Christians and Jews in the Ottoman Empire* (New York: Holmes and Meier).

Christou, G. (2004), *The European Union and Enlargement: The Case of Cyprus* (Basingstoke: Palgrave Macmillan).

Constantinou, C. and Papadakis, Y. (2001), 'The Cypriot State(s) in Situ: Cross-Ethnic Contact and the Discourse of Recognition', *Global Society* 15:2, 125-48.

Coufoudakis, V. (2007 [2004]), 'Cyprus: The Referendum and its Aftermath', in *Cyprus and International Politics: Essays by Van Coufoudakis* (Nicosia: Intercollege Press), 125-41, first published in *The Cyprus Review* 16:2, 67-82.

Deftereos, G. (2005), 'Tracing a Green Line through Time: Inter-Communal Contestation on Cyprus', in Michael, M.S. and Tamis, A.M. (eds.), *Cyprus in the Modern World* (Thessaloniki: Vanias Press), 139-64.

Demetriadou, E. (1988). *Contested Visions: Colonialist Politics in Cyprus Under British Rule, 1878-1890*. Unpublished PhD dissertation: New York University.

Demetriou, O. (2007), 'To Cross or not to Cross? Subjectivization and the Absent State in Cyprus', *Journal of the Royal Anthropological Institute* 13, 987-1006.

Dikomitis, L. (2005), 'Three Readings of a Border: Greek Cypriots Crossing the Green Line in Cyprus', *Anthropology Today* 21:5, 7-12.

Drousiotis, M. (2005), *The First Partition: Cyprus, 1963-1964* [Greek] (Nicosia: Alfadi).

Faustmann, H. (2004), 'The Reunification Process in Germany: Similarities and Differences with regards to Cyprus', paper presentation at a *Symposium on Aspects of the Reunification in Germany and Cyprus* (Nicosia: Goethe Zentrum, 28 February).

Fisher, R.J. (2001), 'Cyprus: The Failure of Mediation and the Escalation of an Identity-Based Conflict to an Adversarial Impasse', *Journal of Peace Research* 38:3, 307-26.

Fouskas, V. and Tackie, A. (2009), *Cyprus: The Post-Imperial Constitution* (London: Pluto Press).

Giddens, A. (1994), *Beyond Left and Right* (London: Polity Press).

Grillo, R. (1998), *Pluralism and the Politics of Difference: State, Culture, and Ethnicity in Comparative Perspective* (New York: Oxford University Press).

Gutman Killoran, M. (1994), *Pirate State, Poet Nation: The Poetic Struggle Over 'The Past' in North Cyprus*, unpublished PhD dissertation (Texas: University of Texas).

Hannay, D. (2005), *Cyprus: The Search for a Solution* (London: I. B. Tauris).

Hocknell, P.R. (2001), *Boundaries of Cooperation: Cyprus, de facto Partition, and the Delimitation of Transboundary Resource Management* (Netherlands: Kluwer Law International).

Huntington, S.P. (1997), Interview in *Le Monde* 18 November, quoted in Blanc, P. (2002), *The Partition of Cyprus: The Geopolitics of a Divided Island* [Greek] (Athens: Olkos Publications), 15.

Huntington, S.P. (1993), 'The Clash of Civilizations', *Foreign Affairs* 72:3, 22-50.

Hyde-Price, A. and Aggestan, L. (2000), 'Conclusion: Exploring the New Agenda', in Aggestan, L. and Hyde-Price, A. (eds.), *Security and Identity in Europe: Exploring the New Agenda* (Houndmills, England: Macmillan Press), 234-58.

Jennings, R. (1993), *Christians and Moslems in Ottoman Cyprus and the Mediterranean World, 1571-1640* (New York: New York University Press).

Joseph, J.S. (1997), *Cyprus: Ethnic Conflict and International Politics* (London: Macmillan Press).

Karpat, K.H. (1973), *An Inquiry into the Social Foundations of Nationalism in the Ottoman State: From Social Estates to Classes, from Millets to Nations* (New Jersey: Princeton University Press).

Kibrish (2003), 'Denktash's Plan!' [Turkish], 19 March 2003.

Kinross, P. (2001), *Ataturk: The Rebirth of a Nation* (London: Phoenix Press).

Kitschelt, H. and Hellemans, S. (1990), 'The Left-Right Semantics and the New Politics Cleavage', *Comparative Political Studies* 23:2, 210-38.

Kokkinos, S. (2002), *From the 'Green Line' to the Attila Wall* (Nicosia: En Tipis Publications).

Kyrris, C. (1976), 'Symbiotic Elements in the History of the two Communities of Cyprus', *Kypriacos Logos* 46-47, 243-82.

Leontis, A. (1995). *Topographies of Hellenism: Mapping the Homeland* (London: Cornell University Press).

Lijphart, A. (1977), *Democracy in Plural Societies: A Comparative Exploration* (New Haven-London: Yale University Press).

Mitsilegas, V., Monar, J. and Rees, W. (2003), *The European Union and Internal Security: Guardian of the People?* (New York: Palgrave Macmillan).

Neuwahl, N. (2005), 'What Borders for Which Europe', in DeBardeleben, J. (ed.), *Soft or Hard Borders? Managing the Divide in an Enlarged Europe* (London: Ashgate).

Nugent, N. (2003), 'Cyprus and the European Union: The Significance of Being Small', *Centre for Small State Studies* Occasional Paper 1, 1-23.

Palley, C. (2005), *An International Relations Debacle: The UN Secretary General's Mission of Good Offices in Cyprus, 1999-2004* (Oxford: Hart Publishing).

Papadakis, Y. (2004), 'Discourses of "the Balkans" in Cyprus: Tactics, Strategies and Constructions of "Others"', *History and Anthropology* 15:1, 15-27.

Papadakis, Y. (2000). 'The Social Mapping of the Unknown: Managing Uncertainty in a Mixed Borderline Cypriot Village', *Anthropological Journal on European Cultures* 9:2, 93-112.

Papadakis, Y. (1998), 'Greek Cypriot Narratives of History and Collective Identity: Nationalism as a Contested Process', *American Ethnologist* 25:2, 149-65.

Papadakis, Y. (1997). 'Pyla: A Mixed Borderline Village under UN Supervision in Cyprus', *International Journal on Minority and Group Rights* 4:3-4, 353-372.

Peristianis, N. (2006), 'Cypriot Nationalism, Dual Identity, and Politics', in Papadakis, Y., Peristianis, N. and Welz, G. (eds.), *Divided Cyprus: Modernity, History, and an Island in Conflict* (Bloomington, IN: Indiana University Press), 100-20.

Peristianis, N. (2000), 'Boundaries and the Politics of Identity', *Chypre et la Méditerranée* 31, 185-95.

Peristianis, N. (1999). 'A Federal Cyprus in a Federal Europe', in Theophanous, A., Peristianis N. and Ioannou, A. (eds.), *Cyprus and the European Union* (Nicosia: Intercollege Press), 125-37.

Peristianis, N. (1995), 'Right-Left, Hellenocentrism-Cyprocentrism: The Pendulum of Collective Identities Post 1974', in Peristianis, N. and Tsangaras, G. (eds.), *Anatomy of a Metamorphosis: Cyprus After 1974* (Nicosia: Intercollege Press), 123-56.

Persianis, P. (1978), *Church and State in Cyprus Education: The Contribution of the Greek Orthodox Church of Cyprus to Cyprus Education During the British Administration, 1878-1960* (Nicosia: unpublished).

Phileleftheros (2003), 'Denktash now opens the "Borders" for T/Cs' [Greek], 20 March 2003.

Politis (2003), 'He looks to Brussels! Denktash will use T/Cs as a Bridge' [Greek], 20 March 2003.

Politis (2003), 'Waiting Stance: Nicosia Watches Denktash's Moves' [Greek], 21 March 2003.

Pollis, A. (1996), 'The Social Construction of Ethnicity and Nationality: The Case of Cyprus', *Nationalism and Ethnic Politics* 2:1, 67-90.

Republic of Cyprus (2003), 'The Cyprus Question', *Press and Information Office* 215/2003-5.000 (Nicosia: Press and Information Office).

Stamatakis, N.A. (1994), *History, Language and National Rituals: The Construction of Modern Greek-Cypriot Identity*, unpublished PhD dissertation (New York: State University at New York).

Stavrianos, L.S. (2002 [1958]), *The Balkans since 1453* (London: Hurst).

Storrs, R. (1945), *Orientations* (London: Nicholson and Watson).

Theodoulou, G. (2005), *The Origins and Evolution of Church: State Relations in Cyprus with Special Reference to the Modern Era* (Nicosia: Kailas).

Webster, G. and Dallen, T. (2006), 'Travelling to the "Other Side": the Occupied Zone and Greek Cypriot Views of Crossing the Green Line', *Tourism Geographies* 8:2, 162-81.

Wimmer, A. (2002), *Nationalist Exclusion and Ethnic Conflict: Shadows of Modernity* (Cambridge: Cambridge University Press).

Yeniduzen (2003), 'Suggestion for "Free Movement" from DP' [Turkish], 19 March 2003.

Post-Soviet Boundaries: Territoriality, Identity, Security, Circulation

Vladimir Kolossov

Dozens of thousands of kilometers of new state boundaries have emerged as a result of the disintegration of the USSR. The adaptation of the population and the economy to the new boundaries is a long process, which is not over yet. Since the 1990s, and especially in the last decade, Russian scholars published the first theoretical works and a number of detailed case studies on most sections of Russian boundaries. A special attention was paid to the theory of cross-border natural and socio-economic systems as the basis of conflicts and cooperation, especially in the eastern part of Russia. A relatively great number of scholars – mainly political scientists but also geographers – studied different sections of the new boundaries between Russia, Ukraine, Belarus and EU countries, especially since the EU enlargement in 2004. These studies were often carried out in cooperation with European experts and supported by different international foundations. Geographers and historians showed the origin of different boundaries, their role in state- and ethnic building and considered the role of political discourse in cross-border cooperation (CBC). Nevertheless, many parts of the new post-Soviet borderland are still to be carefully described, analyzed and mapped.

The objective of this chapter is two-fold: first, to reveal the main specific features of post-Soviet borders in the light of contemporary theoretical approaches developed in border studies (*limology*) and, second, to consider the symbolic role of bordering, and the importance of social perceptions and territorial identities in legitimation and securitization of new boundaries. Under the term 'post-Soviet boundaries' I understand 'internal' (new) boundaries between 15 former Soviet republics, including the boundaries of Baltic countries, but not the former external boundaries of the USSR. I could not pay much attention to the current development, institutes and perspectives of CBC between post-Soviet countries and their neighbours, which is a major theme. In the first section, I highlight some notions and approaches of border studies which can be applied to the study of post-Soviet boundaries. In the second section, I propose a short review of their main features.

Finally, in the last two sections, I analyze the perceptions of boundaries and their impact on border security in different parts of the post-Soviet space.

Border studies and post-Soviet boundaries

Carl Grundy-Warr and Clive Schofield have distinguished two main traditions in contemporary border studies. The first of them is state-centric and interprets boundaries as fundamental elements of international peace and order. The second, 'post-modern' tradition, developed since the 1990s on the basis of post-modern philosophy, considers boundaries as a dynamic and multidimensional social construct: dividing lines are created first in the social consciousness and only then allocated and delimited (Grundy-Warr and Schofield 2005).

In the framework of *the first tradition*, boundaries are primarily understood as lines fixing the limits of a state's sovereignty. Their allocation, delimitation, demarcation, and management are in the focus of analysis (Prescott 1965). This tradition includes four approaches: (1) historical mapping of the evolution of boundaries, their morphological features and geographical patterns of border regions; (2) boundaries' typology; (3) analysis of their functions and (4) their role in international relations (Kolossov 2005).

Countless *typologies* of political boundaries have a history just as long as their mapping. Geographers and politicians have distinguished numerous types of boundaries by their morphology; natural features; origin, history and 'age'; historical circumstances of allocation and delimitation (for example, post-war, colonial, imposed, and so on), and functions. They attempted, on the one hand, to combine various characteristics of boundaries and contributed to a better understanding of the impact of physical and social characteristics of a region, history and politics of neighbouring states on the boundary's allocation and delimitation; and on the other hand, of the boundary's influence on human life and on the physical and the social landscape.

Special attention was paid to the *functions* of boundaries and to the political and territorial factors that determine them. The functional approach usually accepts the allocation of a boundary as a given reality, and focuses on its permeability for different flows in both senses and on its impact on economy and society.

The second tradition in border studies is focused on perceptions of the boundaries, the social construction of border security, borders' role in the hierarchy of territorial identities, symbolic meaning and its creation and diffusion, in particular, via historical narratives and with the markers of political landscape. If there is no stable political (inter-ethnic) identity, there are no stable boundaries and state territory, no state as a whole.

People's ideas about boundaries are an intrinsic element of political identity. Representations about them are inseparable from the geopolitical imagination, that is, a set of popular images, conceptualizations and discourses about the positioning of a state in the world system, the belonging of that state to a particular community of states (Ó Tuathail 2006). So, the discourse about state boundaries is founded upon a basis of state-building. State symbols, signs and narratives are extremely important in bordering. In many regions of the world the situation in border areas is determined by the geopolitics of memory. Cultivating certain representations, they distinguish key periods of common history with neighbouring countries or regions. A negative interpretation of such periods helps to oppose an identity under construction to the identity dominating on another side of the boundary, to deepen a new cleavage, while a positive attitude forges the feelings of solidarity or reconciliation with the neighbour. Geopolitics of memory includes the change in museums' expositions, the erection or the destruction of monuments, the renaming of streets or even towns, and so on.

Studies of bordering and social representations on boundaries are successfully combined with the analysis of their functions, the role in international relations, and so on. So, the first tradition in border studies is not out-of-date and can be successfully used together with the second, more recent one. There are convincing attempts to suggest an approach synthesizing two traditions – for instance, the so called 'PPP approach' ('Practice – Policy – Perception') developed by J. Scott and H. van Houtum. This approach consists in a combined analysis at different spatial levels: First, of the practice related with cross-boundary flows and developed under the influence of the boundary. Border activity is determined by the regime of the boundary, but, on its turn, has an influence on it. Second, border policy is considered at different scales – the international, state and regional institutional and legal infrastructure determining the relationship between barrier and contact functions of the boundary. Third, they study the perception of the boundary, that is, social representations on the boundary, relations between neighbouring states and regions, and CBC (Scott 2000; van Houtum 1999).

J.-M. Blanchard combined two traditions in border studies in distinguishing five main functions of a state boundary: (1) military-strategic, including defense and security, an access to the sea and the control over transit routes; (2) economic (the control over capital flows, the use of resources, trade and national market); (3) constitutive (the maintenance of a state's sovereignty and of its legal space, the regulation of its relations with the outer world); (4) national identity functions (the legitimation of a state to both its citizens and the international community, as well as the separation of kin groups living on the other side of the boundaries), state-building on the basis of socialization, national iconography, historical myths, and regulation in the linguistic, religious and cultural fields; (5) domestic political functions: boundaries structure economy, education, transportation, energy, application of standards, and so on (Blanchard 2005).

The importance and priority of the functions of different boundaries depend on the size and the nature of the state and the historical stage of its development. Not all boundaries have the same importance for a state (Moisio 2002). Moreover, different boundaries have a different meaning from different perspectives. Weak states have 'strong rationales to advance or protect boundaries that execute preferred constitutive and national identity functions because these boundaries affirm the state's right to exist' (Blanchard 2005, 694). French geographer and diplomat

M. Foucher distinguished three types of states: 'regular' sovereign states, 'states under construction' and 'empires' and, respectively, divided world boundaries into six types: between empires, between an empire and a 'regular state', between an empire and a state under construction, and so on (Foucher 1991). He called 'empires' the USSR and USA and under the term 'state under construction' meant an entity with a weak national identity which failed to fully control their territory. This is the existence of empires which determined the persistence of the so-called frontal boundaries with dominant barrier functions.

In the next sections, I attempt to apply both traditions of border studies in characterizing the diversity of situations and different permeability of post-Soviet boundaries and their relations with territorial identities.

The main features of post-Soviet boundaries

Natural and morphological diversity

The enormous differentiation of post-Soviet boundaries by functions and types is determined by the diversity of natural conditions, morphology, the density of population and economic activities on the territories they cross. Only the new Russian boundaries add up to more than 12,000 km. Some of them match important natural limits like watersheds or big rivers (for example, a section of the boundary with Ukraine along the river of Seversky Donets or a boundary with Lithuania along the Neman). The boundary with Georgia follows the Main Caucasian range, though a small part of Georgian territory (the district of Kazbegi) is situated on the northern side of the range. There are very few passes that are suitable for the construction of modern roads or railways in that area. However, dozens of thousands of post-Soviet boundaries pass by relatively flat plains, especially in the zones of steppes and deserts. It favours everyday interactions between neighbouring regions, but also makes border security more challenging.

The system of communications, which is dramatically not well-adapted to the configuration of new boundaries

Political boundaries have a strong influence on the pattern of communications. The transportation system of the Soviet Union has been a single, integrated mechanism created as a result of a long historical development. Most sections of post-Soviet boundaries suddenly became important barriers for the first time in history. It provoked a fast disintegration and serious transformation of transportation systems on both sides of new dividing lines.

The disintegration of the Soviet transport network is classified as polycentric (into three and more parts), in contrast to bi-centric (into two parts, like in Korea) or monocentric disintegration (a split of a part, like a separation of Finnish railways from the Russian network in 1918). The polycentric disintegration provoked by the creation of new *foci* can have particularly negative consequences in peripheral parts of the former network which had a simple topological structure. Such parts may for a long time remain 'stamps' of a disappeared big network suffering from important disproportions (Tarkhov 2005).

However, sooner or later, transport networks are adapted to new political boundaries and a new location of the capital. This process can be analyzed in terms of the so-called nationalization theory explaining the spread of communications, social and political organizations over the territory of a newly emerged country or after a drastic change of political regime (Deutsch 1966). According to Jean Gottmann, circulation understood as different kinds of interactions between political-territorial units is a necessary element of a political community or country's social and political cohesion and development (Henrikson 2003).

But this adaptation can take a long time. The degradation of transport networks was the strongest in Central Asia and some parts of Kazakhstan. As almost all their communications with the outside world passed through Russia, the organization of alternative transit routes toward the ports of the Pacific and the Indian oceans meant the assertion of sovereignty and identity for new independent countries. Another problem was the mutual dependence on transit.

For example, after independence, the direct line from Dushanbe (the capital of Tajikistan) to the boundary of Russia crossed five sections of the Uzbekistani territory. Between them, for several hundred kilometers it went through the territory of Turkmenistan. In Uzbekistan, new state boundaries have cut the railway network into five autonomous components (Ferghana valley, the central part from Tashkent to Samarkand and Bukhara, Surkhandaryah region, the oasis of Khorezm and Karakalpakia). For getting from the west to the east of the country it was necessary to cross the territories of either Tajikistan or Turkmenistan. Several new lines were built for overcoming these problems. Now, Ferghana remains the only component of the national railways that is separated from the rest of the network by high mountains and the territory of Tajikistan (Thorez 2005).

The lack of inter-regional communication provoked by a specific pattern of new boundaries, and the need to transit via neighbouring countries is a major threat to the territorial integrity of Tajikistan or Kyrgyzstan. The very existence of these countries, the poorest in Central Asia, depends on the communication between their northern and southern regions, which have a different economic specialization, ethnic structure, cultural and religious features. In Kyrgyzstan, the south and the north are separated by high mountains. The railway communication between its capital, Bishkek, on the north and one of the main centers of the south, Djelal-Abad, was stopped in the mid-1990s because even the shortest route crossed seven boundaries and resorted to sections of Kazakhstani, Uzbekistani and Tajikistani railways. 1,200 kilometres of this route of 1,375 kilometres pass through the territory of other countries. For the same reason, there is no railway communication between Dushanbe and the north of Tajikistan (the cities of Khojent and Penjikent).

The situation in the South Caucasus is also far from normal. Since the beginning of the Georgian-Abkhazian war in 1992, the direct railway connecting Russia with Georgia and Armenia along the Black sea via Sochi has been completely blocked beyond Russian boundaries. Another line from Armenia and Russia follows the Caspian coast via Baku and is also blocked as a result of the conflict around Nagorno-Karabakh. The Trans-Caucasian roads were closed or used only part of the year even before the 2008 war in South Ossetia. So, communication between Russia and Armenia is possible only by air. Isolation was one of the major factors slowing down restoration of the Armenian economy.

Russia was less concerned by the deformations of transportation networks caused by the establishment of new boundaries. Still, the eccentricity of the railways' system increased, and the connectivity of their European and Asian parts diminished. The North-Caucasian network is transformed into a sort of peninsula. The railways of the Kaliningrad region are totally separated from mainland Russia.

Russian eastward strategic railway communications cross the Kazakhstani territory. More than 100 km of the Trans-Siberian's main branch (all branches merge near Novosibirsk) between Kurgan and Omsk pass through Kazakhstan. Another two branches cross 700 to 1,200 kilometres of Kazakhstani territory. The only branch which passes only through Russia is not able to carry the traffic between the European part of the country, East Siberia and the Far East. Transit through Kazakhstan is critically important for communication between Russian regions.

At the border between the Volgograd region of Russia and the West Kazakhstan region, the railways cross the boundary many times. They were built in order to connect the settlements on both sides of the former line of delimitation between the territories colonized by Russian Cossacks and settlers, and the lands used by Kazakh and other nomad tribes southward. This line was initially protected by the chains of fortresses transformed into towns – administrative centers. On the southern side, with the transition to the common administrative-territorial division in the late nineteenth century, permanent settlements hosting local governmental bodies also grew. So, about 500 kilometres of railways in Kazakhstan belong to the state society 'Russian Railways'. Similar problems can be observed with the roads and at the local level.

Kazakhstan also depends on transit through Russian territory. In total, more than 300 km of railways in the Russian borderland are managed by the society 'Kazakhstan Temir Joly'. But Kazakhstan is actively building the bypasses through its own national territory.

At the borderland of Russia and Ukraine, the shortest line from Moscow to Rostov and North Caucasus, which in the Soviet time has been most often used by fast passenger trains, passes through East Ukraine (Kharkiv and the Ukrainian part of Donbass). Now, trains spend about four hours at border stations because Russian and Ukrainian services control them separately at both the entry and exit from Ukrainian territory. Since the mid-1990s, dozens of passenger trains connecting Saint-Petersburg and Moscow with the South and resorts on the Black sea go via Voronezh to avoid these stops, even though this route is longer. But even this line belonging to 'Russian Railways' crosses small sections of Ukrainian territory. This problem is not legally settled yet, and 'Russian Railways' plan to build a bypass.

The different origin and 'age' of boundaries

As a rule, the longer a political boundary exists, the more closely it is incorporated into national and ethnic identity, and the better adapted to new realities of population and the economy of border regions. State and administrative boundaries constitute an integral system (Kolossov and Mironenko 2001). Under certain historical circumstances, state boundaries can become administrative boundaries, and vice versa. Redistribution of functions within the single system of political and administrative boundaries resulting from globalization, integration and fragmentation of political space is called de- or re-territorialization (Newman 2001). Boundaries often change their status and functions, but not their allocation. Usually, the more recently a boundary is allocated, the less it matches ethnic and linguistic limits.

For example, the northern part of the Russian-Ukrainian boundary is relatively stable because it gravitates around the division between ancient historical-geographic regions – the 'lands' within principalities. The boundary now almost perfectly matches the ethnic border. According to the 1989 census, on the Ukrainian side the share of Russians in population decreases by the ratio of 1:2 and the share of Ukrainians on the Russian side – even more.

On the contrary, the centre and the part to the south of the borderland, the so-called Wild Field, was regularly devastated by nomads and later by Crimean Tatars supported by the Ottoman Empire and was settled by Ukrainian and Russian peasants mostly only in the seventeenth century, after the securitization of these lands by the Russian state. In this historical region called Slobozhanshchina, now divided by two countries, the administrative boundaries changed much more often. These changes occurred within the same state, depending on the gravitation areas of main cities, and *not* on ethnic or linguistic limits. Besides, Russian and Ukrainian villages often neighboured each other. There has never been distinction between Russian and Ukrainian lands. Basically, administrative boundaries inherited the seventeenth to eighteenth centuries' separation lines between the so called regiments – the military-territorial units around the towns-fortresses used for territorial governments and for the organization of self-defence.

The southernmost part of the borderland is the territory of the most recent mass colonization. The share of Russians there diminishes by the ratio of only 2:3, though the share of Ukrainians changes more significantly (Kolossov and Turovsky 1998). This borderland embraces historical steppe lands of the Don Cossack Army, now also divided by the boundary. But its most densely populated and urbanized part is the Donets coal basin (Donbass): most of it belongs to the Ukraine, but a smaller eastern part is in Russia. It is an area of the late nineteenth century industrialization whose population came first from Russian and then from Ukrainian provinces. Mixed marriages were very frequent: the recognition of 'us' and 'them' followed kin and other social dividing lines, and not ethnic ones. Not surprisingly, Ukrainian Donbass was a territory with a strong regional identity.

Mixed, blurred and dynamic border identities

Most of the more than 48 thousand kilometers of new post-Soviet land boundaries still separate 'states under construction'. With the partial exception of Turkmenistan and Baltic countries, all post-Soviet states consequently experience a crisis of identity, which can be defined as a period when ethnic or other regionally-specific sub-national segments of a society create obstacles to national unification and the identification with a certain political community. The existence of self-proclaimed republics in Georgia (Abkhazia and South Ossetia), Moldova (Transnistria) and Azerbaijan (Nagorno-Karabakh) provides evidence of this. Therefore, a considerable part of the population does not recognize the boundaries of the territorial state as a legitimate political unit (Kolossov 2003).

The new independent states inherited the boundaries from the Soviet Union which were often drawn more or less arbitrarily under Stalin for geopolitical reasons. Given the varied and overlapping ethnic structure of the population, political and ethno-cultural borders never completely align, though Stalin's ethnic engineering tried to make it so in some circumstances. Some scholars are prone to explain the complicated administrative-territorial structure of the former Soviet Union as a divide and rule strategy (Carrère d'Encosse 1993). In fact, the reasons were more complicated. Bolshevik leaders believed in the role of knowledge in modernizing economic production, social structures and human consciousness. They tried to eliminate traditional institutions and loyalties, and to delimit new territorial divisions and subdivisions on the basis of commissioned studies conducted by leading experts and planners (Hirsch 2005).

Moreover, the ethnic heterogeneity of the post-Soviet space increased dramatically in the Soviet years because of the industrialization of peripheral areas, which involved the import of labor, mainly Slavs and particularly Russians, so that the major cities in all the republics came to have a higher percentage of Russians than other regions (Kolossov 1992).

It has been already well demonstrated that the relationship between identity and territory is becoming more complex (Newman and Paasi 1998; Paasi 1996) and that the 'deterritorialization' of the state leads to the creation of multi-layered and mixed identities, especially in border regions. For example, in East Ukraine political geographers identified in the early 1990s up to six identities – Soviet, Ukrainian national, Ukrainian ethnic; Russian national and ethnic, and then regional and local ones layered within each like the dolls (Pirie 1996).

The question about the relationship between boundaries and identities is a question of which came first, the chicken or the egg. Although the boundaries between the republics were totally transparent in Soviet times, they clearly had an important impact on the evolution of identities. Ethnic boundaries are a territorial manifestation of dynamic identities and evolve also as a result of migrations and natural movement of the population. In areas with a culturally close population, ethnic boundaries have a tendency to approach political boundaries over time. Even in its most rudimentary forms like in former Soviet republics, the state is usually the most powerful driving force of ethnic and nation-building.

In the case of the Russian-Ukrainian neighbourhood, the 1926 census in three districts of the former Kursk province nowadays bordering Ukraine (a part of Slobozhanshchina) registered 1,268,000 Ukrainians, or 26 to 55 per cent of the population. But in 2002, they accounted for only 5 to 10 per cent of the inhabitants. Neither minor adjustments of the boundary before World War II, nor migrations can explain such changes. Naturally, local Ukrainians did not disappear: keeping souvenirs about their Ukrainian background, they now consider themselves Russians. In 1934, the Stalin regime abolished the so called national-cultural districts with significant ethnic minorities. Since that time, unlike neighbouring Ukrainian regions, education and local media were only in Russian, which was also the language of social promotion.

The same process is quickly developing now on the Ukrainian side as a result of the policy of accelerated Ukrainization. In the city of Kharkiv, the second largest in Ukraine, which is situated only 25 kilometres from the boundary with Russia, about a half of population declared themselves ethnic Russians, but teaching at higher education institutes must be exclusively in Ukrainian. Since the creation of Union republics in the Soviet period, most dwellers on both sides associate themselves respectively with Russians and Ukrainians. However, about 40 per cent of the population have close relatives across the boundary (Kolossov and Vendina 2002).

So, the identity of the population in ethnically mixed areas is ambiguous, and no administrative boundaries match ethnic limits. The most striking example is *Central Asia* where political life before the allocation of today's boundaries by Soviet authorities was determined by cooperation and conflicts between sedentary agricultural and nomad cattle-breeding, Turkic- and Iranian- speaking groups reunited by the common confession – Islam. Interactions between them were structured by the loyalty to different khanates – kingdoms with cross-sectional boundaries. Sovietization has broken this system, but kept the unity of the region, because the boundaries between the republics were transparent. But the disintegration of the Soviet Union has cut integrated systems of settlements and infrastructure, reanimated old disputes over water and land resources, and provoked competition for hegemony not only between new independent countries but also between regional clans within them. It gave rise to sharp political crisis and even to the civil war in Tajikistan.

The situation is aggravated by the mosaic ethnic structure at the edges of the countries. Ferghana valley, the most fertile area and the heart of Central Asia, is divided between three countries – Uzbekistan, Tajikistan and Kyrgyzstan, despite common irrigation and communication systems. Each of them has a multi-million minority which constitutes the titular people in the neighbouring country. Central Asia is one of few regions of the world where there are several exclaves separated by the mainland territory by the territory of another country.

In the Ferghana valley there are 8 exclaves – pieces of land totally encircled by the territory of another state: one of them belongs to Kyrgyzstan, four to Uzbekistan, and three to Tajikistan. Their total estimated population is about 83,000 inhabitants (Gonon 2003). The most known are Sokh and Shakhimardan, parts of Uzbekistan within the Kyrgyz territory. Problems of their communication with the mainland Uzbekistan contributed to the deterioration of the relations between the two countries. Uzbekistani border guards and paratroopers were sent to 'protect' the exclaves. In 2001, Uzbekistan tried to pressure Kyrgyzstan into closing transit roads connecting its north and south. The objective was to impose Uzbekistani proposals on the boundary delimitation and in particular, to connect the Ferghana region and Sokh by a corridor. Nowadays, even if the cross-boundary roads are open, bribes to customs and long waiting times considerably increase transaction costs.

Instability in border areas

The neighbourhood with 'states under construction' may mean permanent instability in border areas. The territorial proximity to areas of ethno-territorial conflicts and, in particular, to self-proclaimed states provokes an unavoidable involvement in their affairs (Kolossov and O'Loughlin 1999). It is statistically proven that if a country borders a neighbour at war, the probability of being involved in military actions is three times higher than for other countries (Siverson and Starr 1991). In other words, only boundaries with stable and peaceful countries are truly reliable. The 'instrumentalist' theory explains that the escalation of local conflicts is due to their being used by neighbouring countries as a card in a large-scale political game. The territorial factor is particularly important in the case of closely inter-depending regions with a complicated and mosaic ethnic structure like the Caucasus. It represents a single ethno-political system because kin or even the same ethnic groups live on both sides of the boundary between Russia, Georgia and Azerbaijan.

A shared border with a country at war can increase the risk of the neighbour's territory being used as a base for supplies and resort. Chechen separatists penetrated the neighbouring valley in Georgia settled by ethnic Chechens. Since the beginning of the 'second' Chechen War (1999) Russia asked the Georgian government to allow Russian border troops to control the boundary from the Georgian side, like during the 'first' war (1994-1996) (Trenin and Malashenko 2002). When Georgia declined this claim, relations between the two countries have sharply worsened. In particular, it pushed Russian leadership to establish the visa regime with Georgia.

In order to prevent the movement of terrorists between some Caucasian regions of Russia itself, their administrative boundaries are almost as strictly controlled as state boundaries. The boundary between Chechnya and neighbouring regions, of course, is not an ordinary administrative boundary. Permanent police check points are established at the boundaries of the republic of Dagestan, and so on.

The value of the common boundary between Russia and Georgia is quite different for each side respectively. For Russia, which for a long time hasn't been able to cope with instability in a part of the North Caucasus, its security functions are clearly much more important than its role as an economic interface and a symbol of national identity. On the contrary, Georgia cannot become a stable state without restoring its integrity, and the boundary with Russia is a symbol of its sovereignty. Since the establishment of the visa regime between Russia and Georgia in 2000, even those dwellers of South Ossetia and Abkhazia, who are not Russian citizens, do not need Russian visas. After the five-days war with Georgia in August 2008, when Russia officially recognized the independence of South Ossetia and Abkhazia; only Nicaragua and Nauru also did so. So, *the de-facto status of many boundaries does not match their formal status.*

The impact of the symbolic role of the boundary with Russia on the legal status, delimitation and demarcation

For a 'state under construction', national identity functions play a primordial role. They build their legitimacy on the basis of a re-interpretation of their history. Therefore, the allocation and the functions of boundaries in the past and nowadays become a highly politicized issue, because they determine the place of the country in the world and the origin of external threats to its security, the selection of political allies, the mission of the state and the preferable model of development. The boundary is the most physically visible symbol of the state, evident for each citizen, its 'skin'.

For this reason, the battles of self-assertive identities between CIS countries at the national level has a direct impact on the legal status of their boundaries, their delimitation and demarcation, and therefore, on the economic situation of border areas. A considerable part of post-Soviet boundaries, especially between the 'states under construction', are not fully legitimized, yet according to the norms of international law, *not delimited and not demarcated.*

The boundary treaty with *Estonia,* ready since 1997-1999, has never been ratified. In the early 1990s, Estonia and Latvia insisted first on the restoration of the boundaries fixed by the Tartu peace treaty, which was signed in 1920 during the civil war in Russia. It meant that Russia should cede two border areas with more than 90 per cent of Russian population. Besides, these areas were not part of the Baltic provinces before the 1917 revolution. Later, when preparing their applications to NATO and EU membership, Estonia and Latvia refused official territorial claims incompatible with the status of these organizations. But Russia continued to connect the boundary problem with the situation of Russian-speaking minorities, a large part of which did not receive the citizenship of Baltic countries. However, the lack of border treaties did not stop their admission to Western unions. Russia and Estonia finally agreed to ratify the treaty. The Estonian parliament adopted it in June 2005, but added a preamble not discussed during negotiations. From the Russian perspective, this preamble allowed, first, consideration of the new treaty as temporary, justification of the return to the Tartu treaty, and potentially opening the way to claims of material compensations from the Estonian side. It meant that the Russian side would agree to interpret Estonia's incorporation to the Soviet Union as annexation. Nowadays, this formula cannot be accepted in Russia. As a result, Russia denounced the treaty.

For a long time, *Latvia* did not show any interest in the progress of the boundary's legitimation. But in contrast with Estonia, the Russian-Latvian boundary treaty, which was ready as early as in 1997, was finally ratified in March 2007, which had an immediate positive impact on transit and cross-border cooperation.

According to the Molotov-Ribbentrop treaty, as a result of its incorporation to the USSR, *Lithuania* got new territories from Poland, and was interested in keeping the existing boundaries. However, delimitation of some sections of the boundary, especially on lakes and along rivers, provoked long debates (Romanova 2006). The treaty on the delimitation of the Russian-Lithuanian boundary was ready in 1997, but the Lithuanian parliament ratified it in 1999, and the Russian State Duma – only in 2003.

Negotiations on the delimitation of the boundary with *Ukraine* lasted for about four years. Fortunately, they did not become a theme of a political discourse, and were considered as technical, not political. As a result, in 2003 the treaty delimiting more than 2000 km of land boundary was signed and ratified.

But a consensus on the demarcation of the sea boundary was not reached. Moreover, in 2003, its politization provoked a serious crisis in Russian-Ukrainian relations. The maritime boundary in the Azov Sea is not yet delimited: Russia claims to apply the same principle as in the case of the Caspian Sea: the bottom should be divided, and the waters remain in common use and have the status of internal waters of both countries. Ukraine firmly insists on the full division of the sea, which could give it the Kerch strait between the Azov and the Black seas. In this case, a Russian ship going from one port to another in the same Krasnodar region should pay taxes to the Ukraine.

Since the accession to power of Viktor Yushchenko and the deterioration of bilateral relations, a solution of border problems has become more difficult. The Ukrainian leadership saw the demarcation of the boundary with Russia, which plays for it a particularly important symbolic role, through the lenses of state-building and the reassertion of independence. From this perspective, it cannot remain 'unprotected' and should match international standards as any other state boundary. Ukrainian political and intellectual elite tried to represent the state of the boundary with Russia as a threat because of illegal migration and the traffic of drugs. It matches the aspirations of the EU, wishing securitization of its eastern borders. Demarcation of the boundary with Russia is seen as proof of its European choice and readiness for the EU integration (Zhurzhenko 2005). At the same time, in Russia there still exists a tendency to assign a special status to boundaries with CIS countries. The transparency of these boundaries and cooperation in defense policy and national security is considered a cornerstone of partnership. Therefore, Ukraine wanted a 'normal' eastern boundary as an attribute of the nation-state, while Russia strives for 'boundaries of trust'.

The delimitation of the boundary with *Kazakhstan*, the longest single land boundary in the world (about 7,000 kilometres), was extremely important for Russia. First, the sides divided the Caspian shelf, which is rich in oil. Delimitation of the land boundary started in 1999. The meetings of the joint commission were often highly emotional, because 18 sections of the boundary were disputed. The two countries exchanged with equivalent pieces of land where it was possible. There were also a number of cases when a part of a large industrial plant or a settlement built for its personnel was located on the other side of the boundary. It also crossed some natural reserves and dams (Golunov 2005). But, unlike the case of Estonia, these problems were not politicized, and the presidents of the two countries signed the treaty on delimitation in January 2005.

It is particularly complicated in cases where the countries concerned do not fully control their territory. *Moldova* tries to further promote a soonest-possible demarcation of the central, Transnistrian, segment of the boundary with Ukraine. The Moldovan-Ukrainian border is 1,222 kilometres long, of which the Transnistrian section, which escapes Chisinau's control, makes up 470 kilometres.

In *Central Asia*, only the boundaries which cross scarcely populated areas are delimited (Uzbekistan – Kazakhstan, Uzbekistan – Turkmenistan, Turkmenistan – Kazakhstan). Sometimes, political instability and speculations on border problems by rivaling clans prevent delimitation. The border treaty between Kazakhstan and Kyrgyzstan was ready in 1999, the heads of the two states signed it in 2001, but the Kyrgyz parliament ratified it only in 2008 because opposition resisted it (Ibraimova 2008). Delimitation of planes, particularly in the Ferghana valley, is going on very slowly. By late 2005, there were 70 disputes between Uzbekistan and Kyrgyzstan. Delimitation of the boundary between Uzbekistan and Tajikistan was stopped for a long time, and re-started only in 2008.[1] In densely populated areas, even if a boundary is delimited and demarcated, like in the case of Uzbekistan and Kazakhstan, it often puts serious problems at the local level, cutting settlements and roads (Thorez 2005).

Perceptions of border threats and the 'circulation – security' dilemma

Border security is an important social and psychological need for the individual. Public opinion has an intrinsic tendency to irrationally perceive political boundaries as the major barrier to any undesirable influence from the outside world. Globalization, economic instability and the increasing speed of social

---

1   The Joint Declaration of Presidents of Tajikistan and Kirgizia, 16 May 2008, see <http://www.ferghana.ru>, accessed 18 May 2008.

transformations put securitization of boundaries and control over migrations in the focus of public debates in most countries. Politicians can transform a regional or local problem regarding only a border area into a 'geopolitical' problem and a threat to the national security – for instance, in interpreting foreign private investments there by an attempt to stimulate a secessionist movement, to colonize new lands abroad, and so on (Wardomsky and Golunov 2002). Therefore, a solution for this problem at the proper level and context becomes more difficult.

Fenced boundaries, visa regime and quotas for immigrants are acts of public communication – a reaction of politicians to fears and phobia in public opinion. Their real efficiency, especially as compared with economic and social costs, is most often rather low. It is known that the real efficiency of boundary control is not high: the bulk of smuggling and the illegal traffic of drugs and weapons pass through official crossing points, most often with the most intense cross-boundary circulation. At best, only a small percentage of drug trafficking is intercepted at the border (Golunov 2007).

The obsession with security has become one of the most typical trends of the post-industrial epoch. In an attempt to stop the illegal flow of migrants, drugs or weapons, to prevent terrorist attack, and to avoid contagion effects conflict areas, all kinds of territorial units – from states to local governments and communities – try to isolate themselves, not only by legal means – 'paper curtains', but also by physical barriers. The reassertion of territoriality in the world is expressed in 18,000 km of fenced boundaries, with the total cost of at least 12 billion dollars (Foucher 2007).

There are no commonly accepted criteria for boundary security. For example, experts of the Federal Border Guard Service in Russia vaguely define it as 'the state of border relations which does not harm the society, the state and its citizen' (Grishin, Gubchenko and Dmitriev 2001). It is not clear whether boundary security is an objective of the state, or a process which should be controlled by it. Therefore, this notion easily becomes a political slogan which is easy to manipulate and can justify any costly and extraordinary measures in sake, for instance, of the 'struggle with international terrorism'. Such measures are based on the traditional understanding of boundary security as, first, prevention of military threat. Border areas become militarized zones, with their own special regime. Second, the traditional securitization of a boundary means taking the widest possible control over any cross-border flow. Third, the boundary is understood as a front line intended to stop the penetration-in-depth into state territory of undesirable individuals, goods, information, and so on. The control of cross-border flow is easier where fewer inhabitants live in the border zone and when economic activity is relatively weak. As a result, these zones eventually degenerate into areas of economic stagnation. Fourth, it is assumed that the security interests of border regions are similar to those of the state as a whole. Geo-economy is subordinated to geopolitics. Interests of populations living in border regions are sacrificed to 'national interests'.

Traditional securitization is hardly compatible with the increasing needs in circulation across the boundaries, in the terms of Jean Gottmann. Well-developed and efficient foreign economic relations are a necessary condition of economic growth. This contradiction can be called a 'circulation – security' dilemma. It cannot be solved only by technological means – in installing the newest equipment for controlling tracks or railway cars, and even less by establishing restrictions in a border area.

Circulation is the best medicine against isolation, which leads to ignorance, ignorance gives rise to mistrust, and mistrust is a key obstacle for CBC. The practice of everyday communications plays a very important role in shaping a positive perception of the neighbouring country. The development of international transport systems, transit flow of people and goods requires the improvement of border infrastructure, and sooner or later will contribute to the development of a good neighbourhood.

The post-modern concept of boundaries is based on their 'desecuritization'. It is based on the assumption that it is impossible to cope with new 'soft' challenges like illegal migrations, or the traffic of drugs and weapons, or the risk of epidemics and environmental disasters by the use of military force. Clearly, the fight against drugs should be 'extra-territorial' and embrace the centers of their production and consumption, and not only the routes of transportation (Laitinen 2003). De-securitization approaches developed by the so-called school of Copenhagen, and in particular by Finnish scholars (Joenniemi 1998; Waever 1995), also presume that border interactions are not focused on territorial disputes and interpretation of the historical past. Instead of territorial claims, dialogue is shifted to the fields of common interest, in particular, on 'soft' security. Reconciliation and cooperation at the local scale are finally reproduced at the national and macro-regional level and strengthen international security as a whole.

The crucial importance of security is clearly seen in the perception of Russian boundaries. If it is impossible to get rid of an undesirable or dangerous neighbour, to subordinate, to control, or to resettle him, the next-best solution is to build a protective fence (Kolossov 2005). Typically, a richer side is afraid of its poorer neighbour, especially of the inflow of economic refugees and cheap labour force, which can undermine the basic elements of the national identity.

Unlike most Western countries, which mostly border each other, Russian neighbours are both 'sovereign states' and 'states under construction'. This division does not fully match the separation of boundaries in 'old' and 'new' (post-Soviet). On the north-west, Russia borders 'sovereign states'. All of them except Norway are now EU members. Though their GDP corrected by purchasing capacity added together they make up less than two thirds of the Russian one, its per capita values are significantly higher (see Table 9.1). Public opinion generally supports the visa regime. For instance, most Estonian experts (officials at different levels, businessmen, NGOs' leaders dealing in the everyday practice with partners from Russia) interviewed in 2004 were in favour of the visa regime. They justified their opinion by a possible increase of the illegal traffic of drugs, migrants, criminals. Receiving information mostly from TV and other media, they evaluated the economic situation in Russia to be much worse that it really was, feared *'the flood of refugees'*. The conclusion was clear: *'without proper police control at the borders, Russia constitutes a threat even for the EU'* (Kolossov and Borodulina 2007).

Ironically, Russian citizens are of the same opinion as concerned migrations from South Caucasus and Central Asia: 90 per cent of them are in favour of a visa regime with them (Kolossov 2003). Neighbours on the south-east can be considered as 'states under construction'. Per capita GDP is much less than in Russia. But China is an economic and demographic giant and has spectacularly high rates of economic growth. However, larger incomes and salaries make Russia attractive for migrants from its neighbours on the south-east.

Table 9.1 Economic Gap between Russia and its Neighbours in 2005, by Country

Neighbouring country	GDP by purchasing capacity, 2005				Comparable prices' level, USA=100%
	billion US dollars	% from Russia	Per capita	Per capita as % from the level of Russia	
Norway	219.8	12.95	47551	400.90	137
Finland	159.8	9.41	30469	256.88	122
Estonia	22.4	1.32	16654	140.41	62
Latvia	30.4	1.79	13218	111.44	53
Lithuania	48.1	2.83	14085	118.75	53
Poland	518	30.52	13573	114.43	59
Belorussia	83.5	4.92	8 541	72.01	36
Ukraine	263	15.49	5 583	47.07	33
Georgia	15.3	0.90	3 505	29.55	41
Azerbaijan	38.4	2.26	4 648	39.19	35
Kazakhstan	131.8	7.76	8 699	73.34	43
Mongolia	6.7	0.39	2644	22.29	35
China	5333.2	314.18	4091	34.49	42
North Korea	No data				
Russia	**1697.5**	1	**11861**	1	**45**

Source: Russian Federal Service of State Statistics, http://www.gks.ru/bgd/free/b02_18/IssWWW. exe/Stg/d000/i040070r.htm, accessed on 7 April 2009.

The strategy of fencing dominates in post-Soviet countries. Its most obvious manifestation is the visa regime. In 1991, when the Soviet Union was dissolved, former republics agreed to maintain the free movement of people across new political boundaries. *Baltic countries* that had declared their independence earlier did not support this principle from the very beginning, and unilaterally established the visa regime with all CIS countries in the summer of 1992. Some years later they made it stricter and started to apply Schengen rules well before their admission to EU and to the Schengen zone.

The policy of enlargement and the European Neighbourhood and Partnership Instrument (ENPI) is focused on the openness of external borders. The objective is to avoid dangerous social contrasts with the neighbours and the appearance of new dividing lines, to develop a prosperity zone along and beyond EU borders – 'the ring of friends', and to incorporate the neighbours with the common legal and economic space in preparing them for integration. On the contrary, the 'pillar of security' is based on a stricter protection of external boundaries, the strengthening of their barrier functions and on the universal character of the Schengen agreement. Demarcation and a better protection of eastern boundaries have for a long time been considered in Brussels as proof of the European choice.

This fundamental contradiction between securitization and the increase of cross-border contacts is proper to all post-Soviet boundaries. *Turkmenistan*, under the dictatorship of Turkmenbashi, closed its borders by a tough visa regime in the mid-1990s. Like in the former USSR, the citizens of Turkmenistan need an exit visa. Trying to protect itself from instability, *Uzbekistan* established a strict visa regime with its neighbours in 2001, to exclude the external support of Muslim fundamentalists and their use of bases abroad, especially in the Ferghana valley. From time to time, as in the autumn of 2007, it totally closes its borders to the movement of people.

Moreover, in 1999, the Uzbekistani military established mine fields around Sokh, in locating them partly on the Kyrgyz territory. Despite the OSCE claims, Uzbekistan refused to deliver their maps to Kyrgyzstan. The boundary between Uzbekistan and Tajikistan has been mined since the early 1990s. Fortunately, in 2007 Uzbekistan agreed to remove mines from some sections of the boundary.[2]

In the *Caucasus*, perceptions of border security have changed dramatically: former Soviet boundaries played a global role and were looking outward as potential front lines. Nowadays, new Caucasian boundaries are looking inward, because their main function is securitization from possible movements of paramilitary units between kin ethnic areas separated between neighbouring states, the illegal traffic of weapons, money, drugs and migrants. It changed 'the scale' and the nature of the boundaries' military function – from the global to local. The task is not to protect the state territory from missiles and long-range fighters, but to control mountain passes that can be used for transporting explosives, light weapons or the wounded. As a reaction to the assumed support of Chechen separatists, Russia imposed the

---

2   Uzbekistan started the works of de-mining the boundary with Tajikistan, see <http://www.ferghana.ru>, accessed 18 October 2007.

visa regime to Georgia in 2001. After the short 2008 war in South Ossetia, Georgia broke diplomatic relations with Russia. There are neither air flights, nor railway communications between these countries.

In *Russia*, the 'circulation – security' dilemma is very salient. The attitude towards border problems is determined by the attempts to reconcile the necessity to regulate the flow of migrants and the need for foreign labor force, the diversity of natural and social conditions in border areas, and the application of the same and insufficiently developed legislation to all situations. On the one hand, federal authorities become gradually aware that security has an important regional dimension, and *the threats for border security are not only from illegal or non-regulated cross-boundary flow, but also from an unfavourable social and economic situation in border areas.* If their population is poor, it is more prone to participate in illegal activities (Golunov 2008). A number of regions participate in recently created Euroregions along the former Soviet boundary and the boundary of Russia with its western neighbours.

On the other hand, geopolitical culture and current geopolitical discourse do not leave doubts that traditional border securitization remains a high priority for federal institutions. A new wave of centralization is hardly compatible with a separation of competences between different levels of government, which is critically important for CBC.

Old securitization approaches gained the upper hand with the adoption by the Duma in 2005 of apparently small amendments to the law on the protection of state boundaries. A year later, the Federal Security Service (FSB) extended the depth of the security zone along all boundaries from 5 kilometres up to about 30 kilometres. In total, the new restrictive border regime is applied to a territory larger than France. For going to a border zone, Russian citizens are requested to apply to a regional branch of the Federal Border Guard Service (now again a part of FSB, like in the Soviet time) for a pass at least a month beforehand. This application must be justified by the invitation from a family member or another person, and certified by local police or by a voucher from a tourist agency, or an order for a mission. Citizens going to a border zone must indicate the exact route and the places of their stay in a border zone day per day. These rules are more severe than even in the Soviet time. In addition, FSB now has the right to control economic and social activity within the border zone. The 'border zone' includes vast northern territories embracing hundreds of thousands of square kilometers, and rich in oil and gas.[3] Still, few exceptions were made: for instance, for the mountain resort of Dombai located not far from the boundary with Georgia. Tourists cannot go anywhere beyond 500 m from the official boundary of this settlement.

These rules were so difficult to apply that in the spring of 2007, FSB withdrew the regions of Kamchatka and Sakhalin from the border zone. In other regions, this zone was reduced to 15 kilometres from the boundary maximum.[4] Obviously,

---

3   Menshikov, A. (2007), 'Yamalo-Nenetz District', *Rossiiskaya Gazeta* 4339, 12 April 2007.
4   *Rossiiskaya Gazeta* 4371, 24 May 2007.

these rules prevent trust and the development of CBC. It was, in particular, noticed by Norwegian officials.[5]

The domination of the traditional approach to securitization results in a great number of consequences. First, the inadequate capacities and number of crossing points, but especially the old technologies used by Russian customs is the major obstacle for the increase of circulation and CBC. Though the turnover of Russian ports was rapidly increasing, they could be more competitive when compared with Finnish ports and the ports of Baltic countries, especially with regards to general goods with a high value added. Customs remain mostly a fiscal institution, and not an instrument regulating foreign economic relations. As a result of long boundary formalities, in 2006 the average distance covered by Russian carriers per day was only about 60 per cent of the distance run by their European colleagues.

Second, the reproduction of old Soviet norms regulating the boundaries' regime slows down local economic development. Most western border regions of Russia are relatively weak, and their border districts, in turn, are most often peripheral to the regional scale. The results of traditional securitization are quite sensible there. For example, the town of Ivangorod (at the boundary with Estonia) possesses an interesting historical monument – the fortress of the sixteenth century. But a strict border regime is a serious obstacle for individual tourists. The plans of local authorities to build a port for sealing boats and an aqua-park in cooperation with their Estonian neighbours from Narva failed because foreign tourists find it difficult to get the permission to enter into Russian internal waters. Thus, internal regulations strengthen the negative consequences of Schengen rules already applied by Estonia for many years.

Traditional securitization and thinking are related to the instability of CBC. It does not yet have autonomous institutions and mechanisms of development and strongly depends on the relations between neighbouring countries, the good will of their leaders, personal interests and sympathies of governors and mayors. A strict border regime is hardly compatible with cooperation between small and medium-sized businesses – one of the main driving forces of CBC. The number of joint ventures is limited; they are mostly specialized in trading operations, and not in production. Respectively, as long as the relations between neighbouring countries remain cold, there are few chances for a successful development of euroregions created on their borders.[6]

Some motives concerning a potential relationship between CBC, border security and territorial integrity regularly appear in the political discourse about Kaliningrad, though they are not dominant. In the early 1990s, a part of local business claimed the status of a republic, or a free zone, or another legal arrangement for acquiring more autonomy in economic relations with the EU countries. Now Kaliningrad region is an island within the EU: the distance to Moscow (1,289 kilometres) is more than twice as long as to Berlin (600 kilometres).

---

5   <http://www.westrus.ru/rus/?article=1893>

6   Mikkenberg, E. 'Russian-Estonian conflict makes people less close to each other', <http://www.veneportaal.ee/politika/09/29090703.htm> [in Russian]

Sociological polls show that since the collapse of the Soviet Union only 45 per cent of young people and 40 per cent of elder generations have been to other regions of Russia, while respectively 54 per cent and 47 per cent of them have been abroad.[7] This personal experience sharply distinguishes the population of Kaliningrad from their other compatriots: in average only 12 to 14 per cent of Russian citizens have ever been abroad (not including CIS countries), and the publication of such data makes the authorities care about communications with the exclave and its economic development.

The contradiction between the two sides of border security – the improvement of the economic situation and well-being of the population in border regions, impossible without circulation, CBC, and better control of cross-boundary flows – is particularly visible in the case of the boundary between Russia and Kazakhstan. This contradiction is strengthened by a high share of Russians in the northern and the eastern parts of the Kazakhstani borderland. This border is to a growing extent perceived in Russia as critical for national security. Indeed, 90 per cent of illegal migrants from Asian countries (Afghanistan, Pakistan, and so on) penetrate Russia through this boundary. Eighty-five per cent of hashish and 78 per cent of opium are brought to Russia via or from Kazakhstan. Drugs and important amounts of smuggling from China and other countries pass mainly by official crossing points (Golunov 2005). There was a proposal to cope with soft security problems in promoting 'the strategy of two boundaries' which considered the boundary between Kazakhstan and Central Asia as the first and the main line of control. Indeed, the southern boundary of Kazakhstan is almost twice as short as the boundary with Russia.

But symbolic and national identity functions of the boundaries were more important than even securitization. Kazakhstan feared the increased dependency on Russia in the delicate field of security, and Russia did not want to take the risk of investing big money in the protection of the external boundary without being absolutely sure of good relations with its ally in the future. This strategy was put under doubt since the withdrawal of Russian border guards from all countries of the region. Tajik authorities recognized that in recent years they could not protect the boundary with Afghanistan – the leading world exporter of drugs.[8]

A high transparency of the boundary with Kazakhstan can hardly be combined with the openness of Russia's western borders and the elimination or the simplification of the visa regime with the Schengen zone proposed by Russia. Globalization and increasing mobility of people transform international boundaries in the east and the west of Europe into a single and highly integrated system.

However, it is proven that many fears are exaggerated: most labour migrants enter the Russian territory legally, and the number of boundary violations is not

---

7   <http://www.edu.baltinform.ru/data/> [in Russian]
8   Russia succeeded in keeping a common external boundary only with Belarus whose customs is supposed to act in the interests of the common 'Union state'. However, Russia's national security boundaries remain partly 'taken out' because of her military presence in a number of CIS countries – Moldova, Ukraine (the naval base in Sebastopol), Armenia, Kyrgyzstan, and Tajikistan.

great, for instance, as compared with the EU. Terrorism is mainly Russia's internal problem. Smuggling is partially explained by the excessive strengthening of the boundary regime and the lack of crossing points. Even an ideal protection of the boundary cannot substitute an efficient regional policy and the benefits of CBC (Golunov 2008). Federal authorities realize that traditional approaches cannot be fully applied to all land boundaries of Russia, and moreover, these approaches are sometimes useless in the face of new threats. The awareness of such threats as international terrorism, the traffic of drugs and weapons, and illegal immigration from third world countries explains the decision of the Federal Border Guard Service to strengthen its forces on the Caucasus and at the Kazakhstani boundary at the expense of more securitized boundaries in the Arctic, Kaliningrad region and the Far East. Paradoxically, western neighbours of Russia – Norway, Finland, Baltic countries, and Ukraine – perceive their eastern boundaries as the most threatened, while Russia believes the same boundaries to be relatively secure, and it was more prone to apply to its protection post-modern, non-military methods.[9]

Conclusions

A complicated hierarchy of territorial identities in the post-Soviet space logically results in the coincidence over time and space of the processes of state- and nation-building. Indeed, the state is not fully established in all new countries – in the terms of M. Foucher, they are still 'states under construction'. A large part of their population, especially in particular regions, does not yet identify with the state-political nation, which presupposes a consensus about the values of common citizenship between all social, ethnic and regional groups. The state has not succeeded in penetrating all ethnic, territorial and social segments of the society to the same degree: the existence of self-proclaimed republics provides evidence of this. It has a deep impact on the legitimation, functions and the regime of post-Soviet boundaries. Almost 20 years since the disintegration of the Soviet Union some of them are not delimited and demarcated yet. Their military, securitarian and symbolic functions dominate over their role in economic relations. Interests of border regions are always sacrificed in favour of 'high geopolitics'.

Different boundaries function in different dimensions. In South Caucasus and Central Asia post-Soviet boundaries are an element of the Westphalian world of sovereign states. While in the North-West the influence of the European world order can be seen in the officially proclaimed objective to abolish the visa regime between Russia and Schengen states, some modest attempts to use new methods

---

9   Interview of the first deputy director of the Federal Border Guards Service general-colonel N.Reznichenko to the review *Bratishka*, May 2002, available at <http://www. fps.ru>. 'How should we arrange the boundary', Interview of the deputy director of the Federal Border Guards Service general-major N.Rybalkin – Krasnaya Zvezda, 13 November 2004.

of boundary protection, and in a relatively favourable attitude to CBC manifested in the creation of a great number of euroregions, not only along the former Soviet boundary on the west, but also all along the western boundary of Russia. But the diversity and the dual nature of Russian borders provokes misunderstandings and misperceptions in the relations between both the federal centre and border regions, and between Moscow and neighbouring countries.

References

Blanchard, J.-M. (2005), 'Linking Border Disputes and War: An Institutional-Statist Theory', *Geopolitics* 10:4, 688-711.

Carrère d'Encosse, H. (1993), *The End of the Soviet Empire: The Triumph of the Nations* (New York: Basic Books).

Deutsch, K. (1966), *Nationalism and Social Communication: An Inquiry into the Foundations of Nationality*, second edition (Cambridge: MIT Press).

Foucher, M. (1991), *Fronts et frontières: un tour du monde géopolitique* (Paris: Fayard).

Foucher, M. (2007), *L'obcession des frontières* (Paris: Librairie Académique Perrin).

Golunov S.V. (2008), *Factors of security in the politic of Russia and Kazakhstan toward their common boundary*, Habilitation thesis, Nizhni Novgorod State University. [in Russian]

Golunov, S.V. (2007), 'The Security of Border Spaces', *Mezhdunarodnye prozessy* (International Processes) 5:14, 27-37. [in Russian]

Golunov, S.V. (2005), *The Russian-Kazakhstani Boundary: Problems of Security and International Cooperation* (Volgograd: University of Volgograd Press). [in Russian]

Gonon, E. and Lasserre, F. (2003), 'Une critique de la notion des frontières artificielles à travers le cas de l'Asie Centrale', *Cahiers de géographie de Québec* 47:132.

Grishin, M.L., Gubchenko, V.N. and Dmitriev, V.A. (2001), *Problems of the Border Policy of the State and the Ways of their Solution* (Moscow: BDC Publishing Group).

Grundy-Warr, C. and Schofield, C. (2005), 'Reflections on the Relevance of Classic Approaches and Contemporary Priorities in Boundary Studies', *Geopolitics* 10:4, 650-62.

Henrikson, A. (2003), 'The Iconography and Circulation in the Atlantic Community', *Ekistics* 70:422/423, 266-70.

Hirsch, F. (2005), *Empire of Nations. Ethnographic Knowledge and the Making of the Soviet Union* (Ithaca and London: Cornell University Press).

Houtum, H. van (1999), 'Internationalisation and Mental Borders', *Tijdschrift voor Economische en Sociale Geografie* 90:3, 329-35.

Ibraimova, E. (2008), *The today delimitation of boundaries corresponds to national interests of Kyrgyzstan* <http://www.ferghana.ru>, accessed 18 April 2008.

International Crisis Group (2002), 'Central Asia: Border disputes and conflict potential', *ICG Asia report* N 33, 4 April 2002 (Osh/Brussels: ICG).

Joenniemi, P. (1998), 'The Karelian Question: On the Transformation of A Border Dispute', *Cooperation and Conflict* 33:2, 183-206.

Kolossov, V. (2005), 'Border Studies: Changing Perspectives and Theoretical Approaches', *Geopolitics* 10:4, 1-27.

Kolossov, V. (2003), 'After Empire', in Agnew, J., Mitchell, K. and Toal, G. (eds.), *A Companion to Political Geography* (Oxford: Blackwell), 251-70.

Kolossov, V. (ed.)(2003), *The World by the Eyes of Russian Citizens* (Moscow: FOM). [in Russian]

Kolossov, V. and Borodulina, N.A. (2007), 'Russian-Estonian boundary: the Barriers of Perception and CBC', *Vestnik Instituta Kennana v Rossii* (Bulletin of Kennan Institute in Russia) 11, 36-51. [in Russian]

Kolossov, V. and Vendina, O. (2002), 'Russian-Ukrainian border: social gradients and Migrations', in Pirozhkov, S.I. (ed.), *Migrations and Border Regime* (Kiev: National Institute of International Security), 21-6.

Kolossov, V. and Mironenko, N. (2001), *Political Geography and Geopolitics* (Moscow: Aspect-Press). [in Russian]

Kolossov, V. and O'Loughlin, J. (1999), 'Pseudo-States as Harbingers of a New Geopolitics: The Example of the Trans-Dniestr Moldovan Republic (TMR)', in Newman, D. (ed.), *Boundaries, Territories and Postmodernity* (London: Frank Cass), 151-76.

Kolossov, V. and Turovsky, R.F. (1998), 'Contemporary State Borders: New Functions Under the Conditions of Integration and Border Cooperation', *Izvestia RAN Geographical Series* 1, 97-107. [in Russian]

Kolossov, V., Glezer, O. and Petrov, N. (1992), *Ethnoterritorial Conflicts in the Former USSR* (Durham: IBRU Press).

Laitinen, K. (2003), 'Post-Cold War Security Borders: A Conceptual Approach', in Berg, E. and Houtum, H. van (eds.), *Routing Borders between Territories, Discourse and Practices* (Aldershot: Ashgate), 13-34.

Moisio, S. (2002), 'EU Eligibility, Central Europe, and the Invention of Applicant State Narrative', *Geopolitics* 7:3, 89-116.

Newman, D. (2002), 'The Lines that Separate: Boundaries and Borders in Political Geography', in Agnew, J. and Toal, G. (eds.), *A Companion to Political Geography* (Oxford: Blackwell).

Newman, D. (2001), 'Boundaries, Territory and Postmodernity: Towards Shared or Separate Spaces', in Pratt, M. and Brown, J. (eds.), *Borderlands under Stress* (London: Kluwer Law International), 17-34.

Newman, D. and Paasi, A. (1998), 'Fences and Neighbours in the Post-Modern World: Boundary Narratives in Political Geography', *Progress in Human Geography* 22:2, 186-207.

Ó Tuathail, G. (2006), 'Thinking Critically about Geopolitics', in Ó Tuathail, G., Dalby, S. and Routledge, P. (eds.), *The Geopolitics Reader*, second edition (London: Routledge).

Paasi, A. (1996), *Territories, Boundaries and Consciousness: The Changing Geographies of the Finnish-Russian Border* (New York: John Wiley).

Pirie, P.S. (1996), 'National Identity and Politics in Southern and Eastern Ukraine', *Europe-Asia Studies* 48, 1079-104.

Prescott, J.R.V. (1965), *The Geography of Frontiers and Boundaries* (Chicago: Aldine Publishing Company).

Romanova, O. (2006), 'The Role of the EU in the Formation and the Development of Russia's North-Western Boundaries', in *Transforming Borders: Global Trends and Regional Dimension* (Saint-Petersburg: Centre of Integration Research and Projects). [in Russian]

Scott, J.W. (2000), 'Euroregions, Governance and Transborder Co-operation within the EU', *European Research in Regional Science* 10, 104-15.

Siverson, R.M. and Starr, H. (1991), *The Diffusion of War: A Study of Opportunity and Willingness* (Ann Arbor, MI: University of Michigan Press).

Tarkhov, S.A. (2005), *Evolutionary Morphology of Transport Networks* (Moscow, Smolensk: Institute of Geography of the Russian Academy of Sciences). [in Russian]

Thorez, J. (2005), *Flux et dynamiques spatiales en Asie Centrale : Géographie de la transformation post-soviétique*, Thèse de Doctorat, Université de Paris-X Nanterre.

Trenin, D. and Malashenko, A. (2002), *Vremya Yuga: Rossiya v Chechne, Chechne v Rossiya* (Time of the South: Russia in Chechnya, Chechnya in Russia) (Moscow: Moscow Carnegie Center).

Waever, O. (1995), 'Securitization and Desecuritization', *Journal of International Affairs* 48:2, 389-431.

Wardomsky, L. and Golunov, S. (eds.)(2002), *Transparent Boundaries. Security and Cooperation in the Belt of Russia's New Border* (Moscow: NOFMO). [in Russian]

Zhurzhenko, T. (2005), 'Europeanizing the Ukrainian-Russian Border: From EU Enlargement to Orange Revolution', *Debate: Review of Eastern and Central European Studies* 13:2.

Polar Regions – Comparing Arctic and Antarctic Border Debates

Lassi Heininen and Michele Zebich-Knos

Early twenty-first century discourse surrounding the Arctic argues that a strategic race on energy resources or even an armed conflict over natural resources within the continental shelf is occurring (for example Beary 2008; Brown 2007; Borgerson 2008). Indeed, in the High North's resource-rich region there is increased competition and use of natural resources, as there has been for fish stocks and marine mammals over the centuries. Furthermore, there are land claims by indigenous peoples, some asymmetric environmental debates and conflicts, and a few marine border disputes between, and new submissions on the continental shelf beyond the 200-mile exclusive economic zones (EEZ) by the littoral states. However, according to the mainstream discourse on geopolitics and security studies in the post-Cold war Arctic there is neither armed conflict nor a strategic race on energy resources, but high stability based on institutionalized, international cooperation. Yet, the Arctic region is not *terra nullius*, or no man's land, but its territories are under national sovereignty with fixed national borders and most maritime boundaries were agreed upon by the relevant littoral states.

Unlike the Arctic, Antarctica has a different set of boundary concerns tied to the fact that it is a continent without countries in its territorial space, and benefits from the Antarctic Treaty System (ATS). This does not preclude traditional territorial conflicts. Argentina and Australia, for example, incorporated their Antarctic claims into the fabric of their own states. Such conflicts allow us to place the polar debate within an environmental security framework. As we will demonstrate with the case of Antarctica, concern over security was indeed the catalyst for creation of the ATS. If it can serve as a model for the Arctic, then environmental security concerns about Arctic waters can also serve as a call to action.

From the Cold War to present, both Polar Regions have remained stable and have enjoyed considerable global cooperation. There is however climate change precipitating physical change and bringing the related uncertainty which contributes to the vulnerability of these two special regions of the globe. Due to the thinning and melting sea ice, climate change has become a security issue in the Arctic that endangers both environmental and human security, and adds options for new global sea routes. This can be viewed as a security threat to native fishing and hunting communities in the coastal areas surrounding the two northern passages; the Northwest Passage in the Canadian Arctic and the Northern Sea route in the Russian North, and even to state sovereignty of Canada and Russia.

As waters have become more passable, the Arctic Ocean littoral states have eagerly extended their rights to utilize natural resources – as Russia did in 2007 on the Lomonosov Ridge – beyond the continental shelf allowed by the United Nations's Convention of the Law of the Sea (UNCLOS). Once a physical rarity, passage makes the Arctic more accessible to those seeking to use its waters for their own benefit. Preservation of state security from *passers-by* in areas heretofore frozen year-round is now a subject of primary concern. Of concern too, is protection of the changing Arctic ecosystem as increased ship traffic makes environmental accidents more likely. This results in a need to create an orderly international regime in which to resolve accidents and disputes, and to create joint rules. We postulate that geographic components subject to climate change affect long-term border behaviour. Our research places the two regions within the international treaty system in order to discuss polar environmental security as a growing global problem. The climate change discourse ultimately links state sovereignty and security concerns to the unique environmental aspects of the poles – polar border security is subject to the movement and shifting behaviour of its ice and its potential mineral resources. The meaning of environmental security, however, can vary, as Dalby notes (Dalby 2002). For our purposes, we use Broadus and Vartanus' definition which asserts that 'environmental security is the reasonable assurance of protection against threats to national well-being or the common interests of the international community associated with environmental damage' (Broadus and Vartanus 1991).

The Arctic Region: A peaceful area with fixed borders and some border disputes

Geographically, the Arctic, or circumpolar North, consists of the Arctic Ocean with its sub-seas, such as the Barents Sea and the Bering Sea, and two rim-lands, the Eurasian North and the northernmost rim of North America. This region of 21 million square kilometres, including about 7 million square kilometres of continental shelves, is about six percent of the Earth's surface. Depending on how one defines the southernmost border, there live from 4-10 million inhabitants representing major nations and indigenous peoples (Bogoyavlenskiy and Siggner 2004).

Politically, the region includes eight northernmost states, or (the) Arctic Eight – Canada, Denmark (Greenland), Finland, Iceland, Norway, the Russian Federation, Sweden and the United States. From a legal standpoint the Arctic Region is divided by the national borders of these states. Consequently, the region's territories and internal waters fall under their respective sovereign control, except the archipelago of Svalbard, which is under the (international) Treaty of Spitzbergen and ruled according to the Norwegian law.

Figure 10.1 The Arctic Region

Source: CIA World Factbook 2009 – available at https://www.cia.gov/library/publications/the-world-factbook/ (accessed 30 January 2010).

This state-centric viewpoint does not represent the whole picture, since in the region there live several indigenous peoples, each with respective claims to land and waters. The first agreements between these peoples and central governments of some Arctic states are already signed. The Saami was the first northern indigenous people to start nation-building and united in 1980-1981 to protest harnessing of northern Norway's Alta River. Although this radical movement lost its fight over the dam, it spawned a national awakening and resulted in Saami self-recognition as a pan-national actor (Heininen 2002). In 1977 the Inuit also built pan-circumpolar connectivity through their own trans-national organization, the Inuit Circumpolar Council (Abele and Rodon 2007). Greenland's nearly 90 percent Inuit population acquired its own home rule government in 1979 and took steps, albeit unsuccessful, towards independence from Denmark (Loukacheva 2007, 30-2). In 2009, Greenland acquired its self-government, but is under Danish rule. The reality is such that national borders still carry weight in dividing indigenous communities (Heininen and Nicol 2007, 158-60).

While indigenous connections remain strong in the north, there exist only a few loosely structured international regimes, such as the Arctic Environmental Protection Strategy (AEPS), and almost no international treaties specific to the region (Huebert 2008). One of the few Arctic international agreements is the Treaty of Spitzbergen, signed in 1920. It declares the entire Svalbard archipelago and nearby waters to be demilitarized. Further, it gives control of environmental protection to Norway. The treaty allows visits and navigation in the archipelago by parties to the treaty and emphasizes their equal right to natural resource use. The treaty has functioned well, since there have been neither border conflicts nor claims around the archipelago. Another international treaty specific to the Arctic is the Agreement on the Conservation of Polar Bears, signed in 1973. This treaty deals with protection of the polar bear population and its physical environment within Canada, Denmark, Norway, Russia and the United States.

The most important treaty in the Arctic today is the UNCLOS. It was signed in 1982, entered into force in 1994. Seven Arctic states have ratified the treaty by 2010. The United States has been concerned about UNCLOS part XI and the transfer of rights to the International Seabed Authority, but ratification now appears imminent under the Barack Obama Administration. The UNCLOS Convention (1985) defines the rights of navigation for everyone, but also gives coastal states the right to establish an EEZ up to 200 nautical miles out to sea and to exploit natural resources within the zone. The UNCLOS is strategically important because it extends state sovereignty onto the northern waters and allows littoral states to expand economic and national interests beyond their internal waters (Macnab 2008).

Relevant to northern sea areas beyond internal waters are the EEZs of the littoral Arctic Ocean states and those of the Norwegian Sea whose management is based on the UNCLOS. Most of the maritime boundaries in the northern seas, excluding the high seas, have already been agreed upon, except for a few disputes over maritime borders. These include the dispute between Canada and the United States in the Beaufort Sea, and the Canadian-Danish dispute on the Hans Island and surrounding waters. These disputes as well as the solved Norwegian-Russian dispute in the Barents Sea are between littoral states on how to draw a line on a continental shelf, when EEZs of two, or more, littoral states overlap. The situation may become even more pronounced in the future due to climate change and thinning of sea ice in these waters (Huebert 2001).

Canada and the United States clash over the Northwest Passage because the U.S. government does not recognize Canadian sovereignty over the passage after Canada established its Arctic straight baselines in 1985 (Pharand 2009). The United States prefers freedom of navigation and in 1969 exercised this freedom by sending the supertanker *Manhattan* through the Northwest Passage. Dispute potential also exists over Bering Sea oil interests and control of the continental perimeter. This largely un-demarcated Canada-U.S. maritime border is critical within the region, and begs a solution which might be to make the Northwest Passage an international strait, open for international navigation, but under Canada's full control.

There was also a long-standing dispute between Norway and Russia in the Barents Sea which concerns how to divide the sea as well as the shelf, and how to draw the dividing line in the Barents Sea, when Norway prefers the median line principle and Russia the sector principle. This mid-Barents Sea disputed area is potentially rich in natural gas and may contain major oil deposits, such as the Fedyn Arch-identified field (Lausala and Valkonen 1999, 99-103). Bilateral negotiations in search of this agreed boundary line – the Norwegians (for example Moe 2009) emphasize that it is a dispute, not a conflict – between Norway and Russia have continued for about 30 years, and finally a principle agreement of the delimitation between Norway and Russia was achieved in April 2010.

There are also new claims by the Arctic Ocean littoral states over natural resource use in the continental shelves on the main Arctic Ocean basin outside the exclusive economic zones (IBRU 2008). This became a sensitive issue after the Russian expedition to the shelf of the Arctic Ocean in Summer 2007 and the reactions by the Canadian and Danish governments. These claims do not necessarily mean a sovereignty conflict exists *per se*, since they occur strictly under the auspices of the UNCLOS (Moe 2009).

As a conclusion, by the early twenty-first century, national borders of the eight Arctic states without border disputes still legally divide the territory of the circumpolar North; however, land claims by indigenous peoples are ever-present. The picture is not so clear for sea areas since there are disputes dealing with EEZ division lines and national claims on the two northern passages. Finally, there are submissions by Arctic Ocean littoral states regarding the continental shelf beyond the EEZs, and possibly more claims will arise in the near future as international interest focuses on energy resources. However, this does not signify a return of the Cold War since '(t)he Arctic is the only NATO region where Russia is participating very constructively with NATO countries' (Störe 2009) and Russia affirms that '(t) he Arctic should remain an area of peace and cooperation' (Medvedev 2009).

Geopolitical changes and sovereignty discourses

State borders in the Arctic are a recent phenomenon, established by events of the nineteenth and twentieth centuries, and are generally associated with colonization and militarization. After World Wars I and II, many northern borders became more pronounced due to growing strategic security concerns. The resulting territories were increasingly controlled by state-actors in response to Cold War ideological and political divisions. However, these political barriers did not end cross-border trade and civil society connections in places like the North Calotte, in north Fennoscandia (Kainlauri 1975).

Since the High North consists of the Arctic Ocean and numerous smaller regional seas and coastal areas, the role of maritime boundaries is as important as land boundaries. Although northernsea areas are strategically important, maritime boundaries often remain poorly defined and are managed by border practices predicated on trans-boundary cooperation that predate the contemporary era. Cold War ideological divisions and increasing scrutiny paid to northern borders could not stop long-range air and sea pollution originating elsewhere from becoming a serious regional problem. This caused the first environmental concerns among non-state actors, and made the discourse of environmental security relevant in the Arctic.

From confrontation to trans-boundary cooperation

The industrialized, militarized and divided Cold War circumpolar North started to thaw in the late 1980s as a result of increased human interaction, intergovernmental cooperation across national borders and region-building with nations as major actors. The end of the Cold War permitted a rebirth of connections between northern peoples and dramatic change as military tensions gave way to an atmosphere of willingness to international and regional cooperation (Heininen 2010).

This new era of circumpolar cooperation owed much to the environment. A 'connectivity' between northern non-state actors, together with a growing concern over the Arctic environment due to increased trans-boundary long-range air and water pollution, pushed the Arctic states to become environmentally active. The first outcome was the Arctic Environmental Protection Strategy (AEPS), which the eight Arctic states signed in 1991 (Rovaniemi Declaration 1991). By 1993, parliamentarians from the eight Arctic states gathered to support the establishment of the Arctic Council which was finally established by the same eight Arctic states and six northern indigenous peoples' organization in 1996 (Ottawa Declaration 1996).

A new kind of regional dynamic was created in which state-centric and military issues that dominated Arctic geopolitics ceded ground to more human-oriented concerns (Chaturvedi 2000) with some concrete results, such as friendship flights across the Bering Strait (Sheldon 1989). The post-Cold War period brought concrete examples of borderlands like the Bothnian Arc between Finland and Sweden, and *Euregio Karelia* on the external border of the European Union between Finland and

Russia. This interpretation of national borders reflects a new and critical approach to geopolitics, where actors and identities, social spaces, and interrelations between knowledge and power play an important role (Newman 1998). It also indicates a de-bordering process that makes it possible to redefine a region, or to create a new kind of virtual region, and brings us to a critical issue – that is, the need to draw a border or not.

Today in the Arctic, we see a rich variety of multi-layered international, mostly multi-lateral cooperation across national borders. It includes tens of intergovernmental and non-governmental organizations, forums and networks, is partly well-institutionalized and official, and partly based on civil society. Some have innovative and flexible, even post-modern structures, but there are also institutional weaknesses. Lurking in the background is whether so-called 'soft' power, that is multilateral cooperation by and between state actors as well as non-state actors is enough, or too little, in international politics, especially when sovereignty and national security, which are often based on hegemonic competition, remain an important way to exert control over the region and Arctic agenda(s).

Sovereignty and national borders

The post-Cold War transition and subsequent international system dynamic influenced how national borders are deconstructed and interpreted, and how geopolitical reinterpretation at borders has changed. The European North is a good example of (national) border deconstruction as well as region-building by nations as major actors. Furthermore, there has been a remarkable shift from peripheral thinking towards 'local identity narratives' across national borders (Koivumaa 2008).

By the early twenty-first century, we might argue that borders in the North are becoming easier to cross and less strategic. It is clear that borderland communities' political clout is an important analytical lens through which to understand the relationship between structure and agency in maintaining border functions (Brunet-Jailly and Dupeyron 2007). They become more like borderlands and less like fences and are increasingly perceived as places that encourage transnational flows from trade, culture, and science. Municipal and regional linkages, growing together across a border now frequently bridge these northern frontiers. Slogans such as 'The Borderless North' indicate how natural it is to (re)define the circumpolar north as an international region based on increased international cooperation.

While there are geopolitical changes and growing global interests to the region from outside, interesting discourses emerge that redefine sovereignty and national borders. Since the late 1980s there have been visionary discourses and political attempts to redefine the Arctic as a distinct international political region (Griffiths 1988). This derives from academic discourse on regionalism and new regionalism leading to a political structure to define borders for governance and development (Hettne 1994), and may be regarded as a new geopolitical state of sovereignty. Region building with nations as major actors then become one of the main trends of circumpolar geopolitics and international relations (Heininen 2004). The post-Cold

War Arctic is a distinctive region in the study of human development, since it exists within an international cooperative region, not only a single country (Heininen et al. 1995). Although the vision has come under criticism, it is supported by northern indigenous peoples' organizations (Abele and Rodon 2007, 57), scholars, and higher-educational institutions with the dual aim of building trust and promoting environmental protection. The discourse, with its potential to secure a stronger voice for Arctic interests in a global context, is also supported by the success stories of Arctic human development. Firstly, northern cultures remain viable when confronted by rapid, multi-dimensional changes; secondly, advanced technologies are applied to address social problems; and thirdly, innovative political and legal arrangements exist to meet resident needs without rupturing the larger political systems (Young and Einarsson 2004).

Recent devolution of power, high activity among indigenous peoples' organizations and non-governmental organizations, as well as region-building and environmental protection as a new field of state foreign policy all reflect different behaviour when compared to the Cold War's normative geopolitical discourse and heightened geostrategic sensitivity in U.S. and Soviet attitudes towards the Arctic (Heininen and Nicol 2007). These processes include different ways and new discourses to redefine region and sovereignty. Although the fundamental geopolitical reality is that the circumpolar North consists of eight sovereign states, the region 'is becoming a spatial entity of political and geographical contiguity between the Arctic states' (Östreng 1999, 45).

The ultimate aim of the establishment of the Arctic Council and the Barents Euro-Arctic Council supports this cooperative spirit previously addressed. The Councils were formed in the 1990s as a setting for decreasing tension, increasing stability, enhancing sustainable development, and furthering trans-national cooperation among the states and peoples of the Arctic.

For example, from a Nordic and Russian Federation viewpoint the Barents Euro-Arctic Council was to decrease tension in the former 'military theatre' through transboundary cooperation. The first years of cooperation are judged a success as the Barents Sea emerged from a period of high tension into a phase of international, mostly inter-regional cooperation (Heininen 2004). In 1989, the Soviet and U.S. governments established a Bering Straits Regional Commission to assist cross-border visa-free travel for Inuit and promote indigenous communities and their resource management (Krauss 1994). The Bering Strait area's cooperation contrasts with the Barents Sea region, since in the North Pacific Rim there is no international body for cross-border institutionalized inter-governmental or regional cooperation.

The main aim of region-building as a working construct by the Arctic state governments is to increase trans-boundary cooperation and lessen the impact of national borders. It also represents an alternative geopolitical approach with a theoretical desire to create a new approach to classical geopolitics dominated by state sovereignty and power, and traditional security. Region-building has supported trans-boundary cooperation and made the national borders lower, but has not demolished them. Behind is the reality that nation-states are the major actors in this quest to achieve regional political and social stability through intergovernmental cooperation, while not weakening national sovereignty. This was seen in the first ministerial meeting of the five Arctic Ocean littoral states in 2008 (Ilulissat Declaration at the Arctic Ocean Conference in Ilulissat 2008) whose *ad-hoc* based arrangement could easily marginalize the Arctic Council. Although the Arctic Council is widely supported and considered a soft-law instrument (Lennon 2008), it has avoided issues dealing with full-scale utilization of natural resources, such as marine mammals and oil or natural gas.

Global interests and options for the circumpolar North

The twenty-first century's circumpolar North is not isolated, but closely integrated into the international community, and indeed, there is manifold growth in its geo-strategic importance in world politics (Heininen 2005). This is largely due to global environmental problems, such as long-range air and water pollution, and global warming. It is also due to growing interest in the region's rich potential energy resources by the Arctic states, because of melting sea ice, and a potentially bigger share of more accessible parts of the maritime Arctic in the global economy. Approximately 90 billion barrels of untapped oil and 1,670 trillion cubic feet of natural gas, and 400 oil and gas fields north of the Arctic Circle exist 'hidden' on the shelf of the Arctic Ocean (Bird et al. 2008). New potential global sea routes interest both the region's states and major powers from outside the region, such as Japan, China and South Korea. The European Union has also shown interest in the region through energy security, environmental protection and climate change.

The United Nations play an important role in the Arctic through UNCLOS and an international scientific body known as the Intergovernmental Panel on Climate Change (IPCC). For ratifying states who have EEZs, UNCLOS includes the option to stake a claim, or submission, extend the borders of their continental shelf and request the right to utilize natural resources in the continental shelf of the high seas (Koivurova 2008a; UNCLOS Convention 1985). Each of the Arctic Ocean littoral states has to make its submission on the main basin of the Arctic Ocean. One exception is the United States which has not yet ratified the UNCLOS, but recently re-emphasized its Arctic maritime presence and sovereign rights (Bush 2009). There are outermost limits to these submissions, either 350 nautical miles from the baselines, or maximum 100 nautical miles from the 2,500 metre isobath. Further, these oceanic ridges cannot become a part of any state's continental shelf, and continental shelves cannot be occupied by coastal states due to freedom of navigation enjoyed by all states (UNCLOS Convention 1985, 265-67).

These submissions have to be made within a ten-year timeframe after the ratification of the Convention and submitted to the UN Commission on the Limits of the Continental Shelf (CLCS) (Koivurova 2008a). Since the deadline for submission of evidence was 2007, Russia undertook an August 2007 scientific expedition onto the Arctic Ocean shelf, the Lomonosov Ridge just below the North Pole. The expedition successfully gathered mineral evidence from the bottom of the high sea basin. Russia argues that the Lomonosov Ridge is a natural extension of the Eurasian landmass, and according to the presidential proclamation on the new Russian Arctic resources law '(t)he continental shelf is our national heritage' (Lomagin 2008).

While there were three international meetings to discuss the issue in 1996, 2000 and 2003 (Macnab 2006, 2), the Russian expedition triggered media rhetoric about a wild Arctic race which many Arctic states took as a hostile provocation (IBRU 2009, 2). This issue deals with a sovereign rights claim beyond the EEZ which is a legal obligation to make a submission to the CLCS and define outer continental shelves in the high seas for the right to use natural resources. Neither the Russian expedition nor other claims are linked to climate-related changes in physical environment, but are more the result of UNCLOS regulations. Though Russia was the first, Canadian, Danish and U.S. estimates based on Arctic Ocean seabed mapping favour Denmark as having the strongest claim for the use of the North Pole's shelf (The Copenhagen Post 2009, 5). In a 2009 UN decision, Norway was already granted right to a bigger area in the Arctic Ocean that is the north from Svalbard.

These submissions and global interest toward the shelves indicate that the Arctic region plays an important role in world politics. Further, the region has entered into a significant, multi-dimensional geopolitical and geo-economical change. This is revealed on one hand, by growing global interest towards the region and its resources, and new options for utilizing them, and on the other hand, by physical and socio-economic impacts of climate change. All of these changes deal with sovereignty and national borders.

Antarctica: A global commons

The icy South: An introduction to the frozen continent

Imagine vast expanses of ice over two miles thick in places, no trees, chilling gale-force winds, and temperatures that can reach minus 47 centigrade. Unlike the Arctic, it is a land mass predominantly covered by fresh-water ice sheets nearly two-miles thick in spots. The continent is divided into East Antarctic and West Antarctic ice sheets. To visualize this think of a top-heavy ice sheet that rests on sunken bedrock located below sea level; that is a picture of the more problematic West Antarctic ice sheet (WAIS).

Ice shelves, on the other hand, are not a mere extension of the continental ice sheet. Instead, they resemble floating ice sheets fed by glacial waters that managed to wedge and attach themselves to coastlines especially around bays and surrounding inlets. Ice shelves are actually floating on the water so alone they do not contribute to sea-level rise even if they break apart into icebergs.

Ice shelf break-up can increase the flow of glacial water into the ocean by unplugging pathways into the sea – and that continental runoff will raise sea levels.

Shelves range from 100 to 600 metres thick and are not nearly as thick as ice sheets, but their role is significant.

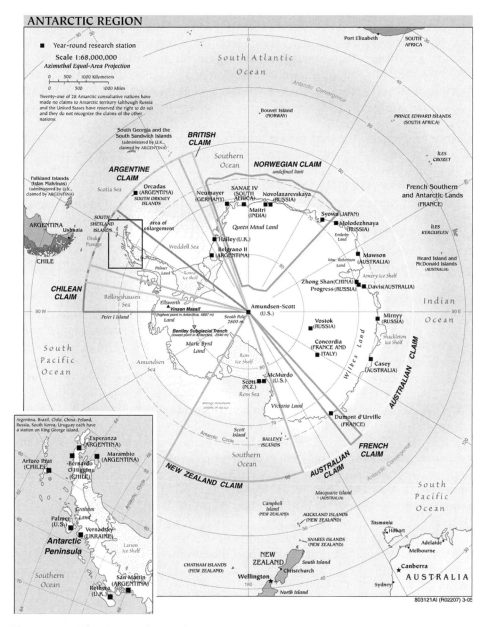

Figure 10.2 The Antarctic Region

Source: CIA World Factbook 2009 – available at https://www.cia.gov/library/publications/the-world-factbook/ (accessed 30 January 2010)

According to the 2001 Intergovernmental Panel on Climate Change (IPCC) report, Antarctica is experiencing a consistent warming trend that is higher than the earth's average. In addition, the ice shelves on the Antarctic Peninsula – seven of them to be exact, appear to be shrinking, or *in retreat*. By 2001, 10,000 square kilometres of ice shelf had melted according to the IPCC report *Climate Change 2001*. Nevertheless, the report qualifies ice-shelf retreat by stating that a West Antarctic ice sheet collapse is unlikely (Houghton et al. 2001). In spite of this we should start thinking about Antarctica and its role in the grander scheme of earth's environmental well-being, because some parts of Antarctica are getting warmer, and ice melt is observed. However, this is not as pressing as what now occurs in the Arctic.

Since Antarctica is the largest ice mass on earth, contains about ninety percent of the world's fresh water, and covers nearly 14 million square kilometres, increased melting could have serious implications for sea levels worldwide, and the well-being of inhabitants of low lying coastal areas.

The continent is inhospitable yet can yield vast knowledge about our overall climate and also holds untapped mineral wealth. Why then do the media focus on Arctic sea ice? The reason remains a people issue – or rather, lack of people, issue. There are four countries in *very* close proximity to Arctic sea ice, namely Canada, Denmark, the United States and Russia, and the Nordic countries with definite Arctic interests. Many of these countries are currently concerned about threats and opportunities for starting and establishing new activities in the Arctic. In short, the Arctic is really a thicket of political activity while Antarctica is largely out of range for the *average* American, Canadian, Russian or Norwegian – or just about anyone else for that matter. While we read almost daily about climate change and the northern ice melt, Antarctic icebergs the size of small countries, or the thinning of Southern Ocean sea ice, receive far less media coverage. Put simply, the world's population lacks a reinforced media link between climate change and Antarctica.

Unlike the Arctic, Antarctica has no indigenous peoples although the Chilean and Argentine governments encourage births at their scientific stations in order to keep alive the claim of having the only true indigenous Antarctic peoples, Argentine or Chilean-Antarcticans. This contrived attempt to populate Antarctica is really not the same as permanent settlements created by the Arctic's indigenous peoples. Those born in Antarctica are few and far between and do not make Antarctica their permanent home. There are also no polar bears in Antarctica. In fact, there are few fauna in Antarctica except those of microscopic portion, while flora consists of lichens, algae and moss. Seals, birds and penguins are considered to be part of the Antarctic marine environment – not part of the continent's fauna.

The Antarctic System creates a global commons in the truest sense of Garrett Hardin's (1968) work. This means that the continent is open to all visitors without significant immigration controls at its border. At most landing spots there are no people on shore – no towns, docks or human-made infrastructure. One simply arrives and walks ashore. Trust is paramount because visitors are generally expected to police themselves.

Antarctica is pristine from both natural and geopolitical standpoints. It is pristine precisely because of its political void and lack of government red tape developed over many years by nations trying to assert their sovereignty and protect their territory. Since there are no states on Antarctic soil, visitors are able to roam about in relative freedom – although Argentines might not agree as they refer to their portion of the continent as 'Antarctica, Argentina'. Apart from this minor exception among claimant countries, the continent is relatively a political no man's land in which visitors operate as if they were in a global commons – even within these claimant areas which we will explain in greater depth later in the chapter. This political void works relatively well because of the development of a complex, albeit imperfect, governance policy surrounding Antarctic management. Management is done at the international level in the form of treaties while states that are party to these treaties create specific laws, regulations and implementation mechanisms about Antarctica. The intent is to apply these laws and regulations both domestically within state borders as they relate to Antarctica, and on the Antarctic continent among its citizens who reside at a state-sponsored scientific bases or research stations.

A history of exploration sets the agenda

Antarctic policy owes its beginnings to the explorers who first set foot on the continent and hence sparked interest in getting Antarctica on the agenda in political circles worldwide. British Captain James Cook's trip around the Southern Ocean between 1772-75 places him as one of the first explorers to venture into Antarctic waters, and was followed by the exploits of Russia's Thaddeus von Bellingshausen who is thought to be the first explorer to sight Antarctic land during his 1819-21 voyages (Hanessian 1965). Inhospitable weather turned British explorer Robert Falcon Scott's expedition to the South Pole into a deadly journey. Instead of being the first group to reach the South Pole on 17 January 1912, Scott discovered that, just one month earlier, Norwegian explorer Roald Amundsen beat him to the pole on 14 December 1911 (Scott 1964). Scott's crew ultimately met a tragic end – all of Scott's team perished yet were carrying mineral samples in their packs (Williams 2005). Also Sir Ernest Shackleton's voyage in 1919 on the *Endurance* met an unfortunate fate although Shackleton and his crew survived (Shackleton 1998, 115).

Proceeding farther from these historic examples we can hypothesize that such extreme conditions are conducive to international polar regime creation and hence diminish states' propensity for conflict, and encourage cooperation. Any vessel voyaging to the Antarctic may need to rely upon another state for search and rescue assistance. Hence, harsh weather conditions may serve as predictor to regime formation.

Most early to mid-twentieth century interest focused on scientific understanding, charting of the Antarctic continent and its surrounding waters, *and* potential mineral exploitation. For example in his *New York Times* article Professor David (1929) expressed confidence that Byrd would find both coal and gold, and was confident that 'if alluvial gold were found in payable quantities it should be possible to work the deposits by thawing them with steam jets, as is practiced in the Winter in Klondike'. Never mind that coal or gold might prove difficult to extract, if they existed at all. The real problem had become one of people management – how to manage all those who just kept coming. And what if resources were numerous and ready for extraction? Should there be a joint global structure to manage such extractive efforts and protect the continent from exploitation?

From exploration to policy formulation

Terra nullius or no man's land, which prevailed in the nineteenth century, gave way to the exercise of sovereignty over portions of the continent in the early twentieth century. This era marked the beginning of Antarctica's political character and, by 1907, seven governments created pie-shaped slices of Antarctica which they claimed as their own territory. These governments include Argentina, Australia, Great Britain, Chile, France, New Zealand, and Norway. Thus began an unusual legal limbo of *claimed* territory which, by the way, is not recognized by other states in the global arena (Joyner 1998).

The claims issue, coupled with increased human presence on the continent, became so contentious that many in policy making circles worldwide agreed that an international effort was needed to jointly work out a management plan for Antarctica to protect it from human expansionist incursions and possible destruction from war. A drastic scenario might even lead to war if one state decided to explore, or eventually extract minerals, within another state's claim area.

Tensions mounted as expeditionary teams explored Antarctica for minerals and to reinforce their state's claims. The 1957-58 International Geophysical Year (IGY) marked a turning point for Antarctic policy making because it was the first global attempt to paint Antarctica as a place for cooperative scientific endeavours among nations rather than for claims-staking political aggrandizement. It also facilitated the creation of concrete mechanisms such as the Antarctic Treaty that would formalize a cooperative Antarctic policy – one that seeks to avoid war over contentious issues like claims, minerals, and nuclear energy.

While states conducted previous scientific endeavours for individual gain, IGY explorations were touted as cooperative undertakings. Findings were to be shared by all participant states. Such cooperation provided a method of politically defusing Cold War tension between the United States and the Soviet Union. Soviet interest in Antarctica was cause for US concern. Would the Soviets establish a military base in Antarctica? The IGY resulted in a flurry of cooperation and activity not the least of which was to create permanent bases in Antarctica. US President Dwight D. Eisenhower labelled the IGY participants in the base-building process as pioneers who contributed to 'the peaceful advancement of the world ... and to the cooperative study of man's environment' (Eisenhower 1957). Despite the existence of claims, such activity contributed to the belief that Antarctica was indeed a borderless continent. Ultimately, the IGY set the stage for dealing with the world's coldest continent in a multinational, United Nations forum that momentarily set aside Cold War animosities.

Global cooperation and the Antarctic as a model

Antarctica holds the possibility of serving as a model to the Arctic. Yet before applying Antarctic border models to the Arctic, we need to acquire a big picture understanding of Antarctic policy. It was not just luck that led to the signing and ratification of the Antarctic Treaty (1959). Rather, there was recognition that historic activity described above could lead to increasingly complex situations that might ultimately harm Antarctica and its surrounding Southern Ocean.

How do we get political leaders to pay attention to the problem, and through which policy means do we solve the problem? In this case, it was through security issues and concerns about increased militarization of the continent. This explains why the first sentence of Article I (1) of the Treaty states that 'Antarctica shall be used for peaceful purposes only' and shall prohibit '... any measure of a military nature, such as the establishment of military bases and fortifications, the carrying out of military manoeuvres, as well as the testing of any type of weapons' (Antarctic Treaty 1959). Cold War fears about the spread of nuclear weapons testing in the Antarctic as well as radioactive waste disposal were assuaged in Article V.

The issue of pre-existing claims presented a sovereignty issue, but was resolved by adding the following words to Article IV (1)(a): 'Nothing contained in the present Treaty shall be interpreted as (a) a renunciation by any Contracting Party of previously asserted rights of or claims to territorial sovereignty in Antarctica' (Antarctic Treaty 1959). Prior claims were neither recognized nor denied and sovereignty issues were essentially put aside in hopes that they would not be raised again.

The Antarctic Treaty (1959) forms the basis for what we term the Antarctic Treaty System (ATS) and is supported by other relevant treaties such as the Agreed Measures for the Conservation of Antarctic Fauna and Flora (1964), Convention for the Conservation of Antarctic Seals (1972), the Convention for the Conservation of Antarctic Marine Living Resources (1980) (CCAMLR), and the Protocol on Environmental Protection to the Antarctic Treaty (1991). This latter treaty is also referred to as the Madrid Protocol. This comprehensive system sets the groundwork for maintaining peaceful coexistence in Antarctica and is one of the most successful environmental endeavors, or international *regimes*, in recent treaty-making history.

A regime is simply a term for a set of rules, norms, and procedures around which the expectations of global actors – or players like countries or nongovernmental organizations (NGOs) converge in a certain topic area (Young and Levy 1999). Global actors unite under the Antarctic Treaty and the other treaties mentioned above to deal with Antarctic-related issues such as wildlife conservation or management of natural resources. In practice, the Antarctic Treaty serves as an umbrella treaty under which other related treaties fall. The Treaty calls for a Secretariat (Antarctic

Treaty Secretariat 2009), headquartered in Buenos Aires, Argentina which monitors relevant Antarctic activities as they apply to the overall Antarctic Treaty System including its array of its above-mentioned treaties.

While states have postured in the past, no state has ever acted in a manner that would project its sovereignty in an extreme hostile manner – although Cold War tensions could have steered us in that direction. For example, the U.S. Palmer Station on the Antarctic Peninsula is located within the Argentine, Chilean and British overlapping claim area and business proceeds as usual. Perhaps out of sheer necessity, cooperation prevails and decisions are made without provocation, although scientific tempers do flare every so often. The case for the sub-glacial Lake Vostok debate over drilling techniques illustrates that point.

Of treaties, protocols and laws

States that are *party* to the Antarctic Treaty – that is, they signed and ratified it, have also adopted laws and regulatory mechanisms designed to harmonize with this international regime. This is important because there is no international police force to enforce treaties. No ice police exists in Antarctica as they do within a country's borders. Instead, states enact domestic laws. For example, the United States signed into law the Antarctic Conservation Act of 1978 and the Antarctic Science, Tourism, and Conservation Act of 1996, and the National Science Foundation's (NSF) Office of Polar Programs is responsible for monitoring the well-being of U.S. run research stations.

If the international community was to protect Antarctica, it had to recognize that the most devastating of humankind's ventures tend to focus on acquisition of natural resources. The creation of a mining structure in the form of the Convention on the Regulation of Antarctic Mineral Resources (CRAMRA) failed in the 1980s when Australia and France withdrew their support. CRAMRA lent credence to the fact that future commercial mineral extraction will occur and that a procedural framework should be enacted in advance of such extractive activities. Article 3 called for the prohibition of mineral resource activities outside the convention. Administrative structure would rest in the Antarctic Mineral Resources Commission while Article 29 provided for a Mineral Resources Regulatory Committee. Unfortunately, CRAMRA fell apart in 1988 (United Nations 2005).

While CRAMRA never entered into force, the Antarctic regime persisted, and member states went on to create a stop-gap mechanism called the Protocol on Environmental Protection to the Antarctic Treaty, or Madrid Protocol. Article 7 prohibits 'activity relating to mineral resources except scientific research activity' (United Nations 1998). The protocol does not expire until fifty years after its entry into force in 1998 and is sometimes referred to as a moratorium on mining. Claimants include Argentina, Australia, Chile, France, New Zealand, Norway, and the United Kingdom. In reality, the protocol could be amended or modified at any time, so it is not a moratorium in the strict sense of the word (Joyner 1998, 14-9).

The most contentious Antarctic issue is that made by the seven countries that staked claims to parts of Antarctica starting in 1907. As a result, they are neither deferred nor resolved. Without a solution in hand, talking about claims might only aggravate the problem so Article IV of the Antarctic Treaty helped create the current environment of issue avoidance in which overlapping claims exist and states build bases on territory claimed by others. Today, states function openly on the continent as if claims did not exist. Ironically, Argentina includes Antarctica in its southernmost province *Tierra del Fuego, Antarctica, and the South Atlantic Islands*, and refers to Antarctica, *Argentina* as the street sign-post photo reveals (see Figure 10.3). The overlapping nature of Argentina's claim not withstanding, the Argentina's National Antarctic Institute considers the claim area part of its national territory.

Figure 10.3 Sign Post in Ushuaia, Argentina referring to the fact that Argentina claims Antarctica to be part of its southernmost province Tierra del Fuego, Antarctica

Source: M. Zebich-Knos.

Australia refers to its claim as Australian Antarctic Territory and so does the United Kingdom with its British Antarctic Territory while France created a formal Overseas Territory, *Terres Australes et Antarctiques Françaises* (*TAAF*) for maintaining French sovereignty over its claim. In short, states work around the sovereignty issue because it is simply too complex and could escalate into armed conflict. However, accidents can, and do, occur and raise liability issues for harming the environment. Article 16 of the Madrid Protocol creates 'rules and procedures relating to liability for damage arising from activities taking place in the Antarctic Treaty area' (United Nations 1998).

Conclusions

Based on the Antarctic Treaty System (ATS), many scientists argue the need for an Arctic Convention or international regulatory regime for the region (for example Harders 1986; Loukacheva 2007), and there is also a proposal for a legally binding instrument (Koivurova and Molenaar 2010). The creation of an international treaty is seen to have benefits such as a legal status to environmental standards, to regulate the use of natural resources and 'to address the sensitive issues of the future' (NRF 2004); and possible downsides, such as a creation of yet another complex treaty organization. Finally, climate change is seen as that ultimate challenge beckoning an international regulatory regime, since the Arctic Council has neither become, nor might become, a regulatory body for challenging issues (Koivurova 2008b).

The fact that the ATS 'has worked very successfully' since its 1961 entry into force (Macnab, Lokin and Anad 2007) is used as a reason for creating an international treaty for the Arctic. Yet, is an international Arctic Treaty System possible given the close proximity of countries that not only want to preserve their territorial security, but also enlarge their continental shelf? Holmes (2008) sees a new Arctic Treaty as a means for providing 'a binding legal framework for resolving overlapping continental shelf disputes in the Arctic'. There are no signs from either the Arctic states or within the Arctic Council, indicating they would be ready to support this approach; and, it is unclear where the recently started cooperation between the five littoral states of the Arctic Ocean will lead to, if anywhere.

The Arctic represents a high stakes game with immediate security concerns while Antarctica's land-based claims are easier to downplay. A treaty signed by thirty-four states most of whom are thousands of miles from the South Pole is well-suited to these circumstances. Conversely, polar ice long served as a security barrier as well a sanctuary for nuclear submarines for the littoral states of the Arctic Ocean which have also other common interests. Today the notion that large parts of the Arctic could be ice free year-round is a high security concern for bordering states and strikes at the very core of their sovereignty; a similar situation does not exist at the South Pole. The Arctic states are less likely to accept an international treaty with many signatories – they would lose too much control and freedom to implement their national interests.

While it is unrealistic to think that an Arctic Treaty System would designate the Arctic as a 'natural reserve, devoted to peace and science', it can borrow from Annex V of the Madrid Protocol to create Specially Protected or Managed Areas (SPAs/SMAs) SPAs are intended to protect areas that hold environmental, scientific, historic, esthetic or wilderness value and must be kept free from human interference (Zebich-Knos 2007). Entry into SPAs is prohibited without a special permit granted by one's country of origin while SMAs are loosely defined as areas where 'activities are being conducted or may in the future be conducted ... to assist in the planning and coordination of activities, avoid possible conflicts, improve cooperation between Parties or minimize environmental impacts' (United Nations 1998). Entry into SMAs does not require a special permit.

Specially Protected Areas are created for environmental conservation, are jointly administered and represent a multiparty effort to govern together in order to protect and preserve. Such procedures could be adapted to parts of the Arctic seas that merit such protection like for example, leading with the continental shelves of Canada and Russia.

While this does not preclude the creation of a regional Arctic Treaty System, would not such a system be more effective if it were inclusive and multilateral, rather than regional? The UNCLOS and its CLCS may be a better framework for resolving border issues and a more realistic means to set clear rules for natural resource use on the continental shelf, territorial waters and high seas. To be effective the United States would have to ratify UNCLOS in its entirety, and then all the five littoral states of the Arctic Ocean would be parties of the convention. The UNCLOS was also mentioned as a key framework for marine cooperation during the 2009 Arctic Council Ministerial meeting (Tromsö Declaration 2009).

Unlike Antarctica, immediacy is the main issue in the Arctic today, and all states involved must work together to create a regime with teeth so that climate change does not precipitate insecurity and harm the polar environment. This leads us to another possible conceptualization of northern issues and redefines them within a global commons similar to that of Antarctica.

References

Abele, F. and Rodon, T. (2007), 'Inuit Diplomacy in the Global Era: The Strengths of Multilateral Internationalism', in *Canadian Foreign Policy* 13:3, 45-63.

Antarctic Treaty (1959), treaty available at <http://www.ats.aq/e/ats_treaty.htm>.

Arctic Ocean Conference in Ilulissat (2008), *The Ilulissat Declaration* (Greenland, 27-29 May 2008), 12-3.

Beary, B. (2008), 'Race for the Arctic. Who owns the Region's undiscovered oil and gas?' *Global Researcher. Exploring International Perspectives* 2:8, 213-42, available at <www.globalresearcher.com>.

Bird, K.J. et al. (2008), 'Circum-Arctic Resource Appraisal: Estimates of Undiscovered Oil and Gas North of the Arctic Circle', *U.S. Geological Survey Fact Sheet* 2008-3049, available at <http://pubs.usgs.gov/fs/2008/3049/>.

Bogoyavlenskiy, D. and Siggner, A. (2004), 'Arctic Demography', in *Arctic Human Development Report (AHDR)* (Akureyri: Stefansson Arctic Institute), 27-41.

Borgerson, S.G. (2008), 'Arctic Meltdown: The Economic and Security Implications of Global Warming', *Foreign Affairs* March/April 2008.

Broadus, J. and Vartanus, R. (1991), 'The Oceans and Environmental Security', *Oceanus* 34:2, 14-9.

Brown, P. (2007), 'Melting ice cap brings diamond hunters and hopes of independence to Greenland', *The Guardian* 4 October 2007, available at <http://www.guardian.co.uk/environment/2007/oct/04/1>.

Brunet-Jailly, E. and Dupeyron, B. (2007), 'Introduction: Borders, Borderlands, and Porosity', in Brunet-Jailly, E. (ed.), *Borderlands. Comparing Border Security in North America and Europe* (Ottawa, Ontario: The University of Ottawa Press), 1-17.

Bush, G.W. (2009), *National Security Presidential Directive/NSPD* 25, 66 (Washington DC: The White House, Office of the Press Secretary), 12 January 2009.

Chaturvedi, S. (2000), 'Arctic Geopolitics Then and Now', in Nuttall, M. and Callaghan, T.V. (eds.), *The Arctic: Environment, People, Policy* (Amsterdam: Harwood Academic Publishers), 441-58.

The Copenhagen Post (2009), 'Mapping support claims', 20-26 Mar 2009, 5.

Dalby, S. (2002), 'Environmental Security', *Borderlines 20* (Minneapolis: University of Minnesota Press).

David, E. (1929), "Expects Byrd To Find Coal Fields And Gold," *New York Times*, 6 January 1929, 60.

Eisenhower, D.D. (1957), 'Amundsen-Scott IGY South Pole Station', *Letter dated 11 January 1957* (Abilene, Kansas: Dwight D. Eisenhower Presidential Library).

Griffiths, F. (1988), 'Introduction: The Arctic as an International Political Region', in Möttölä, K. (ed.), *The Arctic Challenge: Nordic and Canadian Approaches to Security and Cooperation in an Emerging International Region* (Boulder and London: Westview Press), 1-14.

Harders, E.J. (1986), 'The Arctic Ocean: Environmental Cooperation in the Northern Seas', (Norway: Miljövern departementet, Ministry of Environment).

Hardin, G. (1968), 'Tragedy of the Commons', *Science* 162, 1243-8.

Hanessian, J. (1965), 'National Interests in Antarctica', in Hatherton, T. (ed), *Antarctica* (New York: Praeger).

Heininen, L. (2010), 'Globalization and Security in the Circumpolar North', in Heininen, L. and Southcott, C. (eds.), *Globalization and the Circumpolar North* (Fairbanks: University of Alaska Press), 221-63.

Heininen, L. (2005), 'Impacts of Globalization, and the Circumpolar North in World Politics', *Polar Geography* 29:2 (London: Taylor and Francis), 91-102.

Heininen, L. (2004), 'Circumpolar International Relations and Geopolitics', *Arctic Human Development Report (AHDR) 2004* (Reykjavic, Iceland: Akureyri Stefansson Arctic Institute), 207-25.

Heininen, L. (2002), 'The Saami as a Pan-national Actor', in Karppi, K. and Eriksson, J. (eds.), *Conflict and Co-operation in the North* (Umeå: Kulturens frontlinjer. Skrifter från forskningsprogrammet Kulturgräns Norr), 223-38.

Heininen, L., Jalonen, O.-P. and Käkönen, J. (1995), 'Expanding the Northern Dimension', *Tampere Peace Research Institute, Research Report* 61 (Tampere: Tampere Peace Research Institute, University of Tampere, Jäljennepalvelu).

Heininen, L. and Nicol, H. (2007), 'A New Northern Security Agenda', in Brunet-Jailly, E. (ed.), *Borderlands. Comparing Border Security in North America and Europe* (Canada: The University of Ottawa Press), 117-63.

Hettne, B. (1994), 'The New Regionalism: Implications for Development and Peace', in Hettne, B. and Inotai, A. (eds.), *The New Regionalism Implications for Global Development and International Security* (Helsinki: United Nations University, World Institute for Development Economics Research).

Holmes, S. (2008), 'Breaking the Ice: Emerging Legal Issues in Arctic Sovereignty', *Chicago Journal of International Law* 9, 323-51.

Houghton, J.T., Ding, Y. et al. (2001), 'Climate Change 2001: The Scientific Basis', *Contribution of Working Group I to the Third Assessment Report of the Intergovernmental Panel on Climate Change* (New York: Cambridge University Press), 239-88.

Huebert, R. (2008), 'Multilateral versus Unilateral Action: Balancing the Needs for International Governance in the New Arctic', *Seeking Balance in a Changing North. The Proceedings Papers from the 5th Northern Research Forum Open Assembly* in Anchorage, Alaska, 24-27 September 2008, available at <http://www.nrf.is/index.php/publications>.

Huebert, R. (2001), 'Climate Change and Canadian Sovereignty in the Northwest Passage', *Isuma* 2:4, available at <http://www.isuma.net/v02n04/huebert/huebert_e.shtml>.

International Boundaries Research Unit (IBRU) (2009), *Borderlines* 8 (Durham: Department of Geography, Durham University).

Joyner, C.C. (1998), *Governing the Frozen Commons: The Antarctic Regime and Environmental Protection* (Columbia, SC: University of South Carolina Press).

Kainlauri, E.O. (1975), *Multinational*, dissertation submitted in partial fulfilment of the requirements for the degree of Cooperation in Regional Planning for Lapland Doctor of Philosophy (Natural Resources) (Michigan: University of Michigan).

Koivumaa, J. (2008), *Geopoliittista kuvittelua Pohjois-Suomen raja-alueilla. Tutkimus perifeerisyyden purkamisesta kylmän sodan jälkeisessä kansainvälisessä järjestelmässä 1995-2004* (Rovaniemi: Lapin yliopiston yhteiskuntatieteiden tiedekunta).

Koivurova, T. (2008a), *Background paper*, prepared for the joint seminar of the University of the Arctic Rectors' Forum and the Standing Committee of the Arctic Region on 28 February 2008 at the Arctic Centre in Rovaniemi, Finland (Rovaniemi: University of the Arctic).

Koivurova, T. (2008b), 'Limits and possibilities of the Arctic Council in a rapidly changing scene of Arctic governance', *Polar Record* November 2008.

Koivurova, T. and Molenaar, E.J. (2010), *International Governance and Regulation of the Marine Arctic. A Proposal for a Legally Binding Instrument* (Oslo: The WWF International Arctic Programme).

Krauss, N. (1994), 'Crossroads? A Twentieth-Century History of Contacts across the Bering Strait', in Fitzhugh, W.W. and Chaussonet, V. (eds.), *Anthropology of the North Pacific Rim* (Washington D.C.: Smithsonian Institution Press), 365-79.

Lausala, T. and Valkonen, L. (eds.)(1999), 'Economic Geography and Structure of the Russian Territories of the Barents Region', *Arctic Centre Reports* 31 (Rovaniemi: Finnbarents Project).

Lennon, E. (2008), 'A Tale of Two Poles: A Comparative Look at the Legal Regimes in the Arctic and the Antarctic', *Journal of Sustainable Development Law and Policy* 8, 32-6.

Lomagin, N. (2008), 'Russia's Perception of the Arctic. Seeking Balance in a Changing North', *The Proceedings Papers from the 5th Northern Research Forum Open Assembly* in Anchorage, Alaska, 24-27 September 2008, available at <http://www.nrf.is/index.php/publications>.

Loukacheva, N. (2007), *The Arctic Promise. Legal and Political Autonomy of Greenland and Nunav-ut* (Toronto: University of Toronto Press).

Macnab, R. (2008), 'Coastal State Sovereignty in the Arctic Offshore: Is it Compatible with the Concept of a Borderless North', in Heininen, L. and Laine, K. (eds.), *The Borderless North* (Oulu: The Thule Institute, University of Oulu and The Northern Research Forum), 83-9.

Macnab, R. (2006), 'Outer Continental Shelves in the Arctic Ocean: Sovereign Rights and International Cooperation', *Meridian* Spring/Summer 2006, 1-3.

Macnab, R., Loken, O. and Anad, A. (2007), 'The Law of the Sea and Marine Scientific Research in the Arctic Ocean', *Meridian* Fall/Winter 2007, 1-6.

Medvedev, D. (2009), *The Fundamentals of State Policy of the Russian Federation in the Arctic in the period up to 2020 and Beyond*, available at <http://www.scrf.gov.ru/documents/98.html>.

Moe, A. (2009), 'Perspectives on the development of Russia's northern offshore energy resources: Ambitions, capacities and international law', *presentation in the workshop 'Arctic Resource Policies in Russia'* at The Finnish Institute of International Affairs, Helsinki, 3 March 2009.

Newman, D. (1998), 'Geopolitics Renascent: Territory, Sovereignty and the World Political Map', *Geopolitics* 1998, 1-16.

Northern Research Forum (NRF) (2004), 'Northern Dimensions – Expanding Circumpolar cooperation', *Symposium in Brussels on 3-4 June 2004 by the Northern Research Forum in cooperation with the Canadian Mission to the EU and Canadian Embassy in Helsinki*, available at <http://www.nrf.is>.

Östreng, W. (ed.)(1999), 'National Security and International Environmental Cooperation in the Arctic – the Case of the Northern Sea Route', *Environment and Policy* 16 (Dordrecht: Kluwer Academic Publishers).

Ottawa Declaration (1996), *Declaration on the Establishment of the Arctic Council*, 19 September 1996 in Ottawa, Canada, available at <http//www.arctic-council.org/establ.asp>.

Pharand, D. (2009), 'Canada's Arctic Sovereignty and the Northwest Passage', *Meridian* Spring/Summer 2009, 1-5.

Rovaniemi Declaration (1991), *Rovaniemi Declaration*, signed by the Eight Arctic Nations, 14 June 1991 in Rovaniemi, Finland.

Scott, R.F. (1964), *Scott's Last Expedition: From the Personal Journal* (New York: Dodd, Mead and Co.).

Secretariat of the Antarctic Treaty (2009), 'Parties', available at <http://www.ats.aq/devAS/ats_parties.aspx?lang=e>.

Shackleton, E. (1998), *South: The Last Antarctic Expedition of Shackleton and the Endurance* (New York: Lyons Press).

Sheldon, J.F. (1989), 'Across the Ice Curtain: Alaska-Siberia Visits', *Polar Record* 25, 154-219.

Störe, J.G. (2009), 'Challenges in the High North', *statement by the Minister of Foreign Affairs at NATO Seminar*, Reykjavik, 29 January 2009, published online on *M2PressWIRE*.

Tromsö Declaration (2009), *Tromsö Declaration*, on the Occasion of the Sixth Ministerial Meeting of The Arctic Council, 29 April 2009, Tromsö, Norway.

UNCLOS Convention (1985), 'United Nations Convention on the Law of the Sea', in Degenhardt, H.W. (ed.), *Maritime Affairs – A World Handbook* (London, Essex: Longman), Appendix 1, 247-357.

United Nations (2005), *Convention on the Regulation of Antarctic Mineral Resources*, Register of International Treaties and Other Agreements in the Field of the Environment, UNEP/Env.Law/2005/3 (Nairobi, Kenya: UNEP).

United Nations (1998), *Protocol on Environmental Protection to the Antarctic Treaty*, treaty available at <http://www.ats.aq/e/ats_protocol.htm>.

Williams, D.B. (2005), 'Restoring Explorer's Good Name', *Seattle Times* 9 January 2005.

Young, O.R. and Einarsson, N. (2004), 'Introduction: Human Development in the Arctic' and 'A Human Development Agenda for the Arctic: Major Findings and Emerging Issues', *Arctic Human Development Report (AHDR)* 2004 (Akureyri: Stefansson Arctic Institute, Reykjavik, Iceland), 229-42.

Young O.R. and Levy, M.A. (1999), 'The Effectiveness of International Environmental Regimes', in Young, O.R. (ed.), *The Effectiveness of International Environmental Regimes* (Cambridge, MA: MIT Press).

Zebich-Knos, M. (2007), 'Conflict Avoidance and Environmental Protection: The Antarctic Paradigm', in Ali, S. (ed.), *Peace Parks: Conservation and Conflict Resolution* (Cambridge, MA: MIT Press).

Spaces, Territorialities and Ethnography on the Thai-, Sino- and Indo-Myanmar Boundaries[1]

Karin Dean

Introduction

Epistemologically postmodern, the currently dominating imagination of the world becoming borderless premises on the *view that the world space has so far been divided up by borders* – the free flows of people, goods and information become *challenges* only if the state is regarded as a fixed territorial unit. The rhetoric of increasing flows of people, goods and information *challenging* the states and their borders emanates from the elites at the position of power who construct and disseminate discourses – and declare the world borderless just as they did when constructing the past (modernist) images of a bordered and compartmentalized world. Connected by information superhighways today, this tightly-knit community imagines that electronic propinquity and other fast communication are making the world increasingly smaller and borderless by shrinking distances and wiping out borders. The catch-terms in a large volume of academic (and popular) literature of late twentieth century are 'flows,' 'permeability,' 'fluid,' 'porous,' 'conflation,' 'fragmentation,' various '-scape' and 'trans-' words, to which cultural anthropology adds 'hybridization,' 'creolization,' 'multiculturalism,' 'transversal solidarities' and 'intercultural reflexivity' (Bloul 1999). Political geography has used the notion of 'territorial trap' (Agnew and Corbridge 1995) in a critical reference to the state – which has also been attributed various 'leakages' (Taylor 1995), including the leaking away of sovereignty (Marden 2000, 66-7).

---

1   In 1989, Burma was renamed Myanmar by the military government. In this chapter, the name Myanmar is used as the official name of the country, while Burma is used in historic references.

That territorial boundaries are artificial human constructs no matter how natural some might seem (for example following rivers, watersheds, mountain ranges or shore lines of lakes and seas), is a long-established starting-point in political geography:

> *Simply because a line is marked by nature does not necessarily imply that it is a 'natural' thing to utilize it for boundary purposes or that it may constitute a desirable or 'natural' line of separation between neighbouring peoples* (Boggs 1940, 23).

Borders are not palpable in the lived space, or the life-world, but these can effectively be *manifested* by boundary posts, gates, signs and flags that introduce and reinforce the boundary that is otherwise 'not there'. Fencing in all states – reproducing the *de jure* political maps in lived space – is unrealistic and nonsensical, although both the past and present provide a few of such attempts. Thus in most cases, borders are substantiated at states' entry and exit points on the (larger) roads that cross from one state into another, at areas close to human habitation or where military patrolling of the border is deemed necessary. For the rest, the states must rely on people's socio-spatial consciousness – an abstraction to conceptualize the social and historical construction of spatial (and social) demarcations (Paasi 1996) – for enforcing the perceptions of borders.

Relevant to people's socio-spatial consciousness are the meanings attached to the manifestations of state authority by the *local* – not global – villagers. Many local people have seen the boundaries established during their lifetime – out of the 200 or so states in the world today, 120 were created after World War II. The hasty establishment of new boundaries, mostly as the result of decolonization, has left many of the borders deeply and often incessantly wrapped up in tension and incompatible views contingent on historical legacies, states' politics, geopolitics and individual interests.

The focus of the paper on Myanmar – a state conceived in 1948 and since then enjoying external sovereignty, while being territorially and socially enforced upon spaces and peoples and ruled through coercion by military regimes since 1961 – poignantly illustrates the above.[2] The ethnocentric and military vision of Myanmar by the ethnic Bamar leadership, representing the majority ethnic group in Myanmar, is contested and as militantly resisted by an array of actors that have created spaces of their own, mostly at its vast borderlands. These often violently carved out spaces are temporary and fragile. The type of spaces at Myanmar's extensive land borders – and the flows in and out of the state – range from those controlled by the Myanmar military to those 'liberated' by the political armed resistance forces. Earlier spatial practices combined with processes unique to the time-space specific

---

2   A political geographer Peter Taylor (1995, 6) distinguishes between 'external sovereignty' (the recognition by international community) and 'internal sovereignty' (the effective control of a territory), while he points out that only 'external sovereignty' is necessary to consider a state sovereign in international relations.

local contexts are generating peculiar and creative new dynamics – which only open up to a researcher amidst. These practices may circumvent or bend the knowledge informed by laws of citizenship and sovereignty, dominating discourses on ethnicity and language, or on economy, politics and governmentality – the kind of normative knowledge that then deems such practices as *challenges*, or straightforwardly illegal. Thus ethnography is highly relevant to studying such versatile life-worlds, and one of the purposes of this chapter is to highlight its role, particularly since the 'classical' ethnographic field data features in a minuscule amount of human geography research.[3] Political geography ranks the lowest: between 1993 and 1998, less than one per cent of research articles in the flagship journal *Political Geography* used primary ethnographic data, while another central journal, *Geopolitics*, did not have a single piece between 1996 and 2000 (Megoran 2006).

Institutional setting situates the academic in the elite community trusted by society to produce knowledge. The subscribers to this knowledge range from individual scholars to educational establishments to think-tanks, international organizations and policy-makers to the agents of most mass media – all who create, popularize and distribute, and thus shape, fix and normalize the dominating discourses. This is a crowd of explicit global villagers, now immersed in postmodern borderless world in terms of their frequent travel and enjoyment of free flows of information, money and goods. 'There is a complex "geosociology" of political identities emerging, particularly within the European Union, as globalization, emergent regionalisms and localisms combine to generate multiple, fluid, spatial and non-spatial identities within and across political scales', Grundy-Warr and Schofield (2005, 654) point out.[4] They invite to think about different scales of social life and conclude that many parts of the 'Third World' have been left out. Paasi and Prokkola (2008, 26) point out that scholars, often presenting 'rough generalizations and interpretations...' neglect their context-bound character.

This chapter highlights the need to use ethnography in political geography to study the 'context' of the border in order to, in Megoran's (2006, 623) words, '... enrich and vivify the growing, but somewhat repetitious, body of scholarship on both critical geopolitics and international boundaries'. It is argued here that ethnography at the sites of the conceived borders approximates more closely the various 'realities' and dominating perceptions. The general aim of the chapter is to argue against the supraterritorial borderlessness discourse effectively constructed and distributed from the 'global village'. The chapter discusses the mosaic of spaces and contested territorialities at the boundaries of Myanmar that are hidden from the view by the normalized political maps and the dominating discourses. Specifically,

---

3   Herbert (2000, 550) in *Progress in Human Geography* reports that between 1994-1998 only 3.5 per cent of articles published on human geography topics in *Annals of the Association of American Geographers* used ethnographic field data and only five per cent did so in the *Environment and Planning D: Society and Space*.

4   They refer to Berezin, M. and Schain, M. (eds.)(2003), *Europe Without Borders. Remapping Territory, Citizenship, and Identity in a Transnational Age* (Baltimore, MD: The Johns Hopkins University Press).

the purpose is to show that the complex on-the-ground political geographies stipulate the use of ethnography for scrutiny. A failure to include in analysis the lived spaces *challenged and inspired by* the international boundaries risks not only producing repetitious normalizing research that bolsters the normative discourses but a straightforwardly inaccurate one. The chapter concludes that the resulting blurring of the legitimate and illegitimate realities at Myanmar's borders – by both the military regime *and* the international community – will continue to prolong its protracted armed conflicts that already have brought misery to millions of people.

The chapter will first sketch the emergence of the 'geo-body' of Myanmar, a term coined for Thailand by Thongchai (1994), through highlighting the relevant moments in the evolution of borders, while implying that this is by far an insufficient knowledge for imagining the multiple realities at borderlands. It will then discuss ethnography as representing a theoretically driven empirical work that is sensitive to complexity and difference, and that is not bound up in the universalizing discourses. Some important points from research conducted at all Myanmar's land borders during 2000-2005 while living and working at the Thai-Myanmar border, and consequently in 2010, will be highlighted. Then the contested territorialities at Myanmar's borders, based on ethnographic fieldwork, will be discussed and juxtaposed to the grander narrative constructions.

Emergence of the 'national' territory in Myanmar

The so-called *national territories* of modern Southeast Asia were drawn after the withdrawal of the colonial powers only about 60 years ago, when the new 'developmental states and postcolonial imaginaries' (Sidaway 2007) also adopted the full package of Western governmentality, including the ideas of strict sovereignty and territorial delimitation.

Modern Myanmar is the largest state in continental Southeast Asia, sharing thousands of kilometers of land borders with its neighbours – about 2,400 kilometers with Thailand, 2,190 kilometers with China, 1,300 kilometers with India, less with Bangladesh and a stretch along the Mekong River with Laos. All borders cut through many hundreds of kilometers of mountainous jungle areas – some of the wildest, roughest and remotest landmass in Asia, distant from larger regional centers or seats of power. These borders would appear as extreme peripheries from Bangkok, on average 430 kilometers away, New Delhi over 2,300 kilometers away and Beijing even further – while the state borders were also far from Yangon, Myanmar's capital until 2005.[5] There were no pre-existing cultural, economic

---

5   One of the arguments by the military regime for its relocation of the capital to
     Naypyidaw – into what may appear as 'in the middle of nowhere' – were strategic
     considerations to move to more 'centrally' located area with quick access to all parts of
     the country, according to Myanmar Information Minister Kyaw Hsan, reported by BBC,
     available at <http://news.bbc.co.uk/2/hi/asia-pacific/4416960.stm>.

or geographical affiliations between these borders and the above named power centers – the perspective of which has become the basis for 'national' histories. At these borders, now delineating Myanmar's ethnic nationality states from Thailand, India and China, people of many large ethnic groups predominate and inhabit both sides of the international boundaries. In Myanmar, 'ethnic minorities', that is, non-Bamar peoples, constitute an estimated third of the state's population of 56 million (Smith 2008).

Some territories that constitute modern Myanmar have historically emerged, rivaled, declined and/or expanded as various kingdoms (the 'Mon,' the 'Shan,' the Bamar, the Arakan); others have been loosely connected tribal territories, areas of Bengali, Chinese or Siamese (Thai) highly fragile and fluctuating influence. All have had buffer zones of multiple, hierarchical and overlapping loyalties. The more powerful dynasties, albeit loosely connected as political units, emerged at the lowland plains of large rivers where fertile soils allowed for cultivation of rice resulting in sedentary life style. Geo-politically different were spatial practices at the mountainous terrain inhabited by swidden agricultural groups, where various trade routes criss-crossed the terrain. The hill-valley relationship was marked by unique socio-spatial interaction – but not that of political dependency (Leach 1954). At Myanmar's western and northwestern margins, maintaining corridors of empty space as buffer zones was the deliberate strategy of the rival Burmese and Siamese powers (Thongchai 1994).

The British used force to annex most territories of modern Myanmar between 1826 and 1888 in three Anglo-Burmese Wars. The initial conquests in the early nineteenth century prompted the British to turn to the Siamese court with the request to demarcate borders between its colonial territory and that of Siam (Thongchai 1994). Thus the Thai-Myanmar border emerged slowly from peaceful delimitation preceded by inquiry and negotiation in 1890-1893, during which the Siamese and the British colonial authorities interrogated the local people to find out where their loyalties belonged (ibid., 107-9).

The Indo-Myanmar border was originally an administrative line between the provinces of British India, Burma and Assam – until in 1937 Burma became a British self-governing colony and the border became to separate the colonial Burma from the rest of British India. This line was materialized into the present international Indo-Myanmar border upon India's and Burma's independence in 1947/1948 respectively. The British administrative line had paid no respect towards the traditional socio-spatial practices and relations in the lived space. For example, the lived space of the hilly territory of the people speaking various Chin dialects was divided up between three British provinces, Burma, Bengal and Assam, such designations simply based on the stationing of the different military fronts of the British armed forces. What became today's Mizoram in India had been administered by the British governors from Assam. What became today's Chin state in Myanmar had been administered from Yangon, the colonial capital of Burma. A small southwestern portion of the Chin inhabited area is now in Bangladesh. The imposition of states with distant power centres fueled resistance movements on both sides of the Indo-Myanmar border, and the latter has had a facilitating role in this. The border has been criss-crossed for military operations, garnering support, food, recruits or weapons, or for fleeing or avoiding the offensives either by the state (India or Myanmar) or by other ethnic armies. By crossing the border, the civilians have escaped fighting or persecution – in both directions but at different stages of the political resistance. The movement lead by the Mizo National Front (MNF) in and against India was largely based in Chin state (Burma), and joined by many Chin – until a peace agreement with the Government of India in 1986, after which statehood was granted to Mizoram.

To the north from the Chin 'homeland', the Naga lived space was brought under five administrative units by the British – who today are in Burma's Kachin state and Sagaing district, and in India's Assam, Manipur, Nagaland and Arunachal Pradesh states.

The Sino-Myanmar border, a colonial heritage imposed by the British on China was settled between Beijing and Rangoon, both thousands of kilometers away, only on 28 January 1960, after difficult negotiations between the governments of China and the independent Burma (see Figure 11.1). Burma had inherited from the British a partially defined border, and even this was not satisfactory to the Chinese who viewed it as an imposition from the British position of power and superior might (Ghatate 2000, 445-6). By 1911, the British had occupied a vast area of approximately 200,000 square kilometers north of Kachin state capital Myitkyina and west of the Salween and N'Mai Kha watershed. China was claiming these areas, albeit based on ambiguous historical assertions. In the above named border settlement, China 'gave up' this claim and was given three strategically located Kachin villages in exchange for a Burma's 'right' to retain another area (the 220-square-kilometre Namwan Tract) that the British had 'leased perpetually' from China. There was very strong Burma-wide public opposition to the cession of the three Kachin villages, particularly in Kachin state and from the people of that area. Burma's Prime Minister U Nu failed in his numerous efforts to win public support, and made several trips to China to explain the domestic obstacle. Nevertheless, he finally managed to pass the necessary resolution through in the Kachin National Council, whose consent was a constitutional precondition for cession of the area (Ghatate 2000, 445-6).

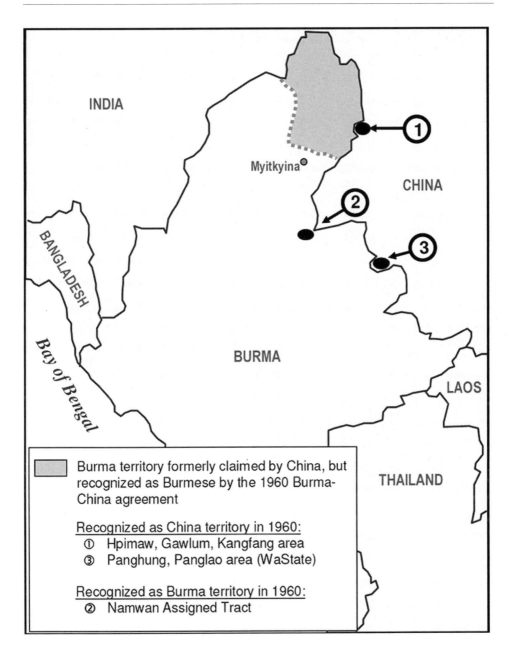

Figure 11.1 The Burma-China Boundary Dispute

Source: adapted from Tegenfeldt 1974.

Myanmar today: still 'just' a geo-body?

Thus the 60 years of British colonialism created boundaries for a future Burma, and established a geo-body – and a nation in need of history and shared traits. All peoples at Myanmar's borders have been faced by three parallel and interrelated processes – the territorial bounding, the nation-building driven by the new state, and their own nationalist projects from within the multiple previously loosely affiliated but culturally related tribes. Just as the first maps of bounded Siam lead to the political construct of modern Thailand in the end of the nineteenth century, Myanmar faced the same prospects in the 1950s. The Burmese nationalists lead by Aung San, inheriting the British colonial administration, conceived of a federal Union in pact with ethnic representatives of some but not all larger groups. In Thailand, state- and nation-building has been a very successful top-down endeavor of 'intellectual indoctrination', whereby the history was 'plotted and remade' retrospectively (Thongchai 1994, 129) – resulting in the Thai language, the Thai culture, the Thai food, the Thai etiquette, entering not only speech but also the consciousness of the people of *Thai*-land. In Myanmar, not only nation-building has failed but the territory itself continues to be contested to the point of violence. The longest armed resistance movements in Asia – those of the Karen and the Naga – continue at Myanmar's borders. While some of the largest ethnic groups (for example the Karen) did not agree to join the Union, others (for example the Shan, the Kachin, the Chin) who signed the pact were disappointed in what they viewed as increasing Bamarization and centralization during the first Burmese (democratic) government. Protracted warfare over contested territories is persisting, although in greatly reduced capacity and by some new or transformed actors. The different historical evolutions of the boundaries is but one factor among the state policies, changing geopolitics and related local practices and new twists in local border dynamics that define spatial practices and even determine what is legitimate and illegitimate. This all establishes the context that matters.

Myanmar has been named an authoritarian 'ethnocratic' state (Brown 1994), an 'illiberal' and uncertain 'unitary state' (Tin 2004), a juridical state rather than an empirical state (Rajah 2001, 14), a failed or weak state, or a strong regime where the military has managed to hold onto power. By 2007, Myanmar was estimated to have fallen to fourteenth place in the 'Failed States Index' and per capita GDP to less than half that of the neighboring Bangladesh or Cambodia (Smith 2008, citing the United Nations Country Team in Myanmar). The military governments in Myanmar have for long failed to capture the mechanism of a modern state agency like the monarchial and military elites in the neighbouring Thailand effectively did – as did the other authoritarian governments in Southeast Asia following independence. While the colonial inheritances continue to menace Myanmar just as other postcolonial 'new nations', Callahan (2003) through her thorough and exceptional study of the evolvement of the Myanmar military argues for the role of contingency that has turned the authoritarian rulers into warmongers with the people mapped onto its geo-body. Many complex dynamics, geopolitical events and developments at the state and local levels have facilitated the evolvement of the military-as-state (Callahan 2003) in Myanmar/Burma. 'In this solution, citizens became barriers to the army's consolidation of political power and national sovereignty', Callahan (2003, 206) points out.

The representation of Myanmar by the unelected military governments during 1961-2010 in international relations and diplomacy has extended 'legitimacy' to the military's performance of state functions. Further propping up the regime was its inclusion in 1997 in the Association of Southeast Asian Nations (ASEAN) that has maintained a strict policy of non-interference. The abundant natural resources and location between the geopolitical rivals of China and India that compete for its oil and natural gas, earn the regime millions of dollars of hard currency and solid political capital that have effectively overturned the western economic and political sanctions.[6]

This blurring of the 'legitimate' and 'illegitimate' sets the scene for further fusions when figuring in the political geographies of lived spaces at Myanmar's borders.

What can lived space tell?

At Myanmar borderlands, the cross-border dynamics, and the survival or livelihoods of its inhabitants are defined by a combination of historical contingencies and twisted political geographies, in which the normatively 'illegitimate' may appear as legitimate and the 'legal' often as 'illegitimate,' and many versions still in between these two ends of the binary. A diversity of reasons and vicissitudes, unpredictable and not necessarily related to the dominating discourses, may determine the lived realities and processes.

Arguing for complementary approaches of discursive analyses of geopolitical texts and detailed ethnographic investigation, Megoran (2006) points to the striking discrepancies between elite and popular political geographical imaginations vis-à-vis the Ferghana Valley, disclosed during his long-term ethnographic fieldwork.[7] Through a spectacle of herd of cows being smuggled across the international boundary for grazing, Megoran shows explicitly how the designation of 'resistance' in the scholarly language is romantic but misleading. The Ferghana villagers are not committed to subvert the order but protect their livelihoods that have been abruptly cut by the establishment of an international boundary.

Academia is in a great position of being a link between normative conceptions and the socio-spatial processes in life-worlds. Academics have the means to engage

---

6   China, upon which the regime is dependent for international political support, is planning to buy oil from Myanmar and pipe it from Middle East via the ports it is constructing on the coast of Myanmar's Arakan state. This would help to solve some of China's dependence on the Strait of Malacca for oil.

7   Megoran's research has been in the Ferghana Valley, a cross-border region between eastern Uzbekistan, Kyrgyzstan and Tajikistan.

in systematic and reflective work at the out-of-the-way places to contribute insight into the academic and international understandings of geopolitics, states and boundaries. A methodology whereby the researcher spends considerable time observing and interacting with a social group is participant observation – the most common method in ethnographic fieldwork (Herbert 2000, 551). Several other social scientific methods, such as interviews and surveys, can be combined with participant observation in the 'field' to enhance observations, obtain additional systematic insights and hidden meanings, and to counter the latter's disadvantages regarding subjectivity, ethical considerations and claims that 'observations are not data' (Dewalt et al. 1998, 271).[8]

In the life-world of the informants of this research, the same border, putatively porous in the general borderlessness declarations, can be startlingly impermeable when considering the territorial sovereignty it provides in granting the military regime impunity and creating those who 'have' and those who 'have not'. The latter in Myanmar context does not refer to material wealth or access to global village but to having the right to live – the most basic human right. Criticizing the limited political commitment among contemporary academics who value 'intellectual autonomy', Routledge (2001) calls for much more than neutral or ambivalent representation. He believes that critical collaborative methodologies that can integrate theory, politics and ethics are crucial because '… to fail to engage is to risk a retreat into bourgeois intellectualism that threatens to make geography irrelevant to the struggles of resisting others and, at worst, *complicit with the regimes of control that critical geographers purport to be so critical of* (Routledge 2001, 118, *emphasis added*).

Some points on doing ethnographic research on Myanmar

Attempts to grasp the contested territorialities at Myanmar's borderlands hidden from the view by the normalized political maps and the dominating discourses, involving international relations and politics between the states and their contestants, and above all, the *de jure* 'illegitimacy' of the large share of de facto phenomena, stipulate extensive participant observations by the researcher.

During 2000-2005, I lived near the Thai-Myanmar border, during which I also spent five months on both sides of the Sino-Myanmar border between Kachin state and Dai-Jingpo Autonomous Prefecture of China, and one month along the Indo-Myanmar border. I have also spent time in Myanmar government controlled territories in Kachin state between 2000 and 2010.[9]

---

8   The chapter will not discuss the changing locations of 'the field' and the issues of moving in and out of the field. See Caputo (2000) on reconfiguring the field in anthropology.

9   I was doing Ph.D. fieldwork in 2000-2003 on the Sino-Myanmar border, while simultaneously, and until 2006, worked for an international organization on conflict resolution, mostly on Thai-Myanmar border.

At Myanmar's borders, information can be misunderstood, misinterpreted or obscured, and is often used for political ends by all parties. Thus any purposeful inquiry needs long-term investment of time to build trust, familiarity with the relationships, sensitivities and rules of conduct, and confidentiality that first has to be proved. Avoiding being a burden or imposing on the informants, and not jeopardizing their security and networks have to be the priority at the expense of valuable information and research interests. An oversupply of information is thus never the case, compensated, though, by the extensive stay and involvement, and development of my own sense and judgment.

The question of ethics, specifically in regards to disclosing the identity of the researcher and the purpose of research, emerges occasionally. The ethics of the researcher in terms of disclosing his/her research interests has been an aspect of debate in the theory of fieldwork. It is held here that overt research is ethical and respectful towards the subjects, while it also helps to ask questions more effectively as the informants know about the research (Berg 1995, 89-91). At Myanmar's borders, changing contexts, not locations, compel different approaches. My identity occasionally shifts between that of a Western tourist, English teacher, cultural anthropologist (popularly perceived as non-political), Ph.D. student, researcher, political geographer, an NGO worker and a friend. The considerations for the 'identity change' are not so much to decrease the level of subject reactivity but for security considerations of the informants and myself due to the sensitiveness and political character of the research. 'Undercover field techniques' – where the researcher does not reveal his/her true identity or research purpose (Eley and Northon 2001, 398) – were utilized at some contexts for political/security reasons. Amongst the immediate informants, which community is tight and exclusive, 'undercover research' is not pursued for ethical considerations.

Recognition of the sensitivities of most issues and the absolute right of the respondents to avoid or divert a topic, or 'not feel like explaining', even if there are no obvious (to me) reasons, are the most important factors for the fieldwork to be successful. After identifying sensitive issues I rather listen to what is narrated than demand answers to questions. I consider the time spent with respondents (friends) chatting, dining, joking or watching videos – or the live broadcast of the 2010 World Cup – as valuable as obtaining answers to formal research questions through interviews. I acknowledge that with a more aggressive approach I can pry out more facts and inside politics but that would sacrifice the deeper tacit relationships with individual respondents that I value the most. By no means is this a unique approach – many researchers recognizing the specifics of culture and/ or circumstances have remained modest. Hyndman (2001, 268), doing research in a refugee camp near Kenya-Somalia border, accounted: 'Listening and probing proved more insightful than any of the interview schedules I had circulated to the research ethics committee prior to my departure. By engaging with people on their terms, doors were opened and invitations extended'. Similarly, Del Casino (2001, 456) writes: 'Choosing to be as unobtrusive as possible, I tried not to disturb the work of the organization or its staff. I certainly did not want to be a burden. I was, as the Thais might say, employing my own understanding of the [Thai] concept of *krengjai* (a reticence to impose one's self on others)'.

Under such circumstances, a very useful method has been collecting themes from popular rhetoric, local narratives and conversations. The strong recurrence of certain themes has been highly relevant to understanding the socio-spatial relationships and phenomena, and useful in interpreting observations and interview responses. Definitely, the clearly changing dominant narratives between 2000 and 2010 speak volumes about the concerns and constructions within the respondent communities. Rapport (2000, 93) has stressed the role of the narrative in anthropological study, arguing that all other methods that "translate experience into static and essential abstractions like 'culture,' 'social structure,' 'habitus' do not capture the mobility and change. He argues that the individuals' 'sense of orders-within-change' is located in their narratives. He backs up his arguments with psychologists' studies, which show that when narrating, individuals tend to talk more to themselves rather than to the researcher. Weller (1998, 373) also suggests that narratives can be used to learn about a topic, and then common themes collected and studied from textual materials. Thus a very common reference in my research is 'Fieldwork Communication, Name [changed or missing for security reasons], Location and Date'.

And finally, not just extracting invaluable material from the life-world but also giving back something to the community and to the people to 'repay kindnesses' (Price 2001, 145) should be part of academic research. The depth of reciprocity depends on the ethical considerations of the researcher and on his/her skills in establishing rapport and relationships but also on the length of the project/research that determines the levels of involvement. Academia owes – and thus should be reciprocally linked – to the lived space and the informants amongst the people it studies.

The contested territorialities at Myanmar's boundaries[10]

Territoriality has been viewed by political geographers as a tool to create and maintain the state and its order (Johnston 1995, 213-25), and as the effective force that explains why territorial states would not (yet) demise (Taylor 1995, 1). Territoriality in the words by Sack (1986, 19) is '… the attempt by an individual or a group to affect, influence, or control people, phenomena, and relationships, by delimiting and asserting control over a geographical area'. Although more flexible ideas on territoriality have been suggested more recently (see El Ouali 2010, Paasi and Prokkola 2008), at the heart of territoriality is the control over territory (space). In Myanmar the conflict is shaped by highly contested territorialities between

---

10   Due to scope, the chapter will not discuss the Bangladeshi-Myanmar border, where the situation remains highly vulnerable for the Rohingya, without citizenship and subject to Myanmar Army persecution, who have fled to Bangladesh in many waves since 1978.

the state versus the ethnic groups that have mobilized into political parties with armed wings – that has lead to institutionalization of the military (way of life). All armed actors at Myanmar's borders strive for the establishment of a territory with active boundaries to affect control. Thus multiple co-existing contested, competing, clashing and overlapping territorialities persist. Obscuring the clear dichotomy are the ambiguous and continuously shifting rivalries and allies between the ethnic groups and other actors contributing to the highly complex mosaics of spaces.

The main contestants for territorial control are different ethnic political organizations and armies. They view the state of Myanmar as encroaching on their 'historic homeland' towards which it has no justified claim, and thus refer to the territories under their control as liberated areas. At the very basic, the spaces can be divided into those of non-ceasefire zones (the zones of actual, low-impact guerilla war) and those of ceasefire zones (post-war areas?).[11] Initially fighting for independence, all significant ethnic organizations have since 1990s 'downgraded' their demands to asking for political, economic and cultural autonomy. In the following sections, the listings of the ethnic organizations are not intended for confusing the reader but rather to demonstrate the sheer amount of actors that establish perhaps one of the most complex sets of territorial and social dynamics in the modern South and Southeast Asia. Although the violence involved in the attempts for solution require all sides to compromise, the state seems to perceive it is cornered to opt for using its military power as a means for any solutions.

At the non-ceasefire areas the ethnic based Karen National Union (KNU), the Karenni National Progressive Party (KNPP), the Shan state Army South (SSA-A) on the Thai-Myanmar border, and the National Socialist Council of Nagalim, Khaplang faction (NSCN-K) and the Chin National Front (CNF) on the Indo-Myanmar border, are the largest groups engaged in armed resistance. In retaliation, in Eastern Myanmar, the Myanmar Army forces entire ethnic villages to relocate to the strategic hamlets that are under its control. In order to ensure that the villagers do not return to their native place, the original village area is then (land)mined and declared a free-fire zone where the Myanmar Army warrants its soldiers to shoot on sight (Grundy-Warr and Wong 2002). According to the Thailand-Burma Border Consortium (TBBC), at least 3,000 ethnic villages have been destroyed since 1996, affecting over one million people. Probably more than 300,000 have fled to Thailand as refugees (the majority being Shan and not recognized by the Thai government). TBBC estimates that in 2006 there were conservatively still some 500,000 IDPs in Eastern Burma.

11　Although this division is widely used in various popular, academic and diplomatic literature, it should be highly contested. First, ceasefires are highly fragile arrangements, and in Myanmar, these do break down with the actual guerilla war continuing. Second, as Kirsch and Flint (2011) argue, there is a false dichotomy between periods and spaces of war and peace, and that the spaces of conflict and reconstruction are inter-twined and constructed through narrative and practice – with the power relations formed in periods of war shaping social practices in post-war settings.

Between 1989 and 1995, a total of fifteen insurgent organizations agreed to brokered ceasefire arrangements with the then 'Prime Minister' General Khin Nyunt that allowed them autonomy on rather generous terms, including maintaining their armies and weapons and *the right to administer international boundaries* (Smith 1999; Oo and Min 2007, *emphasis added*). Not only the non-ceasefire areas but also the territories controlled by the ceasefire groups are generally out of the reach for the Myanmar military government, although the ceasefire groups are confronted by the increasing proximity and political pressure by the Myanmar Army.

In addition, there are semi-autonomous areas for the splinter groups from the ethnic political organizations/armies that under the aegis of 'peace and development' carry out various 'economic', 'trade' and 'business' activities, involving also legal/illegal cross-border trade. The territories of these groups are smaller and less clearly demarcated, and the authority of their leaders overlaps with that of the regime with who the latter closely collaborate in exchange for privileges. The Myanmar government has set these groups on high pedestal in the country, engaging them as the main representatives of the country's ethnic minorities, confusing the less informed international community. Groups such as the Karenni National People Liberation Front, the Democratic Karen Buddhist Army (DKBA), the Mon Peace Armed Group, the Kayinni National Progressive Party, Kayinni National Solidarity Organization, to name a few, belong to this type. This is not the end of the list of important actors. A unique entity due to its history of formation, past and present geopolitical ties with China, and sheer size and wealth from widely documented opium production and the indictment of a number of its leaders by US law enforcement authorities for alleged drug-trafficking, is the United Wa State Army (UWSA).[12] There are other groups gaining influence and enforcing good relations with the military junta for various privileges (for example the Pa-O National Organization).

The ongoing Naga insurgency at the Indo-Myanmar border precedes India's and Burma's independence. The 3.5 million Naga live on both sides of the international boundary, and the primary objective of the existing rival political organizations is reunification of all Naga dominated territories – although also aware that neither India nor Myanmar would cede territory. Linguistically related Chin (numbering 500,000) and the Mizo (700,000) have fought for independence in their respective states, Myanmar and India, and collaborated in supporting each others' insurgencies. The Mizo were granted the state of Mizoram in 1987 by the federal Indian government.

---

12   In 2005, the United Wa State Army (UWSA) banned opium cultivation in the Wa region, following earlier such bans by the other main large opium-growing groups such as the National Democratic Alliance Army (NDAA), that banned opium in the Mongla region in 1997, and the Myanmar National Democratic Alliance Army (MNDAA) enforcing opium ban in the Kokang region in 2003. As a result, opium cultivation in Myanmar has shifted from the traditional Shan state's Wa and Kokang areas to southern Shan state in 2007. These bans were attempts to gain international political recognition and support for the development of their impoverished regions after decades of war and isolation (Jelsma and Kramer 2008).

Lived spaces at Myanmar's boundaries

Lived space often constitutes forms of struggle over the meanings of processes such as democracy and development, material struggle over resources, subsistence livelihoods, basic rights and cultures, while the abstract space of the state often stands against the lived space of indigenous and local communities (Routledge 2001, 115). Research has shown that rather than contesting the border, however, local inhabitants creatively adapt to the existence of the international border and use it as a resource in their spatial practices (see also Paasi and Prokkola, 2008). This section will discuss the rather varying socio-spatial outcomes of the contested territorialities at Myanmar's different borders, all based on fieldwork.[13] None of the borders are continuously demarcated in lived space, while the state manifestations are limited to certain roads and the border-crossings that are controlled by the state, and to the increased army presence near the borders.

Locally embedded spaces at the Thai-Myanmar border

The Thai-Myanmar border, once absolutely irrelevant to the distant centers of power due to its peripheral location, has shifted to become central in many important aspects.

First, it has become the line between death and survival for the hundreds of thousands of refugees fleeing the war or forced relocation, or for those avoiding arrest at Myanmar's urban areas. It is the place where the Karen, the Karenni and the Shan armies can intercept the Myanmar Army planned attacks of their ethnic villages in order to protect their civilian populations, while inflicting 'as much trouble and casualties on the Myanmar Army troops as possible' (Fieldwork Communication, Mae Sot, March 2005). It is also the line that is vital for relief and medical work as the centre for coordinating cross-border humanitarian assistance. The proximity to the border of the normatively illegitimate 'liberated zones' – referred to as insurgent areas by the internationally recognized Myanmar government – enables the passage for well-organized cross-border relief operations to reach the Internally Displaced Persons (IDPs) 'inside' Myanmar's free-fire zones created by the 'legitimate' state institution.[14] Mobile medical relief teams with medical supplies but also with equipment to document and record the silent war, even mobile teachers – all convoyed and protected by the 'insurgents' – cross the Thai-Myanmar border while their lives depend on the local knowledge of the time-

---

13   Thus references to fieldwork are omitted in this section to avoid repetition, with the
      exception of quotes or references to particular sources of information.
14   The specific layout of territorialities does not allow for an access to all IDP population
      from the Thai-Myanmar border. Some IDPs are better (or only) accessible from inside
      the country, that is, from Myanmar Army controlled territories – but any help must be
      extended without being caught by the 'government'. This is done along the invisible
      Buddhist and Christian grassroots networks.

specific patchwork of territorialities and landmine geographies. An encounter with the Myanmar Army or its proxy may easily turn deadly for the providers of such humanitarian assistance. A step into a wrong place continues to maim and kill large numbers of people due to the landmines planted by all parties. There is a subtlety regarding the tactics of planting landmines, as noted by fieldwork informants – that of planting these to secure an area from the attacking troops (attributed to ethnic armies) and that of planting these massively in the rice fields and riverbanks to stop the fleeing villagers (attributed to the Myanmar Army). 'If you face an enemy of 400,000, what do you do?' (Fieldwork Communication, Thai-Myanmar border, March 2005).

It is amazing how close yet separately all the different actors operate. For example, very often almost from the same spot I saw the Thai army, the DKBA and the Myanmar Army camps while the KNU troops were pointed to be just 'behind the mountain'. With the ease that *all* actors cross the border river Moei (or Salween) – facilitated by the drought of the dry season, the border almost ceases to be relevant in this aspect of lived space. Simultaneously, it is reinforced in everyday speech and meanings, where the single reference 'inside' distinguishes – for those who know – the dangerous and complex spaces in Myanmar from the freedoms and life 'outside'.

Second, the border has generated vigorous small scale two-way economic activities between Thailand and the territories under the control of various parties including the Myanmar government, the New Mon State Party (NMSP) ceasefire group, the DKBA, the UWSA, and the non-ceasefire KNU, the KNPP and SSA-S. The character of the cross-border flows of goods and people depends strictly on the type and needs of the group. The one-way flow of drugs into Thailand, mainly amphetamine-type-stimulants produced from the opium grown in Shan state, adds a dimension with long and unique history, geopolitics and dynamics that is beyond the scope of the chapter. A comment by a local Lahu villager from Mong Ton township, Shan state, which grows opium for subsistence, summarizes the complex situation:

> Sometimes, we have to pay to the UWSA, the SSA-South, Wa militia, SPDC militia, or Burma army. Sometimes, we have to pay to two or three of these groups because they are wandering into our areas all the time and they are armed. So if our farm is too small, there is no money left for us (Jelsma and Kramer 2008).[15]

Third, the relevance of the Thai-Myanmar border – as all other Myanmar borders – for the access of information, knowledge and empowerment cannot

---

15 In addition to the UWSA, NDAA and MNDAA that have officially banned opium cultivation, several smaller groups have been implicated in production and smuggling, notably the DKBA (Fieldwork conversations, Thai-Myanmar border, 2003-2004). Drugs are smuggled across all Myanmar's borders. See Soe Myint (2005) for a report on the Indo-Myanmar cross-border smuggling.

be underestimated.[16] It is highly relevant to understanding the struggle to *see* the low-profile offices of *countless* grassroots non-governmental organizations, at all Myanmar's borders, working on strengthening Myanmar's civil society, democracy, documenting human rights abuses; training in social work, counseling, media reporting, international relations or diplomacy; involving in environmental and women activism, and so on.[17] Importantly, these spaces often bring together people of different ethnicities of Myanmar, while information flows are two-way. Here the civilians and refugees fleeing atrocities, arrest or the economic collapse in Myanmar provide accounts that are analyzed and publicized to the outside world. Training courses in the above described knowledge, on the other hand, are provided for people who come from 'inside' to take this back for dissemination. Most of such grassroots organizations are designated as 'illegitimate' by the normative international system of states, since the vast majority of their members and staff has neither passports nor other vital documentation. They nevertheless operate, concealed from view, in lived spaces.

Locally embedded spaces at the Sino-Myanmar border between Kachin state and Yunnan province

Deep-rooted networks of flows and relations amongst the people who are now known as the Kachin have for centuries criss-crossed the mountainous terrain, and these have not withered away as a result of the arbitrary line drawn on the map in 1960. The area intersected by the Sino-Myanmar boundary continues to be tightly incorporated in a web of spatial practices. These include but are not limited to five-day markets rotating between villages on both sides of the boundary, spatial flows and trajectories in the form of travel, visits and commuting that are enshrined through the Kachin trade and kinship/marriage bonds, while boosted further by the presence of ceasefire territories controlled by the Kachin Independence Organization (KIO) and its armed wing, the Kachin Independence Army (KIA).

The Kachin inhabiting both sides of the border have adjusted to the boundary by including new politico-geographical notions such as the 'border', 'China-side', 'Kachin-side' and 'Burma/Myanmar' into their vocabulary. 'It's good to have a border. The border identifies what happens where', a local Kachin pastor who services churches on both sides of the border thus crosses the border several times

---

16 It is beyond the scope of this chapter to discuss how various media organizations operate at Myanmar's borders, providing information that shapes the knowledge and policies of international community vis-à-vis Myanmar's military regime.

17 Many of these groups have had profound impact on the knowledge construction about Myanmar. Perhaps the most spectacular has been the international passage of the report 'Licence To Rape', by Shan Women's Action Network and Shan Human Rights Foundation, documenting incidents of rape and sexual violence involving 625 ethnic Shan women/girls, mostly during 1996-2001, by Myanmar Army.

a day, noted (Fieldwork Communication, Lahtaw Naw Ding, Man Hai, October 2000).

The KIO maintains its army and weapons, and controls and administers territories in Kachin state and along the 'international' boundary with China through the system of state-replicating institutions overseeing education, health, communications, public and external relations. The KIO/KIA army camps and the headquarters are strategically located on the hilltops near the Chinese border. Near the same hilltops, on the 'China-side,' are cell site towers erected by the Chinese mobile network providers, providing access as far as Kachin State capital Myitkyina at the Myanmar military controlled territory, and used by the Kachin, the Chinese and the Myanmar government officials alike. Among the many 'freedoms' in the KIO 'liberated' zones, the Kachin national flag is hoisted daily, education and printed matter are provided in the Kachin national language (Jinghpaw), and access to internet and mobile phones is unrestricted.

While during the KIO armed resistance (1961-1994), all kinds of commodities and supplies were imported from China, today China is the provider of continuous electricity, internet and mobile network, and a formidable 'business' partner in trade, infrastructure development and resource 'export' destinations for the KIO and the Myanmar military alike.[18] An alternative border has emerged inside Myanmar – that between the KIO controlled territory and the rest of the state under the control of the Myanmar Army. The KIO border with the Myanmar Army is guarded much more zealously than the international Kachin-China border (Dean 2005). This border is more 'inter-national', more controlled and guarded than the Kachin-China border, although neither political maps nor dominating discourses acknowledge it.

Locally embedded spaces at the Indo-Myanmar border

The tri-junction between China, India and Myanmar is not demarcated. None of the three countries hold a permanent presence at the tri-junction due to the high mountainous terrain and the near absence of settlements, while both the Chinese and Indian army units occasionally patrol the area (Fieldwork Communication, Indian Army lieutenant, Indo-China border, February 2004). The Myanmar troops do not patrol the tri-junction because 'they do not really care' (Fieldwork Communication, Assam Rifles major, Indo-Myanmar border, February 2004).

Both sides of the Indo-Myanmar border have been connected for centuries by many well-maintained trade routes that even used to have guesthouses along the

---

18   Logging in Kachin state has resulted in extensive deforestation, fueled by the Chinese ban on logging in Yunnan (1996) and nationwide (1998). Large projects in the Myanmar Army controlled areas of Kachin state, such as mining concessions and the development of large hydropower dams to transmit electricity back to China, have been granted by the junta to the Chinese companies, increasingly overriding the KIO and the Kachin (Kachin Development Networking Group 2007).

way. After independence, trade was curtailed between Burma and India – however, neither state has managed to halt the local connections. The most recent and well-disguised statist project is India's 'Look East' policy and its powerful discourses of opening-up borders for trade and new opportunities – most often denoted as 'new gateways of Indo-Myanmar trade'. In locally embedded spaces this translates into the past territorialities being now hijacked by the state for control and profit. Informal trade is being 'legitimized' – if we use the statist vocabulary – through opening *formal* (that is inter-state) checkpoints for channeling trade upon which tax can be collected. A response from an ethnic Chin trader from Mizoram (India), whose trade route extends as far as the Sino-Myanmar border, via Mandalay, exemplifies well what the new opening-up-of-border rhetoric means for local people, as well as how the powerful discourse has entered the traders' consciousness:

> *Before [the opening of the Zakhawthar/Champhai gate] we could do as we liked. Now we have to go through the gate. Before the trade was* illegal, *now it is* legal (Fieldwork Communication, Chin trader, Aizawl, February 2004, emphasis added).

For centuries multiple tribes and clans living in the hilly areas covering today's Mizoram State in India and Chin State in Myanmar, were referred to simply as *khua-chak*, southerners, or *khua-thlang*, northerners. Although today most of the Chin resistance against Myanmar government is based in Mizoram 'illegally,' a large portion constitute a mix of economic migrants and political refuge seekers. Generally, the Mizo recognize that Myanmar's military government is responsible for the exodus of the Chin into India, yet many Mizo see the Chin who reside in Mizoram as nothing but beggars and street laborers. From their traditional reference as *khua-chak*, the Chin have now become to be known as *Burma-ho*, a strongly derogative term for people from Myanmar. 'The Mizo look down on the Chin' (Fieldwork Communication, Pi Par, Indo-Myanmar border, March 2004). The relations have been strained in recent years, and many Mizo are distancing themselves from the Chin. The Chin and Mizo are growing apart. In this case, has the border indeed created two 'separate nations'?

Conclusions

The chapter first looked 'backwards', into history, by discussing the establishment of the geo-body of Myanmar, and then 'inwards'-'outwards' by turning the political map inside out to draw attention to 'hidden de facto geographies that are not reflected in the brightly colored blocks of sovereign territorial states' (Grundy-Warr 1998, 733-74). It argues that to declare a political map insufficient for understanding what it presents entails reliance on participant observations and other fieldwork techniques for mapping and understanding the lived realities. The chapter then discussed the contested, competing and clashing territorialities at

Myanmar's borders, which spatial outcomes affect millions of people, based on my daily engagements with the border during 2000-2005, and again during fieldwork in 2010. The subsequent section on the locally embedded lived spaces showed how the (often deadly) struggle on the ground – revealed only through ethnography – is simultaneously a contest between the meanings of illegitimate and legitimate as these 'fixed' concepts are imposed by the often ignorant but powerful normative discourses.

The mutual but exclusive enhancement between the modes of globalization and the communities these cater, have speeded up the discursive shift from modern to postmodern more so than the (post)modernization in lived spaces. Regardless of the international power elites' pretense of the expanding borderless world, the flows of goods, money, information and people have always existed as an integral part of the social economy of the vast, mainly mountainous borderlands of modern Myanmar. The designation of 'cross-border' holds true for conceived space as the result of the establishment of the state and its boundaries in 1948. In lived spaces the borders have been 'porous' and criss-crossed ever since their conception, while it is within the last decades that state has come closer than ever to controlling its borders in lived spaces, contrary to the 'borders-opening-up' discourses. This has been achieved through force, while the legitimacy of the state and its territoriality continues to be violently contested. The spatial outcomes, however, are contingent on varying evolutions, geopolitics and shifting local/state interests in reaction to geopolitical, political, trade and business opportunities, and local dynamics. It thus is that the Thai-Myanmar border, for example, has become to determine over life and death for many, while the Indo-Myanmar border is creating new nations as is the case of the Chin and Mizo. The continuously changing mixes of 'past' and new territorialities created by the border establish highly complex and locally embedded mosaics of spaces.

The practices discussed here as embedded in lived spaces are those that have been denoted as 'challenging' and 'defying' the international boundaries – regardless that the actors of these lived spaces have apprehended the establishment of the state as challenging and interfering with their territorialities at every level. It is the 'postmodern' discourse that is 'imposing' its rhetoric of challenges to the state and its borders, and academia is in many ways complicit in this.

The geo-body of Myanmar as the effect of the British colonial efforts to rule and administer 'for convenience' has found its borders designated by the British to a large although not exclusive extent. The socio-political context affecting Myanmar's borders has evolved over time as a consequence of successive historical events and fluid combinations, alignments and patterns of a multitude of actors and factors, where contingencies and contexts assume an important role. A thorough study of the evolution of a given boundary may appear to provide an understanding of the relationships. But this may prove to be in direct contradiction with the feelings and practices in lived spaces. All Myanmar's borderlands present quite specific patchworks of spaces, resulting from local evolutions, geopolitics and contingencies at each of its borders. These have lead to a multitude of different political organizations and groups, some of which have mobilized and others regrouped with shifting interests and in reaction to the geopolitics, politics, trade, business and personal opportunities. The lack of internal sovereignty and the military (dis)order in Myanmar constitute both a cause and the effect that in combination with the above factors are responsible for outcomes that neither are predictable by studying wider geopolitics or local histories – but may simply bear no 'logic' at all.

It is *the lived realities* stemming from the particular evolvement of the border or its effected dynamics that seriously challenge the dominating discourses based on sweeping generalizations. Myanmar's lived borderlands provide a good case for demonstrating the need to incorporate the local, contextual dynamics into theory and analysis.

References

Agnew, J. and Corbridge, S. (1995), *Mastering Space: Hegemony, Territory and International Political Economy* (London and New York: Routledge).

Berg, B.L. (1995), *Qualitative Research Methods for the Social Sciences* (Boston: Allyn and Bacon).

Bloul, R.A.D. (1999), 'Beyond Ethnic Identity: Resisting Exclusionary Identification', *Social Identities* 5:1.

Boggs, W.S. (1940), *International Boundary: A Study of Boundary Functions and Problems* (New York: Morningside Heights, Columbia University Press).

Brown, D. (1994), *The State and Ethnic Politics in Southeast Asia* (London and New York: Routledge).

Callahan, M. (2003), *Making Enemies: War and State Building in Burma* (Ithaca and London: Cornell University Press).

Caputo, V. (2000), 'At "Home" and "Away": Reconfiguring the Field for Late Twentieth-Century Anthropology', in Amit, V. (ed.), *Constructing the Field: Ethnographic Fieldwork in the Contemporary World* (London and New York: Routledge).

Dean, K. (2005), 'Spaces and Territorialities on the Sino-Burmese Boundary: China, Myanmar and the Kachin', *Political Geography* 24, 808-30.

Del Casino Jr., V.J. (2001), 'Decision Making in an Ethnographic Context', *Geographical Review* 91:1-2.

Dewalt, K.M., Dewalt, B.R. and Wayland, C.B. (1998), 'Participant Observation', in Bernard, R.H. (ed.), *Handbook of Methods in Cultural Anthropology* (California: Altamira Press).

El Ouali, A. (2010), 'The Flexibility of Territoriality from Early States to Globalisation: Making States Survive Through Territorial Autonomy', *Geopolitics* 15, 82–108.

Fley, T. and Northon, C. (2001), 'Geography Undercover', *Geographical Review* 91:1-2.

Ghatate, N.M. (2000), 'The Sino-Burmese Border Settlement', in Grover, V. (ed.), *Myanmar: Government and Politics* (New Delhi: Deep and Deep Publications).

Grundy-Warr, C. (1998), 'Turning the Political Map Inside Out: A View of Mainland Southeast Asia', in Savage, V.R., Kong, L. and Warwick, N. (eds.), *The Naga Awakens: Growth and Change in Southeast Asia* (Singapore: Times Academic Press).

Grundy-Warr, C. and Schofield, C. (2005), 'Reflections on the Relevance of Classic Approaches and Contemporary Priorities in Boundary Studies', *Geopolitics* 10, 650-62.

Grundy-Warr, C. and Wong Siew Yin, E. (2002), 'Geographies of Displacement; The Karenni and the Shan Across the Myanmar-Thailand Border', *Singapore Journal of Tropical Geography* 23:1.

Herbert, S. (2000), 'For Ethnography', *Progress in Human Geography* 24:2.

Hyndman, J. (2001), 'The Field As Here and Now, Not There and Then', *Geographical Review* 91:1-2.

Jelsma, M. and Kramer, T. (2008), 'Withdrawal Symptoms: Changes in the Southeast Asian Drugs Market', *Transnational Institute Debate Papers* 16.

Johnston, R.J. (1995), 'Territoriality and the State', in Benko, G.B. and Strohmayer, U. (eds.), *Geography, History and Social Sciences* (Dordrecht, The Netherlands: Kluwer Academic Publishers).

Kachin Development Networking Group (2007), *Damming the Irrawaddy*, available at <http://www.kachinnews.com/DtheI/Damming-The-Irrawaddy.html>.

Kirsch, S. and Flint, C. (eds.)(2011), *Reconstructing Conflict: Integrating War and Post-War Geographies* (Farnham: Ashgate).

Leach, E.R. (1954), *Political Systems of Highland Burma* (Boston: Beacon Press).

Marden, P. (2000), 'Mapping Territoriality: the Geopolitics of Sovereignty, Governance and the Citizen', in Graham, D.T. and Poku, N.K. (eds.), *Migration, Globalisation and Human Security* (London and New York: Routledge).

Megoran, N. (2006) 'For Ethnography in Political Geography: Experiencing and Re-imagining Ferghana Valley Boundary Closures', *Political Geography* 25, 622-640.

Myint, S. (2005), 'Illicit Narcotics on the Indo-Burmese Border and India's Role in Combating Drug Smuggling', in Jelsma, M., Kramer, T. and Vervest, P. (eds.), *Trouble in The Triangle: Opium and Conflict in Burma* (Chiang Mai: Silkworm Books).

Oo, Z. and Min, W. (2007), 'Assessing Burma's Ceasefire Accords', *Policy Studies* 39 (Washington: East-West Center).

Paasi, A. (1996), *Territories, Boundaries and Consciousness: The Changing Geographies of the Finnish-Russian Border* (Chichester: John Wiley).

Paasi, A. and Prokkola, E.-K. (2008), 'Territorial Dynamics, Cross-border Work and Everyday Life in the Finnish-Swedish Border Area', *Space and Polity* 12:1, 13-29.

Price, M.D. (2001), 'The Kindness of Strangers', *Geographical Review* 91:1-2.

Rajah, A. (2001), 'Burma: Protracted Conflict, Governance and Non-Traditional Security Issues', Institute of Defence and Strategic Studies Working Paper 14 (Singapore: Nanyang Technological University).

Rapport, N. (2000), 'The Narrative as Fieldwork Technique: Processual Ethnography for a World In Motion', in Amit, V. (ed.), *Constructing the Field: Ethnographic Fieldwork in the Contemporary World* (London and New York: Routledge).

Routledge, P. (2001), 'Within the River: Collaboration and Methodology', *Geographical Review* 91:1-2.

Sack, R.D. (1986), *Human Territoriality: Its Theory and History* (UK, US, Australia: Cambridge University Press).

Sidaway, J. (2007), 'Spaces of Postdevelopment', *Progress in Human Geography* 31:3.

Smith, M. (2008), 'Ethnic Challenges and Border Politics in Myanmar/Burma', in Skidmore, M. and Wilson, T. (eds.), *Myanmar – the state, Community and the Environment* (Australian National University: E Press), available at <http://epress.anu.edu.au/myanmar/pdf_instructions.html>.

Smith, M. (1999), *Burma: Insurgency and the Politics of Ethnicity* (Dhaka: The University Press; Bangkok: White Lotus; London and New York: Zed Books Ltd.).

Taylor, P.J. (1995), 'Beyond Containers: Internationality, Interstatedness, Interterritoriality', *Progress in Human Geography* 19:1.

Tegenfeldt, H.G. (1974), *A Century of Growth: The Kachin Baptist Church of Burma* (California, South Pasadena: The William Carey Library).

Thongchai, W. (1994), Siam Mapped: A History of the Geo-body of a Nation (Chiang Mai: Silkworm Books).

Tin, M.M.T. (2004), 'The Essential Tension: Democratization and the Unitary State in Myanmar (Burma)', *South East Asia Research* 12:2.

Weller, S.C. (1998), 'Structured Interviewing and Questionnaire Construction', in Bernard, R.H. (ed.), *Handbook of Methods in Cultural Anthropology* (California: Altamira Press).

PART III
BORDER ENFORCEMENT
IN THE 21ST CENTURY

The Emerging Politics of Border Management: Policy and Research Considerations

Jason Ackleson

Introduction

How can we take stock of the politics of border management around the world today?

Conventional wisdom in and outside the academic community suggests that borders generally have been 'hardened' or 're-territorialized' in the post-September 11 period due to concerns about national security (Andreas and Biersteker 2003). This is being done, the narrative goes, in the face of countervailing pressures forcing *de-territorialization* such as globalization and free trade which make border control in the twenty-first century a difficult and dilemma-wrought challenge. I accept that this trend has been the case but would like to make the argument here that this remains only one part of the larger picture of contemporary border management around the world. In my view, it is not really a question of if borders are getting 'harder' (they are) or 'softer' (they are) but rather how, why, and when this is taking place – and if any broad generalizations can be made about these dynamics. The overall picture that emerges, I submit, is really one of border policy regime *differentiation* – between, within, and beyond states. These differentiated and uneven regimes manifest themselves in different functional ways in different areas of the world – for example, to serve military or policing ends – some of which will be explored briefly in this chapter.

I connect the term 'regime' with 'policy' here because regimes, as understood in the public policy literature, consist of elements such as power, ideas, interests, actors, and institutions. Bringing this concept into the discussion offers us a clearer way to study policy *change* – for example why governments adopt certain policies over time. I submit that in order to have more meaningful and robust analysis of these regimes, scholarship needs to move beyond the de/re-territorializing duality and consider a hierarchy of border security threats that are dealt with by state border security policy regimes. In doing so, we may be able to separate 'problems' from 'threats' and, in turn, prioritize policy objectives for what hopefully may be more effective outcomes on the ground.

This chapter will offer some basic comparative policy analysis but also commentary on some important theoretical and research approaches to these issues. Specifically, I want to suggest here that it is potentially helpful to look at border security in three ways: (1) as an output of complex and differentiated 'policy regimes' which are evolving in different ways, both within North American and elsewhere in the world; (2) in terms of a hierarchy that can help us isolate and prioritize security concerns; and, finally, (3) from a comparative interdisciplinary perspective that employs insights from a number of academic traditions, including Political Science, Geography, and Economics. Such a perspective offers potential for further empirical research within this framework.

To explore these three components, the chapter proceeds as follows. First, I take a brief survey of some of the more interesting conceptual work inside and outside of the discipline of International Relations (IR) which analyzes the dynamics of contemporary border controls. Second, I examine some of the prevailing de- and re-territorialization impulses on borders in several key parts of the world today. It is impossible to offer a comprehensive, global survey of border security practices. This is, thus, by necessity, a limited, inductive exercise that seeks to make some generalizations based on several individual key cases around the world. Specific attention is paid to the dynamics of post-September 11, 2001 securitization practices, mainly in North America. I make some reference to comparative examples in Europe and elsewhere in the world. In the third section, I deal with two theoretical considerations, first making a case for looking at 'policy regimes' to analyze these matters and then, second, suggesting a hierarchical mechanism to help differentiate border security priorities. Finally, the conclusion argues for an interdisciplinary and comparative research approach to these topics.

Borders in Transition?

Scholars, citizens, and policymakers often drift towards the common practice of reifying our social and political worlds. This is no less the case when many of us think of borders: we tend to accept the prevailing definitions of lineal international political boundaries and the nation-states they tend to inscribe. However, as K.J. Holsti reminds us, while 'one essential attribute of our definition of statehood is fixed territoriality ... this is a relatively new phenomenon, one that is historically unique' (Holsti 2004, 73). In his survey of territoriality across history, Holsti finds that ideas about territory have changed, particularly from the pre-modern to the modern period (see also Sack 1986). Because pre-modern societies organized themselves according to different principles, such as religion, few firm or exclusive notions of citizenship, territory, or even borders as we understand them today existed. As modernity gradually enveloped the West – accompanied by new technologies of mapping and modes of political organization (chiefly, the nation-state) – rules and norms (such as border patrols) developed to enshrine the territorial practices that dominate our contemporary world: strict, mutually defined borders that correlate with and support state sovereignty. This can be understood as a process of *territorialization*.

The larger discourse on globalization is built on the idea that even these modern state borders are becoming less relevant as *de-territorialization* becomes the *de rigueur* mode of spatial organization. Kenichi Ohmae's *End of the Nation State* (1995) is perhaps the most famous popular tract in this genre. Stephen Krasner's more scholarly work on sovereignty (1999) points out the sovereign state was never absolute, even from its origins; he argues that four primary compromises of modern territorial Westphalian state and its borders – conventions, contracts, coercion, and imposition – have occurred throughout history. This is certainly true when one looks at the economic realm, for instance in terms of trade. The multilateral trading system underwritten by the World Trade Organization (WTO), for example, has indeed been successful in tearing down trade barriers, dramatically reducing average tariff levels worldwide (prompting a corresponding increase in world trade volumes). This increase in world trade volume, when twinned with the strong forces of economic globalization, has prompted significant economic activity and integration across and pressures upon state borders. This is especially the case in certain integrated regions of the world such as the European Union (EU) and North America.

Holsti's study, and other work within the border literature corpus by scholars such as Martinez (1994), Newman (2006), and others, is helpful in not only reminding us of the historical peculiarity of our current system of borders but also typologies of the general functions that borders continue to provide. In that regard Holsti argues, for example, that 'it is certainly a myth that borders today are more "permeable" *than ever*' (2004, 109).

One of these functions is *screening*, an attempt to resist penetrability: on a very fundamental level, border controls often serve to regulate (or at least generate the appearance of regulating) the flows of goods and individuals between states. Particularly in the some parts post-9/11 world, this border function of screening has taken on a strong *security* dimension, be it for public health, migration control, counter-terrorism, or other defined concerns. This has been called 're-territorialization', a term contextualized within globalization and capitalism derived originally from Deleuze and Guattari (1987) and further developed in border studies by Paasi (1998), Albert (1998), O Tuathail (1998) and others.

While these and other scholars have evaluated this process, within the goals of this chapter and volume, it is worth taking a step back and asking, from a research perspective, how we are to make sense of this development and how it may be evaluated. In an era of globalization, for example, how effectively can states really be in regulating movement of people or goods across their borders? What threats do transnational actors such as criminal and terrorist networks pose to national borders? When states attempt to regulate their borders to mitigate against these and other risks, what do the emergent border security regimes look like? Does traditional, territorially-driven border conflict – over boundary demarcation, for example – persist?

There is a body of work that is surfacing which begins to answer some of these important research questions. Some of the more interesting literature in this regard seeks to re-conceptualize territorial regulation and mobility. Scholars such as Shamir (2005), for instance, are theorizing an emergent 'mobility regime', particularly in regards to persons, maintaining it is organized by a 'pervasive paradigm of suspicion' that manifests itself through technologies of social screening. In other work, Turner (2007, 287) suggests we are moving towards 'The Enclave Society' where the 'securitization of modern societies … create[s] significant forms of immobility' for certain groups of individuals but not necessarily goods and services. He cites examples that include profiling technologies and quarantine practices in Europe, Israel, and the United States, suggesting these are sovereignty practices which resist market forces and actually resemble certain types of pre-modern territorial regulatory practices.

Given the contradictions between the economic drive for open borders and the state's tendency in a highly securitized age to 'push-back' this trend though reinforced sovereignty and re-territorialization, it is clear that more flexible concepts of border management appear appropriate. Moreover, a close look at how borders appear to be operating around the world reveals that a simply de- and re-territorializing duality falls short of accurately capturing what is going on. I turn to this idea in the following section of this chapter.

Towards Differentiated Border Management Regimes

Rather than generalizing that borders are simply opening or closing, I want to suggest here that differentiated border control regimes are emerging worldwide. These policy regimes may include de-territorialization (in-line with globalization), traditional re-territorialization, or even regulatory and functional mechanisms for screening that are deployed *within* a state's interior to deal with undocumented migrants or other security threats. Any individual state's border policies may, even at the same time, exhibit each or all of these characteristics. To illustrate how this is happening, in the next section I will briefly explore a handful of cases around the world, with a particular focus on the North American case.

North America: 9/11 and the (Re)-emergence of Border and Migration Securitization

Turning first to North America, as I have argued elsewhere, a number of interesting dynamics of border management within the continent appear to be emerging in the post-September 11 period (Ackleson 2007). Borders within the continent experience sometimes contradictory impulses of regulation and openness, leading to an evolving but uneven and tenuous border and mobility management regime that increasingly favours certain economic classes and trade interests but marginalizes 'exceptions' such as economic migrants, refugees, and other identity-based groups. It is thus not simply a case of the border becoming 'harder' or 'softer' but rather the interesting issue is how and why each impulse is occurring.

To understand the trajectory of contemporary border management in North America, one need only consider the major border control-related policy developments of the post-September 11 period (Migration Policy Institute 2005). The United States in particular, undertook a number of key initiatives in the service of national security, operating under the assumption its borders were 'vulnerable' to terrorists, weapons of mass effect, and migrants. Peter Andreas (2003) has characterized these threats as 'Clandestine Transnational Actors' or CTAs which comprise a wide range of 'non-state actors who operate across national borders in violation of state laws and who attempt to evade law enforcement efforts', including terrorist networks, criminals, smugglers, and undocumented migrants.

Such CTAs undoubtedly pose problems for states across the world today. In the American context, however, one should note that the National Commission on Terrorist Attacks Upon the United States (also known as the 9/11 Commission) concluded that none of the 9/11 hijackers illegally crossed US frontiers (Commission 2004). Even if one discounts the possibility of illegal entry, the *legal* entry of terrorists and criminals into the US, prior to 9/11, was, and remains, a troubling possibility. In response to some of these vulnerabilities posed by CTAs, the 9/11 Commission recommended extensive reforms to the US border control and immigration system, including tighter inspections, more law enforcement resources, stricter enforcement of immigration violations, better visa screening measures, new screening and identification technologies, and other initiatives. In the terms of this chapter, this can be seen as clear cases of border re-territorialization and concomitant securitization of migration.

In the period since the attacks and the release of the Commission's report, the US government began work on implementing some of these measures. I classify these efforts in two broad categories: (1) material or physical bordering measures and (2) 'virtual' or technology-driven initiatives.

In the first category falls the construction of border walls and vehicle barriers as well as the use of the military and increased law enforcement resources – very traditional ways of imposing territorial control. In the United States today, the border wall construction business is booming. According to estimates by the US Congressional Research Service (CRS), approximately 700 miles of US-Mexico border fencing – comprised of vehicular, pedestrian, and other barriers – was completed as of early 2010 (Nuñez-Neto and Kim 2008). These measures and other plans are part of DHS's 'Secure Border Initiative', a multi-billion dollar effort that combines physical and virtual infrastructure systems along with new law enforcement efforts at and away from the border, including new detention and expedited removal policies (Philpott 2006). In 2006, U.S. President George W. Bush deployed the US military (via the National Guard) to the US-Mexico border to assist with infrastructure and enforcement efforts. In addition, 'boots on the ground', for example, law enforcement resources devoted to border protection and border management, have increased dramatically in the post-9/11 period with appropriations more than doubling (U.S. Customs and Border Protection (CBP) alone now commands a USD 9.3 billion annual budget) and thousands of new U.S. Border Patrol and other agents are currently deployed to both the northern and southern border zones (the Border Patrol is now near 18,000 total agents) (U.S. Customs and Border Protection 2009). A limited number of bi-lateral border management mechanisms are also in place in North America. The United States and Canada, for instance, are using Integrated Border Enforcement Teams (IBETS) to cooperatively deal with security issues on their common frontier.

The impact of all this on migration and other CTA flows remains mixed (Cornelius and Salehyan 2007). The American public generally supports the border build-up, with majorities in favour of border fences and increased border patrols (Associated Press 2008). However, empirical evidence suggests that migrant flows from Mexico have not decreased as a result of major US border control policies dating to the early 1990s but have rather been re-organized and re-distributed, for example, through smuggling operations (Cornelius and Lewis 2007). The popular 'image', however, of physical bordering measures such as walls remains a potent political mechanism in the United States and elsewhere.

In the second category of 'virtual' bordering measures fall several key initiatives, including the information technology-driven United States Visitor and Immigrant Status Indicator Technology (US-VISIT) which is meant to collect biometric entry and exit data and the Western Hemisphere Travel Initiative (WHTI) which now requires all travellers to show a valid passport when entering the United States from areas within the Western Hemisphere (Hale 2006; Koslowski 2005). As follow-up report cards to the 9/11 Commission recommendations have indicated, the slow progress on these initiatives is emblematic of larger problems in homeland security reform (Carafano and Heyman 2004; Kettl 2007).

Virtual border security measures in the post-9/11 period are also key elements within major bilateral and trilateral mechanisms developed by the United States, Canada, and Mexico over the past decade that seek to help regulate the continent's shared frontiers. The 'Smart Border' and *Security and Prosperity Partnership* accords, among others, for instance involve cross-border information and intelligence sharing, cargo preclearance procedures, 'e-passports' (biometrically enhanced documents), 'e-manifests' (which requires truckers to transmit cargo information electronically to U.S. Customs and Border Protection, now in effect for Mexico and most of Canada), and other similar systems (Ackleson and Kastner 2006). As many of these initiatives involve more than policing at the physical frontier, *non-territorial* border control appears to be emerging in North America, just as it has, in somewhat different ways, in Europe. Through an analysis of US control practices away from its frontier, such as interior immigration policing, Matthew Coleman has similarly identified this emergent non-territorial logic of border control in the US, particularly oriented towards counter-terrorism and migration control ends (Coleman 2007).

While Mexico has offered cooperation on several of these counter-terrorism initiatives, it remains concerned about other security matters – particularly the record levels of narco-trafficking that have recently ravaged its northern frontier zone. This public security issue in Mexico has complicated that country's border control efforts. This is clearly exemplified in the case of Mexico's loosely guarded southern frontier with Guatemala. That frontier has received additional attention in the post-9/11 era due to worries it is a 'soft' entry point into North America (Castillo 2003). Despite law enforcement efforts in the region by the Mexican government, the area remains a transit point for a variety of CTA flows and is an item of concern in U.S. negotiations with Mexico. Thus, we can conclude that, even in the post-9/11 security environment, border management practices in North America remain inconsistent and differentiated.

The European Union: Redeploying Borders

As Peter Andreas (2003) and Malcolm Anderson (1996) note, border management in Europe has seen a dramatic turn away from military purposes, often their primary historical function. With the process of European integration accelerating over the past few decades, on the surface, it is clear that internal borders in the European Union have in some important ways become less salient, particularly under the expanding Schengen agreement which has now dissolved internal borders between most EU states (Migration Policy Institute 2007). While border checks in this zone are now rare, EU states now rely increasingly on cross-border policing methods and intelligence to monitor their shared and open frontiers. In effect, many functional dimensions (such as policing) of previous (pre-Schengen) internal border control forces and policies have not necessarily been eliminated but rather simply *redeployed* in different ways. The 'Schengen Information System (SIS)', and its successor SIS II, for example, contain a shared database of millions of records of non-EU citizens linked with immigration and law enforcement data. Additional biometric identifies are to be added to the system. Thus, rather than borders in the EU disappearing, one can instead see the production of new kinds of borders. In concert with this, as Didier Bigo (2000) suggests, internal and external security in the EU are increasingly becoming merged. Indeed, as the recent *European Security Strategy* acknowledges, 'the post-Cold War environment is one of increasingly open borders in which the internal and external aspects of security are indissolubly linked' (European Council 2003, 2).

This dynamic is occurring just as the *external* frontiers of the European Union continue to be reinforced and cooperatively policed. The EU has set aside 1.82 billion Euros between 2007 and 2013 to help member states patrol the EU's external borders (EU Commission 2006). In 2005, it also launched the European Agency for the Management of Operational Cooperation at the External Borders of the Member States of the European Union or Frontex. Frontex uses intelligence-sharing, risk assessment, and coordination of Member State border management activities (Donoghue et al. 2006).

Frontex represents an outcome of collective EU efforts to deal with migration flows and border control measures generally. These policies involve a multi-layered approach, including external border checks, policing CTAs within and without the EU area, common third-country treatment, and interagency coordination. EU policies have, according to Sergio Carrera (2006, 2), involved a 'reinforcement of the security rationale at common EU external territorial borders – through the development of a discursive nexus between an integrated approach on borders (IBM) – and a global approach on migration'.

For large portions of the world such as the global South, the events of 9/11 have had a relatively marginal impact on border control practices. The rising toll of migrant flows (and deaths) of Africans attempting to enter the EU through Spain, eastern Europeans entering the EU through new member states, and other CTA flows, attest to public and political concern about mobility. The Canary Islands, for example, are facing new, record influxes of migrants seeking access to the EU (Carling 2007). Such cases attract significant media attention, leading to the creeping societal 'unease' about migrants that exists in some communities of the European Union. These developments attest the existence of what some scholars have called an 'internal security deficit' discourse in Europe (Bigo 2001). This has led to the securitization of migration – particularly concerning certain components of the migrant community such as Muslims and the EU's enlargement eastward. As Javier Solana, the EU's former High Representative for Common Foreign and Security Policy clearly put it in a speech to the European Parliament: 'massive flow of drugs and migrants are coming to Europe and affect its security. These threats are significant by themselves, but it is their combination that constitutes a radical challenge to our security' (2003).

Such statements serve to securitize migration and border control in the EU, just as they do elsewhere (Buzan et al. 1998). They speak to the fact that, as Bigo, Carrera, and Guild (2008) argue, the issues of migration and borders will remain 'key dimensions' of the EU agenda. The European Parliament passed a controversial set of EU rules for dealing with illegal immigration; under the new rules, illegal immigrants can be detained for up to 18 months and face a five-year re-entry ban (BBC 2008). It is clear that migration and security will be linked and related to border management issues in the EU for the foreseeable future. Despite this general trend, as Berg and Ehin argue, the EU's external border regime remains fragmented and differentiated, in and of itself (Berg and Ehin 2006).

Other Areas: Traditional Border Practices and Problems Persist

Beyond the highly developed economies of North American and Europe, for a good part of the world, particularly the global South, the events of 9/11 have had a relatively marginal impact on border control practices. In some places border control as it is understood in the West is non-existent, with loosely controlled, or in some cases, non-demarcated borders; in this sense, de-territorialized practices remain relevant to study. This historically was the case in Africa, for example, as

Englebert, Tarango, and Carter argue, suggesting that 'boundary zones were fluid as jurisdiction faded from the centre toward the periphery' and 'the concept of territorial delimitation of political control was by and large culturally alien' (2002, 1095). Nevertheless, as the process of bordering by modern nation-states in Africa accelerates, scholarly attention is required and, unfortunately, often absent from the literature.

In other places, traditional, military-driven border security practices remain important. While the placement of most of the world's land boundaries are now commonly accepted, a strain of research often led by the International Boundaries Research Unit (IBRU) at the University of Durham continues to examine persistent territorial boundary disputes. For example, states such as Ecuador and Peru have, as recently as the late 1990s, contested the placement of their common international border, resorting to violence to do so (Radcliffe 1998). The war between Ethiopia and Eritrea that began in 1998 was largely over border demarcation; while a peace agreement was signed in 2000, tensions remain and sporadic violence occurs despite the deployment of a UN peacekeeper force (Jacquin-Berdal and Plaut 2004). Such conflicts are but a few examples of border-related disputes that are charged not only with power dynamics, resource demands, geopolitical factors, as well as national identity, history, and remain a testament to the power of territorial attachments and security considerations (Mandel 1980). For these actors, border management remains a largely military matter.

The security function of borders is salient in another region of the world: the Middle East. There, hard international barriers remain popular; the Israeli security barrier is but the most prominent example of re-territorialization there. Officials in Egypt and Israel are negotiating a new fence in the Sinai desert between the two states; Egypt is also building a ten foot-high concrete wall along its border with the Gaza Strip in a bid to prevent a repetition of a January 2008 incident which saw Palestinians flood into Egypt (Makovsky 2004; Rynhold 2004). The US military is paying increasing attention to the border between Iraq and Syria and has constructed numerous security barriers in ethnically-contested areas of Iraq. Just east of the region, India remains committed to a project begun in the 1980s to seal its entire 1,800-mile border with Pakistan with high-tech surveillance equipment and an electrified fence; India is also at work on a USD 1 billion project constructing a steel barrier right along its 2,500-mile border with Bangladesh (Lakshmi 2003; Prasad 2005).

These short vignettes are but a few of the many complicated examples of border management issues facing policymakers and scholars today. They illustrate the diversity of border management issues facing political leaders worldwide and further suggest the conclusion drawn here regarding differentiated border policy regimes, and as I argue below, signal the need for refocused and comparative research frameworks.

Research Considerations

The Framework of Policy Regime Analysis

While it may be of interest to catalogue the various empirical dynamics of border security today, a perhaps more important issue is how we understand the *politics* behind these border security initiatives. Unfortunately, research in the border management realm may be theoretically narrow, be overly tied to narrow disciplinary perspectives, or limited to certain geographic areas. Too often students and scholars do not engage the examination of the social and political processes which underpin all border management efforts. Part of the issue in doing that is locating appropriate research frameworks that may offer robust theoretical power to explain differentiated border management policies.

While many approaches exist, one way of approaching research in this area is to look at border security in terms of *policy regimes*. The concept of regimes is well-known to students of International Relations, connoting international 'governing arrangements constructed by states', often around an issue area (Kratochwil and Ruggie 1997). In terms of policy, regimes are defined and explored somewhat differently in the public policy literature as well as in the discipline of Economics. The concept emerged, as Wison (2000) argues in an influential piece, due to dissatisfaction with the mainstream policy change literature because each approach in that genre (such as the ideological, elitist, advocacy, and the political process models) highlights one dimension of change but disregards others. In my view, the complicated and interrelated nature of border control processes do not lend themselves to such mono-dimensional modes of analysis and thus fit well within Wison's policy regime approach. His conception of a policy regime consists of four elements: (1) the arrangement of power (which involves interest groups, the state, and other actors); (2) a policy paradigm (which defines the problem and solutions and includes public and academic discourses); (3) the government organization and implementation structures; (4) the policy itself (the goals of the policy regime and rules of implementation) (2000, 258).

Policy regimes, defined as such, bring important and inter-related components into our view for analysis, such as ideas, interests, actors, and institutions. Most critically, integrating this concept into the discussion offers us a clearer way to study policy regime *change* – for example, why governments adopt certain policies over time. Such an analysis may include factors such as crises (for example 9/11), power shifts (for example a change in political parties), 'stressors' (for example societal pressures) and organizational changes (for example the creation of the U.S. Department of Homeland Security). Using models of these interests and factors, we can explain why border security responses are playing out in different ways in each state and for different actors. This research framework may pave the way forward for a more in-depth analysis of the emerging politics of differentiated border security policies. While that analysis is beyond the scope of this chapter, it may be appropriate to consider in future research endeavours.

Towards a Border Security Hierarchy?

In addition to thinking about a framework centred on policy regimes, I want to add one additional thought regarding research in this area: the issue of defining and appropriating the concept of 'security'. Barry Buzan has famously suggested that security is an 'essentially contested concept' (1991, 7; Lipschutz 1995). This is the case not only among scholars but also of course among policymakers. One need only look at the application of the word 'security' to ever-more expanding domains, including 'human' security, 'economic' security, 'environmental' security, and other areas (Mathews 1989). Moreover, there is a clear bifurcation of how 'security' is understood throughout the world. For most citizens and many policymakers not in the developed world, the word tends to connote 'food security', 'public security', and other human rights-related concerns. This is clearly illustrated within North America, as noted above: Mexico's chief 'security' problems revolve around law and order; the US is broadly concerned with terrorism; and Canada, while also pursuing counter-terrorism policies values highly its 'economic security' provided by a (relatively) open border with the United States.

As demonstrated in the discussion here, most border scholars agree that the events of September 11, 2001 and subsequent policy changes in North America and Europe signalled the (re)-emergence of border securitization often coupled with a securitization of migration. Much work has emerged to examine this process (Bigo 2002; Doty 1998; Huysmans 2000). In some of the American and European political discourse during the years following these events, however, it became clear that border security has become a kind of foil for a sundry list of other 'security' concerns, some of which are directly related to terrorism threats but many others which are not. Both policymakers and academics have been responsible for this misappropriation of the terminology of 'security'. Part of this tendency can be traced to the expansion of security into the multiple domains; much more, however, can be identified with particular political projects, especially efforts to curb immigration that are often thinly disguised as 'national security' concerns. As Martin Heisler (2006) has argued, however, the nexus between migration and security, in these terms, is not particularly robust in either practice or theory.

Is there any way to achieve a clearer view of what border security threats really are in today's international environment? When considering security, it is natural to turn to the International Relations paradigm which takes security as its central problematic: realism. In that regard, we might consider John Mearsheimer's *Tragedy of Great Power Politics* (2001), an analysis of international politics and security that is strongly oriented towards security vis-à-vis offensive realism (Mearsheimer 2001). His work in particular is clearly identified with neo-realism as he is concerned with the nature of the anarchical international system that conditions state behaviour. Mearsheimer's theoretical orientation establishes what he calls 'First Order' security problems critical for survival and 'Second Order' threats which are problems that do not really threaten a great power. In the category of First Order problems of current concern to the United States, for instance, Mearsheimer and others have clearly identified the rise of China. The George W. Bush Administration's 'War on Terror' also fell into this category. Both types of threats are instrumental in presenting the case for 'insecurity' in the international system, thus leading to a standard set of realist prescriptions: the accumulation and expansion of power, self-help, and so on.

Many critical IR scholars have taken issue with Mearsheimer and other realist accounts of security, including his hierarchical approach to security concerns. Lacy's (2005) work on climate change and security, for instance, offers a critique of Mearsheimer's approach. He argues that Mearsheimer's categorizations and prescriptions are built by and on 'networks of power' that legitimate this particular politics of security (ibid. 2005, 11-12). That politics of security limits our ability to see and deal with non-traditional (including second order) problems, such as climate change.

While I certainly take issue with Mearsheimer's neo-realist approach, I want to suggest here that developing a hierarchy of security concerns regarding border politics may actually make some sense because it can offer a more clear-headed view of what we mean by security and how we ought to approach border management. Certainly there will be much disagreement on how that hierarchy might be constructed. It will be necessarily political. But I think it may need to be done.

I should also note that this approach moves beyond the basic outlines of Waever's (1993) original conception of securitization theory, which as Taureck (2006) points out, in and of itself is not a political or normative theory. Rather, a hierarchical approach rests, in part, on an understanding of 'securitization as normative practice', that is, that we can make moral and ethical, as well as pragmatic, policy-based claims about security discourses and practices (Aradau 2004; Huysmans 1995).

In doing this, I think it makes sense to distinguish between border *threats* and border *problems* within First and Second Order issues in the hierarchy. In this regard, one can clearly place traditional military threats, transnational terrorism, weapons of mass destruction, virulent public health concerns such as high-pathology avian influenza in the broad category of 'threats' (and likely 'First Order' ones). However, we might not include migration as a border 'threat', and as such, de-securitize it within border politics, potentially opening up different ways to deal with it within policy regimes. In this regard, we would seek to alter the 'policy paradigm' component of the policy regime which defines the issue – in this case as a problem, not a threat, thus leading to different solutions.

Such a categorization is undoubtedly controversial and rife with problems because no consensus exists on many border or societal security issues. The problem, of course, in doing this is that it likely will remain an academic exercise which may make sense but does not impact how border policy regimes are playing out on the ground. The reason for this is that political actors and systems convert problems into 'threats' in the securitization process for largely interest-based reasons. Nevertheless, additional work to develop a hierarchy – and then apply it – may be useful for both researchers and policymakers given the limited resources available to police borders and the difficulties of achieving full or absolute 'border security' as such.

Conclusions: Towards an Interdisciplinary Dialogue

This chapter has offered some reflections on the empirical changes underway in border management policies in several parts of the world. More than a question of open or closed borders, the picture is, I argue, complex, differentiated, and often unclear.

As discussed at the outset of this chapter, innovative research on the dynamics of mobility, borders, and security under globalization is underway. As I have argued, however, too often our research focuses on describing change or continuity in border management (the de- and re-territorialization duality) but does not adequately explain the reasons *why* such change or continuity exists. Therefore, there are still important gaps in our understanding. I suggested here that we may need re-organized and re-energized research frameworks to move forward. Those frameworks might include the idea of *policy regimes* and *security hierarchies* of first and second order problems. Policy regime analysis, along with securitization theory, and normative securitization theory in particular, can help us make sense of the process of how 'problems' become 'threats' within the political sphere. The normative dimension of this approach can allow researchers to offer judgments about the political and ethical basis of these moves.

In order to tackle the complexity of diverse border security policy regimes, the best meta-approach to studying these questions may be grounded in an interdisciplinary research (IDR) framework. Such a framework is compatible with the tenor of the genre of 'border studies' which may be traced to the late 1980s. That highly interdisciplinary enterprise included contributions from Political Science, Political Geography, Literature, Anthropology and others. The problems borders and border management present, particularly the growing complexity of issues underneath differentiated control regimes, in my view, demand analysis from multiple disciplinary perspectives.

This assertion is confirmed for science in general by a major study conducted by the US National Academies entitled *Facilitating Interdisciplinary Research* (National Academies 2005). While advances in IDR appear to be occurring, particularly in science and engineering, it is not clear that a robust and sustained effort is being made in the area of border studies. This may be the case due to a number of important barriers that the National Academies report points out, including institutional, cultural, administrative, publication and other barriers. The same study concluded that 'the success of IDR groups depends on institutional commitment and research leadership. Leaders with clear vision and effective communication and team-building skills can catalyze the integration of disciplines' (ibid., 2).

Accordingly, strong efforts to foster these qualities should be a prerequisite for organized research along these lines. I would conclude then by making the case for more *comparative* border management research. Too often, border security research is done on a handful of cases globally – the European Union and the U.S.-Mexico border, for instance, receive far too much attention relative to other areas of the world. (This chapter is no exception to this trend.) We know far too little about border management practices in Africa or Asia. And, worse still we have very few rigorous comparative analyses beyond treatment of North America vis-à-vis the EU. Insights and advances are possible with a broader border research agenda. Solid, policy-relevant research from international scholars in border studies may help address these gap as well as explain the larger reasons behind today's border management policies.

References

Ackleson, J. (2007), 'Mobility and North American Border Security', in Mace, G. and Durepos, C. (eds.), *The New Security Equation in the Americas* (Quebec City: Université Laval), 189-203, published online May 2007 <http://www.cei.ulaval.ca/recherche_et_publications/autres_publications/>.

Ackleson, J. and Kastner, J. (2006), 'The Security and Prosperity Partnership for North America', *American Review of Canadian Studies* 36:2, 207-32.

Albert, M. (1998), 'On Boundaries, Territory, and Postmodernity: An International Relations Perspective', *Geopolitics* 3, 53-68.

Anderson, M. (1996), *Frontiers: Territory and State Formation in the Modern World* (Cambridge: Policy).

Andreas, P. (2003), 'Redrawing the Line: Borders and Security in the Twenty-first Century', *International Security* 28:2, 78-111.

Andreas, P. and Biersteker, T.J. (eds.)(2003), *The Rebordering of North America: Integration and Exclusion in a New Security Context* (New York: Routledge).

Aradau, C. (2004), 'Security and the Democratic Scene: Desecuritization and Emancipation', *Journal of International Relations and Development* 7:4, 388-413.

Associated Press-Ipsos Poll (2008), conducted 3-5 March 2008, results available at <http://www.pollingreport.com/immigration.htm>.

BBC News (2008), 'EU Approves Illegal Migrants Plan', 18 June <http://news.bbc.co.uk/2/hi/europe/7460007.stm>.

Berg, E. and Ehin, P. (2006), 'What Kind of Border Regime in the Making? Towards a Differentiated and Uneven Border Strategy', *Cooperation and Conflict* 41, 53-71.

Bigo, D. (2002), 'Security and Immigration: Toward a Critique of the Governmentality of Unease', *Alternatives: Global, Local, Political* 27, 63-92.

Bigo, D. (2001), 'Migration and Security', in Guiraudon, V. and Joppke, C. (eds.), *Controlling a New Migration World* (New York: Taylor and Francis).

Bigo, D. (2000), 'When Two Become One: Internal and External Securitizations in Europe', in Kelstrup, M. and Williams, M.C. (eds.), *International Relations Theory and the Politics of European Integration: Power, Security, and Community* (London: Routledge).

Bigo, D., Carrera, S. and Guild, E. (2008), 'What Future for the Area of Freedom, Security and Justice? Recommendations on EU Migration and Borders Policies in a Globalising World', *Centre for European Policy Studies Policy Brief* 20 March 2008, available at <http://shop.ceps.eu/BookDetail.php?item_id=1627&>.

Buzan, B. (1991), *People, States, and Fear* (Boulder CO: Lynne Rienner), 7.

Buzan, B., Waever, O. and de Wilde, J. (1998), *Security: A New Framework of Analysis* (Boulder CO: Lynne Rienner).

Carafano, J.J. and Heyman, D. (2004), 'DHS 2.0: Rethinking the Department of Homeland Security', *Heritage Foundation Special Report* 2, 13 December 2004, available at <http://www.heritage.org/Research/HomelandDefense/upload/72759_1.pdf>.

Carling, J. (2007), 'Migration Control and Migrant Fatalities at the Spanish-African Borders', *International Migration Review* 41:2, 316-43.

Carrera, S. (2007), *The EU Border Management Strategy: FRONTEX and the Challenges of Irregular Immigration in the Canary Islands* (Brussels: Centre for Euopean Policy Studies), 2.

Castillo, M.A. (2003), 'The Mexico-Guatemala Border: New Controls on Transborder Migrations in View of Recent Integration Schemes', *Frontera Norte* 15:29, 35-65.

Coleman, M. (2007), 'Immigration Geopolitics beyond the US-Mexico Border', *Geopolitics* 12:4, 607-34.

Cornelius, W.A. and Lewis, J.M. (eds.)(2007), *Impacts of Border Enforcement on Mexican Migration: The View from Sending Communities* (Boulder, CO: Lynne Rienner Publishers, Center for Comparative Immigration Studies).

Cornelius, W.A. and Salehyan, I. (2007), 'Does Border Enforcement Deter Unauthorized Immigration? The Case of Mexican Migration to the United States of America', *Regulation & Governance* 1:2, 139-53.

Deleuze, G. and Guattari, F. (1987), *A Thousand Plateaus: Capitalism and Schizophrenia* (Minneapolis: University of Minnesota Press).

Donoghue, J., Ryan, J. and Vent, A. (2006), 'Report on Frontex: The European Union's New Border Security Agency' (Dublin: Institute of European Affairs), available at <http://www.iiea.com/images/managed/news_attachments/Frontex.pdf>.

Doty, R.L. (1998), 'Immigration and the Politics of Security', *Security Studies* 8:2, 71-93.

Englebert, P., Tarango, S. and Carter, M. (2002), 'Dismemberment and Suffocation: A Contribution to the Debate on African Boundaries', *Comparative Political Studies* 35:10, 1093-118.

EU Commission (2006), *Communication from the EU Commission to the Council – Reinforcing the management of the European Union's Southern Maritime Borders*, Document COM/2006/0733, 30 November 2006, available at <http://eur-ex.europa.eu/smartapi/cgi/sga_doc?smartapi!celexplus!prod!DocNumber&type_doc=COMfinal&an_doc=2006&nu_doc=733&lg=en>.

European Council (2003), *A Secure Europe in a Better World: The European Security Strategy*, 12 December 2003 (Brussels: European Council), available at <http://www.consilium.europa.eu/cms3_fo/showPage.ASP?id=266&lang=EN&mode=g>.

Hale, G.E. (2006), 'Western Hemisphere Travel Initiative: Now for the Hard Part', *Fraser Institute Forum Report* December 2006, available at <http://www.fraserinstitute.org/commerce.web/product_files/Dec06ffHale.pdf>.

Heisler, M. (2006), 'The Migration-Security Nexus after 9/11: The Securitization of Regional Migration in North America in Comparative Perspective', *paper presented at the annual meeting of the International Studies Association* 22 March 2006 (San Diego).

Holsti, K.J. (2004), *Taming the Sovereigns: Institutional Change in International Politics* (Cambridge: Cambridge University Press), 73.

Huysmans, J. (2000), 'The European Union and the Securitization of Migration', *Journal of Common Market Studies* 38:5, 751-77.

Huysmans, J. (1995), 'Migrants as a Security Problem: Dangers of "Securitizing" Societal Issues', in Miles, R. and Thraenhart, D. (eds.), *Migration and European Integration: The Dynamics of Inclusion and Exclusion* (London: Pinter), 53-72.

Jacquin-Berdal, D. and Plaut, M. (eds.)(2004), *Unfinished Business: Ethiopia And Eritrea At War* (Trenton NJ: Red Sea Press).

Kettl, D.F. (2007), *System under Stress: Homeland Security and American Politics*, second edition (Washington DC: Congressional Quarterly Press).

Koslowski, R. (2005), *Real Challenges for Virtual Borders: The Implementation of US-VISIT* (Washington DC: Migration Policy Institute).

Krasner, S. (1999), *Sovereignty: Organized Hypocrisy* (Princeton: Princeton University Press).

Kratochwil, F. and Ruggie, J.G. (1997), 'International Organization: The State of the Art', in Diehl, P.F. (ed.), *The Politics of Global Governance: International Organizations in an Interdependent World* (Boulder CO: Lynne Rienner), 32.

Lacy, M.J. (2005), *Security and Climate Change: International Relations and The Limits Of Realism* (London: Routledge).

Lakshmi, R. (2003), 'India's Border Fence Extended to Kashmir: Country Aims to Stop Pakistani Infiltration', *The Washington Post* 30 July 2003.

Lipschutz, R.D. (ed.)(1995), *On Security* (New York: Columbia University Press).

Makovsky, D. (2004), 'How to Build a Fence', *Foreign Affairs* 83:2, 50-64.

Mandel, R. (1980), 'Roots of the Modern Interstate Border Dispute', *The Journal of Conflict Resolution* 24:3, 427-54.

Martinez, O. (2006), 'The Dynamics of Border Interaction: New Approaches to Border Analysis', in Shofield, C. (ed.), *World Boundaries – Volume 1: Global Boundaries* (New York: Routledge).

Mathews, J. (1989), 'Redefining Security', *Foreign Affairs* 68:2, 162-77.

Mearsheimer, J.J. (2001), *The Tragedy of Great Power Politics* (New York: WW Norton), 3.

Migration Policy Institute (2007), 'Europe's Internal Borders Disappearing', *Migration Policy Institute Fact Sheet*, available at <http://www.migrationpolicy.org/pubs/FS20_SchengenDisappearingBorders_121807.pdf>.

Migration Policy Institute (2005), 'Independent Task force on Immigration and America's Future: Appendix A: A Selected Timeline of Events that Relate to Border Enforcement', *MPI Insight 7* (Washington, DC: Migration Policy Institute).

National Academies of Science (2005), *Facilitating Interdisciplinary Research*, Committee on Facilitating Interdisciplinary Research (Washington DC: The National Academies Press).

National Commission on Terrorist Attacks Upon the United States (2004), *Entry of the 9/11 Hijackers into the United States: Staff Statement No. 1*, available at <http://govinfo.library.unt.edu/911/staff_statements/staff_statement_1.pdf>.

Newman, D. (2006), 'Borders and Bordering: Towards an Interdisciplinary Dialogue', *European Journal of Social Theory* 9, 171-86.

Nuñez-Neto, B. and Kim, Y. (2008), 'Border Security: Barriers Along the U.S. International Border', *CRS Report for Congress* RL33659 (Washington, DC: Congressional Research Service), available at <http://fpc.state.gov/documents/organization/105162.pdf>.

Ohmae, K. (1995), *End of the Nation State: The Rise of Regional Economies* (New York: Free Press).

O Tuathail, G. (1998), 'Political Geography III: Dealing with Deterritorialization', *Progress in Human Geography* 22, 81-93.

Paasi, A. (1998), 'Boundaries as Social Process: Territoriality in the World of Flows', *Geopolitics* 3, 69-88.

Philpott, D. (2006), 'Securing the Nation's Borders', *Homeland Defense Journal* 4:7, 20-26.

Prasad, R. (2005), 'India Builds a 2,500-mile Barrier to Rival the Great Wall of China', *The Times London* 28 December 2005, available at <http://www.timesonline.co.uk/tol/news/world/asia/article782933.ece>.

Radcliffe, S.A. (1998), 'Frontiers and Popular Nationhood: Geographies of Identity in the 1995 Ecuador-Peru Border Dispute', *Political Geography* 17:3, 273-93.

Rynhold, J. (2004), 'Israel's Fence: Can Separation Make Better Neighbours?', *Survival* 46:1, 55-76.

Sack, R. (1986), *Human Territoriality: Its Theory and History* (Cambridge: Cambridge University Press).

Shamir, R. (2005), 'Without Borders? Notes on Globalization as a Mobility Regime', *Sociological Theory* 23:2, 197-217.

Solana, J. (2003), *Address to the European Parliament*, Document S0137/03, 18 June 2003 (Brussels), available at [http://www.consilium.europa.eu/ueDocs/cms_Data/docs/pressdata/en/discours/76240.pdf].

Taureck, R. (2006), 'Securitization Theory and Securitization Studies', *Journal of International Relations and Development* 9, 53-61.

Turner, B. (2007), 'The Enclave Society: Towards a Sociology of Immobility', *European Journal of Social Theory* 10:2, 287-304.

U.S. Department of Homeland Security (2005), *Fact Sheet: Secure Border Initiative* 2 November 2005, available at <http://www.dhs.gov/xnews/releases/press_release_0794.shtml>.

U.S. Customs and Border Protection (2009), *Snapshot: A Summary of CBP Facts and Figures*, available at <http://www.cbp.gov/linkhandler/cgov/about/accomplish/facts_figures.ctt/facts_figures.pdf>.

Waever, O. et al. (1993), *Identity, Migration and the New Security Agenda in Europe* (New York: St. Martin's Press).

Wison, C.A. (1991), 'Policy Regimes and Policy Change', *Journal of Public Policy* 20, 247-74.

Building Borders the Hard Way: Enforcing North American Security Post 9/11

Heather Nicol

Introduction

While Ohmae (1990) contended that the pressure of global trade, flows of information, people and goods within a world economy and global market place could not sustain the impediment of borders, this borderless world has yet to materialize. Instead, the North American states, which sustain the world's largest trade flows among themselves, have built ever-higher fences, ostensibly by U.S. interests in protection of the American 'homeland'. But also it would appear that these fences are designed to include neighbours, through harmonization processes, while fortifying the continental American 'homeland' from the broader reach of globalization. These walls facilitate interaction with states whose foreign policies, security programs, ideology and 'values' correspond to American ones. The danger posed for Americans is not from their 'near neighbours', and for these states the walls are there to build or force compliance, rather than exclusion. Indeed, neighbours are encouraged to replicate U.S. security standards and to merge with U.S. homeland interests. In other words, U.S. security policies are implemented through agreements and border controls meant to incorporate neighbours rather than exclude them, but to incorporate them under the terms of U.S. domestic security agendas instead of through foreign policies, diplomacy or broader treaties and international agreements.

Thus, while the phrase 'partnership' currently characterizes the discourse of North American policy-makers involved in building secure borders, this partnership is not particularly accurate. The response to the December 2009 'Christmas Bomber', for example, was to encourage the future use of full body scanners of all air travelers to America. This full body search is in addition to other forms of surveillance and documentation recently imposed through the Western Hemisphere Travel Initiative (WHTI), the PATRIOT Act, as well as various other post 9/11 policies and legislation. While the latter effectively fortifies borders in North America from the outside, its biggest impact is within North America and upon North Americans, as they are the travelers who most frequently cross U.S. borders. These practices and policies fix bordering practices firmly in U.S.-centered ways, rather than in terms of the joint security concerns among North American nations – if we understand North American security in broader terms to include Canada and Mexico, both of which have very different security priorities than the United States (Konrad and Nicol 2008).

Rather than a neutral and consensual process of applying 'best-practices' along border lines (as the process is often defined by policy-makers), the real result of post 9/11 in North America has been its contribution to the hegemony of U.S. securitization and management practices continent wide. These security practices have been loaded-on at North American border sites, and have become, in effect, hegemonic. Resulting from the landscape of post 9/11 U.S. domestic politics and obsessed with 'total security', North American border management today reflects an evolving landscape of state-centered interest in building both physical and virtual walls. Significant political pressure, as well the fear of limited access to the U.S. markets, have proven to be important incentives for neighbourly cooperation. Canadian policy-makers would not, for example, want to be seen as negligent, or as responsible for a security breech, mainly because of its implications for Americas relations. In this way, Canadian security needs are recast as being the same as American. North American countries other than the U.S. do not have a real voice in setting common, or continental, security measures – there is nobody to represent or discuss these continental issues outside of a series of bilateral negotiations. There were hopes that the now defunct Security and Prosperity Partnership (SPP), initiated in 2005, would implement trilateral security cooperation, but even then there was no binding agreement. And, as we shall see, the SPP was never intended to offer an alternative to U.S.-style security, but rather to implement it more quickly.

Even the recently implemented Western Hemisphere Travel Initiative (WHTI), is not a Western Hemisphere Initiative at all, but a U.S. law universalizing documentation protocols of American security to which Canadians and Mexicans must conform. Americans seemingly now believe unilateralism is the most efficient approach to securitization, and security measures have tightened, rather than loosened, under the current Obama Administration. Even security measures implemented by neighbouring states are still considered to be 'weak links'.[1] Harvey (2004) argues that American unilateralism has consistently eschewed the building of alliances with democracies for more specific goals of the war on terror, despite such initiatives as the SPP or other 'partnerships'. Indeed Sokolsky and Legassé comment that 'above all the United States, the loudest promoter of a North American security perimeter, is the least inclined to depend upon a trilateral regime to protect the American homeland' (Sokolsky and Legassé 2006, 15).

This chapter explores some of the recent ways in which border security has been theorized with respect to North America in general, and the Canada-U.S. border

---

1   This was the basis, for example, of Department of Homeland Security (DHS) Secretary Janet Napolitano's mistaken comments in 2009 (still circulating a full eight years after 9/11!), suggesting that the 9/11 terrorists had crossed over Canadian border.

in particular, and evaluates the role of these U.S. security frameworks in orienting twenty-first century North American border practices. How does border security implement U.S. hegemony? Is the delivery of heightened levels of border security linked to substantive changes in the power and role of the U.S. state post 9/11?

We begin with an evaluation of two important frameworks for understanding border control and emerging management practices in North America. The first situates the security power of North American borders within the framework of risk assessment and neoliberalism (Dillon 2008; de Goede 2008; Sparke 2005). The second situates it within what Walters (2006) has called control society, implemented through diffuse modes of power (Deleuze 2008). We then link these frameworks of risk assessment and border control to emerging border cooperation in North America along the Canada-U.S. border and explore how new hegemonic and diffuse border practices have developed, themselves the product of new forms of governance, themselves diffuse and expansive and implementing new forms of control incrementally, without real public debate. Arguing that the concentration of U.S. hegemony impulses at North American borders, under conditions of neoliberal trade, is a relatively new development which coincides with new forms of governance, the second half of this chapter thus explores next the way in which state structure, neoliberalism and governance are important to understand the rise of diffuse security power through the U.S. 'homeland security' bureaucracy. All of these factors, I argue, are responsible for the rise of a securitization discourse as the fundamental discourse for North American relations. This discourse eschews foreign relations and cooperation, and demands walls, even in the face of a continental market and a tremendous degree of cultural and economic integration.

Neoliberalism, Premediation and Control: Theorizing the Framework of North American Borders

Today, the United States, the European Union, as well as many other western (neo)liberal states take border security very seriously. The United States, in particular, situates border management firmly under the rubric of 'national security', and border enforcement is increasingly oriented towards 'domestic' or 'homeland security'. This focus on 'homeland security' and the associated rise of the Department of Homeland Security (DHS), has, in turn, facilitated an obsessive concern about cross-border management and enforcement strategies. The events of 11 September 2001 seem to have ushered in a new security era.

But is this new era really only the latest stage in a continuing series of clear historical phases in the implementation of U.S. border strategies and management policies? Payan (2006) identifies four phases in the mobilization of different U.S. domestic concerns over time along the U.S.-Mexican border, beginning with a nineteenth century focus on customs and revenue enforcement, continuing through a period of immigration control, followed by an obsession with criminality, 'law and order', to an early twenty-first century obsession with homeland security. The latter phase results from a discourse of insecurity, emanating not just from fear of terrorism, but from the perceived organized crime and illegal immigration along this border.

For Payan, each phase in border perception and management corresponds to broader discourses about foreigners, Mexicans, criminality and security and it is very clear from Payan's work, that there exists a state of general anxiety about the Mexican. This, he claims, has become the dominant border motif in recent years, bundling together the disparate issues of criminality, immigration and terrorism, and counterpoising them against the perceived absence of border control. This approach is reminiscent of Pickering and Weber's (2006) argument that discourses identifying borders as a space for 'criminality' are recent, and that the 'intersections of legitimacy, force, sovereignty and resistance at the border', make the border itself a force of control in unprecedented ways (Pickering and Weber 2006, 4).

Yet Payan's observations are by no means exhaustive of the way that North American border management has been framed. Other researchers suggest that rather than dividing communities by nationality or race, there is an evolving link between current border management policies, neoliberal and corporate policy agendas pushing for continental integration, and broader patterns of risk management (de Goede 2008; Isin 2004; Sparke 2005). Sparke argues, for example, that '[t]he deeper and more complexly inter-scalar issues raised by the intersection of homeland securitization and economic facilitation at the border concern the transformation of citizenship on a continent shaped by a notably neoliberal nexus of securitized nationalism and free market transnationalism' (Sparke 2005, 153). The result is the biopoliticization of risk within North American contexts: biopoliticization in the sense that Dillon (2008, 310) suggests that these transformative neoliberal pressures now 'take "life" as their referent object'. Because 'the biopoliticization of security installs risk as one of its single most important devices', risk assessment techniques originally developed for the securitization of financial markets become the measure of individual security (ibid. 2008). In this way, post 9/11 de-securitization protocols continue the implementation of a continental neoliberal agenda, working towards the creation of a hegemonic North American business class, and, by extension, the creation of a North American neoliberal space (Sparke 2005). As Dillon asserts, 'risk has become a universal feature of biopolitical governance' (Dillon 2008, 329).

But for others, the application of risk management strategies to the pre-9/11 border meant that by the end of the first decade of the twenty-first century risk assessment had become almost impossible, an exercise in calculating for infinite scenarios – or a 'premeditation problem' (de Goede 2008). Premeditation is more than a technical problem, however. It is also both a political and cultural process, and it lies at the juncture of politics and culture. De Goede defines premeditation as the way in which security managers, news media and cultural industries all 'map out as many of the possible worlds, or possible paths, as the future could be imagined to take' (de Goede 2008, 158):

What about poison in the New York reservoir system? What about a private plane flying into a nuclear reactor? ... Such imaginative practices respond to the 9/11 Commission's call for scenario testing and are thought to enable the pre-emption of security threats ... Though not new, the political importance of premeditation and its ability to inform security action in the present has significantly increased in the post-9/11 context. (De Goede 2008, 158)

It is exactly this normalization of the practice of premeditation which fuels insecurity, so that premeditation itself has increased to the point where uncertainty itself is a threat and where the 'security of everything' is the answer (Isin 2004). In such a world uncertainty is pervasive, and itself constitutes a threat 'because we don't have any clear basis for making such a judgment' (Homer-Dixon 2008). While the normative application of risk assesses likelihoods or probabilities in terms of risk categories or classes, premeditated risk does not. It is firmly focused on the individual's body, on the individual's biometrics and individual's personal data. It looks for certainty, for possibility, rather than probability. In this sense, the new role of technology is to replace the process of premeditated risk, to 'discover the wolf in sheep's clothing'. But is also makes all sheep suspect.

The end result has been a shift in the way in which risk is assessed and policed in border areas. While Spark's analysis concerning the role of borders in effectively disciplining a North American neoliberal citizenship has currency, particularly when coupled with recent literature on premeditation, it is important to note that for others, these new bordering practices and rationalities represent a broader management of uncertainty which potentially replaces, rather than continues, risk management strategies and corresponding neo-liberal frameworks. Walters (2006), for example, suggests that recent border enforcement practice reflects the fact that we are witness to an age of 'control borders' and 'control society' which he reduces to the motif of 'border/control'.

The role of technology, in the form of full body scans, iris scanners, biometric readers, machine readable passports, linked data sets and other detectors and devices reduce individuals to specific sets of data, or even bits of data and codes (see de Goede 2008; Deleuze 2008; Sparke 2006). This means that the process of control is not only diffuse, but disaggregated, focused on individuals and pieces of individual data rather than the holistic individual who steps forward with a passport (see Salter 2004). As Deleuze reminds us '[t]he numerical language of control is made of codes that mark access to information, or reject it. We no longer find ourselves dealing with the mass/individual pair. Individuals have become *"dividuals"*' (Deleuze 2008 in Walters 2006). Walters argues that this change is significant and societal because control society is strongly linked to communications and information technologies rather than bounded institutional enclosures. Indeed, Walters reminds us, as a result of technological dividuation, there is a disaggregation of border functions away from the border itself (Walters 2006, 196).

This diffusion which Walters, Deleuze and others attribute to new forms of societal control, power relations and border security practices is a crucial condition for U.S. hegemony at North American borders; it is performed and reproduced through the practices, discourses and performances of border security. Security is thus more than simply a generic power. In North America, at least, security is the agent of hegemony, and as such its performance at borders reifies place-specific, hegemonic relations through the 'exceptionalism' which Salter (2008) identifies. Indeed, Salter (2008) links securitization to the exercise of sovereignty, suggesting that '[t]he border is a permanent state of exception, which makes the "normal" biopolitical control of government inside the territorial frontier of the state possible' (Salter 2008, 365). Yet the point that Salter raises is how this extraordinary occurrence is now nothing 'extra-ordinary' at all, not temporary or transient, but permanent.

Yet whose extraordinary power has become permanent? Current power relationships within the North American continent ensure that U.S.-style security will be practiced within neighbouring countries as well as between them. This not only creates new types of hegemony in border practice by challenging the sanctity of territorial sovereignty, it also reflects the way in which power itself has been remapped. Ultimately the changing internal landscape of control along borderlines and beyond borders requires rather new ways of structuring the state and its bureaucracy.

Indeed, the legitimacy of the power of security is derived from what Foucault has called 'the coupling of a set of practices and a regime of truth from an apparatus (dispositive) of knowledge and power that effectively marks out in reality that which does not exist and legitimately submits it to the division between true and false' (Foucault 2007, 19). It is here, also, where the 'Christmas Bomber', who set himself on fire during a flight to the U.S. on Christmas Day, 2009, has special relevance. North American border discourses, practices and relationships, do much more than symbolically reinforce the fences which facilitate continental divide. They facilitate a disciplinary effect for citizens and foreigners alike. They also enforce more general patterns of U.S. hegemony through mobilization of diffuse border management processes increasingly embedded in biometric and biopolitical processes. In this sense border control is a permanent state of exceptional power which is linked to the performance of sovereignty itself (Salter 2008). This facilitates a new border discourse of 'defend and extend', and it is now at the heart of North American border management. Indeed, all of the frameworks for understanding current North American border security so far discussed in this section attempt to identify how processes such as sovereignty and neoliberalism are institutionalized through borders and how they survive and even thrive, as resilient frameworks which condition the formation of international boundaries.

So it is not just raw sovereignty power that is currently performed at borders of North America, it is also hegemonic power rooted in North American relations. Although current North American border security practices have been presented as discourses which reflect joint security concerns among North American nations, consensual and cooperative, they are more accurately seen as a manifestation of the statist expressions of territorially sovereign power (Pickering and Weber 2006, 4; Salter 2008), and more specifically, U.S. power. Much as Pickering and Weber have suggested, these territorially sovereign borders have also produced malleable borders which 'unlock powerful new expressions of jurisdictionally-free political power' (Pickering and Weber 2006, 4).

Hegemony and the Canada-U.S. Border

In North America, as in the EU, there is a strong correlation between the production of a new security agenda implemented through firm borders, and new technologies such as biometrics and counter-terrorism agendas (Vaughan-Williams 2008). The hardening of borderlines and their simultaneous territorial dispersion also requires the deployment of a compelling popular discourse concerning the idea that borders are being technologically 'facilitated' rather than fortified, in order to garner widespread support by citizens and politicians, policy-makers and media.

It is this discourse of 'facilitation', cooperation and partnership which has been used to describe changes in border management and protocol along the Canada-U.S. border and to garner political support for the process. In this section of the chapter I would like to look more critically at this 'cross-border partnership' and examine how contemporary border practice and security governance, has resulted in the reorganization of the Canada-U.S. border in ways which reinforce U.S. security power rather than Canadian sovereignty and autonomy. Since the late twentieth century, the mode of border control and the rationale for control in Canadian border practices has been linked to U.S. security practices, and implemented through bilateral agreements on border management and protocol. Yet we should not lose sight of the fact that while the U.S. determines the nature of border management and securitization practices, Canadians have found themselves implementing and reinforcing U.S. policies. Indeed, there has been a real process of compliance, for reasons which reflect a Canadian tradition of economic and security-oriented dependency, rooted in an asymmetrical political relationship with North America (see Clarkson 2003).

For this reason we need to examine the way in which the Canada-U.S. border is important to, or embedded within an ongoing U.S. hegemony project, in which border security is but the latest stage. This involves understanding how control is executed at the Canada-U.S. border in ways which reflect compliance *and* hegemony. We can then move towards understanding how, and why, the border security of the Canadian state has recently been rewritten in U.S. terms, and how such terms are framed for Canadians.

The success of the common security cooperation which U.S. policy-makers have built is leveraged not because of common agreement about security agendas *per se*, but because of Canadian and Mexican concerns about economic security and market access, stemming from their reliance on U.S. markets. This economic dependency has intensified through free trade agreements in the form of the Canada-U.S. Free Trade Agreement (FTA) and later the North American Free Trade Agreement (NAFTA) which included Mexico. But it is also predicated on a much longer history, marked by historical struggles over reciprocity or free trade and market access which date, in Canada case, to the mid-nineteenth century.

Thus, even though 11 September 2001 is constantly cited as the date when 'everything changed' with respect to border management in North America, it might be more accurate to say that this date marks the acceleration of, rather than the beginning of, hegemony in border practices. Hegemony has been a condition of Canada-U.S. relations for over a century. Canada was the target of a concerted American bid for 'Manifest Destiny' in the early nineteenth century. Despite Canada's Confederation in 1867 and despite Canada's open rejection of annexation to the United States, Americans have alternatively attempted to coax or conquer a hegemonic relationship with its northern neighbour since then. In the early nineteenth century, Americans described the British North American border as a natural source of friction with Britain. Later they said the same of the border with an independent Dominion of Canada, as a protracted desire for the annexation of Canada, continued long after the U.S. Annexation Bill of 1866 had failed. As late as February 27, 1891 the Boston Globe reported that 'The fact is that annexation is a partially accomplished fact'.

But while Canada was never overtly annexed, the U.S. desire for territorial hegemony, in the form of Manifest Destiny, was to re-emerge in other ways. The establishment of military bases within Canadian territory, the negotiation of common defense agreements, and even the creation of the Distant Early Warning Line (D.E.W. Line) in the Cold War era, are examples of the ongoing tendency. In the late twentieth century it was rounds of neoliberal institution-building, including the NAFTA. Thus, the latest round of hegemonic agreements, of the implementation of common security through the adoption of U.S. style borders and border accords, reflects a process with significant historical depth. These included the Shared Border Accord of 1995, the Border Vision Agreement of 1997, and the Canada-U.S. Partnership (CUSP) in 1999. All such agreements created a mechanism for harmonization of border management practice, in accordance with U.S. protocols and concerns. For Canadians access to large American markets, a must for a nation with such an open and dependent economy, created the impetus for co-operation. But it was also mixed with a degree of admiration for U.S. style administration, as well as an inherent uneasiness about whether Canadian concerns would be trampled roughshod by their large southern neighbour if cooperation was not forthcoming. Moreover, historical experience had made Canadians relatively expert at facilitating U.S. concerns, while navigating an independent national agenda. It was, for Canadians, a familiar problem, and in the case of security issues, Canada fell back on a strategy of building cooperative relations, hoping for some degree of consultation in the process, isolating and minimizing what were considered as intractable differences. Beginning with the border security agreements negotiated in the mid-1990s, Canadians attempted to negotiate the terms of hegemony; with the idea of softening the impact when and if it fell.

So in short, securitizing the Canada-U.S. border is an issue which has always been as much related to American strategic and continental interests as it is to building friendly principles of Canada-.U.S. cooperation. Indeed, as we have seen, the latter has relatively shallow historical depth, and while there is a Canadian literature which describes the 'remarkable relationship' between Canada and the U.S. in terms of cooperation and common values, this is of relatively recent origin. Much of the preceding century or two of Canada-U.S. relations had been coached in terms of reciprocity failed and annexation frustrated. The discourse of 'partnership', the dominant motif of border security relations today, thus developed relatively recently.

So when we speak of cooperation, we mean a brief Cold War military alliance, followed by an era of free trade which manifest itself first, as the Canada-U.S. Free Trade Agreement (FTA) of the mid-1980s, and then as the 1994 North American Free Trade Agreement between Canada, the U.S. and Mexico. It is important to remember, however, that these were economic, not political agreements – meaning today that political pressures among the three NAFTA partners, of which the U.S. is the largest, are primarily identified in terms of market-access conditions, and thus filtered through economic leveraging (Moore 2004; Nicol 2008). Because of this, the NAFTA agreement has proven very useful in fast-tracking security arrangements in cooperation with the U.S., because of the immediate way in which border security impacts upon transportation of goods within the North American market-place. The NAFTA thus facilitates cooperation in border security, although it is not an agreement that deals with security *per se*. This has created some important parameters for leveraging U.S.-style border security in North America.

Indeed, the NAFTA was the most important leveraging point for various security and border management protocols which ensued between Canada and the U.S. pre 9/11. All such agreements created a mechanism for harmonization of border management in intent, if not practice, in accordance with U.S.-centred concerns. For example, the Canada-U.S. Partnership (CUSP), a security agreement which followed the NAFTA, was designed to act as a 'mechanism for the two governments, [Canada and the U.S.], border communities, and stakeholders to discuss issues of border management' (Seghetti 2004, 4). The 'guiding principles' that evolved, included streamlining, harmonizing and collaborating on border policies and management. This also included expanding cooperation to increase efficiencies in the areas of customs, immigration, law enforcement as well as environmental protection, and collaborating on common threats from outside the United States and Canada' (ibid. 2004).

The CUSP, like the Shared Border Agreement and other late twentieth and early twenty-first century 'partnership agreements' which followed, has been represented by governments of both countries as the natural (or naturalized) continuation of a remarkable friendship between likeminded nations, and the natural extension of the NAFTA. Under the auspices of these various accords and agreements, the idea of economic integration which we have seen began in earnest under the FTA and then NAFTA, was appended to a harmonized border security project even before 9/11. Security and economic prosperity were linked in a powerful way, meaning that Canadians, like their counterparts to the south, were already feeling a degree of political coercion for more stringent border control and greater degrees on harmonization in border practices before the Twin Towers fell in New York

City. Indeed, a report on the comments of the U.S. Ambassador Paul Celluci on 13 August 2001, one month before 11 September occurred, noted: 'Talks of even closer economic ties with the States than under the current free trade agreements already include a suggestion ... of redesigning border controls' (McDuff 2001, 1).

All of these pre-9/11 agreements laid the groundwork for those which followed. In December 2001, for example, the Smart Border Agreement between Canada and the U.S. was signed. It clearly build on the CUSP, and also moved border cooperation more closely to U.S. standards, incorporating plans to implement the technology for biometric scanning and identity verification, documentation confirmation and detection of dangerous cargos which the U.S. desired. Canadians were told that 'since signing the Smart Border Declaration, Canada and the United States have proven that tremendous progress can be made through close cooperation and a commitment to an effective philosophy of risk management' (Government of Canada 2002, 1). The Smart Border Agreement laid out specific types of technological interventions that were to guide future cross-border relationship between Canada and the U.S., through a thirty-point 'Action Plan'. Key pillars of the agreement included addressing 'security risks' while 'efficiently expediting' the 'legitimate flow of people and goods' across the Canada-U.S. border. Canada and the U.S. signed the border agreement and announced that a new era in security had begun (ibid. 2002).[2]

And yet this was not enough. There was also an increasing degree of pressure, for Canada (and Mexico) to develop policies in other areas which were more synchronized with U.S. policy-makers, and considered critical to U.S. security interests. This was to come in the form of the Security and Prosperity Partnership of North America (SPP) in 2005. The latter was a politically expedient document whose end goal, the Canadian government declared, was 'to improve the safety and enhance the prosperity of the citizens of Canada, the United States and Mexico. This partnership promotes ways for the three countries to work together in areas as diverse as national security, transportation, the environment and public health' (Office of the Prime Minister 2004).

But SPP continued the process of U.S. unilateralism, rather than inserted Canada or Mexico as an equal partner in North American security agendas. It conjoined North American security harmonization with continued market access through a process coordinated and directed through the U.S. In fact, the U.S. Department of Commerce stressed that the SPP was a 'Washington-led' initiative designed among other things to 'coordinate our security efforts to better protect U.S. citizens from terrorist threats and transnational crime and promote the safe and efficient movement of legitimate people and goods' (SPP 2009). And while the SPP is now defunct, its demise created scarcely a ripple. Its demise amounted only to a note on a website, possibly because, as activists claim, the SPP's underlying principles

---

2   The plan looked vaguely familiar, including its provisions for infrastructure and technology development. Nine of the 30 points it embraced had already been set out in the Shared Border Accord of 1995 and the 2000 CUSP Forum.

– integrating energy and electricity markets – still remain in place as official North American priorities (see Trew 2009).

Thus, for Canadians, the most important current incentive for ongoing cross-border cooperation today remains the NAFTA. This is because free trade, first with the FTA, and then the NAFTA, significantly elevated cross-border trade, it also elevated access to U.S. markets, making 'cordial' Canada-U.S. relations, one of, if not *the* most important Canadian foreign policy concern. It reified access to American markets as a key element of Canada's economic security and well-being. Speaking more generally about Canadian and Mexican border policies, Morales has emphasized the importance of economic dependency and unequal power to the North American security relationship, noting that the 'pervasive asymmetric imbalance existing in the North American space explains why the regionalism experience in the northern part of the Western Hemisphere has remained subordinated to the changing strategic interests of Washington at the global and regional levels' (Morales 2009, 3).

What this means is that using border security as a rationale for control, the U.S. has translated its hegemonic control of North American markets into a border securitization discourse which, beginning with the integration of North American markets and economies, universalizes U.S. standards and management protocols, linking security and economy in agreements like the SPP. In the aftermath of 9/11, countries like Canada or Mexico generally yield to American concerns in order to retain close relations and maintain economic partnerships (Moore 2004). A number of researchers have argued that the governments of these nations are increasingly compromising their distinctive foreign policy perspectives to more smoothly facilitate new U.S. security and border imperatives, in order to save their continental trade relationships from further damage. John McDougall (2006) suggests that the Canadian government is now much more likely to engage in policy harmonization for just this reason. But others are more cynical: '[S]ome advocates have suggested the [Canadian] government is using the recent terrorism incident to justify its plans to introduce the machines that could invade personal privacy without ensuring they actually improve airport security… It has not been properly debated, and it has not been properly vetted by independent security experts' (de Souza 2010, 1).

Regardless as to motivation, the end result has been that the negotiation of any number of agreements and practices since 9/11 has been undertaken to ensure that Canada is not the main object of American security concerns. This means that all possible 'bells and whistles' associated with U.S. border control have been adopted on the Canadian side, with little public debate or consultation. Canadian border guards now carry guns, deploy multiple means of surveillance, have access to, and share, U.S. data bases, and work in integrated border enforcement teams (IBETs), often at joint border posts. In this way, control borders have emerged along the Canada-U.S. border, in a way which takes its lead from Washington and the Department of Homeland Security.

State, Security, Foreign Policy and Borders

It is obvious that these types of developments conform, closely to the framework of border control elaborated by Walters (2006), Deleuze (2008) and others. Diffuse power, border security, partnership agreements and border technologies which increasingly focus upon individuals rather than nationalities, are part and parcel of the restructured Canada-U.S. border and extent power beyond borders in diffuse ways. But this is not the end of the story, because such developments are only possible with a corresponding change to the structure and external power of hegemonic states. In the following sections we explore the idea that the restructuring of the U.S. state bureaucracy has had profound impact on the way in which U.S. hegemony has been practiced through its international borders. It reflects the way in which foreign relations and domestic policies are now conflated, and extended, through U.S. security discourses.

This is partly because while globalization suggests the operation of forces which exceed control of the state and operate in a virtual global economy, or operate in a space outside of the control of the nation-state, the experience of political globalization also sees the increasing role of domestic political institutions in incorporating the broader world within new types of domestic political structures, as has been the case, for example, with the development of a U.S. security initiative. The qualitative state, as O'Neill (2003) defined it, has now also been charged with the task of securitization.

This means that the state which brings us neoliberalism is more than simply a container for devolutionary processes associated with the post-foundational condition: it is also a venue for the development of security as Sparke (2005) reminds us. The point is, then, that the qualitative, neoliberal state also provides the structure for the diffuse state, and diffusion creates its own syntax of power. Jessop (2004) has argued that with an expansion of government practices into so many different spheres there has been a 'dramatic intensification of societal complexity' (ibid. 2004, 2). This complexity is reflected in overall concerns about 'the governability of economic, political, and social life in the face of globalization and conflicting identities' (ibid. 2004).

This diffusion in the power of state, when coupled with border control, create what Pickering and Weber (2006, 3) call politicized borders – 'sites and symbols of power', which 'may be reinforced or neglected by states depending upon circumstances': they have put pressure 'upon the machinery of governments themselves to adapt both quantitatively and qualitatively to the new security imperative discourses' (Dicken 1998, 80). In the U.S., the machinery of government has adapted qualitatively, if not quantitatively, to these new security imperative discourses, specifically the way in which post 9/11, domestic security imperatives identified by the Department of Homeland Security (DHS) have actually eclipsed the discourse of foreign relations in the U.S., at least in relation to North American border management. The result has been not just a reorganization of government bureaucracy to facilitate these transnational security discourses, but as the following discussion will suggest, the development of security discourses as foreign policy, and as bureaucratic, rather than legislative areas of concern. In a series of self-perpetuating bureaucratic concatenations, North American security measures are rarely debated nor politicized in terms of their impact upon foreign (continental) relations. They are rather, perceived as technological and incremental measures, imposed by bureaucracy (or even executive order) rather than legislation. They are often surrounded by secrecy. This is also very true for issues related to border management and control. The new border enforcement regime emanates mainly from the concerns of the U.S. DHS and is managed in ways which restructure the way in which borders serve less as territorial markers and more as sites for the projection of continental power, reframing the way in which foreign relations are understood and conducted. Canadians, for example, are informed of the presence of U.S. surveillance balloons watching their border towns by DHS bureaucrats and the media. Mexicans (and Canadians) wake up to find visa requirements have been imposed on Mexicans by Canada, with virtually no political discussion. The deal-breaker, however, has been U.S. discomfort with Canada's visa waiver program which is not in compliance with its own program.

The Rising Star of the Department of Homeland Security

The trend towards unchecked continent aspirations for hegemony in U.S. homeland security are directly related to the way in which the strategic reorganization the U.S. Government has allowed 'Homeland Security' to emerge as its most powerful department. Although previously the mandate of a number of different divisions and departments of the U.S. government, post-9/11 all aspects of border security have essentially been subsumed by the DHS, along with enormous budget appropriations suitable to support its large and expanding bureaucracy. Today the DHS both establishes and implements virtually all U.S. national security practices. It is also heavily invested in the USA PATRIOT Act and the more recent Western Hemisphere Transportation Initiative (WHTI). The latter, with its documentation requirements and surveillance tools, has supported this massive reordering of the machinery of state, creating the need to place U.S. domestic security concerns at the forefront of political discourse, government bureaucracy, and budget appropriations.

Effecting compliance to U.S. norms, but oftentimes inventing these norms, it ensures the centrality of U.S. border control in its security discourse, effectively creating a 'transnational security field'. In this sense DHS both constructs and defines broader issues of security, often reducing them to a homeland security more narrowly conceived (i.e. the Hurricane Katrina fiasco). Waugh acknowledges this, and suggests that 'the values of transparency, cooperation, and collaboration that have come to characterize emergency management over the past decade seem to be supplanted in the new command-and-control-oriented Homeland Security system' (Waugh 2003, 373).

Thus, the U.S. government, in its creation of DHS has affected a major structural challenge to existing governmental organization. This department has assumed the role of management for much of the North American borderlands, as well as defining what indeed constitute security threats (see U.S. Government, Department of Homeland Security, 2008). By its own definition the DHS's role is all encompassing. For example, among its self-described mandates are: 'Protecting the Nation from Dangerous People' and 'To Protect the Nation from Dangerous Goods', both of these requiring no end of 'premediated' risk calculations. In its efforts to protect, the DHS and the U.S. Customs and Border Protection (CBP) which it oversees, have been responsible for constructing more miles of border fencing in the past five years, than in the history of the U.S. It has also developed towers equipped with radar and communications systems and automated ground sensors, as well as linked these to command and control centers, Border Patrol vehicles and unmanned surveillance 'drones' (Konrad and Nicol 2008). Surveillance balloons, joint border posts, shared data, and other means of 'cooperation' link the two sides of the Canada-U.S. border. A new cadre of border guards, a new security mandate, and a compelling set of criteria about cross-border interactions, flows of people and goods across borders, while spontaneous travel among the two nations plummets. To the many Canadians and Americans who rely upon cross-border trade and tourism, this represents, *de facto*, a new foreign policy towards Canada, as well as Mexico.

Initially, of course, security was much-debated within Congress. Even the WHTI stimulated debate and oversight. Today, however, while House Committees like the House of Representatives' Committee on Foreign Affairs, or the Senate Committee on Foreign Relations are technically responsible for the oversight of policies which have a foreign relations impact, for the most part, border issues are dispatched under various committees and sub-committees on Homeland Security – that is to say they are regarded as a domestic security issue. Even immigration issues and policies can be dealt with this way, outside of the purview of the Judiciary Committee.

This means that while Congressional and Senate Committees hold hearings and meetings to discuss foreign policy issues, to make recommendations, and to encourage international policies consistent with U.S. interests, the management of border relations is effectively left to the Homeland Security committees and the Department of Homeland Security bureaucracy. This thrust to securitizing all border discussion is reflected, for example, in the committee allocation of hearings in the past five years, where DHS and Homeland Security Committees assume virtually all responsibility for discussing these issues. A review of this Committee's discussions over the past five years reflects the way in which North American relations have become security issues, while an overwhelming concern with Iraq, Iran, Korea, China and the Pacific Rim define foreign relations. There is less substantial interest in border management issues as objects for foreign policy-making.

The negotiation of the SPP is a case in point. It was, by its own admission, a 'White House-driven initiative' in which the Department of Commerce coordinated the 'Prosperity' component, while the Department of Homeland Security coordinated the 'Security' component, and the Department of State ensured that the two components were 'coordinated and are consistent with U.S. foreign policy' (SPP 2009). The result was a foreign policy driven by bureaucratic oversight. In fact, the involvement of both House and Senate foreign affairs committees in the review of the WHTI, and their July 2005 discussion concerning North American Cooperation on the Border, are perhaps the major exception to this profile of decided lack of foreign policy involvement in Canada-US border management. For the most part, rather than foreign policy, building border relationships and security cooperation with neighbouring North American countries is now more apt to be determined by the actions of bureaucrats in Departments like DHS or the State Department, or an executive decision emanating from the U.S. President, rather than by broad-based government debate and diplomatic engagement.

Moreover, even in cases when the Congress has addressed border-related issues under the various committees and sub-committees dealing with foreign affairs, such discussion often takes within such sub-committees as Terrorism, Nonproliferation and Trade or Homeland Security. So, where previously the relationship between North American countries was mediated by state, diplomacy and foreign policy, today the driving force of the new rhetorical cause is more lined to the rising star of the Department of Homeland Security (DHS), or Homeland Security Committees in Congress and bureaucratic governmental institutions which provide 'experts' advice. North American relations have become, as a result, concerned mainly with security issues broadly defined, in terms of terrorism, immigration and criminality.

Thus, American governmental institutions have developed and implemented what is tantamount to policies which are ultimately rooted in domestic concerns and U.S. political interests. They are unilateralist and devoid of systematic understandings of the nature of the international context in which they are implemented. In a relatively routine briefing, DHS spokesman Jackstra (Verdery 2004) told the Subcommittee on Western Hemisphere, Peace Corps and Narcotics Affairs, that security cooperation really meant working with Canada and Mexico, under the Partnership and Prosperity Agreement, to ensure that US standards were applied to North American states.

This propensity towards security unilateralism was recognized by Manley et al. (2005) who argued that the U.S. must build better bridges with its North American neighbours. Pastor noted that Canada and Mexico maintain a developed 'foreign policy' approach to US relations, having 'organized their governments to give priority to their bilateral relationships with the United States. Washington alone is poorly organized to address North American issues'. In 2005, he suggested that 'to balance U.S. domestic interests with those in the continent, President Bush should appoint a White House adviser for North American affairs'.

But no such advisor has appeared. The universalization of American values, choices and beliefs continues to be a force in continental securitization. The new thrust to US relations with its North American neighbours, reinforced by changes to governmental structure, has had the consequence of often reducing the practice of foreign affairs to the level of promoting of unilateralist border management policies. It is a hegemonic discourse supported by assumptions about the central role of the U.S. within the Western Hemisphere, if not the world, meaning that border issues are rarely addressed as more than domestic policy issues to be 'briefed upon'. Security initiatives are now embedded in complex networks and interdependencies within the DHS and within government itself, as DHS effectively tightens its hold upon any and all activities with a security component. Moreover, these security interdependencies ultimately blur the boundaries between what were traditional and separate constituencies of power and responsibility.

There are, as a result, great pressures for neighbouring countries for convergence in areas which have not been addressed in any bilateral or trilateral forum, despite the promise of the previously mentioned SPP. With the onus on individualized security documents, and with the responsibility for security programs design and implementation left to DHS, traditional structures of power and control, for example those which differentiate between foreign and domestic affairs, are challenged by broader sets of imperatives mandating security, and reinforce the legitimacy of extraterritorial nature of domestic security itself. Walters' (2006) control society itself has thus flourished because of restructured security concerns which realign territorial processes, state bureaucracies and networks of power and control.

Some of the incentives for this governmental restructuring are based upon ideology, but in many cases such motivations are enhanced by the politics of departmental power and bureaucracy. For example, DHS has set the terms for border management, and the many identifiable 'threats' it identifies (premeditation scenarios) are essential as the Department vies for domestic funding. Increased appropriations are a measure of departmental prestige and power. In this sense, DHS becomes a department whose mandate is focused upon linking domestic discourses of terror and domestic political landscapes to the appropriation of funds. In this way, the hard lines between domestic and foreign policies are increasingly blurred within the U.S. government approach to border management. After all, it is DHS, more than any other department, which is involved in the construction of hard-wiring borders. Its political mandate is specific and focused upon the concept of 'securing the homeland', above all other political mandates, but its broader goal is to ensure the broader application of 'U.S.-style' standards and the legitimacy of US concerns in continental, if not global contexts. Regardless as to any other qualification, it is clear in this sense that the landscape of border management and enforcement practices in North America cannot be understood without reference to the landscape of domestic politics within the United States.

Conclusions

One of the most obvious results of 9/11 has been the rising star of the Department of Homeland Security and the reorganization of North American security interests, borders and national policies. No amount of discussion promising 'partnership' among the NAFTA partners is likely to change this fact. Some would argue that the agenda of foreign affairs is increasingly dominated by unilateralism, resulting from an increasingly fundamentalist ideology. And that fundamentality is legislated in the sense that the USA PATRIOT Act ensures that the firm connection is made between security and patriotism. This act not only reorganizes a plethora of existing acts which deal with 'global connectivity', it is the essential act which allows 'Enhanced Surveillance Procedures' for the purposes of fighting 'terrorism'.

The dominant security discourse in the U.S. has thus hard-wired the Canada-U.S. border experience in a fundamentally new way, taking it outside the domain of public or even foreign policy debate within governance, and into the realm of domestic policy developed and implemented internally and bureaucratically. It suggests a profound reordering of priorities, paradigms and indicates that cumulatively, the various new anti-terrorist and Western Hemisphere Travel Initiatives, border management accords, or even the Department of Homeland Security is more than a domestic political reorganization of bureaucracy within the US governmental machinery with implications primarily for internal political landscapes. These events signal a geopolitical change which has tremendous consequences for a world order whose foundations have been, until recently, based upon facilitating frameworks for neoliberal globalization. The new discourses represent, perhaps, an emerging challenge to neo-liberalism, rather than a process complementary to furthering elite neo-liberal relations as Sparke (2005, 2006) suggests.

In effect, we are left with the age-old question of 'chicken' and 'egg'. Is control society a catalyst or a product of new securitization discourses? And while the answer is not necessarily clear, it is important to understand new border control dynamics within this framework or context. If control society is the catalyst, rather than the product, then its orchestration is linked to broader geopolitical discourses, govern mentalities and structures which stimulate or orchestrate, rather than react to new global flows and terrorist fears.

The way in which risk definitions and security scenarios develop and play out in international context reflects, to large extent, the way in which such processes have become internalized within national, and within North American, governmental structures. In the U.S., the highly ideological, polarized and competitive structure of intergovernmental relations, supported by a broadly-defined security discourse has created a problematic process along at the U.S.-Canada border at the 49th parallel. And while it is true that the management of the border is a two-sided affair, current management strategies on the U.S. side, while ostensibly developed to deal with the inherent contradiction between security and trade operational under the NAFTA, are more interested in security than integration. This, of course, has tremendous consequences for Canadians, Mexicans as well in borderlands and other geographical spaces which serve as the conduits for cross-border flows.

Thus, there is an increasing propensity for U.S. domestic security issues to become the 'deal-breaker' in the organization of North American foreign relations. The discourse which drives the orientation and organization of border management strategies is security. While today the implementation of initiatives like the contentious WHTI is complete, it has not occurred without collateral damage to

North American foreign relations. The U.S. has been consistent in its assertion that Canada should bring its immigration policies in line with that of the U.S., particularly in the area of visa waivers, and the Mexican Visa was a concession to this pressure. In this sense, we have witnessed the elevation of border management and enforcement themselves to the status of 'foreign relations' policies, and as such they have pre-empted more broadly defined or comprehensive or continental human security themes in North America.

Thus, in the twenty-first century, the success of a transnational security discourse, in terms of its legitimization of governmental power at various levels, is predicated upon the ability of the state to project power through vastly reorganized institutions and discourses which at the same time maintain the closure required to defend and extend their territorial-based power. Security is inimical to this closure, while risk assessment technologies are inimical to its openness. In North America, the dual nature of borders, both open and closed, have been complicit in the political and functional 'deterritorialization' of U.S. domestic instruments and institutions of control, or more precisely, borders have been complicit in the extension of a catch-all, U.S.-style 'homeland security' to all quarters of the continent. The recent history of North America is thus one of building borders the hard way – metaphorically-speaking, but also, increasingly in a tangible way.

Acknowledgement

The author acknowledges the support of the Social Science Research Council of Canada in undertaking the research for this chapter.

References

Clarkson, S. (2003), 'The View from the Attic, Towards a Gated Continental Community', in Andres, P. and Biersteker, T.J. (eds.), *The Rebordering of North America* (New York: Routledge).

De Goede, M. (2008), 'Beyond Risk: Premediation and the Post-9/11 Security Imagination', *Security Dialogue* 39, 155.

Deleuze, G. (2008), 'Society of Control', *L'autre journal* 1, available at <http://www.nadir.org/nadir/archiv/netzkritik/societyofcontrol.html>.

De Souza, M. (2010), 'Full-body scans coming to Canadian airports: Baird', *National Post* 5 January 2010, available at <http://www.nationalpost.com/story.html?id=2407341>.

Dicken, P. (1998), *Global Shift: Transforming the World Economy* (New York: Guilford Press).

Dillon, M. (2008), 'Underwriting Security', *Security Dialogue* 39, 309-32.

Foucault, M. (2007), 'Security, Territory and Population: Lectures at the Collège de France, 1977-78', in Sellenart, M. (ed.), translated by Burchell, G. (Basingstoke: Palgrave Macmillan).

Government of Canada (2002), *Governor Ridge and Deputy Prime Minister Manley issue one-year status report on the Smart Border Action Plan* 6 December 2002, available at <http://geo.international.gc.ca/world/site/includes/print.asp?lang =en&print=1&url=%2Fcan-am%2Fmain%2Fborder%2Fsmart_border_12_02-en.asp>, accessed 4 February 2010.

Harvey, F.P. (2004), *Smoke and Mirrors: Globalized Terrorism and the Illusion Of Multilateral Security* (Toronto: University of Toronto Press).

Homer-Dixon, T. (2008), 'Global capitalism teeters on the brink: We've moved from a world of risk to a world of uncertainty', *Globe and Mail* Report on Business, 8 March 2008, available at <http://www.globeinvestor.com/servlet/story/ RTGAM.20080319.wxcofinance19/GIStory/>.

Isin, E.F. (2004), 'The Neurotic Citizen', *Citizenship Studies* 8:3, 217-35.

Jessop, B. (2004), 'Governance and Metagovernance: On Reflexivity, Requisite Variety, and Requisite Irony', in Bang, H. (ed.), *Governance, as Social and Political Communication* (Manchester: Manchester University Press), 142-72, available at <http://eprints.lancs.ac.uk/215/>, accessed 31 March 2008.

Konrad, V. and Nicol, H. (2008), *Beyond Walls: Reinventing the Canada–U.S. Borderlands* (Aldershot: Ashgate).

Manley, J. et al. (2005), 'Building a North American Community', *Report of an Independent Task Force,* Council on Foreign Relations, May 2005.

McDougall, J. (2006), *Drifting Together, the Political Economy of Canada-US Integration* (Peterborough: Broadview Press).

McDuff, G. (2001), 'As the U.S. becomes Fortress America, Canada will have to pay more attention to its own interests', *Issues Network* 13 August 2001, available at <http://www.issuesnetwork.com/articles/mcduff20010813.html>.

Moore, K. (2004), 'Cuba in the Wake of NAFTA', *Revista Mexicana de Estudios Canadienses* September-October, 145-61.

Morales, I. (2009), 'Post NAFTA North America: Three Scenarios for the Near Future', *UNU-CRIS Working Paper* W2009/19.

Nicol, H.N. (2008), 'U.S. Hegemony in the twenty-first Century: Cuba's Place in the Regionalizing Geopolitics of North America and Caribbean Countries', *Journal of Borderlands Studies* 23:1.

Office of the Prime Minister (Canada) (2004), 'Government of Canada releases comprehensive National Security Policy', news release 27 April 2004, available at <http://pm.gc.ca/eng/news.asp?id=186>, accessed 30 April 2007.

Ohmae, K. (1990), *The Borderless World* (New York: Harper Collins).

O'Neill, P. (2003), 'Bringing the qualitative state into economy geography'. in Lee, R. and Wills, J. (eds.), *Geographies of Economies* (London: Arnold), 290-301.

Payan, L.P. (2006), *The Three U.S.-Mexico Border Wars Drugs, Immigration, and Homeland Security* (Santa Barbara: Praeger Security International).

Pickering, S. and Weber, L. (2006), *Borders, Mobility and Technologies of Control* (Dordrecht: Springer).

Salter, M.B. (2008), 'When the Exception becomes the Rule: Borders, Sovereignty, and Citizenship', *Citizenship Studies* 12:4, 365-380.

Salter, M.B. (2004), 'Passports, Mobility, and Security: How Smart Can the Border be?', *International Studies Perspectives* 5:1, 71-91.

Security and Prosperity Partnership of North America (SPP) (2009), *SPP Myths vs. Facts: Security and Prosperity Partnership of North America*, available at <http://www.spp.gov/myths_vs_facts.asp>, accessed 25 January 2009.

Seghetti, L.M. (2004), *Border Security: U.S.-Canada Immigration Border Issues*, CRS Report for Congress Received through the CRS Web, Order Code RS21258, updated 28 December 2004.

Sokolsky, J. and Legassé, P. (2006), 'Suspenders and a Belt: Perimeter and Border Security in Canada-U.S Relations', *Canadian Foreign Policy* 12, 15-29.

Sparke, M. (2006), 'A Neoliberal Nexus: Economy, Security and the Biopolitics of Citizenship on the Border', *Political Geography* 25:2, 151-80.

Sparke, M. (2005), *In the Space of Theory: Postfoundational Geographies of the Nation-state* (Minneapolis: University of Minnesota Press).

Trew, S. (2009), 'The SPP is dead: so where's the champagne?', *rabble.ca* 19 August 2009, available at <http://www.rabble.ca/news/2009/08/spp-dead-so-wheres-champagne>, accessed 30 January 2010.

United States Government, Department of Homeland Security (2008), *Preserving Our Welcome to the World in an Age of Terrorism*, available at <http://www.dhs.gov/xlibrary/assets/SBODAC_011608-Accessible.pdf>, accessed 31 March 2008.

Vaughan-Williams, N. (2008), 'Borderwork beyond Inside/Outside? Frontex, the Citizen-Detective and the War on Terror', *Space and Polity* 12:1, 63-79.

Verdery, S. (2004), 'Finding the Needle, Facilitating the Haystack', *remarks to U.S. Department of Commerce Conference 'International Travel to the U.S.: Dialogue on the current state of play'* 10 June 2004 (Washington, DC: Department of Commerce), available at <>, accessed 17 May 2008.

Walters, W. (2006), 'Border Control', *European Journal of Social Theory* 9, 187-203.

Waugh Jr., W.L. (2003), 'Terrorism, Homeland Security and the National Emergency Management Network', *Public Organization Review* 3, 373.

Blurring Boundaries/Sharpening Borders: Analysing the US's Use of Military Aviation Technologies to Secure International Borders, 2001-2008

Alison J. Williams

Introduction

> *At twilight on a clear November evening, CBP-104 rolls onto the tarmac at Fort Huachuca, Ariz., revs its 900-hp turboprop engine and takes off into the ruby desert sky. Banking left, it straightens and climbs on a southerly heading, levelling off at 19,000 foot. For the next few hours, CBP-104 will patrol a 30-mile stretch of the US-Mexico border, its video and infrared cameras trained on the rugged landscape below.*
>
> *In some ways it's a normal border patrol flight, much like the hundreds conducted every day by Custom and Border Protection (CBP), which maintains a fleet of 243 aircraft. But this one is different from most in one important way: CBP-104 has no pilot on board. The plane is a Predator B, a sophisticated unmanned aerial vehicle (UAV). (Wise 2007)*

With their ability to loiter undetected for hour upon hour, the UAVs of the US military provide it with an unparalleled Intelligence, Surveillance and Reconnaissance (ISR) edge (see Blackmore 2005). The US Air Force's Predator UAV aircraft have become battle-hardened in the skies above Afghanistan and Iraq in recent years, providing the US military's eyes in the sky. However, these aircraft are now being put to a number of different uses, so impressed have politicians and military personnel been by their abilities. One of the most significant of these roles is that of border enforcement with these craft deployed within and outside of the US to secure international boundaries. UAVs are well suited to this task with their ability to sit and watch over the border, replacing the border patrol agents as the primary watchers of remote and inaccessible stretches of international boundaries. Controlled by a pilot located several miles away, the sensor arrays that the Predators carry provide real time imagery, and video streaming. Although not the first and only aircraft to be used to provide aerial surveillance in this way, the inherent characteristics of UAVs have resulted in their significant move from a military to civilian law enforcement tool in a way that has not been witnessed before.

This chapter analyzes security and surveillance policies practiced by the US during the Presidency of George W. Bush, on both its Mexico border and along Iraq's international borders. It focuses specifically upon the identification of the vertical element of these borders and provides case studies of the deployment of a variety of UAVs by the US to secure these boundaries. Its aim is to investigate the extent to which the deployment of ever-more militarized forms of border securitization technologies, such as UAVs, are having a two-fold impact: serving not only to blur the boundaries between military and civilian law enforcement agencies, but also conversely to sharpen the borders which they patrol, making them ever more impenetrable to a host of perceived threats.

Constructing the post-9/11 border

In his useful overview of the 'recent rise in security measures along disputed and undisputed boundaries' Donaldson comments that;

> The tearing down of the Berlin Wall and emphasis on cross-border cooperation within a globalized world was believed in the 1990s to have harkened in an age when the inclination was to be towards new ideas and practices which sought to distance the notion of the international boundary as a linear barrier. (Donaldson 2005, 173)

However, he notes;

> Even in the midst of presumed 'de-territorialization', many nation-states and their populations remained passionate about territory. However, the pervading sense of global insecurity in the wake of the 11 September 2001 attacks has led many more states to re-examine their territorial boundaries less as areas of interaction with neighbouring states, and more as areas that need to be monitored and secured. (ibid. 2005, 174)

Here, Donaldson neatly sums up the ways in which the major geopolitical changes of the last twenty years or so have influenced the ways that states perceive their borders. His views (see also Laitinen 2003; Zureik and Salter 2005), illustrate the disjuncture between a post-Cold War breaking down of boundaries and freeing up of inter-state movement, and the post-9/11 desire to re-secure boundaries and restrict such movements. As Caparini and Marenin (2006) note, this can be linked to 'Security Sector Reform', which they argue has produced an increasingly networked, systematic, approach to border securitization. This concerns the incorporation of border security activities under the larger umbrella of state security provision and provides for the use of military technologies to achieve these aims. This chapter illustrates these developments within the US context.

The construction and representation within the Bush administration of the threat posed by unsecured and porous borders to the security of the United States illustrates the administration's strategy of taking any and all steps necessary to 'secure' the US and prevent the possibility of another 9/11. This has been manifested in a number of securitization policies, both within and beyond the US's international borders, which are central to the overarching ideology that has become known as the 'war on terror'. At the heart of this is a perceived need to identify non-desirable elements whilst they are still outside of the country and to prevent them traversing the state's boundaries. This straightforward statement brings the inside/outside dynamic to the fore. This is nothing new in US border policies, but the 'war on terror' has led to a re-working of this notion, extending it to encompass any person who is deemed a potential threat to the US (see Zureik and Salter 2005).

This chapter illustrates that as the desire to keep those deemed unwelcome beyond the boundary becomes more and more important, so it is increasingly being realized through the use of evermore militaristic techniques in the name of 'policing'. Thus, we are witnessing the maturing of an important linkage between the identification of an external 'other' to be kept at bay, and the use of the armed forces and the physical presence of the territorial boundary to achieve this aim. These perspectives have been in evidence to varying extents on the US-Mexico border for several decades. Strategies such as the US government's border enforcement operations 'Gatekeeper', 'Hold the Line', and 'Rio Grande', and a more recent redoubling of efforts to construct a barrier fence along specific high-risk sections of the boundary, illustrate that the US pursued policies aimed at identifying and blocking threatening 'others' from attempting to enter the US illegally over a number of years during the later part of the twentieth century (see Andreas 2000; Dunn 1996; Meyers 2005; Nevins 2002).

This construction of a feared 'other' that has to be kept outside has also led to the blurring of another set of boundaries between civil law enforcement agencies and the military in relation to border policing and border security. Work by Kraska (2007; see also Kraska and Kappeler 1997) and Dunn (1996; 1999) illustrate the militarization of the US police and the utilization of US military forces to secure the US's international boundaries.

The significance of the vertical dimension

Work by Weizman (2002, 2007), Graham (2004), and Williams (2007, 2010) has sought to argue that there is a prescient need to acknowledge and analyse a specifically vertical geopolitical dimension. Graham has commented that, during the Cold War, the projection of military power was planned 'across an essential flat and featureless geopolitical space ... made up of contiguous territories separated horizontally by geopolitical borders' (Graham 2004, 13). Weizman (2002) has also invoked a politics of verticality. In work focusing upon the Israel-Palestine situation, he has taken this notion of a vertical dimension further, considering the numerous verticalities that are at work in the Israeli government's approaches to maintaining control over the occupied territories (see Weizman 2007).

Graham has further argued that we need to take account of the works of French theorists Virilio and Deleuze, to truly 'inscribe the vertical into ... notions of power' (2004, 20). Certainly Deleuze's work with Guattari can be profitably utilized to critique the significance of the vertical to understandings of boundaries. Their work on the identification of smooth and striated space (1988) encourages us to construct airspace not as a single homogenous space, uninterrupted by lines of control, but rather as numerous distinct, overlapping and intermeshed bounded spaces which in turn create vertically and horizontally bounded no entry zones and identifiable zones of control. In this chapter I argue that the vertical element of international boundaries is increasingly being secured to provide such limits for states and enable them to protect themselves against perceived threats.

Weizman illustrates the significance of acknowledging the role of this vertical space in relation to the creation and securitization of borders when he notes that control of airspace provides states with 'a vantage observational point on the terrain underneath it, denying that position to others' (2002). This idea has specific relevance to the securitization of international boundaries; through claiming control of the airspace above these sites not only can a state observe what goes on at ground level, but it can also act to deny access to that airspace. I argue that by claiming and militarizing this airspace, the US seeks to utilize it specifically to secure its boundaries, denying not only access to the airspace above the boundary line, but also through the deployment of aerial technologies to use this airspace to deny access to the horizontal border zone at and below ground level. In boundary studies, therefore, the vertical dimension needs not only to be acknowledged, but also to be problematized and analysed. It seems almost too simplistic to note that international boundaries, be they on land or at sea, have vertical elements, yet the significance of this has yet to be considered widely, Brunn et al being amongst a small number to recognize that borders do 'exist in three dimensions' (2005, 382). Perhaps this is because political geographers have tended to think about our world, as Graham (2004) notes, in terms of horizontal land and sea masses separated by two-dimensional boundary lines (confer Donaldson 2005, 175). The vertical aspect of these lines has not been deemed important because the majority of the potentially problematic traffic attempting to cross these boundaries has been at ground level. Yet this approach provides only a partial consideration of boundaries; the vertical element is significant, and as aerial technologies continue to advance, it is becoming ever more so.

In terms of the securitization of international boundaries and their resultant borderlands it is necessary and productive to consider them in the wider context of the territorial integrity of a state. This notion, enshrined in the UN Charter provides states with the ability to act as sovereign within their own boundaries (the notion of territorial sovereignty) and gives them the right to maintain their boundaries as fixed entities (the notion of territorial preservation) (see Elden 2006). Some definitions of territorial integrity in international law have, significantly, signalled the importance of recognizing the vertical dimension of boundaries. The Encyclopaedia of Public International Law (2000, 813) states that: 'the notion of territorial integrity refers to the material element of the State, namely the physical and demographic resources that lie within its territory (land, sea and airspace) and are delimited by the States frontiers and boundaries' (quoted in El Ouali 2006, 632).

Bounding the air

The limits of this vertical dimension are enshrined in a number of legal treaties that govern the use of air spaces. The concept of territorial integrity is implicit within many of these documents, and as such plays a significant role in how states consider the vertical element of their borders, and thus how they can be secured, and used to secure their boundaries on the ground.

Kaplan has noted that 'the air, as well as water and land, [is] a form of national property' (2006, 398). Whilst discussions on territory may not agree with this perspective the utilization of the term 'property' in this context implies ownership and control of this space; thus illustrating that it is not open to all users (see Banner 2008). The delimitation of this aerial 'property' is contained in a raft of international legal frameworks, and domestic policies, that seek to identify specific airspaces and define both their vertical and horizontal limits, thus creating numerous distinct, bounded, zones of control.

We are all aware that boundary fences, lines, and other demarcation features are common indicators of land boundaries. Of course at sea and in the air such physical demarcation is not achievable. However, the treaties that delimit international land and sea boundaries also affect a state's aerial extent. The 1982 United Nations Convention on the Law of the Sea (UNCLOS), for example, provides a number of measured limits which states with coastlines are entitled to claim. To illustrate, Article 2 of UNCLOS stipulates that 'the sovereignty of a coastal state extends beyond its land territory and internal waters ... to an adjacent belt of sea, described as the territorial sea' (UNCLOS 1982, Article 2.1). The article goes on to clarify that 'this sovereignty extends to the airspace over the territorial sea' (UNCLOS 1982, Article 2.2). This concept is further reinforced by a number of specific airspace treaties which, taken together with relevant land and sea space treaties such as UNCLOS (see Ash 1987), serve to set the limits to the vertical dimensions of international boundaries – the horizontal limits of a state's sovereign airspace.

The notion of aerial sovereignty was first codified internationally in the 1919 Paris Convention for the Regulation of Aerial Navigation; Article 1 of which stipulated that 'the high contracting parties recognize that every power has complete and exclusive sovereignty over the airspace above its territory' (quoted in Kyriakides 1998, 82). This initial treaty, whilst acknowledging the right to aerial sovereignty failed to adequately identify the limits of this control. Whilst the general principle of aerial sovereignty was reasserted in a number of inter-war agreements and conventions (see Butler 2001), it was not until 1944 that an international legal definition of aerial sovereignty was agreed upon at the Chicago Convention on International Civil Aviation. This treaty provides sovereign states with the right to 'complete and exclusive sovereignty over the airspace above [their] territory', defining that territory as 'the land areas and territorial waters adjacent thereto under the sovereignty, suzerainty, protection or mandate of such state' (quoted in Kyriakides 1998, 83). This convention, which has 190 contracting states, thus provided the first definite delimitation of the physical dimensions of a state's airspace, ensuring that they correspond to the legal territorial boundaries of each state. This has been subsequently further reinforced by other international agreements, such as UNCLOS noted above, and taken in concert these provide a comprehensive description of the horizontal extent of airspace.

The vertical extent of airspace is also worth mentioning here because if states are truly interested in securing the totality of their aerial boundaries, the vertical limit of these is also relevant. According to Weizman (2002) and Pascoe (2001) the upper limit of 'controlled' airspace is set at approximately 60,000 feet. However, the full vertical extent of airspace is set at an altitude of 100 kilometres above the earth's surface. This is known as the Karman line and is recognized by the *Fédération Aéronautique Internationale* (FAI), the governing body for aeronautical world records, as the upper limit of airspace. The line defines the altitude at which air becomes too thin for conventional aircraft to fly through (FAI 2004). The relevance of this line for boundary securitization is significant because theoretically a state can claim that its territorial boundaries reach this altitude, providing the notional ability to hermetically seal a state should it have the logistical ability to enforce its boundaries to this height.

The legal regimes enshrined within these treaties also provide states with the ability to secure their land boundaries from the air. The deployment of ever more sophisticated Intelligence Surveillance and Reconnaissance (ISR) technologies, most obviously realized in military-issue UAVs, has the ability to provide a discreet new aspect to the enforcement and maintenance of international boundaries. As the following two examples show, US military hardware is increasingly being brought to bear in this role. These developments cause us to critically question the extent to which this engenders a blurring of the boundaries between civil and military space, at the same time as it sharpens the physical borders being patrolled.

UAVs above the US-Mexico border

It would be short-sighted and erroneous to argue that the securitization and enforcement of the US's border with Mexico was bereft of a military component prior to 9/11. Work by Dunn (1996), Nevins (2002), Andreas (2000) and Meyers (2005) is illustrative of a number of writers who have sought to analyse the militarization of US border patrol techniques to fight both drug smuggling and people trafficking during the latter decades of the twentieth century. Meyers describes a number of initiatives set up during the Clinton administration, including the IDENT automated fingerprint recognition system, that made use of 'technologies [that] originated from the military' (2005, 8). Meyers notes that 'the military continued to assist with the construction, maintenance and operation of [this] equipment' (2005, 8) thus indicating that the military was involved on more than just a provision of equipment basis. Indeed, it was becoming ever more integrated into the day to day workings of the civilian border enforcement agencies that were tasked with securing the US-Mexico border.

Unquestionably, the events of 9/11, and the changes in the organizational structures within the US government that they heralded, had significant impacts upon the structure, remit and technologies of the US's border enforcement agencies, and the role and place of the military and military technologies therein. Whilst many of the changes to the US-Mexico border since 9/11 focused upon developing tools to increase information gathering and sharing abilities at official points of entry (see Meyers 2005, 13-19), this section uncovers the effects of 9/11 specifically upon the developing role and place of military UAV technologies within the US's civilian border enforcement agency, and illustrates how these machines have been increasingly used to secure the vast expanses of relatively un-secured border along the US's southern boundary.

In 2002 the White House published The National Strategy for Homeland Security which signposted a new focus for the policing of the US's international borders – that of seeking to prevent those 'others' capable of providing a terrorist threat to US national security from gaining entry to the country (White House 2008). The securitization of the boundary between the US and Mexico has become emblematic of the desire within the US to create a physical, impenetrable, boundary between the supposedly safe, internal, domestic space of the US and the potentially threat-harbouring, external, space across the boundary into Mexico and beyond.

A re-organization of the civil enforcement agencies tasked with securing and patrolling the US's international boundaries took place in 2003 with the creation of the US Customs and Border Protection (CBP) force. As part of the newly-formed Department of Homeland Security (DHS), CBP was integral to a plan to unify 'all frontline personnel and functions with law enforcement responsibilities' for the US's borders under one agency (Office of Border Patrol 2004). Composed of three sections; Field Operations, Air and Marine, and Border Patrol, CBP's aim is to secure the US's border and prevent terrorism (CBP Air and Marine 2007). By the end of 2007, there were over 41,000 CBP employees working out of 20 Field Operations Offices, staffing 327 official ports of entry into the US, and seeking to secure over

7000 miles of international boundary (CBP 2008). The significance of the national security element of CBP's raison d'être, its origins in the fall out from 9/11, and the significance of the threatening 'other' are proudly described in its literature;

> As a sovereign nation, it has always been important that we control our borders. But after the attacks of September 11, with the threat posed to our country by international terrorists, it is essential that we do so, and it is essential that we have a coherent and understood strategy for doing so. (Office of Border Patrol 2004)

Significantly, the role of UAV technologies is also explained;

> We will use unmanned aerial vehicles (UAVs) where they can assist. In fact, in 2004 the Border Patrol became the very first civilian law enforcement agency in the world to use UAVs to carry out a civilian law enforcement mission. (Office of Border Patrol 2004)

These two quotes clearly illustrate the linkage between the terror prevention element of border security procedures and the use of military technologies to carry out these tasks. The blurring between military and civilian technologies and enforcement strategies is beginning to be brought into focus.

The technology at the cutting edge of this strategy is the General Atomics MQ-1 Predator UAV (see General Atomics 2008a). The Predator first saw active military service in 1995 and has been deployed in the Balkans, Middle East and the Horn of Africa on a variety of covert and regular missions (BBC News 2002). The MQ-1 has become one of the US military's most favoured ISR, and strike, options in combat zones whilst recent advances have produced the MQ-9 Reaper – the first 'hunter-killer' UAV variant (General Atomics 2008b).

The first UAVs deployed by a civilian law enforcement agency were Hermes 450 and Hunter craft which entered service in 2004 as part of the US Immigration and Customs Enforcement service's Arizona Border Control Initiative and were tasked with providing 'border surveillance of illegal activities' (ICE 2004; see also DHS 2005; CBP 2006). The first CBP Predator entered service in 2005 with its Air and Marine section. Since then the UAVs of the CBP have been primarily deployed along the vast open stretches of Arizona's border (see Bush 2005; Wise 2007). To date, the role of the Predator above the US-Mexico border has been one primarily of information gathering, utilizing its ISR capabilities to locate and track illegal immigrants. With a maximum altitude of 25,000 feet and an endurance of up to 40 hours the Predator provides the CBP with the ability to deploy almost constant ISR functions over more remote, and less secure, sections of the border.

One of the most important developments in terms of the US's aim of securing its southern border has been the implementation of the Secure Border Initiative (SBI). Touted as a 'comprehensive multi-year plan to secure America's borders and reduce illegal immigration' the SBI aims specifically to 'improve security in the areas between ports of entry by integrating and coordinating the use of technology including more Unmanned Aerial Vehicles, aerial assets, Remote Video Surveillance camera systems, and sensors' to create 'an integrated border security system' (DHS 2006). Of specific interest is the SBI's stated aim to; 'partner with the Department of Defense to utilize advanced but proven military technologies to help us with our border security mission' (DHS 2006).

This quote clearly reveals that the US implemented policies that blurred the boundaries between its military and civilian law enforcement agencies in order to succeed in its all-encompassing aim of sharpening its borders and securing itself against the threatening external 'other'.

Between 2004 and 2008 ever more funding for the deployment of CBP UAVs was approved by the US Congress. In the December 2007 round of appropriations Congress reserved approximately USD 100 million for the Department of Homeland Security to extend its UAV fleet. Congress noted its support for the use of these combat-capable vehicles to achieve 'the goal of obtaining operational control of the nation's borders' (quoted in Strohm 2007). This operational control was to be achieved, according to CBP, by the purchase of three more Predators during 2008 bringing the total fleet to six and expanding their geographic spread from Arizona to Florida and the North Dakota section of the US-Canada border (see Broache 2007). Between 2005 and 2008 the CBP's UAV complement amassed over 1300 flying hours over the US-Mexico border (Kostelnik 2007).

This expansion of CBP's UAV capacity occurred in tandem with the development of increasingly strong linkages with the US military. In 2005 the US Army instigated a training regime at its Unmanned Aircraft Systems Training Center in Arizona to provide a training facility for CBP personnel (CBP Today 2005b). The CBP's Unmanned Aircraft Systems Operations Center is situated at the same airfield as the Army's training facility (Libby Army Airfield in Sierra Vista, Arizona). These facts illustrate the intertwined nature of the relationship between the US military and the CBP to secure the US's international borders through the use of UAVs.

Arguably, the deployment of UAVs to help secure the US-Mexico border stems in no small way from the reaction to the attacks of 9/11, but it also reflects the successful use of these craft to carry out similar missions in the US's current combat operation zones in the Middle East. Whilst Afghanistan has long-standing security issues along its Pakistan border, it was arguably in Iraq that the US faced more pressing border security concerns, and where US UAVs saw concerted combat action in the prosecution of operations aimed at enforcing and maintaining these boundaries.

UAVs on Iraq's borders

When US-led coalition forces successfully deposed the regime of Saddam Hussein in mid-April 2003, the entirety of Iraq's military and security forces were abolished 'at the stroke of a pen' (Bateman 2006, 43). Included within this was the Iraqi Border Army. This action left Iraq's 2,281 miles of international borders unguarded and unmanaged – something which the US administration seemingly failed to realize – and people and material free to cross in and out of Iraq without official sanction.

It was not until 24 August 2003 that the Coalition Provision Authority (CPA) issued Order 26 which provided for the creation of the Department of Border Enforcement (DBE) (CPA 2003). This order allowed for the merging of the five different border control entities that had, under the previous regime, jointly administered Iraq's international boundaries with Jordan, Syria, Turkey, Iran, Kuwait and Saudi Arabia. In keeping with the US's war on terror-driven focus upon securing its borders, the CPA sought to put in place a strong administrative body that would eventually be capable of enforcing and maintaining Iraq's borders. The primary role of the new department was thus to 'monitor and control the movement of persons and goods to, from, and across the borders of Iraq' (CPA 2003). In order to fulfil this role the new department requisitioned all,

> the facilities, equipment and vehicles engaged in border-related functions that were previously under the authority of the Ministry of Foreign Affairs, the Ministry of Finance, the Ministry of the Interior, the Ministry of Defense [and] the Presidential Office. (CPA 2003)

This illustrates the power that the new department was being given by the CPA and alludes to the importance of this department and its duties to the CPA and the US. Indeed, a press release from the White House, dated 15 March 2004, highlights the extent to which the same border securitization rhetoric being deployed to justify the militarization of the US-Mexico border was also being used with regard to Iraq's borders. In its 'Iraq fact of the day' the White House proudly announced that there were '8,000 border personnel in Iraq', that 'the Iraqi Border Police force will soon double', and most significantly that these forces were charged with keeping 'Iraq's borders open to legitimate travel and commerce, while helping to prevent terrorists and foreign fighters from entering the country' (White House 2004). While Iraq may have had a more pressing need to prevent potentially threatening 'others' from entering its territory, the employment of the language in this press release illustrates the extent to which the Iraq border was represented in a similar manner to the way in which US Department of Homeland Security and the CBP literatures represented the US-Mexico border.

Between 2004-2008 Iraq's border forces grew to a reported 39,752 total personnel (Multi-National Force – Iraq 2008). According to Elliott and Radin's (2008) overview of Iraqi forces, by 2008 the DBE boasted five border police regions, each composed of a number of special troop and commando battalions, although some had not progressed past the planning stage. In addition, the DBE had engaged in a systematic campaign to construct several new border forts to create a chain of almost 300 of these compounds in order to generate a more visible border security presence (Garamone 2006; Multi-National Force – Iraq 2008). However, the most visible aspect of Iraq's border enforcement since 2003 was not carried out by the Iraqis themselves but by US and allied military forces who engaged in a number of operations to secure problematic sections of the border. These actions can be linked to US border policies along its problematic boundary with Mexico in two specific ways; firstly both seek to identify and prevent a designated 'other' entering the state, and secondly; both illustrate the US's desire to provide a military-led solution to securing borders.

The use of aircraft by an imperial state to control the population of its overseas territories is not a new phenomenon; nor is it even a new strategy in Iraq. The British Royal Air Force's used the tactic of 'air policing' to enforce and maintain order in Iraq during its Mandate (see Cox 1985; Omissi 1990). These tactics can be understood as seeking to preserve 'the integrity of a specified airspace' (US Defence Technical information Center 2006) which can be mapped directly onto the ground below. Thus, these types of deployments have been tasked at least in part with enforcing the extent of imperial control over these territories, which in turn provides the vertical and horizontal extent of that space. Therefore, a historical precedent exists for the use of aircraft to enforce and maintain the international boundaries of subjugated states. In more recent times, the no-fly zones imposed over Iraq during the 1990s can be seen in a similar light.

After the 2003 invasion, military aircraft played a significant role in efforts to re-secure Iraq's borders; yet their use by military forces in Iraq once more illustrates the blurring of the boundaries between civilian law enforcement agencies and military forces in the completion of this task. According to reports, the US military employed upwards of 400 UAVs, of various different sizes, ranges and capabilities across Iraq. These ranged from the high-altitude, long-range Global Hawk, through the Predator, to the hand-launched, short-range Desert Hawk (Air Force Print News Today 2005a: 2005d: 2006). The individual capabilities of these aircraft make them suitable for a host of different types of border enforcement and maintenance duties.

Given the political leanings of the Syrian government and the US's identification of the state as a potential adversary (Bush 2002), the desire to secure Iraq's border with Syria was a high priority for US forces. To this end, several large-scale operations were conducted in the Al Qa'im sector of this border in an effort to stem the flow of what the US military termed 'insurgents' entering the country. Operations 'Matador', 'Spear', and 'Steel Curtain' were all conducted in this area during 2005 in a concerted attempt to secure and enforce the border. Although these offensives were primarily ground-based each included a significant UAV component.

In each of these three operations, which are indicative of types of tactics in place within Iraq that combine US military and Iraqi forces to secure Iraq's international boundaries, MQ-1 Predators were utilized in collaboration with manned aircraft. Operation Matador saw 'coalition air forces ... postured to respond to anti-Iraqi forces' activities' in the Al Qa'im region (Air Force Print News Today 2005b), in Operation Spear Hellfire missiles were launched from a US UAV (Air Force Print News Today 2005c), whilst the stated aim of Operation Steel Curtain was to deploy a host of manned and unmanned aircraft to 'restore Iraqi control along the Iraq-Syria border' (Air Force Print News Today 2005e).

One of the most interesting illustrations of the ways in which the efforts to secure Iraq's border mirror the increasingly militarized nature of the US-Mexico border was the deployment, by the Department of Homeland Security, of a number of CBP Support Teams to 'mentor and monitor' Iraqi DBE personnel working at critical points of entry into the country (CBP Today 2005a; Day 2003; Report to Congress 2006, 37). These teams were tasked with ensuring that the Iraqi personnel were fully trained and able to effectively manage their border areas. In addition, a number of private security companies have employed former CBP officers as consultants for the DBE (DynCorp International 2008). However, in contrast to the developments in technology provision at the US-Mexico border, the UAV technologies used along Iraq's border were under the control of the US military.

In an account of the use of the intelligence gathering Global Hawk in Iraq, Butler discusses the role played by these technologies in Iraq and their place within US strategy. 'The push to secure Iraq's borders with Syria and Iran is putting the young Global Hawk unmanned aerial vehicle (UAV) program squarely in the center of President Bush's Iraq strategy' (2007). Butler reinforces this link, noting that the factional insurgency in Iraq was deemed to be being fed through illegal men and materiel crossing Iraq's borders and that only by stopping this, through the use of soldiers, Marines and Global Hawks, could Iraq be secured. This illustrates succinctly the link between border security and the use of military technologies in Iraq. Although the Global Hawk only provides an ISR capability, its use as a front line 'weapon' in the strategy to secure Iraq's borders bears witness to the Bush administration's desire to put whatever tools it had at its disposal to securing Iraq, and by extrapolation, itself, against the risk posed by threatening others who seek to cross international boundaries and harm the US.

In January 2008, the newly appointed Director General of the DBE released a three-year plan for the continued development of the department, in which he stated that he wished to construct and operate 'additional border forts and annexes to establish a line-of-sight perimeter around Iraq' (Report to Congress 2008, 42). This would require the DBE to operate a total of 712 forts, giving a five to six kilometre line of sight facility, requiring a total of 46,000 personnel (Report to Congress 2008; Multi-National Force – Iraq 2008). This would provide a real ability to protect Iraq's borders and prevent the cross-border flow of foreign terrorists that posed a significant threat to Iraq's stability as a state. If this system of forts is duly constructed then Iraq will have successfully sharpened its borders, and interestingly enough it will have attained this without the need to purchase expensive aerial ISR technologies. However, the line-of-sight strategy employed here reinforces the same notion of ocular primacy in terms of surveillance that UAVs extend into the airspace.

Blurring boundaries/sharpening borders

This chapter has sought to analyse the US's utilization of its UAV technologies to support border security actions between 2001 and 2008, and show how this illustrates its aim to re-secure its international boundaries (both at home and those it had de facto control over abroad) in order to prevent threats to US security from those seeking to cross those borders. In this sense the US actively engaged in policies that led to the sharpening of these boundaries in two, interlinked ways.

The first of these is through a physical, visual, sharpening of the boundary through the use of the hi-tech ISR arrays fitted onto Predator UAVs. The utilization of these sophisticated sensors provided those tasked with securing the US's border with Mexico, and Iraq's borders, with an unmatched ability to see potential threats from above. Much of the publicity material from the Bush administration's Secure Border Initiative for the US-Mexico border talks about the functionality of UAV's to provide an eye in the sky, sweeping the border, searching for threats, and directing ground-based units to intercept them.

The second aspect of this sharpening focuses upon the utilization of the combat features of these craft to prosecute actions against these threats once they have been identified. To date these functions have only been carried out above Iraq's border with Syria, and there is no indication at present that armed UAV's would be deployed in the southern US, but this ability has created a sharper boundary in terms of the possible consequences for those un-desirables who seek to cross it.

The focus of this chapter has been to illustrate how this sharpening has itself been caused at the expense of a blurring of the boundaries between the military and civilian law enforcement agencies tasked with securing the US's boundaries. The intertwining of the US Army and the US Customs and Border Protection service (CBP) in the latter's UAV programme on the US's southern border is all too obvious to see. This is mirrored by the deployment of CBP agents to train Iraq's border enforcement personnel and the role of the US military as the sole provider and operator of UAV technologies along Iraq's boundaries. Whilst some of these linkages have been temporary in nature, the possibilities for further interconnections are obvious to see, and it is likely that the intertwining of military and civilian agencies and technologies in border enforcement work will continue and increase within the US.

Analysis of these two inter-linked aspects of the US's all-encompassing 'war on terror' illustrates the importance of understanding the significance of the vertical dimension of international boundaries. The continual development of UAV technologies and the construction and representation of a threatening 'other' that must be kept beyond its gates suggests that the US will continue to blur the borders between its civilian and military agencies whilst it strives to sharpen its international boundaries in order to secure its territory, both on the ground and in the air.

References

Air Force Print New Today (2006), *Global Hawk UAV 'Arrives'*, available at <http://www.af.mil/news/story_print.asp?storyID=123014297>, accessed February 2006.

Air Force Print News Today (2005a), *Desert Hawk UAV Patrols Tallil*, available at <http://www.af.mil/news/story_print.asp?storyID=123009700>, accessed February 2006.

Air Force Print New Today (2005b), *Coalition Aircraft Support Troops in Operations Matador*, available at <http://www.af.mil/news/story_print.asp?storyID=123010534>, accessed February 2006.

Air Force Print News Today (2005c), *Predator Provides Close-Air Support to Embattled Marines in Iraq*, available at <http://www.af.mil/news/story_print.asp?storyID=123010823>, accessed February 2006.

Air Force Print News Today (2005d), *UAV Mission*, available at <http://www.af.mil/news/story_print.asp?storyID=123012615>, accessed February 2006.

Air Force Print New Today (2005e), *Air Force Fighters Strike Insurgents*, available at <http://www.af.mil/news/story_print.asp?storyID=123012970>, accessed February 2006.

Andreas, P. (2000), *Border Games: Policing the US-Mexico Divide* (London: Cornell University Press).

Ash, Major G.W. (1987), '1982 Convention on the Law of the Sea – Its Impact on Air Law', *Air Force Law Review* 26, 35-82.

Banner, S. (2008), *Who Owns the Sky? The Struggle to Control Airspace from the Wright Brother On* (Cambridge: Harvard University Press).

Bateman, R. (2006), 'Iraq and the Problem of Border Security', *SAIS Review* XXVI:1, 41-47.

BBC News. (2002), *US Drones Take Combat Role*, available at <http://news.bbc.co.uk/1/hi/world/2404425.stm>, accessed June 2008.

Blackmore, T. (2005), *War X: Human Extensions in Battlespace* (Toronto: University of Toronto Press).

Broache, A. (2007), *More Aerial Drones Coming Soon to US Borders*, available at <http://www.news.com/newsblog/8301-10784_3-9757070-7.html>, accessed March 2008.

Brunn, S.D., Watkins, J.F., Fargo, T.J., Lepawsky, J. and Jones, J.A. (2005), 'Towards and Geopolitics of Life and Living: where boundaries still matter', in Zureik, E. and Salter, M.B. (eds.), *Global Surveillance and Policing: borders, security, identity* (Cullompton: Willan Publishing), 381-99.

Bush, G.W. (2005), *President Discusses Border Security and Immigration Reform in Arizona*, available at <http://www.dhs.gov/dhspublic/display?theme=44&content=4951&print=true>, accessed January 2006.

Bush, G.W. (2002), *State of the Union Address*, available at <http://www.whitehouse.gov/news/releases/2002/01/20020129-11.html>, accessed June 2008.

Butler, A. (2007), 'Global Hawk UAV Supports Border Ops in Iraq', *Aviation Week*, available at <http://integrator.hanscom.af.mil/2007/March/03082007/03083007-22.htm>, accessed March 2008.

Butler, D. (2001), 'Technogeopolitics and the Struggle for the Control of World Air Routes, 1910-1928', *Geopolitics* 20, 635-58.

Caparini, M. and Marenin, O. (2006), 'Introduction to Borders and Security Governance', in Caparini, M. and Marenin, O. (eds.), *Borders and Security Governance: Managing Borders in a Globalised Network* (Zurich: Lit Verlag Gmbh and Co), 9-16.

CBP Air and Marine. (2007), *CBP Air and Marine Unmanned Aircraft System (UAS) 101 Brief*, available at <http://www.cbp.gov/linkhandler/cgov/border_security/air_marine/uas_program/uas_presentation.ctt/uas_presentation.pdf>, accessed June 2008.

CBP Today (2005a), *CBP Trains Iraqi's to Secure their Borders*, available at <http://www.cbp.gov/xp/CustomsToday/2005/March/other/iraq_training.xml>, accessed May 2008.

CBP Today (2005b), *Unmanned Planes a New Weapon in Controlling Remote Border Locations*, available <http://www.cbp.gov/xp/CustomsToday/2005/nov_dec/unmanned.xml>, accessed January 2006.

CBP (2008), *Protecting Our Borders Against Terrorism*, available at <http://www.cbp.gov/xp/cgov/about/mission/cbp.xml>, accessed June 2008.

CBP (2006), *UAS Overview*, available at <http://www.cbp.gov/xp/cgov/border_security/air_marine/uas_program/uasoverview.xml>, accessed June 2008.

Cox, J.L. (1985), 'A Splendid Training Ground: The Importance to the Royal Air Force of its Role in Iraq, 1919-1932', *Journal of Imperial and Commonwealth History* XIII:2, 157-84.

CPA (2003), *Coalition Provisional Authority Order Number 26 – Creation of the Department of Border Enforcement*, available at <http://www.iraqcoalition.org/regulations/20030824_CPAORD_26_Creation_of_the_Dept_of_Border_Enforcement.pdf>, accessed May 2008.

Day, T. (2003), 'Customs Agents Help Guards on Iraq Border', *Army Public Affairs*, available at <http://www4.army.mil/ocpa/read.php?story_id_key=5402>, accessed April 2008.

Deleuze, G. and Guattari, F. (1988), *A Thousand Plateaus: Capitalism and Schizophrenia* (London: Athlone Press).

DHS (2006), *Fact Sheet: Secure Border Initiative*, available at <http://www.dhs.gov/dhspublic/display?theme=43&content=4922&print=true>, accessed January 2006.

DHS (2005), *A Review of Remote Surveillance Technology along US Land Borders* (Washington DC Department of Homeland Security).

Donaldson, J.W. (2005), 'Fencing the Line: analysis of the recent rise in security measures along disputed and undisputed boundaries', in Zureik, E. and Salter, M.B. (eds.), *Global Surveillance and Policing: borders, security, identity* (Cullompton: Willan Publishing), 173-93.

Dunn, T. (1999), 'Military Collaboration with the Border Patrol in the U.S.-Mexico Border Region: Inter-Organizational Relations and Human Rights Implications', *Journal of Political and Military Sociology* 27:2, 257-78.

Dunn, T. (1996), *The Militarization of the U.S.-Mexico Border, 1978-1992: Low Intensity Conflict Doctrine Comes Home* (Austin: University of Texas Press).

DynCorp International (2008), *Border Police Advisor – Iraq*, available at <http://www.dyncorprecruiting.com/civ/detail.asp?dyn639>, accessed May 2008.

El Ouali, A. (2006), 'Territorial Integrity: rethinking the territorial sovereign right of the existence of the states', *Geopolitics* 11:4, 630-50.

Elden, S. (2006), 'Contingent Sovereignty, Territorial Integrity and the Sanctity of Borders', *SAIS Review of International Affairs* 26:1, 11-24.

Elliott, D.J. and Radin, C.J. (2008), *Iraqi Security Forces Order of Battle – Department of Border Enforcement*, available at <http://www.longwarjournal.org/multimedia/OOBpage11-DBE.pdf>, accessed May 2008.

Encyclopedia of Public International Law (2000), *Encyclopedia of Public International Law*, published under the auspices of the Max Planck Institute for Comparative Public Law and International law under the direction of Bernhardt, R. (North-Holland: Elsevier), 813.

FAI (2004), *100km Altitude boundary for Astronautics*, available at <http://www.fai.org/astronautics/100km.asp>, accessed April 2008.

Garamone, J. (2006), 'Border Police take on mission of Securing Iraq's Frontier', *American Forces Press Service* <http://www.defenselink.mil/news/newsarticle.aspx?id=15842>, accessed April 2008.

General Atomics (2008a), *Predator*, available at <http://www.ga-asi.com/products/predator.php>, accessed May 2008.

General Atomics (2008b), *Predator B/MQ-9 Reaper*, available at <http://www.ga-asi.com/products/pdf/Predator_B.pdf>, accessed May 2008.

Graham, S. (2004), 'Vertical Geopolitics: Baghdad and After', *Antipode* 36:1, 12-23.

ICE (2004), *US Immigration and Customs Enforcement - Arizona Border Control Initiative*, available at <http://www.ice.gov/graphics/news/factsheets/bordercontrols_031604.htm>, accessed March 2006.

Kaplan, C. (2006), 'Mobility and War: The Cosmic View of US "Air Power"', *Environment and Planning A* 38, 395-407.

Kostelnik, Major Gen. M.C. (2007), 'Unmanned Aircraft Systems in Homeland Security', available at <http://www.cbp.gov/linkhandler/cgov/border_security/air_marine/uas_program/uas_dhs_kostelnik.ctt/uas_dhs_kostelnik.ppt>, accessed June 2007.

Kraska, P. (2007), 'Militarisation and Policing – Its Relevance to 21st Century Police', *Policing* doi:10.1093/police/pam065, 1-13.

Kraska, P. and Kappeler, V. (1997), 'Militarising American Police: The Rise and Normalisation of Paramilitary Units', *Social Problems* 44:1, 1-18.

Kyriakides, K.A. (1998), 'Air Power and International Air Law', in Peach, S. (ed.), *Perspectives on Air Power: air power in its wider context* (Bracknell: Joint Services Command Staff College).

Laitinen, K. (2003), 'Geopolitics of the Northern Dimension: A Critical View on Security Borders', *Geopolitics* 8:1, 20-44.

Meyers, D.W. (2005), *US Border Enforcement: from horseback to high-tech* (Washington DC: Migration Policy Institute).

Multi-National Force – Iraq (2008), 'Iraq Division of Border Enforcement graduates 160', available at <http://www.mnf-iraq.com/index2.php?option=com_content&task=view&id=16867&p>, accessed April 2008.

Nevins, J. (2002), *Operation Gatekeeper: The Rise of the 'Illegal Alien' and The Making of The US-Mexico Border* (New York: Routledge).

Office of Border Patrol (2004), *National Border Patrol Strategy* (Washington DC: US Customs and Border Protection).

Omissi, D.E. (1990), *Air Power and Colonial Control: the Royal Air Force, 1919-1939* (Manchester: Manchester University Press).

Pascoe, D. (2001), *Airspaces* (London: Reaktion Books).

Report to Congress (2008), *Measuring Stability and Security in Iraq – March*, available at <http://www.defenselink.mil/pubs/pdfs/Master%20%20Mar08%20-%20final%20signed.pdf>, accessed April 2008.

Report to Congress (2006), *Measuring Stability and Security in Iraq – November*, available at <http://www.defenselink.mil/pubs/pdfs/9010Quarterly-Report-20061216.pdf>, accessed April 2008.

Strohm, C. (2007), *Funding is Reserved for UAVs to monitor borders*, available at <http://www.govexec.com/story_page_pf.cfm?articleid=38905&printerfriendly vers=1>, accessed March 2008.

UNCLOS (1982), *United National Convention on the Law of the Sea* (London: HMSO).

US Defense Technical Information Center (2006), *Air Policing*, available at <http://www.dtic.mil/doctrine/jel/doddict/natoterm/a/00083.html>, accessed February 2006.

Weizman, E. (2007), *Hollow Land: Israel's Architecture of Occupation* (London: Verso).

Weizman, E. (2002), *The Politics of Verticality*, available at <http://www.opendemocracy.net>, accessed October 2006.

White House (2008), *Homeland Security*, available at <http://www.whitehouse.gov/infocus/homeland/index.html>, accessed June 2008.

White House (2004), *Iraq Fact of the Day – Securing Iraq's Borders*, available at <http://www.whitehouse.gov/news/releases/2004/03/20040315-2.html>, accessed April 2008.

Williams, A.J. (2010), 'A Crisis in Aerial Sovereignty? Considering the Implications of Recent Military Violations of National Airspace', *Area* 42: 1, 51-59.

Williams, A.J. (2007), 'Hakumat al Tayarrat: The Role of Air Power in the Enforcement of Iraq's Boundaries', *Geopolitics* 12:3, 505-28.

Wise, J. (2007), 'Civilian UAVs: no pilot, no problem', *Popular Mechanics*, available at <http://www.popularmechanics.com/science/air_space/4213464.html>, accessed March 2008.

Zureik, E. and Salter, M.B. (2005), 'Introduction', in Zureik, E. and Salter, M.B. (eds.), *Global Surveillance and Policing: borders, security, identity* (Cullompton: Willan Publishing), 1-10.

A Retrospective Look at the Nature of National Borders in Latin America

Edgardo Manero

Introduction

The purpose of this chapter is to contribute to a better understanding of borders in Latin America, and how they are related to conflict over sovereignty. The chapter will present an account of the paradoxical process the borders in Latin America have undergone after being, during modernity, more or less subjective mode of delimitation of the political power that made possible the monopoly of legitimate violence and the constitution of semi closed spaces of social conflicts. These borders are now strongly called into question at the same time as they have become a strategic priority.

In the post-Cold War era we find ourselves facing a new vision of the territory-security relationship, a vision that radically changes the traditional strategic representations built on the basis of territorial neighbourhood, all of which affects the more general definition of a border as the boundary we wish to defend. Still, Latin American border areas, which have not been well-defined or integrated since colonial times, continue to be peculiar territories where conflicts proliferate. This is the case despite the relative stability that has been established due to the change in classic war hypotheses of armed conflict based on geopolitical thinking and historic animosities.

Sensitive as always, the issue of the control of borders and territories of necessity continues to reappear on the scene of a deep territorial, social and political reorganization. Such repeated re-emergence of sovereignty conflicts cannot be explained merely by the residual weight that the territory has in the collective imagination, by the fact that the states have not yet completely resolved the issue of colonial heritage, or by the interest in re-igniting the conflict for purposes of internal politics. In post-Cold War times, these conflicts must be analysed in relationship to the importance that the issue of control of flows and stocks, both legal (raw materials) or illegal (for example drugs, smuggling, immigrants) has acquired.

The end of the Cold War was accompanied not only by the prevalence of territorial disputes, but also by a recovery of the strategic importance of the strict, linear border defined by the Roman *limes* concept, a definition which has persisted despite numerous changes. These changes include global issues such as globalization's permeability with its increased mobility of capital, merchandise, and persons the paradigms based on the replacement of the nation-state concept; and the institution of new forms of membership. The strict, linear definition has also persisted despite questions of amore regional nature, such as the resolution of disputes over territories linked to the establishment of post-colonial states; making progress on the regional integration process, which has led to the establishment of supranational spaces; and the consolidation of democracy and the weakening of the military.

This chapter should enable us to analyse the trends observed in the current developments concerning borders. It also offers a prospective view of the possible outcomes of sovereignty conflicts in Latin America in relation to world-level changes. Two chronological stages will be reviewed using a comparative rather than a developmental approach, from the consolidation of the nation-state throughout the end of the Cold War and the post-Cold War.

Territorial Neighbourhood

Neighbourhood geography has strongly influenced decision-making in Latin America since the establishment of the post-colonial state. The geopolitical and strategic representations of Latin American nations are essentially terrestrial as a result of the adaptation of the European paradigm of strategic interaction to the neighbouring communities. However, Latin America has developed a heterodox conception of neighbourhood. The logic of territorial neighbourhood has been modified by the effect of the ideological dimension of the threat – the enemy within – and by the presence of extraterritorial powers, basically the United States of America, affecting the relationship among the region's states. Territorial conflicts were the most frequent and visible way to challenge a state's sovereignty in Latin America. Rivalry concerning power over the different territories developed independently from political ideologies, and reappeared in a diversity of situations. This illustrates a trend that goes beyond Latin America. In general, the ideological variable is not central to territorial conflicts. Sovereignty conflicts may emerge among ideological and military allies or among commercial partners, such as the controversy between the United States of America (USA) and Canada; they can be handled in a peaceful manner among ideological rivals, as shown by the negotiation of a maritime border agreement between the USA and Cuba. Moreover, politicians of opposing ideologies may instrumentalize conflicts in the domestic arena; for example, Venezuelan Presidents Luis Herrera-Campins and Hugo Chávez have both used the dispute between Venezuela and Guyana concerning the Esquibo region.

Thus, border problems, that is, problems generally inherited from the establishment of the post-colonial state, have traditionally been revived by economic questions. Conflicts between Nicaragua and Honduras are an example. In the 1980s, the flow of Nicaraguan refugees into Honduras and the presence of anti-Sandinist groups operating from there created great tension between the two Central American nations. Since the end of the 1990s, the border problem between Honduras and Nicaragua has been linked to two priority issues of the 'new international order': natural resources and economic migrations.

The post-Cold War era illustrates this special feature of territorial conflict. In Central America, border conflicts are mixed with ideology. Tension between Managua and Bogota coincides with tension between Venezuelan President Hugo Chávez and his Colombian counterpart Alvaro Uribe, concerning mediation in the conflict with the the Revolutionary Armed Forces of Colombia – People's Army (FARC) guerrilla. Daniel Ortega, President of Nicaragua, is Chávez's main political ally in Central America and close to the FARC.[1] On the other side of the spectrum, the conflict between Argentina and Uruguay about the installation of cellulose manufacturing plants on the banks of the Uruguay River illustrates the manner in which the geopolitical variable and the 'national interest' are elements affecting the relationship between political actors who view themselves as progressive and who share a political space with common characteristics as well as a community of political representations.[2]

The establishment of territorial boundaries is a key issue in the formation of the nation-state. In Latin America, the modern linear-type border marked by a line of posts or border markers was late to appear and it is particularly linked to the constitution of the nation-state. The North American notion of frontier, developed by Turner for the Far West, does not apply in a homogeneous and general way to Latin American history. Places used as borders are areas where people meet, where there may be confrontations but where also exchange and mingling take place. Relations of complementarity between the populations of the two sides are more important, at least at the local level, than differences, rivalry and conflicts among the countries. In Latin America, the border has been porous and friendly, but also hostile. It has encouraged exchanges, and at the same time it has helped obstruct them.

In peripheral countries, the representation of the border area is much more restricted and local. Frequently, the border representation refers only to the physical border area. As a consequence of the lack of integration of national areas,

---

1   Relations between Colombia and the Sandinista governments have always been problematic. During the 1980s Nicaragua claimed sovereignty over the San Andres and Providencia archipelago, and denounced the Esguerra-Bárcenas treaty (1928). The archipelago has been under Colombian control since the treaty's final ratification in 1930. Nicaragua considered the treaty invalid and argued that it was signed during the American occupation of Nicaragua.

2   Another example is the relationship between the PT administration in Brazil and president Morales of Bolivia.

it is often difficult for the border area to enclose the total area of the national state, and it even happens, in the case of certain populations, that it does not go beyond the local space, the region or even the village. However, an Ecuadorian Indian or a Bolivian peasant who can hardly conceive a national border area becomes aware of it when they enter into contact with the action of transnational firms or with foreign powers that affect their interests.[3]

By contrast in hegemonic countries[4] – especially those with a 'colonial tradition' – the border area does not end where the national space of the metropolis ends. The nation's border is not limited by the national physical border. The border can be extended to any point that a transnational company, a soldier, a foundation or an NGO can reach, which is to say that it is set wherever there may be interests, with which the nation in question identifies itself. This does not necessarily imply expansion of the physical border. The case of the United States of America is paradigmatic. Its idea of limits, in contrast to the idea shared by other new nation states such as the Latin American states, was not about finiteness. Thus, at the end of the nineteenth century, the 'conquest of the frontier' was followed, through expansion towards the outside, by the annexation of Cuba, Puerto Rico, and the Philippines. Such expansion, which had its roots in the 'Manifest Destiny' ideology, sought support in the myths of the frontier of the pioneers and settlers. The border was also set as far away as the national interest would permit. For the United States in the post-Cold War era, the border was inseparable from the 'enlargement' of liberal democracy and the market economy.

A Latin American paradox: While border conflicts are relatively frequent and the military hypotheses of conflict are built upon the idea of a menacing neighbouring community, a central element of regional strategic cultures is that war among states is rare,[5] and co-operation among the states as well as the sense of belonging to one single cultural entity are a constant. Conflicts due to the setting of territorial boundaries do not hinder good relations among the states.

In general, Latin Americans do not feel threatened by their neighbours. It is difficult, in Latin America, other than for territorial affairs and the quest for regional hegemony, to channel hostility vis-à-vis the neighbouring state because of cultural similarities among most countries. On the other hand, the presence of extraterritorial powers – which are culturally different – in territories over which the countries of the region claim rights has not unleashed any wars. With the

---

3   Pollution of the land by oil companies in Ecuador or demands for eradication of coca crops in Bolivia by the United States of America are two examples.

4   This is the case of a member country of the 'Group of Eight' but also of several other countries emerging and re-emerging as 'powers', such as China and India.

5   According to Domínguez, J.I. (2003b), the structure of the international system in the American continent and its relations with the somewhat distant global system and the inter-American procedures and institutions explain the rareness and short duration of wars.

exception of Argentina and Britain in 1982, no country has militarily placed the status quo in doubt.

The states in Latin America have many militarized disputes on their records; nevertheless, they have good relations among themselves and cooperate closely with each other. Although the use of force to determine certain aspects of bilateral relations is a constant, transforming words into action is less so.[6]

Although during the second half of the twentieth century the main armed conflicts among states were linked with territory – whether by force of war (El Salvador-Honduras 1969, Argentina-Great Britain 1982, Peru-Ecuador 1995) or by force of a military confrontation (Colombia-Venezuela 1987, Nicaragua-Honduras 2000), or by the possibility of war (Argentina-Chile 1978), the level of violence reached in territorial neighbourhood-related conflicts cannot be compared in importance to that of other regions.

The history of borders in Latin America and the Caribbean has been relatively peaceful, except at rather localized geographical points, and most of the disputes have finally been solved by negotiation or arbitration. A large number of conflicts have been dormant for a long time. These conflicts result from de-colonization itself. Latin American countries have made efforts to define their territorial sovereignty according to the *Uti possidetis juris* doctrine, a principle establishing that a state liberated from colonization inherits the colonial administrative boundaries that it had when it acquired its independence. The independent republics would be the inheritors of the territories that were under colonial administration. The application of this doctrine consisted in keeping the old administrative borders and creating international borders. It should be noted that there is a long-standing discussion as to whether this principle is applicable to regions where there was no effective occupation during colonial times, such as Patagonia. Territorial conflicts – and irredentism – reappeared with the independence of Guyana (1966) and Belize (1981) as the consequence of a new de-colonization process.

The presence of extra-regional powers such as Great Britain or the USA is a major fact in the territorial picture in Latin America. The latter have participated in separatism, as in the cases of Uruguay in 1828 or Panama in 1903; they have occupied and continue to occupy territories claimed by Latin American states, such as Guantánamo or the Malvinas Islands; and have used dissuasion as a consequence of military asymmetry vis-à-vis the demands of a Latin American state, as in the case of Belize. Closely related to the preceding issue, territorial disputes among the Latin American nation-states can be covers for a 'conflict by delegation' among multinational companies – oil companies, in the Paraguay-Bolivia case[7] and banana companies between Guatemala and Honduras.[8]

---

6   For Domínguez, J.I. (2003b, 16), this is a Latin American dilemma.

7   In the Chaco War (1932 to 1935), the two countries wanted to gain control over the Chaco Boreal section where oil was believed to be, which turned out to be false. Bolivia was supported by U.S. oil companies, and Paraguay by British oil companies.

8   In 1928, these two countries entered into a confrontation with military mobilization in support of the opposing demands of the United Fruit Company and the Cuyamel

The United States has participated in various ways in sovereignty conflicts[9]. At the end of the nineteenth century, the United States became involved in the conflict between Venezuela and Great Britain and repeated its involvement in the 1930s during the conflict between Guatemala and Honduras, in the 1980s between Argentina and Great Britain, and in the 1990s, between Peru and Ecuador.

However, U.S. hegemony is not adequate to explain the perspectives of inter-state war and peace in Latin America. Within a North American hegemony scenario, the second half of the twentieth century has seen territory-related, open armed conflicts erupt among close allies of the hegemonic power: Honduras-El Salvador (1969), Argentina-Chile (1978), Guatemala-Belize (1981), Argentina-United Kingdom (1982), and Peru-Ecuador (1995).

Neither hemispherization of the armed forces nor U.S. influence through the National Security Doctrine have been able to eradicate neighbourhood rivalries; neither readiness to set up military alliances among the region's authoritarian regimes to fight against international communism, nor strategic and political representations close to the international system have impeded traditional rivalry (see Manero 2007b).

Every strategic analysis of the second half of the twentieth century must consider the regionalization of security dynamics in the Southern Cone, in progress since World War II under the influence of the United States, as the persistence of a regional power-balance system resulting from regional rivalries and organized around the logics of a menacing territorial neighbouring community.

The Inside-Outside Dimension in Border Conflicts

Two basic types of reason account for the permanence of border problems in Latin America. Primarily, there are space reasons: Reference is made to the geography of the continent, with its jungles and mountains, making border demarcation difficult; to a weak, inaccurate cartography; and to the existence of enormous empty expanses. These reasons then become political: the weak presence of the state in the territory; the fact that the national states of the American sub-continent were formed by the disintegration rather than by integration of the internal market; the lack of continuity in the territorial delimitation processes associated with political instability; the importance of the armed forces in decision-making; and the fact that territorial conflicts may be used to serve domestic political objectives.

Border conflicts appear as a form of socialization and intensification of group cohesion, an element that reinforces collective cohesion. From the time this mechanism for cohesion was used routinely as a resource by the Somozas in Nicaragua in the conflict with Costa Rica to the Malvinas war, it has been a constant.

Fruit Company.

9   According to Mares, D. (2001), the United States has played a limited role as an intermediary.

Behind the concept of a neighbouring community menacing a state's territory, we can see a system of representation of the antagonisms in which the border dispute is most useful for channelling the conflict out of the nation-state framework. The creation of an external neighbourhood attempts to eradicate the existence of an internal neighbourhood. The principle according to which external 'threat' is the basis of internal political 'friendship' causes external conflict to become the axis of a greater social cohesion. Traditionally, this principle has been used to justify the imposition of limitations on dissidents.[10]

The use of the 'displacement' mechanism in Latin America is clearly an operation within a cost-benefit relationship. This mechanism works very well in a region where the probability of arriving at an open conflict is rather low, given the characteristics of the Inter-American System.[11] This low probability lies upon one characteristic of the region: the mediating role of both the states and the regional institutions for maintaining the peace in any such occurrence.[12] The intervention tradition has made possible the progressive institutionalization of an inter-American conflict-resolution system. One example is the role played by the Rio Group and, to a lesser extent, by the Organization of American States in the Colombia-Ecuador dispute in March 2008.

The available arsenal of inter-American procedures and institutions explains not only the absence or the short duration of inter-state wars, but also plays a role in the instrumental utilization of the territorial neighbourhood and certain defiant behaviours in the pursuit of domestic political objectives.

The 'displacement paradigm' is always tempting as an analysis and explanation of the phenomenon of nationalism. To a certain extent, it is even appropriate for interpreting a great number of border conflicts. However, this analytical perspective cannot be mechanically applied to the populist movements, which are the most important manifestation of Latin American nationalism. For them, the threat does not come from a neighbouring state but from 'Imperialism'. From Perón to Chávez, integration thus appears as an element of *Realpolitik*. For this type of nationalism, the defence of national interests necessarily falls into the framework of regional integration.

---

10 While extreme conflict may be an important integration factor, it is not the only one. Shared beliefs and values and the expectation of mutual benefits from living together as a community are also important integration factors. Agreement on values reinforces a community.

11 According to Domínguez (2003b, 30), states can behave carelessly in order to serve national political objectives, under the assurance that the international institutions will intervene to settle the dispute.

12 Thus, during the 1930s, the Chaco war between Paraguay and Bolivia generated a general concern. Argentina played a leading role in this conflict and foreign affairs minister Saavedra-Lamas was in fact awarded the Nobel Peace Prize for his intervention towards a solution of it. Another example is the decisive role played by Argentina, Brazil, Chile and the United States of America in the various conflicts between Ecuador and Peru (1940, 1980 and 1990).

Nevertheless, the logic of displacement quickly shows its limitations. The attitude of the Guatemalan military vis-à-vis the decision of President Jorge Serrano to change a secular, century-old political position by recognizing, the existence of Belize in 1991 illustrates this. The army, which supported the president, was satisfied with such a decision, which allowed the military to acquire greater control on internal security tasks, while reducing the risk of war against the British guarantors of Belize's sovereignty (Mares 2003, 81).

Conflicts Associated with the Management Limitations of State Power

International political and economic processes and the current hemispheric dynamics are eroding the pre-existing *status quo* in Latin America, despite the persistence of 'archaic' border-type conflicts. This does not imply denial of the inertia that preserves regional rivalry or the importance of territory that may remain in the collective imagination, as can be observed in the relationship among Chile, Bolivia and Peru.[13]

However, beyond the change experienced with respect to the menacing neighbouring community, Latin America continues to be a setting for local and regional crises; one example is the escalation, in March 2008, of the conflict among Venezuela, Ecuador and Colombia as a consequence of the Colombian military entering into Ecuadorean territory to destroy a provisional camp of the FARC and killing one of their leaders, Raul Reyes.

Crises and factors of political instability are among the sources of conflict, the type of open conflict whose final settlement is a prerequisite for achieving co-operation. While the disagreements between Alvaro Uribe and Hugo Chavez did not stop bilateral trade, they paralysed the resolution of the border dispute, the energy integration project, and the consolidation of the Andean Community of Nations.

In the 1990s, the array of inter-American procedures and institutions as well as the hegemonic political and strategic representations attempted to defuse border conflicts. A shared vision concerning integration into the international system, the role of markets and the value of liberal democracy accompanied the decision to deactivate conflicts so as to give priority to common economic interests. This was based on a 'utilitarian' logic that the costs of disagreements are greater than the price to be paid for solving the conflicts. Solving a conflict would thus become part of a macro strategy.

Thus, while the Argentine-Chilean case is a good example, the Peruvian-Chilean case shows the unpredictable nature of the initiative. Although in 1999 Chile and

---

13   This case concerns a legacy of the War of the Pacific (1879-83), during which Peru lost the province of Tarapacá and Bolivia the province of Antofagasta.

Peru made progress on the imposition of the 1883 and 1929 treaties, which marked the end of the 'War of the Pacific,' the conflict re-emerged in 2007 with respect to maritime borders. Nevertheless, the Peruvian demands did not affect bilateral relations.

A final solution to the main border problems generated by the colonial heritage in South America was found at the end of the twentieth century (Argentina and Chile, Ecuador and Peru). Only four classic, non-maritime conflicts are still being dealt with. Three among them are related to de-colonization as a consequence of British colonial advances after the independence of Latin America. They are sources of conflict between Venezuela and Guyana, Guatemala and Belize, and Argentina and the United Kingdom. The first two conflicts reappeared at the end of the 1990s, the third in 2007. The fourth one is a question of irredentism mixed with new problems: renewed efforts by Bolivia seeking an outlet to the Pacific Ocean.

However, at the same time Latin America has witnessed the emergence of 'new' disputes and the reactivation of the old ones, which to a large extent are related to new disputes: Guyana-Surinam, Nicaragua-Colombia, Honduras-Cuba, Nicaragua-El Salvador, Nicaragua-Honduras, Nicaragua-Costa Rica, Argentina-Uruguay, Peru-Chile, Colombia-Ecuador, Colombia-Venezuela, Honduras-Guatemala, Venezuela-Trinidad and Tobago, Honduras-El Salvador, and Panama-Colombia. With the exception of some islands of the Caribbean (Bahamas, Dominica, Jamaica, San Cristobal, Saint Kitts and Nevis and Saint Lucia), all other member countries of the Organization of American States (OAS) are involved in at least one international border conflict. In addition, if disagreements over the rules that regulate actions in territorial waters and national air space are included in the disputes over sovereignty, the United States has conflicts with almost the entire American continent. However, the asymmetry of power makes it difficult for this type of dispute to become a serious conflict.

One characteristic of these conflicts is the fact that they can be unilateral. Thus, while Bolivia and Peru maintain that they are in conflict with Chile, the latter does not acknowledge that there is such a conflict. The situation is similar in the case of Colombia. In response to criticism from Nicaragua's president Daniel Ortega, the Colombian minister of foreign affairs, Fernando Araujo, has stressed on several occasions that his country is not in any situation of conflict with any state.

Such comeback of territorial conflicts within a political context characterized by the hegemony of the democratic system, the market economy, the regional integration process, and by the hegemony of the United States of America seems to question the traditionally-established relationship between the regime-type variable and territorial rivalry in Latin America, a distant by-product of the notion that democracies do not fight each other.

Without a doubt, the existence of a democratic framework and procedures plays a role in the solving of border and territorial conflicts. The Argentine-Chilean case is a good example. These countries cooperate with each other in every field, including defence and security. For them, their relations constitute a strategic alliance. However, the intensification of the sovereignty conflicts in Central

America since the 1990s among democratic states illustrates the autonomy of this type of dispute in relationship to the political system.

The resurgence of borders as strategic priorities must be viewed in relationship with new problems. Poorly determined border lines and unfinished agreements are combined with the political use of the conflict and interests such as access to natural resources, management of border areas, problems like migration, the development of various transnational criminal organizations, and the effect of strategic representations and doctrines which relativize traditional national sovereignty.

Thus, at the start of the twenty-first century, the most important border conflict, Colombia, is not related to disputes over the border line, but to the action of various actors (guerrillas, paramilitary forces, the armed and security forces of Colombia and of the neighbouring countries, criminal organizations, displaced populations, and the United States of America), and diverse interests ranging from illegal and legal traffic – evidenced by the size of the underground economy in Colombia – through the activities of transnational companies that exploit oil or that provide security to the national interests of the regional and extra-regional nation-states.

In the Post-Cold War era, sovereignty problems in Latin America are related to the significance of the control of flows and stocks, whether legal (raw materials) or illegal (for instance, drugs, smuggling, and immigrants). Diverse, heterogeneous actors are involved in such control. They could be criminal or political-military organizations, but also nation-states or transnational corporations seeking to acquire control over natural resources.

The consolidation of new forms of border problems, which are related to the limits of managing state power and of the state's capacity to prevent crime and guarantee a legal framework, has been accompanied by the development of legal and illegal organizations – to a large extent transnational – that are perceived as a threat. These trends are already taking shape. The real or assumed absence of 'effective sovereignty' allows for criminal organizations and transnational corporations to be active and the USA to intervene. During the post-Cold War era, territory-related conflicts in Latin America are not due to the power of the neighbouring states, but to the weakness, whether real or assumed, of the state in question vis-à-vis actors as diverse as multinational corporations, criminal organizations or the hegemonic power.

The Latin American state was drastically put to the test during the neoliberal cycle by the intensity with which the new forms of mobility and circulation that characterize the contemporary experience manifested themselves. From this point of view, probably the most important phenomenon marking this experience is that which affect borders, where the architecture of defense and security has traditionally been anchored.

Transnational Flows

In South America, not all flows and stocks have the same strategic importance. The circulation of illegal products such as cocaine stands in contrast to the increase in importance of the illegal circulation flows of legal goods, which is taken into consideration but does not constitute a major strategic concern or a cause of conflict. The 'triple border' is a case in point. Brazil's unilateral project to build a wall along the border with Paraguay between the towns of Foz do Iguaçu and Ciudad del Este has not created a conflictual situation. The illegal circulation of legal merchandise crosses a series of countries around the 'triple border,' from Paraguay to Foz do Iguaçu and Puerto Iguazú to then go on to the rest of the territory. However, the 'triple border' region, considered by the USA as a no-law zone where various criminal organizations, especially 'narcos' and 'terrorists' are established, has a high strategic priority.

Inside Latin America, population flows have a considerable impact on the reshaping of security spaces, even though national societies are not internally affected by intensive migration flows that would result in a flow over territorial borders producing a mingling of socio-cultural identities. The scale and dynamics of human displacements in Latin America cannot be examined on the basis of the classic research terms developed in and for European and North American societies. In the region, migration as a strategic problem implies matters as diverse as refugee issues resulting from the spill-over of inter-state conflicts (Colombia is an example); the containment of flows towards developed countries, particularly the United States of America; and holding foreign elements responsible for the increase in crime or unemployment[14] or for settlements in border areas. However, in the twenty-first century this has been oriented towards prohibiting the purchase of land in border areas or of land considered strategic by foreign corporations rather than to citizens settling in the neighbouring country, as had been the case during the geopoliticism of confrontation in the twentieth century.

Migration as a cause of conflict in Latin American inter-state relations was an issue at a very early stage. Repeated tension cycles upset official relations between Haiti and the Dominican Republic with occasional tragic outcomes; such was the case, in 1937, of the massacre of thousands of Haitians in the Dominican Republic under the Trujillo regime. In 1969 the flow of Salvadorians who crossed the border into Honduras was one of the main causes for the war.

In the Post-Cold War era, the issue of refugees and displaced populations is of paramount importance in the Colombian conflict, but this is also true in Central America. Guatemalan populations that occupy virgin lands in Belize and the migration of Nicaraguans into Honduras are two examples. In 2006-2007, the possibility of a conflict in Bolivia has been a matter of concern in the neighbouring

---

14   In the Argentina of the 1990s, it is possible to find a common denominator with the European experiences in the manner in which Latin American immigrants were reclassified in a security sense by the receiving populations, the political establishment and the press. See Manero (2007a).

states given the possible increase in the number of seasonal immigrants and refugees. In Latin America, an increase in the displacement of populations must be visualized in the context of the expansion of monocultures, especially of soybeans and palm oil. As part of the global trends towards the production of bio fuel and supplying an international food market under pressure on demand, monocultures destroy peasant cultures and forces migration. Such 'internal' migrations could become 'transnational', flowing not only to the United States of America but to Europe as well. The case of Ecuadoreans, Colombians and Peruvians in Spain illustrates this point since they constitute human flows of significant importance from Latin America to Europe on the basis of already established networks.

From a strategic point of view, the borders between Latin America and the United States of America are a basic element in this analysis. The U.S.-Mexican border is the point where the immigrants from all of Latin America converge. The reinforcement of restrictions to the circulation of migrant populations dates back to the 1980s. The installation of metal barriers in the Tijuana-San Diego region was encouraged by the free trade agreements among the United States of America, Mexico, and Canada. It is less likely for the flows of capital and goods to be accompanied by displacement of the work force. The other side of the agreements for the circulation of goods and capital is the setting up of barriers to the circulation of the labour force. This is not particularly characteristic of the United States of America. The images of African immigrants trying to make it through the different defensive systems – metal barriers, electrified link fences, security forces – at the Spanish exclave Melilla resemble those of Latin American immigrants at the U.S.-Mexican border. Since 9/11, the aspect of security regarding migrations is no longer an explicit taboo. It is on the basis of a terrorist threat that the new forms of the control of mobility and the displacement of certain individuals and populations are developed.

Because of NAFTA,[15] the Mexico-USA border is both open to the free passage of goods that are difficult to control and simultaneously strongly fortified; its role is to slow the movement of immigrants and keep them, through its offshore manufacturing operations, on the other side of the border to take advantage of the comparative advantages provided by this labour force, resulting from the development of competitive prices for a displaced U.S. industry. These offshore manufacturing operations are a key element within a more sophisticated logic of containing human flows through the economy. In general, peripheral border regions have an important effect on national economies. Border zone industrial facilities are a source of development that exerts a permanent attraction for populations that seek better living conditions. This is the case of Tijuana and Ciudad Juárez in Mexico, or Tangiers and Tetuan in Morocco. The various governmental bodies tend to be overtaken by the multiple consequences of demographic growth.

---

15   The North American Free Trade Agreement defines a free-exchange zone formed by the United States of America, Canada and Mexico. Signed by presidents George Bush, Brian Mulroney and Carlos Salinas de Gortari on 10 July 1992, the agreement entered into force on 1 January 1994.

Management of Stocks

In the global disorder, some sovereignty conflicts have to do with controversies about the acquisition, control, management of, or access to real or imagined natural resources. The importance that disputes relative to the definition of maritime borders have in comparison to land borders is a case in point. These conflicts are directly related to the exploitation of hydrocarbons and fishing. This is nothing new. The controversy between Colombia and Venezuela over borders in the Gulf of Venezuela is closely related to the discovery, in the 1960s, of oil in this area.

It is also worth noting the disputes between Argentina[16] and Great Britain in the South Atlantic and Antarctica, between Peru and Chile in the Pacific, and in the Caribbean region. In this region, there are various maritime conflicts: Honduras-Cuba, Nicaragua-Honduras, Venezuela-Colombia (Gulf of Venezuela). They may be tripartite as in the case of El Salvador, Honduras, and Nicaragua concerning the Gulf of Fonseca, or also inactive, as is the conflict between Venezuela and Trinidad and Tobago concerning fishing; they may even riddled with ideological issues, which is the case in the dispute between Bogota and Managua concerning their borders in the Caribbean. This is the most interesting conflict, given the number of actors and variables and the level of militarization involved. The government of Nicaragua stresses attempts by Colombia and Honduras[17] to take from it territories in the Caribbean Sea. Nicaragua is also in conflict with Costa Rica over the San Juan River. The common denominators in such border disputes, which are mainly in Central America and in the Caribbean region, are non-observance of treaties and agreements, their long duration, and a low intensity of violence.

Several factors are closely related to the development of this type of conflict. Among them are the increasing importance of the sea to the world economy, the development of new technologies to exploit maritime resources, and changes extending maritime jurisdiction in international maritime law as a consequence of the United Nations Convention on the Law of the Sea (1982).

The oceans are governed by this convention, which sets the extent of the exclusive economic zone of a coastal state at 200 nautical miles. If a state claims seabed beyond that point it must prove with geological profiles that these seabed are an extension of its own continental shelf. Otherwise, the principle of freedom on the high seas is applied. This convention has not been ratified by the United States of America, which causes permanent conflicts in Latin America.

The matter of oceans as open borders where tensions between two coastal states manifest themselves is of a global nature. Thus, the hypothesis according to which the Arctic Ocean releases its summer ice under the effect of climate warming, thus making raw materials in the abyss more accessible will kindle the desire for them. At the end of July 2007, two expeditions, one from Russia and one from Canada,

---

16   Since 2006, Argentina has sought to toughen sanctions against illegal fishing in an exclusive economic zone.

17   The government of Honduras has approved prospecting by oil companies in the region disputed with Nicaragua.

made almost simultaneous claims of sovereignty. Disputes over sovereignty abound in the Arctic zone.

Concerning natural resource management, we can also look back at the conflict between Argentina and Uruguay over the use of the Uruguay River. This conflict put back on the table, in a radically new form, the conflicts relative to the control of rivers and river basins with their tributaries and effluents. With the agreements between Brazil and Argentina in 1979 the matter of the use of water resources was the last expression of the controversy concerning the way in which neighbouring states use the resources in border areas.

At the beginning of the twenty-first century, strong tensions characterized relations between Argentina and Uruguay, although the two countries were governed by presidents who were ideologically close. The origin of the conflict was the installation of two large cellulose manufacturing plants on the banks of the Uruguay River, a bi-national water course that serves as border between the two countries. According to the Argentineans, these industries pollute the river. For diplomatic reasons, an agreement with the Argentine government would have been required, to authorize the installation of these plants in the border area. Uruguay violated the treaty on the river. This conflict is of paramount importance, given the fact that this border has traditionally been characterized by relations of complementariness rather than conflicts and tensions at the local and regional levels. These exchanges have initiated cultural practices rooted in cross-border identities. Encounters and rapprochement have prevailed over conflicts. Tension between the populations along the banks of the Uruguay River is new.

In Argentina, the conflict has produced the emergence of a social movement structured into assemblies, according to the tradition established with the 2001 crisis, which acts not only against the construction of the two cellulose plants, but also against the economic model that these plants represent. In Argentina, the participation of social movements in disputes over natural and mineral resources, water, and land, has been important since the 1990s.

The expression of an intention on the part of the inhabitants to control the development of the space near them is the new characteristic of the conflict. This reveals a new relationship with the territory. It also reveals the effect that civil society has on inter-regional relations, not only with reference to Uruguay, but to other countries of the region, like Chile. The members of the assemblies have blocked not only the bridges between Argentina and Uruguay, but also access routes used by Chilean trucks that transport materials for the construction of the plants. This has created problems in the relations between Argentina and Chile.

On the Uruguayan side, the conflict is presented and perceived as a sovereignty issue. The population feels that the defence of the cellulose plants is a 'national' issue. There is a wide consensus shared even by the left and by the labour-union movement concerning the measures taken by the government. The cellulose plants are viewed as a way out of the employment crisis. The establishment of the cellulose plants and the government's forestry policy are criticised only by ecologists and the extreme left.

At the end of November 2006, the government of Uruguay entrusted protection of the Botnia plant to the armed forces. The measure came in addition to a decree approved in October, which had increased the frequency of patrol missions by the Naval Prefecture along the Uruguay River. While the Uruguayan decision has not militarized the conflict between the two countries, it shows the new strategic condition of the borders. This decision represents not only a change in bilateral relations but also a change in the spirit of the politics of the Uruguayan left. The consequence of controversies over acquisition, control, management of, or access to natural resources may be the redefinition of the external and perhaps also the internal borders of national spaces.

The debate over the appropriation and use of hydrocarbon benefits is associated with the appearance of autonomist movements in the Zulia region of Venezuela and in the Bolivian *Oriente* region. At the beginning of the twenty-first century and by virtue of the stakes associated with hydrocarbons, Bolivia has become the example not only of a relationship between conflict and sovereignty over resources, but also of the durability of certain geopolitical 'tools' of varying degrees of relevance: activism for independence, irredentism, and annexation.

The twenty-first century brought about an attempt on the part of the state to re-appropriate the 'right to manage,' which corresponds to the demand for sovereignty that arose in a large part of the various societies after the 1990s. The strategic representations that began to circulate upon the exhaustion of the neoliberal cycle show that the perception of menace in border territories is not restricted to multiple illegalities – from criminal organizations to illegal immigration through terrorism- as the basis of transnational strategic representations. Strategic representations also turn on a more archaic problem – in the etymological sense of the term – of strategy: natural resources. At the beginning of the twenty-first century, such resources were found, under different forms, at the core of strategic and border questions. Actions by the armed forces were related to the defence of water in Argentina, of the Amazon in Brazil, of oil in Venezuela and in Ecuador, and of gas in Bolivia.

Nevertheless, the strategic dimension of natural resources is a question that acquires different emphasis depending on the definition of national interest and the development model chosen. In Chile and Uruguay in 2006, the governments instructed the armed forces to intervene for the protection of transnational corporations developing activities in the primary sector.

Colombia, Transnational Stakes of a Conflict

The border is a central component of a conflict particularly characterized by its actors' increased autonomy vis-à-vis the state system,[18] their heterogeneity, their command over illegal flows and stocks, and the high level of intervention of the hegemonic

---

18   The FARC have developed an action of a global nature structured by political and military contacts and support from different actors and nations.

power. The different actors in the Colombian conflict frequently cross the border. The dimension that borders have acquired in the relationship between Colombia and its neighbouring states became evident at both the tactical and strategic levels in the diplomatic consequences of the military operation of March 2008.

The bordering countries within the context of 'The Colombian Plan'[19] have expressed their concerns about the porosity of their borders. Governments have grown increasingly worried because of the expansion of the armed struggle, particularly towards the Amazonian basin. Brazil, Peru, and Venezuela have indicated that the military component of the Colombia Plan will eventually affect the whole of Amazonia: expulsion towards their borders of narco-traffickers, guerrillas, the migration of population, action undertaken by irregular military organizations, the expansion of illegal crops, and pollution.[20]

Brazil has militarily reinforced its border with Colombia, which was one of the priorities of the United States of America and has launched the *Calha Norte* plan to keep guerrillas and narcotraffickers from crossing the border. Brazil has also developed the training of anti-drug military units in the jungle. Considering narcotraffic increasingly as a matter of national security, the military has become involved in the fight against criminal organizations related to drugs. However, President Lula's Minister of Defense, José Viegas-Filho, does not want the government to amend the constitution in line with U.S. policy.[21]

Constant penetration of the Colombian army into Ecuador in pursuit of guerrillas, as well as the flow of immigrants, has negatively affected relations between the two countries. Differences became intensified in 2006 when the Uribe government started fumigating drug crops at the border with Ecuador.[22] In 2007, Ecuadorian President Rafael Correa endorsed the statements of his minister of defence indicating that the country's border in the north is not with Colombia but with the FARC guerrilla. He added that the southern Colombian border was not protected by the regular Colombian forces and that the Colombian conflict was very costly for Ecuador. In March 2008 the elimination of Raul Reyes, the number-two man in FARC, by the Colombian Army led to an escalation of tensions, the

---

19 The original version of the 'Colombia Plan' was officially conceived by the administration of President Andrés Pastrana to attain an economic and social revitalization and a strengthening of the state that would make it possible to end both the armed conflict and drug production. Within the framework of the bilateral agreements with the United States as the main supporter of the Plan, the state strengthening and pacification goals started to be increasingly less sought through an institutional reform and an improvement in the social and economic conditions, and more and more through the modernization of the army and the security forces to become the main guarantors of the re-establishment of order and territorial control. The objective of ending drug trafficking resulted in an open war against the insurgent movements. It was no longer related to the original mission that Pastrana had intended to accomplish at the beginning of his term.

20 *Clarín* 1 September 2000.

21 O Estado de S. Paulo 9 March 2003.

22 Ecuadoreans assert that they do not control the border with Colombia.

most serious in the region for many years among the three Bolivarian nations.[23] The violation of Ecuador's sovereignty by Colombia in 2008 not only re-launched the debate in Latin America over the 'no-law zones,' but also introduced the concept of 'preventive war' in the region.

Panama increased the deployment of its security forces along its border with Colombia as well. FARC activities should also be mentioned: organized crime, kidnappings, drug and arms traffic, and illegal immigrants. There is also a humanitarian problem that has two aspects, first, the Colombian refugees in the Darien region, and the elimination of alleged FARC collaborators by paramilitary forces that cross the border also in pursuit of guerrillas. Both the Panamanian and American governments perceive these actions as threats.

The porosity of the border between Colombia and Venezuela is a central element of the 'cold war' between Chávez and Uribe. Miraflores Palace blamed Uribe for the incursions of paramilitary forces into Venezuelan territory, particularly for kidnappings for extortion and the murder of Venezuelan military; Colombians blame the latter on the guerrillas. Sovereignty has been a central issue in the controversy between Colombia and Venezuela because of the capture of FARC leader Rodrigo Granda. Hugo Chavez has accused the Colombian government of having violated territorial sovereignty with the support of the United States of America. The members of the Colombian military forces in general and the Uribe government in particular accuse Venezuela of being a sanctuary for the guerrillas and maintain that this country does not take action against international terrorism. Hugo Chavez regards the FARC neither as a threat against his government nor as a terrorist organization.

The conflictual relationship between Uribe's Colombia and Chavez' Venezuela brought back, at the beginning of 2005, the fear of an arms race in the region. U.S. military support to Bogota via the 'Colombia Plan' transformed the Colombian forces into the second military power after Brazil in which led to the purchase of weapons by Venezuela. The United States underlined its suspicion that Chavez was arming the Colombian guerrilla.[24] Since Alvaro Uribe took office, Colombia, the main ally of the United States in the region, has been playing a central role in the politics of the American continent to contain the Bolivarian republic and its 'radical populism,' defined by Washington as a 'new threat.' George Bush's proposal for U.S. aid to be used against every 'menace against Colombian national security' closes a cycle. Originally intended to be used in the anti-drugs fight and actually used in the 'anti-terrorist' fight, the request of the U.S. president would have permitted the use of such aid in a hypothetical conflict with Venezuela.[25]

The Colombian issue shows that the strategic revaluing of borders must not be related only to the nature of the threats of the Post-Cold War era, to their perception, or to their effects. Revaluing borders must also be associated with the development

---

23   Ecuador and Venezuela concentrated military forces along their borders with Colombia and broke diplomatic relations with Bogota. Liberation 3 March 2008.
24   Clarín 16 February 2005.
25   El Tiempo Bogota 3 March 2006.

of a vision of security that is closely related to hegemonic strategic representations at the base of the international system and supported by the United States. These representations stress the global character of the stakes at play and of the security reactions. They sustain the assertion that the defence of sovereignty shall no longer be limited to the protection of borders and the territory in their traditional forms. The armies must approach the protection of each country on the basis of a regional perspective, working together towards the defence of sovereignty with a regional awareness and with an international solidarity. The argument raised over the fight against terrorism and drugs, which promotes control over the so-called 'porous borders', 'no-law (lawless) zones', and 'failed states' (Manero 2007b), implies a re-definition of the concept of sovereignty. Borders are no longer respected and sovereignty has become a conditioned privilege that depends, ultimately, on the national interest of the USA.

During her trip to Brazil in March 2008, the U.S. Secretary of State Condoleezza Rice proposed a regional combat policy against terrorism and justified Bogota's military incursion into Ecuadorean territory against the FARC as preventive action. The United States defended the concept of preventive attack at the OAS meeting. She proposed that countries in the region join together in the fight against 'narcoterrorism' and suggested that Ecuador and Venezuela were in complicity with the FARC. According to Rice, borders are important but they cannot be a refuge for terrorists who kill innocent people. She stated with assurance that it was time that the region revises the matter of security in the border areas while suggesting that Washington keep tabs on the evolution of the situation, undertaking whatever was necessary.[26] Rice repeated that the FARC is a 'terrorist' organization with which there is no room for negotiation.[27] This position is opposed not only to that of Venezuela. Brazil's foreign affairs minister Celso Amorin reiterated that his government does not characterize the Colombian guerrilla as a terrorist organization. For the USA, transnational threats do not respect geographical limits; they are common to all and confronting them demands group action. In March 2003, Commander Hill of the U.S. Southern Command stated that, according to the United States, the main threat against the countries of the region did not come from the military force of a neighbour or from an invading foreign power. The enemy was composed of terrorists, drug-traffickers, and international crime (false documents, the arms trade, money laundering). He referred especially to the 'narcoterrorist' (Hill 2003). In 2005, his successor reiterated not only how important it was to build a co-operative security community, but also the threat that 'populism' represented for the states of the region, the existence of radical Islamic groups that participate in illegal activities, and support to the Colombian government in the struggle against armed movements (see Craddock 2005).

The case of the 'Triple Border' area is an example. The Triple Border[28] is a security concern based on several menacing situations: criminal networks linked to Islamic

---

26   Página 12 14 March 2008.
27   Página 12 14 March 2008.
28   Since 2002, the Triple Border concept has been used to describe other places, such as the

fundamentalist groups setting up in the region, the presence of sleeping terrorist cells, operation fields for new attacks, activities financed by Islamic contributions, and illegal businesses. In Brazil and Paraguay, migrant colonies from the Middle East (especially Syria and Lebanon) have existed for a long time and increased with the arrival of Lebanese Shiites after the civil war in Lebanon.

The Triple Border consists of three cities: Foz do Iguaçu (Brazil), Puerto Iguazú (Argentina) and Ciudad del Este (Paraguay). The main economic activity of Foz do Iguaçu and Puerto Iguazú is tourism, while in Ciudad del Este, the trade of smuggled goods predominates. This region is a traditional place of intense clandestine activities, where all kinds of global disorder (for example illicit weapons traffic, drugs, stolen cars, kidnapped human beings and animals, fake identity documents, and counterfeit products) can be observed. The Triple Border region, considered by the United States a lawless area where numerous criminal organizations, especially narco-traffickers and terrorists, have settled, has a high strategic priority. The Triple Border is a 'paradigm' of an ungovernable zone. Formed in the 1990s in the context of the Colombian conflict, the Triple Border illustrates the similarities between the Democrat and the Republican strategic representations. In 1999, the anti-terrorism coordinator of the Department of State, Mr. Sheehan, notified the Argentinean government of U.S. concerns about the increasing presence of terrorist and drug-trafficking groups in the region.

In the context of the war against terrorism, the United States has noted that there are Islamic groups in the Triple Border, arguing that the ties between drug dealing and the FARC will be strengthened by the war in Afghanistan. The damage caused to heroin trafficking by the Afghan war has promoted an alliance between Colombian drug dealers and Islamic terrorists in order to develop and maintain the production and commercialization of drugs.[29] In 2003, General Hill of the US Southern Command said that narco-terrorism activity was fuelling radical Islamic groups associated with Hamas and Hizbullah militants who were operating in such places as the triple-border area of Brazil, Argentina and Paraguay and on Venezuela's Margarita Island (Hill 2003).

Since the 1992 and 1994 attacks against the Jewish community in Buenos Aires, the Triple Border zone has been under control. As of 1999, the Argentinean intelligence services have been looking for traces of and connections to Osama Bin Laden. U.S. intelligence services maintain that the authors of the terrorist attack in Luxor, Egypt, in 1997 found shelter in the Triple Border. Hassan A. Mokhler, who was accused of having participated in this attack, was caught on the border between Brazil and Uruguay for carrying fake identity papers; his wife has always lived in the zone. Another suspect in this attack was later arrested in the region.

Under U.S. pressure, a Joint Security Command was created by the countries of the region. Brazil and Argentina have deployed important security mechanisms in order to prevent criminal actions from threatening their vital tourism industries. These mechanisms are used in an integrated way: national and state police forces,

---

area linking Brazil, Bolivia and Paraguay, and Brazil, Argentina and Uruguay.
29   O Globo Sao Paulo 28 October 2001.

intelligence services, customs control and private security agencies for hotels and other tourist infrastructures. A contingent of Argentinean intelligence services staff works closely with their U.S. counterparts.

However, terrorist activity in the Triple Border has never been demonstrated. The United States has been unable to prove the existence of terrorist cells and the local armed forces have denied the presence of terrorists in the zone. The lack of state presence exercising efficient sovereignty does not imply, however, that the Triple Border zone is ungovernable.

According to some political and non-governmental organizations,[30] U.S. interest in the zone is related to the control of natural resources and access to drinking water. Researchers have revealed that there is a huge supply of drinking water in that zone, in the *Acuífero Guaraní*, which is probably the most important reserve in the world.

In the post-Cold War era, the goals of both international policy and security and defence policies encouraged by the United States in the region are inseparable from a conception of the world which tends to dilute national sovereignties into a globality of interests. These policies lie upon a set of principles that serve as a foundation of the 'global civilization', inspired by 'Anglo-Saxon' representations, which antagonize the precepts of the regional political culture. However, in contrast to the conditions prevailing in the 1990s, the United States has encountered resistance to the imposition of its representations.

Conclusion

In Latin America, the conception of defence and security developed during the Post-Cold War era has shattered the geopolitical logic historically accepted by the Latin American armed forces and has caused the collapse of one of the main elements of their traditional strategic representations: the menacing neighbouring community. This geopolitical determinism which has explained all conflicts since post-colonial times by the influence of history itself and out of rivalry for power and territorial rights has become weak.

From the point of view of space, the three traditional geo-strategic logics of conflict – fluvial, maritime, and territorial- sustaining the representations of the menacing territorial neighbouring community were torn apart (see Manero 2002). The patterns and the dynamics of conflicts that now affect land and water are very different. These are fundamental transformations which, because of the scale and speed at which they are occurring, imply consequences for the regional strategic cultures.

---

30   On this topic, see the documents of the first and the second *Foro Social de la Triple Frontera*. Puerto Iguazú, Argentina, June 2004 and Ciudad del Este, Paraguay, July 2006, respectively.

Even when conflict shows a traditional sub-regional polarity in the form of an inter-state confrontation, as in the case of the Colombia governed by Uribe and the Venezuela presided over by Chavez, it is more closely related to the problems of the Post-Cold War era than to a territorial logic based on the historical relationship between power and space or on a territorial redistribution (the Gulf of Maracaibo). Clearly, such a trend manifests itself at different levels. The differences do not exist simply between countries and regions, but also between security institutions and political and social actors. This situation is clearer in the Southern Cone than in Central America.

The de-legitimation of the menacing territorial neighbouring community constitutes a concurrence, although for very different reasons, among radically antagonistic political and ideological positions. This de-legitimation is as much a central element in the security policies encouraged by the United States as it is in those of different and heterogeneous sectors of South American nation-states promote an expansion of the border as the limit of that which must be defended. However, paradoxically, the dismemberment of the menacing territorial neighbouring community is accompanied by the development of strategic representations that continue to attach great strategic importance to borders.

At the beginning of the twenty-first century, border disputes have become more complex in nature than the traditional disagreement over the place where the physical and jurisdictional bordering line must be drawn. The post-Cold War era overdeveloped one of the characteristics of disputes over borders. These disputes, involving a range of problems, generally have characteristics that pertain to more than one type of conflict.

While in Latin America, there is no real possibility of a regional war caused by an indirect spill-over of an inter-state conflict, a fear that conflicts inside the states may spill over is alive in the region. The case of Colombia has been the most evident since the 1990s.

From a strategic point of view, given the end of the concept of space that characterized the nineteenth and twentieth centuries, we are confronted with a break in the logic that created spheres of identification that referred to those evoked by the terms of rivalry of nations over the neighbourhood. We are far away from the 1970s. During the Post-Cold War era, the hypotheses of traditional conflict related to the expansionist territorial ambitions of a country have become devalued.

In the strategic hegemonic representations of the post-Cold War era in Latin America, the threat concerning territory thus no longer appears as the result of state power or of actions of neighbouring national armies fighting for possession of the territory. It appears rather as the consequence of other factors: the loss of the *imperium* capability; a weakening of the exercise of sovereignty; or the loss of the states' monopoly of violence in border regions. This permits both the development of organizations considered a threat and the loss of control over natural resources considered of strategic importance, or the development of interventionist policies on the part of the hegemonic power or a neighbouring state.

The post-Cold War era implies a weakened effect of geopolitical conceptions in their traditional form. However, at the beginning of the twenty-first century, several factors have brought about the reinstatement of the geopolitics felt to be abandoned in the 1990s as a consequence of the 'elimination' of political and social conflicts and the primacy of the economic rationality manifested in the commercial agreements that sought insertion of the region into globalization. These include the end of consensus on the policies of the hegemonic power, the revaluing of the national interest and of nationalism as well as 'high politics', the importance of natural resources, the militarization of U.S. policies in Latin America, the establishment of political projects with a hegemonic spirit in Brazil and Venezuela, and the transnational character of the Colombian conflict.

Global disorder redefined in Latin America security practices and destabilized traditional strategic references and identities as it established new problems and other fields of experience of 'collective survival'. However, a de-naturalization of the defensive function of its borders, redrawn and redefined in various ways, cannot be discerned. At a time when national borders lose their original function in favour of a unification of markets sought everywhere, they necessarily acquire a new strategic dimension. This dimension should grow with the risks and threats that climate change has brought with it. Floods and droughts cause a reduction in the amount of arable land, a lack of water, and a shortage of food supplies. The cycle closes with massive migrations, the collapse of states, political radicalization of conflicts over the control of territories rich in natural resources, and the increase in the military capacity of developed countries in response to the situation.

Translation from the original French into English by Orlando García-Valverde, Interidiom, S.A., Costa Rica, ogarde@ice.co.cr.

References

Amilhat-Szary A.-L. (2005), 'Géopolitique et frontières en Amérique Latine', in *L'Amérique Latine*, Hardy, S., Medina, L. (dir), Nantes, Editions du Temps.

Craddock, B. (2005), *U.S. Southern Command before 109th Congress Senate Armed Services Committee* 15 March 2005, available at <http://armed-services.senate. gov/statemnt/2005/March/Craddock%2003-15-05.pdf>.

Domínguez, J.I. et al. (2003a), 'Boundary Disputes in Latin America', *Peaceworks* 50 (Washington: U.S. Institute of Peace USIP).

Domínguez, J.I. et al. (eds.) (2003b), *Conflictos territoriales y democracia en América latina* (Buenos Aires: Siglo XXI).

Hill, J. (2003), Posture statement of general James T. Hill, United States Army Commander, United States Southern Command before the 108th Congress House Armed Services Committee, 13 March 2003. Available at http://www. globalsecurity.org/military/library/congress/2003_hr/hill.pdf.

Manero, E. (2007a), 'L'inquiétante étrangeté sociale. Sécurité et altérité dans l'Argentine contemporaine', in *Diasporas, Histoire et Sociétés* 10.

Manero, E. (2007b), 'Strategic Representations, Territory and Border areas: Latin America and Global Disorder', in *Geopolitics* 12:1, 19-56.

Manero, E. (2002), *L'Autre, le Même et le Bestiaire* (Paris: L'Harmattan).

Mares, D. (2003), 'Conflictos limítrofes en el hemisferio Occidental', in Domínguez, J.I. et al. (eds.), *Conflictos territoriales y democracia en América latina* (Buenos Aires: Siglo XXI).

Mares, D. (2001), *Violent Peace: Militarized Interstate Bargaining in Latin America* (New York: Columbia University Press), chapter 3.

Musset A. (dir.), Géopolitique des Amériques, Nathan.

The Inter-Korean Border Region – 'Meta-border' of the Cold War and Metamorphic Frontier of the Peninsula

Valérie Gelézeau

Introduction

Set around the 38th parallel, and dividing the Korean peninsula into two parts similar in size, the inter-Korean border separates the two states born after the division of the Korean peninsula following the colonial rule of the Japanese (1910-1945) defeated in World War II: the Republic of Korea (ROK or South Korea) in the South, former a newly industrialized country, now a developed and post-industrialized society that has encountered rapid democratization since the end of the 1980s; in the North, the Democratic People's Republic of Korea (DPRK or North Korea), a reforming socialist country, non-democratic, facing a grave crisis of its politico-economic system since the mid-1990s. Still one of the most closed and heavily armed borders on the planet, seemingly a perfect example of a 'hot border' crystallizing probable conflicts (Foucher 1991), the inter-Korean border thus remains an awkward outcome of the Cold War in the 'post-Cold War' world of the beginning of the twenty-first century.

The relationships between the Koreas, the two competing nations of the 'long partition' (Zamindar 2007[1]) of the peninsula, which remained difficult with scarce communication for many decades, have nonetheless significantly changed since the end of the Cold War. The inter-Korean rapprochement, symbolized in the South by President Kim Dae-Jung's so-called 'Sunshine Policy' launched in 1998, the outcome for which was widely mediatized during the first inter-Korean summit

---

1   Used by the anthropologist V. Zamindar to refer to the partition of India, this expression well suits the idea of how division becomes imprinted in the national and social landscape, way beyond the political border.

in June 2000, triggered economic exchanges and cooperation, of which some came to focus around the inter-Korean border, such as the symbolic projects of Mount Kŭmgang[2] Tourist Zone and Kaesŏng Industrial Complex operated by South Korea and located in the North. Indeed, and contrary to the simplistic representation of this border in the international media staging since the end of the 1950s the usual guard-posts, barbed wire and patrolling troops of a closed and fossilized border, the inter-Korean border region structurally changed over the years and continues to transform itself.

How did the change in inter-Korean relations materialize in and around the inter-Korean border? Does the current management of the border in South Korea, which is the only directly accessible side for field research, reflect those changes? How do greater regional transformations, such as the geopolitical evolution in North East Asia, the crisis and reforms in North Korea, and the development of inter-Korean exchanges, get articulated on the national and/or local management policies of the border in South Korea?

This chapter will discuss these issues while trying to develop the hypothesis of a frontier-type development at the border – that is a dynamics of settlement and occupation in the border region, which is sustained, at least in South Korea, by designed policies from the state. Written in 2009, just following a harsh shift back in inter-Korean relations since the second inter-Korean summit in October 2007, it also offers a welcome chance to reconsider the effect that the interstitial opening of the border had on the border regions, defined as territories affected by the proximity of the border itself,[3] during the past ten years (1998-2007). At the same time, it will provide a fresh interpretation of the recent 're-closing' of the border concretized by the termination of the Mount Kŭmgang tour and the present hardships of the Kaesŏng industrial complex.

Using a methodology elaborated in previous research,[4] the chapter is based on several case studies of border settlements that have been conducted between September 2004 and April 2009, in the two South Korean border provinces of Kyŏnggi and Kangwŏn.[5] It will first discuss the very nature of this border which,

---

2   The transcription of Korean refers to the McCune-Reischauer system, but for well-known geographical names (ex. Seoul), and proper names standard spelling formats are used throughout (ex. Park Chung-hee, which would be Pak Chŏnghŭi in McCune transcription).

3   See Guichonnet et Raffestin (1974), Renard (1997), Rumley (1991).

4   See Gelézeau (2008a and 2008b) for most recent articles. The methodology involving direct fieldwork is based on two types of primary sources: a heterogeneous body of written primary sources (statistics, reports, maps, and so on), gathered locally, and the production of original primary sources via an ethnographic approach sustained by interviews with inhabitants and actors of development.

5   In Kyŏnggi province: Paengnyŏn Island (the Northernmost Island of the Kyŏnggi Bay) in 2004, Pa'ju city (a fast growing border city) and Yŏngch'ŏn county (a rural county of Kyŏnggi located next to P'aju) in 2008; in Kangwŏn province, Ch'unch'ŏn City (the provincial capital, farther away from the border but still influenced by it) in 2007, and Ch'ŏrwŏn county (a divided border county transferred from North to South between

still a 'demilitarized zone' (DMZ) on both sides of a cease fire line, created a complex spatial region irrigated by various limits and scattered by ambiguous territories (part one). It will then describe the general transformation of the border region, in connection with both the change in inter-Korean relations and in broader peninsular dynamics (part two). Finally it will illustrate how those transformations articulate with specific border management policies and features that may, or not, express what could be labelled a 'frontier drive' at the regional or local scale in South Korea.

The inter-Korean border: The complex 'meta-border' of a long partition

A fossilized 'meta-border' of the Cold War?

The inter-Korean border is, as several borders of the world were and still are, a post-colonial border born from the Cold War equilibrium. In his recent work describing the bordering of the world since the 1990s, the French geographer and border specialist Foucher elaborates on the concept of 'meta-border' (Foucher 2007): not a conventional land border, but a border that goes way beyond the local or the national scales, and refers to, or even creates, a system at large. Foucher identifies a few meta-borders in the World History; among them the one established by the 1495 Tordesilla Treaty splitting between Spain and Portugal the New World and future territories to conquer, or more recently, the so-called Iron Curtain, which was a meta-border of the Cold War. Since its disruption after the fall of the Berlin Wall in 1989 and the dislocation of the USSR in 1991, the inter-Korean border still remains one of the last dividing fault lines of the two great political, economical and social systems that structured the twentieth century and, as such, appears as a fossilized meta-border of the Cold War. For example, geopolitical work shows that the opposition between capitalism and socialism is still very alive between the two Koreas, from both sides, and it is very evident in the Northern propaganda (Bleiker 2005).

Technically, the division of the peninsula at the 38th parallel was sealed during the night of 10-11 August 1945, by two American colonels who were given 30 minutes to find a line parting American and Soviet occupation to disarm defeated Japan (Cumings 1997, 186-92). This emblematic moment symbolizes now, in both South and North greater narratives, the unjust and somewhat hazardous division of an ethnically homogenous proto-nation-state considered unified since at least the fifteenth century. But in fact, the process of border formation is much more complex and has to be understood at a longer time scale that also identifies Korean roots during the colonial time and the anti-Japanese guerrilla fighting which radicalized

---

1945 and 1953) in 2009.

local conflicts between political parties. Furthermore, the symbolic moment of partition has to be replaced in the broader geopolitical context: at the end of World War II, the Allies failed to reach an agreement upon the future of colonized Korea while the fracture between the U.S. and the Soviet Union was deepening. In their competition triggered in Asia to disarm Japan, the latter indeed agreed upon the 38th parallel proposed as the dividing line by their soon to be enemy only to bargain for other territories, such as the Kouriles islands. As a result, and after being ruled by two foreign-military led governments between 1945 and 1948, separate elections held in respective zones eventually gave birth to the ROK on 15 August 1948, and to the DPRK on September 9 the same year; after a period of repeated incidents and guerrilla fighting at the border that culminated in important border battles during the summer of 1949, the two countries clashed in the Korean War (1950-1953), one of the 'hottest' wars of the Cold War. At the end of the Korean War, the border was set: although geographically approximate to the previous 38th parallel division line, it was now determined by the cease fire line close to the 38th. This is not just a detail: it reflects that during the years between 1945 and 1953, the 38th parallel was the epicentre of a division in the making, of the war violence and the focal points of the great migrations triggered by this period of havoc on the peninsula which contributed to creating the '10 millions separated families of the peninsula' often referred to by South Korean media. The War cost about 3 million Korean lives (military and civilian) and created major forced migrations: the major flux happened between 1950 and 1951, drawing about 1 million persons from North to South.[6]

In this rather long process, regions changed sides, sometimes several times. Now located in the DPRK and bisected by the 38th parallel, Kaesŏng, the most famous historical capital of medieval Korea, shifted from South to North. Now located in the ROK, Ch'ŏrwŏn county, which was a very busy town in pre-modern and colonized Korea, shifted from North to South; it still bares numerous heritage sites of its former Northern episode such as the famous Korean Workers Party Building.

One border, multiple limits for a complex spatial structure

As a result of its lengthy time formation process, the inter-Korean border is, contrary to most linear political borders, a composite spatial region organized by several limits in direct connection to the 1953 Armistice Agreement signed between North Korea, China and the United Nations to end the Korean War and fix the cease-fire line.

---

6   The actual number of separated families is not only the result of the war, but also the result of previous migrations in the late nineteenth and early twentieth century (including the migrations triggered during the colonial rule of Japan). As James Foley argues, it is pointless to calculate numbers of separated families (Foley 2003): it is both impossible to come up with an accurate figure, and to point to any specific period in particular.

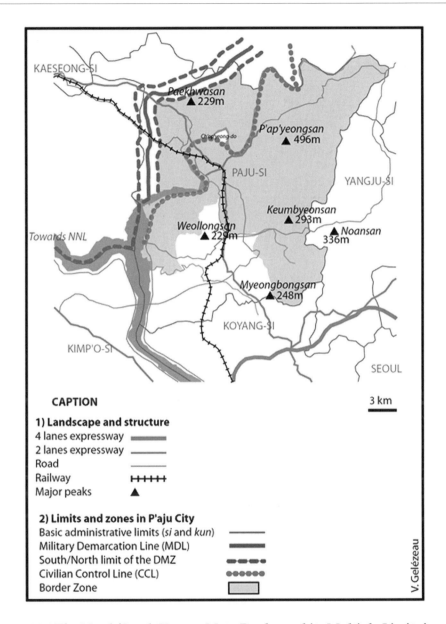

Figure 16.1 The North/South Korean Meta-Border and its Multiple Limits in P'aju City

Source: Kyŏnggi-do haengjŏng toro chido – administrative and road map of Kyŏnggi Province, Chungan chido-sa 2007, 1:200,000; P'aju-si cheondo – general map of P'aju City, SJMaps 2006, 1:50,000; P'aju kwan'gwang annae-do – tourist map of P'aju 2007, not scaled; Atlas of Korea, Sung Ji Mun Hwa Sa 2000; Fieldwork in P'aju 2007 and 2008; edited by V. Gelézeau).

The Military Demarcation Line (MDL: *kunsa pun'gye sŏn*), as well as the Northern Border Line (NBL, *pukpang han'gye sŏn*) located two kilometers North of the MDL and Southern Border Line (SBL, *nambang han'gye sŏn*), two kilometers South, are the core limits of this composite border. Between the Northern and Southern Border Lines lies the four kilometre wide DMZ (Demilitarized Zone, sometimes called *pimujang chidae* in Korean), which is supposed to be a neutral and disarmed territory devoid of any human settlement. On the ground, the DMZ has in fact shrunk in many of its portions, resulting from when both North and South tried to push its limits to expand their territories.

Beyond the two border lines, the territorial limits have been established by the national governments of North and South Korea, respectively. In North Korea, the border region within fifty kilometers from the border line is a special military region. In the South, the South Korean Secretary of Defense established the Civilian Control Line (*min'ganin t'ongje sŏn* or *mint'ongsŏn* – CCL): running South ten to fifteen kilometers away from the MDL and limiting the Civilian Control Zone (*min'ganin t'ongje chiyŏk*), where civilian access and settlements are strictly controlled.[7] Also delineated by the Secretary of Defense, the Military Installations Protection Districts (*kunsa sisŏl poho kuyŏk*) are special districts (usually including military bases and neighbouring settlements) designated within areas of up to fifty kilometers away from the MDL.

A border that is not a border and its questioned territory

Last but not least, the legal nature of the inter-Korean border is rather peculiar: as explained in the previous section, it is not a border but a cease-fire line between two countries that are still technically at war – no peace treaty has been signed yet between the two Koreas. As a consequence, the border itself being a simple cease-fire line and generating around it multiple limits of different status and origins, the larger inter-Korean border region also includes territories of questioned and contested status, which characterizes military border areas (see for example Chang 2005, 57-118). The case of Paengnyŏng Island, combining the constraints of a border location with an extremely strategic and symbolic location as an outpost of South Korean national territory, provides a clear example of such a situation.

Located just below the 38th parallel, less than 25 kilometers from the North Korean coast, Paengnyŏng Island is part of a group of South Korean islands included in one rural county (*kun*) of Inch'ŏn Metropolitan City located 250 kilometers away. In 1953, the Armistice Agreement did not determine maritime limits beyond the estuary of the Han River, and neither North Korea nor South Korea could agree on one until now: they did not negotiate after the 1982 Montego Bay conference changing international maritime law, as all states having such intricate maritime

---

7   For a travel writing account full of historical data about the Civilian Control Zone, see the recently translated work by Lee Si-Woo (2008), whose activist action actually led to his imprisonment for several months in 2007.

limits were supposed to do. The so-called NLL (Northern Limit Line), appearing on South Korean maps and many Western international maps, which is connected to the land MDL and runs northwest in the Yellow Sea, is a 'limit' established *de facto* in 1958 by the ROK, primarily to protect their own fishing boats from sailing into dangerous waters. On its own side, North Korea unilaterally proclaimed in 1977 a fifty mile military sea zone that actually encompasses the five ROK islands (Lee 2001). As a consequence, in the absence of an agreement over the definition of territorial waters, most of the ocean around the five islands is a 'grey area' of very ambiguous status.

- Ocean: national framework, no negotiations

- Continent: international framework negotiations (1953 Armistice Agreement)

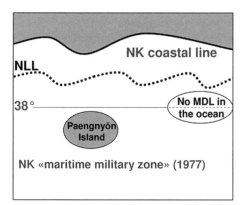

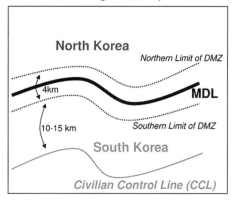

Figure 16.2 Paengnyŏn Island: A South Korean Enclave in 'Grey Waters'
Source: V. Gelézeau.

So, although it is clearly a South Korean territory, Paengnyŏng Island lies in a maritime area of indefinite status regarding both international agreements *and* inter-Korean maritime borders. The island bares the obvious scars of the partition, clearly visible in the barbed wire fences and stakes disfiguring its Northern coast; direct violent encounters between both Koreas are part of the regional landscape, such as the naval clashes that opposed North and South Korean ships in June 1999 and September 2002 (Roehrig 2009), and more recently on 10 November 2009.[8] On 10 November 2009, a North Korean military ship and the South Korean navy were opposed nearby (South) of the NNL in a two minute fire exchange that resulted in one person dead and three injured on the North Korean side. On 13 November, the North Korean government disclosed the statement that the only valid border for

---

8   Most recently, in March 2010, the sinking of the South Korean corvette Ch'ŏnan happened in the vicinity (see Kim 2011).

North Korea is the one defined by the North – and that they would take 'implacable measures' to defend it.

This particular and recent example, of which the particular circumstances remain unclear (each side blaming the other one for triggering the hostile fire exchange) shares with the other two naval clashes common features exposing the unclear status of the maritime border region. First of all, they are related to a broader competition over non-delimited fishing territories, involving Chinese boats in the area. In 1999 and 2002 for example, the battles occurred during the busiest blue crab fishing season in the summer. During my interviews in Paengnyŏn Island, all the fishermen mentioned the illegal penetration of Chinese boats in the Korean waters as a problem; in the November 2009 incident, the North Korean navy argues that they were indeed chasing a Chinese fishing boat that was illegally fishing in North Korean waters, when they crossed the NNL. In the current state of affairs, and the impossibility for both Koreas to settle their maritime borders without a peace treaty, those ambiguous maritime territories are the weak points where the border actually becomes hot and incidents may happen, despite of the state of inter-Korean relations: in 1999 and 2002, the relations of the two countries were facing some tension, in a broader period of rapprochement; on the contrary, 2009 is a phase of improvement within a general trend of cold relations since 2007.

A 'hot' border and its militarized culture

The intense degree of militarization on both sides of the border is one obvious aspect of the cultural identity of the border regions. In the North, this identity is for example quite well described in the movie *Nae kohyang-ŭi ch'ŏnyŏ-dŭl* ('The girls in my hometown', 1991), which takes place in Kangwŏn province and is dedicated to disabled soldiers and their patriotic wives. Although the topic of the border is not touched upon as such, and although the army plays a significant role everywhere in North Korea, this movie, which is focused on the military's civil accomplishments in the province such as the construction of a dam, shows quite well the crucial importance of the military in this border region close to the DMZ and how they intermingle with the peasants' daily life.

In South Korea as well, the border region is characterized by the importance of the military population, which actually does not completely appear in local or regional statistics: professional military personnel only appear in the figures which do not count conscription soldiers, who are in fact the great majority, and as a consequence, basic demographic figures can be highly misleading. To take only here the example of population numbers, none of the public servants I interviewed in Paengnyŏng Island could (or would) provide an exact figure of the military personnel on the base, of which the main quarters occupy most of the central part of the island. But the estimated number amounts for about 4,000 soldiers, which actually roughly doubles the population of the island (4,280 inhabitants in 2003). It means for example that the population density given by using the official population (census data) is twice as low as the density calculated when aggregating military personnel: to some extent, there are two different Paengnyŏng Islands. Likewise, in P'aju City, the exact military population was not disclosed (or unknown) by my informants who were all civil servants at the city governments, but they acknowledged there were about 50,000 soldiers, which accounts for a sixth of the city population of 305,000 inhabitants in 2008.

The military is also involved in the civilian tasks, through the so-called *taemin chiwŏn saŏp* (civil support operations). In Paengnyŏng Island for example, during the busy farming seasons, the peasants receive considerable help from the base. Each village registers everyday with a request for workers and the local administrator passes on the information to the base that then sends the required work force to the villages. The military also provides support in case of an emergency or crisis situation such as flooding or fire. Last but not least, the military presence in the South Korean borderlands is also symbolized by the figure of the *kijich'on*, designating in Korean US military camp town areas. Among the six largest *kijich'on* in South Korea, five are located in the Kyŏnggi province or in Seoul and they do crystallize the many problems linked to the presence of foreign troops on the South Korean territory such as prostitution that is a particularly sensitive issue in those military camp town areas (Moon 1997; Yea 2008).

Living in the border zone is not only living around soldiers, working for them by providing mundane services from clothing and food to entertainments, and sometimes with them (through the *taemin chiwŏn saŏp*); to some extent, it seems that the people living in the border region assimilate with the military, even though they only work in civil society. As can be expected, many civilians interviewed in the border zone and particularly islanders, discussed about stressful military-like life and strong anti-communist education and training. In Paengnyŏng Island, stress and tension were naturally related to the North's proximity and everyone talked about the naval clashes of 1999 and 2002. Of course, anti-communist education was common everywhere in Korea until the late 1980s. But the connection is clearly made to what is considered and experienced by the inhabitants as a specific 'border mentality' and closeness to the North which recalls, directly or not, a military experience. For a significant number of informants, this is taken to the point that they consider themselves as performing a military duty, by their very presence on this Northern extreme of the South Korean land. The military are the first 'to guard the land' (*nara-rŭl chik'inda'*), but the people also stand there in front of the North, as it was expressed by several of them.

Inter-Korean relations and transformation of the border region since the 1950s

Although it is still a 'hot' border and a (fossilized) 'meta-border' of the Cold War (Foucher 1991 and 2007), the inter-Korean border has deeply changed in its structure and use since 1953, along with the change of the inter-Korean relations that reached an important turning point in the early 1990s toward rapprochement reflecting the broader geopolitical transformations of the post-Cold War era.[9] This part may demonstrate that, in this general realm of events, the inter-Korean border actually expresses one interesting feature of inter-Korean relations: even during *'détente'*, tensions remain and clashes may occur at the border as it has been the case for the naval clashes in 1999 and 2002; similarly, during periods of tensions, relationships continue and the border continues to change as we will see here.

Inter-Korean relations and the border until the early 1990s: between détente and tensions

In the 1950s and 1960s context, the only place of contacts at the border was the so-called 'Joint Security Area' (JSA), an enclave located within the DMZ at P'anmunjŏm, where the Armistice Treaty had been signed, and which was occupied by the army of both Koreas, in addition to the UNCMAC (United Nation Command Military Armistice Commission) and the NNS (Neutral Nations Supervisory Commission) whose duty was to monitor the due respect of the armistice and, if necessary, arbitrate its violations. The inter-Korean dialogue started at the beginning of the 1970s and resulted in the opening of liaison offices of the Red Cross within JSA as well as to the establishment of cross-border phone channels between the two Red Crosses, expanding the contacts from exclusively military to also civilian personnel.

This first step in inter-Korean relations in the early 1970s, occurred in the broader context of Nixon's Guam doctrine of *détente* with China and the USSR, and led the U.S. to disengage troops in Vietnam. In 1970, the South Korean CIA (KCIA) exchange visits with its North Korean counterpart resulted in the 4 July 1972 'common declaration for pacific reunification' stipulating the three basic principles of a reunification to be reached 'independently', 'peacefully', and for the sake of 'great national unity'.[10] During the same period, seven consecutive meetings of separated families were organized by the Red Cross offices from both sides, between August 1972 and May 1973, alternatively in Seoul and Pyongyang. However, these reunions were interrupted, while both Koreas entered a period of reinforced dictatorship, which enhanced mutual distrust: in South Korea, President Park Chung-hee declared martial law with the introduction of the Yushin regime (or 'Revitalization' Constitution) in late 1972, while in North Korea the new 1972 constitution officially introduced the concept of *juche* (self-reliance) as its basic ideology. The following 1980s were a rather dark decade for inter-Korean relations, marked by two terror attacks from the North, one of which was set in Rangoon in 1983 and the other a Korean Airlines (KAL) airplane bombing organized by the North Korean female agent Kim Hyunhee.

---

9   A huge body of scholarly research describes inter-Korean relations and their transformation since 1953 (see Kim 2004).

10   The full text of the declaration was published in *The Korean Quarterly* (Autumn 1972, 58-60).

As a consequence, the high level of military tension between both Koreas between the mid-1970s and the late 1980s, lead to renewed surveillance and reinforcement of the border. This is well illustrated by the direct aftermaths of the so-called 'Axe Murderer incident' of August 1976, which changed the structure of the JSA by reinforcing the North/South partition within the area itself, and triggering the construction of yet another secondary dwarf-wall within the jointly managed enclave (see Kirkbride 1985 and 1994). During those decades, transformations of the border were indeed almost exclusively related to war type strategies: for example the Southern side actively strengthened its defensive apparatus by constructing an anti-tank 'concrete wall' in open plain areas (such as the Ch'ŏrwŏn plains), between the Southern limit of the DMZ and the CCL; while North Korea started to build several invasion tunnels underneath the DMZ designed to ferry troops and war material across the border. The first three tunnels were discovered by the South near the DMZ in 1974, 1975 and 1978 respectively, a fourth was discovered more recently in 1990.

But at the end of the 1980s, the dark decades of inter-Korean relations seemed to take a new path opened by South Korean President Roh Taewoo (1987-1991). After the German reunification and the fall of the Soviet Union, his so-called 'Nord Politic' – inspired by 1960s Willy Brandt's *Ostpolitik* towards East Germany – led the ROK to develop economic ties with the USSR and China, while normalizing its diplomatic relations with the USSR in 1990 and China in 1992.

A limited opening of the border region after the 1990s and during the Sunshine policy era (1998-2007)

In this post-Cold War *détente* context in North East Asia, the 1990s opened a new era for inter-Korean relations with eight meetings between both prime ministers between 1990 and 1992 and the signing of the 'Basic Agreement' on 13 December 1991. This 'Agreement on Reconciliation, Non-Aggression, Exchange and Cooperation' reaffirms the principle of the 1972 declaration while adding important dispositions regarding concrete exchanges between both countries, among which: the establishment of a direct phone line between the two governments; measures regarding the circulation of people (including the meetings of separated families), and future cooperation projects including the reconnections of the land routes (train lines and roads). This direction was reinforced by the so-called Sunshine Policy (*Haetpyŏt chŏngch'aek*), launched by South Korean President Kim Dae-Jung after he came into office in 1997: the Sunshine Policy consisted of a resolute engagement with the DPRK, and opened the path to the historical June 2000 summit marking the first meeting between the two State leaders (Kim Dae-Jung and Kim Jong Il) since the partition of Korea. The several inter-ministry meetings that followed discussed the future concrete terms of the rapprochement: development of economic exchanges and investments in the brother country, reconnection of the Seoul-Sinŭiju train line, reopening of the Munsan-Kaesŏng land route, the construction of a joint North-South industrial zone in Kaesŏng, and some flood prevention projects in the upper

Imjin basin. In this context, the era of the Sunshine Policy significantly improved inter-Korean exchanges:[11] for example, the share of South Korea in North Korean international trade jumped from negligible values in the mid-1990s to 25 per cent in 2005 (Ducruet and Gelézeau 2008).

The Sunshine Policy era also triggered a gradual opening of the border, which began after the mid-1990s. It first started in 1998 with the development of the Mount Kŭmgang Tour that was operated by Hyundai Asan, a branch of South Korean conglomerate Hyundai specifically created to help developing North Korean projects. This tour, which at the time consisted in an exclusive cruise bringing a few South Korean tourists from the east coast port Sŏkch'o to a North Korean harbour connected to a tourist enclave in Mount Kŭmgang, was mainly the result of the personal action of Hyundai conglomerate owner and general manager Chung Ju-Hyun (who did so partly because of his Northern origins[12]). But in 2002, the enclave was expanded and designated the 'International Tourist Zone' (*kukche kwan'gwang chigu*) by the North. However, the tour still took a maritime path then and the border was still largely an uncrossed line.

The 2000 summit launched a new moment of border opening with the reconnection of railways achieved in 2002 and that of the roads in 2003. This allowed the transformation of the Mount Kŭmgang trip into a bus tour in September 2003 and in the fall of 2004, the opening of the Kaesŏng Industrial Complex, also developed by Hyundai Asan, to host South Korean and international factories employing North Korean workers. One of the concrete consequences of the development of border-crossing movements was the construction of two CIQ (Customs, Immigration and Quarantine) offices on land routes to filter those first border movements.

Tested in May 2007 for regular cargo use across the border, the railway liaison contributed to increase the land border-crossing movements that had developed little by little since the reconnection of the highway between Seoul and Kaesŏng along with the development of the industrial zone. Also highly symbolical of this opening of the border was the land border-crossing staged by South Korean President Roh Moo-Hyun in October 2007 when he went to the North for a second (and last) inter-Korean summit. Unfortunately, the summit was soon followed by a shift back in inter-Korean relations reflected by the rise of the conservatives in both Koreas. As an expression of increasing tensions, the Mount Kŭmgang Tour came to a brutal stop after 11 August 2008, when both Koreas found themselves unable to deal with the consequences of a tragic accident: early in the morning

---

11   A comprehensive assessment of the result of the 10 years of the Sunshine Policy (1998-2008) was made by an international symposium held in December 2008 at the École des Hautes Études en Sciences Sociales in Paris ('North/South Interfaces in the Korean Peninsula', 17-19 December 2008, more information on <http://lodel.ehess.fr/crc/document.php?id=467> and on the EHESS Centre for Korean Studies' website <http://crc.ehess.fr/>.

12   Recent research has illustrated the role of elite families of Northern origins in the development of inter-Korean ties (Rivé-Lasan 2008).

and, while detailed circumstances remain unclear, a South Korean tourist had trespassed a military area and was shot and killed by a North Korean soldier posted in the tourist enclave. Until the recent degradation of the border crossing activities triggered by this accident, the land route had been supporting increased flows of merchandise and people. Between the launch of the Sunshine Policy in 1998 and July 2008 (before the incident at Mount Kŭmgang) about two million people had visited Mount Kŭmgang, and another half a million had crossed the border for business purposes, mainly in Kaesŏng (Petrov 2008).

Dreamed Peace Belt and spatial enclaves of the DMZ: the border imagined and managed

Stated in South Korean discourse, whether they come from national research institutes' blueprints or from local public servants, to prepare 'for the peaceful reunification of the peninsula', the South Korean 'Peace Belt' project for the management of the regions around the DMZ is part of the Fourth Comprehensive National Territorial Development Plan of South Korea (2000-2020) prepared by the Korean Research Institute for Human Settlement (KRIHS).

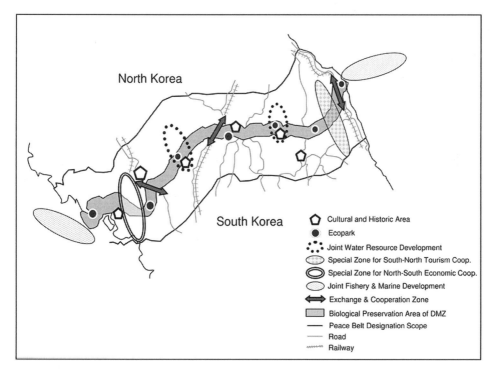

Figure 16.3 The KRIHS 'Peace Belt' Project

Source: KRIHS 2004; edited by V. Gelézeau.

This project envisions several phases of territorial reintegration based on the gradual opening of the border and the development of cooperation projects around it, while the DMZ, where unique ecological niches have developed during the last 50 years (Kim 2001[13]), is to become a protected area. The scheme shows a planned region densely connected by the reconstruction of the former pre-Korean war roads and train lines, as well as by the cooperation in natural resource management; the planned region would include several zones of economic cooperation (agricultural in Ch'ŏrwŏn, or industrial in Kaesŏng), and would support the development of inter-Korean tourism based on the natural and historical heritage of the DMZ. Needless to say, this blue print is far from territorial realities – although some inter-regional cooperation projects did develop between 2000 and 2005 in Kyŏnggi or Kangwŏn provinces (Kim Jeong-Ho 2008).

In reality, and contrary to this fluid and global vision of the 'Peace Belt', a fragmented spatial structure emerged since the early 2000s, based on the emergence of several types of enclaves around the border. The first type is represented by tourist enclaves such as the six 'Observatories' (*chŏnmangdae*) and tourist areas that have been gradually developed after the late 1990s in South Korea's Civilian Control Zone. Since the 2002 easing of regulations requiring a week pre-registration for a visit, they are largely accessible Southern enclaves within the South. The two other enclaves, Kaesŏng Industrial Complex and Kŭmgang Tourist Zone, are restricted Southern enclaves within the North of which only Kaesŏng is still in operation since the closure of Mount Kŭmgang in the summer of 2008.

Until the freezing of the inter-Korean relations since the fall of 2008, Kaesŏng was the symbol of the Sunshine Policy and possible cooperation between the two states. Located in the outskirts of Kaesŏng city, in an area that actually jeopardized valuable archaeological heritage for both North and South, the industrial complex was leased by the North for 50 years to Hyundai Asan, the South Korean developer.[14] The land was developed along with the Korea Land Corporation, and the first South Korean factories started to function in late 2004. At the end of 2008, covering 250 hectares, the complex hosted over 80 South Korean factories, employing close to 40,000 North Korean workers under over 1,500 South Korean managers. The development of the project lead to the opening in December 2007 of yet another bus tour, that allowed South Korean tourists to visit the historical highlights of the City of Kaesŏng, the centre of which still holds a unique heritage of traditional Korean houses. Twenty buses filled with South Korean tourists have made the daily trips between December 2007 and the brutal ending of the trip that occurred in November 2008 with the degradation of inter-Korean relations and after the Kŭmgangsan incident, a total of about 100,000 South Korean tourists visited the North Korean city.

---

13   See also Choe and Yang (2008) for an extraordinary photographic and artistic account of the ecological resources of the DMZ.

14   For an exhaustive presentation of the Kaesŏng industrial complex history, development and features, see Lim Eun-Chul (2007).

The inter-Korean border in broader dynamics of a greater western central region?

Although the transformation of the border is far from meeting the vows of the planned 'Peace Belt' project, it seems to indicate a gradual structural and functional transformation that has to be replaced in greater peninsular dynamics.

First of all, the opening of the two Northern enclaves of Kŭmgang and Kaesŏng is directly linked with the North Korean development policy of Special Economic Zones (SEZ) close to the borders; in particular the SEZ close to the South Korean borders were enhanced after the political and economic reforms of 1998 and 2002 (Frank 2005). This policy goes along with the change of the North Korean territory that occurred after the so-called 'Arduous March' of the North Korean famine (1995-1998), and led to the degradation of the economic activities of the industrial east coast corridor and the concentration of the major economic activities on the west coast around the Pyongyang and Hwanghae regions (Ducruet, Gelézeau and Roussin 2008). This was first noticed through an analysis of the maritime connections between North and South Korea showing that the direct connection between Inch'ŏn and Nam'po (that was non-existent before the mid-1990s) emerged as the main maritime connection between both countries after the 2000s (ibid.). It seems that deeper spatial dynamics for the border region are now more determined, in the South and in the North by the growing opposition between East and West (Kangwŏn vs. Kyŏnggi and Hwanghae) and the concentration on both capital regions (Kyŏnggi/Seoul and Hwanghae/Pyongyang), connected to the emergence of a new western central region in the peninsula. I may argue here that these structural and functional transformations involving the development of activities in the border region express a 'frontier drive'; not only for the South, but also for the North where the policy of the Special Economic Zones, located far away from the political centre to keep at bay the testing areas of capitalist introduction, led to the *de facto* development of the borders.[15]

In this broader backdrop, the case studies provide interesting material to observe the spatial and social feature of the border at the micro-local scale, expressing the various aspects of the 'frontier drive' through economic change and development projects and testing the hypothesis of a rising greater western central region.

---

15   See Colin (2008) on the Sino-North-Korean border.

Regional border management and local features of the 'frontier drive' in South Korean provinces of Kyŏnggi and Kangwŏn

Demographic change in rural border counties: 'frontier drive' or rural exodus?

The inter-Korean border still being, as we saw, the border of a war regime, the settlement logic of such a region is characterized by a number of specific features. Control and regulation on settlements by the army, and incentives given to civilians to occupy the territory are among the classical features of such a border. As a consequence, the demographic change in many rural counties of the border region differs to more general national features. Whereas most rural counties faced an intense rural exodus from the mid-1960s, in many rural counties of the border, the population decrease started only after 1995 when local autonomy and subsequent reforms were implemented in the ROK. Before that year, the settlement policies were defined by the state and, especially during the years of the harsh military rule of the 1970s and the 1980s, migration from such counties was made administratively difficult and relocation there was encouraged.[16]

The particular example of Paengnyŏng Island shows the consequences of such incentives given to occupy the territory. Looking from South Korea, Paengnyŏng-*do* would technically be located in the area of a maritime Civilian Controlled Zone – that is to say in a territory where only rare settlements should be allowed and where access would be highly restricted. In the absence of such a thing as a 'maritime DMZ', because of this territorial ambiguity, the access to the island is 'abnormally' open, with no particular control for South Korean or foreign tourists; as a consequence, and despite of the restrictions imposed on economic activities, it is a lively settlement.

The twelfth largest island in South Korea, Paengnyŏng Island is a farmers' island. In 2004, 60 per cent of the active population was engaged in farming, 7 per cent were fishermen, the rest (33 per cent) was involved in various service activities (mainly commercial and/or related to tourism). The importance of farmland is obvious in the spatial organization of the island, where large areas of paddy fields have been created by land reclamation projects. The dominating farming economy and the importance of reclaimed surfaces (more than 1,700 ha have been created since the 1970s, which is more than a third of the island's some 46 square kilometers!) are a direct result of the border location. While the fishing activities are restricted by various military regulations (a curfew from sunset to sunrise, the ban on sailing beyond 1 nautical mile up North), important reclamation projects have been developed thanks to the provision of special government funding devoted to the border region, in order to keep permanent South Korean settlements in the area. On Paengnyŏng Island, the conjunction of the military constraints with a 'frontier'

---

16 For example, victims of several typhoons in the 1970s were relocated to Ch'ŏrwŏn-*gun*.

type national management, meant to ensure and develop the territorial occupation of the island, created this situation which contradicts the more balanced economy between farm and sea of other South Korean coastal or island villages.

Meanwhile, the demographic destiny of border cities of the Kyŏnggi province was totally different. In that case, the demographic change reflected strong national tendencies such as the completion of the urban transition in South Korea between 1960 and the mid-1990s. For example, fast urbanizing P'aju City almost doubled its population during the same period of time and, with 305,076 inhabitants in 2008 and 6.3 per cent of average growth rate between 2000 and 2005, is at the beginning of the twenty-first century one of the fastest growing cities in the Capital Region. The momentum of demographic growth accelerated after 2000, which may be connected as one of the practical consequences of the June 2000 summit, and the implementation of the 2000 border law.

The Border Zone Support Law of 2000 and recent local development projects

In January 2000, preceding the historical summit by about six months, the South Korean government voted on the 'Border Zone Support Law' (*chŏpkyŏng chiyŏk chiwŏn pŏp*) defining a 'border (planning) zone' (*chŏpkyŏng chiyŏk*) including settlements located within 20 kilometers away from the Civilian Control Line. Contrary to the limits and areas presented previously in this chapter, the definition includes data related to the economical and functional profile of the localities (importance of Military Installations Protection Districts), and recent (in last five years) growth criteria on various aspects (demographic, infrastructures, productive functions) (see Park Sam-Ock 2005, 11). In short, the border zone (*chŏpkyŏng chiyŏk*) is defined as an area suffering from development problems and economical stagnation due to the numerous restrictions related to such a border location, in the context of a closed and militarized border.[17] Implemented from 2003 on, the support law is specifically meant to correct the under-development due to that location.

So, what the Border Zone Support Law puts at stake in Kangwŏn and Kyŏnggi provinces is totally different. In Kyŏnggi province, the border location has created yet a secondary discrepancy, between South Kyŏnggi, where the spatial dynamic of growth was primarily directed, and North Kyŏnggi, where the proximity of the border zone created underdevelopment or tension in the development: although not visible in national statistics, the difference is considerable.[18] Now Kangwŏn province has long been seen as a peripheral province in South Korea:

---

17 Most contemporary research on border regions shows, on the contrary, how an opened border triggers economical exchanges and cultural acculturation (see for example Amilhat-Szary and Fourny 2006; Chen 2005; Vélasco-Graciet and Bouquet 2006, 2007). In that sense, the Korean case stands for one of the few exceptions in the contemporary world.

18 See figure in Sam-Ock Park (2005, 200), and related chapter; Hwang Kŭmhoe (2007).

rural, mountainous, struggling with the closing of most of its mining activities in the 1980s and trying to market its various mountainous and coastal amenities to develop tourism. As such, the border zone is marketed as the rest of the province, and the military colour of the area does not impede on that project (Ji Kyoung Bae 2007; Kim Tae Dong 2006; Ŏm Suwŏn 2001).

In both Kyŏnggi and Kangwŏn province, the current law opened to a number of research projects handled by the Gyeonggi Development Research Institute (GDRI) or the Gangweon Research Institute (GRI), and connected to the larger Peace Belt project mentioned previously in the chapter. In Kyŏnggi province, the project of a so-called 'Eco-peace park' to be built within the DMZ is one example of what is currently being considered by the province. The park would actually be developed on both sides of the military demarcation line (MDL), with the park administrative buildings and visitor's centre on the southern side, and excursion areas to observe wildlife on the northern side of the MDL. Needless to say, because of the ongoing war regime, this park is still a blueprint and might remain so for the foreseeable future. But according to the researchers in charge of the project at the GRI, one of the obstacles to the finalization of the project is the vigorous opposition of P'aju City against having the park developed in its premises. The city's planning bodies seem to call for more industry and services, for more economic activities and less green belt regulations – which means that the peace park is considered by them as a mere abstract project that might counter future development.

Indeed, along with a steady demographic growth, economic development appears quite dynamic in P'aju, despite of the restriction imposed on 623 square kilometers (area including Military Installations Protection Districts) out of a total surface of 673 square kilometers. Several industrial complexes have recently emerged, among them the 'LG Cluster' including a Philips factory. The development of Kyohwa New Town (Kyohwa *sin tosi*) reflects both the demographic growth and economic vitality of P'aju. The New Town, which is to eventually accommodate 250,000 inhabitants in both collective high rise housing complexes and detached homes areas, is planned to compete with Ilsan New Town.

Furthermore, in P'aju, the future of military bases is of crucial importance and, then again, greater political agenda has a strong impact on the local development. South Korean government actions to reduce the role of U.S. military role in Korea lead to the very significant agreement whereby South Korea will take back wartime operation control of their own troops from the U.S. military by April 2012.[19] This will also include the reduction of U.S. military personnel stationed in Korea, which was already reduced from 37,000 to 28,500 between 2001 and 2005. As a consequence, the total or partial removal of military bases in P'aju City is already part of the present development plan and city planning – to the point that the city published a brochure presenting the different bases and the possible opening for land development and acquisition. Two famous Seoul based universities have already officially announced that, by 2010, they would develop new campuses in liberated military bases: Ewha Womans University at Camp Edward, and Sogang University

---

19   This was postponed until 2015 after the sinking of the Ch'ŏnan in March 2010.

at Camp Giant. More generally, the interviews conducted in P'aju confirmed that the present issues for the city are more typical of a fast growing city – such as urban renewal, development of infrastructures (transportation, sewage facilities, and so on), rather than the worries of a border zone location, the proximity of the North, and even the future of the border exchanges. The dynamic of growth is clearly coming from the capital region at a larger scale and pushing towards the North because the pressure in the South part of the region is too important.

Not surprisingly, the situation is quite different in rural areas, such as nearby Yŏnch'ŏn rural county, where the law triggered hope that the incentives could allow for diversification of the county's economic functions, in connection with its current rural character and its traditional location on the Kyŏngwŏn line, which was an important route connecting Kyŏnggi province to the North-East (Wŏnsan). Since 98 per cent of the county's territory is restricted by the Military Installations Protection Districts, a project launched in 2006 intends to create a small scale and local techno-pole, with a technical university and a research centre focusing on light industries, especially agro-industries. In the wake of the contemporary attention devoted to organic food and health issues, the research team came up with the label 'Slow Food' as one of the identity icons for this techno-park. This recalls similar projects in the Kangwŏn province, where local resources advocate for similar development projects, promoting the preservation of rural landscape and traditional rural habitat, the use and management of forest and the development of small scale community projects supporting research and development (R&D) in light industries connected to rural and local development as is analyzed in Ji Young Bae's study of 100 villages in Kangwŏn-do (Young Bae Ji 2007; see also Han Suck Ho 2007).

Tourism: practical and symbolic aspects of the 'frontier drive' in South Korea

In all cases, and particularly in rural districts, tourism is one interesting marketable asset of the border – then considered as a product – and the inter-Korean border region is no exception to this primary use of borders, which is often linked with the presence of foreign troops in the US military camp towns (*kijich'on*) mentioned previously (Moon 1997 and Yea 2008). The development of tourism in the border zone has thus been of particular importance not only in Kyŏnggi province where most of the *kijich'on* are located, but also in Kangwŏn province, where lots of tours and infrastructures were developed and connected to the issue of national security (Plaza of Peace in Chŏlwŏn, Hills of Peace in Inje, DMZ Museum in Kosŏng). However, it seems that between 2004 and 2008, during the short apogee of Kŭmgangsan Tours, border tourism in Southern Kangwŏn was rather low (Ponghŭi Yi 2007).

Paengnyŏng Island is a very good example illustrating the symbolic and practical power of tourism as an efficient 'frontier drive'. Indeed, even in this traditionally farmer's island I described above, tourism appeared to be one big concern for most of the informants. To sustain that, the opening of the Mandarin maritime liaison in the summer 2004 (cutting down by more than half the journey to the island: five hours instead of the previous ten or twelve) has benefited from incentives by Inch'ŏn city, which in addition provides a 30 per cent subsidy on the ship fare to local inhabitants. The island itself is very active in promoting the tourist industry, and several actions were undertaken by the local government over the recent years, such as the publication of a tourist brochure of the island. When I visited the charming village of Tumujin, raw fish restaurants (*hoetjip*) were lined up along the harbor as in any South Korean coastal village. While there, I happened to interview a fisherman who was constructing a prefab building, and we conducted the interview in that rather noisy environment. He explained that he was erecting the building to compensate for the fall in his revenue coming from the fishing activity. Here, as in many other villages and towns in the border region, the interface position actually gives way to the business of 'border tourism', which can be interpreted as a very significant 'frontier drive' emerging around the inter-Korean border, at least from the South Korean side.[20]

Conclusion

Despite the South Korean dream of a Peace Belt on the 38th parallel, the Korean border is still a militarized 'hot' border, deeply embodied in the spatial organization of the region (scattered by various military enclaves, either off-limit military zones, or *kijich'on* that is US military camp towns), in its management frameworks (regulations and control on human settlements), and its way of life (largely determined by and oriented towards the military presence). However, the border region is far from being a simple buffer zone dividing the peninsula and putting the South in an insular position.

The analysis of the spatial features of the inter-Korean border region and their recent transformation allow interesting conclusions regarding the territorial structures taking shape. The existence of South Korean 'enclaves'-type of territories in the border region is one of them, whether these enclaves are inland, such as Kaesŏng or Kŭmgangsan special zones in the North, or tourist enclaves in the South (such as the DMZ tourist spots), or located in an ambiguous territory of 'grey waters', such as Paengnyŏng Island. It is here worthwhile to recall that in the historical process of the construction of modern borders in the European context, the enclaves which were usually spatial structures around pre-modern borders were mostly eliminated during the eighteenth century along with the emergence of new theories regarding borders especially in their philosophical meaning, juridical status and technical aspects (Nordman 1998). However, in Korea the persistence, the development and the continuous emergence of enclaves around the inter-Korean border suggests that despite its apparent frozen nature this border can also

---

20 This interpretation of the tourism as a symbolic 'frontier drive' is developed by D. Nordman about Alsace-Lorraine after 1871 (Nordman 1986).

be analyzed as a 'frontier' – at least one that is driven by a South Korean push towards the North.

In the context of a militarized 'hot' border, the 'frontier drive' takes various forms. Its grassroots are probably to be found in the continuous efforts to maintain some sort of civil settlements along with the military presence. Tourism development along the DMZ is one important support of this drive, in Kyŏnggi as well as in Kangwŏn provinces, but obviously the most significant expression of it is the cluster that has been developing in the recent years around P'aju / Kaesŏng. This cluster is set on deep tendencies in the territorial architecture of the peninsula, with the growing emergence of a western central region and the relative loss of importance of the east coast.

In this context, the harsh restriction of border movements since the winter 2008 is of great significance. This radical re-bordering after a short episode of de-bordering signifies that the spatial contacts worked only too well and that – as it is the case between the U.S.-Mexican border, or in Europe after the fall of the Berlin Wall – the re-bordering is meant to keep at bay exchanges and activities developing at the border during the de-bordering phase – including legal borderline activities (Andreas 2000a and 2000b; Chen 2005). Of course, in the inter-Korean border, illegal migration and smuggling can hardly take place inland, but the importance taken of the Southern activist balloons floated across the border to North Korea may well be the sign of what is at stake: countering the frontier-building for the time being. Will this border become a fossilized frontier of post-Cold War dynamics, in addition to being one fossilized outcome of the Cold War? Or will deeper tendencies determining spatial structures continue to make it a pioneering region, at least in the South? My hypothesis is that these deeper spatial tendencies are now more determined, in the South and in the North by the growing opposition between East and West (the east coast becoming more and more a periphery) and the concentration of both capital regions connected to the emergence of a new western central region in the peninsula.

References

Amilhat-Szary, A.-L. and Fourny, M.-C. (2006), *Après les frontières, avec la frontière. Nouvelles dynamiques transfrontalières en Europe* (Paris: Les Editions de l'Aube).

Andreas, P. (2000a), 'Introduction: The wall after the wall', in Andreas, P. and Snyder, T. (eds.), *The Wall around the West: State Borders and Immigration Controls in North America and Europe* (Lanham: Rowman & Littlefield), 1-11.

Andreas, P. (2000b), *Border Games: Policing the U.S.-Mexico Divide* (Ithaca: Cornell University Press).

Bleiker, R. (2005), *Toward a Culture of Reconciliation* (Minnestoa: University of Minnesota Press).

Chang, Y. (2005), *Chŏpkyŏng chiyŏk p'yŏnghwa chidae-ron* (Theory of border zones and peace regions) (Seoul: Yŏn'gyŏng Munhwasa).

Chen, X. (2005), *As Borders Bend* (Lanham: Rowman & Littlefield Publishers).

Choe, S. (pictures) and Yang, H. (text) (2008), *DMZnŭn sala itta* (Lively DMZ) (Seoul: Humandom).

Colin, S. (2008), 'The Sino-North Korean border and its adjacent areas in China: interface's places between both Koreas?', *paper presented at the international symposium 'North/South Interfaces in the Korean Peninsula', EHESS-CNRS 16-19 December 2008 (Paris).

Cumings, B. (1998 [1997]), *Korea's Place in the Sun* (London and New York: Norton Paperback).

Ducruet, C., Gelézeau, V. and Roussin, S. (2008), 'Les connexions maritimes de la Corée du Nord. Recompositions territoriales dans la péninsule coréenne et dynamiques régionales en Asie du Nord-Est', *L'Espace géographique* 08:03, 208-24.

Foley, J. (2003), *Korea's Divided Families, 50 Years of Separation* (New York and London: Routledge, Curzon).

Foucher, M. (1991 [1988]), *Fronts et frontières* (Paris: Fayard).

Foucher, M. (2007), *L'obsession des frontières* (Paris: Perrin).

Frank, R. (2005), 'Economic reforms in North Korea (1998-2004): Systemic Restrictions, Quantitative Analysis, Ideological Background', *Journal of the Asia Pacific Economy* 10:3, 278-311.

Gelézeau, V. (2008a), 'Changing Socio-Economic Environments, Housing Culture and New Urban Segregation in Seoul', *European Journal of East Asian Studies* 7:2.

Gelézeau, V. (2008b), 'From Paengnyŏng-*do* to P'aju-*si*: The inter-Korean border region, new frontier of the peninsula?', *paper presented at the international symposium 'North/South Interfaces in the Korean Peninsula', EHESS-CNRS 16-19 December 2008 (Paris).

Gelézeau, V. (ed.)(2004), *La Corée en miettes. Régions et territoires* (Paris: L'Harmattan).

Guichonnet, P. and Raffestin, C. (1974), *Géographie des frontières* (Paris: PUF).

Hwang, K. (2007), 'Chŏpkyŏng chiyŏk chiwŏn pŏp-ŭi kyŏnggi-do hyogwa punsŏk-kwa kaesŏn pangan yŏn'gun' (Evaluation and alternatives for Kyŏnggi-do of the act supporting for the national border area in South Korea), *GRI Report* 10.

Ji, K.B. (2007), *Kangwŏn-do nongch'on ŏmenit'I chiwŏn silt'ae mit hwalyong pangan yŏn'gu* (Study on rural amenities and possible use of these ressources in Kangwŏn-do), (Kangwŏn: Kangwŏn paljŏn yŏn'gu-wŏn (Gangwon: Gangwon Development Research Institute)).

Kirkbride, W.A. 1996 [1994], *North Korea's Undeclared War: 1953-* (Séoul: Hollym), 95.

Kirkbride, W.A. 2003 [1985], *Panmunjom. Facts about the Korean DMZ* (Seoul: Hollym), 97.

Kim, C. (2003), 'Chŏpkyŏng chiyŏk-ŭl chungsim-ŭro han nambuk kyoru pangan' (Project of North/South cultural exchanges centered on the border zone), *T'ongil-gwa kukt'o* (Reunification and territory), 4-21.

Kim, C.-H. (2001), *The Korean DMZ – Reverting beyond Division* (Seoul: Sohwa).

Kim, J.-H. (2008), 'Inter-Korean Socio-economic and Cultural Exchange and Cooperation Programs of 2000-2005: the Case of South/North Gangwon

Province, Korea', *paper presented at the international symposium 'North/South Interfaces in the Korean Peninsula'*, *EHESS-CNRS* 16-19 December 2008 (Paris).

Kim, N. (2011), 'Korea on the Brink: Reading the Yŏnp'yŏng Shelling and its Aftermath', *Journal of Asian Studies*, 70:2, May 2011.

Kim, S. (2004), *Inter-Korean Relations. Problems and Prospects* (London: Palgrave).

Kim, T.D. (2006), *Kangwŏn kukche lejŏsŭp'och'ŭ & kwan'gang p'eŏ-ŭi silt'ae punsŏk mit paljŏn pangan* (Kangwŏn international fair of tourism and leisure sports: reality and development perspectives), (Kangwŏn: Kangwŏn paljŏn yŏn'gu-wŏn (Gangwon: Gangwon Development Research Institute)).

Kim, Y.-B. (1997), *Chŏpkyŏng-ŭi hyoyuljŏk kwalli pangan* (Strategic Proposals for an Efficient Management of the Border Zone) (Seoul: Korea Research Institute for Human Settlements).

Kim, Y.-B. (2006), 'Building a Peace Belt in the South-North Korean Border Region', *KRIHS Special Reports* 5 (Anyang: KRIHS).

Lee, J.M. (2001), 'History of Korea's MDL and Reduction of Tension along the DMZ and Western Sea through Confidence Building Measures between North and South Korea', in Kim, C. (ed.), *The Korean DMZ: Reverting Beyond Division* (Seoul: Sohwa), 79-125.

Lee, S.-W. (2008), *Life on the Edge of the DMZ* (Folkestone, UK: Global Oriental).

Lim, E.-C. (2007), *Kaesŏng Industrial Complex. History, Pending issues, and Outlook* (Seoul: Haenam Publishing Co).

Matsuda, H. (2007), 'A Clash of Empire in East Asia: the Geneva Conference on Korea, 1954', *Seoul Journal of Korean Studies* 20:2, 193-211.

Moon, K.H.S. (1997), *Sex Among Allies: Military Prostitution in US-Korea Relations* (New York: Columbia University Press).

Nordman, D. (1986), 'Les Guides-Joanne, ancêtres des Guides Bleus', in Nora, P. (ed.), *Les lieux de mémoire. II La nation* (Paris: Gallimard), 529-67.

Nordman, D. (1998), *Frontières de France. De l'espace au territoire, XVIe-XIXe siècles* (Paris: Gallimard).

Ŏm, S. (2001), 'Nambuk kyoryu hwansŏnghwa-wa chŏpkyŏng chiyŏk-ŭi t'oji iyong.kwalli pangan' (Project for the land use and management in the border zone through the activation of North/South cultural exchanges), *T'oji yŏn'gu* (Land) 12:2, 71-93.

Park, S.-O. (ed.)(2005), *Sahoe.kyŏngjekongan-ŭrosŏ chŏpkyŏng chiyŏk. Sooesŏng-gwa nak'usŏng-ŭi hyŏngsŏng-gwa pyŏnhwa* (Economic and social geography of the border zone. Aspects and change of backwardness and alienation) (Seoul: Sŏul Taehakkyo ch'ulpan-bu (SNU Press)).

Park, S.-O. (ed.)(2004), 'T'ŭkchip nonmun: chŏpkyong chiyŏk yŏn'gu' (Special Issue on the Border Region), *Han'guk kyeongje chirihak-hoeji* (Journal of the Economic Geographical Society of Korea) 7:2, 117-244.

Petrov, L. (2008), 'Political Factors and Socio-economic Influence of Inter-Korean Cooperation', *paper presented at the international symposium 'North/South Interfaces in the Korean Peninsula'*, *EHESS-CNRS* 16-19 December 2008 (Paris).

Renard, J. (ed.)(1978 [1979]), 'Réflexion et contributions à propos des frontières, seuils, limites en géographie et aménagement régional', *Cahiers nantais* 15, 191; 16, 125.

Renard, J. (ed.)(1997), *Le géographe et les frontières* (Paris: L'Harmattan).

Rivé-Lasan, M.-O. (2008), 'Northern Natives within the South Korean Elites', *paper presented at the international symposium 'North/South Interfaces in the Korean Peninsula', EHESS-CNRS* 16-19 December 2008 (Paris).

Roehrig, T. (2009), 'North Korea and the Northern Limit Line', *North Korean Review* 5:1, 8-22.

Rumley, D. (1991), *The Geography of Border Landscapes* (London: Routledge).

Shin, S. (2003), *Oettan kosŭ-roŭi yŏhaeng* (Seoul: Random House).

Son, K.-Y. (2006), *South Korean Engagement Policies and North Korea: Identities, Norms and the Sunshine Policy* (New-York: Routledge).

Vélasco-Graciet, H. and Bouquet, C. (eds.)(2006), *Tropisme des frontières. Approche pluridisciplinaire* (Paris: L'Harmattan).

Vélasco-Graciet, H. and Bouquet, C. (eds.)(2007), *Regards géopolitiques sur les frontières* (Paris: L'Harmattan).

Yea, S. (2008), 'Marginality, transgression, and transnational identity negotiations in Korea's *kijich'on*', in Tangherlini, T.R. and Yea, S. (eds.), *Sitings. Critical Approaches to Korean Geography* (Honolulu: University of Hawaii Press).

Yi, H. (1999), *Paengnyŏndo, Taech'ŏngdo, Soch'ŏngdo* (Inch'ŏn).

Zamindar, V.F.-Y. (2007), *The Long Partition and the Making of Modern South Asia. Refugees, Boudaries, Histories* (New York: Columbia University Press).

PART IV
BORDERS AND
TERRITORIAL IDENTITIES:
THE MECHANISMS
OF EXCLUSION AND
INCLUSION

National Minorities in European Border Regions

Jan D. Markusse

Introduction

Most states in Europe have autochthonous minorities. Since the 1990s these groups are mostly referred to as national minorities. The concept of national minority covers a diverse category of population groups. They are not all perceiving the same profoundness of their distinction. Some consider themselves as inheritors of a different language, others as people with a different nationality. They vary substantially in size and the corresponding scale of their area of habitation, from some tens of thousands or even less in a rural locality to hundreds of thousands or more in a regional homeland. These last minorities are the native population of a region with cities and a diversified economic structure. Because of this wide variety, it can even be argued that the linguistic groups in multilingual federations have the characteristics of national minorities. Most national minorities have their homeland in the peripheries of the state, in coastal regions or border regions. Some groups live entirely within the boundaries of a single state, but others are ethnically akin to the population across the border. Because of their diffuse institutional and cultural relationship with both sides of the boundary these minorities can be called interface minorities. Among the interface minorities are some that share their culture with a minority on the other side, but most belong to the titular nationality of a neighbouring state.

Relations between minorities and the states where they live are often a compromise between the ideals and ambitions of the minorities and those of the state. These compromises can vary between harmonious and tense. The way minorities are incorporated in the state and its national society is changeable. Like the fundamentals of states itself, such as national and state ideologies, also relations with minorities are regularly reconfirmed or renegotiated and revised. The past few decades have seen a general tendency to extension of rights of national minorities. This tendency must be attributed to activism, assertiveness or even struggles from the side of the minorities, as well as to changes in the attitude of states. Sometimes, there is a link with a regime change towards democracy. But this cannot explain many other cases. These developments have also affected minorities in border-regions and are part of the dynamics in these regions.

Set in a wider perspective, many dynamics of border zones are part of changes due to macrosocial developments such as globalization and European integration. In contrast with initial speculations, these are not inducing a decline of states and irrelevance of borders and territories. Nevertheless, they are leading to drastic adaptations and changes, particularly in the area of the European Union. The role of the states as bounded containers has shifted in the direction of a participant in the common policies at the European scale (Brenner 2004). This has led to permeable state borders, but it does not imply that borders and boundaries are disappearing from border zones. Instead, the border zones are more evolving into zones of transition with multiple boundaries, which have different functions and relevance. This applies in particular for border zones with minorities, which can contribute an extra source of internal boundary-making. Next to the internal boundaries on both sides of the border, emerge the boundaries of territories with cross-border cooperation in so-called Euroregions. In zones with interface minorities, this trend seems to open opportunities for demarcation of territories expressing ethno-national kinship across borders. The concept of ethno-nationalism was coined by Connor. It refers to the loyalty to ethnic groups or nations deprived from a state embodied in specific states (Conversi 2004). The concept of ethno-regionalism is mostly used to refer to regional claims to ethnic distinctiveness (Hechter and Levi 1979).

This chapter will focus on the role and development of territorial boundaries in border regions with national minorities, more in particular the state boundaries, regional boundaries and the boundaries of the Euroregions. In short, the trends can be summarized as follows. State boundaries are loosing traditional functions. Boundaries of internal regions and Euroregions are increasingly relevant for the national minorities, because they enclose the territories for realization of their aims and ambitions. Although these tendencies manifest themselves in most border regions with minorities, the outcomes are different. They depend on the interplay between regional and national actors and the context of inherited institutional structures and conditions. In the past, it has been argued that the regional actors are becoming increasingly relevant (Keating 1998). In similar vein the phenomenon of the Euroregion has even been interpreted as a manifestation of extra-state regionalism (Murphy 1993). However, the territoriality of the states has not ceased to exist. The state borders are not deprived from their meaning as separator between unique inherited institutional structures. Moreover, despite transfer of competencies to the European level and pressures that have to be taken into account, they have not completely given up direction over regional and minority politics in their territories (Le Galès and Lequesne 1998; Markusse 2004).

The following part of this chapter starts with an overview of national minorities in Europe, in particular those in the border zones. Next, the general trends in the relation of national minorities with the state and the outside world are elaborated and related with the development of the various territorial boundaries in European border regions. Thereafter follow three cases of multiple boundary-making in border regions with interface minorities. These are the Basque Country, the former

Habsburg *Kronland* of Tyrol and the Slovak-Hungarian border region. Finally, the cases are compared and commented upon.

The combination of these three border zones covers an interesting variety of relevant conditions. Ethno-regional activism varies from relatively moderate in the Slovak-Hungarian border region to the more extreme ethno-regionalism in the Basque Country. The concerning minorities have different degrees of identification with the population across the border. The concerning states have different structural characteristics and national self-perceptions. Also geographical conditions are different. In the Slovak-Hungarian border region infrastructural and functional relations are embedded in a lowland area. In the other two the Pyrenees and the Alps are physical barriers. The border zones are in different parts of Europe. Transborder cooperation in the concerning border regions dates from different stages of European integration.

National minorities

The concept of *national minority* is used in Europe to grasp the diverse groups of autochthonous minorities, which are considered as a different category to the immigrant minorities. With the elaboration of international law on the rights of these minorities it is adopted in international diplomacy as a more accurate concept than alternatives which had sometimes been used before, such as linguistic, religious or ethnic minorities, or even just minorities. The adjective *national* is not uncontroversial (Benoît-Rohmer 1996). By origin, it refers to an ethnic notion of a nation as it is quite common in Central and Eastern Europe. This view does not match very well with more civic conceptions of a nation in some other parts of Europe and the World (Brubaker 1992; Parekh 2002; Schöpflin 2000).

The Council of Europe has defined a national minority as a group of persons in a state with the following characteristics: First, they should reside there and be citizens; second, they should maintain long-standing, firm and lasting ties with that state; third, they should display distinctive ethnic, cultural, religious, or linguistic characteristics; fourth, they should be sufficiently representative; and fifth, they should be motivated by a concern to preserve together that which constitutes their common identity, including their culture, their traditions, their religion, or their language (ECDL 1994). The rather open characteristics of fourth and fifth can avoid that the status of a national minority has to be recognized when it is claimed on behalf of very small groups or on behalf of groups with low levels of awareness and mobilization. Historical immigrants, such as Roma and Jews, are considered to fulfil the condition of having long-lasting ties. Following this definition, more than a hundred subgroups in the populations of the European states have the characteristics of a national minority.

From the point of view of the idealized nation state, national minorities are an anomaly (Jackson Preece 1998; Flint and Taylor 2007). Despite their long standing and long-lasting ties with the state in which they live, they have not been assimilated into a homogeneous nation. National minorities have obtained and preserved their distinctive characteristics from the majority in the context of a state. This has not happened for all minorities in a similar way. Three different types can be distinguished. In the different parts of Europe national unification and state formation has followed a different historical development path (Kohn 1944; Krejci and Velimsky 1981; Rokkan and Urwin 1983; Sugar 1969). In relation the types of minorities are not evenly spread over Europe (Markusse 2007).

The first type of national minorities are those which are the offspring of historical migrants. These people were settlers and refugees, such as Germans in Hungary and Albanians in Italy. Sometimes they were representatives of a dominant group, such as the Swedes in Finland. Most of these minorities have the titular national identity of a state. In some states Jewish communities should be included, but in many European states Jews are considered as a religious group rather than a national group. A few groups of historical settlers have a regional cultural identity, such as the Lemko in Poland and the Catalans and Occitans in Italy. Only the Roma communities have a minority identity that is not affiliated with a state or a region. This type of minorities can be found in the eastern half of Europe, in the area of the former empires and also in Italy. Many are relatively small. They have been able to preserve their identity because they live concentrated in localities. Also the ethnic conception of national identity, which has evolved in this part of Europe, may have contributed to the survival of a distinctive national identity. The national minorities of this type are not necessarily living at borders with neighbouring states, most of them are not.

A second type of national minorities represent the indigenous regional groups that have no kinship with the titular national population of another state. A few of these minorities are relatively small such as the Saami in the Nordic countries, the Sorbs in Germany and the Ladins in Italy. However, the most well-known representatives of this type are larger population groups such as the Bretons, Catalans, Frisians and Scots. With the exception of the Frisians these larger groups are found in the large old states of Western Europe. Some consider themselves rather nations than minorities (Malloy 2005). Population size and scale of their homelands have contributed to their capacity to resist complete political integration and cultural assimilation. Also divergent institutional structures have played a role (Cole and Williams 2004; Lecours 2000). The concerning states have applied differing strategies and policies to achieve and maintain their internal coherence, with differing effects for the territorial and cultural distinctiveness of these minorities. Most of the indigenous regional minorities have a homeland in the periphery of a state. The Catalans and the Basques on both sides of the Spanish-French border are interface minorities.

A third type represent the national minorities that live in the vicinity of another state of which they have the national cultural identity. Also these minorities are interface minorities. Usually, their national identity had already developed before they were separated from the rest of their national group. Their homelands were cut off by borders drawn when states were founded or when boundaries were revised. Though the oldest states and the oldest borders can be found west of the zone from

Germany to Italy, this type of minority is not unevenly concentrated in the East. In the twentieth century state foundations took place in Central Europe but also at the Atlantic side. The twentieth century border shifts were most drastic in the east, but nevertheless they also affected the northern border of Italy and the western borders of Germany. As a result, interface minorities with the national cultural identity of a neighbouring state, such as the Älanders in Finland, the German-speaking in Belgium and the Roman Catholic Northern Irish in the United Kingdom are found in different parts of Europe.

Table 17.1 Borderland Minorities of 50,000 and more in European Union Member States

Minority	Member State	Type	Population size	Autonomous territory (since)
Flemish	Belgium	3	5,500,000	Yes (1993)
French	Belgium	3	3,000,000	Yes(1993)
German-speaking	Belgium	3	70,000	Yes (1993)
Polish	Czech Republic	3	50,000	No
Alsatians	France	2	>100,000	No
Basques	France	2	>100,000	No
Catalans	France	2	>100,000	No
Danes	Germany	3	60,000	No
Sorbs	Germany	2	50,000	No
Turks (incl. Pomaks)	Greece	3	130,000	No
Macedonian Slavs	Greece	3	50,000	No
South Tyrolese	Italy	3	300,000	Yes (1972)
Valdotian French	Italy	3	200,000	Yes (1948)
Slovenes	Italy	3	100,000	Yes (1948)
Friulians	Italy	2	600,000	Yes (1948)
Polish	Lithuania	3	235,000	No
Germans	Poland	3	300,000	No
Byelorussians	Poland	3	200,000	No
Lemko (Ruthenians)	Poland	2	50,000	No
Hungarians	Slovakia	3	550,000	No
Hungarians	Rumania	3	1.500.000	No
Catalans	Spain	2	>1,000,000	Yes (1978)
Basques	Spain	2	>1,000,000	Yes (1978)
Tornedal Finns	Sweden	3	60,000	No
Irish Northern Irl.	United Kingdom	3	600,000	Yes (1921)

Notes: Types: 2: Minorities living in their historical homeland, not having national identity of another state; 3: Minorities living in their historical homeland, having national identity of another state.

Source: © Markusse 2007.

Table 17.1 lists the 25 borderland minorities of 50,000 and more in the member states of the European Union. It appears that 13 of the 27 European Union members have one or more of these groups among their population. Eight are regional groups, 17 have the national identity of a neighbouring state. There are no historical migrants among these borderland minorities of 50,000 and more. Also when the small groups are left out, there are borderland minorities of all size scales. Ten of the 25 groups live in an autonomous territory. It appears that enjoying territorial autonomy is hardly connected with a more substantive population size of the minority. However, it should be taken into account that several minorities share their autonomous territory with others. Moreover, also minorities without an autonomous homeland can exercise territorial political control when their homeland is a regular self-governing administrative unit. Table 17.1 also indicates the year that the present autonomy regulation was introduced. Although it should be taken into account that the ten cases are concentrated in only four states, it is still indicative that in 1960 only four of the ten cases had their present degree of autonomy.

Relations with the state and the outside world

In the past half century national minorities have frequently asserted claims to facilities and rights which should conserve and reinforce their distinctive language and secure or increase political influence on affairs in their homelands. The explanation is multifaceted (Agnew 2001). Among the heterogeneous category of national minorities there are considerable differences regarding aspirations. Phenomena at local scale as well as at regional scale are relevant. Causal conditions may have changed over time. In the past five decades the macrosocial context that plays a role in most explanations has evolved. Some of its components, such as globalization, European integration and proliferation of democracy, may have gradually proceeded. But a discontinuous development such as the shift from the welfare state in Western Europe to neo-liberal economic relations, points at different episodes.

For larger, more mobilized minorities sociologists and political scientists have come out with cultural explanations (see Connor 1977). Others have stressed structuralist explanations and elaborated on struggles for political and economic resources in welfare states (see Hechter 1975; Hechter and Levi 1979). The alternative approach of historical institutionalism does not generalize one of these essentialist interpretations (Lecours 2001a, 2001b). In the theoretical context of Giddens' thoughts on societal evolution, minority politics could also be explained as a manifestation of people's increasing reflexivity and assertiveness (Flint and Taylor 2007).

In a more geographical multi-scalar perspective, consequences of globalization and European integration have to be emphasized. These processes are resulting in a smaller visibility of the state, and a declining position of dominant national culture and national cultural institutions (Keating 2004). Due to global communication with the outside world, significance of local identities and places of identification is rising. In several cases minority identity politics is overlapping with regionalism. Analogous with the decreasing significance of national culture and its institutions, also significance of national economies with national networks of economic power and distribution of resources is on the wane. Regional actors require more independency to participate in alternative networks and improve their competitive qualities in the neo-liberal environment of the *single European market* and the wider global economy.

In relation, enabling conditions and opportunity structures for successful minority politics is improving. After the fall of authoritarian and totalitarian regimes, first in Southern Europe then later in Central and Eastern Europe, virtually all European states are democracies. Democratic states have restricted possibilities to neglect minority demands. Nevertheless, between the European states with their different national self-images and state traditions are considerable variations in the degree to which they are inclined to grant or resist rights for minorities (Brubaker 1996; Knippenberg and Markusse 1999; Loughlin and Mazey 1995; Markusse 2007).

There is a common understanding that dogmatic policies to promote national unification are incompatible with principles of democracy and civil liberties. This is not only playing a role in domestic politics, but also in global and European politics (Jackson Preece 1998). Already after World War I several minorities were protected with special arrangements supposed to be supervised by the League of Nations. In the 1960s, the United Nations laid down rights of autochthonous minorities. In the 1990s the Council of Europe developed international norms for minority rights, which are more geared to regulate the position of minorities in Europe. The concept of *national minority* was introduced. *The European Charter for Regional and Minority Languages* lays down cultural linguistic rights. *The Framework Convention for the Protection of National Minorities* tends to go further and stipulates that minorities should have 'appropriate local or autonomous authorities or a special status' in regions where they are a majority (Framework Convention, Article 11).

The binding legal force of these documents is relative. *The Charter* offers the possibility of opt-outs and a compliant of the *Framework Convention* may self indicate which domestic population groups enjoy the status of national minorities. The two agreements primarily aimed to address the Central and Eastern European states in transition to democracy. Here effects are the most manifest, in particular because the European Union has in fact adopted the *Framework Convention* in its criteria for membership. However, the importance of these documents is wider. They are also a contribution to setting minimal standards for proper democratic minority politics. As such they play a role in international diplomacy and political pressure from activists and interest organizations.

Many minority rights are associated with delimited territories. In principle, rights can be organized on a territorial or a non-territorial basis (McRae 1975). However, the range of non-territorial rights, such as optional use of a minority language or guaranteed representation in governing bodies is restricted. Moreover, also non-territorial rights can seldom be enjoyed in a whole country but they are mostly confined to the administrative territories of a homeland. Matters of inclusion and exclusion in administrative territories where minority rights are exercised are relevant. A prominent field of struggles is the interdependence between delimitation of territories and population composition. The last can be relevant for the election of local and regional bodies or for necessary threshold population shares.

Developments above are relevant for all national minorities. For the minorities in the border zones they are combined with developments along the inter-state borders. As a result of European cooperation and integration many traditional boundary functions have disappeared or been transferred to outward borders. Initially, this process followed the Cold War division, later mainly the expanding European Union. Inter-state boundaries are no longer seriously contested. Relaxation of relations with neighbouring states goes together with relaxation of relations of states with their borderland minorities (Keating 2004). Opportunities for interface minorities to rely on resources of a neighbouring state have also contributed to relaxation of tensions (Bufon and Minghi 2000; Markusse 1999).

In all European border zones transborder local and regional cooperation has emerged in the territorial frame of so-called Euroregions. In the course of time, their number has increased to well over a hundred. Originally, the Euroregions were initiatives from below by non-central authorities. Involvement of the organizations for European cooperation followed relatively late. In 1980 the Council of Europe's Madrid Convention was a significant political incentive for national governments to remove legal obstacles. Since 1989 the European Interreg programs for transborder cooperation in the *single European market* have also stimulated formation of Euroregions (Perkmann 1999). In recent history several stages of Euroregionalism can be distinguished. The first Euroregions in the 1960s and 1970s were located along the borders in the historical core of the European Union and its external borders with Switzerland. In the late 1980s foundation of Euroregions in other parts of the extending European Union received a new impetus by the introduction of the first Interreg program. Soon after the fall of the iron curtain this was followed by the introduction of Euroregions along borders of the new candidate member states.

The Euroregions have multiple objectives. One of the main aims has been to break down barriers that put the territories on either side of a border in a peripheral position, hinder them from taking advantage of complementarities and handicap joint action to deal with shared problems. In the larger frame of the *single European market*, the alliances play also a role in promoting common interests. Euroregions are also aimed as territories of common identity. In everyday language, this aim has been summarized as the creation of a *we feeling* that goes beyond national boundaries (Weyand 1997). The idea of an identity community is promoted in order to improve mutual understanding and to mitigate nationalist alienation. In border zones with interface minorities Euroregions seem to offer opportunities for local actors to establish or re-establish cross-border territories with a strong ethno-national profile.

However, it has been argued that Euroregionalism is not as uniform as its general presence may suggest (Kepka and Murphy 2002; O'Dowd 2002). In the next sections it will be demonstrated how the general tendencies above are affecting boundaries and boundary-making in the three border zones with different institutional structures and conditions.

The Basque Country

Basque is spoken by people in the Basque Autonomous Community and in the northern part of the adjacent, autonomous Foral Community of Navarre in Spain, and by people in the territory of three historic provinces in France, which are now part of the department of the Pyrénées-Atlantiques (see Figure 17.1). Together these territories have a population of almost three million, of whom 250,000 live in France. It is impossible to clearly delimitate a territory of Basque speakers or even a Basque cultural area, as the Basque language is not widely spoken and alternative common cultural characteristics are hard to determine. (Mansvelt Beck 2005). The extension of the Basque Country is defined by the Basque nationalist ideology as a historical homeland of seven provinces. In nationalist discourses, the *Greater Basque Country* includes the three provinces of the Basque Autonomous Community, Navarre and the three former provinces in France (Raento 1999). However, Basque identity is professed by only one third of the population of Navarre, as opposed to three quart of the Basque Autonomous Community. In the part on the French side of the border, half of the population profess Basque identity (Mansvelt Beck 2005).

There is great asymmetry in the political status of the relevant administrative units on both sides of the border. On the Spanish side, the post-fascist constitution of 1978 stands for a non-centralist approach in the relation with regions and national minorities. The Basque Autonomous Community and Navarre have autonomous governments with ample competencies. Their natural counterpart on the French side is the region of Aquitane. This territorial body is of comparable size and has an elected government with competencies to participate in the control of institutionalized transborder cooperation. The region embraces five departments. At 250,000 inhabitants, the population of the Basque lands numbers only 10 per cent of the total population of the region of Aquitane and still less than half of that of the department of the Pyrénées-Atlantique. Basque demands for an own separate department have always been refused by central authorities. In the 1980s the French socialist government even broke an earlier promise concerning the matter (Douglas 1998; Letamendia 1997). As a soft alternative, the French Basques are allowed to have themselves represented by a Basque Country Development Council with membership from different sectors in public life and a Council of Elected Representatives with members recruited from the departmental and community councils.

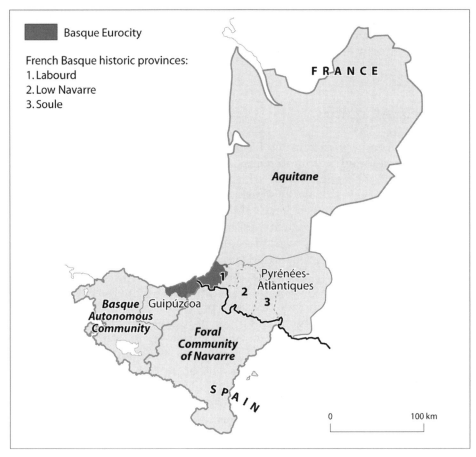

Figure 17.1 Aquitaine-Euskadi-Navarra

Source: Cartography: Uva-kaartenmakers.

The regional authorities in this area embarked on transborder cooperation at the end of the 1980s. In 1989, the foundations for a Euroregion were laid by a collaboration protocol between the Basque Autonomous Community and the region of Aquitane. The Basque Autonomous Community has only a short border with France (see Figure 17.1). In 1992, they were joined by the Foral Community of Navarre (Latamendia 1997). As a result of the incorporation of the whole region of Aquitane, the territory of the Aquitaine-Euskadi-Navarra Euroregion by no means coincides with the Greater Basque Country. This is strikingly expressed by an unofficial website of the Greater Basque Country Euroregion, showing a map of the Basque Autonomous Community and Navarre with only the Basque historical lands on the French side of the border.[1] In fact, the French Basque territory is not a

---

1   <http://www.euskalherria.org>, accessed 24 June 2008.

constituent part of the transborder regional alliance between Aquitane and the two Spanish regions because it lacks a necessary territorial governmental institution. An important motivation for Aquitane to co-operate with the Basque Autonomous Community and Navarre is the expectation of regional economic benefits. The discourses on transborder cooperation focus on transforming this peripheral area in the south-west of France into a node in a future *Axe Atlantique* that can compete with the axes of economic gravity and dynamism further to the east (Mansvelt Beck 2005; Lamentadia 1997).

In 1993, local authorities and sponsoring higher authorities agreed upon the foundation of a *Basque Eurocity* in the zone along the Atlantic coast stretching from the French city of Bayonne to the Spanish city of San Sebastian. This inter-regional alliance aims to form a transborder urban zone in the infrastructural corridor between France and Spain west of the Pyrenees that is to be developed into a zone of economic dynamics (Raento 2002). Evidently, the territorial extent of this transborder region covers only a smaller part of the Greater Basque Country as a whole, as well as of the French Basque lands.

It is obvious that the absence of a Basque territorial authority on the French side of the border is a major obstacle to the formation of a Basque Euroregion. The French central government has always been able to resist Basque regionalist demands for an own Basque department at relatively moderate costs. Although there are some radical activist groups who adhere to the ideal of a Greater Basque Country, the level of mobilization and of pressure and violence is not comparable to that on the Spanish side of the border (Mansvelt Beck 2005). Basque nationalism is from the late nineteenth century, and developed from quite different conditions on both sides of the seventeenth century border. French Basque regionalist demands seem to be much more inspired by cultural protectionist and regional welfare considerations rather than by nationalist ideology (Douglas 1998).

Moreover, also on the Spanish side of the border there is too much difference of opinion to firmly associate transborder regional alliance with a Greater Basque Country discourse (Bray 2004). This idea is the most rigidly embraced by the radical factions of the Basque nationalist movement. In Navarre, radical Basque nationalism has limited support. A considerable share of the population and the elected autonomous bodies adhere to a Navarrese regionalism that does not regard this region as a part of a unified Basque Country (Mansvelt Beck 2005). In the Basque Autonomous Community, Basque nationalism has much broader support, but there is a marked division between the radical wing and the circles of the moderate Basque nationalist party, which has decisive participation in the autonomous government. Although this party still puts forward claims that would bring them closer to Basque sovereignty, it does not demand the immediate realization of a Greater Basque Country.

The former Habsburg *Kronland* of Tyrol

After World War I, the Habsburg *Kronland* of Tyrol was divided between Italy and the new Austrian Republic. The Austrian part is now the *Land* of Tyrol with a population of 670,000, while the Italian part has become the autonomous region of Trentino-Alto Adige. This Italian region is subdivided into two provinces: Alto Adige or South Tyrol[2] in the north bordering Austria, and Trentino in the south (Figure 17.2).

Figure 17.2 Tyrol-Alto Adige/South Tyrol-Trentino

Source: Cartography: Uva-kaartenmakers.

The 470,000 strong population of Trentino is Italian-speaking. In South Tyrol, 70 per cent of the 460,000 inhabitants are German-speakers. Here is a large minority of Italian-speakers with an immigrant background, which is a legacy of Italianization policies under fascism. These population numbers imply that the German-speakers

---

2   Alto Adige is the Italian name, South Tyrol is the English transcript of the German name Südtirol. Here Trentino-Alto Adige is used for the region and South Tyrol for the province.

are a majority in the province of South Tyrol but a minority in the region. After firm ethno-nationalist resistance from the German-speakers in the 1950s and 1960s, far-reaching autonomous competencies were granted to the two provinces that now have the status of autonomous provinces within the autonomous region. The region of Trentino-Alto Adige remained as a rather hollow overarching institution. The autonomy statute of 1972 brought political stability to this border zone after a period of conflict and terrorist violence (Markusse 1997). In South Tyrol the statute decrees proportional power sharing between the German-speaking and the Italian-speaking in the autonomous provincial government and in public institutions according to their shares in the population. The agreement is sustained from the German-speaking side by the ethno-regionalist party SVP that has always got an overwhelming majority of the votes cast by German-speaking in subsequent elections. A number of Italian-speakers in the province tend to be dissatisfied with the ethnic German domination of affairs enforced by proportionality principle.

The German-speaking population in the province of South Tyrol and in Austrian Tyrol profess a common Tyrolese identity. The historical Tyrol includes the territory and Italian-speaking population of Trentino, but there is in fact an ethnic cleavage between the German-speakers and the Italian-speakers in the region (Cole and Wolf 1974). Ethnic affinity is restricted to the German-speaking Tyroleses in Italy and Austria. The Italian-speaking population of Trentino does not participate in Tyrolese nationalism, but is inclined towards Trentino regionalism.

Since the end of World War II, there have been special relations between Austrian Tyrol and the province of South Tyrol. The linguistically German university in the Austrian Tyrolese capital of Innsbruck is officially considered on both sides of the border as an institution for the whole area of Austrian Tyrol and South Tyrol. Here one can graduate in Italian law, and Austrian medical qualifications are recognized in Italy.

The regional political structures on both sides of the border are much more symmetric than they are in the Basque Country. The Austrian *Land* of Tyrol and the autonomous provinces of South Tyrol and Trentino participate in *Arge Alp* and in *Alpen-Adria* – two macro-regional transborder alliances founded in the 1970s (Perkmann 1999). The participants are the relatively autonomous regions in the German, Swiss, Italian and formerly Yugoslavian parts of the central Alps and the adjacent Adriatic. These large-scale transborder alliances have facilitated transborder cooperation between different regional authorities in the territory of the former *Habsburg Kronland of Tyrol,* but cannot be considered as emerging Tyrolese transborder regions.

A transborder region at the lower scale level of the historical Tyrol was established much later. Since the beginning of the 1990s, the concept of a Tyrol Euroregion has been increasingly used in the smaller variant of Austrian Tyrol and South Tyrol, as well as in the larger variant that includes Trentino. In 1995, the name Tyrol Euroregion was used for the joint representation of the three territories to the European Union commission in Brussels (Markusse 1999). In 1998, the Tyrol-Alto Aldige/South Tyrol-Trentino Euroregion was proclaimed by the joint assembly of their three parliaments. The new Euroregion is not attributed with institutions. The only institutionalization is in the form of the triennial joint meetings of the regional parliaments; however, this symbolic cooperation antedates the proclamation of the Euroregion (Südtiroler Landesregierung 2007).

In contrast to the Euroregions in the Basque Country this Euroregion coincides with a historical region with an inherited identity that is still strong. Also the majority of its population can identify with this region. While the former case has manifest structural obstacles to the formation of a Euroregion with a strong identitiy, here we can identify obstacles raised by the prudence of regional actors who want to avoid discourses on a restored historical Tyrol within a unified Europe.

Although most of the German-speakers in South Tyrol seem to be satisfied with the present situation, the fear of latent German-Tyrolese nationalist aspirations is not completely unrealistic. Ethnic Italian politicians criticized political statements on a unified Tyrol in a Europe of regions. Discussion of the issue is thought to raise tensions between the German-speaking and the ethnic Italian community.

The moderate German-speaking Tyrolese nationalists, who control the governments in South Tyrol and in Austrian Tyrol, seem to be satisfied with the situation of substantial autonomy for the province of South Tyrol, which implies a dominant position for the German-speaking majority. They are reluctant to discursive actions that may be interpreted as irredentist aspirations of German-Tyrolese nationalists, which would lead to reactions at the Italian side. Although these risks are diminishing, they still played a role in discussions on the establishment of a Euroregion when Austria joined the European Union in the early 1990s.

From a governance point of view, there is no urgent need to establish a Euroregion as an instrument to promote cross-border cooperation. German-Tyrolese politicians and officials from South Tyrol and Austrian Tyrol have always maintained friendly and co-operative relations. Moreover, since the 1970s they have had a formal platform for cooperation in the framework of *Arge Alp* and *Alpen-Adria*.

When incentives to establish an Euroregion in Tyrol increased in the 1990s, there were good reasons to avoid an exclusive union of Austrian Tyrol and South Tyrol with a dominant majority of German-speakers with a Tyrolese identity and a significant minority of ethnic Italians. The inclusion of the whole of historical Tyrol with Trentino neutralizes the ethnic German-Tyrolese nationalist meaning of the new Euroregion.

The Slovak-Hungarian border region

On both sides of the Slovak-Hungarian border the Hungarian [Magyar] language is spoken. The 550,000 Hungarians on the Slovak side are the largest minority in Slovakia. They make up 10 per cent of its population. Until the end of World War I, the present Slovakia belonged to the territory of the historical Hungarian kingdom, which was at that time a constituent part of the Habsburg dual monarchy. The Trianon Treaty of 1920 has drastically reduced the size of Hungary. Slovakia and

Ruthenia, the present Transcarpathian oblast in the Ukraine, became parts of the newly founded state of Czechoslovakia. The new border-line should more or less separate Slovaks and Hungarians and cut across former counties and functional regions (Hardi 2005; Sikos and Tiner 2008). For a part it followed the rivers of Danube and Ipoly. In fact a sizable area with Hungarian communities was incorporated in Czechoslovakia.

The Hungarian minority and the Czechoslovak and Slovak states have known episodes of uneasy relations. During World War II southern Slovakia was annexed by Hungary, which was a German ally at that time (Dostál 1994). In the aftermath of the war Czechoslovak authorities decided to expel the Hungarian minority. Repatriation of Hungarians is only partly executed but the number of Hungarians in Czechoslovakia was drastically reduced. During communism, anti-Hungarian policies were stopped and the Hungarian minority enjoyed cultural rights. However, by the end of this period rights for the Hungarians came under pressure. In a reaction, the illegal *Committee for the Protection of the Rights of the Hungarian Minority in Czechoslovakia* was founded (Bakker 1997). After independence in 1993, Slovakia was governed for five years by a populist and nationalist coalition. This period in the middle of the post-communist and post-Czechoslovak transition was characterized by tensions with the Hungarian minority and Hungary (Schöpflin 1996, 2000). There were struggles about new laws with unfavourable consequences for the Hungarians. A treaty for cooperation with Hungary could not be ratified until it was confirmed in an annex that the Hungarians in Slovakia should never have collective rights or autonomy. Since a change of government in 1998, relations have considerably improved. The Hungarian political party SMK and its successor PHC participated in the national government. In 1999, a more generous language law was passed, which fulfils the criteria of the *Framework Convention* (Meijknecht 2004). A few years later the Slovak parliament decided to found a Hungarian university in Komárno, which can co-operate with universities in Hungary (Sikos and Tiner 2008).

Mutual identification between Hungarians in Slovakia and in Hungary is still strong. In 2001, Hungary unilaterally launched the so-called *Status Law* that allowed the Hungarians across the borders a number of rights in Hungary. Initially the law was contested by Romania and Slovakia, but after some time the matter has been settled in bilateral agreements.

Slovak-Hungarian political activity and organization resumed after the period of communism. In 1994 just after the break up of Czechoslovakia, a local initiative from 500 villages and towns demanded independence for the Slovak-Hungarians. This was followed by a demand for autonomy by the Hungarian parties in parliament and eventually led to some cultural concessions. But in general, the Slovak-Hungarians are not aiming at collective political rights in a Hungarian territory. They try to exercise political influence on their affairs by participation in national governments. In the context of the small Slovak state their relative weight in the national parliament is significant. Under the pressures of the former coalition, the Hungarian politicians have bundled their forces in one party. Moreover, the Hungarians in Slovakia live in an extended not even completely contiguous zone along the border, which has little functional coherence. In many municipalities they live together with Slovaks.

Yet, territorial demarcations are playing a role for the Hungarian minority politics. The necessary reorganization in the territorial system of government raised controversial issues. Apart from the relevance of the population composition for elected institutions, there is also the relevant threshold of a Hungarian population share of 20 per cent for the provision of bilingual facilities. The most decisive adaptation of administrative territorial boundaries was realized in 1996 under the old coalition. A tier of eight non-self-governing regions was introduced and the tier of districts was completely revised. The operation evoked Hungarian accusations of gerrymandering tactics to divide the Hungarian territories and keep their population shares as low as possible (Mezei 2005). The tensions arose again in 2002 when the system was reformed by the new coalition. Regional self-government was implemented in the existing eight regions. An alternative plan providing for 12 self-governing regions, which would have given better opportunities for the Hungarians to pass the 20 per cent threshold, was rejected. In reaction the Hungarian party temporarily withdrew from the national government.

Figure 17.3 Slovak-Hungarian Euroregions

Source: Cartography: Uva-kaartenmakers.

In Slovak-Hungarian border region is covered by several Euroregions (Mezei 2005). There are no major physical obstacles and historically, areas on both sides have had functional relations. Scale asymmetries between the two administrative systems are relatively small. Hungary knows a tier of 19 counties with elected bodies, which are combined in seven regions for economic planning. Authorities and organizations from both sides of the border are involved in transborder regional cooperation at two different scale levels. Two Slovak regions and five Hungarian counties with four independent city authorities participate in the Carpathian Euroregion (Figure 17.3). This large conglomerate of 26 regions further extends into Poland, Romania and the Ukraine. The Carpathian Euroregion has been compared with *Arge Alp* and *Alpen-Adria*, however in contrast with these last two the participant regions lack the competencies to develop political cooperation. Obviously, at this larger scale Hungarian identity hardly plays a role. Moreover, most Slovak-Hungarians live further west.

The lack of a regional authority and the functional fragmentation of the elongated homeland make it virtually impossible that the Hungarian minority participates as a whole entity in Euroregions. The Slovak-Hungarian border region is covered with a string of smaller scale Euroregions that seek to retake advantage from regional complementarities. Two of these small scale transborder regions, *Sajo–Rima-Slana-Rimava* and *Neogradiensis*, are covering the territories of historical counties. Some other Euroregions are not even having a territorial delimitation. The *Miskolc-Kosice Euroregion* is an alliance between the two cities, and the *Ipel'-Ipoly Euroregion* is a corporation of civil organizations for environmental protection and rural development. In all these small-scale Euroregions Hungarians co-operate with Slovaks, none can be considered as a Hungarian transborder region.

Conclusions

General contemporary trends can be easily traced back in the three different border regions. In all these cases minority rights and related territorial demarcations have been reconsidered and in all, state borders have opened up and Euroregions are founded. However, comparison of the three border regions also demonstrates that the outcomes are very diverse because similar trends are embedded in different situations and inherited structures within the European Union collection of states.

In the matters of minority rights and related internal boundaries the differentiating force of path dependent development is evident. All minorities in the border zones have seen their rights improve. But there is a considerable difference between the South Tyroleses and Spanish Basques who have a firm territorial autonomy, and the French Basques and Slovak-Hungarians who have only cultural rights. Next to differences on the side of the minorities themselves, different national and state ideologies are manifested. These different attitudes seem to be more decisive than size and distance between centre and periphery. Both France and Slovakia have been much more reluctant to grant territorial autonomy than Spain and Italy. France still fosters the Jacobin ideal of a uniform state and a homogeneous civic nation (Loughlin and Mazey 1995). In Slovakia, inclination to a defensive variant of ethnic nationalism might have played a role. Spain and Italy have chosen for decentralism and autonomous regions after a radical break with centralist authoritarian regimes.

In all cases internal territorial boundaries proved to be an essential element of minority rights. As such, they are often a subject of disagreement. The broken promise for territorial delineation as a department for the three French Basque provinces, the disputes about the Slovak regions and districts, and the struggles to transfer autonomous competencies from the region Trentino-Alto Adige to the province of South Tyrol are all examples of territorial strategies applied by the states, which are contested by national monitories. In the case of the Basque Country, radical activists aim at a Greater Basque Country and are contesting the more realistic confines of the Autonomous Basque Community.

The situational differences between the three border regions are also reflected in the characteristics of their Euroregions. But among the great variety of trans-national regions there are no examples which are aimed to unite the interface minorities with their kin across the border. The nature of Euroregions is different from intra-state regions and incentives to initiate ethno-national Euroregions are probably weak. Moreover, the three border regions have shown that the obstacles are manifold. The Basque case clearly indicates that the asymmetry between different systems of regional government is a source of obstacles. In the Slovak-Hungarian case the systems of regional government are more symmetric and national affiliation of the Slovak-Hungarians with Hungary is still relevant. Here, the territorial incongruence between the regions and the homeland of the Hungarian minority is a major obstacle. Euroregions do not necessarily comprise whole regional entities, but it is unrealistic to assume that firm, ethno-national Euroregions could be bilaterally or unilaterally built up form the municipal level under the auspices of non-ethnic regional actors. The case of Tyrol demonstrates most explicitly that important categories of minority actors are not always inclined to challenge the status quo in their states by insisting on ethno-national Euroregions. Here, the internal relation with the Italian-speaking population in South Tyrol is a complicating factor.

Finally, all cases have demonstrated that the opening of the internal boundaries in the European Union has brought about drastic changes, but it has not undermined the relevance of the state borders. They are still the most significant lines of divide between different inherited institutional systems and ideological approaches. It may even be assumed that the loss of traditional border functions contributes to the consolidation of this pattern of boundaries, in the sense that the permeable borders are no longer contested.

References

Agnew, J. (2001), 'Regions in Revolt', *Progress in Human Geography* 25:1, 103-10.

Bakker, E. (1997), *Minority Conflicts in Slovakia and Hungary*, PhD thesis (Capelle a/d IJssel: Labyrint Publications).

Benoît-Rohmer, F. (1996), *The Minority Question in Europe. Texts and Commentary* (Strasbourg: Council of Europe Publishing).

Bray, Z. (2004), *Living Boundaries: Frontiers and Identity in the Basque Country* (Brussels: P.I.E. Peter Lang S.A.).

Brenner, N. (2004), *New State Spaces: Urban Governance and the Rescaling of Statehood* (Oxford: Oxford University Press).

Brubaker, R. (1996), *Nationalism Reframed: Nationhood and the National Question in the New Europe* (Cambridge: Cambridge University Press).

Brubaker, R. (1992), *Citizenship and Nationhood in France and Germany* (Harvard: Harvard University Press).

Bufon, M. and Minghi, J. (2000), 'The Upper Adriatic Borderland: From Conflict to Harmony', *Geojournal* 52, 119-27.

Cole, A. and Williams, C. (2004), 'Institutions, Identities and Lesser-used Languages in Wales and Brittany', *Regional and Federal Studies* 14:4, 554-79.

Cole, J.W. and Wolf, E.R. (1974), *The Hidden Frontier: Ecology and Ethnicity in an Alpine Valley* (New York: Academic Press).

Connor, W. (1977), 'Ethnonationalism in the First World: The Present in Historical Perspective', in Esman, M.J. (ed.), *Ethnic Conflict in the Western World* (Ithaca: Cornell University Press), 19-45.

Conversi, D. (2004), 'Conceptualizing Nationalism: An Introduction to Walker Connor's Work', in Conversi, D. (ed.), *Ethnonationalism in the Contemporary World. Walker Connor and the Study of Nationalism* (London and New York: Routledge), 1-23.

Dostál, P. (1994), 'De lange weg naar Slowaakse onafhankelijkheid', *Geografie* 3:3, 29-31.

Douglas, W. (1998), 'Pyrenean Borderland Cultures', in Wilson, T. and Donnan, H. (eds.), *Border Identities: Nation and State at International Frontiers* (Cambridge: University Press).

ECDL (1994), 'The Protection of Minorities. Collected Texts of the European Commission for Democracy through Law', *Collection Science and technique of democracy* 9 (Strasbourg: Council of Europe).

Flint, C. and Taylor, P.J. (2007), *Political Geography: World-economy, nation-state and Locality* (Harlow: Pearson).

Hardi, T. (2005), 'Borders and Regional Co-operations', in Fekete, E., Kukorelli Szörényiné, I. and Timàr, J. (eds.), *Hungarian Spaces and Places: Patterns of Transition* (Pécs: Centre for Regional Studies), 502-25.

Hechter, M. (1975), *Internal Colonialism: the Celtic fringe in British National Development 1536-1966* (London: Routledge).

Hechter, M. and Levi, M. (1979), 'The Comparative Analysis of Ethnoregional Movements', *Ethnic and Racial Studies* 2, 260-74.

Jackson Preece, J. (1998), *National Minorities and the European Nation-States System* (Oxford: Clarendon Press).

Keating, M. (2004), 'European Integration and the Nationalities Question', *Politics and Society* 32:3, 367-88.

Keating, M. (1998), *The New Regionalism in Western Europe: Territorial Restructuring and Political Change* (Cheltenham: Edward Elgar).

Kepka, J. and Murphy, A. (2002), 'Euroregions in Comparative Perspective', in Kaplan, D.H. and Häkli, J. (eds.), *Boundaries and Place: European Borderlands in Geographical Context* (Lanham: Rowman & Littlefield), 50-69.

Knippenberg, H. and Markusse, J.D. (eds.)(1999), 'Nationalising and Denationalising European Border Regions, 1800-2000', *The GeoJournal Library* 53 (Dordrecht: Kluwer Academic Publishers).

Kohn, H. (1944), *The Idea of Nationalism* (New York: Macmillan).

Krejci, J. and Velimsky, V. (1981), *Ethnic and Political Nations in Europe* (London: Croom Helm).

Lecours, A. (2001a), 'Political Institutions, Elites, and Territorial Identity Formation', *National Identities* 3:1, 51-68.

Lecours, A. (2001b), 'Regionalism, Cultural Diversity and the State in Spain', *Journal of Multilingual and Multicultural Development* 22:3, 210-26.

Lecours, A. (2000), 'Ethnonationalism in the West: A Theoretical Explanation', *Nationalism & Ethnic Politics* 6:1, 103-124.

Le Galès, P. and Lequesne, C. (eds.)(1998), *Regions in Europe* (London: Routledge).

Letamendia, F. (1997), 'Basque Nationalism and Cross-Border Co-operation between the Southern and Northern Basque Countries', *Regional and Federal Studies* 7:2, 25-41.

Loughlin, J. and Mazey, S. (eds.)(1995), *The End of the French Unitary State? Ten Years of Regionalization in France (1982-1992)* (London: Frank Cass).

Malloy, T. (2005), *National Minority Rights in Europe* (Oxford: Oxford University Press).

Mansvelt Beck, J. (2005), *Territory and Terror: Conflicting Nationalisms in the Basque Country* (London: Routledge).

Markusse, J.D. (2007), 'Are National Minorities in the EU Progressing Towards the Acquisition of Universal Rights?', *Environment and Planning A* 39:7, 1601-7.

Markusse, J.D. (2004), 'Transborder Regional Alliances in Europe: Chances for Ethnic Euroregions?', *Geopolitics* 9:3, 649-73.

Markusse, J.D. (1999), 'Relaxation of Tensions in the Multi-ethnic Border Province of South Tyrol: The Importance of cross Border Relations', in Knippenberg, H. and Markusse, J.D. (eds.), *Nationalising and Denationalising European Border Regions, 1800-2000* (Boston: Kluwer), 133-51.

Markusse, J.D. (1997), 'Power-sharing and "Consociational Democracy" in South Tyrol', *Geojournal* 43:1, 77-89.

McRae, K. (1975), 'The Principle of Territoriality and the Principle of Personality in Multilingual States', *Linguistics* 158, 33-54.

Meijknecht, A. (2004), *Minority Protection: Standards and Reality: Implementation of Council of Europe standards in Slovakia, Romania and Bulgaria* (The Hague: Asser).

Mezei, I. (2005), 'Hungarian and Slovakian Cross-Border Relations', in Fekete, E., Kukorelli Szörényiné, I. and Timàr, J. (eds.), *Hungarian Spaces and Places: Patterns of Transition* (Pécs: Centre for Regional Studies), 544-78.

Murphy, A. (1993), 'Emerging Regional Linkages within the European Community: Challenging the Dominance of the State', *Tijdschrift voor Economische en Sociale Geografie* 84:2, 103-18.

O'Dowd, L. (2002), 'Transnational Integration and Cross-Border Regions in the European Union', in Anderson, J. (ed.), *Transnational Democracy: Political Spaces and Border Crossings* (London: Routledge), 111-28.

Parekh, B. (2002), 'Reconstituting the Modern State', in Anderson, J. (ed.), *Transnational Democracy: Political Space and Border Crossings* (London: Routledge), 39-55.

Perkmann, M. (1999), 'Building Governance Institutions across European Borders', *Regional Studies* 33:7, 657-67.

Raento, P. (2002), 'Integration and Division in the Basque Borderland', in Kaplan, D. and Häkli, J. (eds.), *Boundaries and Place: European Borderlands in Geographical Context* (Lanham: Rowman & Littlefield), 93-115.

Raento, P. (1999), 'The Geography of Spanish Basque Nationalism', in Herb, G. and Kaplan, D. (eds.), *Nested identities: Nationalism, Territory and Scale* (Lanham: Rowman and Littlefield).

Rokkan, S. and Urwin, D. (1983), *Economy, Territory, Identity* (London: Sage).

Schöpflin, G. (2000), *Nations, Identity, Power: The New Politics of Europe* (London: Hurst).

Schöpflin, G. (1996), 'Nationalism and Ethnic Minorities in Post-communist Europe', in Caplan, R. and Feffer, J. (eds.), *Europe's New Nationalism: States and Minorities in Conflict* (Oxford: Oxford University Press).

Sikos, T. and Tiner, T. (2008), *One Town–Two Countries: Komárom–Komárno* (Komárom: Research Institute of J. Selye University).

Südtiroler Landesregierung (2007), *Südtirol Handbuch 2007* (Bozen, Autonome Provinz Bozen).

Sugar, P. (1969), 'External and Domestic Roots of Eastern European Nationalism', in Sugar, P. and Lederer, I. (eds.), *Nationalism in Eastern Europe* (Seattle: University of Washington Press).

Weyand, S. (1997), 'Inter-Regional Associations and the European Integration Process', in Jeffery, C. (ed.), *The Regional Dimension of the European Union: Towards a Third Level in Europe?* (London: Frank Cass).

The Borderland Existence of the Mongolian Kazakhs: Boundaries and the Construction of Territorial Belonging

Alexander C. Diener

By profoundly altering the world map, the collapse of the Soviet sphere in 1991 implicitly highlighted the enduring significance of borders. Vast opportunities for research rapidly emerged in this region among an array of new states, new governments, historic homelands, old diasporas, new diasporas, and shifting patterns of social, economic, and cultural interaction. This chapter focuses on a group of Kazakhs living in the western reaches of Mongolia's territory for multiple generations. Alongside 'western Mongols' practicing a similar form of pastoralism, they have stalwartly endured the challenges of harsh climate, the national bounding of the steppe, the rise of communism, collectivization, and the decline of communism. Today, however, Mongolia's Kazakhs stand at a crossroads.

For the last two decades, competing social discourses of identity and place attachment have flowed into and out of their semi-autonomous province. These discourses are comprised of: First, stories from recent emigrants pertaining to venues of resettlement abroad; second, rumors of new attitudes from the Mongolian capital; and third, inconsistent migration/settlement policies of the Kazakhstani government. In combination, these discourses leave Mongolia's Kazakhs torn between bonds to their local territory, allegiance to the Mongolian state, and the allure of an independent, historic-homeland offering prospects of 'modernity' and the benefits of titular status. Borders play profoundly into this complex negotiation of competing territorializations and nationalisms by creating new and reflecting old landscapes of belonging and alienation.

In the sections that follow, I analyze the construction of territorial belonging among the various components of this minority community. This analysis reveals how Mongolia's Kazakhs are negotiating their place in the world amidst an unprecedented confluence of nationalism, transnationalism, diasporism,

THE ASHGATE RESEARCH COMPANION TO BORDER STUDIES

emigration, hybridity, and hegemony. Their struggle to attach appropriate meaning to places at various scales speaks to a *bordering process* by revealing how 'social actors not only refract changing state borders and geopolitical conditions but recast or accommodate with the dominant state projects' (Razsa 2004, 162). The concept of *borderland* offers a potent lens through which to consider the complex processes of constructing territorial belonging among *dispersed peoples* in the marginal spaces of Eurasia and, more broadly, the world.

Theoretical Framework

The main strains of inquiry in border studies decreasingly focus on the issue of 'borderless-ness' and are more attentive to the manner in which borders reinforce the state-nation-citizen nexus; while simultaneously acting as spaces of connectivity and interaction (Diener and Hagen 2009). Scholarly reflections on the state-centered naturalization of space aggressively problematize traditional conceptualizations of human territoriality and political spatiality by revealing contingent and relational flows of power that extend beyond territorial containers (Agnew 2009). Nevertheless, traditional geopolitical perspectives remain persistent aspects of much research. John Allen (2003) notes: 'It seems that much easier to see the association of power and geography through the odd tall fence, high wall and exclusionary boundary marker than it is to recognize that the many and varied modalities of power are themselves constituted differently in space and time.' Central to new perspectives on borders and state sovereignty are the manifestations of different forms of power – 'over, with, through, proximate, dispersed, hierarchical, associational, networked' (Grundy-Warr 2009). These varied forms of power are readily approached through the concept of *borderlands* and the alternative ideas it generates regarding intersections of space and identity (Diener and Hagen 2010). It also offers a de-centered mode of thinking about a whole range of socio-spatial practices.

Carl Grundy-Warr (2009) adroitly suggests that we 'turn the political map inside out' and produce 'historically informed political geography which examines the contradictions of national geo-bodies with reference to previous social relations and polities'. Nick Megoran's (2006) ethnographic approach to political geography heeds this call, by exploring indigenous spaces plowed under with the creation of the modern political map. Such scholarship reveals how traditional concepts of homeland derive from highly selective historical geographies of 'nation' and enable us to uncover a variety of counter-mappings associated with local belonging and indigenous forms of sub-national sovereignty.

Research into borderlands and the creation of spaces betwixt and between, inherently confronts the representational quality of boundaries and how the symbolic processes of inclusion and exclusion relate to identity and belonging. We may better understand the manner in which borders underline existing differences and engender new 'others' through historically informed analysis of a particular borderland group. Mongolia's Kazakhs provide an ideal case for considering the interrelations of varied discourses formulating and problematizing territorial belonging within a borderland community. Recent changes at larger scales of place (global, national, regional) have dramatically alerted this group's perception of homeland. What shall become eminently clear from the following case study, however, is that territorial belonging is not a simple relational juncture between ethnicity (or any other identity) and place – but a daily performance of history, economics, politics, and socio-cultural behaviors that is affected by and in turn affects the border.

Mongolia's Kazakh Community – History, Geography, and Culture

The rise and fall of the Turkic Khaganates (551-742), the formation and splintering of various tribal alliances (Pechaneg, Kipchak, Oghuz, Uzbek, Uighur), and the eventual advance of the Mongol armies and their successors distributed Turkic speaking peoples across the vast grasslands of Central, Southwestern, and Northern Eurasia. The formation of the Kazakh ethnic group is, however, generally dated to the fifteenth century defection of the princes Kerei and Janibek from the Uzbek confederation. Remaining nomadic, while the majority of tribes and clans followed the Uzbek banner south to sedentarize within the failing Timurid states, Kazakh confederations dominated in the steppe until invasions by Jungarian (Mongol), Kalmyk (Mongol) and Kokandian ('Uzbek') forces compelled alliances with the Tsarist regime in the eighteenth and early nineteenth centuries. Alliance soon gave way to Russian rule and the European style bounding (demarcation of borders) of the steppe. Even though this process was slow and subject to fluctuations in power amongst the major players (Russia, China, Bokhara, Khiva, Samarkand, Kokand), the confluence of the Altai, Pamir, and Tien Shan mountain ranges was eventually viewed as a 'natural' territorial demarcation between Russian lands and the territory of the Qing dynasty (that is Manchurian Empire – see Bureau of Intelligence and Research 1984, 1966).

The Kazakh community currently occupying the territory east of the Altai Mountains traces its origins to the mid-eighteenth century. Having assisted the Qing war effort against the Jungar (Oirat or western Mongol) confederation, Kazakhs were granted grazing rights on pastures of western Mongolia and northwestern China (1758). In 1881, the Russian Tsar handed authority over these Kazakhs to the Qing. This component of the Kazakh community remained under the dominion of the Manchurian leadership until the establishment of the Bogd Khan's theocracy in 'Outer' Mongolia (1911-21). Periodically, bolstered by migrations from lands west of the Altai and western China during the early to mid-twentieth century, the Mongolian-Kazakh leadership petitioned for Mongolian citizenship in 1917. The Bogd Khan (ruling Lama of the Buddhist-based Mongolian state prior to the 1924 declaration of Mongolia as the world's 'second socialist state') granted this request and ethnic Kazakhs have been part of the broadly defined Mongolian nation ever since. Solidification of the borders between Soviet Union, Mongolia, and China, eventually led to the isolation of Kazakh communities and gave rise to distinct identities that reflect a measure of hybridity with their respective host-national cultures. Here we see an early sign of borders affecting identity.

Over the course of the twentieth century, Kazakh communities in all three states suffered along with their 'host' populations during various periods of revolution and the establishment of communist rule. Within Mongolia, the Stalinist inspired repressions of the 1930s saw Kazakhs (along with the Urianghai Mongols) compactly settled first informally within the Chandamani Uul *aimag* (province) and Khovd *aimag,* and later formally within the semi-autonomous, western-most province of the state, Bayan Olgi *aimag* (established 1940). Here the process of demarcating territory, even for the purpose of accommodating an 'other' within the national state, suggests an impact of borders (albeit provincial boundaries) on identity. A similar impact is even more evident in the Soviet Union proper.

Within the USSR, various reconfigurations of provincial administrative units (most notably the creation of the Kyrgyz Autonomous Soviet Socialist Republic or ASSR within the Russian Federation in 1920 – later renamed the Kazakh ASSR in 1925, and finally designated as the Kazakh SSR – Soviet Socialist Republic in 1936) established a modern political territory bearing the Kazakh name. As argued by Robert Kaiser (1994), the formation of such territorial units was integral to the nationalization of the various Central Asian ethnic groups. Within provincial homelands of the federated Soviet Union, these groups were vested with governmental structures and subjected to expedited modernization. From this process a nationalized-elite emerged to sow the seeds of national identity and eventually lead the independence movements of the region. Provincial borders concomitantly offered a territorial frame into which the societies of the region are currently attempting to grow.

A detailed historical analysis of the process by which the various borders of the region were demarcated is beyond the scope of this chapter. Suffice it to say that it involved a series of bilateral treaties and intra-state gerrymandering (see Bureau of Intelligence and Research 1984, 13-6; Bureau of Intelligence and Research 1966, 8-12; Hirsch 2000, 200-16). Ultimately, the aforementioned provincial allocations (that is within Mongolia and the USSR) resulted in the Kazakhs of Mongolia existing across from the Soviet territory of their co-ethnic kinsmen (see Figure 18.1). As these provincial borders morphed into international borders, they gave rise to an odd nexus of four states within roughly 100 kilometres of each other.

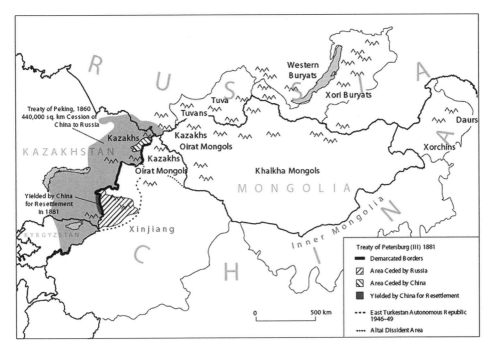

Figure 18.1 The Evolution of the Russo-Chinese-Mongolian Border

Source: Wisconsin Cartography Laboratory; edited by A. Diener.

A story relating to the convergence of these four states was told to me by a Kazakh herdsman while gazing west across the Altai highlands towards Kazakhstan. He said:

> *One day the Chinese came to the nomads of our region with maps. They were great, large papers showing the whole territory of Mongolia with all its lakes and mountains and pastures. One of these Chinese asked our fathers (ancestors) if, in the interests of peace, we would be willing to cede a matchbox size of land to China. Nomads, you must understand, are not accustomed to maps – we know our land in our heads and hearts. We are not so used to looking at the world in such a way (two dimensions). Also, nomads are generous people and like to show guests hospitality. So, they agreed to give the Chinese the land of a matchbox size. The Chinese then placed the matchbox on the map and traced its edges. The land beneath it was the great gold producing territory southwest of the Mongolian Altai range. They took the city of Alotai, the clean rivers of that region and, of course, the gold. What's more, they created this infernal gap. I can almost throw a stone to Kazakhstan, but must have so many papers to travel there.* (Author interview with Kazakh herdsman 2002)

This story hints at Mongolian-Kazakhs' attitudes toward the Chinese and the meaning of the roughly 100 kilometre gap between the borders of the western-most *aimag* (province) of Mongolia and the eastern-most *oblast* (province) of Kazakhstan. This gap constitutes an isolated meeting point between Russia and China, as well as a complex spatial, geopolitical, and bureaucratic chasm between Kazakhstan and Mongolia. Though affecting the Kazakhs of Mongolia for generations, this gap has become particularly problematic since the 1990s. Bayan Olgi essentially exists as a Kazakh borderland between Mongolia and Kazakhstan without actually touching Kazakhstan. It is an enclave of Kazakh culture within the Mongolian state but does not constitute a Kazakhstani exclave.

A wave of nationalistic exuberance relating to Kazakhstan's emergence as an independent state catalyzed an estimated 60,000 or roughly half of the 120,000 Kazakhs existing in Mongolia in 1989, to migrate to their historic homeland.[1] The gap, along with a lack of modern communication technology within Bayan Olgi, limited the capacity for interaction between the now separate components of the Mongolian-Kazakh community. Over the past 20 years a complex negotiation of territorial belonging has occurred, whereby those who migrated and crossed the borders into Kazakhstan, as well as those who remained within Mongolia, find themselves betwixt and between national projects. They, along with the land they occupy, are subjects of competing narratives of ownership, identity and belonging. The remainder of this chapter will attempt to unpack the thicket of claims and counter claims that cast the Mongolian-Kazakhs as a borderland people both within Mongolia and, ironically, within their historic-homeland of Kazakhstan.

Mongolian Kazakhs – Diaspora or Borderland Minority

Forming the largest non-Mongol minority in the state – at roughly 5.9 per cent of the population in 1989 (120,000) and 4.3 per cent in 1999 (103,000), Kazakhs have settled compactly for decades. Their primary locales of concentration are Bayan Olgi (91 per cent Kazakh in 1989, 88.7 per cent Kazakh in 2000) and Khovd *aimag* (only 16.7 per cent of the total *aimag* population in 1989 but roughly 96 per cent of the Khovd *soum* or county),[2] with additional pockets of ethnic Kazakhs in the capital city of Ulaan Baatar (0.61 per cent Kazakh) or in mining towns such as Nalaikh (26 per cent Kazakh). Nevertheless, it is estimated that 78 per cent of Mongolia's Kazakhs live in Bayan Olgi.

---

1 The number of Kazakhs in Mongolia is debated. Some experts place the 1990 population at 150,000. The number of migrants to Kazakhstan is also in question. The Kazakhstani census of 1999 indicates that 42,426 Kazakh migrated to Kazakhstan from Mongolia but Zhusupov (2000, 2) puts the number at 63,500. This number differs from the Mongolian population statistics which suggest a reduction of 17,500 persons.

2 A *soum* is akin to a *county* within an *aimag* [province]. A gradual decline in this percentage has occurred over time (see Finke 1999, 112).

With relatively few ethnic Mongols living within the Bayan Olgi *aimag*, the great distance between it and the capital city of Ulaan Baatar has enabled equilibrium of distinction to be created and maintained between the Kazakhs and the general Mongol population. In terms of culture, there are both major differences and considerable similarities between the groups. Both share a proud nomadic heritage, which readily lends itself to contemporary overlaps in traditions, values, and technologies. Differences, however, are profound and made even more so by changes in the region over the last 20 years.

The Kazakh people are traditionally Muslim and speak a Turkic language that, while sharing an Altaic root with Mongolian, radically differs from the language of the predominantly Buddhist Mongols. Such differences could represent a pretext for tension, especially considering the global discord that currently revolves around actual and perceived threats from radical Islamists. But it should be noted that both groups contain large numbers of atheists and some shamanistic/animistic practices occur as well. Also, most Mongolian-Kazakhs have at least a rudimentary command of Mongolian, and often the educated elite speak Russian. I contend that tensions between Mongols and Kazakhs have, for the most part, fallen short of conflict because of the condition of 'isolation' and 'insulation' in which Mongolia's Kazakhs have lived.

Bayan Olgi is some 1,500 kilometres from the capital city of Ulaan Baatar and, while possessing a regional airfield, it is not on any rail line, nor is it formally connected to a paved highway network. As noted above, the province's borders abut remote regions of China and Russia, and it has lost much of its industry since the early 1990s. The friction of distance that gave rise to the 'isolation/insulation' conceptual rubric of Kazakh marginality in Mongolia is, however, shrinking due to a variety of intervening factors.

With the collapse of the Soviet Union, new processes of modernization emerged. Formerly tied to the truncated global-communist economic system, Mongolia was thrust onto the post-modern global stage in 1990. This process entailed the introduction of a variety of new technologies and the advent or reification of ideologies relating to identity and territorial belonging. In terms of technologies – Mongolia saw the mushrooming of internet cafes that, while slow to come to the western portion of the state, have recently provided this once isolated/insulated region with a window onto the world. Cell phone towers are also under construction, along with the increasingly common sight of satellite television dishes mounted on *Ger* [Yurt] roofs (Barcus and Werner 2007). On the horizon, however, is a mega-project having a potentially far greater impact.

Where no permanent transportation infrastructure (neither rail nor paved road) currently spans Mongolia east to west, the proposed 2,400 kilometre *Millennium Highway* will eventually convert the Mongolian steppe into a major transportation corridor for Northeast Asia and rupture the insulation buffer of distance between Bayan Olgi and Ulaan Baatar (Diener 2011). One need only to look at China's example of 'developing the west' (its predominantly Turkic Muslim *Shinjiang* province) as a potential model to be followed once modern transportation infrastructure has penetrated a region. This is especially significant given the emergence of independent Kazakhstan some 100 kilometres away from the border of Bayan Olgi. The completion of the *Millennium Highway* could facilitate unprecedented flows of people to Bayan Olgi, but also from the *aimag* should links be established with Russian and/or Kazakhstani road networks. The precedent for out migration already exists as transnational flows of information in the early 1990s catalyzed a national awakening among Kazakhs in Mongolia and altered the sense of territorial belonging among much of the population. The very nature of the gap and the borders that constitute it are subject to change as 'territorial borders both shape and are shaped by what they contain, and what crosses or is prevented from crossing them' (Anderson and O'Dowd 1999, 594).

Projecting the Historic-Homeland

With the advent of the Soviet Union, the borders of Northeast Asia became more impermeable than at any time in history. Throughout much of the twentieth century, Moscow limited contact between the Kazakhs of Mongolia and Kazakhstan. Exchanges of teachers/students and textbooks were sporadic and, with time, relative rigidity of the border reset the cultural trajectories of the co-ethnic peoples it divided. Some elites in Bayan Olgi have positively interpreted this process as 'insulating' Mongolia's Kazakhs from Russification occurring in the Kazakh SSR and thereby preserving the cultural purity and authenticity of Mongolia's Kazakhs. To this day, many claim that the Bayan Olgi Kazakh community alone remains knowledgeable in the pastoral ways and language of their ancestors; whereas other Kazakh groups, including those in Kazakhstan, have been 'corrupted'. Other elites, however, interpret this new trajectory as a product of 'isolation', whereby the group had only limited opportunities for modernization and economic development throughout much of the 1990s and early 2000s. It is within this social and geographic context that Kazakhstan's emergence as an independent state (1991) profoundly problematized the, heretofore, stable existence of Mongolia's Kazakhs.

Ousted from the Soviet Union in 1991, the independent Republic of Kazakhstan faced an uncertain future. Its head of state was a savvy, former apparatchik that seamlessly converted his Soviet First Secretary post into a Presidency. The country, over which he ruled, however, was not so seamlessly evolving into a functional national-state. Within its borders, inherited from the Soviet territorial administrative system, an ethnically diverse population (over 100 ethnic groups) struggled to reconcile their identities to the new socio-political structure of Kazakhstan. Most citizens of the Kazakh SSR had not fully succumbed to a Soviet identity and retained a sense of their ethno-national selves. Given the ethnic core of their new state name (Kazakhstan = land of the Kazakhs), many took to reifying historic homeland conceptions and reconsidering their current place attachments at every scale. This is not to say that every group reacted identically to their new circumstances, but Kazakhstani officials were quick to recognize the vulnerability of a state named for a 'minority' community (Kazakhs = 38 per cent in 1989).

Their policy responses to this condition were often dichotomous. They included establishing Kazakh as the 'official state language', while giving Russian (the most commonly spoken language of the Kazakh SSR) the status of 'language of international communication'. They launched media campaigns to promote a civic national and multicultural status of citizenship while simultaneously making educational, political, and cultural structures more Kazakh-centric. Large-scale emigration of certain non-titular groups (Russian, German) bolstered the demographic advantage of ethnic Kazakhs, and a campaign to summon 'home' the Kazakh *diaspora* helped recast the social positions of Kazakhs within the state. This had a rather ironic correlated effect on those abroad.

'Kazakh' identity was portrayed in the public discourses exported to dispersed co-ethnic communities as tied to the new 'nation-state'.[3] No longer forbidden from 'returning' to the lands of their ancestors, the Kazakhs of Mongolia were now recast as a *diaspora*. Such a social category was, for many, quite new, and, for some, not wholly comfortable. Simply by virtue of occupying a new social category, the group was tacitly impelled to transcend a condition of 'exile' and give up the lands they had occupied for multiple generations. A process of de- and re-territorialization of identity was thereby catalyzed by the very prospect of border crossing ('return' migration).

The educated elite were the initial component of the Mongolian Kazakh community to embrace the idea of migrating to Kazakhstan – particularly those academics with access to Kazakh nationalistic literature and discourses on self-determination following the collapse of the Soviet Union. From this foothold, Kazakh nationalism and the idea of migration was disseminated among the isolated pockets of Kazakhs in Mongolia, as they were considered to be the most fearful of losing (or their children losing) their 'Kazakh' identity and cultural heritage. Gradually, the process of de-territorialization reached Bayan Olgi and manifested in public critiques of the condition of the semi autonomous Kazakh *aimag*. Articles in major Mongolian language newspapers advanced the conception of the province as 'isolated' and argued that the community was being ruptured by the migration of people (particularly educated and artistic elites) to Kazakhstan (see Hahaar 1993; Huandag 1991; Sultan 1993; Unen 1993).

In 1993, this discourse took tangible political form, when the Bayan Olgi Governor Mizamkhan and chief of the Citizens Representative Board sent a letter to then Mongolian President Ochirbat requesting the following: First, permission to expand trade with neighbouring regions of Kazakhstan, Russia and China; second, completion of an unfinished felt factory and return of the Nbuurst hotgor Coal mining facility (which had been given to the Uvus *aimag*); and third, subsidies of cattle feed for livestock during the drought and *zhut* seasons (Mizimkhaan and Murat 1993, 5). While such a request suggested an interest in remaining in Bayan

---

3 An example is available in the *Resolution of the 1992 World Kuraltai of Kazakhs*, President Nazarbayev appealed to 'all Kazakhs to unite under a single flag on the soil of Kazakhstan' (Kazakhstanskaya Pravda 1991, 1).

Olgi, it also cultivated awareness of the problems faced by Kazakhs in the region, thus making the idealized (historic homeland) alternative appear more attractive.

The aforementioned discourses targeted different groups of Kazakhs within Mongolia and offered de-territorialization arguments specific to their conditions. For example, acculturation to Mongol ways was presented as a reason to migrate to Kazakhstan among Kazakhs dispersed throughout Mongolia, while for the people in Bayan Olgi, migration was presented as a means of escaping economic woes and accessing modernity.

As a result of these de-territorialization discourses, Kazakh emigration from Mongolia was estimated in 2001 to have reached 60,000. Though not overtly pushed from Mongolia, nearly half of the Kazakh community opted to migrate from the lands of their birth. Mongols were at times puzzled by this reaction. Most had considered Kazakhs welcome neighbours and had sanctioned accommodation of this group. Many even felt that Kazakhs had been favourably treated during the Soviet era and pointed to the provincial boundaries that symbolized the semi-autonomous status of Bayan Olgi as evidence.

The process of nationalization occurring within the Kazakh population during the early 1990s was paralleled among Mongols. Elites from both groups advanced ideas on the social boundaries of the state and sought to negotiate a place for Kazakhs within a now truly sovereign Mongolia. A series of articles in major Mongolian newspapers pointed to the predominance of ethnic Kazakhs in Bayan Olgi and raised the prospect of a 'Mongolization' of the province. Several articles from this period lamented the decreasing number of Mongols in Bayan Olgi (see Chuluunbaatar and Onjoon 1990, 2; Huandag 1991, 3; Tuyabaatar 1991, 3) and others contested the level of autonomy held by the Kazakh minority (see Hudulmur 1990, 2; Tuyabaatar 1990, 3).

This debate came to a head when Kazakh elites proposed new Turkic names for mountains, rivers and other landforms in their province. Proposed conversion of the *aimag* name from Bayan Olgi to Bai-Olke ultimately spurred Mongol political elites to create laws requiring the retention of Mongol names for natural features (mountains, rivers and so on) and state level territorial entities (*aimags*). However, these same Mongol elites acceded to the Kazakhizing of street names in the city of Olgi (the *aimag* capital) and many of the *soum* centers (small towns serving as the rough equivalent to 'county seats'). The Kazakhs' efforts to assert their ethnic identity in landscape is reflective of both an interest in remaining in Mongolia and a rising sense of Kazakh-ness that stems, at least in part, from the emergence of a state bearing their name just a 'stone's throw away'.

The Kazakhs of Mongolia along with their Mongol neighbours were compelled to ask 'for whom is Mongolia a homeland?'. For many, the mere existence of an independent Kazakhstan answered this question. Evidence of longstanding 'return myths' is somewhat limited, but clear evidence of recent attempts to construct a bond between Mongolia's Kazakhs and their historic homeland can be found in textbooks on Kazakh history published after 1990 (see Babaev 1995). These books portrayed the evolution of the Kazakh people within the borders of contemporary Kazakhstan and promoted the conceptualization of genealogical links between all Kazakh peoples. They quickly became popular in Kazakh-Mongolian schools, initiating a process of de-territorialization (in relation to Mongolia) at an early age.

It should be noted that stoking the fires of Kazakh nationalism worked congruently with the prospect of titular advantage. The new social concept of Mongolian-Kazakhs as a *diaspora* lent itself to idealized notions of living as a Kazakh within a Kazakh state. Adding to this motive were, at times, somewhat pejorative statements as to the cultural or economic level of Kazakhs abroad. An anonymous 1991 article in the Mongolian language newspaper *Ardyn Erkh* entitled 'No Interest in Staying There' attributes the following comments to Kazakhstan's President Nursultan Nazarabayev: 'The majority of Kazakhs migrating to Kazakhstan are from Mongolia and they are not interested in living there (Mongolia) ... Livestock herding is the main occupation of these people and their cultural stage is rather poor' (Ardyn Eerkh 1992, 3). Such statements contradict others that praise the retention of Kazakh culture in Mongolia,[4] nevertheless, some Kazakhs of Mongolia came to regard their borderland province as a 'cultural artifact' and longed to see their children raised with the opportunities afforded by a 'modern, sophisticated country' (that is Kazakhstan).

Labour contracts served as the primary mechanism for movement of diasporic Kazakhs to Kazakhstan and offered benefits for those willing to migrate. These contracts offered housing, employment, education (for the young), pension support (for the elderly), animals and a minor stipend to cover initial settlement costs. Unfortunately, the construction of an idealized historical homeland does not always match its lived reality. For many of Mongolia's Kazakhs, crossing the gap and settling in the Republic of Kazakhstan only restated the questions of territorial belonging that compelled their migration.

Negotiating the Historic-Homeland

Believing that *diasporic* peoples remain territorialized to their historic-homeland, nationalist elites within Kazakhstan assumed that 'return' migration of dispersed Kazakhs would result in their seamless integration with the 'co-ethnic' population. Such thinking reflects a 'primordialist' mentality to identity and territory, whereby generations abroad and high levels of cultural hybridity would be trumped by the very idea of being a 'Kazakh' in Kazakhstan. They discovered, however, that dispersed ethnic communities can possess intense feelings of place attachment for regions outside of the 'historic homeland' and that nominal co-ethnicity is not sufficient to engender a clear sense of social or territorial belonging.

Returning Kazakhs from Mongolia often displayed cultural practices and attitudes that problematized the very concept of *diaspora* as a social category

---

4   Citing their retention of eagle hunting, pastoral nomadism, animal husbandry, language purity, and art forms, President Nazarbayev declared Mongolian-Kazakhs the most culturally authentic Kazakhs at the World *Kuraltai* of Kazakhs in 1992.

innately linked to a condition of placeless-ness and dispersal. In other words, their 'borderland existence' had not been placeless. De- and re-territorialization of identity was required despite their 'return migration' to an historic-homeland and titular status.

'Return myths' regularly portray the historic homeland in idealized terms (Safran 1991). The discourses of de/re-territorialization discussed above openly advanced an image of Kazakhstan as modern, economically viable, and culturally welcoming to all Kazakh peoples. Upon their arrival in Kazakhstan, however, many Mongolian-Kazakhs were dismayed by barriers to their integration. Such barriers included socio-economic issues such as unemployment, housing problems, governmental shortcomings in the area of allowances, pensions, and other forms of material support. Difficulties in the citizenship/naturalization arena and barriers to communication between the various returning groups (for example those from Mongolia, Afghanistan, China, and so on) also ranked quite high. Particularly surprising to some returnees was their subjection to resentment by Kazakhstani citizens (Diener 2005a, b). Labeled, *Oralmandar* (returnees/repatriates) or referred to as titular members of their former 'host state' (that is Mongols or Mongolians), many Mongolian-Kazakhs found themselves in a social position ironically akin to that of a *borderland people* within their historic homeland (Diener 2005a, 2009).

The term *Oralmandar* constitutes a label that many return migrants regard as pejorative; while other returnees consider the *Oralmandar* label a badge of honour. For this latter group the label marks their distinction from Kazakhstani Kazakhs and the years of Russification endured as direct subjects of Soviet rule. Cultural purity is a point of pride for some returnees, while others fear their differences will prevent them from becoming full-fledged members of the 'Kazakh nation'. From this dichotomy of perceptions, the complexity of hybridity is clearly evident.

Some Kazakhstani-Kazakhs have impugned return migrants as culturally corrupt due to their enacting traits learned from their former 'host' societies. Simple examples include accents and loan words that reflect a measure of linguistic hybridity (Maukaruly 1997, 2). The response of returnees has involved assertions of 'pure' Kazakh culture and by consequence the inference of cultural corruption among their ethnic kinsmen in the historic-homeland. Russian loan words and the limited knowledge of Kazakh among many urban co-ethnics (particularly in the 1990s) have coupled with a general loss of pastoral-nomadic practices to provide material for *counter othering*. By tapping into an already existent social discourse vilifying the hybridity of russified Kazakhs,[5] return migrants are often seen as natural supporters of Kazakh ethno-nationalism. Such a position can place them at odds with non-titular peoples within the state.

Another societal cleavage that predated the arrival of Mongolian Kazakh 'returnees' but into which they have been embroiled reflects a pattern common to relations between core and borderland peoples. The urban-rural divide is a rather prominent social distinction in Kazakhstan. Migrants from the far abroad

---

5   See Chingiz Aitmatov's metaphoric categorization of the sovietized/russified Turkic peoples of Central Asia as *Mankurttar* (see Aitmatov 1988).

(that is not from former Soviet republics) have generally been settled in rural regions and on state farms in accordance with the labour contracts that brought them to Kazakhstan. Though troublesome in economic terms (particularly during the slowdown of the late 1990s), these locations are advantageous to returnees in that rural Kazakhs have proven more familiar with the traditional cultural practices and the Kazakh language than their urban counterparts. Unfortunately within Kazakhstan a pejorative attitude is often levied against 'village Kazakhs'. By association, returnees are often regarded by Kazakh and non-titular urban elites as unsophisticated siphons of government funding and blights on the urban landscape.

Particularly during the first years of independence, when dispersed communities of the far abroad were most prominent in the migration stream to Kazakhstan, animosity manifested between returnees and the Kazakhstan-born components of society. Returnee reactions to these problems have, at times, taken a territorial form. Reflecting the capacity of boundaries to be used in the construction of belonging, returnees have requested and in some cases simply created small scale *borderlands* within Kazakhstan.

Karakalpak-Kazakh, Afghanistani-Kazakh, Chinese-Kazakh, Iranian-Kazakh, Turkish-Kazakh, and Mongolian-Kazakh returnees have each manoeuvred for specific territories, arguing that adaptation into Kazakhstani society of current and future migrants would be eased by this cultural 'half-way house' within their historic-homeland (see Karzhowbai 1992, 4). By living in one area, the return migrant communities hope to recreate the intimacy of their formerly *diasporic* existence, complete with social structure and cultural hybridity. Mongolian Kazakhs performance of a *Naadam* festival in the Kokshetau oblast is a clear manifestation of such cultural hybridity.

Held every summer throughout Mongolia, *Naadam* celebrates a unique Mongolian/nomadic heritage. Three nomadic sports (wrestling – males, archery – both male and female, and cross-country horse racing – for children) constitute the core of the festival. Through their shared nomadic traditions and years of coexistence with Mongols, Kazakhs in Mongolia have become equally involved in *Naadam*. Even within Bayan Olgi, local *Naadam* festivals are held in almost every *soum* [county]. The performance of this ostensibly 'Mongol festival' in their historic-homeland, signifies this group of returnees as 'Mongolian-Kazakhs' possessing a deep-seated and valued cultural hybridity. Clustering in one area is seen as a means of controlling their assimilation to a largely foreign society. In essence, they are seeking to recreate the *borderland* within their historic-homeland.

Kazakhstan's leadership has however expressed concern that the provision of such borderland-like settlements to in-migrants could set a precedent for other ethnic communities within the state and delay their social integration. Economic instability and rising discontent relating to unfulfilled promises of government support of returnees catalyzed a clear *scale down* of return migration to Kazakhstan during the second half of the 1990s from 10,000 families in 1990 to 600 families in 2001 (see Agentstvo Respubliki Kazakhstan po Informatsi 2003).

This *scale-down* was achieved by providing dispersed Kazakh communities a more realistic picture of the conditions within the historic homeland. The countering of nationalistic 'return myths' problematized homeland conceptions among dispersed groups. This tension was heightened by the reverse migration of some 10,000 Mongolian Kazakhs, whose sense of territorial belonging within their historic-homeland failed to trump that of the land of their birth. With this group we return to Bayan Olgi and the efforts by these and remaining Kazakhs to reconcile their ethnic identity to their sense of territorial belonging outside of Kazakhstan and membership in the Mongolian civic nation.

Projecting the 'New' Homeland

Migration studies have only recently begun to appropriately consider those opting to remain in place (see Cohen 2005; Fischer et al. 1997; Heleniak 2009). This group is of particular interest in cases of 'return migration', where a component of a dispersed group decides to remain within a borderland existence. Such components of dispersed groups make clear that not all of peoples labelled *diasporas* are equally disposed to 'the call' of the historic-homeland. In the case of Mongolia's Kazakhs some have migrated because of economic ambition or hardship, and others by virtue of conceptualizing their ethnic identity as inextricably linked to Kazakhstan, but a large percentage of Mongolia's Kazakhs have opted to remain in Mongolia. Rather than de-territorializing from their current places of residence, clear attempts have been made by both Kazakhs and Mongols to construct a distinctly 'Kazakh-Mongolian' identity and affirm the community's territorial belonging within Bayan Olgi and Mongolia.

These efforts occurred during the 1990s within the complex socio-political environment of a 'Mongol renaissance'. Long contained within the political sphere of the Soviet Union and at times serving as a buffer between its patron and the Peoples Republic of China, Mongolia emerged on the world scene in 1990 as a fully independent state. Resetting the trajectory of the nation involved major decisions as to who belonged within the state and who did not.

Once again, the role of borders in identity formation emerges as a 'territorial' or civic principle established as the criterion for inclusion within Mongolian nationalization.[6] As a result, Kazakhs have often been afforded greater legitimacy in their claims to belonging within Mongolia than even ethnic 'Mongol' peoples living beyond the state's borders. The reason for this territorial or civic national structure is multifold but may reflect parochial concerns of specific elites. The incorporation of all ethnically Mongol peoples into the 'Mongolian nation' or 'pan-mongolism' was seen as problematic by the reigning Khalka Mongol elite in that the inclusion of

---

6   A 1995 law on citizenship states that every person who was a citizen of Mongolia on and after 11 July 1921 and has not relinquished their citizenship will be considered as a citizen of Mongolia.

Buryats, Tuvans, Kalmyks, and other groups currently living in Russia would bolster the political power of the western Mongols. Socio-cultural divides between eastern (mostly Khalka) and western (Oirat) Mongols are long standing. While not overtly divisive since the nineteenth century, they can be argued as factoring into current conceptions of the Mongol nation. Though inclusion of the predominately Khalka Inner Mongols (for example Chinese Mongols) would improve the percentage of Khalka Mongols in the state, fear of the Chinese demographic dilution of Mongolia makes this highly unlikely. Ultimately, the idea of Khalka hegemony[7] has proven rather non-threatening for the Kazakhs. This may be argued to relate to borders in that Kazakhs have no desire to be considered Mongols and those remaining within their semi-autonomous *aimag* appear rather accepting of a 'second among equals' status within Mongolian society. Many residents hope that transnational contacts will increase between Kazakhstan and Mongolia, and the borderland of Bayan Olgi will serve as a bridge between the two societies.

One may posit that by virtue of their long cohabitation, history of cooperation (particularly during World War II), and shared suffering under Stalin's representative Khorloogiin Choibalsan (1895-1952) – head of Mongolia's Communist Party, Kazakhs have become valued contributors to Mongolian society. Add to this a revival of nomadic traditions and pastoralist self conceptions, and the notion of Kazakhs belonging in Mongolia as 'fellow felt tent dwellers' [*tuurgatan*] makes sense. Components of both the Kazakh and Mongol communities within Mongolia share a concern for modernity's capacity to eradicate a traditional pastoral lifestyle (see Diener 2007).

While the spatial isolation and cultural insulation of Bayan Olgi from the rest of Mongolia enabled the retention of a distinctly Kazakh identity, many of Mongolia's Kazakhs suggest that their shared nomadic heritage with Mongols is an equally important factor in the retention of true 'Kazakh-ness' and the value they place in their borderland existence (Diener 2007). As shall be discussed in greater detail below, this notion of cultural purity outside the historic homeland speaks directly to territorial belonging at a scale beneath the nation-state. Simply stated, to remain in Mongolia's borderland is to remain truly Kazakh for many of those living in Bayan Olgi.

Negotiating the 'New' Homeland

While most of those opting to remain sent their relatives off with best wishes, a powerful sense of loss set in after the departure of their ethnic kinsmen. Because of the gap between Kazakhstan and Mongolia, the Mongolian-Kazakhs, at least

---

7   Khalka, Mongols constitute 81.5 per cent of the total citizenry of Mongolia. It is relatively common to hear the term *Mongol* used in reference to the Khalka, while other *Mongol* groups are referred to by their ethnonym (Uriangkhai, Durvut, etc.) or grouped into a category of *Western Mongols* or Oirats (see Bulag 1998).

for the near future, face a division of their community between two states and the likelihood of widening social boundaries between those choosing to remain in the land of their birth and those opting to resettle in the land of their ancestors. The expanse of this social gap is dependent on the evolving meaning of the nexus of borders between China, Russia, Kazakhstan and Mongolia, and by consequence the group's negotiation of belonging within Mongolia. This section outlines the evolution of this process. I begin with efforts to cast Kazakhs firmly within the evolving narrative of the Mongolian nation.

In the wake of tensions arising from reports of Kazakh nationalism in the early 1990s and the seeming evidence of this identity shift through migration during the same period, a series of articles in Mongolian language newspapers promoted the territorial belonging of Kazakhs in Mongolia. In the article entitled 'We Have Only One Homeland', Kazakh writers Hurmetbek and Minis (1990, 8) stated 'Mongolia is our homeland, where we were born and drink its water. We Kazakhs have only one homeland that cannot be replaced'. A Mongol writer named Huandag followed with an article entitled, 'No One Possesses Dual Homelands' and criticized attempts to overtly Kazakhize place-names in Bayan Olgi. He implored Kazakhs, as 'fellow-countrymen to understand and trust us (Mongols) ... as we have lived together in peace and will be together for all time' (Huandag 1993, 3).

Public demonstrations relating to both groups' concerns over their status in the west eventually compelled a visit by then Mongolian President Ochirbat in 1994. During this visit, the President stated 'I do not want the Kazakhs to leave. The plan to establish a pan-Mongol state will never materialize and if it does, it will push the country to its destruction' (Ganhuyag 1994, 7). These words were later backed with actions that demonstrate the Mongol leadership's commitment to limiting citizenship to those within the current borders of the state and by consequence including Kazakhs within the Mongolian national conception. Examples of such efforts include establishing the category of 'Mongolian Citizens of Kazakh Descent' as the official designation of Kazakh peoples in Mongolian state documents and a variety of institutional and iconic symbols of Kazakh ethnicity in the social and physical landscapes of Mongolia.

Attention to Kazakh symbols in the landscape relates not solely to recent iconography but extends to the reification of 'indigenous' histories of the Naiman and Kerei tribes and a revival of interest in the Turkic totems and graves scattered throughout Bayan Olgi. Taken as a whole, these efforts speak to a conscious desire to justify the community's remaining in Mongolia. A risk, however, must be acknowledged in such efforts. Symbolizing primordial belonging of Kazakhs in Mongolia can stand in direct opposition to Mongol assertions of homeland priority, as well as Kazakhstani generated return myths and projections of the 'historic homeland' in the Republic of Kazakhstan.

Two related themes of re-territorialization within Mongolia emerged over the last 20 years. These involve the negation of the idealized 'return myths' and an active assertion of belonging within Mongolia. Both themes celebrate traditional 'Kazakh' culture (uncorrupted by Russification and modernization), as well as the history of long-term cooperation between Mongols and Kazakhs. Among the most prominent themes in the process of negating return myths has been the depiction of a dispersed settlement pattern of the Mongolian-Kazakhs within Kazakhstan. Shynai states 'our people are strewn throughout Kazakhstan and will soon forget their traditions' (Author Interview in Bayan Olgi 2002). The loss of community cohesiveness is seen as a major blow to Mongolia's Kazakhs who put great stock in their distinct social network. By publicly contrasting their strong ties within Mongolia to the weak ties of a larger Kazakhstani society, the migration process is cast in a negative light. With articles depicting Mongolian-Kazakhs as 'scattered to every corner', 'strewn throughout fifteen provinces', 'spread out over nineteen provinces', an image of Kazakhstan emerges in contrast to that offered by return myths (see Hahaar 1993, 3; Natsagdorj 1993, 3; Otgonbayar 1992, 4).

Through this process, the 'Kazakh' homeland has become something malleable, transferable, and contingent upon the values of the people defining it. In one sense, the Kazakhs of Mongolia have sought to protect and preserve a distinct sub-culture (perhaps even a new ethnos) that has developed in Bayan Olgi. Integration into a broader Kazakhstani society may be seen as a relinquishing of cultural purity and a loss of the 'real' Kazakh identity. This attention to authenticity attaches great value to the land and boundaries that facilitated its preservation.

Reverse migration of some Mongolian-Kazakhs that attempted to resettle in Kazakhstan in the early 1990s reinforced this view of Kazakh culture and the value of a small-scale Mongolian homeland. It also provided tangible evidence of the realistic and at times negative view of return migration. The return of some 10,000 people to Mongolia along with newspaper articles describing these 'reverse migrants' as 'destitute' brought into question the fulfilment of the labour contracts and the degree to which Kazakhstan truly wants its dispersed ethnic kinsmen to 'return' (Huandag 1992, 7; Sarai 1993, 2; Shynai 1998, 3).

Conclusion

Until recently surpassed by the movement of Uzbekistani Kazakhs to Kazakhstan, this migration was the largest of all the dispersed Kazakh communities. The fact that some Kazakhs remained in Mongolia and some 10,000 migrated back across the gap after an attempted (re)patriation to Kazakhstan suggests that not all Kazakhs are equally disposed to the call of the historic homeland or the label diaspora. Such a condition speaks to the importance of territorial belonging in the construction of identity. Traditional definitions of *diaspora, nation,* and *homeland* become problematized by the policies of governments and the choices of individuals relating to the meaning of place at various scales. This chapter has offered analysis of the complex relationship between borders and the construction of territorial belonging.

Where borders give the impression of discreet, integrated socio-political, cultural, and economic units, non-titular people's lives in border regions regularly involve a triangulated relationship between state government, minority leadership, and an external national homeland (Brubaker 1995). The concept of scale is therefore central to understanding how place, in both the lived and abstract senses, serves as a repository of socially and politically relevant traditions. Place mediates between local and national social fields as well as supranational institutions, thereby enabling a multiplicity of identities and conceptions of belonging. This is especially so in post-colonial/imperial borderlands where the national quality of individuals and territories are in high relief due to the active processes of insulation/isolation and inclusion/exclusion. Mismatches of cultural and political boundaries combine with reified or invented ideals of group spatiality to raise questions of a place's viability in terms of individual and group survival, ambition, potential, and legacy. The matter of signifying belonging is thus vital to those wielding power at every scale. Belonging is manipulated through the border's role as a site of vulnerability and a marker of security. Tension constantly exists due to the contradiction between the border's representation of the finite – as limits of power and authority, and the cultural and social processes of bordering and re-bordering catalyzed by migration, diaspora, and the creation of trans-national, hybrid identities.

Traditional meanings of terms such as nation, diaspora and transnationalism are problematized by the increasing prevalence of overlapping and penetrative social fields. These fields shatter the conception of assimilation and transnationalism as binary opposites. They cross borders and create multilayered, multi-cited matrices of belonging that incorporate migrants, those who stay behind, state actors/ structures, as well as supranational and non-governmental institutions. In this process, borderlands emerge as primary sites of identity renegotiation. As this chapter suggests, the physical gap between the borders of Bayan Olgi and the East Kazakhstan Oblast has come to symbolize distinction between the groups.

However, rather than evolving to a condition of animosity, Mongolia's Kazakhs greatly appreciate and even revel in the existence of an independent Kazakhstan. They are, nevertheless, openly rejecting the notion that all Kazakhs must reside within that state. Instead, they assert their territorial belonging within Mongolia and seek to reconcile their identity as ethnic Kazakhs within the structure of a Mongolian civic nation.

In this sense the *aimag* of Bayan Olgi constitutes an enclave of Kazakh ethnicity within Mongolia but does not signify a Kazakhstani national exclave. The division of Mongolian-Kazakh community between two states has compelled the creation of a transnational social field that bridges the spatial gap that divides them. As technology becomes more available to those in Bayan Olgi and former Mongolian-Kazakhs become more integrated into Kazakhstani society, more dense interactions will likely develop between the two groups. The close-knit community in Mongolia is being, at least partially replaced by a more abstract bond to remote clusters of dispersed Mongolian-Kazakhs and, by consequence, to Kazakhstan more generally.

Territorial belonging may therefore be viewed as a discursive condition that is affected by contingent events that strengthen, weaken and shift meaning relating to specific portions of the earth's surface. The central point here is that neither borders nor homelands are immutable facets of specific groups or even humanity at large. Individuals and groups are not born with blood linked to soil. This bond is constructed and must be analyzed in relation to specific narratives of community, society, and state – each of which are performed with profound impacts around political borders.

References

Agentstvo Respubliki Kazakhstan po Informatsi (2003), *Decree of Oralman Migration 2003* (Almaty: Agentstvo Respubliki Kazakhstan po Informatsi).

Agnew, J. (2009), *Globalization and Sovereignty* (New York: Rowman & Littlefield Publishers).

Aitmatov, C. (1988), *The Day Lasts More than a Hundred Years* (Bloomington: Indiana University Press).

Allen, J. (2003) *Lost Geographies of Power* (London: Blackwell)

Anderson, J. and O'Dowd, L. (1999), 'Borders, Border Regions and Territoriality: Contradictory Meanings and Changing Significance', *Regional Studies* 33:7, 593-604.

Ardyn Erkh (1992), 'Any News in Kazakhstan', *Ardyn Erkh* 16 October 1992, 3.

Babaev, D. (1995), *Kazakhstan Tarikhy* [History of Kazakhstan] (Almaty: Rauan).

Barcus, H. and Werner, C. (2007), 'Transnational Identities: Mongolian Kazakhs in the 21st Century', *Geographische Rundschau: International Edition* 3:3, 7-10.

Brubaker, R. (1995), 'National Minorities, Nationalizing States, and External National Homelands in the New Europe', *Daedalus* 124:2, 107-32.

Bulag, U.E. (1998), *Nationalism and Hybridity in Mongolia* (Oxford: Clarendon Press).

Bureau of Intelligence and Research (1984), 'China-Mongolia Boundary', *International Boundary Study* 173.

Bureau of Intelligence and Research (1966), 'China-USSR Boundary', *International Boundary Study* 64.

Chuluunbaatar, S. and Onjoon, Sh. (1990), 'Where are the native Urianghai?', *Hudulmur* 24 April 1990, 2.

Cohen, J.H. (2005), 'Non-migrant Households in Oaxaca, Mexico: Why Some People Stay While Others Leave', in Trager, L. (ed.), *Migration and Economy: Global and Local Dynamics* (Lanham: Altamira Press), 103-26.

Diener, A.C. (2011), 'Will New Mobilities Beget New (Im)Mobilities?: Prospects for Change Resulting from Mongolia's Trans-State Highway', in Brunn, S. (ed.), *Engineering Earth: The Impact of Mega Projects* (Kluwer and Springer Press), 627-642.

Diener, A.C. (2009), *One Homeland or Two? The Nationalization and Transnationalization of Mongolia's Kazakhs* (Stanford CA and Washington DC: Stanford University Press and Woodrow Wilson Center Press).

Diener, A.C. (2007), 'Negotiating Territorial Belonging: A Transnational Field Approach to the Mongolia's Kazakhs', *Geopolitics* 12:3, 459-87.

Diener, A.C. (2005a), 'Kazakhstan's Kin-State Diaspora: Settlement Planning and the *Oralman* Dilemma', *Europe Asia Studies* 57:2, 327-48.

Diener, A.C. (2005b), 'Problematic Integration of Mongolian-Kazakh Return-Migrants in Kazakhstan', *Eurasian Geography and Economics* 6, 465-78.

Diener, A.C. and Hagen, J. (2010), *Borderlines and Borderlands: Political Oddities at the Edge of the Nation State* (Lanham: Rowman & Littlefield).

Diener, A.C. and Hagen, J. (2009), 'Theorizing Borders in a Borderless World: Globalization, Mobility and Scale', *Geography Compass* 3:3, 1196-216.

Finke, P. (1999), 'The Kazaks of Western Mongolia', in Svanberg, I. (ed.), *Contemporary Kazakhs: Cultural and Social Perspectives* (Richmond: Curzon Press), 112-34.

Fischer, P.A., Martin, R. and Straubhaar, T. (1997), 'Should I stay or Should I Go?', in Hammar, T., Brochmann, G., Tomas, K. and Faist, T. (eds.), *International Migration: Immobility and Development: Multidisciplinary Perspectives* (New York: Berg), 49-90.

Ganhuyag, N. (1994), 'Resettlement of the Kazakhs has Stopped', *Mongol Messenger* 24, 7.

Grundy-Warr, C. (2009), *Commentary for Blackwell Virtiual Conference* 19-30 October 2009, available at <http://compassconference.wordpress.com>.

Hahaar, O. (1993), 'Insomnia Caused by Unstable Condition', *Ardyn erkh* 13 October 1993, 3.

Heleniak, T. (2009), 'The Role of Attachment to Place in Migration Decisions of the Population of the Russian North', *Polar Geography* 32:1-2, 31-60.

Hirsch, F. (2000), 'Toward an Empire of Nations: Border Making and the Formation of the Soviet National Identities', *The Russian Review* 59, 201-26.

Huandag, Sh. (1993), 'Scream Afterwards', *Ardyn Erkh* 19 June 1993, 3.

Huandag, Sh. (1992), 'Kazakhstan is not a Paradise', *Il Tovchoo* 1-10 March 1992, 7.

Huandag, Sh. (1991), 'None Posses Dual Homelands', *Ardyn Erkh* 4 January 1991, 3.

Hudulmur (1990), 'Reply to the Article 'Where Are the Native Urianghai', *Hudulmur* 21 June 1990, 2.

Hurmetbek, B. and Minis, A. (1990), 'We Have One Motherland', *Ardyn Erkh* 20 December 1990, 8.

Kaiser, R.J. (1994), *The Geography of Nationalism in Russia and the Soviet Union* (Princeton: Princeton University Press).

Karzhowbai, M. (1992), 'Kazakhstan Respublikasynyhg Elteresi Prezidenti Nursultan Abiwuly Nazarbayevka Mongholiyaghy Kazakh Zhurtynyhg Otinish Khat', *Letter-Request to the President of the Republic of Kazakhstan N.A. Nazarbayev from the Mongolian Kazakh People* 28 April 1992.

Kazakhstanskaya Pravda (1991), 'Reprint of Speech by President Nazarbayev', *Kazakhstanskaya Pravda* 23 November 1991, 1.

Maukaruly, A. (1997), 'Kazakh Repatrianttarynyng Bugim taghdyry Kandai?!' [How is the Destiny of Kazakh Repatriates at Present?!], *Kazakh Eli* 4, 1-4.

Megoran, N. (2006), 'For Ethnography in Political Geography: Experiencing and Re-Imagining Ferghana Valley Boundary Closers', *Political Geography* 25:6, 622-40.

Mizimkhaan, M. and Murat, B. (1993), 'Letter On Behalf of the *Aimag* Population to President of Mongolia N. Bagabandi and P. Jasrai', *Zagyn Gazryn Medee* 6 April 1993, 5.

Natsagdorj (1993), 'They are not Emigrants', *Ardyn Erkh* 20 April 1993, 3.

Otgonbayar (1992), 'Need of a refugee camp in Kazakhstan', *Il Tovchoo* 35, 3-4.

Razsa, M. (2004), 'Regionalism, Memory and the Belonging at the Frontiers of the Nation-State', *Anthropological Quarterly* 77:1, 161-5.

Safran, W. (1991), 'Diasporas in Modern Societies: Myths of Homeland and Return', *Diaspora* 1:1, 83-92.

Sarai, A. (1993), 'Who Are the Victims of a Huge Migration?', *Ardyn Erkh* 26 September 1993, 2.

Shynai, K. (1998), 'Who Caught Luck Migrants or Residents?', *Ardyn Eerkh* 9 July 1998, 4.

Sultan, T. (1993), 'Shortcomings of Remote Areas', *Ardyn Erkh* 21 July 1993, 1.

Tuyabaatar, L. (1991), 'If the Nest Was Not Set Up', *Hudulmur* 4 January 1991, 3.

Tuyabaatar, L. (1990), 'Orgoo ger dotroo oor ger barih hereg baina uu?' [Do We Need to Set Up Another Ger Inside Our Ger?], *Hudulmur* 28 July 1990, 3.

Unen (1993), 'An Urgent Issue: Seven points to Save Bayan Olgi', *Unen* 23, 1.

Zhusupov, S. (2000), 'Immigration Policy in Kazakhstan: Case of Repatriates', *KISEIF – Kazakhstan Institute of Social and Economic Information and Forecasting* (Almaty: SOROS Foundation - Kazakhstan).

Borders and Territorial Identity: Persian Identity Makes Iran an Empire of the Mind

Pirouz Mojtahed-Zadeh

Introduction

To a mind not trained in academic subjects like political geography or international law there are little differences between the terms *border, frontier* and *boundary*. Fascinated by impressive lip forward in information technology of recent decades some seem to have gone so far in their socio-political philosophizing of spatial concepts related to matters of *state* and *territory* as to declare the end of all that is related to *state, territory, boundary,* and geography much the same way as Francis Fukuyama declared the *end of history* in the 1990s (1). Some seem to have gone even further in their fascination of these developments as confusing themselves between actual meanings of the concepts related to human space and thinking of human, economic, political and spatial *barriers* in terms of geographical *border*. The political geographer however, cannot be too careful in his use of geographical concepts. To him (her) the terms *border, boundary* and *frontier* constitute for a three-dimensional spatial concept that deals with the task of defining peripheries of the territories of a given state. In a recent slogan advertised in CNN network (February 2011) individuals of varying ethnic/national background appear to invite viewers to '*go beyond borders*'. But listening to their reasoning no doubt remains that they mean to encourage their viewers to cross human, economic, political, and geographical barriers. Otherwise not even CNN can invite its international viewers to cross US boundaries or borders to its headquarters in Washington without obtaining proper visa permission from US border authorities.

When the peripheral line separating the realm of one state from that of others is concerned, *boundary* is the core of the discussion. This line of separation can at the same time be described as a line in space drawn to manifest the ultimate peripheries of the state and/or a line in space to show the ultimate limitations of the territory.

Whereas in the ancient world, people were preoccupied with the idea of establishing the *frontiers* of their realms, the main concern of modern peoples regarding the peripheries of their dominions is to define their *boundaries*. *Boundary* in the modern sense of the word did not exist until the nineteenth century. Ancient peoples considered the end of their conquest as the *frontier*. *Frontier* is, therefore, ancient and *boundary* is new (Mojtahed-Zadeh 2002), but what might look more current in a multi-disciplinary approach to the concept is that the idea is represented by the term *border*, which gives more socially oriented meaning to the concept.

Moreover, this concept, just as ubiquitous as the terms, also manifests in many different ways and has many different functions and roles. Scholars have, for instance, argued the case for the term *border* as being a peripheral line or zone of separation between states in the form of a socially constructed phenomena in order to distinguish between the internal society – people of a given territoriality – and those outside its borders, eventually culminating in the concept of separation, that is, the notion of 'us' (our society) separate from 'them' (their society). People living inside bounded territories who may collectively represent some form of nationhood are consequently spatially socialized as members of the territorial entity they live in.

Endeavouring to distinguish frontiers from boundaries, geographers have used various etymologies. Peter J. Taylor (1989) quotes Kristof (1959) that the etymology of each term derives their essential difference and that while *frontier* comes from the notion of *in front* as the 'spearhead of the civilisation'; boundary comes from 'bounds' implying territorial limits. Taylor then observes that 'frontier is therefore outward-oriented and boundary inward-oriented' and 'whereas a boundary is a definite line of separation, a frontier is a zone of contact'.

As mentioned above, political geographers have variously described the term *boundary* as *a line in space drawn to manifest the ultimate peripheries of the state and/ or a line in space to show the ultimate limitations of territory* (Mojtahed-Zadeh 2005, 51-8). The terms *frontier* and *border* normally represent two variations in defining the same concept. While the term *frontier* represents the notion of 'in front' of the peripheral line of limitation of a territory, the term *border* normally refers to a strip of land around that line of territorial limitation and is normally used in association with term 'area'. Hence, one can state that it is within the framework of this kind of conceptualization that the term *border area* normally describes the land area as a distinct territorial identity surrounded by the peripheral line of boundary that separates it from 'others', especially in terms of culture and civilization, whereas the term *frontier* represents a zone of contact between two states (Kristof 1959).

While the etymology of each of the three terms can be explored further, in this study, the term *border* will be adopted to represent a combination of all of the three interrelated concepts explaining the line of separation between states. Prominence will be given in this chapter to the study of the idea of *territorial identity* within well-defined boundaries in association with the concepts of *state* and *territory*.

Today's movements towards regional or even continental integration and the formation of bloc identities such as EU, NAFTA, and MERCOSUR, are concurrent with the globalization of the market economy and the triumphant advance/march of cyberspace; the political map of the world has, as Anssi Paasi reminds us, undergone significant changes (Paasi 2005). Many boundaries have become more permeable for people, goods, capital, and a revolutionized information technology that recognizes no boundary limitation. This rapid movement in border functions has encouraged some scholars specializing in economy and information sciences to argue their case for a unified world of geopolitics by using phrases like 'borderless world' and political 'deterritorialization'. In response, David Newman (2006) argues from a geographer's point of view that despite these trends, human activities continue to take place within well-defined territories. He furthermore points out that the notion of a 'borderless world' has been coined by the West, specifically by a Western European perspective in which the permeability of borders is currently being actively promoted. Nevertheless, this trend has not gained ground around the globe. For example, in the post-9/11 era, borders are being re-erected or reinforced in many places. Hence, the current political situation in the world characterized by the prevalence of fear of terrorism can be interpreted as a sign for a *reterritorialization* rather than a *deterritorialization* of the world.

Indeed it seems that several factors have prompted such ideas as a 'borderless world' and 'deterritorialization' to arise. Among these factors has been the general promotion of permeable borders, the lifting of economic barriers inside the European Union (EU) by thirteen members in 1997, and the later creation of the Schengen area followed by monetary union and the creation of the Euro zone by 15 EU member states in 2002. A geographer, however, can hardly overlook the fact that, despite lifting economic barriers in the Schengen area of the European Union, legal and cultural borders are firmly in place and borders have in fact been strengthened between the Schengen area and the rest of the EU; borders have also been fortified between the European Union and various states surrounding it, especially those south of the Mediterranean.

In his *Iconography*, Jean Gottmann, the internationally respected political geographer of the late twentieth century, described iconography as the 'glue' which binds individuals together in order to form political societies, each related to its own portion of space (Prevelakis 2003). This triangular relationship is an exponent of the human state of mind rather than physical expediency. Peers like W.A. Douglas Jackson (1958) refer to Jean Gottmann as the father of modern geography because he brought back political geography to the mainstream of social science after its near demise in the wake of wartime German geopolitics. Gottmann accomplished this by using his *circulation* and *iconography* to put the main emphasis on the territorial identity of the state and has stated:

> To be distinct from its surroundings, a region needs much more than a
> mountain or a valley, a given language or certain skills: it needs essentially
> a strong belief based on some religious creed, some social viewpoint, or some
> pattern of political memories, and often a combination of all three ... The
> most stubborn facts are those of the spirit, not those of physical world ...
> And while history shows how stubborn are the facts of the spirit, geography
> demonstrates that the main partitions observed in the space accessible to man

are not those in the topography or in the vegetation, but those that are in the minds of the people. (Gottmann 1964)

Gottmann's earlier statement that '… to be different from all others and proud of one's special features is an inborn trait of man', tells us that as long as humans are concerned with their own identities independent of all others, borders will remain in place to proclaim the human desire for independence, and as long as humans want to be independent in their spheres of life, human nature needs that line in space called *border* to separate one group of humans from others. Thus, *border* is a human state of mind that cannot be marred by material desires to allow notions like *borderless world*, *global village* and/or *deterritorialization* of human's political life to exceed the bounds of virtual reality.

In a historical approach, it is hard to confine our thoughts to the idea that the emergence of the interrelated notions of *state*, *territory* and *boundary* date back to the Treaty of Westphalia in 1648 overlooking the fact that these modern notions are rooted in periods prior to the emergence in Europe of nation-states. There are indications that ancient civilizations were familiar with the notion of *state* in connection with the concepts of territory and boundary. Early texts reveal that this basic principle existed in ancient Persian literature in respect of matters of state, territory, and boundary. Similarly, the likelihood exists that these Persian notions could have influenced Roman civilization.

It is widely believed that a combination of ancient Greco-Roman and Persian civilizations is a major contributor to what culturally constitutes 'West'. Later in the Sassanid period, the inter-linked notions of *state*, *territory*, and *boundary* developed substantially, coming quite close to their contemporary forms. On the other hand, considering that 'justice' was the corner stone of ancient Persian political philosophy, the idea that the ancient Persian spatial arrangement might have contributed to the evolution of the concept of democracy in the West may not be too difficult to contemplate.

Whither Iran?

Before engaging in the main discussion about the evolution of the *idea of Iran* and its *territorial identity*, it seems appropriate to briefly see what Iran is and what constitutes Persia and why there is variation (Kamiar 2007).

The term *Iran* has constituted the official name of the country or state known by that name at least since the emergence of the Achaeminid federative state in the sixth century BC. The term first appeared in pre-Achaeminid antiquity as *Aryana* meaning the land of the Aryan race. Later at the time of the Achaeminids, this term was simplified to *Irana* and later still became *Iran Shahr* during the Sassanid period, meaning the country of Iran. The West came to know this country as *Persia* through the Greeks of the city-states, which in the sixth century BC, were not as yet familiar with the concept of a state of multitude of cities = country. They named

Iran Persia in accordance with their on-going tradition of naming places after the name of the dynasties or the ethnicities ruling them, in much the same way that Iranians – and through them, the entire Muslim world – named Greece *Yunan* in their historiography of that entity, simply because in antiquity, the Iranians first came into contact with the *Ionian* ethnicity of Greece. Thus, it is obvious why the Greeks named Iran *Persia*, which originally was and still is but a province in southern Iran where the ancient Achaeminid and Sassanid dynasties had emerged. The term *Persia*, however, became more solidly founded in Western culture when it entered biblical texts and became somewhat sanctified. Nevertheless, the term *Iran* maintained its place in Western cultural thinking in more obscure forms such as a feminine name; that is *Iran* in the Persian language; *Irene* in Latin, Germanic, Armenian, and other Western languages, while its prefix 'ir' representing the mysticism of *the land of Aryans*, is to be seen in country names like *Ireland*, which comes from *Éire* of Proto-Celtic origin, reflecting its Proto-Indo-European roots. In today's common and official usage of the variation, it is worth noting that while the language and literature, art and culture are all *Persian*, the civilization and the name of the country are attributed to the term *Iran*.

Border, an ancient Iranian concept

The concept of *state* seems to be much older than its contemporary variation since its modern version exists only because its legitimacy is tied to normative territorial ideas; as Alexander Murphy (2003) reminds us, '… (t)he pattern of modern states reflects the pattern of nations'. Hence, there is little doubt that modern concepts of *state* and *territory* developed in medieval Europe; nevertheless, it is difficult not to note that they are rooted in the periods prior to the emergence in Europe of nation-states. There are indications that ancient civilizations were familiar with the notion of *state* in connection with an elementary form of territoriality and its *frontier* characteristics. The Great Wall of China, the Hadrian Wall of Roman Britain, and Sadd-e Sekandar (Alexander's Wall) in northeast Iran[1] might indeed have been parts of wider peripheral zones of contact in the ancient world (Taylor 1989), yet, it is certain that even in that capacity, these walls represented the notion of a 'line' in space designed to separate the proverbial 'us' from 'them'. Indeed, there are references in ancient Persian literature to modern-like conceptions of state, territory, and border. Similarly, when considering the extent of both belligerent and peaceful contacts between Rome and Iran, the likelihood exists that these Persian notions could have influenced Roman civilization.

A mixture of ancient Greco-Roman and Persian civilizations seems to have been a major source of contribution to what culturally constitutes *West* in our time. Taking into consideration the extent to which Greek and Roman civilizations

---

1   This wall was built at the time of the Parthian civilization (247 BC to 224 AD) in Iran to separate that civilization from the Turans of the East.

interacted with that of ancient Iran, little doubt remains as to the validity of Jean Gottmann's assertion in his letter (1978) to the author that:

> *Iran must have belonged to the 'Western' part of mankind, and I suspect that this was what Alexander the Great of Macedonia, a pupil of Aristotle, therefore, in the great Western philosophical tradition, found in Iran and that attracted him so much that he wanted to establish a harmonious, multinational cooperation between the Iranians and Greeks within the large empire he was building.*[2]

Verification of this can be sought in historical events. For example, when Alexander the Great conquered Iran, he claimed in Persepolis that he was the 'true successor to the Achaeminid Darius III'. Ferdosi (1020 AD), the famous epic poet of Iran, says of this in his *Shahnameh* (book of kings)[3] that having conquered Iran, Alexander wrote to the nobles of the country apologizing for having done away with their king. Moreover, Alexander reassured them that, '(i)f Dara is no more, I am here and Iran will remain the same as it has always been since its beginning'. He adopted the existing political organization of space, later modified by his successors. Alexander also proclaimed 'justice' to be the goal, the attainment of which would be his mission in Iran:

منم ارا کشآ ناهن دش وا رگ   منم اراد زورما هک دینادب

تسردنت و لد ناداش دیشابب   تسخن زا دوب هک نار یا تسا نامه

---

2   Professor Jean Gottmann, whose student the author of this chapter was at Oxford University in late 1970s, authorized this quotation from the said letter, in a separate note dated 19 May 1992.

3   *Shahnameh* (book of kings) of Abul-Qassem Ferdosi (d. 1020 AD) is widely praised as the only reliable source in Persian literature that studies parts of the pre-Islamic history of Iran and its association with other ancient political entities, but hitherto little attention has been paid to the way it describes political relations in association with the political organization of space in the ancient world. Popularly regarded as an epic account of ancient Persian history, especially of the Sassanid period (224 to 651 AD), the *Shahnameh* provides a remarkable description of the development of the concept of state in ancient Iran. It carefully describes how the idea of a vertically organized state evolved in ancient Iran with clearly demarcated boundaries, which influenced such western political conceptions as 'state', 'territory', 'boundary', and 'democracy'. Ferdosi's description of the political geography of the ancient world bears a remarkable resemblance to the modern concepts of political geography that evolved in post-Westphalian Europe. Is it, however, possible that he, who lived a thousand years ago, well before the Treaty of Westphalia of 1648, had learnt these ideas from modern Europe or is it rather that what Ferdosi described in terms of the evolution of political thought and geography in ancient Persia influenced medieval Europe? This is certainly a fascinating question deserving further exploration with the help of the reliable analysis of the socio-political developments in the ancient world.

داي ديريگم یتيگ راتفر ز   داد و گن‌هرف و یمانک‌ين ز از زج

Be informed that today Dara is me
*   If he has disappeared, I am to be seen*
Iran is as has been from the start
*   Do remain healthy and happy in heart*
But of good name, culture and justice
*   Learn not from the ways of this life*
                 (Ferdosi 1985, 330)

State, territoriality and border in ancient Iran

Although the Achaemenids waged wars and captured territories, their concept of state was more culturally oriented than concerned about the exactness of physical space. Various satrapies were defined along the lines of cultural and ethnic divides. Indeed, eminent scholars like Will Durant (1988, 412) and Pio Filippani-Ronconi (1978, 67) maintain that the concept of 'state' is an original Iranian invention, which was later adopted by the West through the Romans. A.H. Nayer-Nouri, an eminent writer on ancient Persian civilization, quotes T.R. Glover on Persian civilization:

> *The Persians set new ideas before mankind, ideas for the world's good government with utmost unity and cohesion combined with the largest possible freedom for the development of race and individual within the larger organization.* (Nayer Nouri 1971, 196)

Ancient Greek historian-geographers like Herodotus (approximately 484 to 425 BC) and Xenophon (approximately 430 to 355 BC) confirm that the Achaemenids (559 to 330 BC) founded a kind of federal state, a vast commonwealth of autonomous nations, aided by a state apparatus, thus making *state* and *federalism* central to Iran's governance from earliest times. The founder of the federation, Cyrus (*Kurosh*) the Great (559 to 529 BC) together with his successors substantially expanded their domain and divided it into many satrapies (thirty to forty at times), each governed by a local *Satrap*, a *Khashthrapavan,* or a vassal king. This was a federation of global proportions, which included the lands of Trans-Oxania, Sind, and Trans-Caucasus as far as what are now the Republic of Moldavia, Jordan and Syria, Macedonia and Cyprus, Egypt and Libya. This was a political system of universal aspirations ruled by a *Shahanshah* (king of kings). Thus it could also be referred to as the *Shahanshahi* system. The king of kings in that system was not a lawgiver but the defender of laws and the religions of all in the federation (Templeton 1979, 14). Moreover, T. R. Glover (ibid.) described the state created by the Achaemenids as *good government*;

in accord with Cyrus's proclamation in Babylonia[4] that all were equal in his realm, ethnic and cultural groups enjoyed a large measure of independence in the practice of their language, religion, and economies. To uphold religious, cultural and political independence of the various peoples in the federation, the king of kings did not lay claim to any specific religion. Consequently, the peoples of conquered territories were free to keep their religions, laws and traditions. Having conquered Babylonia, for instance, Cyrus the Great found thousands of Jews in captivity there. His response was to free them and send them back to their place of worship. He did not proceed to conquer their land, but his respect for their religious freedom guaranteed their good will towards the Iranians. He became their prophet and they became the voluntary citizens of his federation. Cyrus commissioned the building of their temple and their reaction was to assess his work as the fulfilment of the prophecy of Isaiah (Isaiah 44): 'I am the lord … that saith of Cyrus, he is my shepherd, and shall perform my pleasure: even saying to Jerusalem, thou shalt be built: and to the temple, thy foundation shall be laid' (Lockhart 1953, 326).

Many have tried to attribute a 'dark side' to this early form of federative state and/or *good government*. In our time, possibly the worst imaginable characterization by those who were politically motivated, such as the former Baath Party in Iraq has been to equate Cyrus with a warmongering king who supported the Zionists (captive Jews in Babylonia). They condemn Cyrus for using the sole force of arms to create the vast commonwealth of the Achaemanid state. These are blatant inaccuracies since Babylonia was not an Arab state but rather an Akkadian civilization; according to Arab historians like Masudi (1977) and Maqdasi (1906), the Arabs first appeared in Mesopotamia when the Sassanid state created the vassal kingdom of Hirah; these historians have also indicated that Arab settlement of southern Mesopotamia began after the advent of Islam. Furthermore, the captive Jews in Babylonia could not possibly have had anything to do with *Zionism*, because it is a phenomenon of the twentieth century. Moreover, war has always been an inherent aspect of human political behaviour. Even in the age of modernity when 'war' is detested as an act of immorality in the domain of human behaviour, there are moralists who defend the so-called 'just war'. Babylonia was an Akkadian civilization ruled by tyranny according to biblical texts, thus Cyrus's war on Babylonian tyranny easily qualifies as a just war.

On the other hand, our knowledge of ancient Iran and its role in the ancient world is largely shrouded in obscurity and our information as scanty as it is, is derived from foreign sources (Iliff 1953) who tell us that the decree Cyrus issued in Babylonia concerned freedom and equality for all, Babylonians and captive Jews alike; it was for this broad-minded policy that he is so praised in the biblical literatures of the West and Islam. Additionally, it was because of this broad-minded policy of the Achaeminid king that he won the allegiance of many peoples, including the Greeks of Ionian cities (Templeton 1979), Cyprus and Jerusalem who joined their federation; for these peoples to join this system of governance voluntarily

---

4   The text of this proclamation is in cuneiform Acadian (Akkadian), inscribed on a clay cylinder now in the British Museum's Persian section.

rather than by force of arms, the federation must have held a certain attraction. This attraction was the justice on which Iran's federal tradition of statehood was based and which, by the time of the Christian era, had become Iran's spirit and its territorial identity. This process turned the idea of Iran into a distinct state of mind.

Justice as the cornerstone of the Iranian state system

Considering that *justice* was the cornerstone of ancient Iranian political philosophy, the idea that ancient Iranian spatial arrangements have contributed to the evolution of the concept of democracy in the West cannot be too difficult to contemplate. Some claim that when Cyrus founded the federative state of many nations in what was to become known in the West as the Persian Empire, he did not invent righteousness and tolerance from his own genius but rather that he followed a deeply-rooted, age-old tradition of how an ideal king should behave. He had inherited the tradition of *good government* based on *justice*, toleration of others and respect for varying religious beliefs from the Medes whose king Deicos (Diaxus) had gathered all Iranians into one nation (Nayer-Nouri 1971, 188). Nevertheless, the earliest available evidence suggesting that *justice* formed the foundation of good governance in the ancient Iranian tradition of statehood is Cyrus's decree of *freedom* and *equality* when opening Babylonia in 539 BC.

According to the stone inscription left for posterity at *Naghsh-e Rostam* in western Iran, Darius the Great (Dariush I, 521 to 486 BC) left a remarkable heritage. He organized thirty satrapies, each under an autonomous king assisted by a Satrap representing the central authority of the king of kings. He appointed army commanders and secretaries of political affairs. He fixed the tributes of each satrapy by appointing tribute collectors and travelling inspectors called the *eyes and ears* of the great king to watch over the Satraps and army commanders. He introduced currencies of gold *darics* and silver *siglus* that facilitated trade exchange in the federation (Nayer-Nouri 1971, 221); he also built the 2,700 kilometre long Royal Road from Susa, northwest of the Persian Gulf, to Sardis on the Aegean Sea with branches to Persepolis and other political and commercial centres (Von Hagen 1974). To enhance the state apparatus, Darius ordered the map of this road and civilized countries alongside it to be engraved on a plate of bronze,[5] which was perhaps the first detailed geographic map in history. He established a postal

---

5   A plate of bronze or other metals is called *jam* in Persian. Similarly a goblet of metal or crystal is *jam*. On the other hand, Ferdosi's *Shahnameh* speaks of legendary Jamshid Shah, the founder of Iran, who had a *jam* showing the world. From this concept comes the mystical crystal ball in almost all cultures, yet this author is of the opinion that Jamshid Shah was none other than Darius the Great who had the bronze disc *jam* showing the map of the civilized world. A discussion of further evidence supporting this theory goes beyond the scope of this chapter.

service with relays of men and horses at short intervals and ordered a canal to be dug in Egypt to link the Red Sea to the Nile (Arberry 1953).

In matters of state politics, while the Athenians were busy with their peculiar version of citizenship-oriented democracy, the Achaemenids were forging a state system based on independence for cultural groups or nationalities; this federative system granted peoples of varying ethnicities the right of governing their affairs autonomously and respected their religion and cultural identity. Thus it seems quite plausible that equality and justice were the essence of governance in that ancient tradition of statehood. The administration of justice, however, reached its zenith in the Sassanid period in the person of Anushirvan the Just, and it might be plausible to assume that these early Iranian traditions of political philosophy have contributed to the development of modern concepts of democracy in the West. Some have suggested that the concept of *empire* is perhaps a Roman adoption of Iranian *Shahanshahi* system (Tavakoli 1993, 828-30). However, the difference between the two is that while various nations and ethnic groups lived autonomously in the Iranian *Shahanshahi* order, peoples of varying ethnicities enjoyed no autonomy or self-rule in the *imperial* system that the Romans developed. Given this, it may not be difficult to assume that the Romans evolved their idea of *Senate* on the basis of ancient Parthian *Mehestan*, the House of the Elders, or vice versa.

Evolution of the state and territory under the Sassanids

The Parthians (247 BC to 224 AD), who succeeded the Macedonians in Iran, created two kinds of autonomies in the federation: the internal satrapies and the peripheral dependent states, 18 of which enjoyed greater autonomy (Vadiei 1974, 186). This system of diffusion of power was revived by the Safavids of sixteenth-century Iran in the form of *ialats* and *biglarbeigis*.

About the dawn of the Christian era, the concepts of state and territoriality assumed greater sophistication with the advent of the notion of border. This was primarily the result of the greater centralization of power *vis-à-vis* new threats from powerful adversaries such as the Roman Empire to the west and the Turans to the east. The political organization of space in the Sassanid federation (224 to 651 AD) was marked by the development of such concepts as inner and outer frontier-keeping states, buffer states, and boundary pillars. There are even hints in the ancient literature of a river boundary between Iran and Turan in Central Asia.[6]

A look at the works of Persian literature relevant to Iran's ancient political geography like *Shahnameh* reveals that the Sassanids successfully developed the

---

6   Turan is a term used by Ferdosi (d. 1020 AD) in his *Shahnameh*, the greatest piece of epic literature in the Persian language, in reference to the Turkic peoples originating on the eastern fringes of Iran. What now constitutes 'Central Asia' was 'Greater Khorasan' in most post-Islamic Iranian geography; prior to that, Turan formed the easternmost boundary.

concept of *territory* within the bounds of defined borders. They created an elaborate system of the territorial organization of state. To begin with, the founder of the dynasty revived the Achaeminid political organization of the state, but divided it into twenty autonomous countries. He initiated a government-style cabinet by assigning ministers of state like Bozorg-Mehr the philosopher and then revived the ancient notion of the 'Four Corners' of the world (four quarters of the federation) by creating four separate armies for the realm. He also created an advisory board of nobles by dividing the political structure into seven classes: ministers, the priesthood, supreme judges, and the four generals commanding the four armies (Masudi 1977, 464-5). Anushirvan the Just (531 to 579 AD), whose administration of justice is widely praised by early Islamic historian-geographers,[7] lent a more practical meaning to the Achaeminid concept of the 'four corners' of the realm by placing the twenty countries of the federation in four vast *Kusts* or *Pazgous*. Each of these divisions was ruled by a viceroy or regent called *Pazgousban* or *Padusban* and a general called an *espahbad* commanded the army of each Pazgous. In his epic *Shahnameh*, Ferdosi lists these *Kusts* or *Pazgous*: 1) *Khorasan*, including *Qom* and *Isfahan*; 2) *Azarabadegan* or Azerbaijan, including *Armanestan* (Armenia) and *Ardebil*; 3) *Pars* (Persia) and *Ahvaz* as well as territories of *Khazar* (most likely *Khuzestan*); and 4) *Iraq* and Roman territories (Syria and Anatolia) (Ferdosi 1985, 415).

The development of the concept of territory in the Sassanid era went hand in hand with the evolution of the concept of border. It is noteworthy that the term 'border' existed in ancient Iran. The Persian equivalents for territoriality and border, attributed to the Sassanid period by Ferdosi, appear synonymous with middle Persian *Marz-o Boum* – موب و زرم literally meaning border and nativity. But in Ferdosi's idiosyncratic manner of using these terms, together they assume the meaning of 'border that contains the native homeland'. *Marz* – زرم , meaning border or frontier, however exists in Persian on its own, whereas another middle-Persian term for boundary is also in use in the form of *saman* ناماس- mostly in reference to a boundary line separating houses from one another. Both concepts of border and frontier were in practical use in the Sassanid era. While appointing governors or *Padusbans* – نابسوداپ for the vassal states, they appointed mayors or *shahrigs* – گيرهش for the cities. They created frontier zones in the west of their federation and border lines to its east.

In the west of their federation, the Sassanids appear to have developed two kinds of frontier-keeping states: the internal frontier-keeping states within their

---

7   On Anushirvan's administration of justice, see many early Arab and Islamic works of history and geography including: a) Tabari, M. (1974), *Tarikh-e Tabari*, Persian translation, 11 volumes (Tehran: Bongah-e Tarjomeh va Nashr-e Ketab); b) al-Beshari, M. (1906), *Ahsan at-Taqasim fi Marefat al-Aqalim* (Leiden); c) Abu-Reihan, B. (1955), *Qanoun-e Masudi* (Dakan); d) Ibn al-Faqih, A.M. (1885), *Moktasar-e al-Boldan* 279 AH (Leiden); e) Ibn Huqal, M. (1938), *Surat al-Ardh* (London); f) Eslakluri, E. (1889), *Al Macalek val-Mamalek* (Leiden); g) Hamavi, A.Y. (1906), *Mo'jam al-Boldan* (Cairo); h) Masudi, A.-H.A.I.H. (1997), *Moravvege az-Zahab*, Persian translation, Bongah-e Tarjomeh va Nashr-e Ketab, (Tehran).

four *Kusts*: and the external ones, the most famous of which was the state of *Hirah* or *Manazerah* in Mesopotamia (Masudi 1977).

On the north-western corner of the Persian Gulf, where Iranian borders met those of the Romans, the vassal kingdom of *Hirah* – حيره was created in fifth century by the Sassanids on the river Tigris not far from their capital Ctesiphon. This frontier-keeping state, which was funded and protected by the Iranians, effectively formed a buffer state, thereby defusing pressures emanating from the Romans (Masudi 1977, 240). In a similar move, the Romans created the vassal kingdom of *Ghassan* ناصق in the region now known as Syria (Masudi 1977, 467). Moreover, it should be noted that by virtue of its struggle against Arab rule, Iran played the role of a cultural barrier throughout the Islamic era, which guaranteed Iran's cultural survival in subsequent periods. The precise location of the line of this cultural barrier can be defined somewhere around the western peripheries of the Iranian Plateau in Mesopotamia, which played the same role in the pre-Islamic era between the Persian and Roman empires. Here, David Mitrani's theory of 'middle zone' – defined as somewhere in Central Europe, around the river Danube (Mitrani 1950) – can be applied to the status and implications of the geographical position of Mesopotamia as a buffer between Iran and powers to her west. This geography prevented the total predominance of other cultures over the Iranian Plateau throughout history.

To their east, the Sassanids faced the Turans. Like the Romans, the Turans also engaged in numerous wars with the Iranians. But unlike their buffer-zone arrangements with the Romans in the west, the Iranians created, at least in one instance, a border line with the Turans in the east. This must have resulted from the degree to which rivaling powers to their east and west exerted pressure on their federation. While rivalries with the Romans to the West were of a geopolitical nature which evolved into a situation similar to the Anglo-Russian Great Game of the nineteenth century in Central Asia, rivalries with the Turans to the east were of an intensely strategic nature culminating in many wars, which in turn necessitated demarcation of the border lines that separated the two.

It is noteworthy that not only did the Sassanids revive the Achaemanid organization of the state and territory, but they also fashioned the term *Iranshahr* – ايرانشهر (the country of Iran), which must arguably have been the first time that a state or a nation had assumed an identity embodied in a name independent of the names of its ruling dynasties (Mojtahed-Zadeh 1999, 147-8). Ferdosi detailed Bahram's debate with a Roman emissary on the subject of varying Roman and Persian styles of *statesmanship* and *diplomacy*, he then asserted that Bahram (420 to 438 AD), victorious in his campaign against the eastern Turks, commissioned construction of border pillars between the two countries. He decided that the river Oxus (*Jeyhun*) would form a river boundary between the two sides. In Ferdosi's account of this, he says:

جلخ و كرت و ناريا ز ار سك هك   چگ ز و گنسز يليم دروآ رب

هار هب يیجنايم نوحيج زين هنامه   هاش نامرفب ز-ج رذگ يدوبن

Translated literally:

> (he) constructed pillars of stones and plaster, ensuring that no Iranians or Turks or other nationals would pass beyond unless permitted by the Shah, who had also made Jeyhun (the river Oxus) a medium in the way. (Ferdosi 1985, 394)

While earlier in his *Shahnameh*, Ferdosi referred to the issue of defining the borders of Iran in terms of the range of the bow shot by Arash the Archer from the top of the Damavand peak in the Elborz range, lands that mark the border between Iran and Turan according to the legendary beginning of Iran, in the historical part of the *Shahnameh*, he explicitly referred to the process of boundary demarcation. Thus it is Ferdosi who asserted 1,000 years ago that boundary pillars had been erected 600 years earlier, and that Iranians, Eastern Turks, and third-party nationals were prohibited from going beyond them unless permitted by the king himself. The king, victorious in his campaign against the eastern Turks, had also defined the river Oxus as part of the border (river boundary) between the two countries. This may be seen as a clear example of the creation of a border line in ancient Iran corresponding to the modern understanding of the concept. Royal permission for passing beyond the border might also be considered the initial form of a passport in today's terms.

Impact on western civilization

There is no doubt that the Athenians initially developed the concept of 'democracy'. However, their practice of democracy was limited to the various social strata of a city. A nationwide application of democracy had to wait until Alexander the Great of Macedonia conquered Iran and adopted the Persian way of organizing political space, that is, as a quasi-federal 'state' divided into discrete territories. The Achaemenids no doubt developed the original concept of state, but the idea of a vertically organized state with distinct and clearly demarcated boundaries matured under the Sassanids and began to influence Western civilizations.

When assessing the influence of Iran on the concepts of 'state' and 'boundary' in medieval Europe, one might point to the biblical references to Persian statehood and its tradition of respect for the rights of varying peoples (see, for instance, Isaiah 44, Esther 1, Ezra 1). According to these testimonies, despite spearheading military campaigns against the Greek cities and the Turans, the state organization created by the Achaeminid kings was essentially culturally-based and not grounded in rigid territorial conquest. This was particularly manifested in the Achaemenids' universal aspirations of statehood and good government. By developing their own version of a 'federative state' based on the notion of justice for all, the Iranians created a commonwealth of semi-independent nations or a federation of autonomous states, and arguably laid the foundation for the idea of *state democracy* or *democratic state*.

This political structure of statehood was taking shape in Iran simultaneously with the advent of the Greek version of citizenship-centered democracy. In this regard, it is important to note that Cyrus issued a charter in Babylonia (the text of which is now kept in British Museum) declaring *equality* and *justice* for individuals as well as freedom for religious-cultural 'organization' in the realm. These notions formed the political fabric of the Persian state since or because Darius the Great also frequently referred to *justice* in the stone inscriptions he bequeathed to posterity. This is to suggest that while the Athenians were concerned about the rights of individuals in society, the Persians were anxious to promote the rights of communities within their state system.

There are few other sources explaining the extent to which these ancient Persian traditions influenced the evolution of the Western concepts of *state, boundary,* and *democracy*, save for the works of scholars like Will Durant (1988). Even a philosopher as widely misrepresented as Friedrich Nietzsche, whose writings many philosophers have found difficult to take seriously, seems to have formed his view of the civilized Western citizen under the influence of the ancient Persian philosophy of life (Nietzsche 1892). R. Ghirshman (1962), for instance, states that '... under Alexander, "monarchy by divine right" of the Iranians became an institution of Hellenism and later was taken up by many European states' (cited in Nayer Nouri 1971, 152).

R. Levy (1953, 61), on the other hand, identifies the Arab Caliphate as an intermediate culture through which the Persian tradition of statehood influenced the modern world. Quoting early Arab and Islamic records, he argues;

> ... the Fakhri, an early fourteenth-century manual of politics and history, relates how the caliph, Umar, when at his wit's end to know how to distribute the spoils of war which were pouring in, sought the advice of a Persian (Iranian) who had once been employed in a government office (of the Sassanid time). His suggestion was that a divan, a register or bureau, should be instituted for controlling income and this became the germ out of which grew the government machine that served the Caliphate some hundreds of years.

Of the influence of the Iranian legacy of statehood and statesmanship on the Arab Caliphate, an early Islamic historical account quotes Caliph Umar as saying, *Verily have I learnt justice from Kesra* (Khosro Anushirvan the Just) (Maqdasi 1906, 18).

In his writings on the tradition of sacred kingship in Iran, Filippani-Ronconi, basing himself on reliable Roman sources, states that;

> ... if we want to look into the successful diffusion in the Western world of certain institutions connected with kingship, in either the religious or the lay domain, we must go back to the Roman Empire, which was the first Western state to absorb a great deal of such outside influence, especially in its political and administrative institutions regarding the status of the Emperor.

He then proceeds to cite examples of the influence of the Iranian tradition of statehood on the Western civilization by asserting:

> *The heritage handed down by Iran to the West and still living in its ideological conceptions and cultural institutions is manifold. If its patterns are sometimes difficult to recognize and trace back to their origin, that is due to the fact that this legacy has been received through intermediate cultures and westernized models ... The leading elements of what we could call the vertical organization' of the state are part of this age-old heritage. They were handed over to the modern world through the late Roman imperial structure and its medieval renaissance: through the institutions of chivalry and knighthood that, obscurely transmitted to European society in a Celtic-Germanic garb, were later Christianized ...* (Filippani-Ronconi 1978, 67)

The post-Islamic identity

Exactly what happened to these concepts in post-Islamic Iran might be of some interest. With the arrival of Islam, Iran disappeared as a country from the political map of the time. Though the Arab Caliphate of Baghdad (Abbasid Caliphate 750 to 1258 AD) mimicked the Sassanid organization of territories almost in its entirety, the territorial identity that had evolved over the previous millennium vanished into thin air. Nevertheless, Iran as a fundamental cultural heartland remained to shape the political geography of the Islamic world for centuries to come. This was because, in the words of Professor Rice (1953, 41);

> *(the spirit of Iran) was not to be destroyed in a day ... Persian art, Persian thought, Persian culture, all survived to flourish anew ..., and impelled by a new and powerful driving force, their effect was felt in a widely extended field from the early eighth century onward ...*

Iran as a country disappeared and was replaced by a number of ethnic authorities of Turkic and Iranic background who ruled the Iranian plateau on the strength of what they could remember of Persian cultural and political heritage of the pre-Islamic Achaemanid and Sassanid eras. Even when Timberline's grandson Babur established the vast Mongolian empire in India, he adopted Persian as the official language of the state and by the time of Akbar the Great India became the main centre of Persian language, literature, and arts. In a similar fashion, Persian was adopted by the vast Ottoman Empire as the official language of the state for some time, which strengthens the idea that Iran had become a powerful empire of the mind in its post-Islamic experience of living out of its geographical existence. The Iranians' embrace of Shiite Islam over Sunni Islam of the Arab Caliphate was essentially a desire to revive Iran's cultural and national identity. The ancient Persian concept of justice gained new currency by transmuting into one of the five basic principles of Shia Islam. In the following centuries, the expansion of Shiite faith in Iran merged with other notions of identity, paving the way for the eventual revival of the concepts of Iranian territoriality and statehood (Mojtahed-Zadeh 2007, 26).

The phoenix rises again

In *The evolution of the concept of territory*, Professor Jean Gottmann reminded his audience at the IPSA round table discussion of January 1975 held at the *Institut D' Etudes Politiques* in Paris, in reference to this author's presence among the participants, that Iran represented a good example of his 'iconography'. In his explanation, Gottmann invoked the legend of the phoenix (Persian, *Samandar*) as the symbol of Iran, which has risen from its ashes so many times in its thousand years of statehood.

Iran's re-emergence in the post-Islamic era as a vast federative *Shahanshahi* with its powerful sense of identity had to wait until the emergence on the political scene of medieval southern, central and western Asia of a 13-year-old *protégé*, Esmail Safavid, who led an army of ten thousand devout Shiite Sufis and at the age of sixteen proclaimed in 1501 that he had descended from the heavens to revive the *Shahanshahi* of Iran (Filippani-Ronconi 1978). However, what the Safavids (1501-1722) revived in terms of the territorial organization of space was but a vague adaptation of the Abbasid Caliphate's interpretation of the Sassanid system of statehood, and not the original version (Mojtahed-Zadeh 1995, Introduction). This vagueness of the new state structure suggests that Iran had departed from its own ancient traditions of statehood and border arrangements. This proved to be a powerful handicap that manifested itself later, especially in the face of the conceptual and physical onslaught of modern European versions of nationality and statehood which resulted in comprehensive territorial dismemberment. By the 1920s, no less than 14 countries, including the modern nation-state of Iran, emerged from the Safavid federative *Shahanshahi*.

Iranian identity in the era of modernity

By the late nineteenth century, Iran was among the first nations in Asia to undergo a major revolution to adopt modern ideas of constitutionalism and democracy. Adoption of western-style democracy has proved to be a painful experience throughout the twentieth century but considerable progress has been made towards a home-grown democracy which has been preceded by a number of adjustments in its national and territorial identities. These occurred in two different movements. The first move for modernism was made by Reza Shah Pahlavi, who established the Pahlavi dynasty in 1924 and successfully sacked regionalism of a separatist nature as well as put an end to the old and decadent federative system that had, by the turn of the twentieth century, been reduced to mere feudalism, which was the cause of the country's territorial dismemberment. Reza Shah Pahlavi also laid the foundation for the growth of a modern and industrial Iran and constructed/designed/crafted/founded a modern nation-state based on the former feudal state's core areas with tangible Iranian territorial identity. His great emphasis on pre-Islamic ideas of Iran left some with the thought that Reza Shah's emphatic reliance on pre-Islamic Iranian identity resulted in fundamental neglect of the country's millennial Islamic identity. An Islamic revolution thus took place in 1979 to address that shortcoming, but its complete reversal of emphasis was aimed at denying Iran's pre-Islamic existence. The Islamists first started to construct a state of Islamic *Ummah* in the lands of Iranian territorial identity. This was an ideological approach based on the notion of the universality of Islam that defies ideas any idea of border and territorial identity. However, twentieth-century realities have fundamentally modified this approach so that the Islamic Republic of Iran has successfully translated itself into a territorial identity within the confines of a nation-state.

The national awakening in Iran today has motivated demands for democracy throughout the society. Today the elite, along with ordinary citizens, speak the same political language with the same purpose. Both the elite and ordinary citizens demand the kind of reforms that are fundamental and far-reaching, the kind of reforms that could address the problems that prevent or at least delay the implementation of democracy in Iran. The demand for democracy has gained ground in Iran at the grassroots level and by the national election of 1997, passed the point of no return. The tree of democracy in Iran now appears to be growing with its roots firmly placed in its home culture, fed by the values that form the Iranian identity.

Today, the Iranians seem to have awakened to the realities and challenges of the globalized twenty-first century world. They seem to have set in motion all the mechanisms needed for progress towards democracy. When the mechanism of political supply and demand begins to move, it also sets in motion the mechanism of the clash of political views that is essential for striking a balance of power in society. This in turn gives birth to the dialogue necessary among the forces shaping political events.

Iranian society is presently experiencing this clash of views and opinions among political forces which have begun a far-reaching dialogue. Two main groups have emerged, the traditionalists and the reformists. The emergence of real and effective political parties has been delayed, however, because it seems that the political elite have not as yet awakened to the reality that, without the functioning of real and well developed political parties, democracy cannot function in the true sense of the word. At the same time, the Iranians are working hard to strike a balance between their pre-Islamic territorial identity and their post-Islamic cultural pride as well as their desire for a home-grown democracy. This balance is being challenged both internally and externally, including recent threats of war and economic sanctions by an axis of US, EU and Israel for concerns over Iran's nuclear energy ambitions and the occasional expression of Arab territorial ambitions against Iran. If the balance is achieved, it will undoubtedly be Iran's secret to a successful future and, allow the Iranians to build on their national dialogue for democracy, a dialogue badly needed for the settlement of the strong revolutionary fervor nurtured by these foreign threats and challenges. Such a balance will provide for Iran's domestic piece of mind as well as an improved sense of stability in its neighbourhood.

References

Arberry, A.J. (1953), *The Legacy of Persia* (Oxford: Clarendon Press).

Durant, W. (1988), *Tarikh-e Tamaddon* (History of Civilization), translated into Persian (Tehran: Enqelab-e Eslami Publications).

Douglas Jackson, W.A. (1958), 'Whither Political Geography', *Annals of the Association of American Geographers* 1958:2, 178-83.

Ferdosi, H.A.-Q. (1985 [1364]), *Shahnameh*, in Persian, Javidan publication, fourth print, volume III (Tehran).

Filippani-Ronconi, P. (1978), 'The Tradition of Sacred Kingship in Iran', in Lenczowski, G. (ed.), *Iran Under the Pahlavis* (Stanford University: Hoover Institution Press).

Ghirshman, R. (1962), *Iran, Parthes et Sassanides* (Paris: Galliard).

Glassner, M.I. and de Blij, H.J. (1989), *Systematic Political Geography* (New York: John Wiley and Sons).

Gottmann, J. (1964), 'Geography and International Relations', in Jackson, W.A.D. (ed.), *Political and Geographic Relationships* (Englewood-Cliffs New Jersey: Princeton Hall Inc.).

Gottmann, J. (1975), 'The evolution of the concept of territory', *paper presented at the IPSA Round Table, held at the Institute d'Etudes politiques* January 1975 (Paris).

Iliff, J.H. (1953), 'Persia and the Ancient World', in Arberry, A.J. (ed.), *The Legacy of Persia* (Oxford: Claredon Press).

Kamiar, M. (2007), 'Country Name Calling: The Case of Iran vs Persia', *Focus on Geography* 49:4, Special Country Issue: Iran, 2-11.

Kristof, L.D. (1959), 'The Nature of Fontiers and Boundaries', *Annals of the Association of American Geographers* 49, 269-82.

Levy, R. (1953), 'Persia and the Arabs', in Arberry, A.J. (ed.), *The Legacy of Persia* (Oxford: Claredon Press).

Lockhart, L. (1953), 'Persia as Seen in the West', in Arberry, A.J. (ed.), *The Legacy of Persia* (Oxford: Claredon Press).

McLachlan, K. (2006), 'Traditional Regions and National Frontiers of Iran – A General Overview', in Mojtahed-Zadeh, P. (ed.), *Boundary Politics and International Boundaries of Iran* (Boca Raton: Universal Publishers).

Maqdasi, al-Beshari (1906), *Ahsan at-Taqasim fi Marefat al-Aqalim* (Leiden).

Masudi, Abul-Hassan Ali Ibn Hussein (Arab geographer-historian of the 4th century AH, *Moravvege az-Zahab* (Propagator of the Way), Persian translation 1977 by Abul-Qasem Payandeh, Bongah-e Tarjomeh va Nashr-e Ketab (Tehran).

Mitrany, D. (1950), 'Evolution of the Middle Zone', *Annals of the American Academy of Political and Social Science* 271:1, 1-10.

Mojtahed-Zadeh, P. (1995), *The Amirs of the Borderlands and Eastern Iranian Borders*, (London: Urosevic Foundation Publication).

Mojtahed-Zadeh, P. (2002), *Joghrafiay-e Siasi va Siasat-e Joghrafiaei* (Political Geography and Geopolitics) (Tehran: SAMT official publishers of text books), 43.

Mojtahed-Zadeh, P. (2005), '"Boundary" in the Ancient Persian Tradition of Statehood', *GeoJournal* 66:4, 273-83.

Mojtahed-Zadeh, P. (2007), 'Iran, an Old Civilization and a new Nation State', in *Focus on Geography of the American Geographical Society* 49:4, Special Country Issue: Iran, 13-20.

Murphy, A.B. (2003), 'Dominant Territorial Ideologies in the Modern State System: Implications for Unity within and beyond the Islamic World', *paper presented to the second International Congress of the Geographers of the Islamic World* 16-17 September 2003 (Tehran).

Nayer Nouri, A.H. (1971), *Iran's Contribution to the World Civilization*, volume II (Tehran).

Newman, D. (2006), 'The Resilience of Territorial Conflict in an Era of Globalization', in Kahler, M. and Walter, B. (eds.), *Territoriality and Conflict in an Era of Globalization* (Cambridge: Cambridge University Press).

Paasi, A. (2005), 'Generations and the "Development" of Border Studies', *Geopolitics* 10:4, 663-71.

Prevelakis, G. (2003), *Jean Gottmann's Relevance in Today's World* (Paris: Sorbonne University).

Rice, T. (1953), 'Persia and Byzantium', in Arberry, A.J. (ed.), *The Legacy of Persia* (Oxford: Claredon Press).

Tavakoli, A. (1993), 'Emperaturi Ya Sahahnshahi', *Ayandeh monthly Journal*, 19, 828-830.

Taylor, P.J. (1989), *Political Geography*, second edition (London: Longman Scientific and Technical).

Templeton, P.L. (1979), *The Persian Prince* (London: Persian Prince Publication).

Vadiei, K. (1974), *Moghadamehi bar Joghrafiay-e Ensaniy-e Iran* (An Introduction to the Human Geography of Iran) (Tehran: Tehran University Press).

Von Hagen, V.W. (1974), *The Golden Man: The Quest for El Dorado* (Farnborough, Saxon House).

PART V
THE ROLE OF BORDERS IN A SEEMINGLY BORDERLESS WORLD

Waiting for Work:
Labour Migration and the
Political Economy of Borders

Roos Pijpers

Introduction

This chapter presents a review of literature on borders and labour migration, with a particular regional focus on the European Union (EU). Partly as a consequence of the globalization and security discourses that have emerged in the past decades and years, the academic community continues to portray a strong interest in migration across international borders. Within the EU, this interest is further constitutive of the recent eastward expansion and the migration pressures on the internal borders this event allegedly has caused. Many scholars have expressed their concern about the territorial exclusion that, in their view, is the result of the migration controls put in place by the EU and its Member States (Amato 2002; Bigo 1998, 2005, 2008; Bigo and Guild 2005; den Boer 1995, 2002; Guild 2005a, 2005b; Guild and Bigo 2002; Jileva 2002; Kostakopoulou 2000; Mitsilegas 2002; Pastore 2002; Puntscher Riekmann 2008; Thränhardt and Miles 1995; Verstraete 2001). In general, this literature points to what is seen as a fundamental 'contradiction between greater openness of internal borders and the reinforcement of controls at the external borders' (Foucher 1998, 242). The internal borders of the EU have disappeared for citizens of Member States only to reappear for *aliens*: 'Freedom of mobility for some could only be made possible through the organized exclusion of others forced to move around as illegal aliens, migrants, or refugees' (Verstraete 2001, 29).

As regards the stratification of status rights that became visible in the course of the recent enlargement rounds, the EU is reproached for obliging new Member States to adopt the well-known Schengen regime and its visa directives, while creating *second-class* EU citizens at the same time (Jileva 2002). In December 2007, only nine of the twelve new Member States (Cyprus, Romania and Bulgaria not included) accessed the Schengen area. Meanwhile, the right to seek paid employment in many *old* member states is suspended for workers from Romania and Bulgaria. Germany and Austria are still suspending this right for workers from all new Member States.

The discontent expressed with regard to the legal injustices identified here underexposes, to some extent, the geopolitical and politico-economic motives that lie behind these injustices. It has been argued, for example, that scholarly celebrations of notions like *global nomadism, free mobility* and *moral equality* for nationals and non-nationals do not keep pace with *developments on the ground* (Favell and Hansen 2002, 581; see also Anderson and Bort 2001; Brown 2002; Favell 2009; Jordan and Düvell 2003; Peixoto 2002; Samers 2004; Walters 2002, 2004). In particular, two claims stand out here. The first is that not only the state, but also market actors are willing and able to (re)direct migratory movements through the use of borders. As will be described on the pages that follow, market demand does exert an important influence on the ways in which borders are erected and for whom they are erected, how they are enforced, and how they are bypassed. The second claim, especially pertinent to neo-Marxist inspired literature, follows from the first one and entails that EU borders can be conceptualized as networked power instruments by which the risks posed by global capitalism are managed in much the same ways as are security risks (Mitchell 2001; Sassen 1988, 1996). In reviewing the literature that sustains these claims, I argue in that the ensemble of border management practices in the EU qualifies as *queue tactics* (Crowley 2005), or, on a less metaphorical note, as *the political economy of waiting*.

Two caveats apply. Whilst the reader of a research companion to border studies might expect an overview that reflects at least the author's attempts to be objective and all-inclusive, for a number of reasons, I make no pretensions to completeness. Inevitably, the chapter's regional emphasis on Europe/the EU is prone to culminate in a one-sided, Eurocentric perspective on borders and labour migration. Clearly, this does not do justice to the important insights revealed by experts on labour migration from Mexico and Central America to the United States, interregional migration in Southeast Asia and Africa, and transit migration in Central Asia and West Africa. Furthermore, as this is an overview of academic literature on borders and labour migration, references to past or present policy frameworks will be made only when they are considered functional for the broader argument outlined.

A very short history of the migration state

The question of why states control migration can be traced back to classic political philosophical thought, in which the notion of statehood is famously equated with territorial sovereignty (Crowley 2005). The sovereign has the exclusive authority to enact laws on its territory, as well as the moral responsibility to ensure that these laws are just. When laws are obeyed, hence when people submit to the sovereign, sovereignty is exercized and the state is strengthened (Crowley 2005; Foucault 1991; Walters and Haahr 2005). This means that the ultimate end of sovereignty is sovereignty itself. However, in his seminal work, Michel Foucault has challenged this circularity, arguing that statehood carries with it a certain sensitivity to tactics, to the *arrangement of things* (Foucault 1991). Authority can also be maintained by opening up the black box that is the inside of the state (Walters and Haahr 2005). To some extent, therefore, the traditional reading of legal statehood is eroded by what Foucault has called *governmentality*:

> When states negotiate with powerful corporate interests, conduct public-health campaigns using advertising techniques, and use various technical market-based instruments to steer the economy, they are not acting as 'sovereign' in any useful sense of the word. Yet much of what contemporary states routinely do is, precisely, either non-authoritative or non-legal, or both. This was the point of Foucault's notion of 'governmentality', which he counterposed to legal statehood, and resurfaces under a different guise, but with similar analytical implications, in the currently fashionable notion of 'governance'. (Crowley 1995, 146-47)

Over time, the population has become an effective means with which to arrange things and to achieve specific ends: 'to those in political power, the control of territory now seems less important than the control of those who claim the right to move about within it' (Foucher 1998, 237-38). Indeed, the term *population management* has been coined to appropriately describe the ultimate end of government (Foucault 1991; Foucher 1998; Walters 2002). According to Foucault (1991), regulation in the realms of health (health care campaigns), education (public schooling) and employment (taxation, social security leverage) target the increase of welfare of the native population yet can be exposed as control techniques with intended and unintended disciplinary effects. One of these is that people's room to move is restrained. For the well functioning of property rights laws, population censuses and welfare institutions, in short for people to become visible in statistics, they must be place-bound. The sheer amount of space occupied by the institutions and apparatuses of the modern state has left little room for people to be on the move without the intervention of some governing authority. Even mobility within the confines of the nation state is framed by a *sedentarist metaphysics* (Cresswell 2006).

One legal institution accompanying the rise of the modern state, to the purpose of which passport and visa systems were created, was nationality (Hollifield 2004).[1] In the late nineteenth and early twentieth centuries, these systems were relatively open, receptive to the migratory movements caused by industrialization, international trade and demographic change. During and following World War I, this slowly but dramatically changed when stronger forms of nationalism arose and decolonization started. It can be ascertained that the *liberal paradox* (that is economic forces requiring the openness of borders and security concerns that promote their

---

1   Nationality laws are based on either of two principles: the *jus sanguinis*, which defines nationality as ethnicity, or the *jus soli*, which refers to the territory where one is born (Hollifield 2004).

closure, Hollifield 2004) in which contemporary migration states find themselves trapped finds its origins in this period.

After World War II, the guest-worker recruitment schemes processed in various western European countries attracted workers from Mediterranean countries such as Algeria, Morocco and Turkey (Castles 2006). As a consequence of the economic downturn in the early half on the 1970s, and as an immediate result of the 1973 oil crisis, the schemes were put to halt (Castles 2006). Other initiatives took over the regulation of labour migration in the European migration contexts. Arguably the most prominent are the bilateral recruitment schemes that supply national labour markets with migrant workers of various skills and professions. Many of these schemes take on the form of Temporary Migrant Worker Programmes, which solicit workers for specific job vacancies for specific, limited, periods of time. According to a recent overview, these programmes are not very successful in achieving the economic objectives predefined, and, moreover, they are not contributing to decrease the large numbers of undocumented workers in the EU (Castles 2006).

As of the 1990s, through the construction of a neoliberal-inspired Internal Market, the EU has aimed to create a cohesive, internally borderless economic space furnished to compete with the United States, Japan and Southeast Asia's large, rapidly developing economies. To this end, in accordance with neoclassical economic theory, institutional barriers to the free movement of capital, labour, goods and services between Member States are brought down. This theory, also known as *marginalist* theory (Gidwani and Sivaramakrishnan 2003), represents a very influential academic perspective on the relationship between borders and labour migration. It explains international migration through the existence of initial differences in marginal returns to labour (Borjas 1989). That is to say, one extra *unit* of labour put to work in all countries yields different amounts of additional national output. In order to unveil how migration processes work, the theory draws on highly stylized dual economy models which assume a binary distinction between labour-intensive and technology-intensive countries. The initially low marginal value product of labour in the labour-intensive countries provides an incentive to relocate to places where extra labour inputs are needed. Eventually, marginal returns to labour equalize across countries; an *equilibrium* state is reached. Importantly, neoclassical or marginalist theory regards the border as a discontinuity in an economic space that is ideally free of discontinuities. As they increase the marginal cost of interaction, borders, in this theory, are seen as barriers (van Houtum 2000).

The free movement of labour in the Internal Market is facilitated by the abolition of work permit requirements and, under the auspices of the Schengen regime, by the abolition of passport controls. Over time, Schengen has become strongly associated with the external border of the EU. Today, its principal goals are the co-ordination of visa, work and residence permits for non-EU citizens as well as the creation of a common asylum policy. Furthermore, internal security concerns have committed the Schengen external border regime to the detection and prevention of illegal migration. Some say that security and migration issues in the EU and its Member States have been integrated to such an extent that migration policies are effectively being *securitized*, and that similarly discursive, illegal migrants are being *criminalized* (Bigo 1998, 2001; Huysmans 1995, 2000; Kostakopoulou 2000).

It is against this backdrop that the following sections can be read.

Geostrategies: organizing the space of the border

While academic debates over which model of state the EU may take on at some point in the future is far from decided, there has been a tendency among politicians and opinion makers to name, term and label the allegedly static nature of the EU's external border and the social space that this border contains. Immigration and asylum issues have been thankfully used as a lens for this, largely instigated by political and public debates. The two best-known names reflect a confrontation between those who expected the intensity of border controls at the external border of the enlarged EU to become excessive (*Fortress* Europe) or insufficient (*Sieve* or *Maze* Europe, see Bigo 1998; Brown 2002). In general, the academic literature has held a much more nuanced view vis-à-vis both of these extremes, although Sieve/ Maze Europe, that is the idea that the external borders are porous and people *leak* through seems to attract more consent than Fortress Europe. The argument here is that the controls are so immensely time, money and resource consuming that a fortress-like external border is not feasible (Bigo 1998; Christiansen and Jørgensen 2000; Favell and Hansen 2002). At best, the fortress resembles an asymmetrical, neo-medieval empire (Pastore 2002; Zielonka 2001, 2006, 2008) with characteristically overlapping spheres of governance and concomitant *fuzzy borders* (Christiansen, Petito and Tonra 2000).

However, the developments at the borders of the EU have invoked border metaphors that are much richer and much less static. Take for instance the notion of *Ban-opticon*. Giving a contemporary twist to Foucault's classic notion of the *Panopticon* – the prison-like form of governmentality by which the modern society disciplines its population – in the Ban-opticon, it is not so much 'the population' that is managed as 'the unease with possible harm done to the population' (Bigo 2005; Bigo and Guild 2005). The identity of those who are thought likely to commit any kind of *next crime* is traced, filed and distributed. Thus imagining different possible futures, proactive policing and, if needed, pre-emptive military strike is launched to prevent these next crimes from actually happening (Bigo 2005). This concern with risk management requires particular ways of organizing the space of the border (Walters 2004). Following Michel Foucher, Walters has identified these ways as *geostrategies*:

> *Drawing upon historical precedents and examples, geostrategies have the potential to offer a much more nuanced and topographical account of the production of geopolitical space in Europe than do concepts like fuzzy borders or Fortress Europe.* (Walters 2004, 693)

Of the four geostrategies, the first – the *limes*, meaning *boundary* – is used to refer to the boundary of the Roman Empire, especially that in the north of Europe (Foucher 1998; Walters 2004). It refers to the relatively stable, quasi-permanent frontier that separates an empire-like power from its constitutive outside. In the south, the border of the EU resembles the limes: membership has explicitly been ruled out for the EU's non-European partners there.

The limes is closely related to the second geostrategy identified by Walters: That of the colonial frontier, offering a more discursive interpretation of the EU as an empire and surrounding third countries as its cultural other. Contrary to the limes, the colonial frontier is less fixed, as it is prone to changes in cultural identity and, above all, in the sociocultural features ascribed to identity by those inside. Identity markers, in turn, are inextricably linked to the question where the European enlargement project will eventually end.

Whereas the limes and the colonial frontier still dominantly express spatial containment as a means to manage risk, the third and fourth geostrategies combined suggest a tendency towards networked spatiality. The geostrategy of the *march* – once a neutral zone separating Roman from enemy powers and awaiting occupation by either one of them – has a 'very long, historical association with Central and Eastern Europe', too (Walters 2004, 684). Already a buffer zone in the Versailles Treaty, and later during the Cold War, the region comprising the EU's new Member States (as well as Belarus, Moldova and Ukraine) now re-emerges as a 'space in-between' (ibid.), awaiting candidate membership, full-fledged membership, the application of Schengen and the coming into force of freedom of labour in the Internal Market. The geopolitical in-betweenness of the countries in East-Central Europe has become institutionalized in the European Neighbourhood Policy (ENP). In its Wider Europe Communication (2003), the EC explores far-reaching ideas with regard to the relations between the EU and nations on its eastern fringe (Russia and the above-mentioned Western Newly Independent States). In the Communication, the likely ineligibility of these countries for EU membership is positively phrased by expressing the aim to construct its *near abroad* (Christiansen, Petito and Tonra 2000) as 'a zone of prosperity and a friendly neighbourhood – a "ring of friends"' (EC 2003, 4). The movement of persons is one central element of the ENP. Explicit references are made to the future need for skilled migrant labour due to demographic change (ageing), conclusive readmission agreements in order to combat illegal and transit migration, and joint cooperation in the fields of human trafficking, organized crime and security matters (EC 2003).

The march can also be found at the micro-political level, namely at international airports and on the territories of municipalities across the Member States. On many occasions, the march here takes the form of fenced *zones d'attente* located in remote areas where people can do little else but wait. In these 'spaces of indistinction', be they refugee camps or migrant detention centres, one awaits transit, access to asylum procedures, the outcome of such procedures, or expulsion and return (see also Guild 2005a). Sometimes, protective national jurisdiction does not apply: These spaces of indistinction have the legal status of an exclave (Walters 2004).

These contemporary appearances of the march introduce the fourth geostrategy: The *networked (non)border* (Walters 2004). This concept aims to capture the changing spatiality of border control activities in the EU from physically concentrated at the border to country-internal networks of regulation and cooperation, implying a 'reconfiguring of the border from a space of lines and edges to one of nodes' (Walters 2002, 577). Interconnected nodes and networks are complementing and even replacing controls enforced at the border proper: National territory is increasingly treated as an extended frontier zone, wherein border guarding is taken over by migration managers (Foucher 1998). Upon entering the Netherlands, for instance, migrants and asylum-seekers access the *migration chain*, an institutional network consisting of ministries, the immigration and naturalization services, institutions responsible for the issuance of work permits as well as the aliens police. The immigration and naturalization services within this Dutch chain also partake in the European Migration Network (EMN), a network of national contact points designated by the Member States with the objective to systematically collect and analyse migration data (EC 2005). Other examples of the networked (non)border in the EU are the police networks that face networks of organized crime and human trafficking in strategic games or even openly fought battles (Walters 2004).

The limits to state migration control

State migration control, however, is neither confined to the borders of the state, the inside of the state, nor the state itself. To illustrate this, again the EU and its members serve as a telling example. The global economic and political developments in the second half of the twentieth century pose challenges to the regulation of migration by national states. These multifaceted challenges are eloquently summarized by Jordan and Düvell, who argue that 'new forms of global economic nomadism have outstripped the capacities of national migration management to adapt to the requirements of international capitalism' (2003, 87). In their view, *global nomads* are labour migrants who are pushed forward by ongoing worldwide economic restructuring and at the same time are driven towards the neoliberal collaborative projects currently being undertaken in the EU and elsewhere. At the same time, flexible labour demand soars, particularly in the high-skilled and low-skilled segments of national labour markets (Menz 2002; Peixoto 2002). Since many labour migrants are able, or forced, to offer this flexibility, the demand for their labour is soaring too (Jordan, Stråth and Triandafyllidou 2003a; Sassen 1988, 1996). In this global migration order, the state must continuously redevelop regulation for labour migration.

Virginie Guiraudon has argued that although a 'denationalization of migration control' is by all means taking place, this does not necessarily imply that the state incurs a loss of authority (2000, 2001). The Member States cope with a growing dependency on the decisions of the European Court of Justice, and with an increased obligation to answer to supranational representative bodies such as the

European Parliament. Having in many individual cases overruled state verdicts to deny access to would-be migrants or to expel asylum-seekers, these institutions have encouraged decision-making actors at the national level to seek new partners in order to retain dominantly restrictive migration policies. 'Transnational cooperation in the fields of immigration and asylum is increasingly taking on the characteristics of a multilevel governance regime' through the entry on stage of these partners (Guiraudon 2001, 37). Currently in the EU, migration control shifts up, down and out in a fashion that has been called *venue shopping* (Guiraudon 2000, 2001; Lahav 2000; Lahav and Guiraudon 2006). When venue shopping, the state searches for alternative institutional loci to take over governmental and managerial functions.

Shifting up refers to the incorporation into policy frameworks of third countries (countries of origin and transit). Under the auspices of return or readmission agreements, third countries are urged to readmit people (Guiraudon 2001). Also, customs agents are stationed at major transport hubs in these countries (Samers 2004), and information films specifically made to discourage migration are distributed among their native resident population. These latter ways of establishing translocal linkages with third countries have been referred to as *remote control* (Samers 2004; Zolberg 2003).

Responsibilities in terms of migration control are being shifted down as well, that is, they are being transferred to the subnational level. This concerns, for example, family reunification (*in casu* the prevention of bogus marriages) and the access by not legally residing immigrants to the welfare state. Also, local governments may be contracted to manage migration detention centres (Guiraudon 2001). Balancing between an economic demand for flexible migrant labour and nationalist desires to protect native workers, local immigration and welfare officers have considerable discretionary powers. Generally, migrants are the *weak users* of these administrative systems. Important considerations about difficult cases have to be made under great time pressure, implying that people improvise and prioritize certain tasks over others (Jordan, Stråth and Triandafyllidou 2003a). As a consequence, the translation of policy imperatives 'into a bureaucratically streamlined algorithm' creates inequalities between applicant migrants, regardless of their eligibility for the requested privileges (Crowley 2005, 155). Also, this suggests that the functions of police forces and welfare agencies may converge when migration control is shifted down (Jordan, Stråth and Triandafyllidou 2003a).

Thirdly, through shifting out, non-state actors emerge in migration control processes. This relates to, for example, the *de facto* transfer of authority to transport carriers as agreed upon at the level of the EU, and to the development that individual employers in the Member States are increasingly being held responsible for the presence of illegally employed labour migrants at the workplace (Guiraudon 2001; Lahav 2000; Lahav and Guiraudon 2006). Shifting out may imply that returns to capital are realized by the participating non-state actors. In her case study of the Belgian seaport of Zeebrugge, Verstraete (2001) reports about companies that specialize and invest in, and indeed gain from the production of technological devices that detect the presence of stowaways. It could be argued that borders actually help to *produce* illegal immigration: the insides and outsides created in and by the various European border treaties and migration policy narratives reify through private capital investments in border technology (Samers 2004; Verstraete 2001;). Contemplating the fate of the stowaways detected in Zeebrugge, Verstraete conceptualizes the production of the illegal migrant as follows:

> *Once the 'alien' is thus translated – objectified – within the parameters of physical science, once s/he is reduced to the generic polar electrical view of a heartbeat, another mode of polarisation comes into view, that of 'man' versus animal ... Along the way, the stowaway is reproduced along a set of Western cultural relations – man versus animal, the law versus the criminal, technology versus humans, movement versus location – that situate him/her at once inside and outside the capitalist nation, inside and outside European territory. S/he is, in one and the same breath, the target of the gun-shaped Life Guard, of national security, of police officers, of Europe's external frontiers, and of global capital investment.* (Verstraete 2001, 40-1)

Ever since the remarkable decision made by the European Court of Justice back in 1990, 'which explicitly permitted the posting[2] of workers from low-wage Portugal *within this framework of the provision of services*' (Menz 2002, 727; italics in original), the policy framework defining the freedom of services in the Internal Market has opened up alternative ways for employers to bypass restrictions on labour migration than to illegally enter and put to work people. Yet, not only the employers benefit from the posting of workers and other practices developed within the realm of freedom of services: There is a burgeoning market for consultancy and legal firms that specialize in, and indeed also gain from advising client firms on how to legally or semi-legally bypass migration restrictions (Pijpers and van der Velde 2007). Apart from the use of the services framework, these advisory activities include tax and welfare issues, and, where the entry and employment of migrant workers is concerned, state-specific issues of labour law.

It is against the backdrop of these and similar examples that the idea has been raised to rethink the role of private actors in academic discussions on the governance of migration in a European context:

> *Scholarly reflection on these issues, however, has not kept pace with developments on the ground. Driven by a normative attentiveness to the*

---

2   Posted workers remain on the pay list of their home country-based employer, while carrying out a service in another country. Hence they are not moving with the purpose of seeking paid employment abroad, which they would be if they were migrants. Depending on international laws, bilateral agreements and the duration of stay, when employers apply the posting concept, taxation and social security leverage may remain under the auspices of the sending country – which makes this kind of labour mobility easier to organize.

> negative and exclusionary aspects of both current governmental policies and
> hostile public opinion ... (Favell and Hansen 2002, 581)

Developments on the ground are the reason that policy makers and implementers, who are struggling to meet populist anti-immigration sentiments, are unable to prevent large inflows of migrants who perform unskilled seasonal labour and increasingly also skilled work in local labour markets across the Member States. Venue shopping may encourage migrants to employ trial and error, hence to try first what they see as the most beneficial recruitment channels, implementation practices or travel routes within or into the Member States, and to try elsewhere and otherwise if the preferred strategy fails (see also Peixoto 2002). The involvement of employers and their ancillaries may allow migrants to circulate between home and the country, or countries, of destination. Favell and Hansen (2002) argue that, by acknowledging the limits to state migration control and by allowing market actors into migration selection processes, the EU and its Member States may actually create new opportunities for migration.

The border as an instrument of weakening and disempowerment

Whereas the work referred to in the previous section may remind border scholars of the fact that borders, as barriers to labour migration, are strategically used both by states and markets, Marxist-inspired literature stresses their weakening power. For Michael Samers, the Marxist-inspired perspective on borders and labour migration entails that an overly deterministic account of political economy is avoided, but its *spectre* is recognized (Samers 2003, 575). In a nutshell, this boils down to the following.

Places, in more radical versions of Marxist theory, are *spatial fixes* that can effectively be drawn into the circulation process of capital, to be left behind again when crisis strikes. These more radical versions harness a structural determinism that implies these migrants will emerge as the victims of the economic development of core areas (Gidwani and Sivaramakrishnan 2003). The EU's Internal Market thus features core areas, thriving with economic activity and always in need of labour migrants from peripheral areas.

A milder version of this argument has famously been adopted by dual labour market theorists, who argue that a *built-in demand* for migrant labour stems from the rigid occupational hierarchies that society constructs institutionally as well as socially (Massey et al. 1993). According to these theorists, the *bottom* of the labour markets concerns those jobs that will be insusceptible to demands to increase wages, in order not to surpass the institutionally fixed wages of jobs that are higher on the hierarchical ladder. As a consequence, native workers will not accept these dead-end jobs for doing so would lower their social status. This encourages employers to hire labour migrants, who are not bothered by the hierarchy and are desperately in need of work (Kraler and Parnreiter 2005). Moreover, as opposed to capital, labour is a flexible production factor that can easily be dismissed in times of scarce product demand: 'The inherent dualism between labour and capital extends to the labour force in the form of a segmented labour market structure' (Massey et al. 1993, 443). Migrant workers hardly ever move up across the occupational boundary between the capital-intensive primary sector and the labour-intensive secondary sector.

Marxism-inspired studies try to show how the – geographically uneven – spread of capitalist economic development is sustained by a wide range of institutional and regulatory practices, state borders, recruitment schemes and work permits included. Labour migration, as a direct result of uneven development, is structured, in the sense that the scope of action of migrant workers is both constrained and enabled by these practices. In the words of Saskia Sassen:

> *National boundaries do not act as barriers so much as mechanisms reproducing the system through the international division of labor ... Border enforcement is a mechanism facilitating the extraction of cheap labour by assigning criminal status to a segment of the working class – illegal immigrants. Foreign workers undermine a nation's working class when the state renders foreigners socially and politically powerless. At the same time, border enforcement meets the demands of organized labour in the labor-receiving country insofar as it presumes to protect native workers. Yet selective enforcement of policies can circumvent general border policies and protect the interests of economic sectors relying on immigrant labor.* (Sassen 1988, 36-7)

This statement speaks to the broader neo-Marxist[3] argument that global capitalism *weakens* labour (Comaroff and Comaroff 2002). According to this argument, the traditional workplace – which provides stability in terms of income and entrenchment in local communities – is relocated or closed down. As a consequence, the migrant comes to resemble a zombie, a spectral figure whose speech is impaired due to unfamiliarity with the language of the receiving country, pushed away from shrinking national labour markets and pulled towards temporary job openings abroad (Comaroff and Comaroff 2002). Public hostility, illegal employment and the inability to communicate render migrants invisible: They are territorially present but socially absent (Crowley 2005). Their labour degenerates into ghost labour. In such circumstances, the border is a *revolving door* that invites people and pushes them back at the same time (Mitchell 2001). However, the invisibility of migrants' bodies and migrant labour to some extent problematizes the very notion of the border as a line of exclusion: What is absent cannot be excluded (Saybasili 2004). In this view, the border is also a *performative space*, in the sense that only the apprehension of illegal migrants who attempt to cross it makes it real (Saybasili

---

3   The term 'neo-Marxism' refers to Marxist-inspired critiques of contemporary manifestations of capitalism, particularly those associated with globalization.

2004, 5). When recognizing its *spectre* – a term by which Samers refers to the first words of Marx' Manifesto, a political economy of borders not only takes into account what we can still learn from the more radical versions of Marxist theory, but also that migrants may actually further challenge the idea that borders are barriers, by bypassing them or by not getting caught.

In the first post-Wall years, migrant workers from new Member States in the Netherlands personified ghost labour, being subjected to acts of violence with regard to working, payment and housing conditions. These were the heydays of *witch hunts*: attempts by the labour inspectorate to catch illegal migrants while working in the open fields, pursuing people into nearby woods if necessary. Fortunately, today, recruitment and employment practices have improved. The workers are now increasingly visible in the Dutch landscape, working, consuming, being driven around by recruiting agents. It is important to note that settings can change for the better: The border is always 'a political technology which records the balance of power *at a particular time* in space' (Bigo 1998, 149; *emphasis added*). Nevertheless, illegal and semi-legal employment remains, in this case and in the many other instances of labour migration in the EU. These migrants find themselves trapped in *networks of violence*, comprising the workplace, the country of origin and, of course, the border:

> The border stands as the primary regulator of this system, the primary point of passage in the network of violence that drives migrant ... workers underground, and stigmatizes them so thoroughly that their labour becomes ever cheaper, ever more pliable. (Mitchell 2001, 57)

As was discussed above, the networked spatiality of borders in the EU currently encompasses a plethora of physical nodes and administrative structures. Yet, from a neo-Marxist perspective, these borders exist by virtue of unequal and sometimes physically offensive power relations between the involved actors: labour migrants, employers, recruiters, human traffickers, migration managers, the labour inspectorate, the aliens police, the border guards. Following Sassen (1988, 1996), more than a mechanism by which capitalist relations are reproduced, the border is a management instrument by which the risks posed by global capitalism are controlled.

Migrant agency and the transgression of borders

Despite substantial ideological disagreements about the nature of borders, the neoclassical (marginalist) and neo-Marxist perspectives share a materialist bias (Gidwani and Sivaramakrishnan 2003; Silvey 2004). Both approaches assume that economic motifs are the key factors that make people move. As a consequence, for Gidwani and Sivaramakrishnan, they are two sides of the same coin, *progress*:

Neither the marginalists nor the Marxists question the Eurocentric, historicist metanarrative of 'modernity' that undergirds their models of migration, and that has taken the form of Orientalism under colonialism, Modernization under imperialism and nationalism, and Globalization under late capitalism ... In this universalized story of Progress, migration and its upheavals are reduced to a necessary, if sometimes unfortunate, subplot in the unfolding of History in Europe's image. (Gidwani and Sivaramakrishnan 2003, 189)

According to the marginalists, once barriers are overcome, international migration ultimately benefits the migrants as well as the sending and receiving countries. For the Marxists, 'migration is a natural outgrowth of disruptions and dislocations that inevitably occur in the process of capitalist development' (Massey et al. 1993, 445). As a result of its febrile search for new spatial fixes, global capital penetrates into a great many underdeveloped areas, thereby transferring economic and bodily risks to people who are forced to migrate across borders (Kraler and Parnreiter 2005; Massey et al. 1993).

At this point, I shall turn to another set of thoughts that have influenced migration studies and, albeit less strongly, border studies. These thoughts do not centre on the prediction of spatio-temporal outcomes: The migration *process* is what matters, and so are the borders that are crossed in this process. The 1990s witnessed a growing awareness among migration researchers that many international migrants are part of networks between places of origin and destination. Newly arrived migrants may find homes and jobs using such networks, and potential migrants may perceive the threshold to actually migrate as considerably lower knowing that they will be received by fellow compatriots, or even by next of kin. Importantly, the literature suggests that through migrant networks, international migration flows are being reproduced (Kraler and Parnreiter 2005; Massey et al. 1993). According to Thomas Faist, the notion of social capital – which he defines as 'the arrangement of resources wielded by social and symbolic ties' (2000, 117) – is of great help in understanding how these networks function. These resources include intra-group solidarity as well as reciprocal obligations. They may lower transaction costs and facilitate coordination. The concept of social capital thus links actions undertaken by individual migrants to wider institutional structures that impede or facilitate international migration (Faist 2000).

Faist's work is an outstanding example of what have become known as *transnational migration studies*. Arguing that technological developments and global capitalism have greatly improved the opportunities for people to cross borders, circulate, stay in contact and remit money, transmigration researchers try to explain how migrants increasingly engage in activities that transcend the boundaries of the state (Waldinger and Fitzgerald 2004). From transnationalism, *transnational social spaces* arise, disrupting geographical and social space and connecting migrants to their countries and regions of origin while temporarily or permanently making a living in a host society (Faist 2000; Guarnizo 2003; Pries 2001; Waldinger and Fitzgerald 2004). Transnational migration studies devote a great deal of attention to entry and survival strategies, the hybrid and sometimes fractured social identities of transmigrants, and to specific transnational actions such as the participation in migrant representative organizations and migrant entrepreneurship (Guarnizo 2003; Pries 2001). They include meticulous reconstructions of the onset of migrant networks, tracing the subsequent events that connect small groups of pioneer migrants to vibrant ethnic communities in countries of destination.

The knowledge accumulated within the perspective of transnational migration studies is relevant to border scholars for two main reasons (Mitchell 1997). First, there is now a convincingly large body of empirical literature demonstrating that borders can be overcome, and, moreover, that also individuals, migrants and local actors in countries of destination alike, can gain from borders. In the Netherlands, for example, when you want to have your photograph taken in order to obtain a visa for a specific destination country, you may find that you can only approach some local photographers, namely those who have been contracted by the embassy in question. Second, and on a more theoretical note, the act of overcoming borders has been associated with post-structural and post-colonial scholarship dedicated to ideas like hybridity, identity, and migrant subjectivity (Gidwani and Sivaramakrishnan 2003; Mitchell 1997; Silvey and Lawson 1999). Since migration implies an unsettling of one state of mind and a transgression to another, circumscribed identities (often, that is, circumscribed not by the migrant him/herself but by the *Eurowest* observer) dissolve, and, under the influence of the various cultures he/she enmeshes him/herself in, become hybrid. The statement that a border is a performative space, as voiced in the previous section, is an example of how the – widely accepted – meaning of a border as a barrier, or a power instrument for that matter, is productively destabilized.

Like marginalist and Marxist theories and research, also the field of transnational migration studies has received criticism over the years. Stories of international migrants shaping and reshaping transnational social spaces often leave untold the multiple political constraints stemming from the national and supranational levels between which these same migrants normally hover. Yet, transnational practices are partly also contingent outcomes of these political constraints (Waldinger and Fitzgerald 2004).

The political economy of waiting

Characteristically, the modern state negotiates, regulates and allocates wage levels, labour rights, labour duties, social security benefits, pensions and tax deductions. In the EU, at present, a harmonized system of labour laws and welfare entitlements does not exist, nor does a uniform system to coordinate what currently amounts to 27 national systems (Douven et al. 2006). As a consequence, the more mobile workers are, the more difficulties can be expected with regard to their legal, social and fiscal status. For example, a Polish migrant worker hired by a Dutch recruitment agency and put to work in the Netherlands, then in Belgium and then in Germany is a much greater source of legal anomalies and conflict than cross-border commuters between the Netherlands and Germany. Some of the literature presented in this chapter suggested that for some actors and collectives of actors – who are very differently empowered but invariably creative – the border of the migration state is not a barrier at all. As alternative pathways are explored, precisely the incompatibilities between state control systems that are encountered when moving along these pathways allow migrants, but above all employers, recruiting actors and advisory firms, the latter being somewhat hidden in the current migration discourse, to obtain significant cost advantages and even profit. In turn, these observations suggest that the border to some extent creates what it is supposed to prevent: unfair competition for native workers as well as below standard payments and unacceptable working conditions for migrant workers.

Today, labour market deregulation is an issue of considerable political priority and societal uproar even in the continental EU Member States. In the Netherlands, there is growing awareness of the low degree of competitiveness of strongly protected Dutch workers vis-à-vis semi-legally entered and employed migrant workers. In France, the publication of the posting directive (as part of the liberalization of the movement of services in the EU) in its unabridged version (EC 2004a) stirred an intense moral panic about service providers from new Member States, personified by the figure of the cheap and flexible Polish plumber, supposedly threatening French workers of various professions.

One can detect an uneasy fusion between supranational attempts to foster freedom of movement and national struggles to prevent too great a loss of decisive power. The Member States are challenged by plans to *Europeanize* migration policy and of the various appearances of global nomadism, and other institutional sites emerge to take over the control of migration. Foucault's memorable observations regarding the management of the population as the ultimate end of government come to mind here; even more so when one realises how present concerns over internal security only reinforce the tendency to control migratory movements. The literature has given a variety of names to the ensemble of control practices, most recently *the Ban-opticon*. The bureaucracies accompanying this ensemble have invoked a renewed attention for the territorial border spaces within which migration control develops and is implemented. Sure, notions such as the march and the networked (non)border are not new, for *zones d'attente*, monitoring institutions and welfare agencies concerned with migrants have existed in Western Europe's managerial states for quite a while. Yet, these are the spaces where the collaborative efforts to achieve a maximum controllability of *next crimes* and of global capitalism are now the most overtly manifest, which justifies their conceptual reuse.

Drawing the threads together, it could be argued that the ensemble of border control practices finds expression in the metaphor of the *queue* (Crowley 2005). In the literal sense of the word, a queue is a line of people who are waiting. And precisely waiting is what many migrants do. Migration chains are so complex that those passing through them may spend weeks, months or even years waiting. Final decisions related to the acceptance or refusal of a specific status right, and hence about inclusion or exclusion to a society, are amenable to randomness, subjectivity, prejudice, the nature of contacts with migration managers, and erratic judgement resulting from the hasty allocation of resources. The anticipation of significant time delays may even discourage otherwise eligible people from applying for work permits, residence permits, insurance and so on. As such, the queue can never be fair to everyone 'in any but the crudest sense' (Crowley 2005, 154). A perhaps provocative but nonetheless important question to ask, bearing in mind the observed institutional inertia and bureaucratic slowness, is whether the migration state actually functions by virtue of waiting. Is waiting *just* a by-product of state institutions and bureaucracies or might it be a tactic, a management technique that is not outside but fully part of the state, struggling as it does to strike a balance between sedentarist and flexible ideologies?

As was the case with the concept of the march, the queue is very much about micro-management, too. Illustrative for this is the existence of *queuing theory*, the mathematical study of waiting lines. Its practitioners construct mathematic models in order to minimize waiting times, given that the positions of subjects or objects in the queue are arbitrary. The models are applied in the realms of logistics, (public) transport and industrial production, where strives to minimize storage time and the time between input and output have become known as *just-in-time management* and *real-time processing*, respectively. From my research, I am tempted to draw the conclusion that the way labour pools of migrant workers from new Member States are organized could qualify as an application as well. Among employers, these people are known as highly flexible workers, where flexibility is understood as the ability to swiftly move between different job placements. Flexibility is therefore associated with notions such as mobility, activity, and productivity – not with waiting. However, since employers indicate the labour they wish to hire from recruitment agencies on a very short notice, there are time intervals when the workers are actually out of work. On these occasions, they are not usually given permission to return home or to enjoy leisure time. Rather, they have to stay in the often semi-closed premises arranged by the agencies, where they can be called to work at any moment. For migrant workers, having to wait not knowing in which workplace you will be toiling next, and if you will be earning money at all, can be a frustrating experience. Here, the queue relates to the whole of management practices of spatially contained – bordered – labour pools. One question to address in this regard would be how precarious work, precarious at least in part because it entails being in a waiting room, inflicts on the subject position of migrant workers.

Conclusion

While this review chapter did not offer a clear-cut listing of research perspectives, their associated literatures and their main criticisms, at least not in a very well structured manner, for the sake of clarity, an attempt to summarize these will be made in this final section. Surely, there is no dominant perspective on the relationship between borders and labour migration, not least due to the fact that views on what exactly a border is have not been fleshed out in traditions pertinent to academic disciplines as diverse as legal studies, economics, geopolitics, political economy, and migration studies. It can be ascertained, though, that some perspectives have had more influence than others in specific realms of political life. Whereas the EU's neoliberal market ideology relies in no small part on the premises of neoclassical economic theory, political economic accounts of work in the new capitalism continue to attract the political Left, activists included.

Exceptions aside, many a key publication within the neoclassical or marginalist perspective pictures issues of mobility and migration in an abstracted fashion, stripped of its social meaning (Gidwani and Sivaramanakrishnan 2003). Flowing from the discussion on how the modern state, and hence most if not all EU Member States have found themselves trapped in contradictory desires to open and close borders (the liberal paradox), it was shown that, at least according to the common interpretation by border scholars, to a majority of marginalists a border is a barrier to mobility. Indeed, borders as institutional and corporeal barriers can be challenged by rational action, another premise held in this perspective, albeit for many migrants at the peril of losing their invested money, personal freedom or even their lives. The thematic literature reviewed subsequently discusses how the EU and its Member States, in their contemporary geopolitical manifestations extending beyond state borders proper, aim to retain control over who enters and leaves their spheres of jurisdiction at many borders sites and spaces. The telling names given to these sites and spaces evince that notions of border, boundary and frontier are powerful metaphors, lastingly impressing the exclusionary nature of spatial containment and alternative modes of control in the memory of its readership.

Having reviewed these conceptualizations from a geopolitical perspective, the attention turned to the political economy of borders in the EU. Specifically, it turned to the pleas that have been made to rethink *the more fundamental labour market dynamics* underpinning the expectations that the capacities of state migration control are *outstripped* or that its *current limits* are in sight (EC 2004b; Favell 2009; Favell and Hansen 2002, 597; Jordan and Düvell 2003; Peixoto 2002). Within this neo-Marxist perspective, reflections on migrant selectivity and illegal migration are approached from the stance that non-state demand actors, hence the market, matter in steering these processes. As power instruments, borders may discursively and materially produce people as illegal migrants, labouring under substandard conditions or being hunted down by innovations in biotechnology (Mitchell 2001; Sassen 1996).

Partly Marxist-inspired, but also influenced by transnational migration studies, a perspective with a strong emphasis on the sustainable cross-border ties between migrants and hometown actors in different places, is the literature that offers a reconsideration of the (state) border. Importantly, this literature reminds us that the border is first and foremost an ontological category, yet a category that can be unsettled by transnational action as well as theoretical exercise, reshaping it as a space of possibility (Mitchell 1997).

With these perspectives having passed in review, perhaps a final task for the author of this review piece is to formulate a challenge for border researchers interested in labour migration. While this challenge is certainly multifaceted, one interesting issue would be to scrutinize to what extent the perspectives and their associated literatures (reading borders as barriers, power instruments and performative spaces, and emphasizing states, markets, agency, and subjectivity) speak to one another. Although at this point I must restate that the listing offered is contingent upon the context within which its author has been trained as a border researcher, the bordered labour pool might be graspable enough a physical and analytical space to start from. The queue, the waiting line in the waiting space, may prove a surprisingly functional bordering tactic contributing to the control of economic and security risks felt by the state, and to the elimination of business risks. This, and what this may mean for labour migrants, however, is not a premise but an open question. Interdisciplinary by definition, border researchers, I feel, should not hesitate to be at the forefront of this interrogation.

References

Amato, G. (2002), 'The Long Term Implications of a New EU External Border', in Anderson, M. and Apap, J. (eds.), *Police and Justice Cooperation and the New European Borders* (The Hague: Kluwer), 1-9.

Anderson, M. and Bort, E. (2001), *The Frontiers of the European Union* (Basingstoke: Palgrave).

Bigo, D. (2008), 'EU Policy Cooperation: National Sovereignty framed by European Security?', in Guild, E. and Geyer, F. (eds.), *Security versus Justice?* (Aldershot: Ashgate), 91-108.

Bigo, D. (2005), 'Frontier Controls in the European Union: Who is in Control?', in Bigo, D. and Guild, E. (eds.), *Controlling Frontiers: Free Movement into and within Europe* (Aldershot: Ashgate), 49-99.

Bigo, D. (2001), 'Migration and Security', in Guiraudon, V. and Joppke, C. (eds.), *Controlling a New Migration World* (London: Routledge), 121-149.

Bigo, D. (1998), 'Frontiers and Security in the European Union: The Illusion of Migration Control', in Anderson, M. and Bort, E. (eds.), *The Frontiers of Europe* (London: Pinter), 148-164.

Bigo, D. and Guild, E. (2005), 'Introduction: Policing in the Name of Freedom', in Bigo, D. and Guild, E. (eds.), *Controlling Frontiers: Free Movement into and within Europe* (Aldershot: Ashgate), 1-13.

Borjas, G. (1989), 'Economic Theory and International Migration', *International Migration Review* 23:3, 457-85.

Brown, D. (2002), 'Storming the Fortress: The External Border Regime in an Enlarged Europe', in Ingham, H. and Ingham, M. (eds.), *EU Expansion to the East* (Cheltenham: Edward Elgar), 89-109.

Castles, S. (2006), 'Guestworkers in Europe: A Resurrection?', *International Migration Review* 40(4): 741-66.

Christiansen, T. and Jørgensen, K. (2000), 'Transnational Governance "Above" and "Below" the State: The Changing Nature of Borders in the New Europe', *Regional & Federal Studies*, 10(2): 62-77.

Christiansen, T., Petito, F. and Tonra, B. (2000), 'Fuzzy Politics around Fuzzy Borders: The European Union's "Near Abroad"', *Cooperation and Conflict* 35:4, 389-415.

Comaroff, J. and Comaroff, J. (2002), 'Alien-Nation: Zombies, Immigrants, and Millennial Capitalism', *The South Atlantic Quarterly* 101:4, 779-805.

Cresswell, T. (2006), 'The Right to Mobility: The Production of Mobility in the Courtroom', *Antipode* 38:4, 735-54.

Crowley, J. (2005), 'Where Does the State Actually Start? The Contemporary Governance of Work and Migration', in Bigo, D. and Guild, E. (eds.), *Controlling Frontiers: Free Movement into and within Europe* (Aldershot: Ashgate), 140-60.

Den Boer, M. (2002), 'To What Extent Can There Be Flexibility in the Application of Schengen in the New Member States?', in Anderson, M. and Apap, J. (eds.), *Police and Justice Cooperation and the New European Borders* (The Hague: Kluwer), 139-61.

Den Boer, M. (1995), 'Moving between Bogus and Bona Fide: The Policing of Inclusion and Exclusion in Europe', in Miles, R. and Thränhardt, D. (eds.), *Migration and European Integration* (London: Pinter), 92-111.

Douven, C., Essers, G., Houwerzijl, M. and Smits, J. (2006), *De Grensoverschrijdende Werknemer* (The Hague: Sdu Uitgevers).

European Commission (2004a), *Proposal for a Directive of the European Parliament and of the Council on Services in the Internal Market* (Brussels).

European Commission (2004b), *Study on the Links between Legal and Illegal Migration* (Brussels).

European Commission (2003), *Wider Europe - Neighbourhood: A New Framework for Relations with our Eastern and Southern Neighbours* (Brussels).

Faist, T. (2000), *The Volume and Dynamics of International Migration and Transnational Social Spaces* (Oxford: Oxford University Press).

Favell, A. (2009), 'Immigration, Migration and Free Movement in the Making of Europe', in Checkel, J. and Katzenstein, P. (eds.), *European Identity* (Cambridge: Cambridge University Press), 167-91.

Favell, A. and Hansen, R. (2002), 'Markets against Politics: Migration, EU Enlargement and the Idea of Europe', *Journal of Ethnic and Migration Studies* 28:4, 581-601.

Foucault, M. (1991), 'Governmentality', in Burchell, G., Gordon, C. and Miller, P. (eds.), *The Foucault Effect: Studies in Governmentality* (London: Harvester Wheatsheaf), 87-104.

Foucher, M. (1998), 'The Geopolitics of European Frontiers', in Anderson, M. and Bort, E. (eds.), *The Frontiers of Europe* (London: Pinter), 235-50.

Gidwani, V. and Sivaramakrishnan, K. (2003), 'Circular Migration and the Spaces of Cultural Assertion', *Annals of the Association of American Geographers* 93:1, 186-213.

Guarzino, L. (2003), 'The Economics of Transnational Living', *International Migration Review* 37:3, 666-99.

Guild, E. (2005a), 'The Legal Framework: Who is Entitled to Move?', in Bigo, D. and Guild, E. (eds.), *Controlling Frontiers: Free Movement into and within Europe* (Aldershot: Ashgate), 14-48.

Guild, E. (2005b), 'Who is Entitled to Work and Who is in Charge? Understanding the Legal Framework of European Labour Migration', in Bigo, D. and Guild, E. (eds.), *Controlling Frontiers: Free Movement into and within Europe* (Aldershot: Ashgate), 100-139.

Guild, E. and Bigo, D. (2002), 'The Legal Mechanisms: Collectively Specifying the Individual: The Schengen Border System and Enlargement', in Anderson, M. and Apap, J. (eds.), *Police and Justice Cooperation and the New European Borders* (The Hague: Kluwer), 121-38.

Guiraudon, V. (2001), 'De-Nationalizing Control: Analyzing State Responses to Constraints on Migration Control', in Guiraudon, V. and Joppke, C. (eds.), *Controlling a New Migration World* (London: Routledge), 31-64.

Guiraudon, V. (2000), 'European Integration and Migration Policy: Vertical Policy-Making as Venue Shopping', *Journal of Common Market Studies* 38:2, 251-71.

Hollifield, J. (2004), 'The Emerging Migration State', *International Migration Review* 38:3, 885-912.

Huysmans, J. (2000), 'The European Union and the Securitization of Migration', *Journal of Common Market Studies* 38:5, 751-77.

Huysmans, J. (1995), 'Migrants as a Security Problem: Dangers of "Securitizing Societal Issues"', in Miles, R. and Thränhardt, D. (eds.), *Migration and European Integration* (London: Pinter), 53-72.

Jileva, E. (2002), 'Visa and Free Movement of Labour: The Uneven Imposition of the EU *Acquis* on the Accession States', *Journal of Ethnic and Migration Studies* 28:4, 683-700.

Jordan, B. and Düvell, F. (2003), *Migration: The Boundaries of Equality and Justice* (Cambridge: Polity Press).

Jordan, B., Stråth, B. and Triandafyllidou, A. (2003a), 'Contextualising Immigration Policy Implementation in Europe', *Journal of Ethnic and Migration Studies* 29:2, 195-224.

Jordan, B., Stråth, B. and Triandafyllidou, A. (2003b), 'Comparing Cultures of Discretion', *Journal of Ethnic and Migration Studies* 29:2, 373-95.

Kostakopoulou, T. (2000), 'The "Protective Union": Change and Continuity in Migration Law and Policy in Post-Amsterdam Europe', *Journal of Common Market Studies* 38:3, 497-518.

Kraler, A. and Parnreiter, C. (2005), 'Migration Theoretisieren', *Prokla* 35:3, 327-44.

Lahav, G. (2000), 'The Rise of Nonstate Actors in Migration Regulation in the United States and Europe: Changing the Gatekeepers or Bringing Back the State?', in Foner, N., Rumbaut, R. and Gold, S. (eds.), *Immigration Research for a New Century* (New York: Russel Sage Foundations), 215-41.

Lahav, G. and Guiraudon, V. (2006), 'Actors and Venues in Immigration Control: Closing the Gap between Political Demands and Policy Outcomes', *West European Politics* 29:2, 201-26.

Massey, D., Arango, J., Hugo, G., Kouaouci, A., Pellegrino, A. and Taylor, E. (1993), 'Theories of International Migration: A Review and Appraisal', *Population and Development Review* 19:3, 431-66.

Menz, G. (2002), 'Patterns in EU Labour Immigration Policy: National Initiatives and European Responses', *Journal of Ethnic and Migration Studies* 28:4, 723-42.

Mitchell, D. (2001), 'The Devil's Arm: Points of Passage, Networks of Violence, and the California Agricultural Landscape', *New Formations* 43, 44-86.

Mitchell, K. (1997), 'Transnational Discourse: Bringing Geography Back in', *Antipode* 29:2, 101-14.

Mitsilegas, V. (2002), 'The Implementation of the EU *Acquis* on Illegal Immigration by the Candidate Countries of Central and Eastern Europe: Challenges and Contradictions', *Journal of Ethnic and Migration Studies* 28:4, 665-82.

Pastore, F. (2002), 'The Asymmetrical Fortress: The Problem of Relations between Internal and External Security Policies in the European Union', in Anderson, M. and Apap, J. (eds.), *Police and Justice Cooperation and the New European Borders* (The Hague: Kluwer), 59-80.

Peixoto, J. (2002), 'Strong Market, Weak State: The Case of Recent Foreign Immigration in Portugal', *Journal of Ethnic and Migration Studies* 28:3, 483-97.

Pijpers, R. and van der Velde, M. (2007), 'Mobility across Borders: Contextualizing Local Strategies to Circumvent Visa and Wok Permit Requirements', *International Journal of Urban and Regional Research* 31:4, 819-35.

Puntscher Riekmann, S. (2008), 'Security, Freedom and Accountability: Europol and Frontex', in Guild, E. and Geyer, F. (eds.), *Security versus Justice?* (Aldershot: Ashgate), 19-34.

Pries, L. (2001), 'The Disruption of Social and Geographical Space: Mexican-US Migration and the Emergence of Transnational Social Spaces', *International Sociology* 16:1, 55-74.

Samers, M. (2004), 'An Emerging Geopolitics of "Illegal" Immigration in the European Union', *European Journal of Migration and Law* 6, 27-45.

Samers, M. (2003), 'Invisible Capitalism: Political Economy and the Regulation of Undocumented Migration in France', *Economy and Society* 32:4, 555-83.

Sassen, S. (1996), *Losing Control? Sovereignty in an Age of Globalisation* (New York: Columbia University Press).

Sassen, S. (1988), *The Mobility of Labor and Capital: A Study in International Investment and Labor Flow* (Cambridge: Cambridge University Press).

Saybasili, N. (2004), 'Crossing Borders'. *paper presented at the ABS 2004 European Conference* (Graz: University of Graz).

Silvey, R. (2004), 'Power, Difference and Mobility: Feminist Advances in Migration Studies', *Progress in Human Geography* 28:4, 490-506.

Silvey, R. and Lawson, V. (1999), 'Placing the Migrant', *Annals of the Association of American Geographers* 89:1, 121-32.

Thränhardt, D. and Miles, R. (1995), 'Introduction: European Integration, Migration and Processes of Inclusion and Exclusion', in Miles, R. and Thränhardt, D. (eds.), *Migration and European Integration* (London: Pinter), 1-12.

van Houtum, H. (2000), 'An Overview of European Geographical Research on Borders and Border Regions', *Journal of Borderlands Studies* 15:1, 57-83.

Verstraete, G. (2001), 'Technological Frontiers and the Politics of Mobilities', *New Formations* 43, 26-43.

Waldinger, R. and Fitzgerald, D. (2004), 'Transnationalism in Question', *American Journal of Sociology* 109:5, 1177-95.

Walters, W. (2004), 'The Frontiers of the European Union: A Geostrategic Perspective', *Geopolitics* 9:3, 674-98.

Walters, W. (2002), 'Mapping Schengenland: Denaturalizing the Border', *Environment and Planning D: Society and Space* 20:5, 561-80.

Walters, W. and Haahr, J. (2005), *Governing Europe: Discourse, Governmentality and European Integration* (London: Routledge).

Zielonka, J. (2008), 'Europe as a Global Actor: Empire by Example?', *International Affairs* 84:3, 471-84.

Zielonka, J. (2006), *Europe as Empire: The Nature of the Enlarged European Union* (Oxford: Oxford University Press).

Zielonka, J. (2001), 'How New Enlarged Borders will Reshape the European Union', *Journal of Common Market Studies* 39:3, 507-36.

Zolberg, A. (2003), 'The Archaeology of "Remote Control"', in Fahrmeir, A., Faron, O. and Weil, P. (eds.), *Migration Control in the North Atlantic World. The Evolution of State Practices in Europe and the United States from the French Revolution to the Inter-War Period* (New York: Bergahn Books), 195-222.

A Cross-boundary Mega City-region in China under 'Two Systems': Multi-level Governance in the Greater Pearl River Delta

Chun Yang

Introduction

The contingent effects of globalization, regionalization and the end of the Cold War have brought about the proliferation of cross-border regions (CBRs), that is territorial units that include contiguous national or subnational units from two or more nation states (Perkmann and Sum 2002). National borders and the associated border regions seem to be deriving new meanings and presenting new opportunities. There are virtually no local or regional authorities in border areas that are not somehow involved in cross-border cooperation initiatives with their counterparts. Since 1990, there has been witnessed a renewed interest in boundaries within a number of different academic fields (Newman and Paasi 1998). However, more empirical case studies in different parts of the world would be helpful for setting up a useful framework for research on borders and cross-border regions (Blatter 2004; Scott 1999; Sidaway et al. 2005).

In comparison with substantial literature on cross-border regions that have primarily concentrated in Europe and North America on supranational levels, the Greater Pearl River Delta region in China provides a salient case of a cross-border[1]

---

1   As Anderson and O'Dowd (1999) have pointed out, terms for borders, boundaries, and frontiers exist in all languages to signify the limits of social groups, but their connotations differ widely from culture to culture. The words 'frontier' and 'border' in English are normally used for international demarcations (though 'border' needs not necessarily have this connotation), while the word 'boundary' is rarely if ever used for

city-region under 'two systems' (socialist and capitalist systems respectively) in a single sovereign country. Since China's Opening and Reform initiated in the late 1970s, the Pearl River Delta (PRD)[2] under the jurisdiction of Guangdong Province, Hong Kong and Macao, the two former British and Portugal colonies have been inextricably integrated into a subnational cross-boundary region, the so-called 'Greater PRD'. It is worthwhile investigating the dynamics, nature and significance of the boundary and the cross-boundary region of the Greater PRD which has demonstrated distinctive characteristics under the unique institutional framework of 'one country two systems' (OCTS),[3] compared with cases in other parts of the world (Yang 2004 and 2006a). This study considers the PRD, rather than Mainland China as a whole, for investigating the evolution of the cross-border region under OCTS. This is because Hong Kong's social-economic interaction with Mainland China has been mainly concentrated in the PRD, which is Hong Kong's immediate geographical and economic hinterland. Since the mid-1990s, especially after Hong Kong's return to Chinese rule and the Asian Financial Crisis in 1997, it is being gradually recognized by the both sides of the boundary that the economic fortunes of Hong Kong and the PRD are inextricably linked in the long run. Well-coordinated regional integration and its implications for enhancing the

---

a line of international demarcation (though in an interesting exception, the Kowloon street marking the northern border of the British colony of Hong Kong in 1860 was called Boundary Street). The term 'border' (*bianjing*), widely used before 1997 to denote the frontier between Hong Kong and Guangdong Province, has been replaced by 'boundary' (*bianjie*) in official documents since Hong Kong's return to Chinese rule, perhaps because the former term was felt to imply an international frontier. I therefore use the terms 'border' and 'boundary' respectively to reflect pre-1997 and post-1997 conditions in this study.

2   The area I have labelled 'the Pearl River Delta' for brevity's sake in this chapter is officially known as the Pearl River Delta Economic Zone (Zhujiang Sanjiaozhou Jingji Qu). The Zone was designated by the Guangdong Provincial Government in October 1994 (Guangdong Provincial Planning Committee and Office for the Planning of the Pearl River Delta Economic Region 1996). In administrative terms, the PRD includes two vice-provincial level cities (Guangzhou and Shenzhen), seven prefecture-level cities (Zhuhai, Foshan, Jiangmen, Zhongshan, Dongguan, Huizhou and Zhaoqing), nine county-level cities (Zengcheng, Conghua, Huiyang, Taishan, Kaiping, Enping, Heshan, Gaoyao and Sihui), two counties (Huidong and Boluo), and a number of city districts (see Figure 21.1).

3   'One country, two systems' is originally proposed by Deng Xiaoping, then Paramount Leader of the People's Republic of China (PRC), for the reunification of China during the early 1980s. In 1984, Deng Xiaoping proposed to apply the principle to Hong Kong in the negotiation with the British Prime Minister, Margaret Thatcher over the future of Hong Kong when the lease of the New Territories (including New Kowloon) of Hong Kong to the United Kingdom was to expire in 1997. The same principle was proposed in talks with Portugal about Macao. The principle is that, upon reunification, despite the practice of 'socialism' in Mainland China, both Hong Kong and Macao, which were colonies of the UK and Portugal respectively, can retain their established system under a high degree of autonomy for at least 50 years after reunification.

long-term competitiveness of the region as a whole is firmly on the policy agendas of the governments both of Guangdong Province and the Hong Kong Special Administrative Region (HKSAR)[4] (Guangdong Provincial Governmental Report 2003; HKSAR Chief Executive's Policy Address 2003). This chapter seeks to enrich the literature of CBRs through the unique case of the PRD-Hong Kong region, but will also deepen the empirical knowledge and raise questions which have policy implications for the governments concerned.

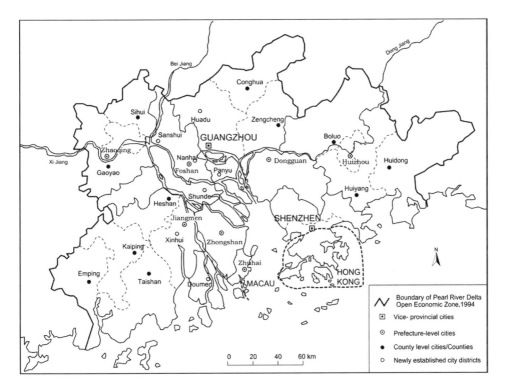

Figure 21.1 Administrative Boundary of the Greater Pearl River Delta, China

Source: ©: C. Yang.

---

4   The Special Administrative Region (SAR) of Hong Kong was formally established on 1 July 1997, immediately after the People's Republic of China (PRC) assumed the sovereignty over Hong Kong. According to Chapter 1, Article 5 of the Hong Kong Basic Law, the constitutional document of the Hong Kong SAR reads, 'the socialist system and policies shall not be practiced in the Hong Kong Special Administrative Region, and the previous capitalist system and way of life shall remain unchanged for 50 years'.

Cross-border regions in the context of globalization and regionalization

So far, cross-border regions (CBRs) have been emerging in very different geographical and geopolitical settings, most prominently within Europe, North America, and recently Southeast Asia. As a consequence, most studies on CBRs have mainly concentrated on supranational paradigms or national-level analyses of specific regional groupings, such as the European Union (EU) (Brenner 1999; Telo' 2001), where typical studies have focused on bilateral cooperation, such as developments in the border regions between Germany and Poland (Krätke 2001), Finland and Russia (Paasi 1999), and UK-France cross-border cooperation (Church and Reid 1996). Outside Europe, studies have focused on the North American Free Trade Area (NAFTA) and the US-Mexico border region (Herzog 1991; Weaver 2001), and the Growth Triangles in Southeast Asia among Malaysia, Indonesia and Singapore (Grundy-Warr et al. 1999; Sidaway et al. 2005).

However, it is argued that the conventional national-based perspectives of CBRs are scarcely applicable in the Chinese context (Breslin 2000). More specifically, in terms of the cross-border regional development between Mainland China and Hong Kong, the difference has tended to be more significant since Hong Kong's transition into a Special Administrative Region (SAR) under the jurisdiction of China in 1997. In order to maintain the prosperity and stability of Hong Kong, upon China's resumption of the exercise of sovereignty over Hong Kong, the HKSAR has been established under the principle of OCTS in 1997. OCTS means literally that the socialist system and policies shall not be practiced in HKSAR and that its previous system and way of life shall remain unchanged for 50 years (The Basic Law of the HKSAR of the People's Republic of China 2003, Article 5). As the unprecedented OCTS principle has only been implemented since 1997, little has been written on the changes of the cross-boundary interaction between Mainland China and Hong Kong in general, and how the unique framework of OCTS has influenced the cross-boundary region evolving between the Pearl River Delta and Hong Kong in particular. This chapter is an attempt to update existing literature on the transformation of the cross-boundary region of the Greater PRD under the OCTS over the past decade and supplement empirical literature on cross-border regions in the world.

Globalization has brought with it a change in the scales at which strategic economic and political processes territorialize. Global cities and global city-regions have emerged as major new scales in this dynamic of territorialization (Sassen 2001). In a world characterized by simultaneous trends towards globalization and regionalization, distinctive subnational social formations in which local characters and dynamics are undergoing major transformations have occurred in global city-regions. As 'a new scale of urban organization' both in terms of its polynucleated but integrated internal structure and its privileged position within far-flung global networks of commercial, social and cultural transactions (Hall 2001), the global city-regions are coming to function as the basic motors of the global economy (Scott

2001). Although rooted in the concept of 'world cities' (Friedmann and Wolff 1982; Hall 1966), and 'global cities' (Sassen 1991), city-regions are more appropriate units or variables of local social organization in the context of the global economy. A global city-region can be defined to comprise any major metropolitan area, or contiguous set of metropolitan areas, together with a surrounding hinterland – itself a locus of scattered urban settlements – whose internal economic and political affairs are intricately bound up with far-flung and intensifying extranational relationships (Scott 2001). A city-region is characterized by the spatial extent of closely linked economic activity, rather than the 'city', or jurisdictional definition of the settlement. Most city regions contain dozens, hundreds or even thousands of political subdivisions. Many of the problems, which settlements face, call for region-wide policies and coordinated action across many jurisdictions. At least eleven global city-regions have been identified by Simmonds and Hack (2000), including Bangkok, Boston, Madrid, Randstad, San Diego, Santiago, Sao Paulo, Seattle, Taipei, Tokyo, and West Midlands.

Along with these dynamic transformations, some fundamental changes have been occurring. Firstly, a huge and growing amount of economic activities emerge in the form of cross-border relationships, including migration streams, foreign direct investment by multinationals, and monetary flows. Secondly, multinational blocs such as the EU, NAFTA, South American Common Market (MERCOSUR), Association of South-East Asian Nations (ASEAN), and many others have proliferated. Thirdly, sovereign states and national economies remain prominent, indeed dominant elements of the global landscape, but they are clearly undergoing many significant changes. Some of the regulatory functions formerly carried out by the central state have been drifting to higher levels of spatial resolution, while other functions have been drifting downward. Fourthly, there has been a resurgence of region-based forms of economic and political organizations, with the most overt expression being the formation of large city-regions. In consequence, the process of worldwide economic integration and accelerated urban growth make traditional planning and policy strategies in these regions increasingly problematic, while more fitting approaches remain at a largely experimental stage (Brenner 1998; Scott et al. 2001).

This chapter attempts to examine the nature and changing patterns of the PRD-Hong Kong cross-boundary region over the past two decades, with particular emphasis on the post-1997 socio-economic integration after Hong Kong returned to China's sovereignty. This case provides an interesting example of microregionalism and sub-national city-regions, with regard to how two different socio-economic-political systems are applied within the same country, exemplifying the OCTS principle applied by the Chinese government to the Hong Kong and Macao SARs.

Emergence and transformation of the cross-boundary integrated region in the Greater Pearl River Delta

Before 1978, Mainland China was closed to the outside world and there was hardly any cross-border development between Hong Kong and the Mainland. The opening and reform policy implemented in China since 1978 brought about a new mechanism for cross-border interaction particularly between Hong Kong and the PRD, which was primarily driven by the transplantation of manufacturing activities from the former to the latter. According to a survey conducted by the Federation of HK Industries, 10.3 million workers were employed in 53,300 manufacturing operations of HK-based companies in the Mainland by the end of 2001 (FHKI 2003). HK-PRD integration was characterized by a locally driven bottom-up mechanism in which initiatives are made primarily by entrepreneurs from Hong Kong and local governments of the PRD, although the central state is responsible for making the necessary institutional changes (Lin 2003; Shen 2003). The governments on both sides of the border were not actively involved in the cross-border interaction. Because of Hong Kong's status as a former British colony, official communications related to cross-border issues were conducted through diplomatic relations between the two sovereign countries, namely China and the United Kingdom. The situation has changed since 1997, with increasing official communications between the HKSAR, Guangdong Provincial and the central governments.

Since 1997, the cross-boundary relationship has decentralized and shifted from the diplomatic relations between China and the United Kingdom to two subnational governments: the HKSAR and Guangdong Provincial governments. Generally speaking, the HKSAR government has been much more proactive in pursuing cross-boundary cooperation compared with the pre-1997 period (Cheung 2002). The Guangdong-HK Cooperation Joint Conference (GDHKCJC) was established to coordinate issues such as infrastructure, environmental regulation, and flows of passengers and freight across the boundary. The GDHKCJC has considered such ad hoc issues as the selective expansion of border control point operations, the improvement of air and water quality, and an increase in the quota of Mainland visitors permitted to enter Hong Kong. Unfortunately, strategic vision and region-wide planning to further economic integration have not been discussed at GDHKCJC.

With China's resumption of sovereignty over Hong Kong, there have been many proposals made by the Mainland to forge closer economic relations between the two sides. When the economy was prosperous, the idea was not particularly attractive to the people and senior civil officials of Hong Kong, who feared that a blurring of their international identity would occur with the colony's further integration into the Mainland. Faced with a very worrying economic downturn since the early 2000s, however, many Hong Kong people are now less hesitating and willing to embrace the idea. On the other hand, China's accession to the WTO, the continuous growth of the Mainland domestic market, and the upsurge of the Shanghai-centred Yangtze River Delta will open up new opportunities for Hong Kong. There is also an anxiety that Hong Kong's middleman role will inevitably diminish given that China's WTO entry and increasingly globalized outlook of the Chinese economy. In order to better position Hong Kong for the change and in anticipation of the increasing competition from the Yangtze River Delta and other neighbouring competitors, many businessmen and citizens feel that Hong Kong must embark on strategic cooperation with the PRD. The outbreak of the severe acute respiratory syndrome (SARS) in early 2003 highlighted the fact that Hong Kong and the PRD are inextricably linked. Following China's accession to the WTO in December 2001, Hong Kong's business sector soon recognized the importance of closer economic cooperation with the Mainland. The Hong Kong General Chamber of Commerce proposed in June 2000 a 'free trade agreement area' with the Mainland in June 2000. The former Chief Executive of the HKSAR government, Tung Chee-hua, submitted the proposal to the Central government concerning closer economic and trade relations. The proposal was later changed to the Closer Economic Partnership Arrangement (CEPA), which was considered to be more suitable given that the Mainland and Hong Kong are independent customs territories and WTO members under the OCTS principle. After 18 months of consultation, the agreement was concluded and signed on 29 June 2003, and came into force on January 2004.

CEPA consists of three parts, that is trade in goods, trade in services, and trade and investment facilitation. The potentially huge market of the Mainland will open in advance of all foreign investors to HK investors with lower entrance thresholds than China's commitments to the WTO. In terms of trade in goods, about 90 per cent of HK domestic exports to the Mainland have enjoyed zero tariffs from January 2004. The annual savings in tariffs are estimated to be HK$750 million (HKTDC 2003). In terms of trade in services, the package is 'WTO-plus', because the concessions go beyond China's WTO commitments. HK businesses will have priority in accessing the Mainland market with lower thresholds, especially a total of eighteen service sectors including banks, insurance, legal services, retailing, and professional services. Taking the banking sector as an example, under CEPA, HK banks will be allowed to open a branch on the Mainland if they have total assets of USD 6 billion or more, significantly lower than the entrance requirement under WTO commitments of total assets over USD 20 billion. In general, CEPA's impact on services is likely to be greater than on manufacturing. This is particularly true when services, accounting for only 34 per cent of China's GDP and 45 per cent of the PRD's GDP, have become a constraint on the country's economic development. Services already contribute 87 per cent to the Hong Kong domestic economy, and will therefore be able to contribute more to the modernization of the country under CEPA. Since June 2003, there are four stages of further improvements of CEPA.

Notably, while the PRD's development was heavily reliant on Hong Kong for investment, trade, and capital, the economy of Hong Kong has become increasingly dependent on the Mainland Chinese visitors, goods, and markets to maintain its status as an international logistics and financial centre. Under CEPA, moreover, the integrated Hong Kong-PRD region is likely to become oriented more inwardly towards the Mainland market than it was oriented outwardly towards foreign exports during the past two decades. The CEPA agreement marked a new milestone in the relationship and will have a fundamental impact on the further economic integration of the Mainland, especially the PRD and Hong Kong. The functional regional integration between the PRD and Hong Kong spontaneously initiated by both entrepreneurs and local governments has been transforming into an institution-based integration via the CEPA (Yang 2004). Obviously, the conclusion of the CEPA agreement represents a pioneering intervention by the central government to coordinate cross-border economic integration more directly. The establishment of the CEPA has marked a milestone of the paradigmatic transition of the cross-border integration between the PRD and Hong Kong (and Macao as well) from the previous informal spontaneous integration driven by market forces, the private sector, and lower-level PRD governments to an institution-based integration driven by the governments.

Multi-level governance in the Greater Pearl River Delta under the 'one country, two systems' framework

While the inter-governmental communication has become more intensive and cross-border integration has turned to institutionalization, the relationship between the PRD and HK has been changing from closer cooperation to fierce competition. The usually cited examples of keen competition are the duplication of infrastructure construction, especially ports and airports. Within the diameter of 100 kilometres, there are five international airports and a similar number of container ports, all vying for the trade of goods in the PRD. In addition, the trinity of the regional centre cities, that is HK, GZ (Guangzhou) and SZ (Shenzhen) are struggling for the region's economic centre or the 'dragon head' in Chinese (Yang 2005a and 2008). HK is clearly the leading metropolitan core for the Greater PRD, and dominates the region's GDP of over 50 per cent. Yet due to the OCTS framework, HK has been mostly isolated from the PRD's regional planning and national planning. In the recent five-year plan and the regional planning of the PRD, both Guangzhou and Shenzhen have been designated as the regional centres. Another case is, the National Aviation Bureau designated three national aviation centres, that is Beijing, Shanghai and Guangzhou, while HK has not yet been taken into consideration under the OCTS. After two decades of rapid growth, Guangdong province and cities of the PRD came to recognize their growing economic strength and had their own plans. They have tended to be reluctant admitting HK as the 'economic engine' in the region. In the past years, Guangdong and Guangzhou municipal governments have made a great deal of efforts, for example the expansion of city proper area of Guangzhou municipality, development of the automobile industry and the Nanasha port in Panyu in southern Guangzhou, to resurrect Guangzhou's former position as the 'dragon head' (that is the leading city of the region) of the PRD and the entire southern China.

Along with the institutionalization of the integration mechanism, the pattern of cross-border governance has been under transformation, in which the central, HKSAR, Guangdong provincial, and the local government of PRD have interacted with each other. It is similar to the perspective of the multi-level governance (MLG), originated in the EU, where decision-making is shared by actors at different levels, rather than monopolized by state executives. Under the unique framework of OCTS, the MLG pattern in the HK-PRD case has demonstrated some distinct characteristics. The PRD is a region in the concept of economic geography, rather than an entity as an administrative region. The same is the Greater PRD. There is no regional institution directly undertaking the coordination of the region's development and planning (Yang 2005a and 2006a). In the PRD, only the Guangdong provincial government is in charge of cross-boundary regional affairs. No governmental communication mechanism with Hong Kong has been established even after 1997. There exists a dilemma, that is local governments of the PRD have established close contacts with entrepreneurs from Hong Kong since the late 1970s when China initiated Opening and Reform, while there is a lack of official relationships with the HKSAR government. Shen (2003 and 2004) argued that the political change, that is the return of Hong Kong to China in 1997 did not alter the demographic-economic linkages between Mainland China and Hong Kong during 1997-2001 significantly as such connections were well-established during the period of 1978-1997.

Notably, the Greater PRD region is characterized by multiple administrations (One Region, Multiple Levels of Administrations). In terms of administration in the Greater PRD, HK and Macao as two SAR, are similar to a province or a centrally-governed municipality, while directly administered by the Central Government under the umbrella of OCTS. The PRD under the jurisdiction of Guangdong provincial government includes two vice-provincial municipalities (Guangzhou and Shenzhen), seven prefecture-level municipalities, nine county-level cities and two counties. In addition, there are 30 city districts ranked the same administrative level. Although the PRD is theoretically under the control of the Guangdong provincial government, regional cooperation and coordination have proven more difficult than expected, owing to the multiple levels of local governments with their individual development goals and strategies. Such diversified administrative jurisdictions and multiple governing bodies have potentially complicated the joint efforts for coordinated regional policies and governing. This study argues that a pattern of MLG, which originates in the EU and its member states to elucidate the dispersion of decision-making across various levels of governments ranging from supranational, national to sub-national levels in the process of regional integration, has been evolving in the Greater PRD (Yang 2005a and 2006a).

Although social and economic interaction between the PRD and Hong Kong has become more intensive, the boundary between Shenzhen and Hong Kong continues to resemble the international border it was before 1997 (Cheung 2002). The physical landscape, management, operation and planning of the boundary area remain much as they were before Hong Kong's return to Chinese rule. Although substantial urban development has taken place on the Shenzhen side of the boundary, a security zone immediately to the south of the boundary on the Hong Kong side is still maintained as a 'frontier closed area'. Only limited and authorized access is permitted to this area, just as under British rule (Shiu and Yang 2002). At present, there are four land control points along the boundary between Hong Kong and Shenzhen: Huanggang/Lok Ma Chau, Lo Wu, Man Kam To, and Sha Tau Kok. Lo Wu is the northernmost Kowloon-Canton Railway (KCR) station in Hong Kong, and the Lo Wu control point serves only train-bound cross-boundary passengers. These account for more than 85 per cent of cross-boundary passengers. The other three crossing points handle cargo and passenger vehicles, and account for the remaining 15 per cent of cross-boundary passengers. Because the vast majority of cross-boundary passengers choose to travel by rail and pass through Lo Wu, the railway station is nearly always congested. There are particularly long queues for customs formalities at weekends and public holidays. While most international border crossings are open 24 hours a day, the Hong Kong-Shenzhen boundary crossings only operate between certain set hours, and are open daily between 15 and 18 hours only (Table 21.1). Although the hours of operation have been extended several times after the Hong Kong-Guangdong Joint Conference, they still fall far short of 24-hour operation.

Congestion of passengers and vehicles is frequent at the control points for custom formalities, especially at the weekend and on public holidays. According to FHKI (2003), 64 per cent of surveyed companies experienced delays, which incurred financial loss while transporting goods across the land boundary in 2001.[5] The median value of annual financial loss reached HKD 100,000. Under such circumstances, Guangdong, especially the Shenzhen municipal government, proposed to extend the operation and further implement 24-hour operation on the eve of Hong Kong's return to the Mainland and in the early 2000s (Guangdong Provincial Development Research Centre 1999; Singtao Daily 2001). It did not receive a prompt and positive response from the HKSAR government, partly because of differences of opinion within Hong Kong. The issue has been put on the agenda of the major discussion topic on the GDHKCJC.

However, there has not been any consensus between Hong Kong and Guangdong, except for several expansions of the operating hours at selective boundary crossings during the past few years. In contrast to the positive attitudes of the Guangdong Provincial and Shenzhen municipal governments, the HKSAR government worries that the 24-hour operation will bring about changes in property values and in the wholesale and retail, food and drink, entertainment, transport, import and export, professional services, and logistics industries. Moreover, it may trigger a series of problems involving employment, family relationships, law and order and juvenile delinquency and so on (OCTSRI 2002). Hence, the HKSAR government declared that the 24-hour operation is a long-term target (HKSAR government press release, 24 October 2001). In recognition of the different views on both sides of the

---

5   The scenario has been changing with the decreasing number of manufacturing firms invested by Hong Kong, Taiwan and other sources of foreign investment as a result of the outbreak of the 2008 global financial crisis.

boundary, both the former governor of Guangdong, Lu Ruihua, and the former mayor of Shenzhen, Yu Youjun, had to readjust their original target to improve the efficiency of population flows during the peak period and to increase the number of channels for cross-boundary passengers.[6]

Moreover, views on the 24-hour operation are disputable among various sectors in Hong Kong. First, there are different views among business actors in Hong Kong. Productive service industries, who served the manufacturing activities in the PRD, were more optimistic than consumptive service industries. A survey of business enterprises' views indicated that more enterprises than average from the wholesale, import, export, and communications industries found, it would be useful to implement the 24-hour operation, whereas more enterprises than average in the retail, recreational, entertainment, and personal service industries held the opposite view (OCTSRI 2002). Productive service industries, such as import, export, financing, insurance and banking, business services, and communications, had a stronger demand for early implementation of the 24-hour operation. The number of business enterprises in the real-estate industry that supported the 24-hour operation was more or less the same as the number of those that held the opposite view. In terms of enterprise size, most large and very large companies had a positive outlook. The survey revealed the worries of the retail, catering, and entertainment industries about implementing the 24-hour operation. More than half of the catering business enterprises expected a decrease in profits. Business operators in recreational and entertainment services (covering billiard centres, electronic game centres, dance halls, and massage parlours) all shared the same pessimistic view.

Second, different views were also held among Hong Kong residents. A household survey revealed that the public in general that travelled between Hong Kong and Mainland China took the view that 24-hour passenger clearance would not be particularly useful to them, given that few of them (2.9 per cent) would cross the boundary during the extended hours. The scenario was, however, a bit different for those whose visits to the Mainland were mainly necessitated by work. Two thirds of them considered that it would suffice to open one land boundary control point to 24-hour operation (MDRT 2002). As a result, in order to balance the interests of different actors, the HKSAR government continues to have reservations about opening the boundary 24 hours a day, which is technically very easy to achieve.

The 24-hour operation has remained an unsolved problem owing to different views between Hong Kong and Guangdong. Under the OCTS principle, any proposals on the management of the boundary should get an approval from the central government. So far, the central government has not been involved in this issue. The decision-making has been horizontally shared by various actors at the same territorial level (for example Hong Kong). Under the existing mechanism of cross-boundary governance (the GDHKCJC), both Guangdong and Shenzhen have failed to communicate with Hong Kong and it is difficult for both sides to achieve

---

6   <http://dailynews.dayoo.com/content/2002-03/12/content397492.htm>, see comment above.

an agreement on the issue. Shenzhen, as one of the members of the GDHKCJC, has weak influence in pushing forward the 24-hour operation. It seems that the issue could be solved only when the Chinese central government becomes involved and plays its somewhat backstage coordinator role. In short, the central government has served as an authority at backstage for cross-boundary governance of the HK-PRD region, which responds to the lack of a regional-level authority in the Greater PRD, if compared to the existence of a supranational institution, that is the European Commission in the EU.

However, no consensus has been achieved on the issue of the 24-hour operation of the Hong Kong-Shenzhen boundary control points between the two sides, except an agreement to extend the operation period to midnight in 2001, except the 24-hour opening in Lo Ma Chau/ Huanggang from January 2003. A comprehensive study on the social and economic impacts of a 24-hour operation of the boundary control points was commissioned by the HKSAR Government's Central Policy Unit, and conducted by the One Country Two Systems Research Institute (OCTSRI) and Marketing Decision Research Technology (MDRT) Limited in 2001 and completed in June 2002. It consisted of a household survey of 5,573 households and an enterprise survey of 1,598 firms. These surveys suggested that the overall economic impact of the 24-hour opening might well be positive and that fears saying that such a relaxation would disrupt the local economy and exacerbate social problems, were much exaggerated. The import and export, transport, communication, banking, financial services and business service sectors, which employed 34 per cent of Hong Kong's total workforce in 2001 and contributed 46 per cent of the territory's GDP in 2000, believed that they would profit from the 24-hour opening. The sectors that expected to lose out (mainly the retail, catering, hotel and entertainment sectors) accounted for only 19 per cent of the total employment and 13 per cent of the GDP. Both surveys suggested that the impact on the property sector would be limited, and some property developers felt, it would be better for the property market for the uncertainty factor to be removed as soon as possible. About 33 per cent of retail operators believed that their profits would suffer, as did a little more than half the catering operations (in particular restaurants, bars, karaoke lounges, massage parlours and billiard halls). There was general concern that 24-hour opening of the land boundary control points could result in an increase in drug abuse problems in Hong Kong, though the household survey findings suggested that border crossing arrangements were not a serious factor in this problem.

There is no evidence that Hong Kong consumers will flock to Mainland China in large numbers if the control points operate 24 hours a day. Indeed, most survey respondents (86.7 per cent) said that they did not consider the 24-hour opening of the control points to be useful. However, the survey identified a group of frequent travelers to Mainland China (visiting at least once a week), who were much better disposed to such an arrangement. The group generates an estimated 46.8 million trips a year, and accounted for 45 per cent of all cross-boundary trips in 2001 and over 60 per cent at the end of 2007 (HKSAR Panning Department 2008). Most of their visits are work-related (66.3 per cent). Nearly half of this group (46.8 per cent) considered the 24-hour operation of land boundary crossings to be useful, compared to 12.5 per cent for the general public as a whole. However, 'reducing congestion during peak hours on weekends, public holidays and weekdays' was ranked above 'opening control points round-the-clock every day', and opening the control points for 24-hour operation will not necessarily provide relief from congestion during peak hours (MDRT 2002; OCTSRI 2002). This is probably also a factor in the caution so far displayed by the governments on both sides of the boundary.

The unbalanced cross-border flows and operating restrictions on the boundary control points represent a potential loss of economic opportunity for Hong Kong, the solution to which lies in the hands of the HKSAR Government. If the HKSAR Government relaxed restrictions on Mainland travel, investment and immigration to Hong Kong, a more balanced flow of economic activities would occur between Hong Kong and Mainland China, and the economic benefits thus derived could help to mitigate losses that certain local business sectors (for example the retail and entertainment sectors) might suffer arising from the 24-hour opening of the control points.

The 24-hour operation of control points is normally discussed from the point of view of Hong Kong residents only, but there are also a number of cross-boundary travelers who do not carry Hong Kong ID cards. The survey indicated that an increasing number of foreign businessmen going to the PRD for business deals and inspection had stopped, using Hong Kong as their business base because of the tiresome queues in Lo Wu. Perceptions of Hong Kong by foreign and Mainland travelers are important, and if this class continues to encounter difficulties at the boundary, Hong Kong's role as an international trading platform will be tarnished and its attraction for tourists diminished (OCTS 2002).

In a word, the return of Hong Kong to Chinese sovereignty (to the Mainland China) has not necessarily changed the nature and management of the boundary between Hong Kong and the Mainland, especially Shenzhen. The Greater PRD as a sub-national cross-border region has not tended to be more easily to be governed as other cross-border regions in a single sovereignty country, owing to the implementation of the unique principle of 'one country, two systems'. Compared with the cases in the other parts of the world, there are distinctive characteristics of the Greater PRD and thus warrant for careful and comprehensive comparative studies for scholars and policy practitioners.

Conclusions

To conclude, the institutionalization of cross-boundary integration between Hong Kong and the PRD has been in line with the global tendency of institution-based integration in the context of globalization and regionalization. Firstly, significant changes have been taking place in various aspects, for example transition from spontaneous and market-driven to institution-based interaction, from entrepreneurial-level to inter-governmental communication-based interaction, from a bottom-up track to dual-track including 'top-down' interaction with the active participation of the Chinese central government, from manufacturing-dominated to service-expanding integration, as well as from export-orientation to targeting the potential domestic market of the Mainland.

Secondly, the Greater PRD has demonstrated critically the explanatory value of the concept of multi-level governance to the cases outside the EU, which originates and has developed extensively in the member states of the EU. I have attempted to contribute to the literature through the empirical study in this chapter. I argue that a pattern of MLG has been emerging in the subnational cross-boundary region, accompanying the transformation of cross-boundary integration from market-led to institution-based. Decision-making in the Greater PRD has been dispersing across multiple levels ranging from the central, Guangdong provincial, HKSAR, to municipal, city and county-level governments of the PRD, as well as concerned stakeholders, for example business, NGOs, and so on. Unlike the case of cross-border integration in the EU, in absence of any regional authorities governing cross-boundary issues, the central government has played a 'backstage' role, for example the central government's involvement in the Bridge debate. Complex and dynamic power struggles in the evolution of the cross-boundary cooperation in the Greater PRD are heightened in the unique and evolving context of OCTS.

Although the alliance of local governments of the PRD and Hong Kong entrepreneurs have played a key role in cross-boundary economic integration, with the limited involvement of the central, Guangdong provincial, as well as the former British-Hong Kong governments in the 1980s and 1990s, I argue that the central, Guangdong provincial, and HKSAR governments as well as other stakeholders, such as the business sector in Hong Kong, have played major roles in the transition of the integration mechanism and cross-boundary governance since the early 2000s. Moreover, it is worth noting that in the relational geometries are not static 'things' fixed in terms of time and space. Power relations among various levels of governments in the Greater PRD have kept changing in order to protect their own interests. Thus, a dynamic approach is essential in understanding cross-border governance of the Greater PRD and work out practical policies to foster cross-border integration and coordinate regional governance. Last but not least, this chapter also urges careful and comprehensive investigation of the needs of establishing a region-level institution to coordinate regional development and planning of the Greater PRD as a multi-level governed cross-boundary region in a single sovereignty country under 'two systems'.

References

Anderson, J., and O'Dowd, L. (1999), 'Border, border regions and territoriality: contradictory meanings changing significance', *Regional Studies* 33:7, 593-604.

Blatter, J.K. (2004), 'From "spaces of place" to "spaces of flows"? Territorial and functional governance on cross-border regions in Europe and North America', *International Journal of Urban and Regional Research* 28:3, 530-49.

Brenner, N. (1999), 'Globalization as reterritorialization: the re-scaling of urban governance in the European Union', *Urban Studies* 36:3, 431-51.

Brenner, N. (1998), 'Global cities, global states: global city formation and state territorial restructuring in contemporary Europe', *Review of International Political Economy* 5:1, 1-37.

Breslin, S. (2000), 'Decentralisation, globalisation and China's partial re-engagement with the global economy', *New Political Economy* 5:2, 205-26.

Breslin, S. and Hook, G.D. (2002), *Microregionalism and World Order* (New York: Palgrave Macmillan).

Cheung, P.T.Y. (2002), 'Managing the Hong Kong–Guangdong relationship: issues and challenges', in Yeh, A.G.O. et al. (eds.), *Building a competitive Pearl River Delta region: cooperation, coordination and planning* (Hong Kong: The Centre of Urban Planning and Environmental Management, The University of Hong Kong), 39-58.

Church, A. and Reid, P. (1996), 'Urban power, international networks and competition: the example of cross-border cooperation', *Urban Studies* 33, 1297-318.

Enright, M., Scott, E. and Chang, K. (2005), *Regional powerhouse: The Greater Pearl River Delta and the rise of China* (Singapore, Hoboken, NJ, Chichester: Wiley).

Federation of HK Industries (2003), 'Made in PRD: The changing face of Hong Kong manufacturers', *Full Report Federation of HK Industries* part II (Hong Kong: FHKI).

Friedmann, J. and Wolff, G. (1982), 'World city formation: An agenda for research and action', *International Journal of Urban and Regional Research* 6:3, 309-44.

George, S. (2004), 'Multi-level governance and the European Union', in Bache, I. and Flinders, M. (eds.), *Multi-level Governance* (Oxford: Oxford University Press), 107-26.

Grundy-Warr, C., Peachey, K., and Perry, M. (1999), 'Fragmented integration in the Singapore-Indonesia border zone: Southeast Asia's "Growth Triangle" against the global economy', *International Journal of Urban and Regional Research* 23:2, 305-28.

Guangdong Provincial Development Research Centre (1999), *Kuayue Shiji Xin Jiyuan:Yuegang'ao Jingji Hezuo Lunwenji* (Across the new era: a collection of essays on economic cooperation among Guangdong, HongKong and Macao) (Guangzhou: Guangdong Provincial Government).

Guangdong Provincial Governmental Report (2003), available at <http://www.southcn.com/news/gdnews/hotspot/gdlh/sjrdychy/200301230268.htm>, accessed on 10 November 2003.

Hall, P. (2001), 'The Global City-Region: Global City-Regions in the Twenty-first Century', in Scott, A.J. (ed.), *Global City-Regions: Trends, Theory, Policy* (New York: Oxford University Press), 59-77.

Hall, P. (1966), *The World Cities* (London: Weidenfeld and Nicolson).

Herzog, L.A. (1991), 'Cross-national urban structure in the era of global cities: the US–Mexico transfrontier metropolis', *Urban Studies* 28, 519-33.

HKSAR Chief Executive's Policy Address (2003), *Capitalising on our advantages, revitalising our economy*, available at <http://www.policyaddress.gov.hk/pa03/eng/index.htm>, accessed on 15 November 2003.

HKSAR Government Press Release (2001), *Transcript of the Chief Secretary*, available at <http://www.info.gov.hk/gia/general/200110/24/1024150.htm>, accessed on 24 October 2001.

HKSAR Planning Department (2008), *North Bound, South Bound: 2007 Cross-boundary Travel Survey* (Hong Kong: Planning Department).

Krätke, S. (2001), 'Cross-border co-operation in the German–Polish Border Area', in Geenhuizen, M.V. and Ratti, R. (eds.), *Gaining advantage from open borders: an active space approach to regional development* (Aldershot and Burlington: Ashgate), 213-32.

Lin, G.C.S. (2003), 'An emerging global city-region? Economic and social integration between Hong Kong and the Pearl River Delta', in So, A.Y. (ed.), China's developmental miracle: origins, transformations, and challenges (New York: M.E. Sharpe), 79-107.

Market Decision Research Technology Limited (2002), *Household Survey on 24-Hour Passenger-clearance at Land Boundary Control Points*, executive summary, submitted to the Central Point Unit, HK Special Administrative Region Government (Hong Kong: MDRTL).

Newman, D., and Paasi, A. (1998), 'Fences and neighbours in the postmodern world: boundary narratives in political geography', *Progress in Human Geography* 22, 186-207.

One Country Two Systems Research Institute (2002), *Socio-economic of 24-hour Operation of Land Boundary Control Points on HK*, executive summary, submitted to the Central Point Unit, HK Special Administrative Region Government (Hong Kong: OCTSRI).

Paasi, A. (1999), 'Boundaries as social practice and discourse: the Finish–Russian border', *Regional Studies* 33:7, 669-80.

Perkmann, M. (2003), 'Cross-border regions in Europe: significance and drivers of regional cross-border cooperation', *European Urban and Regional Studies* 10, 153-71.

Perkmann, M. and Sum, N.L. (eds.)(2002), *Globalization, Regionalization and Cross-border Regions* (Basingstoke, Hants: Palgrave Macmillan).

Sassen, S. (2001), 'Global cities and global city-regions: A comparison', in Scott, A.J. (ed.), *Global City-Regions: Trends, Theory, Policy* (Oxford: Oxford University Press), 78-95.

Sassen, S. (1991), *The Global City* (Princeton: Princeton University Press).

Scott, A.J. (ed.)(2001), *Global City-Regions: Trends, Theory, Policy* (Oxford: Oxford University Press).

Scott, A.J., Agnew, J., Soja, E.W. and Storper, M. (2001), 'Global City-Regions', in Scott, A.J. (ed.), *Global City-Regions: Trends, Theory, Policy* (Oxford: Oxford University Press), 11-32.

Scott, J.W. (1999), 'European and North American contexts for cross-border regionalism', *Regional Studies* 33:7, 605-18.

Shen, J. (2004), 'Cross-border urban governance in Hong Kong: the role of state in a globalizing city-region', *The Professional Geographer* 56, 530-43.

Shen, J. (2003), 'Cross-border connection between HK and Mainland China "under two systems" before and beyond 1997', *Geografiska Annaler B* 85, 1-17.

Shiu, S.P. and Yang, C. (2002), 'A study on developing the HK Shenzhen border zone', in Yeh, A.G., Lee, F.Y. and Sze, N.D. (eds.), *Building a Competitive Pearl River Delta Region: Cooperation, Competition and Planning* (Hong Kong: Centre for Urban Planning and Environmental Management, the University of Hong Kong), 245-70.

Simmonds, R. and Hack, G. (2000), *Global City Regions: Their Emerging Forms* (London and New York: Spon Press).

Singtao Daily (2001), 'Shenzhen Mayor released good news without confirmation of HKSAR Government: extension of border controls to midnight by the end of this year', *Singtao Daily* 31 October 2001, page A01.

Smart, A. (2002), 'The HK/Pearl River Delta urban region: an emerging transnational mode of regulation or just muddling through?', in Logan, J.R. (ed.), *The New Chinese City: Globalization and Market Reform* (Oxford: Blackwell), 92-105.

Sparke, M., Sidaway, J.D., Bunnell, T. and Grundy-Warr, C. (2004), 'Triangulating the borderless world: geographies of power in the Indonesia-Malaysia-Singapore growth triangle', *Transactions Institute of British Geographers*, 29, 485-498.

Telo', M. (2001), *European Union and new regionalism: regional actors and global governance in a post-hegemonic era* (Aldershot: Ashgate).

Weaver, T. (2001), 'Time, space, and articulation in the economic development of the US–Mexico border region from 1940 to 2000', *Human Organization* 60:2, 105-20.

Yang, C. (2008), 'Multi-level governance of the polycentric mega-urban regions in China: the case of the Greater Pearl River Delta' (in Chinese), *Urban Planning International* 23:1, 79-84.

Yang, C. (2006a), 'The geopolitics of cross-boundary governance in the Greater Pearl River Delta, China: A case study of the proposed Hong Kong-Zhuhai-Macao bridge', *Political Geography* 25:7, 817-35.

Yang, C. (2006b), 'The Pearl River Delta and Hong Kong: An evolving cross-boundary region under "one country, two systems"', *Habitat International* 30:1, 61-86.

Yang, C. (2005a), 'Multi-level governance in the cross-boundary region of Hong Kong-Pearl River Delta, China', *Environment and Planning A* 37:12, 2147-67.

Yang, C. (2005b), 'An emerging cross-boundary metropolis in China: Hong Kong and Shenzhen under "two systems"', *International Development Planning Review* 27:2, 195-225.

Yang, C. (2004), 'From market-led to institution-based economic integration: The case of the Pearl River Delta and Hong Kong, China', *Issues and Studies* (A Social Quarterly on China, Taiwan and East Asian Affairs) 40:2, 78-119.

Global City Frontiers: Singapore's Hinterland and the Contested Geographies of Bintan, Indonesia[1]

Tim Bunnell, Hamzah Muzaini and James D. Sidaway

Introduction: Relocating Singapore's urban frontier

> *Borderlands have become privileged in the global narrative as places where local differences may be developed as sites of profitable exchange* (Medovi 2005, 172).

Since the 1980s, Singapore's policy-makers and politicians have argued that further expansion of the Singapore economy required spaces and labour beyond the 680-square-kilometre territorial limits of the city-state. Ambitious land reclamation schemes had their physical limits in terms of their capacity to provide new commercial and residential spaces. Intensive redevelopment and state-finessed (and frequently state-financed) gentrification strategies in locales where 'heritage' could be profitably mobilized also ran up against the sheer density of population (over 5,000 people per square kilometre) and urbanization. With an accumulation and development strategy founded on exports, transhipment and a reputation as

1   This is an updated version of a paper that was first published as 'Singapore's Hinterland and the Contested Socio-political Geographies of Bintan, Indonesia', *International Journal of Urban and Regional Research* 31:1, 3-22. The revised version is published here with permission of Wiley-Blackwell. Our informants are gratefully acknowledged for their time, guidance, information and encouragement during our research in Bintan from May-August 2004. Since many continue to be involved in the struggles that this chapter depicts, all names of interviewees cited in the text have been substituted with pseudonyms. We thank four anonymous reviewers, Henry Yeung and Peter Taylor for their helpful comments on earlier drafts. The research reported here was conducted under the auspices of a research project, 'Accumulation, Regionalization and Sovereignty: The Singapore–Johor–Riau Growth Triangle' (R-109-00-042-112) funded by the Faculty of Arts and Social Sciences at the National University of Singapore. The usual disclaimers apply.

a relatively secure and efficient regional base for services, banking and brokering, Singapore had long needed to import cheap contract labour from elsewhere in Asia (especially from Bangladesh, India, Indonesia, the Philippines, Sri Lanka and Thailand), source skilled workers globally and consume vast quantities of resources and provisions (from foodstuffs, to sand for the construction industry, to drinking water) from elsewhere in Southeast Asia and as far away as Europe and New Zealand. Singapore has hence been particularly active in pursuit of multilateral and bilateral 'free trade' agreements. Since the 1980s, however, a more formal arrangement with Singapore's immediate neighbours has also been sought. The Singapore government fostered deeper economic cooperation with these regional neighbours, most famously in the form of a so-called Growth Triangle (formalized in a tripartite treaty signed in 1989), centred on the city-state, but incorporating proximate areas of Malaysia and Indonesia (see Figure 22.1). In addition to the expectations of resort development and tourists traversing the Growth Triangle's peripheries, corporate and official narratives about the putative complementarities of this triangular arrangement proliferated (see Bunnell et al. 2006; Phelps 2004a; Sparke et al. 2004). These argued that the other sides of the triangle would benefit from inflows of investment and expertise; while the city-state itself would benefit from the availability of relatively cheap land and labour in the Malaysian state of Johor and, more markedly, on the Riau islands (chief among them Batam and Bintan) of Indonesia. In more critical terms, the profound and often contradictory social, environmental and economic consequences of opening vast tracts of land in the island of Batam to Singaporean and other foreign investment have been traced elsewhere (for example Grundy-Warr et al. 1999; Lindquist 2009; Mack 2004; Phelps 2004b).

The transformation of neighbouring Bintan, by comparison, has received relatively little critical scrutiny. Chang (2001) has begun to chart Bintan's place in the contours of 'Singapore's regional tourism forays' (these will also be our primary focus here) and Grundy-Warr et al. (1999) began to map Singaporean investment in Bintan as part of what they term 'fragmented integration' in the Singapore-Indonesia border zone. Chou (2002) and Chou and Wee (2003) describe how the indigenous people of the *Kepulauan Riau* (Riau Archipelago), including those, known as the *Orang Suku Laut*,[2] who live in and around the coasts of Bintan and Batam, have found their presence and especially their access to resources increasingly marginalized and overwritten by new forms of tenure and 'development' propelled by the Indonesian state and bolstered by the Growth Triangle (see also Chou 2006). However, further attention to Bintan offers instructive pointers to patterns of domination and resistance in the 'backyard' of what has come to be regarded as a key node in the world economy, one of the control centres for global accumulation – in short a putative Global or World City (Beaverstock et al. 1999; Friedmann 1986; Sassen 1991; Taylor 2005). In the case

2   The term may be translated as 'people of the sea'. The *Orang Suku Laut* are usually differentiated from *orang kampong* (villagers) and both are now greatly outnumbered by more recent migrants to Riau.

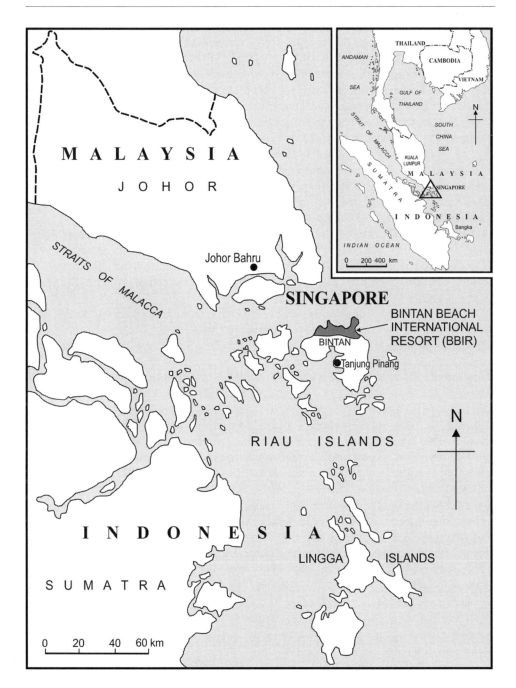

Figure 22.1 The Location of the Bintan Beach International Resort within the Indonesia-Malaysia-Singapore Growth Triangle

Source: ©: T. Bunnell, H. Muzaini and J.D. Sidaway.

of the Growth Triangle, the immediate hinterland of Singapore spans interstate boundaries. It is precisely this complex array of formal boundaries that – together with other (related) processes of demarcating, dividing and bounding space – make this case distinctive. However, we will argue that the complexity and multiplicity of boundaries across the Growth Triangle are an acute expression and combination of wider tendencies. These include the imposition of new modes of conduct increasingly registered in bounded urban sites and zones (what Smith (1996) terms the 'revanchist city' associated with intensified gentrification), the development of planned tourist enclaves (Judd and Fainstein 1999) and the shifting political terrain and reworking of border practices that incorporate both elements of older sovereign practices and new transnational state sovereignties (resulting in what Cunningham (2001) and Coleman (2005) argue is a 'gated globalism').

Also seeking a conceptual vocabulary to locate contemporary globalization and inter-city relations, Michael Peter Smith (2001, 5) coins the productive metaphor of 'transnational urbanism', 'as a marker of the criss-crossing transnational circuits of communication and cross-cutting, translocal and transnational social practices that "come together" in particular [urban] places'.

In the Growth Triangle, however, 'transnational urbanism' appears as a more literal manifestation of transnational territoriality in the form of complex articulations of nation-state and other boundaries. Singapore and its hinterland thus form an interlaced assemblage of border zones. We argue that these are symptomatic of wider tendencies and strategies of rebounding at diverse urban frontiers and transnational spaces of accumulation. This chapter is a grounded attempt to excavate and analyze some of these geographies. It thus takes us into the contested frontiers of Singapore's immediate cross-border hinterland. Following some further background on Bintan (in the remainder of the introduction), we provide an overview of recent conceptualizations of the interactions of global cities, borders and states. Yet we insist that the case we elaborate here in relation to such literatures is one of specifically *human* geographies. What is usually absent from the media reportage on the rise and missteps of Bintan as Singapore's economic playground are the voices and imaginings of anyone other than political and corporate authorities. To the extent that much academic research on regional economic zones relies on similarly selective authoritative material, social scientists – even ostensibly 'critical' ones – have often served to perpetuate the preponderance of views of selected global/world cities and 'from above' (Robinson 2002). Thus, in the second section of the chapter, we complement secondary sources with material from fieldwork[3] in elaborating our arguments on the contested landscaping

---

3   Twenty semi-structured interviews were conducted in Bintan in May-August 2004. Most of these were with activists involved in the demonstrations and struggles over land in Bintan or displaced villagers. All interviews were conducted in Indonesian and selected sections transcribed and translated. All translations here are by the authors. The interviews were conducted without the knowledge or permission of the authorities, and no officials were present at the discussions. In addition to the diverse conceptual literatures cited in the main text, we found some inspiration and encouragement in

of Bintan. We conclude by relating the Bintan case to wider arguments about socioeconomic exclusion in city 'frontier' zones. The issues raised and potential for their exploration in Bintan and other islands of the Riau Archipelago are broad. However, our empirical focus here is necessarily limited principally to the intriguing case of the tourist enclave in Bintan.

Bintan contexts

The contemporary Indonesia-Malaysia-Singapore Growth Triangle overlays both a long history of territorialization and reterritorializations and an array of formal and informal networks. Prior to the 1824 Anglo-Dutch Treaty of London (which demarcated British and Dutch colonial spheres of trade and influence in Southeast Asia), the Riau Archipelago, Singapore and the Malay Peninsula were closely bound by kinship and trade and subject to common political jurisdiction under maritime-orientated sultanates. Subsequently, the borders between the colonial states remained relatively porous and after the interlude of Japanese Occupation this continued into the early post-colonial era. Geopolitical tensions and conflicting claims over the legitimacy of the postcolonial states made the borders much less open in the 1960s (Liow 2005). By the 1970s, the uneven development of Singapore, Indonesia and Malaysia rested upon and reinforced sovereign aspirations (particularly on the part of Singapore) to regulate borders, especially to control labour migration, whilst retaining some flexibility for capital and commodities to flow across them in search of profitable opportunities. The Growth Triangle represents a consolidation of these modes of regulation and control. Thus, whilst Newman and Thornley (2005, 246-7) are able to claim that 'as a city state Singapore is free from the complexities of intergovernmental relations between national and city levels', a host of other complex relations emerge between Singapore and neighbouring territories in Indonesia and Malaysia.

Since the establishment of the Growth Triangle in 1989, Batam has seen the largest transformations. The population there has grown from a few thousands in the 1970s to hundreds of thousands today. Much of the landscape of the island has become densely urbanized (with a mix of industrial facilities, bars, nightclubs[4] and restaurants, informal housing and speculative real estate) and over 400 factories have been established, as well as port facilities, hotels and highways. Over 70 per cent of the foreign capital investment is reportedly from Singapore-based

Routledge's (2001, 2002) critical 'post-development' ethnographies of some similar struggles in Indian resort areas.

4   These facilitate sex tourism (mostly from Singapore), and Batam in particular has acquired the reputation (both in Singapore and to some extent in Indonesia) as a site of sex tourism and more widely as a sometimes 'unruly' place (Lindquist 2009). Although there are some locales for prostitution in Bintan, these are both more partitioned from the main settlements and relatively distant from the enclaved resort that forms our empirical focus here.

companies (including Singapore-based branches of multinationals). However, in the 1990s Singaporean (and other foreign) investments also flowed into two distinct and demarcated zones in Bintan, each of which was intended to perform a specific economic role (see Figure 22.2). The first of these was the Bintan Industrial Estate (BIE) in the northwest of the island, at Lobam. Phase 1 of the estate covering 55 hectares was, as one Singapore *Business Times* (14 June 1996) report put it, 'aimed at traditional low-tech industries like textiles, footwear and woodworking'. While such 'low-tech' and labour-intensive manufacturing could be shifted to Bintan, higher-end manufacturing processes as well as product design, marketing and distribution would be retained in Singapore. The official conception of this S\$ 60 million development, however, emphasized not so much economic division as spatial expansion. With the completion of a direct ferry link from Singapore's Tanah Merah ferry terminal to Lobam, it was even possible for senior staff to commute to BIE within this extended 'transnational' economic space.

A second Singaporean economic zone on Bintan, and our main focus here, comprised a 23,000 hectares resort and tourist complex along the northern coast. On the one hand, this was intended to be (and to be seen as) different from Singapore, a space of salubrious tranquillity in contrast to fast-paced, modern city life. Thus, for Singaporeans, Bintan was to become 'another Bali ... only closer to home' (*Straits Times* 18 October 1996). On the other hand, however, Bintan Beach International Resort (BBIR, as the zone eventually became known) was also conceived as part of an extended Singapore. The combined marketing of Bintan's 'beaches with coconut trees and palm trees' and Singapore's 'city experience' was used to attract international visitors to an emergent transnational tourist region (*Straits Times* 22 January 1996; see also Chang 2001). For the Singaporean market, proposed holiday bungalows in Bintan were likened to New York City residents' country homes 'in the woods in New Jersey' (*Straits Times* 18 October 1996).

Since the mid 1990s, ten resorts and villas have been built on the palm-fringed white sands facing the South China Sea. In terms of security,[5] infrastructure, cleanliness and even roadside landscaping, this zone of Bintan – like the industrial estate at Lobam – was imagined as, and has functioned as part of, a greater Singapore. Partnership with one of Indonesia's largest conglomerates – closely connected with then President Suharto – promised a smooth process of Singapore-led economic transformation in Bintan.

However, almost from their inception, development of the new economic spaces in Bintan was far from smooth. From June 1997, malaria scares led to a collapse of visitor arrivals at BBIR. The environment and ecology of the island itself appeared to defy easy emulation of Singapore. Meanwhile, tourist arrivals across Southeast Asia were also adversely affected by haze attributed to forest fires in other parts

---

5   Since 9/11 and even more so since the foiling of plots to explode bombs in Singapore in 2002 and attacks on clubs and restaurants in Bali in 2002 and 2005, security concerns have grown in Southeast Asian resorts. However, as the chapter details, in Bintan 'security' (and heightened surveillance and border practices) are both wider phenomena than, and predate, these concerns about terrorism.

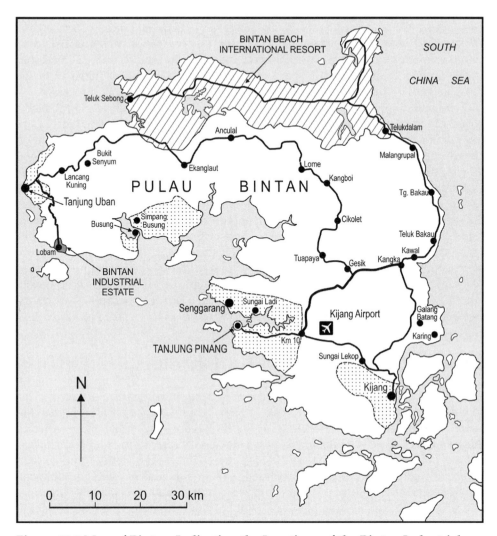

Figure 22.2 Map of Bintan, Indicating the Locations of the Bintan Industrial Estate and Bintan Beach International Resort

Source: ©: T. Bunnell, H. Muzaini and J.D. Sidaway.

of Indonesia. At least Bintan's remoteness from the centres of Indonesian politics appeared to protect Singaporean tourists and investors from the social and political turmoil characterizing many other Indonesian islands and cities. In May 1998, while riots and anti-Chinese pogroms took place in Jakarta, prompting Singaporean expatriates to return home, readers of Singapore's *Business Times* were assured that Batam and Bintan remained 'a haven of tranquillity among the chaos and rampage in Jakarta' (*Business Times* 16 May 1998). Yet later that year, reports surfaced about two demonstrations over land compensation in Bintan. In the second of these, on 19

December 1998, 'angry villagers' blocked access roads to the Bintan beach resorts. While resort representatives stressed that 'the demonstration was not instigated by other unrest in other parts of Indonesia' (reported in *Straits Times* 23 December 1998), 'Singaporean' economic space in Bintan was clearly not isolated from the consequences of the wider political and economic transformation in Indonesia.

Following the fall of President Suharto in May 1998, the new Indonesian government attempted to wrest control of companies owned by Salim Group, one of which (PT Buana Megawisatama [BMW]) had overseen compensation awarded to occupants of the land that became BIE and BBIR. In a subsequent, larger demonstration in January 2000, a crowd of more than 1,000 destroyed the guardhouse at the gates of the resort, while 300 others shut down the main power supply to the industrial estate. Yet perhaps more significant was the re-imagining of Bintan's economic landscapes in the light of the violence. On 17 and 19 January 2000 respectively, images of 'angry mobsters' breaking the gate to BBIR and 'weapon-toting demonstrators' made the front page of the *Straits Times*. Despite a decade of refashioning specially selected zones of Bintan into suitably Singaporeanized economic space and the literal and metaphorical cultivation of a 'peaceful' haven, other views on and of these zones – other social and political geographies – surfaced in the form of unruly, *parang*-wielding demonstrators.

Framing the growth triangle: boundaries and limits

As we have noted, Singapore is designated in academic literature as a world (or global) city, what Taylor (2004) terms a 'regional command centre'. It is important, however, to consider the specificity of the Singapore case rather than reducing this to a generalized singular pathway of global city formation. Yeung (2000) has pointed out how Singapore's determined pursuit of world city status is tied up with an active regionalization drive, involving investments and markets in Southeast and East Asia. More recently, Olds and Yeung (2004) have considered Singapore as exemplifying a distinctive pathway to global city formation. The distinguishing feature of what they term 'Global City-States' such as Singapore and Hong Kong is that they have not had a hinterland within the same national boundaries. Thus, whilst other world cities have developed strong embedded relations in their immediate 'national' hinterlands, in the case of Singapore, a regional hinterland extends across state boundaries. Amidst what Scott et al. (2001) have identified as a range of 'Global City-Regions', Singapore is therefore distinctive. The result is a complex mode of 'fragmented integration' (Grundy-Warr et al. 1999), whereby Singapore's relative economic power extends unevenly into and re-articulates other political spaces within the 'Growth Triangle' and beyond.

Our interest here is at a more truncated scale however: the immediate hinterland of Singapore under formation today in Bintan. Part of the chapter's contribution, therefore, is to detail attempts to shape territory in northern Bintan, Indonesia. This zone is intended to perform a specific role, as a tranquil haven for tourists and global city professionals (both Singaporean and expatriate) and one which is differentiated from the rest of Bintan (Ford and Lyons 2006) and other parts of Indonesia. In tracing this, we follow Smith (2001, 6) in seeking 'an agency-oriented theoretical perspective [towards transnational urbanism] that concretely connects macro-economic and geopolitical transformations to the micro-networks of social action that people create, move in, and act upon in their daily lives'. Notwithstanding the roles of global networks in configuring world cities, Smith goes on to argue for 'the continuing significance of borders, state policies, and national identities even as these are often transgressed by transnational communication circuits and social practices'.

We have also noted that others have referred to 'revanchist cities' to describe the gentrification and political confrontation at the (internal) urban 'frontier' of capital and conflict in western cities (MacLeod 2002; Smith 1996). In our case study, however, the 'frontiers' involve the reworking and replacing of *international* and *intra-national* boundaries within the Growth Triangle. Whilst examining the construction and reproduction of these boundaries, we are also mindful of the limits to, and disruptions of, the smooth space of accumulation (and the neatly bounded BBIR). In particular, in what follows, we recount the roles of, and voices from, struggles articulating other geographies in and beyond these frontiers. Yet as this chapter also begins to detail, this project has not proceeded uncontested.

The 'Singaporeanization' of the Bintan landscape

It is hard not to notice how the BBIR has been refashioned as part of greater Singapore. The clean and immaculate veneering of the roadsides, the streetlights, white lines on the road, smooth tarmac and road signs, the modern – yet localized – architecture of the resorts (the products of investments by Singaporean and other international investors) and the golf courses that line the sandy beaches of Bintan offer a stark contrast to much of the rest of the island, as does, less visibly, the importation of infrastructural facilities (such as a powerhouse and reservoir supplying electricity and freshwater to the resorts). Outside the BBIR (with the exception of the busy provincial capital of Tanjung Pinang, the BIE and other smaller industrial areas), there still exists a landscape of *kampungs* ('villages'), jungle and plantations, unpaved roads and smallholdings. Aside from immigration checks at the Bandar Bintan Telani ferry terminal (the disembarkation point for holiday-makers to the tourist zone), there is little to distinguish BBIR from tourist islands within Singapore such as Sentosa (which has been transformed into a resort with hotels, golf courses, an artificial beach and other tourist attractions). In Bintan, aside from the resort establishments, visitors can watch cultural performances, shop for souvenir items, and sample Singaporean, 'international' or Indonesian food at the restaurants (all priced in Singapore dollars). For Singaporeans the transformation of the landscape also allows them to relate to the site as an extension of 'home', a place where modern city-dwellers can experience a little of the 'rustic' (something that has largely disappeared from 'mainland' Singapore). For Singaporeans and others residing in or visiting Southeast Asia's global city, the proximity of Bintan and the fast ferries – combined with the fact that accessibility, security and local 'authenticity' are tightly managed and circumscribed – make it ideal for weekend getaways.

Yet this space was no *tabula rasa* awaiting an influx of capital, workers and tourists. When the land was acquired in the 1990s, there were already people residing within and moving through what was to become the BBIR. These included both thousands of villagers (*orang kampung*) and the more mobile *Orang Laut* (sea people) whose presence is harder to enumerate, but who had long moved through Riau and beyond (prior to the imposition of border controls), utilizing a diverse range of resources and economic strategies. As Chou and Wee (2003, 332) document, the resort development in Bintan, in tandem with the wider transformations in Riau, have carved up and undermined custodianship and utilization of resources by the *Orang Laut*.

For the villagers (*orang kampung*) of north Bintan, 'development' has also largely been an experience of loss and exclusion. Bintan Resort Corporation (BRC), the main developers of BBIR saw more than 5,000 existing residents from 10 villages as antithetical to the aim of promoting BBIR as a 'world-class' attraction. Virtually all were relocated to new settlements outside the boundaries of the resort area. Land acquisition by BMW thus led to the demarcation of a 'Singaporean' economic space as separate from the rest of Bintan, an area that is reconfigured not only in terms of its physical landscaping but also in terms of permitted people and practices. This is nowhere more visible than at the iron gates of the entrance to the resort premises, with its guardhouse and patrolling security personnel. In addition, a fence circles much of the perimeter of the BBIR and where it does not, there are natural barriers (the sea and steep jungle) and guards patrol to ensure that relatively few people can slip through undetected. Entrance into the BBIR for 'local' people who are not working at the resorts is usually controlled. Those without any official business are frequently refused entry and those working within the resort have to produce a card that identifies them as resort workers. As Rahman, a resident of one of the villages that has been resettled, stated, 'Unless villagers have official business at the resort, or they work there, they are not allowed in … there are guards making rounds to ensure no one goes in illegally'.

Contesting the BBIR: BBIR boundary practices

Notwithstanding attempts to ensure that BBIR is a secure place for visitors, and to regulate entry, a large demonstration took place at the entrance of the BBIR in January 2000.[6] As part of the protest, villagers, 'armed with spears and machetes, overran Singaporean-owned tourist resorts' on the island (*Associated Press*, 28 February 2000). Led by student provocateurs from other parts of Indonesia, more than 1,000 displaced villagers assembled illegally to launch a protest against the BBIR and the

---

6   Prior to the demonstration of January 2000, smaller protests by employees seeking more remuneration and better staff benefits had already occurred (see *Straits Times*, 8 December 2000, for example).

Indonesian authorities. The demonstrators blocked the main entrance, and food and other supplies were disrupted (*Straits Times* 21 January 2000). They were only dispersed when the authorities deployed the military (bringing reinforcements from elsewhere in Indonesia) to put down the demonstration (Figure 22.3, which was supplied by our informants in Bintan shows the police lines behind gates and was taken at the time of the demonstrations). The villagers then had no choice but to leave the area.

In the case of Bintan, media narratives quickly linked the demonstration to the issue of inadequate compensation for the land that had become the resort. According to these press reports, the primary grievance concerned the low level of compensation. Agencies responsible for clearing the way for the resort and industrial estate paid just 100 rupiah (US 1 cent) for each square meter of land acquired (*Agence Presse* 20 April 2000; *Straits Times* 20 January 2000) by agencies. However, our conversations with villagers and activists, many of whom were personally involved in the demonstrations, indicate that these issues of compensation are more complex.

For one thing, some villagers bemoaned that the payment of compensation was not consistent. According to Anwar (one of the students who came to Bintan to participate in the demonstration), 'while most [of the villagers] were only given 100 rupiah per square meter, there are also those who received as much as 4,000 rupiah and also those who only received 75 rupiah or as low as 25 rupiah'. Many of the villagers were also unhappy with the way the *pembebasan tanah* (literally, the 'freeing of the land') was carried out. Some complained that they had not been consulted prior to the act of land acquisition itself, and most had grievances about how the process was undertaken. As Hami, now a resident of Sungei Kechil village, recounted, 'the villagers were forced out of their own houses. They were evicted and not given any choice. Some were injured [during the process of evictions]. When BMW came, they did not care for the villagers, they just wanted the land'.

Understandably, this is also one of the reasons stipulated within the *Ratapan Rakyat Bintan* ('Grievances of the Bintanese Villagers') (Yayasan Tragedi Lagoi 2004) document, outlining the numerous grievances of those affected by the land acquisition:

> *The process and implementation of the acquisition of indigenous land was done in a method that was inhumane, inappropriate and involving the use of intimidation, force and violence. The villagers themselves were never consulted for their views as to whether they wanted their land to be acquired or not, and the value of the land offered as compensation to the villagers was also never discussed before the act.*

Other eviction tactics were also used. As Rahman, a resident of Segiling village, stated:

> *The authorities used other means to get villagers out. The school that used to be nearby was moved to the new settlement. It is now very far for villagers*

**Figure 22.3 Police Lines behind Gates in the Aftermath of the January 2000
Demonstrations in Bintan**

Source: Photograph supplied by our informants.

*who refused to sell their land, about 9km. It is hard for us to send our children
to school. Therefore, to be close to the new school, the villagers eventually
moved.*

Upon being compensated for moving out of their land, villagers were to be
provided with an alternative settlement (*pemukiman*) where each household would
be given a house and a piece of land (*tanah kaplin*) where they could continue
farming. However, according to many of the villagers involved, these promises
never materialized. Instead of just being given new houses, villagers had to pay (in
some cases more than they were originally compensated) to buy them. Some had
to live in tents while their new houses were being built. Even those who secured a
house were far from content with the resettlement. In Hami's words, 'the houses
measured five by six metres, small and hardly enough to live in. The houses did
not have any flooring, just sand and earth. There were no windows. And the
houses were not free. Life was really bad for us'. Many of these houses have, over
time, been torn down or refurbished although a few still stand as testament to the
difficult times that these villagers endured during the initial resettlement period.
According to Hami, at some parts of Sungei Kechil, many of the *tanah kaplin* remain
undeveloped by the villagers due to lack of funds.

The move to the new settlements also affected the livelihoods of the villagers, most of whom are either farmers or fishers. Those who once worked extensive plots now found that the new lands they were provided with were too small or not suitable for planting. The fishermen were the most adversely affected. For many, home used to be by the sea, but, since many of the new settlements were located away from the coast, some fishermen now have to travel far just to get to the sea. At Segiling, for instance, villagers have to travel seven kilometres to the beach each day. In other cases, the water near the settlements is considered unsuitable for fishing. As Kersen, a fisherman at Sungei Kechil, puts it:

> We are near the sea but there are no fish here. The best place to catch fish is within the resort area near Lagoi [where our village used to be]. A lot of the villagers have to go all the way into sea to catch fish. There are no fish here.

Further compounding problems, some fishermen claim that resort activities have adversely affected fishing conditions. As Kersen continues, 'fishing here is bad because of resort developments. There are too many tourist ferries that drive the fish away. The many water-sports activities also mean that benzene is produced that kills the fish here'.

The frustration at being excluded from the prime land and resources appropriated for the BBIR is further aggravated by exclusion from job opportunities within the resorts. For example, many of the villagers are unhappy that workers within the resorts are mostly from other parts of Indonesia. As part of efforts to make the resorts 'world-class', there has been extensive recruitment of Indonesian resort workers who have been trained in other established tourist centres such as Bali (*Straits Times* 20 January 2000). Given that many of the Bintan villagers lack formal qualifications and foreign language skills, they are therefore restricted, at best, to menial jobs such as grass-cutting and sweeping. The employment of workers from other more established tourist areas has also precluded the need to train the local people. As one villager mentioned:

> Many of the original inhabitants here are still fishermen. None of us work at the resorts. If we want to work at the resort, we need to know how to speak English, or have a certificate. The villagers here are mainly the uneducated. The resorts do not even have plans to train us.

Another mentioned that:

> The outsiders working at the resort are paid quite high, about S$500 per month. This is because they are trained. For example, those from Bali or Jakarta, they have been trained and when they come here, their pay is high. But for the villagers, many of them are not trained, so cannot even get a job.

According to villagers, jobs at the resorts are mainly advertised over the Internet (to which the villagers had no easy access). Moreover, according to another villager:

> *At Lagoi, if there is a job opening, the villagers don't know about it. Because of a system of racial bias [sistem suku], many of the employees are from outside Bintan. If superiors are Javanese, they would only select Javanese to work for them, if Bataks, they only employ the Bataks. So Riau people do not get to work at the resorts.*

This ensures a cycle where many feel themselves to be systematically deprived of job opportunities within the resort. In addition, the few attempts to incorporate villagers within the resort activities have also achieved only limited success. For example, at Sungei Kechil, a small-scale BBIR-driven initiative (involving ecotourism, demonstrations of fishing techniques and performances of traditional Malay dances) is not widely felt to have had much positive impact. This is largely due to low earnings (since earnings depend on the number of tourists who come) and the fact that such an initiative only allows for those with certain skills to take part.

It is therefore apparent that the impetus for the demonstration of 2000 extends beyond the issue of compensation *per se*. It is important to note that not all villagers affected by the land acquisition process supported the large-scale demonstrations.

In the issue of how the BMW had 'scared' or 'tricked' the villagers into leaving their homes, Pak Salman also recounted instances where the local villagers themselves had tried to mislead the authorities during the *pembebasan tanah*:

> *During the freeing of the land, villagers were paid for the land as well as for their houses, chicken coops and coconut trees. All trees had their own prices according to their age. There was no cheating. There were villagers in Lagoi and Segiling who, the night before the day the BMW surveyors came, planted new vegetation so that they could get more money. Thus, the villagers also cheated.*

What is clear is that following the demonstration, the boundaries that were implemented as part of the 'Singaporeanization' of the BBIR landscape became more visibly demarcated: barbed wire barricades were installed in front of the entrances to the BBIR (and the BIE); security was stepped up in the form of more guards patrolling (*Straits Times* 1 February 2000); and a sign at the entrance of BBIR warns villagers of the consequences of any future illegal assemblies. While the demonstrations manifested overt expressions of broader grievances, in the next section of the chapter, we consider the more mundane or 'everyday' transgressions and negotiations around the boundaries of the BBIR.

Tactics of negotiation and transgression

One of the outcomes of the January 2000 demonstration was the formation of the *Yayasan Tragedi Lagoi* ('The Organization for Tragedy of Lagoi', hereafter Yayasan[7]), which was aimed at carrying on the struggle over compensation (Yayasan Tragedi Lagoi Indonesia 2004). Anwar, one of the activists working with the Yayasan outlines the organization's primary functions:

> *The Yayasan was set up after the demonstration of 2000. It is an official institution for those involved in the land compensation issue. Our priorities are as follows: (a) to seek suitable compensation for those who have not received appropriate compensation for land taken away from them; (b) to fight for better human rights more generally; (c) to upgrade the status of the local population workforce and get the villagers involved in the authorities' development plans.*

Aside from the eventual formation of the Yayasan, whose activities since then have led to significant progress in terms of acquiring some form of compensation for the local people, resistance took other forms and, indeed, some of the villagers themselves managed to stand their ground. Within the BBIR, there is still one village, Kampong Bahru, where some residents refused compensation and relocation. According to one of these villagers, Yusuf, 'at the time, the military came to force us to move. But my family resisted them because this is our land. Most others have moved to the new *pemukiman*. Here only about six or seven of the original households are left'. He went on to recount the subsequent ways in which BMW had attempted to get them to move to the new *pemukiman* that had been provided for them at Sungei Kechil:

> *In 1995, when the BMW came to develop the golf course, they actually blocked the entrance to the village ... without the entrance we would be trapped here. So a group of the villagers, including those who have moved out of the resort area, about 700 of us, demonstrated against BMW. After that, the blockade was lifted.*

Being within the BBIR prevented these people from taking part in protests including the one in 2000. However, in spirit, they supported these actions:

> *We live within the resort, and our land has not been freed. We have not received compensation, so we have not been cheated. It is difficult because we live within the resort. If the authorities force us to leave for creating trouble,*

---

7   Apart from organizing demonstrations, petitions and protests, the Yayasan also seeks to find a solution to the problems faced by the local villagers by negotiation and discussions with local politicians and resort investors.

> *we may be in a worse state. We support our friends out there. But we do not want any incidents.*

There are some villages in which people have been compensated but have yet to move as their land has not been developed. According to Rehman, a resident of Berakit, for example, 'at Berakit, the villagers whose land had been freed have received compensation but, because a new settlement has not been set aside for them, they have remained where they are. How can they move? They have nowhere to go'.

In the case of the lost lands that were redesignated as the BBIR, the prospect of more systematic and comprehensive compensation became one of these subjects of contest and counter-mapping. As another Berakit villager said, 'our house here is still within the resort area, but developments have not been planned yet. If the authorities want to get this land later, they would have to pay us appropriate compensation. We will negotiate for a higher amount of money'.

In other cases, despite new *pemukiman* having been granted, village land remained undeveloped and so villagers have moved back to fishing. In Segiling, for example, 20 or so former residents have been able to return (even though their homes are no longer standing) and have constructed small huts by the beach. As one of the villagers stated:

> *We moved back here because we are fishermen. It is easier for us to catch fish if we are close to the sea. The land that we have at the new settlement is far from the sea. If the developers decide to develop this land, we will just leave again.*

Some of these villagers now maintain houses at both the old sites and the new *pemukiman*. In other cases, villagers have not moved back to the sites of their old villages, but negotiate with security guards about periodically crossing over into the resort area to fish:

> *There are many more fish within the Sedona area than here. The security at the Sedona Resort knows us, so they let us go into the resort area to catch fish. But we have to be very careful so that we do not disturb any of the resort activities.*

Hence, despite the various security measures that have been emplaced at the BBIR, boundaries are sometimes still quietly transgressed by some of these local villagers.

A few of the villagers have also found other ways of re-inserting their presence within tourism activities from 'below'. At Kampong Bahru, for instance, resort employees sometimes bring tourists to the village within the BBIR as part of an unofficial tour. To cater to these visitors, the villagers put up mini-galleries outside their homes where tourists can learn about seashells and fishing techniques. Yusuf added:

There are many fishermen here. When we go out to sea to catch fish, many resort visitors see us. 'White people' like to see us work and take photographs. In the village, we also have a stage where we practice our dances for visitors. This way, we can earn money from tourists. They also come to eat fresh coconuts for S$ 1-2. We have a gallery where visitors can learn about types of seashells. Some visitors would buy souvenirs from us costing up to $5. This is very good for the villagers.

Part of Kampong Bahru has also been converted into a rustic *kelong* (a wooden pier traditionally used for fishing).

The presence of Kampong Bahru also allows for other boundary-crossings on the part of those who have moved out of the resort area. For example, individuals who have family at the village within the BBIR are allowed to enter the zone (although they still need to report to the guardhouse each time). Movements into the resort are also allowed on other special occasions. As Winarta indicated:

When we were forced to move out, we did not have enough time or money to move the cemeteries. Now it is difficult to go in. But they cannot destroy it. It is important to local villagers [orang orang kampong disini]. Our ancestors are buried there. Once a year ... villagers are allowed in. But we still need permission.

These sacred presences endure. Despite the process of 'Singaporeanization', there are landscape features and presences which predate the formation of the resort. Earlier human geographies have not simply been overwritten or erased by the formal economic development of the BBIR. Alternative views of the land (and continuation of earlier understandings, meanings and 'power' of the space) indicate how, despite attempts to present the resort area as an ordered landscape, other narratives resurface. For many of the villagers, sites and places within BBIR are still seen as sacred[8] and the way they have been developed is perceived to be sacrilegious.

It is clear therefore that, notwithstanding the many measures put in place by the BRC to 'Singaporeanize' the BBIR, it is not possible to eradicate all the local particularities and meanings invested in the land. The process of taming the Bintanscape through specific strategies of boundary-making and the production of a biome for tourists, enabling flows of foreign bodies and monies, thus remains subject to these material and symbolic reworkings.

---

8   See Chou (1997) for further details of how places in Riau have become differentiated as abodes of spirits (*hantu*) that require certain modes of human conduct.

Conclusions: the revanchist global city?

Writing of 'development' strategies elsewhere in Southeast Asia, Cooke (2003, 268) notes how mapping and land-use policy have been used by successive colonial and postcolonial regimes as a strategy of power 'exercised via species control and territory'. Cooke explores how, in response, counter-mappings have sought to assert the customary rights (*adat*) of local communities to land, and the material and cultural resources upon it. Bintan's proximity to Singapore means that low-cost industrial production (at Lobam) and tourism (in the BBIR) are similarly envisioned as niche spaces within the 'global'. In this chapter, we have both detailed aspects of this process and read them through developing literatures on borders, accumulation and city 'frontiers'. We have also documented some of the ways that, in the case of the Bintan resorts, the visions of developers have evoked 'counter-mappings' in the form of other claims and attendant transgressions. The modest efforts by locals to benefit from the tourism economy, to negotiate better prices when their land is taken and, in some cases, to reclaim land and resources, have been described here in a provisional and partial attempt to develop accounts of agency and struggle in the context of ongoing reterritorializations which they can sometimes subvert and disrupt, but ultimately over which they have little control.

As we noted in the introduction, to describe the frontiers of capital and contours of struggle over social space, housing and welfare in cities of the Americas and Europe, critical observers have designated 'revanchist cities', where 'repressive and ideological state apparatuses are folded together in a disciplinary and, at times, penalizing and stoutly authoritarian effort' (MacLeod 2002, 608). In this sense, Singapore's post-independence push for order, development and control looks like a prototype, albeit one mediated through recourse to powerful ideologies of 'Asian values' modernity, nation-building and community and the spectacular redevelopment and reworking of a migrant and colonial city into a model of globalized, networked 'post-colonial' urbanity (Kong and Yeoh 2003). For about the first 30 years following independence, this was confined to the national territory of Singapore; all 'traditional' *kampong* housing was cleared and swathes of the island reordered according to a master plan to build (in the language of the day) a 'world-class' tropical city. By the 1980s, notwithstanding land reclamations (which increased the national territory from 580 square kilometres to more than 710 square kilometres in 2009) and higher skyscrapers, space for extensive further expansion in Singapore had more or less run out. In this context, the visions of a Growth Triangle taking in parts of Johore and Riau were born. Since these visions articulated (albeit not without some tensions) with the elite developmental visions in Malaysia and Indonesia, the Growth Triangle came to be celebrated as an avatar of a new phase of regionalized development. In this, Singapore and its neighbours were amongst the advance guard of a worldwide proliferation of Growth Triangles, Arcs and entrepreneurial cross-border regimes (Neilson 2004). As we have charted here, this rests upon extensive reterritorializations, in particular the reworking of boundaries. Thus capital flows and tourist bodies permeate the Singapore–Indonesia boundary (whilst migrants are blocked), but beyond this postcolonial boundary, other new lines are being drawn and spaces enclosed, as in the fences around the BBIR and the strategy to rework its biome into geometric cultivated landscaping.

These processes have continued in northern Bintan during the five years since the fieldwork upon which this chapter is based was carried out, albeit in ways increasingly subject to the dynamics of political decentralization and democratization[9] in Indonesia. After years during which visitor numbers were said to have been hit variously by the Asian financial crisis, 9/11 and subsequent 'terrorist' attacks in Indonesia, Sars and tsunami fears – not to mention the land compensation protests – the zone appeared finally to be making a 'comeback' (*Straits Times* 31 January 2007). Investments committed by a Malaysian company, Landmarks Bhd, in 2006-7 promised the first significant development in north Bintan since the Banyan Tree Group opened the Angsana Resort in 2000. Not surprisingly, newspaper reports about the proposed tourist complex at 'Treasure Bay' and a range of residential plans in the Lagoi area made much of both the price and abundance of land: reportedly half the price of comparable plots in other tourist islands such as Phuket or Bali; and on a 1,300 ha area said to be seven times larger than Singapore's two upcoming 'integrated resort' (IR) developments combined (*Straits Times* 31 January 2007). No opposition is reported to the residential component of the plans, for the 'cheap and big bungalows' which form part of plans 'to turn north Bintan into a suburb for Singaporeans to live and play' (*Straits Times* 23 June 2009). An improved ferry service will not only speed up access to these homes but will allow airline-style business class passengers to get 'personalized immigration clearance in their own dedicated lounge' on their way into and out of Singapore's gated, cross-border suburbs. This is, of course, an example of a worldwide phenomenon; the firming of new gates, boundaries and fences (Klein and Levy 2002; Sidaway 2007a, 2007b). Business class border crossings exist in a wider context of tightened immigration and 'security' controls everywhere, increasingly revanchist cities and thousands of gated communities. Although some observers locate creative cultural hybridities in cross-border sites of fast urbanization (Dear and Leclerc 2003), the force and exclusions on which such urbanization rests give others much less cause to be sanguine (Coleman 2005).

---

9   The climate of political democratization has expanded the legal possibilities for Indonesian citizen groups to pursue grievances against businesses and state authorities. In the context of the campaign by the *Yayasan Tragedi Lagoi* for compensation and through the organization's cooperation with other institutions – local, regional as well as those based in the Indonesian capital of Jakarta – the BMW recently agreed to further compensation for people in Lagoi who lost land during the development of BBIR and BIE. While the full details were not disclosed, compensations will be awarded according to four main classifications: (1) land that has been officially surveyed and paid for previously albeit without the consensus of the local people; (2) land that has been officially surveyed but not compensated for previously; (3) land that has not been officially surveyed; and (4) land that has not been officially surveyed but has already been built upon (see *Sijori Mandiri* 4 February 2009).

Moreover in Bintan, in the immediate hinterland and – as we have set out here – on one of the frontiers of a world city, there are also suggestive historical parallels which cast such tendencies into a longer-term frame of state–city–capital–societal interactions. Thus in his account of the changing roles of the Straits of Malacca (of which the *Selat Singapura* between the Riau archipelago and Singapore is the narrowest point) in the evolving patterns of regional and global commerce over the past several millennia, Freeman (2003, xvi) points to 'the critical functions of trade facilitation, enhancement, security, and control performed at different epochs by three important gate-keeper entrepots in the region: Melaka (Malacca), British Penang (Pulau Pinang), and Singapore'. In due course, concerns about disruption to these functions (including piracy) lay at the roots of colonial intervention (and are echoed today in discourses about terrorism and piracy in the Straits). Here, other geographies of power and accumulation (those of 'buccaneers' and 'rebels') have long contested the views from those control centres. The contexts may have changed, but the marginal disruptions detailed in this chapter and attempts to extract just a little of the profits of commerce and subvert something of the sovereign power are not unprecedented. Writing about such transgressions and complexities in the past, Eric Tagliacozzo describes how:

> The political economies of the frontier areas between what was emerging as British and Dutch Southeast Asia were complex, and conceptually these spaces looked remarkably like a patchwork quilt in the decades leading up to 1900. By the Treaty of 1871, a line had been drawn bisecting the Straits of Melaka, separating the two colonial possessions by a shallow ribbon of water ... Yet on the ground, in the lands and seas adjoining the frontier regions, this picture was exceedingly more complicated (Tagliacozzo 2005, 29).

Today, for all the apparent significance of the postcolonial boundaries and the apparent rigidity of newer ones, so ongoing struggles threaten to disrupt and transgress the 'smooth' spaces and sharp lines between the multiple territories and boundaries that border the Straits.

References

Beaverstock, J.V., Taylor, P.J. and Smith, R.G. (1999), 'A roster of world cities', *Cities* 16:6, 445-58.

Bunnell, T., Sidaway, J.D. and Grundy-Warr, C. (2006), 'Remapping the Growth Triangle: Singapore's cross-border hinterland', *Asia Pacific Viewpoint* 47:2, 235-40.

Chang, T.C. (2001), 'Configuring new tourism space: exploring Singapore's regional tourism forays', *Environment and Planning A* 33:9, 1597-619.

Chou, C. (2006), 'Multiple realities of the Growth Triangle: Mapping knowledge and the politics of mapping', *Asia Pacific Viewpoint* 47:2, 241-56.

Chou, C. (2002), *Indonesian sea nomads: money, magic, and fear of the Orang Suku Laut* (London and New York: Routledge).

Chou, C. (1997), 'Contesting the tenure of territoriality: the Orang Suku Laut', *Bijdragen tot de Taal, Land en Volkenkunde* 153:4, 605-29.

Chou, C. and Wee, V. (2003), 'Tribality and globalization: The Orang Suku Laut and the 'Growth Triangle' in a contested environment', in Benjamin, G. and Chou, C. (eds.), *Tribal communities in the Malay World: historical, cultural and social perspectives* (Leiden: Institute for Southeast Asian Studies, Singapore and International Institute for Asian Studies).

Coleman, M. (2005), 'U.S. Statecraft and the U.S.–Mexico border as security/economy nexus', *Political Geography* 24, 185-204.

Cooke, F.M. (2003), 'Maps and counter-maps: globalised imaginings and local realities of Sarawak's plantation agriculture', *Journal of Southeast Asian Studies* 34:2, 265-84.

Cunningham, H. (2001), 'Transnational politics at the edges of sovereignty: social movements, crossings and the state at the U.S.–Mexico border', *Global Networks* 1:4, 369-87.

Dear, M. and Leclerc, G. (2003)(eds.), *Postborder city: cultural spaces of Bajalta California* (London and New York: Routledge).

Ford, M.T. and Lyons, L. (2006), 'The borders within: mobility and enclosure in the Riau islands', *Asia Pacific Viewpoint* 47:2, 257-71.

Freeman, D.B. (2003), *The Straits of Malacca: gateway or gauntlet?* (Montreal and Kingston, London, Ithaca: McGill-Queens University Press).

Friedmann, J. (1986), 'The world city hypothesis', *Development and Change* 17, 69-83.

Grundy-Warr, C., Peachey, K. and Perry, M. (1999), 'Fragmented integration in the Singapore-Indonesian border.zone: Southeast Asia's "growth triangle" against the global economy', *International Journal of Urban and Regional Research* 23:2, 304-28.

Judd, D.R. and Fainstein, S.S. (1999)(eds.), *The tourist city* (New Haven: Yale University Press).

Klein, N. and Levy, D.A. (2002), *Fences and windows: dispatches from the front-lines of the globalization debate* (Toronto: Vintage Press).

Kong, L. and Yeoh, B. (2003), *The politics of landscape in Singapore: constructions of 'nation'* (New York: Syracuse University Press).

Lindquist, J. (2009), *The anxieties of mobility: development and migration in the Indonesian Borderlands* (Honolulu: University of Hawaii Press).

Liow, J.C. (2005), *The politics of Indonesia– Malaysia relations: one kin, two nations* (London and New York: Routledge Curzon).

MacLeod, G. (2002), 'From urban entrepreneurialism to a 'revanchist city'? On the spatial injustices of Glasgow's renaissance', *Antipode* 34:3, 602-4.

Mack, J.S. (2004), 'Inhabiting the imaginary: factory women at home on Batam island', *Singapore Journal of Tropical Geography* 25:2, 156-79.

Medovi, L. (2005), 'Nation, globe, hegemony: post-Fordist preconditions of the transnational turn in American Studies', *Interventions: International Journal of Postcolonial Studies* 7:2, 162-70.

Mitchell, D. (2001), 'The devil's arm: points of passage, networks of violence and the political economy of landscape', *New Formations* 43, 44-60.

Neilson, B. (2004), *Free trade in the Bermuda Triangle* (Minneapolis and London: University of Minnesota Press).

Newman, P. and Thornley, A. (2005), *Planning world cities: globalization and urban politics* (Basingstoke: Palgrave Macmillan).

Olds, K. and Yeung, H. (2004), 'Pathways to global city formation: a view from the developmental city-state of Singapore', *Review of International Political Economy* 11:3, 489-521.

Phelps, N. (2004a), 'Archetype for an archipelago? Batam as anti-model and model of industrialization in *reformasi* Indonesia', *Progress in Development Studies* 4:3, 206-29.

Phelps, N. (2004b), 'Triangular diplomacy writ small: the political economy of the Indonesia–Malaysia–Singapore Growth Triangle', *The Pacific Review* 17:3, 341-68.

Robinson, J (2002), 'Global and world cities: a view from off the map', *International Journal of Urban and Regional Research* 26: 3, 531-54.

Routledge, P. (2002), 'Travelling east as Walter Kurtz: identity, performance and collaboration in Goa, India', *Environment and Planning D: Society and Space* 20:4, 477-98.

Routledge, P. (2001), 'Selling the rain, resisting the sale: resistant identities and the conflict over tourism in Goa', *Social and Cultural Geography* 2:2, 221-40.

Sassen, S. (1991), *The global city: New York, London, Tokyo* (Princeton, NJ: Princeton University Press).

Scott, A., Agnew, J., Soja, E.W. and Storper, M. (2001), 'Global city-regions', in Scott, A.J. (ed.), *Global city-regions: trends, theory, policy* (Oxford: Oxford University Press).

Sidaway, J.D. (2007a), 'Enclave space: a new metageography of development?', *Area* 39:3, 331-9.

Sidaway, J.D. (2007b), 'Spaces of postdevelopment', *Progress in Human Geography* 31:2, 345-61.

Smith, M.P. (2001), *Transnational urbanism: locating globalization* (Oxford: Blackwell).

Smith, N. (1996), *The new urban frontier: gentrification and the revanchist city* (London and New York: Routledge).

Sparke, M., Sidaway, J., Bunnell, T. and Grundy-Warr, C. (2004), 'Triangulating the borderless world: globalisation, regionalisation and the geographies of power in the Indonesia–Malaysia–Singapore growth triangle', *Transactions of the Institute of British Geographers* 29:4, 485-98.

Tagliacozzo, E. (2005), *Secret trades, porous borders: smuggling and states along a southeast asian frontier, 1865-1915* (New Haven and London: Yale University Press).

Taylor, P.J. (2005), 'Leading world cities: empirical evaluation of urban nodes in multiple networks', *Urban Studies* 42:9, 1593-608.

Taylor, P.J. (2004), *World city network: a global urban analysis* (London and New York: Routledge).

Yayasan Tragedi Lagoi Indonesia (2004), *Rapatan Rakyat Bintan* (Grievances of the Bintanese People), 15 June 2004 (Tanjung Pinang: unpublished).

Yeung, H.W. (2000), 'State intervention and neoliberalism in the globalizing world economy: lessons from Singapore's regionalization programme', *The Pacific Review* 13:1, 133-62.

Cross-border Cooperation and Regional Responses to NAFTA and Globalization

Vera Pavlakovich-Kochi

Cross-border cooperation in the U.S.-Mexico border region is not a new process; the international boundary between the United States and Mexico, which was finalized in 1854 with the Gadsden Purchase of what is now southern Arizona, has always been considered quite porous and conducive to local cross-border interchanges. For decades cross-border cooperation was mostly local in scope; it was used as the most common strategy in coping with border issues and remoteness from the respective national capitals.

Cross-border cooperation in the U.S.-Mexico border region in the last two decades is characterized by new modalities, new territorial scopes, new agents, and new outcomes – mainly as a result of the North American Free Trade Agreement (NAFTA) and globalization. While the 'whys' and 'hows' of contemporary cross-border cooperation are common to other border regions worldwide, the geography, history and social fabric of the U.S.-Mexico border region have created region-specific contexts which filter and modify global processes, and at the same time produce their own outcomes.

Not long ago, Clement (2001) concluded that despite an outpour of literature on borderlands 'very little attention has been focused on a theory of transboundary collaboration, particularly one that can be helpful to those charged with managing practical projects in transboundary settings'. While we still lack a comprehensive theory of transborder collaboration, important advances have been made since Clement's (2001) statement. This chapter reviews conceptualization of recent trends in cross-border cooperation in the U.S.-Mexico border region, and by using selected examples, demonstrates the complexity of processes and their outcomes. This complexity, in turn, presents challenges for both the academic research and practical decision and policy making.

Conceptualization of Cross-border Cooperation in a Regional Context

In its simplest definition, cross-border cooperation refers to working together, that is collaborating, across national or international borders for the purpose of achieving some common goals. It implicitly assumes benefits to participants on both sides of the border. In theory, cross-border partnership building relies on mutual interests and includes activities that bring or are perceived to bring equivalent benefits to the participants. In reality, cross-border cooperation is a very complex phenomenon; it encompasses a multitude of forms and levels, occurs within and outside institutional frameworks, spans over different timeframes, and consequently produces different outcomes.

Based on OECD (1979) scheme, Lara Valencia (2001) identified three main stages of coalescence in a border context: (1) convergence; (2) collaboration, and (3) co-management. These three stages differ in terms of actions, scope and outcomes. Collaboration is defined as a middle level between convergence – which is mostly based on personal contacts for the purpose of exchanging information about preliminary plans or policies – and the co-management stage, which involves formalized cross-border programs and coalitions. Collaboration may involve exchange of financial and other resources and usually leads to formation of binational groups and mechanisms for consultation with the other side of the border. It is important to stress, however, that delineations between the three stages are not fixed, nor do they necessarily occur in succession. Rather, these different stages may coexist with one another and mutate back and forth through time as the economic, political and societal conditions change.

Rationale for Cross-border Cooperation

The actions, scope and outcomes of cross-border cooperation are intimately related to the existence and type of boundaries. Morehouse (1995, 2004) classified boundaries in order to understand their functions during a particular time in history as barriers, filters, expression of nationalism, points of conflict, or points of contact and cooperation. Consequently, border functions include establishing a territorially based identity (shell function), control/jurisdiction (net function), improvement of administrative/management efficiency (facilitator function), prevention of border crossing (filter function), restriction of passage into certain bounded border spaces (gate function), surveillance inside or outside defined areas (panopticon function) and balancing opposing demands (fulcrum function).

Building on Morehouse's (1995, 2004) framework, Pick, Miggins and Viswanathan (2005) suggest that in modern border exchanges between nations the border interactions that are most likely to be present are those involving control and jurisdiction (net function) and those involving administration and management (facilitator function).

Indeed, the recent dramatic change in border functions of international boundaries is seen as a major driver behind increasing cross-border cooperation in many parts of the world. In general, international boundaries have become more open and present fewer barriers to cross-border activity and the development of transborder regions (Clement 2001). Blatter (2001) stresses that many reasons explain this phenomenon; on one side, global economic, technological, ecological, and social developments all contribute to a rapid increase in interdependence across territorial boundaries. At the same time, factors within political systems, including trends toward decentralization in most Western countries and, more importantly, the political move toward continental integration, such as the North American Free Trade (NAFTA), have created opportunities that are being pursued by subnational organizations and regional actors.

Clement (2001) emphasizes the role of the so-called 'new economy' in the changing functions of international boundaries at the end of the twentieth and the beginning of the twenty-first century. He argues that the new economy is a result of diminished involvement of central governments in attaining full employment and economic growth. Instead, the prevailing conservative ideology emphasizes market-oriented, supply-side economics. This devolution of power, in turn, forces local and regional governments to accept more responsibility for economic development in their own jurisdiction. Especially in border regions, such developments contribute to a rapid increase in interdependence across territorial boundaries and to a political process that Brian Hocking (1993 in Blatter 2001) calls 'localizing foreign policy' or what Clement (2001) refers to as 'regionalized decision making across international boundaries'.

Increasing interdependence in border regions is seen as a major force behind cross-border cooperation. Air pollution, diseases, and river flows have always disregarded political boundaries. As the border population, industrialization and urbanization of border regions increase, so do the environmental problems multiply. Aside from environmental issues, border regional governments are being encouraged to engage in cross-border cooperation in hope of reducing conflict and improving prosperity and quality of life (Clement 2001).

From a policy-making perspective, cross-border cooperation has been touted as the most rational tool for handling border issues. However, as Lara Valencia (2001) argues, participation in transboundary arrangements occurs only after incentives have been carefully weighted and the participants are sure of obtaining certain benefits, or at least perceive a reasonable potential for benefit. The benefits range from tangible gains (such as access to infrastructure or improved air quality) to intangible benefits (such as gaining an ally or avoiding conflict with a neighboring country).

General Conditions for Building Cross-border Cooperation

The complexity of developing cross-border cooperation stems partly from the fact that international borders are simultaneously areas of conflict and collaboration. Indeed, in the U.S.-Mexico border region, two opposing dimensions have coexisted and interacted continually, shaping the nature and depth of transboundary relations (Lara Valencia 2001; Martinez 1988; Wong-González 2004). Given these difficulties and a continuous tension between conflict and collaboration, the question arises: under what conditions does partnership building become the means preferred by border communities for settling differences in addressing environmental problems or planning for economic development? In answering this question, Lara Valencia (2001) identified two approaches – structural variables perspective (based on works by Mumme 1987 and Hansen 1986) and organizational perspective (based on Scherer and Blatter 1994).

From a structural standpoint, cross-border partnerships depend largely on local actors' receptiveness to cooperation, which is determined by those factors within their social and political environment that support the development of interorganizational links across the border. Specifically, there are five factors: (1) a certain level of decentralization and the allocation of certain responsibilities to local and regional authorities; (2) the existence of institutional structures that facilitate participation in transboundary issues; (3) the willingness to accept binational solutions to shared problems; (4) community optimism that embraces a shared vision of the future, and (5) the existence of situations in which cooperation is a feasible and viable way to obtain tangible, equitable benefits for the participants.

From an organizational perspective, four specific factors contribute to developing transboundary cooperation: (1) the commitment that an organization shows to cross-border arrangements as the preferred strategy for handling regional problems; (2) resources allocated to cross-border endeavors; (3) the ability to overcome language and other idiosyncratic cultural differences, and (4) the ability to identify appropriate counterparts on each side of the border.

In fact, argues Lara Valencia (2001), when both perspectives are taken together they provide the basis for responding to the why, when, where, and who of cooperative networks within borderlands.

Actors, Agents and Followers

Cooperation does not occur in a vacuum; rather, as discussed in the preceding section, it develops when certain socio-economic, political and cultural conditions are met. Nor does it happen by itself; it always has a certain mass of main actors, a varied number of followers, and a number of more or less formal agents. Actors define the initial scope and modality of cooperation, while agents and followers influence the implementation of cooperation and its final outcomes. Agents (be it institutions or less formal groups) manage and mediate the process of cooperation, while followers support the cooperation as they see its objectives in full or partial alignment with their own interests. Therefore, in order to better understand goals, interests, objectives, modality and effects of cross-border cooperation, it is critical to gain insights into who are the main actors, how is cooperation being managed, and who might be the followers.

Because the scholarly interest in cross-border cooperation is relatively new, we still lack a full grasp of intricate nature of interaction among actors across the border. Empirical studies suggest that uneven contexts (material and social) along the border present obstacles and challenges for various agents, but not enough is known about how they negotiate those differences. We know even less about how (and if) the followers modify the initial objectives and possibly expand (or limit) the scope (scale) of cross-border cooperation.

Vázquez Castillo (2005) suggests three principal levels at which cross-border cooperation in North American context takes place: diplomatic, bilateral and political mobilization level. At the diplomatic level, the main actors are national and binational governmental institutions. Bilateral cooperation, she argues, is carried out more and more by regional governments and local communities on both sides of the border. At the political mobilization level, the principal actors are non-governmental organizations (NGO) and citizens in border communities.

Blatter (2001) argues that linkages across the border are almost always centered on sectoral focal points and suggests that environmentalists and business groups are generally the two dominant coalitions of actors in any border region area. Typically, business coalitions' objective is to put together the necessary critical mass for the region to become a major player in the new global economy. To 'become a globally competitive community' has been the key unifying objective of every cross-border coalition since the early 1990s (see for example Pavlakovich-Kochi and Walker 1996; PNWER 1997; Wong-González 2004). Environmentalist coalitions, on the other side, are focused on preservation of and management of cross-border region as a bioregion. Thus, the visions of the business and environmental communities are often diametrically opposed although both downplay the future importance of the nation-state in favor of border regions' self-governance (Blatter 2001).

Increasingly, cross-border partnerships range from those in which a single organization interacts with another single organization in the same sector to those in which multiple organizations from different sectors are represented in some ongoing cooperative enterprise (Lara Valencia 2001). The partnerships can become quite complex; they may include a multitude of actors coalesced around a common interest, although they may differ in their larger visions and specific interests. In recent years, one of the most notable characteristics is that cross-border cooperation has expanded between local governments, businesses and non-governmental organizations (NGO), the actors that in the past were often on opposite sides.

In the U.S.-Mexico border region, universities and other higher education/ research institutions have become increasingly active in both economic development and environmental cooperation. As will be shown in more detail later in selected case studies, these institutions not only provide passive expertise (study reports) but are often actively involved as mediators among actors and as participants in decision-making processes.

Cross-border Cooperation, Integration and Transboundary Region-Building

Although closely related, there is a difference between cross-border cooperation, integration and transboundary region-building. Transboundary region-building in North America is commonly understood in terms of formal, government-supported cross-border alliances that gained momentum since the late 1980s (Blatter 2001; Pavlakovich-Kochi and Walker 1996; Swanson 1994; Wong-González 2004).

Formal cross-border region-building, such as the establishment of the Pacific Northwest Economic Region (PNWER), spanning the Canada-United States border is implicitly based on cross-border cooperation. Indeed, cross-border cooperation has been often initiated and encouraged by ongoing economic and territorial integration; and vice versa, cross-border cooperation often has the cross-border economic integration as its primary objective. This close relation persuaded some border scholars, such as Blatter (2001) to argue that cross-border cooperation needed to be renamed cross-border region-building, even though most cross-border institutions might be little more than informal networks. While this statement of calling every mode of cross-border cooperation 'region-building' might be too gallant, there is no doubt that cross-border cooperation is the foundation of any region-building.

Since the 1980s and especially in the 1990s, the local governments have taken on an increasingly important role in fostering cross-border cooperation as a tool in transboundary region-building. The North American regionalism, however, differs from European regionalism in tone, context, and causes. According to Delamaide's (1995, cited in Wong-González 2004), the European trend of 'regionalism' prompted creation of 'super regions' that transcend national borders. They show a paradoxical double trend wherein economic and political integration occur simultaneously with a trend toward greater autonomy at the smallest regional levels, where social and cultural unity is greater.

In North America, it was mainly state and provincial governments (that is subnational entities) that signed cross-border partnership agreements to facilitate communication among private sector business people. A formalization process has spurred the creation of organized territorial forms for regional development management. These transnational economic regions are actively promoted by entrepreneurial boards and groups, community associations, and local government actors. Through these partnerships, initiatives are developed to increase trade flows, attract industries, plan transportation and improve border ports of entry (Wong-González 2004).

NAFTA as a Catalyst of Cross-Border Cooperation

In North America, cross-border collaborative initiatives were greatly fostered by the North American Free Trade Agreement (NAFTA) between the United

States, Canada and Mexico, inaugurated in 1994. As a trade agreement, NAFTA's primary purpose was economic integration of production, consumer and financial markets among the three countries through duty-free movement of goods, services and capital across the borders. Cross-border movement of labor, unlike in the European Union, remained restricted. Attached to the trade agreement are two side agreements regarding the management of border environment and labor standards. Many observers agree that NAFTA, in spite of its focus on economic integration, has become a catalyst that has stimulated and facilitated new subnational cross-border activities over the last decade (Blatter 2001; Lara Valencia 2001; Little 2005).

Blatter (2001) rightly observed that this new momentum of continental integration spilled over into the borderlands and encompassed almost all policy area. Moreover, cross-border activities have extended far beyond free trade policies causing new motivations for what Haeflinger (1996, cited in Blatter 2001) referred to as 'micro-integration.' 'Even more significantly', argues Blatter (2001), 'new initiatives sprang up in almost every border region... A common region became a salient topic in the late 1980s and early 1990s, changing perceptions about both borders and neighbors'.

For example, as a direct effect of the U.S.-Canada FTA, British Columbia signed an agreement with Washington State called Pacific Northwest Economic Partnership. This was a drastic change, according to Blatter (2001), because the region had been characterized by distant cross-border relationships, limited socioeconomic interdependence and pronounced economic competition. Similar formal cross-border partnerships have sprung in other parts of the U.S.-Canada border such as the Northern Plains-Mid Continent Region encompassing Manitoba, North Dakota and Minnesota (Nelson and Twite 1996) and the North-East North America encompassing New England States, Québec and the Atlantic Provinces (Proulx 1996).

Signing of NAFTA encouraged the cross-border cooperation along the U.S.-Canada border. But the major effects were felt along the U.S.-Mexico border. Unlike U.S.-Canada border, the entire U.S.-Mexico border region is highly interdependent with a long history of cross-border interchanges in economic, political and cultural spheres.

Pre-NAFTA cross-border cooperation, however, differs from the more recent collaboration in scope, actors involved and forms of collaboration. On one side, pre-NAFTA cooperation was limited to solving local issues such as cross-border assistance in cases of fire or other elementary disasters. On the other side, the broader 'border issues' were mostly addressed at national/international level; in other words, the destiny of the border region was decided at, what Vázquez Castillo (2005) referred to as diplomatic level. Not surprisingly, many local communities and organizations criticized such national level decisions for not taking into account local needs and local participation.

NAFTA was designed explicitly to encourage free trade and economic integration. However, the negotiations preceding NAFTA created an environment for discussion at the public level about a multitude of border issues. As expressed by Vázquez Castillo (2005), it was at that time that a public conceptualization emerged of a 'border region as a common area apart from the two countries'. In particular, the status of environment in the border region was lifted to the center stage. Although focused on erasing boundaries for the movement of capital and goods, it was largely the opposition to NAFTA that made it possible to reconceptualize environmental planning in a regional and transborder context.

The implementation of NAFTA resulted in direct and indirect changes (Little 2005). First is the direct creation of new formal institutional arrangements for transboundary cooperation, such as that of the Border Environmental Cooperation Commission (BEEC) headquartered in Ciudad Juárez, Chihuahua, Mexico. Another parallel institution, the North American Development Bank (NADBank) was established primarily for the investments in cleaning the environment (Table 23.1).

Table 23.1 Pre- and NAFTA-related Institutions for Environmental Management in the U.S.-Mexico Border

Regime	Main Institutions/Institutional Frameworks for Cross-border Cooperation	Approach
Pre-NAFTA (1848-1993)	• International Boundary Commission (IBC), 1906-1944 • International Boundary and Water Commission (IBWC), 1944 • La Paz Agreement on Cooperation for the Protection and Improvement of the Environment in the Border Area, 1983 • Integrated Border Environment Plan, 1992-94	• Allocative • Territorially defensive • Centrally dominated • Reactive • Fragmentary • Technically oriented
Post-NAFTA (1994-)	• Commission for Environmental Cooperation (CEC), 1994 • Border Environment Cooperation Commission (BEEC), 1994 • North American Development Bank (NADBank), 1994 • Border XXI Program (EPA-SEMARNAP), 1994	• Cooperative • Citizen based • Integrative • Consensus oriented • Binational • Planning oriented

Sources: Author's elaboration based on Spalding (2000); Mumme (1995); Lara Valencia (2000); Vázquez Castillo (2005).

Secondly, NAFTA has had indirect influence in broadening the missions of existing binational entities such as that of the International Boundary and Water Commission (IBWC), with its U.S. component headquartered in El Paso, Texas and its Mexican component headquartered in Ciudad Juárez, Chihuahua.

NAFTA is also credited with initiating new 'border-emphasis' units, which were created within existing government entities, such as the Environmental Protection Agency's border offices located in the major border sister cities. The NAFTA framework also was instrumental in formalizing local-to-local cooperative efforts, such as the Memorandum of Understanding developed between the two water utilities of El Paso, Texas and Ciudad Juárez, Chihuahua in solving the regional problem of water supply (Little 2005).

All of these changes resulted in the emergence of new actors in border spaces. For one, the institutional innovations, such as BEEC and NADBank, intended to strengthen public participation and local involvement in borderlands environmental policy making (Lara Valencia 2001). Changes within existing institutions, such as planning departments, converted local planners into actors who mediated bilateral planning between the two countries at the local scale. This translocal and transborder collaboration represented a new element in the process of bilateral planning between Mexico and the United States (Vázquez Castillo 2005). While many partnerships in the border region were not new, their prominence has also grown as a consequence of institutional innovations introduced by NAFTA and its environmental side agreement (Lara Valencia 2001).

Besides environmental issues, pre-NAFTA discussions have spurred formalization of cross-border alliances in practically every area; a truly new element was the active involvement of state and regional governments in transborder economic development issues in partnership with private sector, and especially with border universities. Table 23.2 shows examples of transborder alliances.

While researchers in the U.S.-Mexico border region have had a long tradition of cross-border collaboration, the NAFTA framework provided opportunities for a more active role of universities in strategic economic visioning processes for border regions. For example, the strategic economic vision project for the Arizona-Sonora Region lead to the formation of the Arizona-Sonora University Consortium, which played a key role in production of a formal binational (and bilingual) document including recommendations for a more economically integrated and globally competitive transboundary region (Pavlakovich-Kochi 2006; Wong-González 2004).

An indirect impact of NAFTA on cross-border cooperation in the U.S.-Mexico border region was that it profoundly increased inter-regional competition. NAFTA not only sanctioned the existing economic integration, but opened up new opportunities for increased trade. The border states felt compelled to carve for themselves the biggest benefits of increased cross-border trade by becoming the most attractive gateways within NAFTA area. Arizona's Governor Janet Napolitano, for example, proclaimed as one of her first goals, making the Nogales port of entry 'the premier port of entry' in the entire U.S.-Mexico border region.

Table 23.2 Selected Transborder Collaboration Agreements between State, Regional and Local Actors in the U.S.-Mexico Border

City, County or State	Type of Collaboration
States of California (U.S.) and Baja California (Mexico)	Joint promotion of investment and economic development: 'Discover the Californias: Two countries, one region'
San Diego (U.S.) and Tijuna (Mexico)	Collaboration agreement between both chambers of commerce; Project to jointly build an efficient high-level international airport in order to promote the region as one of the world's strategic centers for international trade
States of New Mexico (U.S.) and Chihuahua (Mexico)	Cooperation agreement to promote border development, build a large maquiladora city and take advantage of NAFTA related opportunities
Border counties from southwestern United States	Mayors' initiative for creation of a binational city council block that would jointly try to solve common problems, as well as promote regional development
States of Arizona (U.S.) and Sonora (Mexico)	Through a joint strategic economic development vision to develop Arizona and Sonora as an integrated economic region and increase region's global competitiveness; collaboration of states governments, private sector, and universities under the auspices of the Arizona-Mexico Commission and Comisión Sonora-Arizona
States of Texas (U.S.) and Northeast Mexico (Chihuahua, Tamualipas, Coahuila and Nuevo León	Regional integration program for the purpose of achieving regional competitiveness by fostering cross-border cooperation in research and innovation; participant include state governments, institutions of higher education and private sector
Camino Real Economic Alliance (cities of Las Vegas, Santa Fe, Albuquerque, Las Cruces and El Paso in U.S. and Ciudad Juárez in Mexico)	Collaboration between chambers of commerce, universities, local governments and private sector for the purpose of promoting trade and regional tourism
U.S. border states and Mexico border states	Collaboration of ten border states' governors through annual conference regarding joint environmental, economic and security issues

Sources: Based on Wong-González (2004); Mora et al. (2006).

The regional actions played at the international level have generated intense competition among Mexican states, counties, and cities, with regard to expanding exports, and attracting investments. Similarly, competition among U.S. border states has increased with regard to participating in technology transfer activities and signing trade agreements in Mexican territory (Wong-González 2004). Border states compete for both public and private investments. States compete for federal funding from their respective national governments in support of a continuous upgrading of border-ports-of-entry infrastructure in order to improve the efficiency and efficacy of trade flows through their territory. Even more fiercely they compete for national and international private sector investments.

Consequently, cross-border cooperation has become a necessary (although not sufficient) strategy in marketing individual transborder regions as the best places for doing business, access to pool of labor, as well as access to consumer markets.

U.S.-Mexico Border Region: A Laboratory for Myriad of Cross-Border Collaborations

The U.S.-Mexico border (region, area) has been defined in different territorial terms; in its broadest term, the U.S.-Mexico border region encompasses four U.S. border states (California, Arizona, New Mexico and Texas) and six Mexican border states (Baja California, Sonora, Chihuahua, Coahuila, Nuevo León and Tamaulipas). Most commonly, though, it is understood in terms of counties (on the U.S. side) and municipios (on Mexican side) adjacent to the international boundary. There is also a 60-mile (100 kilometres) delineation on each side of the international boundary which is used to determine jurisdiction of international organizations, eligibility for special funding (such as NADBank funds) or border crossing privileges (for example, form I-94 in the past was not required within this zone (Figure 23.1)).

One of the most striking facts is that the border separates a developed country and a developing country, with one of the largest cross-border income gaps in the world. Nevertheless, as Anderson and Gerber (2008) point out,

> ... in every economic and demographic category, the local and regional disparities are less than those between the two countries as a whole: whereas the Mexican border region is wealthier than Mexico as a whole, the U.S. border region is mostly poorer than the rest of the United States, thus bringing communities on either side of the border closer together than the enormous economic differences at the scale of the nation would suggest. (Anderson and Gerber 2008)

These relatively smaller economic differences and greater similarities at the level of communities straddling the border is exactly what makes the U.S.-Mexico border area unique.

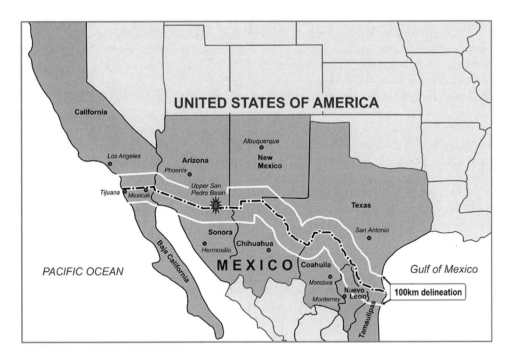

Figure 23.1 The U.S.-Mexico Border Region and the Upper San Pedro Basin

Source: ©: V. Pavlakovich-Kochi.

And yet, despite of or maybe because of this gap, the border region is the area where most of the integration between the United States and Mexico takes place. Integration is rooted in the shared histories, migration and demographic changes, foreign investments, businesses, local governments, and the decisions of millions of families and friends engaging in activities that require border crossing (Anderson and Gerber 2008). This 'ocean of local activity', suggest Anderson and Gerber (2008), is largely beyond the control of national policy makers.

The border region is also the area where the economic integration between the United States and Mexico has caused most dramatic changes affecting the border in the last half-century (Staudt 1998; Anderson and Gerber 2008). The Border Industrialization Program, which introduced assembly plants (maquiladoras) to northern Mexico in the mid 1960s, helped initiate this shift, while NAFTA since the early 1990s, consolidated it (Staudt 1998). Economic integration and free trade are the main forces that will continue to shape the U.S.-Mexico border as a primary region for U.S.-Mexico economic expansion (Herzog 2000).

In the remainder of this chapter, three examples will be presented to demonstrate the multiplicity and complexity of cooperative processes in the U.S.-Mexico border. The case of the Upper San Pedro Basin illustrates cross-border cooperation on a subregional scale with a focus on resolving management of shared water resources. Next, the Arizona-Sonora region demonstrates collaboration on a state level, where two border states on the basis of their long history of cross-border cooperation attempt to carve a more competitive position in the global economy. The last example shows recent attempts in organizing all border states into a single voice different from their respective national territories.

In presenting these three cases, we adopt a template for analysis proposed by Clement (2001) to identify several key elements: history of interdependence/cross-border relationships; problem/rationale for cooperation; principal actors; mode of cooperation; accomplishments and outcomes, and remaining challenges.

Upper San Pedro Basin: The Birth of Cross-border Water-Resources Coordination

The case of the Upper San Pedro Basin (USP Basin) (Figure 23.1) illustrates cross-border cooperation on a subregional scale with a focus on resolving management of shared water resources. This is an example of a growing intensity of cooperation between residents, scientists and water managers, and a key role of a university institution not only in research, but especially as a neutral actor in coordinating binational forums, evolution of the Upper San Pedro partnership, and facilitating binational NGO and governmental agencies working together.

The San Pedro River originates in northern Sonora, Mexico and flows north to Arizona. Approximately 74 per cent of USP Basin is in Arizona and 26 per cent in Mexico (Varady 2006). The Basin is considered to be one of most ecologically diverse areas. The area is outside major north-south trade and transportation corridors, but with increasing cross-border activity and growing urban population. At present, water is used for agriculture, cattle grazing, mining, recreation and growing urbanization.

A specific border issue emerged because of differences between principal users and management practices on each side of the border (Varady 2005). On the Mexican side, growing production of copper from extensive ore reserves limit groundwater availability for municipal and agricultural uses in Mexico; in the U.S. portion of the basin, high population growth rates will result in a major rise in water use to support municipal and domestic use. As water usage has been increasing over last couple decades, and all evidence suggests that it will continue to do so, the allocation of water led to divisiveness among water users and water management entities.

According to the 1906 and 1944 water treaties between the United States and Mexico, any formal binational mechanism that regulates or reallocates water must involve the International Boundary and Water Commission (IBWC) and its Mexican counterpart the Comisión Internacional de Límites y Aguas (CILA) as the lead agencies. As found in other cases, these international agencies have been reluctant to delegate authority and resources at the regional and local level. The NAFTA environmental law, however, made it possible to conduct an initial study of the riparian system.

The University of Arizona, located in Tucson about 75 miles from the border and with long standing collaboration with Mexican researchers, played a key role in the facilitation of cooperation within Arizona's portion of the Basin as well as across the border. Securing the funding from the trinational Commission for Environmental Cooperation (CEC), the University facilitated the public-input process for the 1998 report on water issue in the USP Basin, prepared for CEC. In 1999, University coordinated a binational conference to identify Basin-stakeholder need and concerns, and in 2000, the University conducted surveys of Basin residents regarding their views on water issues and concerns. The survey involved cooperation of local governments, federal agencies and interested citizens (285 in Sonora and 420 in Arizona), as well as interviews with individuals having extensive experience in water research, policy or water management.

Four border 'Environmental Encuentros' (Roundtables) were conducted from 1999 to 2003. They provided opportunities for nongovernmental and community-based organizations to exchange information regarding efforts to improve environmental quality and health in the U.S.-Mexico border region. The specific objective of these roundtables was to strengthen the capacity of nongovernmental and community based organizations.

In the process, new partnerships/institutions were formed. At least four border water-management groups have arisen on the Arizona side (the Sierra Vista sub-basin), with the Upper San Pedro Partnership (USPP) the key group (Varady 2005). The USPP consists of federal, state and local agencies that collectively work to initiate water-research projects in order to implement water-management policies and projects in the Sierra Vista sub-basin. The partnership has evolved from a single body into a commission with a number of subcommittees (advisory, administrative, coordinating, technical advisory and outreach committee). The partnership has become the dominant water-management group; it designates priorities for water research and makes recommendations to the local government.

A special role of the University was to facilitate the establishment of a grassroots watershed association in the Mexican portion of USPP and its collaboration with USPP on the U.S. side. The Mexican coalition originated in 2001 and was organized by a group of teachers; municipal, federal and state agency representatives; mine engineers and lawyers, and other citizens from the Cananea-Naco region in response to concerns about local water-quality and delivery problems. Eventually it extended its scope to other environmental issues. It basically runs as NGO.

Useful experiences were gained with implications for trans-boundary resource management. These include the following (Varady 2005):

- Policy or diplomatic solutions mandated from above may fail without local support;
- Borderlands environmental coalitions initiated by local groups may be more effective at addressing shared problems than national initiatives;
- Economic policies should coincide or at least not conflict with environmental policy;

- Coalitions of local stakeholders need to be inclusive and the process transparent, but this can lead to power struggle;
- Borderlands coalitions as well as national policy initiatives face potential fear of 'outside interference';
- When local environmental groups possess disparate missions or goals it is more difficult for two groups of stakeholders to maintain common dialogue over watershed management;
- More effective decision making occurs when social scientists and natural scientists work together, and
- Knowledge of social history helps understand stakeholders' perspectives.

The University of Arizona remains actively involved as the facilitator of collaboration and coordination among water interests in the USP Basin.

The Arizona-Sonora Region: Builders, Implementers and Followers

This is an example of formal cross-border cooperation between two adjacent border states where an explicit goal was set to, through coordination of economic activities, increase more efficient use of resources on both sides of the border for the purpose of enhancing the region's competitive position vis-à-vis other border states within NAFTA area and global economy.

The states of Arizona and Sonora share a 361-mile stretch of the U.S.-Mexico international boundary. They initiated formal relationships in 1959 when the governors signed the formation of the Arizona-Mexico West Trade Commission for the promotion of economic and cultural ties. Activities included working meetings to jointly discuss topics of common interest related to economy, education, health and communication. The Commission represents the origins of the present Arizona-Mexico Commission and its sister organization, Comisión Sonora-Arizona (Wong-González 2004).

Thus, the basic institutional framework for cross-border cooperation between Arizona and Sonora existed before NAFTA, including the membership structure, binational committees, and working schedule. The membership was drawn from governmental agencies, academic institutions, private sector, nongovernmental organizations, as well as interested citizens. The two Commissions had 12 standing committees co-chaired by one chair from Arizona and one from Sonora; there were two semiannual plenary meetings, one in Arizona and one in Sonora for all members, while committees also met between plenary meetings.

As the discussions about pros and cons of NAFTA intensified, the Commissions took on an active role in order to 'prepare' for the opportunities and challenges of the anticipated framework for conducting cross-border economic activities under free trade. Having the representation of government agencies, private sector and universities, the Commissions were ideally positioned to take a lead and propose formal economic integration between the two neighboring states. At the June 1993 plenary session in Phoenix, Arizona, the governors of Arizona and Sonora announced the initiation of a joint Strategic Economic Development Vision project for Arizona and Sonora as an integrated economic region. With this, argues Wong-González (2004) started a 'new stage' in cross-border relationship between Arizona and Sonora.

Soon after that, the Joint Legislative Protocol Session of the Arizona and Sonora legislative bodies endorsed this initiative. This was the first joint collaborative project based on a shared strategic economic development vision. According to Wong-González (2004), the move marked the beginning of an ambitious process of border integration between the two states. 'Formalizing the integration process through the Strategic Vision project also meant a strong change in emphasis and direction in the relationship between the two states and the work of the two Commissions.'

The new collaboration emphasized strengthening economic, commercial and investment interactions within six main objectives:

1. Develop Arizona and Sonora as a single region with a competitive advantage in the global market;
2. Facilitate movement of goods, service, people and information through the region and promote establishment of a trade corridor with Arizona and Sonora as the hub;
3. Promote stronger linkages and eliminate barriers between both states, to facilitate economic development and to promote complementarity in trade and production;
4. Encourage cross-border cluster development in the Sonora-Arizona region to increase value-added economic activities;
5. Create new external markets and new market opportunities for the Arizona-Sonora region, and
6. Identify and develop economic foundations, infrastructure and services needed to reach the desired level of competitiveness in the region (Wong-González 2004).

Subsequently, the seventh objective was added which addressed the improvement of quality of life for the region's residents (Pavlakovich-Kochi 2005).

Under the auspices of the two Commissions, a tri-pod partnership was formed between governments, private sector and universities. In particular, the preparation of background reports for the SEDV project encouraged the establishment of the Arizona-Sonora University Consortium to conduct research and prepare recommendations in cooperation with governmental agencies and private sector. This was the first time that the region's universities formalized their relationships within their states and across the border at the highest administrative level (presidents' offices).

The Commissions acted as the central, unifying and process overseeing entity. On each side of the border technical advisory committees were established and included representatives of government, private sector, NGO and researchers. They were charged with providing input to research teams working on reports. About a dozen joint reports (in both English and Spanish) were completed outlining the current cross-border linkages in each sector (agribusiness, mining, manufacturing, transportation and distribution services, business services, financial businesses, tourism, trade patterns, quality of life, impact of investments on education, and data exchange).

With the completion of the SEDV project in 1998, when the last of joint reports was submitted, the SEDV recommendations became a blue print for the binational regional economic development. Local and regional economic development organizations and various public-private partnerships adopted the general idea of a transborder region as a necessary new framework for competitive industries and pursued their specific initiatives to strengthen their economic ties across the border. For example, the Puerto Nuevo initiative in Tucson, Arizona, was built on the idea of stronger cross-border ties with Sonora's port of Guaymas in this newly envisioned borderless, single economic region (Pavlakovich-Kochi 2006).

The Commissions remain the major institution of formal cross-border cooperation supported by governments of the two states. The latest joint plenary session in June 2008 in Phoenix, Arizona, was carried under the theme 'The next chapter of collaboration in Arizona and Sonora's history'. Under the theme, the Arizona-Sonora region has been promoted as a place where businesses can thrive on the strong binational relationship with a long history of successful collaboration (AMC 2008).

Just about the time when the NAFTA framework was promising a 'borderless economy', new political developments have created conditions for re-bordering of North America (Andreas and Biersteker 2003). This has slowed the process of decentralization of political decision-making in the region as a result of increasing focus of federal governments on border security in the aftermath of terrorist attacks on 11 September 2001. Another obstacle is the unresolved immigration policy and building of real fences along the border between Arizona and Sonora, the area that became a major gateway of undocumented immigrants into the United States. While 'security' and 'safety' have been added to the Commissions' documents dominated by advancing the region's 'prosperity,' these two areas remain outside the control of regional decision-makers.

One Border Region: A Strategic Vision for Competitiveness

This example illustrates cooperation between four U.S. border states (California, Arizona, New Mexico and Texas) and six Mexican border states (Baja California, Sonora, Chihuahua, Coahuila, Nuevo León and Tamaulipas) through a formal institution of Border Governors Conference.

The first Border Governors Conference convened in Ciudad Juárez, Chihuahua in 1980 with a purpose to enhance communication among border states. A general mechanism involves a conference held each year alternating locations between the United States and Mexico. The organization addresses issues related to water, agriculture and livestock, environment, health, economic development, energy, logistics and international crossings, tourism, and lately, a new emphasis on science and technology, and border security (Border Governors Conference 2007).

Each conference concludes with a joint declaration. In the preamble of the last declaration from the 2007 conference in Puerto Peñasco, Sonora, it is stated that 'current international conditions have magnified the border region's strategic role, uniting our [border] States and compelling us [border states] to cooperate more then ever to ensure greater security and efficiency at the border'. While greater cooperation is being demanded in response to border security issues, it is important to note that the central theme of the 2007 conference was building a common regional vision for the entire border region.

As the host of the 2007 Conference, governor of Sonora requested a background report that was coordinated by researchers at El Centro de Investigación en Alimentación y Desarrollo (CIAD). As a part of the study, the report identified a growing number of successful projects of cross-border collaboration in economic development at different levels in the border region. Based on these experiences, a list of important conditions for successful cooperation includes (Wong-González 2007):

- Permanent binational collaboration between social, corporate, institutional and community actors;
- Development of relationships of trust between the project participants;
- The will to become partners and design strategies under consensus;
- Political and financial commitment to drive projects;
- Wide community participation and collaboration between private and social agents and different government agencies;
- Broad discussion and wide dissemination of the project and its result;
- Having local and regional support networks among the diversity of agents (businessmen, academicians, government officials, NGOs), and
- Transformation of culture of doing business.

One of the most interesting findings in the report is based on a survey of key regional agents in the ten border states. The findings suggest that the ten border states are perceived to make up a region in a 'comprehensive sense of the concept'. The authors of the report argue that this condition is mainly the result of sharing a common natural and geographical environment ('Geographical region'), the intensive interaction and economic interdependency between productive agents ('Economic region'), as well as the existence of strong social and cultural ties throughout the border ('Socially constructed region'). Thus, in functional terms, there is a regional formation. However, the authors conclude, 'the majority of the inhabitants do not feel totally identified as members of a regional community due to the existence of various factors which prevent cohesion and regional identity' (Wong-González 2007).

The Joint Declaration consists of many statements such as 'encourage, support, promote' in regard to ongoing projects at state, regional and local levels, although in no position to offer financial support. Instead, the Conference underscored its commitment to supporting border states in their requests for continuing or new funding by respective federal governments of border region projects. The Conference also demanded that the federal governments (principally the United States government) come up with a 'comprehensive immigration reform'.

One of the more specific recommendations includes the creation of a Statistical and Geographical Information System for the U.S.-Mexico Border Region as a basis for monitoring the competitiveness in the region. For that to happen, border states plan to engage in an agreement with federal agencies on both sides of the border. Also, the creation of a regional fund for Border Competitiveness and Infrastructure was proposed that would eventually bring together the existing resources through international organizations such as International Development Bank, and border-specific, NADBank.

Conclusions

Cross-border cooperation in the U.S.-Mexico border has a long history, but even more importantly, the creation of cross-border institutions and participation in cross-border activities gained momentum in the 1990s. NAFTA and globalization are seen as major forces that redefined the international boundary, and created new conditions and needs for cross-border cooperation. As a direct impact of NAFTA, several new institutions were established to deal specifically with binational cooperation in resolving environmental issues. Indirectly, NAFTA encouraged reorganization in the existing institutions by adding entities with focus on the border.

NAFTA and its side agreements also provided opportunities for local actors to build partnerships with national institutions in solving local problems, as demonstrated in the Upper San Pedro case study. While by no means adequate, the NAFTA-related NADBank provides funding for border environmental clean-up. This is the only formal institution with funds designated specifically for the border region.

The partnerships are increasingly being built among former adversaries, such as environmentalists and business groups, when cooperation promises gains to all. Another trend is a new role of universities in cross-border cooperation. The universities not only provide scientific research, but increasingly act as neutral facilitators of cooperation between diverse actors. This is particularly evident in cross-border partnerships for economic development.

A whole array of new cross-border economic regions have sprung up as local, regional and state governments compete for investments. Because there are no institutions for border economic development that may parallel what NADBank does for border environment, it is left up to local, regional and state agents to attract private and federal government investment to their specific areas. This has amplified regional competition in the border region as every cross-border region claims to be the best location for business in the NAFTA area. The case of the Arizona-Sonora region is an example of such a formal cross-border partnership for the purpose of increasing the region's competitiveness through a better coordination of resources on both sides of the border.

Increasing concerns about border security and unresolved immigration policy regarding Mexican labor to the United States have created new stressors in the border region. Because these are considered national issues, states have little control over them. This has prompted border states in the United States and Mexico to strengthen their cross-border cooperation and act in a more unified fashion, as a 'border region', as demonstrated in the latest Border Governors Conference declaration.

In reviewing literature on cooperation in the U.S.-Mexico border, one conclusion that springs out is that transborder collaboration is multifaceted in nature and requires a multidisciplinary approach. While the academic literature (although still quite fragmented) provides a pretty good understanding of why different actors cooperate, the outcomes and their regional implications are less known and warrant further research. This is also an area of strong ties to public policy. Therefore, we see the future research needs and opportunities especially in the area of 'translating' the academic work into practical uses for decision-makers.

References

Anderson, J.A. and Gerber, J. (2008), *Fifty Years of Change on The U.S.-Mexico Border: Growth, Development, and Quality of Life* (Austin: University of Texas Press).

Andreas, P. and Biersteker, T.J. (eds.)(2003), *The Rebordering of North America: Integration and Exclusion in New Security Context* (New York and London: Routledge).

Arizona-Mexico Commission (2008), 'The Next Chapter of Collaboration in Arizona and Sonora's History', *Arizona-Mexico Commission Summer Plenary Session* 20-21 June 2008 (Phoenix, Arizona), available at <http://www.azmc.org>.

Blatter, J. (2001), 'Cross-border Regions: A Step toward Sustainable Development? Experiences and Considerations from Examples in Europe and North America', in Ganster, P. (ed.), *Cooperation, Environment, and Sustainability in Border Regions* (San Diego: State University Press), 33-59.

Border Governors Conference (2007), *Declaración Conjunta/Joint Declaration*, retrieved on 11 August 2008, available at <http://www.bordergovernors.ca.gov/pdf/22.pdf>.

Clement, N.C. (2001), 'Transboundary Collaboration: Conceptualization and Theoretical Considerations', in Ganster, P. (ed.), *Cooperation, Environment, and Sustainability in Border Regions* (San Diego: State University Press), 17-32.

Delamaide, D. (1995), 'The New Superregions of Europe' (New York: Plume), cited in *Wong-González, P. (2004), Conflict and Accommodation in the Arizona-Sonora Region*, in Pavlakovich-Kochi, V., Morehouse, B.J. and Wastl-Walter, D. (eds.),

Challenged Borderlands: Transcending Political and Cultural Boundaries (Aldershot: Ashgate), 122-51.

Haeflinger, C.J. (1996), 'Microintegration: Sechsmal die "Aussen-Schweitz"', Region-Inform 1:2, 4, cited in Blatter, J. (2001), *Crossborder Regions: A Step Toward Sustainable Development? Experiences and Considerations from Examples in Europe and North America*, in Ganster, P. (ed.), *Cooperation, Environment, and Sustainability in Border Regions* (San Diego: State University Press), 33-59.

Hansen, N. (1986), 'Conflict Resolution and the Evolution of Cooperation in the U.S.-Mexico Borderlands', *Journal of Borderlands Studies* 1:1, 34-38, cited in *Lara Valencia, F. (2001), Crossborder Partnerships for Environmental Management: The U.S.-Mexico Border Experience*, in Ganster, P. (ed.), *Cooperation, Environment, and Sustainability in Border Regions* (San Diego: State University Press), 63-79.

Herzog, L.A. (2000), 'The Shared Borderlands', in Herzog, L.A. (ed.), *Shared Space: Rethinking the U.S.-Mexico Border Environment, U.S.-Mexico Contemporary Perspectives Series, 16* (University of California, San Diego: Center for U.S.-Mexican Studies), 3-15.

Hocking, B. (1993), 'Localizing Foreign Policy: Non-Central Governments and Multilayered Diplomacy' (London and New York: Macmillan) cited in Blatter, J. (2001), *Crossborder Regions: A Step toward Sustainable Development? Experiences and Considerations from Examples in Europe and North America*, in Ganster, P. (ed.), *Cooperation, Environment, and Sustainability in Border Regions* (San Diego: State University Press), 33-59.

Lara Valencia, F. (2001), 'Crossborder Partnerships for Environmental Management: The U.S.-Mexico Border Experience', in Ganster, P. (ed.), *Cooperation, Environment, and Sustainability in Border Regions* (San Diego: State University Press), 63-79.

Lara Valencia, F. (2000), 'Transboundary Networks for Environmental Management in the San Diego-Tijuana Border Region', in Herzog, L.A. (ed.), *Shared Space: Rethinking the U.S.-Mexico Border Environment, U.S.-Mexico Contemporary Perspectives Series 16* (University of California, San Diego: Center for U.S.-Mexican Studies), 155-79.

Little, D.J. (2005), 'Transboundary Cooperation in the U.S.-Mexico Border Region', in Fuentes Flores C.M. and S. Peña Medina (eds.), *Planeación Binacional y Cooperación Transfronteriza en la Frontera México-Estados Unidos* (Tijuana: El Colegio de la Frontera Norte), 51-74.

Martinez, O.J. (1988), *Troublesome Border* (Tucson: University of Arizona Press).

Mora, J.G., Marmolejo, F. and Pavlakovich-Kochi, V. (2006), *Supporting the Contribution of Higher Education Institutions to Regional Development, Nuevo León* (Paris: Organization for Economic Co-operation and Development, Directorate for Education, Education Management and Infrastructure Division Programme on Institutional Management in Higher Education).

Morehouse, B.J. (2004), 'Theoretical Approaches to Border Spaces and Identities', in Pavlakovich-Kochi, V., Morehouse, B.J. and Wastl-Walter, D. (eds.), *Challenged Borderlands: Transcending Political and Cultural Boundaries* (Aldershot: Ashgate), 19-39.

Morehouse, B.J. (1995), 'A Functional Approach to Boundaries in the Context of Environmental Issues', *Journal of Borderlands Studies* 10:2, 53-73.

Mumme, S. (1987), 'State and Local Influence in Transboundary Environmental Policy Making Along the U.S.-Mexico Border: The Case of Air Quality Management', *Journal of Borderlands Studies* 2:1, 1-16, cited in Lara Valencia, F. (2001), *Crossborder Partnerships for Environmental Management: The U.S.-Mexico Border Experience*, in Ganster, P. (ed.), *Cooperation, Environment, and Sustainability in Border Regions* (San Diego State University Press), 63-79.

Nelson, R. and Twite, K. (1996), 'The Northern Plains-Mid-Continent Region', in Pavlakovich-Kochi, V. and Walker, M.P. (eds.), *Transnational Regional Economic Development in North America: Problems, Challenges & Solutions in the 1990s, Proceedings of the Conference held in Tucson, AZ May 9-11* (Tucson: The University of Arizona Department of Community Affairs & Economic Development), 36-43.

Organization for Economic Co-operation and Development (OECD)(1979), 'Environmental Protection in Frontier Regions' (Paris: OECD) cited in Lara Valencia, F. (2001), *Crossborder Partnerships for Environmental Management: The U.S.-Mexico Border Experience*, in Ganster, P. (ed.), *Cooperation, Environment, and Sustainability in Border Regions* (San Diego State University Press), 63-79.

Pacific Northwest Economic Region (PNWER) (1997), available at <http://www. ei.gov.bc.ca/~PNWER/Default.htm>, cited in Blatter, J. (2001), *Crossborder Regions: A Step Toward Sustainable Development? Experiences and Considerations from Examples in Europe and North America*, in Ganster, P. (ed.), *Cooperation, Environment, and Sustainability in Border Regions* (San Diego: State University Press), 33-59.

Pavlakovich-Kochi, V. (2006), 'The Arizona-Sonora Region: a Decade of Transborder Region-Building', *Estudios Sociales: Revista de Investigación Científica* 14:27, 25-55.

Pavlakovich-Kochi, V. (2005), 'Transborder Indicators: Lessons from the Arizona-Sonora Region', in Fuentes Flores, C.M. and Peña Medina, S. (eds.), *Planeación Binacional y Cooperation Transfronteriza en la Frontera México-Estados Unidos* (Tijuana: El Colegio de la Frontera Norte), 29-50.

Pavlakovich-Kochi, V. and Walker, M.P. (eds.)(1996), *Transnational Regional Economic Development in North America: Problems, Challenges & Solutions in the 1990s, Proceedings of the Conference held in Tucson, AZ May 9-11* (Tucson: The University of Arizona Department of Community Affairs & Economic Development).

Pick, J.B., Miggins, S. and Viswanathan, N. (2005), 'U.S.-Mexico Border Planning in the Context of a Theory of Border Interchange', in Fuentes Flores, C.M. and Peña Medina, S. (eds.), *Planeación Binacional y Cooperation Transfronteriza en la Frontera México-Estados Unidos* (Tijuana: El Colegio de la Frontera Norte), 133-63.

Proulx, P. (1996), 'Economic Integration in North America: Formal, Informal and Spatial Aspects between New England, Québec and the Atlantic Provinces', in Pavlakovich-Kochi, V. and Walker, M.P. (eds.), *Transnational Regional Economic Development in North America: Problems, Challenges & Solutions in the 1990s, Proceedings of the Conference held in Tucson, AZ May 9-11* (Tucson: The University of Arizona Department of Community Affairs & Economic Development), 46-47.

Scherer, R. and Blatter, J. (1994), Preconditions for a Successful Crossborder Cooperation on Environmental Issues, Research Results and Recommendations for a Better Practice, available at <http://www.unisg.ch/~siasr/public/cbla5b. html>, cited in *Lara Valencia, F. (2001), Crossborder Partnerships for Environmental Management: The U.S.-Mexico Border Experience*, in Ganster, P. (ed.), Cooperation, Environment, and Sustainability in Border Regions (San Diego: State University Press), 63-79.

Spalding, M.J. (2000), 'The NAFTA Environmental Institutions and Sustainable Development on the U.S.-Mexico Border', in Herzog, L.A. (ed.), *Shared Space: Rethinking the U.S.-Mexico Border Environment, U.S.-Mexico Contemporary Perspectives Series* 16 (University of California, San Diego: Center for U.S.-Mexican Studies), 75-98.

Staudt, K. (1998), *Free Trade? Informal Economies at the U.S.-Mexico Border* (Philadelphia: Temple University Press).

Swanson, L. (1994), 'Emerging Transnational Economic Regions in North America Under NAFTA', in Hodges, M. (ed.), *Proceedings of the Symposium The Impact of NAFTA: Economies in Transition* (London: The London School of Economics and Political Science), 64-93.

Varady, R.G. (2005), 'The Birth of a Mexican Watershed Council in the San Pedro Basin of Sonora', in Fuentes Flores, C.M. and Peña Medina, S. (eds.), *Planeación Binacional y Cooperation Transfronteriza en la Frontera México-Estados Unidos* (Tijuana: El Colegio de la Frontera Norte), 165-83.

Vázquez Castillo, M.T. (2005), 'Planeación Bilateral México-Estados Unidos: Instituciones, Planificadores y Comunidades', in Fuentes Flores, C.M. and Peña Medina, S. (eds.), *Planeación Binacional y Cooperation Transfronteriza en la Frontera México-Estados Unidos* (Tijuana: El Colegio de la Frontera Norte), 243-71.

Wong-González, P. (Coordinator) (2007), 'Competividad y Areas de Oportunidad en la Region Fronteriza México-Estados Unidos: Visión Estratégica Regional', prepared for the *XXV Border Governors Conference, Puerto Peñasco, Sonora, México, September 2007* (Hermosillo: CIAD, A.C. and Consultoria y Estudios Estratégicos).

Wong-González, P. (2004), 'Conflict and Accommodation in the Arizona-Sonora Region', in Pavlakovich-Kochi, V., Morehouse, B.J. and Wastl-Walter, D. (eds.), *Challenged Borderlands: Transcending Political and Cultural Boundaries* (Aldershot: Ashgate), 122-51.

PART VI
CROSSING BORDERS

Everyday Practices of *Bordering* and the Threatened Bodies of Undocumented North Korean Border-Crossers

Eunyoung Christina Choi

Introduction

This chapter explores daily practices of *bordering* that continuously redefine spatial and social boundaries between North Korea and China, and the implications of these practices on the lives of North Koreans who unofficially cross them. What do I mean by *bordering*? Joseph Nevins (2002) argues that the border is continually constructed through the building of not only walls and fences but also national identities and exclusivities. In other words, continual 'dividing practices' over the physical boundary serve to distinguish between those who belong and those who do not, and this process contributes to the construction of subjects and identities (Nevins 2002, 53). Building on Nevins' concept of the border, I use the term *bordering* to refer to the daily dividing practices over the physical territory and the people. By using the concept of *bordering*, I intend to emphasize the historically constituted and on-going nature of the exclusionary practices that affect the lives of undocumented North Korean migrants.

In this chapter, I will examine the everyday bordering experiences of undocumented North Korean migrants and the people who live in the North Korean-Chinese borderland of Yanbian.[1] The Yanbian Korean ethnic autonomous prefecture is situated in the northeastern part of the People's Republic of China (PRC/China), neighbouring the Democratic People's Republic of Korea (DPRK/

---

1   I have followed the McCune-Reischauer system of romanization for Korean words and names. For the names of authors, I use the romanization that appears in their publications. Chinese terms and names are romanized in Pinyin. All translations are my own unless otherwise noted.

North Korea) along the Tumen River; it has a high density population of ethnic Koreans.[2] Most Korean-Chinese (*Chosunjok*)[3] in the Yanbian area speak Korean in their daily lives and are educated in the Korean language in ethnic Korean schools up to the high school level. This prefecture has become an important enclave for undocumented North Korean migrants since the 1990s. Yanbian is geographically close to North Korea, and here, migrants are more likely to find shelter and food, communicate in the Korean language, as well as make an easy transition into Chinese society (Suh et al. 2002, 173-5). It is estimated that around 30,000-50,000 undocumented North Koreans resided in 2007 (Margesson et al. 2007, 4).[4] Despite the fact that North Koreans have recently begun to settle in regions further inland, the majority of undocumented North Korean migrants continue to reside in the three Northeast states (Liaoning-sheng, Jilin-sheng, and Heilongjiang-sheng) where there is a concentration of Korean-Chinese people, in particular, within the Yanbian prefecture of Jilin-sheng (Figure 24.1).

Most scholars agree that the present-day Korean-Chinese community is the result of migrations from the Korean peninsula to Northeast China which began as early as the 1860s (Kwon 2005; Lee 2001), but it is only over the last decade that the border between China and the Korean peninsula has become militarized and highly regulated. In the mid-1940s, during the period of modern Chinese state-building, undocumented Korean migrants living in the PRC would have been granted Chinese citizenship, and incorporated as one of China's 'minority nationalities' (*shaoshu minzu*) (Kwon 2005). Today, however, undocumented migrants from North Korea are considered tentative threats to China, and the Chinese government has militarized the North Korean-Chinese border. Undocumented North Korean migrants are considered 'dangerous others' even by the Korean-Chinese people. These 'illegal migrants' are often forcefully repatriated to North Korea, where they are subject to harsh punishments. Even though undocumented North Koreans and Korean-Chinese are visually indistinguishable migrants or descendents of migrants, their social and legal statuses are extremely different.

The chapter explores two sets of questions: (1) In what socio-economic and political circumstances and through what kinds of daily practices, have the territorial and social borders between Yanbian Korean-Chinese community and North Korea been constructed? (2) How have the multiple forms of *bordering* worked to threaten the bodies of undocumented North Korean migrants who cross the rigid borders

---

2   1,923,842 ethnic Koreans reside throughout China, and among them 43.77 per cent resided in Yanbian in 2000 (The Bureau of Yanbian Statistics 2002).

3   *Chosunjok* (*Chaoxian-zu* in Chinese) means 'the Chosun people'. The term *Chosun* derives from the name of the last dynasty that existed on the Korean peninsula before the Japanese colonization. Currently, *Chosonjok* refers to Korean ethnics in China who have Chinese citizenship (Freeman 2006, 2).

4   Because of the clandestine nature of migration, the collection of accurate statistics is impossible. Estimates of the total number of North Korean migrants vary from 10,000 to 300,000 depending on announcing organizations. China estimates that there may be 10,000 unauthorized North Koreans in the country, while aid groups put the figure at 150,000 to 300,000 (Pomfret 2001).

Figure 24.1 The North Korean-Chinese Borderland

Source: Cartography: O. Kim.

clandestinely? This research proceeds along two lines. First, through archival research and media analysis, I document the histories of Korean migration to China, the North Korean-Chinese border construction process, and the policies and dialogues regarding undocumented North Korean migrants among and within states and international organizations. Second, drawing on ethnographic fieldwork conducted in Yanbian in July 2003, March to December 2005, and August 2006, I analyze the everyday practices of *bordering* by focusing on the individual narratives and daily experiences of North Korean migrants as well as of the local Chinese people who live in this borderland. Drawing on interviews that I conducted while working as a student intern for an international NGO[5] that provided humanitarian

---

5   The organization that I worked with requested anonymity for obvious reasons of political sensitivity. Helping undocumented North Korean migrants is not allowed in

aid to undocumented North Korean migrants in China, I intend to understand the human realities and experiences resulting from border constructions. Efforts to link a top-down approach with a bottom-up perspective have helped me explore the border construction process and its implications at various scales, from body and household levels to regional, state, and international levels.

Narrating the Border

North Korea and China are geographically divided by the Tumen River on the eastern border and by the Yalu River on the western border. In July 2003, I went to the Tumen River. The river was much narrower than I had expected. The width of river is only several meters at some points. If my Korean-Chinese taxi driver who accompanied me to the border area had not pointed it out, I would not have thought that the river was an international boundary between North Korea and China. The border which seems peaceful and quiet during daytime changes at night to a battle-field between, on the one hand, illegal migrants who cross the river without permission and, on the other, border guards who are ready to shoot these migrants. The taxi driver told me how the circumstances around the border had changed. He lived in Gaesantun, a village located beside the Tumen River. He said there was a time when his mother would often cross the river to borrow oil or ingredients from relatives on the North Korean side while she prepared the dinner. Emotionally and socially, he felt closer to the villages on the North Korean side rather than the Han Chinese villages on the Chinese side. He also told me that there were very few interactions between the Han Chinese and the Korean-Chinese because differences in language and culture presented barriers. Border towns across the Tumen River were, therefore, not only connected through blood ties but also through cultural affinities. During his childhood, in the 1950s and early 1960s, even though the border between North Korea and China was clearly demarcated on topographical maps, it was not clearly acknowledged in the everyday lives of the residents of the borderland.

My interview with Mr. Lee, an undocumented North Korean migrant, enabled me to understand with greater clarity that nation states are not naturally bounded places and that it is almost impossible to categorize the people along the border. Mr. Lee is a person who is 'on' the border. He was born in Yanbian in 1939 as a Korean-Chinese. He left for North Korea in 1961 to get more education and received North Korean citizenship after he graduated from college in North Korea. He described that time:

> I crossed the Tumen River in 1961. It was the time of Great Famine. Everybody
> in China was hungry. After the Korean War, North Korea had an office called

China. All the names of places and people, aside from the names of provinces and large cities, are pseudonyms to protect the anonymity of my informants.

the 'Welcoming Office for Korean-Chinese' and allocated houses and jobs to Korean-Chinese who crossed the border and wanted to live in North Korea. As a lot of people died during the War, especially young men, the North Korean government needed people to work for the country. I went to North Korea without any official permission and I could get a college education in North Korea; it was free and the government provided everything. When I graduated, the government asked me whether I wanted to get North Korean citizenship or remain a Chinese citizen. I kept my Chinese citizenship while I was in college, but later I changed my citizenship to North Korea. Before I decided to change my citizenship, I thought about going back to China after graduation. Therefore, in 1965, I secretly crossed the border to Namyang in China. By that time, the situation at the border had changed a lot. That was the time of the Cultural Revolution in China. My family suffered from hunger and my father was killed because of me. Anyone who talked about Korean culture and North Korea was punished as a segmentist or spy. A college degree was useless. Instead, it was a target for blame. Because I had moved to North Korea and had gotten a college education there, my father was considered a political spy from North Korea and was stoned to death by the people. I was afraid of returning to China and asked my family to go to North Korea together with me. But they were afraid and wanted to stay in China. The 'Welcoming Office for Korean-Chinese' along the Tumen River was gone after the Cultural Revolution. But many people still crossed the border to North Korea secretly to escape from the social and economic conditions in China.

I met Mr. Lee in China. He lived in North Korea with North Korean citizenship until 1997 and then returned to China with his daughter, who was born in North Korea. When I asked his nationality in order to check whether he could be in my possible interviewee group or not, he asked me why that information always mattered. Not only had he moved back and forth between North Korea and China holding both Chinese citizenship and North Korean citizenship at different times, but at the time of my interview he said he did not know whether he was Chinese or North Korean. As the following interview with Mr. Lee illustrates, individuals living in the borderlands often keep the ambiguity and experience of bordering throughout their entire lives:

Today, the situation is just the opposite. Now, North Korean people illegally cross the border into China. Now, China is richer than North Korea, and North Koreans are begging for food and money from the Korean-Chinese. My wife died of hunger and I came here to get some support from my brothers and sisters. They feel uncomfortable about helping an illegal migrant like me. They criticize me and blame me as a 'selfish person who moves around for better opportunities without thinking of family'. I know that people think I am someone who ran away to North Korea when China was poor, and came back to China when North Korea was poor. But, I was always discriminated against. Even though I have changed my citizenship from Chinese to North Korean, North Koreans called me Hwa-kyo (Chinese) and called my house Hwa-kyo ne (Chinese neighbour) while I was in North Korea. As I was born in China, I experienced limitations and discrimination when I was working in North Korea. Over here in China, I am an illegal North Korean migrant. I live here with the fear of apprehension all the time. I don't know whether I'm Chinese or Korean. China and North Korea, both countries at one time were my own, but neither now welcomes me, even my Chinese brothers and sisters. There is a border even in my family. I am the same person, but I was a Chinese for a while, and now I'm a North Korean who wants to deny my North Korean citizenship. I'm a criminal in both countries and do not have freedom in either. Among North Koreans who live in China as illegal migrants, many were born in China or have families and relatives in China like me.

The above narrative demonstrates that the North Korean-Chinese border is an unnatural boundary. Nonetheless, the concerned states have repeatedly enacted practices of bordering along this unnatural boundary. Even though Mr. Lee finds it difficult to categorize himself, he has been categorized and discriminated against by others along both sides of the North Korean-Chinese border. The North Korean-Chinese borders that he has experienced are social divisions between North Koreans and Chinese as well as territorial boundaries between two neighbouring states. They exist both at the metaphorical as well as the physical level, and at various scales including the scale of the household. This interview with Mr. Lee gave me insights into the blurred character of the North Korean-Chinese border and pointed out the necessity for understanding the political and social construction of the North Korean-Chinese border. In the next section, based primarily on secondary literature, I will briefly document the history of migration in the Korean-Chinese border and the states' efforts to bind the nations and construct the border in their nation state building processes.

Nation State Building and Identity Construction of Korean Migrants

The border between North Korea and China was formally defined in 1964 (Lee 2004, 233) and the efforts of states to control the flows of people along the border therefore have a variegated history. Mass migrations of Koreans to Northeast China took place several times. As Korea and China are geographically contiguous, there has been frequent human movement and exchanges of culture, politics, and commerce since very early periods, but not much information is available on the early period of migration to China, most of which was seasonal (Koo 2007, 23).

In the mid-nineteenth century, after the Qing dynasty ended the Fengjin policy[6] in 1875, people from Korea's northern provinces began to migrate to Manchuria (currently, the north eastern part of China) in order to escape food shortages and to find land to grow crops (Kwon 2005, 121; Lee 2001, 95). That is considered the starting point of a substantial Korean migration to Manchuria. Others, around 15 million, were forcefully relocated by the Japanese from the southern part of the Korean peninsula to Manchuria in order to expand Japanese colonialism into China after Japan won the war against Manchukuo in 1895 (Kwon 2005, 121). Some voluntarily left Korea due to the harsh rule of the Japanese colonial government, while others left to lead or join the Korean independence movement, which was centred in Manchuria. Most of these resettled Koreans considered themselves temporary residents in China and intended to return to their hometowns. Around 700,000 Korean ethnics among a total of 1,700,000 Koreans in China (approximately 40 per cent of Koreans in China) voluntarily returned to Korea immediately after Japanese colonialism ended in 1945 (Kwon 2005, 1, 123). It is thought that more Korean ethnics in China would have returned to Korea if there had been no sudden political changes on the Korean peninsula after 1945, which included the division of Korea into North Korea and South Korea, and the Korean War.

Kwon (2005, 123) argues that the period between 1945 and 1950 was a 'time of confusion and choices' for ethnic Koreans residing in China. After almost a half-century-long struggle on China's part to build a modern Chinese state, the Communist Party took power and succeeded in establishing the People's Republic of China in 1945 (Freeman 2006, 2; Lee 2001, 91). State nationalism of Communist China was emphasized, and a new form of Chinese nation was invented. According to Lee (2001), the Chinese nation (*Zhongguo-ren*) refers to Chinese citizens' embracing 56 officially recognized sub-nations, including the Han Chinese. The PRC emphasized loyalty to the state and territorial and ideological integration under one nation state. Even though the Chinese government claimed equality between nationalities and regional autonomy, equal relationships between nationalities could not exist given the supremacy of the Han Chinese and China's increasingly narrow and exclusive view of nationalism (Lee 2001, 91-2). In 1945, ethnic Koreans who had migrated to Northeastern China, between the 1860s and the early twentieth century, were officially recognized as one of the 55 ethnic minorities in China under the name of *Chosonjok* (*Chaoxian-zu*) (Freeman 2006, 2; Jung 1998, 24). While *Chaoxian-zu* in Chinese refers to the Korean minority in China, *Chaoxian-ren* refers to Koreans outside China, including Koreans living on the Korean peninsula (Lee 2001, 92). Thus, the Korean minority in China was differentiated from Koreans on the Korean peninsula. This was a big change for Koreans in China, who were now considered foreigners rather than Chinese (Chung 1999, 22).

The Chinese government was quite aware of the arbitrary, political nature of the border and belonging, and quite actively manipulated the official classifications.

---

6   The Qing had prohibited any ethnic groups other than the Manchus from entering Manchuria (where Yanbian is located) because they considered Manchuria a sacred place.

Lee (2001) has provided a thorough documentation of the conflicts between Chinese state nationalism and Korean identity. As the Korean-Chinese (*Chosonjok*) mostly supported the Communist party in internal wars between the Communist Party and the Liberal Party, they received favourable status from the Chinese government. Koreans were granted rights to land during the land reform period, mostly between 1946 and 1948, and also received citizenship (Lee 2001, 105). The Yanbian Korean Autonomous Region was established in 1952, and in 1955 the region was renamed the Yanbian Korean Autonomous Prefecture (Koo 2007). Political purges, however, were also especially severe in the Korean regions because Korean ethnic identity was strong, and there were Korean national revolutionary movements that insisted on 'Korean self-rule' and the 'independence of the Gando Region [Northeastern part of China] from China' (Lee 2001, 101-3). The PRC forcefully suppressed Korean political nationalism and mobilized the Koreans in China to promote socialism and national integration through land reform and land distribution (Lee 2001, 105).

Even though the PRC tried to integrate the ethnic Koreans within China, significant numbers returned to Korea in the 1950s, 1960s and 1970s, specifically during and after the Korean War, the time of the Great Famine of China, and the period of the Cultural Revolution. After the Korean War ended in 1953, many *Chosunjok* soldiers who participated in the Korean War on the Chinese side remained in North Korea. Even after the Korean War, the Korean-Chinese were welcomed by the North Korean government, and they received North Korean citizenship once they arrived in North Korea, as a part of the War Reconstruction Project. It is estimated that during the Great Famine in China between 1959 and 1962, around 300,000 undocumented Korean-Chinese crossed the border, and half of them resettled in North Korea (Democratic Labour Party of Republic of Korea 2004). A similar occurrence of undocumented migration happened again during the Cultural Revolution in China.

The conflicts between Chinese and Korean nationalism climaxed during the Cultural Revolution, which started in 1966 and ended in 1976. *Chosunjoks* were accused of being ethnic nationalists and separatists and were severely punished, more than any other minority group in China (Jung 1998, 38-44; Lee 2001, 114-5; Seong 2007, 85-6). Around 2,000 Korean-Chinese were killed in the Yanbian area during the Cultural Revolution (Jung 1998, 42).[7] Unlike the revolutionary promise of the preceding years, Korean language schools were closed and Korean traditional cultural practices were banned during the Cultural Revolution (Koo 2007, 54). The Chinese nationalism of the PRC required absolute loyalty and this motivated China to block North Korea's political and social influence on the Yanbian area (Seong 2007, 66). Nationalism, which is about identity attached to a defined territory, has worked to strengthen the nation's external boundaries as well as eliminate internal boundaries between members of the nation (Nevins 2002, 157). During this time,

---

7   According to the *Yanbian Legal Statistics*, 175 Korean-Chinese high government officials and policemen – 70 per cent of all Korean-Chinese government officials and policemen – were accused of being political spies for the North, and among them, 12 Korean-Chinese were stoned to death and 82 became handicapped (Jung 1993, 306).

the remaining Koreans who had not applied for Chinese citizenship requested it (Jung 1998, 43) and the people who did not follow this request ran away to North Korea. Significant numbers secretly crossed the border to North Korea but there is no official record of the numbers of migrants because of the undocumented migrations' clandestine character. Pressures on minority nationality were relaxed in 1971 and further eased by the end of the Cultural Revolution in 1976 (Oliver 1993). The new leadership of Deng Xiaoping focused on economic reform rather than revolution and class struggle.

Since the PRC and the DPRK set up formal diplomatic relationship in 1949, they have cooperated economically, politically, and culturally based on the 'China-North Korea economic and cultural collaboration contact' (Chung 2004, 18-22). China sent troops, mostly Korean-Chinese soldiers, into the Korean War between 1950 and 1953 to protect North Korea from the US, their common enemy (Chung 2004, 19). During the Cold War, the relationship between North Korea and China was represented as socialist brotherhood and the countries were considered to be allies of the Soviet Union. However, the broad picture of Cold War geopolitics at the international level often ignores the human faces at the local level. Even though North Korea and China collaborated together to compose the communist block, the continuous separation of the Korean-Chinese territories and North Korea along the border was vividly practiced on a daily basis for the purpose of binding nations and stirring up nationalistic identities.

Binding nations is a process of both (re)creating territorial borders and social borders. The PRC has constructed an identity of Korean-Chinese (*Chosunjok*) and this belonging has contributed to making the social boundaries between Chinese citizens and aliens. Borders create order (Newman 2006, 143). An edited book titled *Korean Chinese Intellectuals' Seminar Papers – the Analysis on Korean Chinese Society's Current Situation and Its Future* shows how the Korean-Chinese understand themselves (Park 1998). In this volume, Korean-Chinese scholar Panryong Jung (1998, 8, 22) describes how the identity of the Korean-Chinese was constructed.

> *The biggest change that happened to us Korean-Chinese during the previous 100 years was that we started to accept ourselves as one of the ethnic groups that make up the People's Republic of China. Unlike the other ethnic groups who have been here from the beginning, we Koreans migrated from the Korean peninsula after we already formed as a modern ethnic group. Therefore, even after we resettled in China, we believed that we were staying temporarily, as migrants, and we considered ourselves the same as the Koreans who lived on the Korean peninsula. However, after we built China, our common nation state, with other ethnic groups, by developing this country and protecting its land from enemies, we received a great deal of credit from other ethnic groups and the Chinese government and assumed a position as one of China's ethnic minorities. Through this process, rather than seeing China as a foreign country, we started to see it as our homeland and one of our motherlands, and also to think of our future in terms of China's future. ... (Beside China), we have two motherlands. One is the 'rich' motherland, South Korea, and the*

> *other is the 'poor' motherland, North Korea. Because we, the Korean-Chinese,*
> *are able to go to both Koreas, we need to contribute to Korean reunification*
> *and reconciliation from our middle position. Even though we live in China,*
> *we Korean-Chinese differ from the Han Chinese. But we also differ from*
> *the Koreans in both the 'rich' and 'poor' motherlands. We are just Korean-*
> *Chinese.* (Jung 1998, 8, 22)

The Chinese government's efforts of binding the nation state along the borders changed the sense of belonging, affiliation, and membership of Korean ethnics in China. As seen in the narrative above, in the wake of the confusion and negotiation that accompanied the PRC's modern state-building process, the Korean-Chinese started to legally and emotionally differentiate themselves from Koreans on the Korean peninsula. Furthermore, they also actively began to produce a space for the Korean-Chinese and the culture of the borderland (Koo 2007). Rather than understanding the borderland as a place of confusion and suppression, the Korean-Chinese began to re-conceptualize the borderland as a privileged locus that contributed to the relationship of the two Koreas. After China opened its markets and established a formal relationship with the Republic of Korea (South Korea) in 1992, economic and social networks between Korean-Chinese society and South Korea started to develop dramatically and the relationship between North Korea and China became more complex. Yanbian became geographically and socially a frontier in the changing geopolitics of Northeast Asia, particularly in the transition from the Cold War period to a period of market-driven neoliberalism. This change contributed to the changing view of the border among the Korean-Chinese who now saw the borderland as a place of advantage and hope for a better world. However, this has accelerated *borderings* between the Korean-Chinese and North Korea, while the connection between the Korean-Chinese and South Korea has strengthened. While it may appear that China's policy of assimilation has been relaxed, bordering practices on the everyday level along the North Korean-Chinese boundary have actually intensified in the changing geopolitics of Northeast Asia.

Militarized Borders amidst Changing Geopolitics

Many proponents of a 'borderless' and 'deterritorialized' world argue that the power of the state has become weakened as borders of nation states have eroded through the movement of capital, goods, and ideas, as well as migrants. However, others (Andreas 2003; Mountz 2010; Newman 2006; Varsanyi 2008) have also noted that the importance of territoriality persists, and who and what is permitted to cross the border is still critically determined by states. Borders are actually more strongly controlled than ever before under neoliberalism, and undocumented migration flows especially have been severely regulated (Ackleson 2005; Coleman 2007; Mountz 2010; Newman 2006; Scarpellino 2007; Varsanyi 2008). Using the concept of the *neoliberal paradox*, Varsanyi (2008, 879) juxtaposes neoliberal forms of economic openness with political closure that denies territorial accesses for undesirable 'others' through maintaining a political distinction between insiders and outsiders. Since the decline of militarized interstate border disputes in the post-Cold War era, borders in the twenty-first century have become more intensively policed in more invisible ways through sophisticated surveillance and information technologies (Andreas 2003).

However, unlike the borders between liberal democratic nation states in Europe and in North America, I argue that the North Korean-Chinese border has not only restricted human movement but has also restricted economic trade and information flows often in extremely oppressive and visible ways. In neoliberal globalization, North Korea has been labeled as a major stumbling block for the global expansion of liberal democracy and market economy (Department of Defense United States of America 2004). The North Korean-Chinese border has become regulated in more visible ways and militarized more heavily since the collapse of USSR and the communist countries in Eastern Europe countries, and the opening up of China's markets. North Korea's isolation became visualized through the concrete walls and fences constructed by the Chinese government along the North Korean-Chinese border. In the decades following their shared fight against US-led U.N. forces in the Korean War, China left the border lightly guarded, but constructions have begun to be erected over the last several years (Guan 2006). China has built wire fences and concrete walls on major defection routes along the Tumen River and the Yalu River mainly for the purpose of blocking the smuggling of North Koreans across the border (Guan 2006).

In addition, in September 2003, up to 150,000 troops from the People's Liberation Army (PLA) were deployed to the border, replacing local armed police (Moore 2008; Kahn 2003). According to US officials, following reports about Kim Jong Il's health problems in September 2008, the Chinese military boosted troop numbers along the border with North Korea in anticipation of a possible regime change of North Korea and an influx of refugees into China (Sevastopulo and Song 2008). Even though China is still North Korea's closest political and economic partner, the construction of concrete walls and the militarization of the North Korean-Chinese border suggest a decline in PRC-DPRK amity and even indicate bilateral tension (Moore 2008). The socialist brotherhood of the Cold War has changed to a strategic partnership amidst a changing geopolitics.

Even in the era of neoliberal globalization, unlike most other international borders, economic trade and information flows are strongly regulated on this border alongside the regulation of human movements. As China opened its markets, North Korea feared the growing capitalist orientation of China and its potential to exert a negative international influence on Kim Jong Il's totalitarian regime. The fear of the flow of capitalist ideologies to North Korea and growing international influences led to the tightening of border controls to further insulate North Korea from the outside world. Today, information from the international mass media and the internet is blocked in North Korea. According to interviewees, any kind of activity considered to be informally influenced by the outside world is regarded 'anti-socialist' and punishable. In order to control the border, the North

Korean government regularly replaces many of the border guards to prevent them from taking bribes to abet illegal activities on the border, including clandestine migrations.

Apart from that, a *bi-sa groupa* (a high level committee to monitor anti-socialist activities, typically comprising senior officials from the Central Committee of the Korean Workers' Party, as well as officials from national security agencies) from Pyongyang has been deployed to the North Korean-Chinese border areas to monitor the possibility of interactions with the outside world, specifically border-crossing activities. What follows is the story of Mrs. Kim, a North Korean woman who left for China out of fear of being arrested by the *bi-sa groupa*.

> *One night, my daughter ran away to China and married a good Chinese man. She sent me money from China regularly. In January 2005, I heard that a bi-sa groupa was going to come to our city. As soon as I heard that I left for China through a migration broker. I came here on January 14 in 2005. According to my neighbour, who also recently came to China, a bi-sa groupa came to my hometown in February 2005 and investigated people who had stayed in China for a long time and returned secretly, people who got help from outside of North Korea, people who watched or listened to foreign broadcasts, and religious believers. Using a cell phone is also punished severely. A bi-sa groupa breaks into houses and hustles people into trucks. Some of them are sent to political prisons and some are relocated in places far from the border. No time is allowed to pack household goods. Everything is left behind. The people are forcefully relocated without any means of livelihood, and no house is provided. Survival itself is hard. The expulsion of anti-socialists from my hometown, the border city, took place in February, in May, and again in November 2005. I heard that the same thing happened in other border cities, such as Shineuiju, Onsung, and Musan. People in the border areas have a high chance of contacting foreign things, and many cross the border to China illegally. Therefore, the bi-sa groupa was sent from Pyongyang to the border area to control the border people.*

As seen in the above interview, North Korea tries to block any kind of informal border-crossings. However, even though the border seems impermeable, it has been a place of severe confrontation between state efforts to control the border and increasing unofficial border-crossings. While the North Korean border is highly regulated, unofficial cultural, economic, and human flows have not only increased but have also become more clandestine. Mrs. Kim explained to me details of unofficial border-crossings on the North Korean-Chinese border:

> *My daughter sent me some money every six months through a Korean-Chinese merchant who takes Chinese products into North Korea and sells them. Whenever my daughter would send the money, the cross-border merchant would take 30 percent and leave me the rest. The ratio of 3 to 7 is almost a rule in the borderlands. I had a small business while I worked*

for a food distribution center for a state construction enterprise in North Hamkyeong province. I was good at business and made quite good money. My daughter also sent me a cell phone from China. She paid the phone bill in China. Chinese cell phones can be used in the North Korean Chinese borderland via Chinese wireless facilities, but using a cell phone is very dangerous. There are detection facilities for wireless phones. I used the phone only in emergencies, as I was afraid of being detected. If someone has money, living in North Korea is much better than living in China with the fear of arrest. Anyway, I knew that I could be arrested by a bi-sa groupa, so I left. I had no intention of going to China.

As the interview above shows, ways of transporting goods, ideas, and human beings have become more diversified and the networks that help those movements have become more densely, delicately, and invisibly organized. Amidst life-threatening food shortages in North Korea, it is almost impossible to prevent cross-border activities along the North Korean-Chinese border. As unofficial flows increase, the state bordering practices have become harsher and more cruel. In the next section, I focus on the North Korean border controls to block undocumented migration flows and the state violence on the bodies of migrants who cross the North Korean-Chinese border without permission.

Threatened or Threatening? Contested Securities between the North Korean State and Migrant Bodies

Paradoxically, North Korea's voluntary and involuntary isolation during a changing geopolitics has resulted in an increase in undocumented North Korean migrations. With the economic difficulties and political instability in North Korea, undocumented North Korean migration has dramatically increased since the 1990s. While the US trade embargo on North Korea has not eased, North Korea has continued to see negative economic growth since the late 1980s. The severe flood and drought damage of 1995 and 1997, and failed economic reform in North Korea, have aggravated the food shortage in the country. Haggard and Noland (2007, 1) estimate that the Great North Korean Famine – beginning some time in the early 1990s and extending into 1998 – killed between three and five per cent of the entire population of North Korea.

Given the life-threatening food shortage, North Koreans choose undocumented migrations as survival strategies. However, North Koreans who are detected and arrested in China as illegal migrants have been forcefully repatriated to North Korea according to the North Korean-Chinese Treaty (Kwak 2005, 38). These forcefully deported North Koreans were defined as 'betrayal against the people and the fatherland' (Article 86 of the old North Korean constitution) (Suh et al. 2002, 176). In the past, repatriated North Koreans were all identified as political prisoners and were sent to political prison camps for special supervision (Suh et al. 2002, 175). They were severely tortured and even executed (United States Committee for Refugees and Immigrants 2001; Yoon 2001, 58). However, as the numbers have increased, the punishment of repatriated North Koreans has decreased (Yoon 2001, 58). Most repatriated North Koreans, who have simply engaged in earning money with the intention of returning to North Korea, are considered minor offenders and are subjected to up to six months imprisonment at extrajudicial detention centers and 'labour correcting centers' (Margesson et al. 2007, 9; Suh et al. 2002, 176). The conditions in those centers are extremely harsh. Numerous interviewees mention that extreme labour exploitation, public torture, and sexual harassment are practiced in those centers. The sick and the elderly have a hard time surviving in these places due to malnutrition and the dirty environs.

Here is an excerpt from an interview with a 34-year-old North Korean woman in Yanji in China who had experienced repatriation and was punished in North Korea. This particular woman revealed how the 'bad' bodies of repatriated North Korean migrants were treated in their relations with soldiers, nurses, and governmental officials who implemented the state's policies in a gendered way. She married a Korean-Chinese man in China, but was forcefully repatriated to North Korea with her unborn baby on 9 October 2002. The following narrative also shows how the unacceptable body, from a Korean-Chinese father, can be discarded like a 'thing' that does not have human dignity.

> I was nine months pregnant when I was deported to North Korea. While I stayed at a National Security Police Camp for 18 days, I ate only half a handful of cold corn porridge with salt everyday. ... Most people suffered from diarrhoea and enteritis because of the dirty water and environment, but could not get any medicine. My room was cold and dirty. People used part of their room as a toilet and there was no toilet tissue. Women, especially, had difficulty during their menstruation. They used their clothes instead of sanitary napkins and reused these as clothes after washing them without soap. ... Eighteen days later, I was sent to a labour correcting centre. People had to do hard labour except for some hours' sleep. For the first few days, I was allowed to take rest with the other pregnant women, while other people worked. But three of the other pregnant women were forced to take some medicine and had induced abortions. ... I thought that my baby would be safe. But after I delivered my baby, some policemen wrapped it in a plastic bag and put it into a waste-basket. They said my baby was a 'dirty one from a Chinese ethnic'. I saw the bag moving. She was alive.

Women's bodies are sites of biological reproduction that demarcate and maintain national boundaries (Mayer 2004, 156). As seen from the interview above, the North Korean government controls pregnant women's bodies. The babies who are offspring of North Korean women and Chinese men are considered to be dangerous bodies that pollute the pure and homogeneous nation; repatriated North Korean women are not allowed to give birth to those bodies. Women are seen not only as biological but also as cultural reproducers (Bracewell 1996). North Korean women interviewees often told me that once they repatriated to North Korea, agencies checked their appearances, and beat the women who pierced their ears and dyed their hair in China. Agencies often said that those styles can damage the pure and natural style of Korean beauty. Repatriated North Korean women's bodies are criminalized as they threaten the nation's identity from the perspective of ruling groups of North Korea.

Chinese Security, Construction of Borders, and Criminalized Bodies

For several years, China informally tolerated the presence of North Koreans and repatriated them only when the North Korean government asked it to do so (Yoon 2001, 69). However, the Chinese government's attitude changed when it became apparent that the illegal migration flow to China would not end soon, and once the human rights situation of undocumented North Korean migrants became a hot topic in international politics. Specifically, Chinese crackdowns on undocumented North Koreans became much severer after the several high-profile incidents since summer 2001, involving undocumented North Korean migrants who entered UNHCR and foreign embassies in Beijing for asylum seeking (Human Rights Watch 2002, 3).

China became sensitive to this issue and officially explained how the Chinese government defines undocumented North Korean migrants. Wang Gwang-ya, the Chinese Deputy Foreign Minister, announced that undocumented North Korean migrants in China are simply illegal 'economic-resettlers' (Suh et al. 2002, 183). Therefore, he argues, China cannot accord them refugee status. If the Chinese government were to grant refugee status to illegal North Korean migrants, a mass influx toward China would ensure and it would cause enormous economic burden and social disorder in the PRC. Thus, in order to avert a possible international dispute, the Chinese government has more actively deported undocumented North Korean migrants (Choi 2000, 64). In this situation, the remaining undocumented North Korean migrants in China became the target of harsh Chinese crackdowns. Chinese government's forceful deportation has become increasingly severe under the name of the 'Strike Hard Campaign' as part of an anti-crime campaign started in 2001 (Pomfret 2001). Chinese security authorities inspect houses, street corners, churches and factories looking for illegal North Koreans, and forcefully repatriated them. Even those who are found to have helped North Koreans in China are subject to large fines or arrest (Yoon 2001). On the other hand, a person who detects illegal North Korean migrants and reports them to the police can get a reward from the Chinese government.

In 2004, the former U.S. president George W. Bush signed *the North Korean Human Rights Act of 2004* in order to foster human rights and democracy in North

Korea and protect undocumented North Korean migrants in China as refugees. The bill also urges Chinese authorities to fulfil China's obligations as a signatory to the 1951 U.N. Refugee Convention and the related 1966 protocol (Hwang 2005). The United Nations Refugee Agency (UNHCR) has appealed for access to unofficial North Korean migrants in China, but China has continued to deny the UNHCR access. The international society exerts pressure on both North Korea and China to consider undocumented North Koreans' human rights, but its attempts are regarded by North Korea and China as political interventions that threaten state sovereignty using the norms of universal human rights (Aaltola 1998; Kang 2001).

The campaign of detecting undocumented North Korean migrants is likely to pervasively continue given the prevailing stigma against them and the Chinese government's continuous efforts to deepen social borderings between Chinese and undocumented North Koreans. The Chinese government has even treated the regulation of North Korean migration as synonymous with a war on international criminal activities, given that the involvement of North Korean migrants in drug dealing, human trafficking, US dollar forgeries, burglary, and murder has been reported in the North Korean-Chinese borderland. Discourses defining undocumented North Korean migrants as threats to China, together with immigration control and border enforcement, have become widely perceived as the basis for the protection and security of the homeland. The North Korean-Chinese border enforcement could have been harshly conducted through the continuous social borderings that divide Korean Chinese as 'our' people and undocumented North Korean migrants as 'dangerous enemies' and 'criminals'.

Kim (2004) specifically argues that when murders and robberies take place in the Yanbian area undocumented North Korean migrants are the first to be suspected by the Chinese authorities. North Koreans therefore often run away from the sites where incidents occur, even when they are not at all involved because they fear forceful deportation. Therefore, it is very common for undocumented North Koreans to be targeted as criminals, and for those living near incident sites to be arrested and deported (Kim 2004). The criminalization of undocumented North Korean migrants and social discrimination toward them make the status of North Korean migrants unstable and more marginalized.

At the beginning of the current undocumented North Korean migration flows in the mid-1990s, most Korean-Chinese kindly assisted undocumented North Korean migrants. Korean-Chinese supported them for a variety of reasons, including family connections, a sense of altruism, and a desire to reciprocate for the help that North Koreans gave the Korean Chinese who escaped from China across the border during the political turbulence of the Cultural Revolution in the 1960s and 1970s (Margesson 2007, 5). Korean-Chinese, however, have become hesitant to support undocumented North Koreans. An interview with a Korean Chinese woman who helped me with the translation illustrates well the difficulties of supporting North Korean relatives:

> My relatives on my mother's side live in North Hamkyung province. It's just across the Tumen River. Very close. As Korean Chinese with relatives in

North Korea we can get official travel permits. When my mother was alive, we siblings collected money once in a while to visit my mother's brother. Whenever my mother would hear that many North Koreans had died of hunger, she would cry from thinking of her brothers and sisters. We sent used clothing, food, some cash into North Korea. However, it has already been more than ten years that North Koreans have suffered from severe poverty. Too many times, my North Korean relatives asked for help. The numbers who ask for help are too many. North Korean aunts, uncles, cousins, nephews and nieces ... they're countless. They often call or secretly visit us, and then ask for money. Maybe they think that every person in China is rich. Several months ago, a relative whom I'd never met before visited my house. She asked for money but I didn't have any. I only gave her some food. When I told her that I didn't have any money, she didn't believe me and told me I was stingy. I knew that she came to China to get help under danger of arrest. But it was beyond my ability to help them continually and I am afraid of helping them because helping North Korean migrants is illegal.

While some Korean-Chinese are afraid of helping North Koreans because of strict regulations, some exploit undocumented migrants' unstable situation for their own ends. Because they can be arrested and forcibly repatriated, undocumented North Koreans in China are vulnerable to abuse. They are controlled, manipulated, and exploited and their everyday activities are highly limited in China. The exploitation of the labour of North Koreans is particularly egregious. Because they are undocumented, sometimes they are not paid at all in China and they cannot call on the government for protection because of their illegal status. Humanitarian activists in China say that more North Koreans are arrested during the winter in rural areas than in any other season. This is because Chinese farmers are more likely to report North Koreans to government authorities so they will not have to pay for them for their labour during the farming season. Above all, women's and children's human rights are severely violated. Most North Korean children in China do not get a proper education and suffer from malnutrition, while North Korean women, especially poor young women, who cross often become part of the trade in trafficked human beings (Choi 2005; Kim and Noh 2003; Muico 2005). Women who are sold as 'brides' to rural households are often treated like slaves, and subjected to confinement, sexual exploitation, and hard labour (Yoon 2001). They are also sometimes sent back to North Korea because they are not offered a residence permit or citizenship by the Chinese government even after they have several children.

Conclusion

In this chapter, through linking various scales, I have attempted to understand how international and national levels of politics are manifested in the local conditions of the North Korean-Chinese border, and the bodies that clandestinely cross that border. Specifically, I have focused on the extent to which the nation-building processes of North Korea and China, and the transition from the Cold War period toward an international system marked by a more market driven neo-liberal imperative, have impacted the daily practices of bordering along the North Korean-Chinese territorial boundary. North Korea and China have been represented as allies in a socialist brotherhood amidst Cold War geopolitics at the international level, and as strategic collaborative partners under neo-liberal globalization. However, even though North Korea and China have maintained strong ties, there has also been a continuous separation of the Korean-Chinese from North Korea along the territorial border, which is part of a daily practice of binding nations and stirring up nationalistic identities. The border between China and North Korea has been created and regulated along with the development of the two modern nation states, and the border control has intensified as Cold War geopolitics in Northeast Asia have been transformed into neo-liberal globalization.

Discriminatory and intensified bordering practices on the North Korean-Chinese boundary have helped to differentiate the Korean-Chinese from North Koreans. Territorial bordering practices, such as building the walls and increasing the military power on North Korean-Chinese border, and social bordering processes that divide ethnic Koreans who have Chinese citizenship and undocumented North Korean migrants mutually reinforce each other, and even threaten the bodies of North Koreans who unofficially cross the rigid North Korean-Chinese border. The bodies of repatriated North Korean migrants have been starved, tortured, imprisoned, made to do hard labour training in North Korea, and have become a target of human trafficking, forced marriage, and labour exploitation in China. Both the state authorities and the people who exploit the unstable status of undocumented North Korean migrants completely ignore the human security of migrants. By highlighting the daily practices of *bordering* and the threat they have posed to the bodies of undocumented North Korean migrants, I argue the security of undocumented migrants needs to be considered as a matter of public concern.

Acknowledgements

I am truly grateful to the North Koreans who so generously shared their experiences despite difficult circumstances. Without help from the NGO where I worked in China, this academic undertaking would not be possible. I also thank Beverly Mullings for taking time to read, and comment on, earlier versions of this chapter. I benefited greatly from discussions with Alison Mountz in writing this chapter. Thanks also go to Ohseok Kim for his cartographic work. I bear full responsibility for any shortcomings.

References

Aaltola, M. (1999), 'Emergency Food Aid as a Means of Political Persuasion in the North Korea Famine', *Third World Quarterly – Journal of Emerging Area* 20:2, 371-86.

Ackleson, J. (2005), 'Constructing Security on the U.S. – Mexico Border', *Political Geography* 24, 165-84.

Andreas, P. (2003), 'Redrawing the Line: Borders and Security in Twenty-first Century', *International Security* 28:2, 78-111.

Bracewell, W. (1996), 'Women, Motherhood, and Contemporary Serbian Nationalism', *Women's Studies International Journal* 19, 25-33.

Bureau of Yanbian Statistics (2001), *The Year book of Yanbian Statistics* (Yanji: Yanbian People's Press).

Coleman, M. (2007), 'A Geopolitics of Engagement: Neoliberalism, the War on Terrorism, and the Reconfiguration of US Immigration Enforcement', *Geopolitics* 12, 607-34.

Choi, C.D. (2000), *Talpukcha ŏtŏke Halkŏsinka?* (What can we do for North Korean Refugees?) (Seoul: Doori).

Choi, J. (2005), *Kukyunŭl Sebŏn kŏnnŏn Yŏcha* (A Woman Who Crossed the North Korean-Chinese Border Three Times) (Seoul: Bookhouse).

Chung, S.C. (2004), *Hanpantowa Chungkuk Chosŏnjok* (Korean Peninsular, China and the Korean-Chinese) (Seoul: Mosinŭnsalamdŭl (The Serving People)).

Chung, S.C. (1999), *Chungkuk Chosŏnjok Sahoeŭi Pyŏnchŏnkwa Chŏnmang* (The Changes in Korean- Chinese Society and Its Future) (Shinyang: Liaoning Korean Ethnic Press).

Democratic Labor Party of Republic of Korea (2004), 'Chae Chung Yipuk Kyungchaeyumin Jinsangchosa kyŏlkwa' (The Paper on Economic North Korean Migrants in China), *Korea Press Release Network: Newswire* 7 November 2004, available at <https://www.newswire.co.kr/?job=news&no=15309>, accessed 14 May 2009.

Freeman, C.W. (2006), *Forging Kinship across Borders: Paradoxes of Gender, Kinship and Nation between China and South Korea*, Ph.D. Dissertation (Virginia: University of Virginia).

Guan, N.H. (2006), 'China Erects Fence along N. Korea Border', *USA Today* 10 October 2006, available at <http://www.usatoday.com/news/world/2006-10-16-china-nkorea_x.htm>, accessed 13 May 2009.

Haggard, S. and Noland, M. (2007), *Famine in North Korea – Markets, Aid, and Reform* (New York: Columbia University Press).

Human Rights Watch (2002), 'The Invisible Exodus: North Koreans in the People's Republic of China', *Human Rights Watch Report* 14:8, available at <http://www.hrw.org/legacy/reports/2002/northkorea/>, accessed 14 May 2009.

Hwang, B.Y. (2005), 'Spotlight on the North Korean Human Rights Act: Correcting Misperceptions', *Backgrounder* 1823 (Washington: The Heritage Foundation).

Jung, P.R. (1998), 'Sekikyochewa Chungkuk Chosŏnjok Kachikwanŭi Pyŏnhwa mit Minchokchŏnilches ŏngmunche' (The Changes in the World View of

Korean-Chinese in 21 Century and the Problems of Korean Unity), in Park, M. J. (ed.), *Chungkuk Chosŏnjok Chisŏngin Seminar Nonmunchip: Chungkuk Chosŏnjok Hyunsangtae Punsŏk mit Chŏnmang Yŏnku* (Korean Chinese Intellectuals' Seminar Papers – The Analysis on Korean Society's Current Situation and Its Future) (Yanji: Yanbian University Press).

Jung, P.R. (1993), *Yŏnpyŏnŭi Munhwadaehyŏkmyŏng* (Cultural Revolution in Yanbian) (Yanji: Minchokchulpansa (Korean Ethnic Press)).

Kang, C. (2001), 'North Korea and the U.S. Grand Security Strategy', *Comparative Strategy* 20:1, 25-43.

Kahn, J. (2003), 'China Sends Troops to Monitor North Korean Border', *The New York Times* 15 September 2003.

Kim, T.H. and Noh, C.Y. (2003), *Chaechung Pukhanital Yŏsŏngdlŭi Sam* (The Daily Lives of North Korean Migrant Women in China) (Seoul: Hawoo).

Kim, Y.J. (2004), 'Chung Talpuk Yŏsŏng Chungŏn Wangchŏng Salinsakŏn Haekyŏl, Ponyinŭn Puk Kangchesonghwan ŭiki' (A North Korean Woman who Helped to Solve the Accident of 'An Murder in Wangquing' in China will be Forcefully Deported to North Korea), *The Daily NK* 4 August 2004, available at <http://www.dailynk.com/korean/read.php?cataId=nk02500&num=9599>, accessed 15 May 2009.

Koo, S.H. (2007), *Sound of the Border: Music, Identity, and Politics of the Korean Minority Nationality in the People's Republic of China*, Ph.D. Dissertation (Hawaii: University of Hawaii).

Kwak, H.R. (2005), *Pukhanitalchumin Hyunhwangkwa Munche* (The Current Situation of North Korean Migrants and Their Problems) (Paju: Hankukhaksuljŏngbo (Korean Academic Information)).

Kwon, T.H. (2005), 'Sahoechŏk Hwankyŏngkwa Chŏngchesŏng' (Social environment and identity), in Kwon, T.H. (ed.), *Chungkuk Chosŏnjok Sahoeŭi Pyŏnhwa* (The changes of Korean-Chinese Society) (Seoul: Seoul National University Press).

Lee, J.S. (2004), *Pukhan – Chungkuk Kwankye 1945-2000* (The Relationship between North Korea and China 1945-2000) (Seoul: Chungsim (The Center)).

Lee, J.Y. (2001), 'The Korean Minority in China: The Policy of Chinese Communist Party and the Question of Korean Identity', *The Review of Korean Studies* 4:2, 87-131.

Margesson, R., Emma, C. and Andorra, B. (2007), 'CRS Report for Congress – North Korean Refugees in China and Human Rights Issues: International Responses and U.S. Policy Options', *US Congressional Research Report* CRS Cod: 34189, 26 September 2007, available at <http://opencrs.com/document/RL34189/>, accessed 14 May 2009.

Mayer, T. (2004), 'Embodied Nationalism', in Staeheli, L.A., Kofman, E. and Peake, L.J. (eds.), *Mapping Women, Making Politics – Feminist Perspectives on Political Geography* (New York and London: Routledge).

Moore, G.J. (2008), 'How North Korea threatens China's Interests: Understanding Chinese "Duplicity" on the North Korean Nuclear Issue', *International Relations of the Asia-Pacific* 8, 1-29.

Mountz, A. (2010), *Seeking Asylum: Human Smuggling and Bureaucracy at the Border* (Minneapolis: University of Minnesota Press).

Muico, N.K. (2005), *An Absence of Choice – The Sexual Exploitation of North Korean Women in China* (London: Anti-Slavery).

Nevins, J. (2002), *Operation Gatekeeper* (New York: Routledge).

Newman, D. (2006), 'The Lines that Continue to Separate Us: Borders in Our "Borderless" World', *Progress in Human Geography* 30:2, 143-61.

Oliver, B.V. (1993), *The Implementation of China's Nationality Policy in the Northeastern Provinces* (San Francisco: Mellen Research University Press).

Park, M.J. (ed.)(1998), *Chungkuk Chosŏnjok Chisŏngin Seminar Nonmunchip: Chungkuk Chosŏnjok Hyunsangtae Punsŏk mit Chŏnmang Yŏnku* (Korean Chinese Intellectuals' Seminar Papers – The Analysis on Korean Society's Current Situation and Its Future) (Yanji: Yanbian University Press).

Park, M. (2000), *Chungkug Chosŏnjog hyŏnsangtae bunsŏg mit chŏnmang yŏngu – Chungkug Chosŏnjog jisŏngin seminar ronmujib* (The Analysis on Korean Chinese Society's Current Situation and its Future – Chinese Intellectual's Seminar Papers) (Yanbian: Yanbian University Press).

Pomfret, J. (2001), 'China Steps Up Repatriation of North Korean Refugees', *Washington Post* 23 July 2001, A16.

Scarpellino, M. (2007), '"Corriendo": Hard Boundaries, Human Rights and the undocumented Immigrant', *Geopolitics* 12, 330-49.

Sevastopulo, D. and Song, J.A. (2008), 'China Increases Troops on North Korea Border', *Financial Times* 13 November 2008.

Seong, G. (2007), 'Munhwadaehyŏkmyŏngkwa Yŏnpyŏn' (The Chinese Cultural Revolution and Yanbian), *Chungkukhyundaemunhak* (The Contemporary Chinese Literature) 43, 57-99.

Suh, H.J., Choi, E.C., Kim, P., Lee, W.Y., Lim, S.H. and Kim, S.A. (2002), *White Paper on Human Rights in North Korea* (Seoul: Korea Institute for National Unification).

The Bureau of Yanbian Statistics (2001), *Yŏnpyŏn Tongkyeyŏnkam* (The Year book of Yanbian Statistics) (Yanji: Yanbian People's Press).

United States Committee for Refugees and Immigrants (2001), *U.S. Committee for Refugees World Refugee Survey 2001 - North Korea*, published online 20 June 2001, available at <http://www.unhcr.org/refworld/docid/3b31e16710.html>, accessed 13 May 2009.

Varsanyi, M. (2008), 'Rescaling the "Alien", Rescaling Personhood: Neoliberalism, Immigration, and the State', *Annals of the Association of American Geographers* 98:4, 877-96.

Yoon, Y.S. (2001), *Chaewyotalpukcha* (The North Korean Refugees outside of Korean Peninsula) (Seoul: Yolrinforum (Open Forum)).

Women and Migration in Asia – Eroding Borders, New Fixities

Parvati Raghuram and Nicola Piper

Introduction

Migration is usually considered to be an archetypal example of border-crossing. However, borders have come to mean different things depending on who you are. Highly-skilled migrants who cross international borders are seen as placing different cultural and economic knowledge in contact, spurring economic growth (Beaverstock 2002). For them, it appears that borders have been transcended and mobility enabled as they are encouraged to move in an increasingly borderless world. Lesser-skilled migrants and refugees have, on the other hand, been largely regarded as threats to borders, seen as crossing borders without appropriate papers and thus spurring a host of technologies for monitoring and controlling border crossings (Bigo 2002; Huysmans 1995). For these migrants, borders have therefore gained in strength and significance in a securitized world (Ibrahim 2005). These two experiences of border also posit migrant destinations in different ways – one in which receiving state and society are seen as victims ('illegal' migration, typically involving the lesser skilled), the other where they are beneficiaries of 'foreign talent'. The same border thus acts differently for different kinds of migrants.

Asia is an important crucible for migrant activity. In 2005, an estimated 53.3 million (or 28 per cent) of the worldwide stock of 191 million international migrants were in Asia (UN 2006, 29). A large number of these were economic migrants: The International Labour Office (ILO) estimates that of the 86 million migrant workers globally (excluding refugees), about 22.1 million were economically active in the Asian region (ILO 2004, 7). Aside from economic migrants, most of whom are migrating within the region, Asia is also a major source region of permanent settlers (mostly family migrants) and students migrating to other regions. In addition, forced migration continues to play a part within the continent. These trends and patterns point to substantial numbers of Asians crossing international boundaries.

Women form an increasingly significant part of these migratory flows. They play an ever more important role in certain sectors such as domestic work and nursing but are also present in considerable numbers within sectors such as manufacturing and agriculture (Yamanaka and Piper 2005). However, in much of the policy-oriented literature on women and migration borders are viewed as preordained or natural. In this chapter, we move away from this tendency to explore some aspects of female migration as they relate to the political, economic and social nature of borders. We suggest that migration studies that focus on women could explore the diverse and dynamic nature of borders as they are construed in the lives of migrant women. We use Asia as a specific example towards this purpose. However, it is important to state at the outset that this chapter does not provide a comprehensive review of the literature on borders as they relate to migrant women in Asia. Rather, we look at how borders manifest themselves in the lives of migrant women displacing some women, and conditioning experiences of both immigration and emigration of others.

In the first section following this introduction, we provide a brief overview of dominant paradigms that emerge from the literature on women's economic migration before moving on to explore how borders are being constructed and negotiated in border zones, in source countries and in destination countries. Our discussion of Asia mostly refers to East, South and Southeast Asia as well as migrants from these areas that are in other parts of the world.[1] Although there is a significant amount of migration in the newly independent post-Soviet countries of Central Asia, their proximity to Eastern Europe and their historical links with that region has meant that they are perhaps best considered separately.

The second section uses two examples to explore the dynamic nature of borders and their role in constructing the identities of female economic migrants. The first example on the historical production of borders in Malaysia highlights the porosity and the constructed nature of borders. It also exemplifies the fertile intersection between borders as metaphorical devices and borders as socially constituted practices showing how the latter invariably interrelates with the former. A second example of the experience of migrants at the Burma-Thailand border suggests the productive nature of borders in producing new forms of labour and political subjectivities.

The third section explores practices of bordering as they pertain to emigration. Most literature on migration focuses on migration as an act of reception, and there is much less work on the devices used to monitor and control border crossings by source countries. We aim to address this gap by exploring how India uses regulations to limit who can find employment where, and how in creating a legislative framework of protection, the government instates a border between the rights of those who are regular and those who are not.

In the last section we look at bordering within the context of sites of destination. Here, we explore two forms of borders, those between skilled and lesser skilled workers and those that are created in temporary labour regimes. We also briefly explore how systems of advocacy are reworking the territorial borders of migrant politics.

---

1   We have used World Bank definitions of different parts of Asia for this chapter.

The small body of work that has explored the conceptual issues surrounding female migration and borders within Asia (see Devasahayam et al. 2004) has assumed that borders are fixed frontiers that women cross. Our approach, on the other hand, emphasizes the constructed nature of these borders, their dynamicity and the multiple sites where bordering is played out. It suggests that borders can simultaneously enforce both mobility and enclosure (Cunningham and Heyman 2004).

Migrant women in Asia – dominant paradigms

Economic migration of women from Asia (both within the region and without) is not a new phenomenon. Some of this movement can be traced to historical processes such as women's involvement in plantation work under colonialism or in the tourism and manufacturing industries as part of export-led industrialization (Ball and Piper 2001; Oishi 2005).

However, in the past couple of decades there has been an overall feminization of migration, which is related to at least four phenomena. First, there has been improved statistical visibility of female migrants in migration streams, partly related to a changed perception of women-dominated migration as 'work migration' in its own right. Secondly, there has been increasing participation of women in most, if not all, migration streams. Thirdly, the increasing inability of men to find full-time employment in the origin countries has meant that female migration has become part of household strategy to overcome the resulting shortfall in income. Finally, the growing demand for feminized jobs in destination countries (Piper 2008a) has also led to increased female migration. The forms of migration depend on the particular situation in specific origin and destination countries, skill level and type of job. These movements of women do not come easily. They are encouraged because of their importance to economic growth but are also regulated because of the securitization of women's bodies and because of the negative effects that the care gap that women's departure produces in both the household and the state.

Broadly speaking, there are two strands to the literature on female economic migration: one that focuses on intra-Asian migration (Chin 2003; Grundy-Warr et al. 1996; Huang and Yeoh 2003; Wickramasekara 2002) and another that follows the broad contours of migration, from countries of the global South to the North (McGovern 2003; Parreñas 2001). The extent of intra-regional migration in Asia, the conditions under which much of this labour is performed and the new forms of political and civil engagements that have emerged as a result have all evoked feminist attention (Barber 2000; Piper 2008b; Piper and Yamanaka 2003). On the other hand, literature on female economic migration from Asia to Northern countries has heavily focused on the relocation of socially reproductive activities globally through the formation of global care chains whereby women move to provide various forms of care such as nursing, domestic work and childcare to households in the richer global North. This relocation leads to a demand for such carework in the households of those who migrate, spurring migration from other parts of Asia (Anderson 2000). In this way, the demand for socially reproductive labour (Kofman and Raghuram 2006) creates what Arlie Hochschild calls a care chain, 'a series of personal links between people across the globe based on the paid or unpaid work of caring' (Hochschild 2000, 131). This form of migration shapes the border crossing of most female economic migrants in Asia today (Espiritu 2002; Parreñas 2001).

In both strands of literature female labour seems to primarily involve body work, work where the female body or *femininity* are implicated in the nature of work provided (see Gulati 1994). Most Asian women labour migrants move to take up jobs as domestic workers, sex workers and nurses, professions that are defined by notions of femininity. As Bowlby et al. (1997) argue such notions can act in oppressive ways to structure women's entry into occupations but also shape the form of international female migration as independent economic migrants and main income earners (UN General Assembly 2004).[2]

However, women who move from the global South to the North as well as those moving within Asia are also taking part in the less feminized sectors of the labour market such as IT and business, where gender exclusivity and male dominance are the norm. But such participation has received much less attention (see Raghuram 2004; Yeoh and Willis 2005). At the same time, the demand for labour in feminized sectors has become so strong that there is some evidence, especially in the Philippines, of male migrants attempting to enter feminized streams (especially nursing) because of the legal channels and breadth of destinations on offer.[3]

In sum, despite the broadening of Asian women's experiences, the bulk of research on female migration has for long focused primarily on a few sectors. The largest volume of work documents the experiences of domestic workers (Heyzer et al. 1994; Huang, Yeoh and Rahman 2005). Entertainers are another category of female migrants who have been widely researched. It has been argued that their migration has typically been subsumed under trafficking rather than migration for work (see Piper 2005). International interest in trafficking has clearly led to the availability of funding for research on this field, and trafficking, particularly in the Greater Mekong subregion, and in South Asia has been researched by international organizations such as the United Nations and by regional bodies (Asis 2008; Lee 2005; Piper 2005; Yea 2006). There has also been some interest in migrant women nurses (Ball 2004; Percot 2005), especially within the context of brain drain and brain waste. Here attention has focused on the deskilling of nurses who are employed

---

2   Arguably, similar processes are at work even in *marriage migration*, especially that between Asian women and Western men where women are less skilled. Here marriage is often among the few options available for securing women's migration status (Piper 1999; Piper and Roces 2003).

3   There is some evidence of men taking up feminized professions in order to migrate (Manalansan IV 2006). In the Philippines, for instance, cases of medical doctors have emerged who retrain as nurses in order to access the international labour market (personal communication, Dr. Maruja M.B. Asis, Scalabrini Migration Center, Manila).

as carers and domestic workers. Oishi's (2005) work on ten countries across the Asian region, covering both sending and receiving countries with its multi-level analysis (globalization, state policies, social legitimacy and individual autonomy) also provides an integrative and comparative perspective on female migration in the region. Such multi-sited, multi-level studies are, however, still quite rare.

Intra-regional borders: borders in flux

Historically, migration has been a central part of the development of Asia even in the pre-colonial period. South East Asia was a crucible where trading links between East and South Asia were played out. Similar links also existed between South and West Asia. However, colonialism changed the nature and quality of migration with large scale redistribution of populations within the region through practices such as indentured labour. Colonial authorities used indenture systems such as the *kangany* and *maistry* to provide a workforce for the labour intensive plantations in South East Asia.

Women were always part of this arrangement. Many women were themselves indentured and worked in the plantations. Some women who were not indentured, but had been allowed to accompany men, entered domestic labour. Others migrated singly either as marriage migrants or in order to seek domestic work although these numbers were small. Thus, of the 74,454 Indian women in Mauritius 868 were reported as domestic workers, 549 as gardeners and 244 as laundresses. Domestic work was thus the largest single occupation for migrant women (Carter 1995). Similarly, Indian domestic workers accompanied soldiers and assistants in 1819 when Sir Raffles first went to Singapore to establish a base there (Ministry of External Affairs 2001). In these flows it is not always clear whether to name the migrants as Indians, or subjects of the British Empire. Their mobility is clearly shaped by both. At that time the borders of the British Empire meant that this migration was easily arranged but as the Empire dissolved borders between these countries were reinstated. Some borders were eroded, others emerged and became fixed. Clearly then, borders are not static – they alter as the logic of bordering itself alters. Empires and nations provide different frameworks for bordering practices.

A historical approach to migration, thus, suggests that migrants do not necessarily transcend borders – rather borders are constructed underneath their feet. Moreover, the borders that women navigate simply find new shape in the post-migration situation. One example of this is offered by Bernard Wilson (2008) in his reflections on K.S. Maniam's text *Between Lives* (2003). Wilson highlights some of the struggles that the texts' protagonists face in producing a polymorphous life within the context of an increasingly ethnicized Malaysia. They live through a range of historical formations, with their own particular boundary making moments – British colonization, Japanese occupation, independence, insurgency, and developmental change in contemporary Malaysia. In these processes new borders emerge and have to be negotiated in independent Malaysia.

One of these new borders arises from the changing status of ethnicity within independent Malaysia. By according Malays the status of Bhumiputra, which means children of the soil, differentiation between different ethnic groups within Malaysia was given statutory recognition. Ethnic differentiation was strengthened so that bordering increasingly occurred within Malaysia. The lives of different ethnic groups became increasingly differentiated. The ethnic heterogeneity of the Malaysian population was an inheritance of the heterogeneity of the Empire, with labour being shipped from one place within the Empire to another, but the 'borderless' Empire became re-bordered as many of the countries became independent. Indentured workers were stranded because of hundreds of years of economic history in countries far away from those they thought of as home. This form of bordering is recounted by Maniam through the protagonist of his text, Sellamma, a Tamil migrant who came to work in Malaysia's plantations. Her life is a struggle to remember, to belong and to find representation. As a young professional urban woman, also of Tamil descent, coaxes Sellamma to adapt to urban development and to become part of the new Malaysia, Sellamma traverses a range of identificatory boundaries, temporal and spatial. She has to negotiate the borders of tradition and modernity as lived out through the processes of modernization and urbanization in an ambitious forward-looking Malaysia. But it is not only the territorial border that has altered but also the social basis of belonging as ethnicity comes together with the tropes of modernity to decide who belongs and where. Sellamma's life is bordered and rebordered in this history of Malaysia. Borders are emergent, physically and metaphorically. The case of indentured Indian female workers in Malaysia provides one example of how the transformation of international geopolitical borders has shaped gendered subjectivities.

The transformations of borders between Empire, nation and ethnic groups also leave behind a trace in the present. In many cases, current movements of women can be understood as an intensification of previous patterns of migration. For example, colonialism laid the seeds for migration from Asia to Europe and in the Philippine case, the US, a trajectory that has continued into the post-colonial period. The direction of labour mobility also follows colonial links in the case of other countries: Indonesia to the Netherlands; South Asia to the UK and so on. What has become international migration often has routes in colonial linkages. Borders have their own fluid histories while bordering as a process is lived out through the lives of these labour migrants.

This dynamicity of borders is not restricted to the past – borders continue to be volatile. In many instances, in post-colonial Asia, borders have not yet stabilized. Borders are often used to mark the limits of national sovereignty, but they also help to construct a socio-cultural imaginary. And in many parts of Asia, geopolitical boundaries do not neatly overlie meaningful social and cultural spaces. Over time meaningful cultural boundaries were cut across by imperial boundaries which then influenced the borders of post-colonial states. On the other hand, different cultural groups were put together in producing new geopolitical entities leading to ethnic conflict within states. Boundary wars have resulted. In these areas borders are clearly not lines on a map; rather they may be better seen as broad zones where border skirmishes are played out. These border zones come to be seen as threatening the territorial integrity of the spaces on either side of the boundary. But they are also zones for population movements of refugees, of people fleeing to find work.[4] Labour migration of women is also widespread in these boundary zones as the economies of these areas collapse through war.

The boundary struggles in eastern Myanmar offer an example of a boundary in the making and the resultant forms of female mobility that mark this conflictual landscape. This border area between Thailand and Myanmar is a zone of movement, produced by the ethnic violence within the latter country and resulting in new forms of ethnicization within the former. Historical affiliations, colonial agreements and postcolonial military dictatorship have together left a legacy of a wide range of political rights and recognition for the many ethnic minority groups within Myanmar. The Shan, the Karens and the Mons are amongst the ethnic groups for whom the search for statehood and national belonging have resulted in widespread displacement and search for new meaningful borders (Grundy-Warr and Wong 2002; Laungaramsri 2006). The Karens, with their claim to territory, spanning international boundary between Myanmar and Thailand, imagine their own borders, of a nascent state which they call Kawthoolei.

> *The processes of demarcating Thailand and Burma territory have established the two nation-states and simultaneously designated the Karens, as well as other ethnic nationalities and indigenous peoples situated in the border zones, as unqualified forms of life. Through this inclusive exclusion, these peoples have been abandoned by the two sovereignties. Being lives without, for the most part, any protection, they are deprived of any possibility of appeal.* (Tangseefa 2006, 411)

This instability has found expression in diverse forms of labour migration from this border zone into Thailand. Domestic work, sex work (Grundy-Warr et al. 1996) and trading (Kusakabe and Mar Oo 2007) have been amongst the occupations in which women have found jobs. However, in a study of Mae Sot town in the Tak Province in Northern Thailand, Arnold and Hewison (2005) found that 95 per cent of the workers in the approximately 200 factories were Burmese, and that about 70 per cent of the migrants in the area were women. Thus, contested borders appear to dispel populations, particularly women.

Yet, these zones can also be sites for the production of new political subjectivities, as exemplified by women from one of the large ethnic minority groups in Myanmar, the Shan. As part of the formation of a unified state, the military government in Myanmar has forcibly relocated many people in the Shan province, destroyed crops and has attempted to subjugate the border zones through a mixture of interventional development projects and military offensives (Laungaramsri 2006). In an insightful analysis, Laungaramsri suggests that Shan women find themselves caught between three nationalist discourses within these territorial imaginaries

---

4   As a result of this Asia has one of the largest numbers of refugees in the world.

and socio-cultural borders. The Myanmar government has evicted Shan women as bearers of non-Burmese identity; the Thai government has refused to give Shan women refugee status and hence made them ineligible for humanitarian assistance, while the Shan nationalist movement has incorporated women as subordinates in a military conflict. The Shan Women's Action Network, set up in 1999, was an attempt by Shan women to find a voice in the marginal space between the three dominant nationhoods. Through research, advocacy and community based action they have attempted to forge a way of defining what it means to be a Shan. They have established educational opportunities, training, health centers and counseling centers for those who face the daily rigours of displacement and exile. Towards this, they have taken part in transnational networks that span many international borders. This type of work not only enables new forms of labour force participation for those whom they support, but is also a source of employment for Shan women. It has become a site of emergent transnational political subjectivities.

Bordering devices in origin countries

From the examples above we get a clear sense of the importance of the state in bordering processes and in creating borderless populations in a bordered world. States are often the architects of the bordering devices and the law and technology through which this bordering is achieved. States decide who should be eligible for protection from the state, and who amongst those within its borders should be protected. As such, we would argue that states continue to play a key part in producing borders.

But within the migration context which state should provide this protection, the state in the source country or the destination country, is also unclear. Moreover, in an increasingly 'networked state' (Cannoy and Castells 2001), most countries have some presence within the borders of other nations' territories. The role of consulates in dispensing protection and legislating on migrant welfare means that the borders of the destination state are interpellated by the juridical borders of the source states.

On the other hand, in source countries some individuals know even prior to migration that were they to migrate they would have greater rights to welfare than others. The boundaries of inclusion, such as rights to welfare, may be demarcated prior to migration. One example of this is through the distinction between skilled and lesser-skilled people. Those with skills know they will have greater rights. Moreover, the source country may also give up offers of protection to citizens. For example, the distinction between regular and irregular migrants and the withholding of legal protection from those who are irregular by both source and destination states. Nikolas Rose argues that this process of exclusion is an example of a global shift from offering welfare to those who are citizens to those who are included within and have passed through (and thus reinforced the power of) contemporary legislative frameworks. Legal protection is often only offered to documented workers, rather than to residents irrespective of status. The border between irregular and regular migrants is thus enacted in the conditions of who can become documented and how. This process of recognition of the right to migrate is thus itself a bordering device that determines who can become regular, who is eligible for protection and for whom the source state's protection can be extended extra-territorially.

Below, we explore this issue through the example of migrant Indian domestic workers. The borders between regular and irregular migrants are particularly significant amongst domestic workers, many of whom are irregular and are therefore not protected by any laws. Moreover, India is only one of several Asian states which has placed limits on women migrating to enter domestic work, limiting the rights to mobility or forcing more and more women into an irregular status on the one hand, and creating new borders between those who are able to migrate legally and those who are not on the other.

There are a range of practices through which these forms of control are materialized. Until October 2007 the possession of skills (those holding graduate degrees, vocational qualifications), wealth (income-tax payers), nature of employment (those working in skilled and semi-skilled sectors, in diplomatic service), nature of employer (those employed as Gazetted government servants) and destination countries (migrants to Pakistan, Bangladesh, Japan, New Zealand, Australia, all countries in North America and in Europe, excluding Commonwealth of Independent States (CIS) countries) were all used to decide who required clearance from the government to emigrate and who did not. Moreover, women under the age of 30 were also not allowed to go abroad to take up domestic work. A range of bordering devices thus, operated to decide who could migrate easily, who on migrating would be considered legally eligible for Government of India protection and who would not. Moreover, for women age acted as a supplementary device making some people who are below that age, irregular and outside the remit of protection from the source country.

Since October 2007, these borders of acceptability around migration have altered. Those seeking employment in 18 Asian countries are now required to obtain emigration clearance, while all other criteria for clearance have been removed, except for women. The symbolic border between those who require protection and those who do not has clearly shifted from those around class (and its proxy measures such as education and wealth) to geographical imaginations of safe and unsafe countries.

Women are, however, a special case, especially if they are entering domestic work. Until 2007, domestic workers were required to obtain emigration clearance through the Office of the Protectorate of Emigrants which is based in some of the major Indian cities.[5] The offices in Delhi and Mumbai deal with the bulk of applications and as such they are of higher status, being led by officials of the rank of Under Secretary (to the Government of India) rather than section officers. The Protector's office aims to determine that there is a demand for the worker and

5   The Protector of Emigrants does not involve itself with helping employees to obtain a visa or to meet regulations set by destination country.

that the conditions under which the worker will operate will be adequate for the worker and equivalent to those that would have been given to local employees, particularly with respect to the period of employment and placement, wages and conditions of work.

The rationale for not allowing domestic workers to seek employment through recruitment agents is that recruitment agents will not have adequate control over employers due to the privatized nature of the employment. The Ministry of Labour aims to strictly control the emigration of domestic workers and to protect the rights of domestic workers by checking that there is a direct relation between the employer and the employee and ensuring that the regulations of the Protector of Emigrants are all being met. Domestic workers seeking to emigrate have, therefore, to be recruited directly by the employer and have to give assurance that they will only work for the foreign employer who has recruited them and will only be engaged in the job for which they have been recruited. Those seeking emigration clearances must come personally to the office of the Protector to make their application to emigrate. A letter stating that the employer will receive them at the point of destination must accompany this application. Domestic workers are also required to produce a medical clearance certificate testifying that they are fit for the job and an employment contract that has been attested by the Indian mission in the country to which the worker is destined. The Emigration Act requires that the employee will be paid at least the minimum salary of the country in which they seek employment and that they will be governed by minimum standards of condition of employment. For domestic workers the contract should stipulate that workers would only work for eight hours a day, six days a week and eleven months of a year. The employees must provide medical insurance in the destination country. Clearly, then

> there is a sense in which today the experience of crossing the border is, for many people, not unlike entering a large corporate building, government ministry, a university library, gated residence or computer network. In each case the subject is scanned, identified and profiled. A databank is accessed, a record created. An entry occurs, or perhaps access is denied. Such is the changing texture of borders. (Walters 2006, 197)

Moreover, these borders clearly exist well inside territorial entities and not just at its limits. In order to obtain clearance, the husband (if married) or parent of the domestic worker must accompany them to the office of the Protector of Emigrants. This practice removes the responsibility of the domestic worker from the office of the Protector to the accompanying person. This form of infantilization of gendered subjectivities is particularly problematic in a context, where it is precisely the failure of the patriarchal family, abandonment by husbands and hence, by both the natal and new families, that spurs migration.

Officially applicants who seek emigration clearance to be employed as domestic workers must also be at least 30 years of age, although this may be relaxed where the employer is themselves an Indian citizen. Apparently the border between employer and employee is muted by co-nationality. However, in such circumstances the office of the Protector seeks an affidavit from the employer to the effect that only they will employ this worker. Until 2002 this rule only pertained to women intending to migrate to West Asia but on the recommendation of the National Commission for Women, this regulation has been extended to those bound for all countries.

The Protector is required to check that the intending emigrant has been informed of any problems or issues that might arise in the country of employment. The prospective worker must deposit an application fee, as well as a sum of money equivalent to a one-way fare from the country of destination. The latter is deposited with the office of the Protector in the name of the employee by the employer in order to fund repatriation of the domestic worker in case any problems arise during the duration of the employment. The money is withdrawn on behalf of the domestic worker by the office and is sent to the Indian mission in the destination country under these circumstances. If no problems arise, this money is returned to the domestic worker once they return to India. In order to keep track of all these issues, the office of the Protector maintains a separate register for those seeking employment abroad as domestic workers.

Here we see a detailed example of how borders are kept intact through a range of regulations. These are the borders of a mobility regime (Shamir 2005) as they ultimately operate to limit access and restrict movement. They are layered – with a range of actors: protectors of emigrants, male members of the household of the prospective domestic worker, employers and so on, well meaning members of the National Commission for Women and so on, acting to control women's cross-border movements and to create and govern difference. We can also see some of the minutiae of how these actors find a role in such bordering activities. Given the context of familial abuse which prevents so many women from accessing familial support for migration and hence a legal route to migration, these processes may well be seen as the 'energies, the practices, the works of division that act upon persons and collectivities such that some ways of being, some forms of existence are cast into a zone of shame, disgrace or debasement, rendered beyond the limits of the liveable, denied the warrant of tolerability, accorded purely a negative value' (Rose 1999, 253).

In 2007, the ways of ordering female workers' mobility altered. Under the new rules, it is not only household service workers, but rather all women who require emigration clearance who will be subject to controls over migration. All women who hold passports requiring emigration clearance will be banned from taking up employment in countries with which India has not yet entered into bilateral agreements. The limits of legal migration have closed in and new borders based on bilateralism have come to be implemented between those who are seen as legal and those who are not.

Moreover, gender has become a guiding principle in this form of bordering, working in consonance with other forms of differentiation. The need for emigration clearance now encompasses all women who require emigration clearance (and see above for how this operates across class boundaries), rather than just domestic workers. The distinction between men and women supersedes that of the conditions of work. Also, the state in taking up the mantle of protecting women appears to have excluded more and more women from state protection by making them irregular. Migrants are, thus, clearly subject to layers of gendered dimensions of state regulation *at home* and *abroad* and the borders between regular and irregular migrants are indelibly gendered.

Borders within the nation

In this penultimate section we want to explore some ways in which borders draw upon other social hierarchies, especially those between different parts of the population. Here, once again we see borders operating as filters, rather than as blockages, selecting out those whose movements will be enabled and those whose mobility will be withheld (Walters 2006). In the first part of this section we discuss the increasing differentiation between the skilled and lesser skilled and how certain versions of skills act as a boundary marker between different populations. Although borders have always divided and sorted populations into the desirable and the undesirable, what is increasingly significant in the Asian context is the extent to which these borders are permanently in place. Asian migration is marked by a host of temporary arrangements so that settlement is never on offer, especially for women who are migrating within the lesser skilled sectors. Such women are only ever reluctantly and contingently admitted into destination countries. In the second part of the section we discuss the entrenchment of temporary migration systems and the *stickiness* of the geopolitical borders of source countries in such systems. We suggest that many Asian countries have failed to expand symbolic or social-cultural borders in line with the resident population within geographical territories but that this is also being challenged by advocacy organizations.

Polarization and stratification

When the monolithic category of female migrant is broken down to explore the differences between the various types of economic migrants, refugee or trafficked women and migrating wives (Piper and Yamanaka 2008), it becomes clear that the increasing polarization between skilled and less skilled migration in the ease of migration between countries has gender implications.

The trend toward increasing diversification and polarization results in highly stratified migratory movements. The notion *of polarization* highlights the differences between the skilled and lesser skilled. *Diversification* refers to intra-group differences (for example Asians in Australia constitute a highly diverse group too, see Khoo et al. 2008) as well as inter-group differences (more source countries have appeared on the migration scene; the number of destination countries has increased with more countries having shifted from being purely sending to both sending and receiving countries).

Gender intersects with other social relations, such as class and/or caste, migration status, ethnicity and/or race, generational cleavages, and so on. Taken together, a complex map of stratification emerges with its own dynamics of exclusion/inclusion and power relations. It is important to highlight these dynamics in both destination and origin countries to emphasize that migrants leave and enter gendered and stratified societies (with qualitative and quantitative differences depending on specific context, Piper 2008; see also Oishi 2005).

Thus, *stratification* emphasizes the combined effects of gender, ethnicity, legal status, skill level, and mode of entry or exit. This is also played out geographically: Migrants with high socio-economic status tend to go to higher income and more developed countries (for example the US, Canada, Europe, Hong Kong, Singapore) as the fees charged and the skills demanded are higher. Religion, and social norms associated with it also plays a certain role with some Muslim countries giving preference, and being preferred, by migrants of the same faith (for example Indonesian domestic workers going in larger numbers to West Asia than elsewhere). Asian women migrating within Asia tend to be less qualified and many of them belong to the lower middle class or working classes, hence many of them migrate to closer destinations within the region (Oishi 2005, 111). The gendered and geographic stratification of migration has implications for labour market experience, entitlements and rights. Thus, social and cultural identities as well as class backgrounds influence who migrates, where, as well as what rights migrants can then subsequently have. It appears that borders within the country are extended out into destination states, being mapped out onto where women can go and to define their employment and residence rights.

In opposition to the narratives of lesser skilled Asian women workers travelling around Asia, is the finding that according to the OECD (2002), women play a significant role in skilled migration flows. 'Indian IT specialists and doctors, Filipino nurses or Chinese professionals are emblematic of this phenomenon' (Dumont et al. 2007, 10). When zooming in on women in specific, the Philippines take lead position as origin country for tertiary educated women in OECD countries (Dumont et al. 2007).

Closer examination of skilled migration through a gender lens shows that, ironically, many skilled women become less skilled migrant workers purely because of the lack of demand in the jobs they are qualified for – a phenomenon referred to as *de-skilling* (see Dumont et al. 2007; McKay 2003). This has in particular been noticed with regard to two highly feminized jobs: nursing and domestic work. Despite their classification (by immigration policies) as skilled migrants, de-skilling has been highlighted by existing studies as a common phenomenon experienced by foreign nurses. Women who enter skilled sectors such as nursing may become deskilled and have to work as say care home workers where their medical qualifications are devalued, yet their ability to get to the OECD countries has been dependent on accessing the right skills set prior to migration. Moreover, with domestic work constituting the major legal channel available to women in most regions of this world, including West and Southeast Asia, it is not rare to find fairly well-educated women taking on this type of job which is categorized as *unskilled* by immigration policies.[6] Yet we note that very often the class stratification in being able to access higher education can be played out in the international borders that migrants can then cross so that where you perform lesser skilled jobs may also depend on the social borders within home countries.

At the same time, there are less skilled women who are turned into skilled migrant workers because of the otherwise controversial nature of their jobs or of their physical mobility. For instance, in the Philippines, the government classifies women departing to Japan, Korea and Taiwan on the entertainer visa as *professional overseas performing artists*. A recent study by the International Organisation for Migration (IOM) (2003, 65) describes the classification of entertainers as professional or skilled as an anachronism because most of the women are rarely trained as professional entertainers or performing artists. At the same time this raises a feminist concern about reproductive or care work often not being considered as requiring skills. Another example is provided by the case of Bangladesh: as the out-migration of less skilled Bangladeshi women is banned by the government, female factory workers in Malaysia are classified as skilled to allow them to migrate legally.[7] Thus, the official categories of skilled and unskilled need deconstruction to expose their social embeddedness (Dodson 2008). Commonly used classifications do not always reflect or recognize the actual level of skills or professionalism but are rooted in the economic and gender disparities that exist between origin and destination countries as well as within societies.

This exploration of the distinction between skilled and lesser skilled highlights 'the notion of unequal passages and delineates how power works through borders as distinctive spaces connecting and regulating movement across the different fragments of globalization' (Cunningham and Heyman 2004, 300). Moreover, these differences really matter because the emerging policies by destination governments also result in increasingly stratified rights and entitlements. Citizenship is becoming less important for the skilled who obtain most rights via permanent residency status. At the same time, changing citizenship is becoming easier for the privileged and the toleration of dual citizenship is increasing (Dauvergne 2009). For the lesser skilled, citizenship is of less immediate importance than accessing overseas employment in general (Briones 2006). International migration of both the skilled and lesser skilled is set up increasingly as circulatory and, therefore, not closely in tune with citizenship. The skilled, however, enjoy a greater range of benefits and choices to do with unequal access to the Permanent Residency (PR) status and the (eventual) opportunity to settle (as in the U.S., Canada, Australia and New Zealand in particular), which is largely denied to the lesser skilled, although it has been noted that even the permanence of PR is being affected by pressures of globalization (Dauvergne 2009).

---

6   Domestic work is the single most important job category in the Gulf States mostly taken up by Indonesians, Sri Lankans and Filipinas. There are 250,000 Foreign Domestic Workers (FDWs) in Hong Kong, and of 500,000 foreign workers in total, 150,000 in Singapore are FDWs.

7   Personal e-mail communication with Dr. Petra Dannecker, 10 November 2005.

Temporary migration

As temporary contract workers with legal employment permits, both male and female migrants are often tied to one specific employer in one specific line of work – and when this is a job classified as *unskilled* and is linked to the informal sector of the economy, this results in limited wage earning power, little if any upward or sideward mobility, and, thus, implications for sustaining family members back home. It also leads to the disciplining of migrants into compliant and docile workers. This is compounded by the emergence of a complex *migration industry* with the involvement of brokers and recruiters who often charge fees that exceed *legal* ceilings (Verité 2005). Furthermore, labour laws are often not enforced, freedom of association is widely violated, and undocumented migration is tacitly approved and legal status denied by many receiving states (Piper 2008b). While two of the male-dominated sectors are classified as the most dangerous types of work – construction and agriculture – domestic work has been recognized as one of the most vulnerable types of employment with high levels of isolation and widespread occurrence of abusive practices (ILO 2004). As women in lower skilled jobs often end up in (certain) reproductive spheres of the labour market (as domestic workers, sex workers), they work in jobs that are socio-legally not recognized as *proper* work.

Temporary migration schemes, however, do not only concern the lesser skilled. Even when classified as skilled workers, this does not automatically come with a permanent residence permit. In Europe, many jobs in the health and education sectors are contracted and highly dependent on the labour market situation, as exemplified in the recent changes in the United Kingdom's hiring procedure. Although family reunification is in principle an entitlement skilled migrants have, temporary status renders the uprooting of a family a complex decision to be made by individual migrants.

In Asia, where most receiving countries operate with strictly temporary migration schemes, research on the social costs of this type of migration has begun to expand, especially on the issue of transnational parenthood/motherhood and transnationally split family life. Also, there is more and more evidence of short-term stays turning into longer term arrangements, with migrants extending their contracts several times ending up being absent for many years, if not decades, yet without the prospects of uniting with their families at the destination (Piper 2008). Thus, in a world of temporary migration, crossing borders does not entail any rights to social inclusion. The social border of the nation is, in many ways, held intact while the territorial border is crossed.

Despite these physical and social borders, there are also rising forces from within society in both origin and destination countries to 'deborder' states (Rumford 2006), and that is through ordinary citizens taking up advocacy on behalf of migrants and also by migrants' forming their own associations. There is an evolving literature now on so-called 'transnational political activism' and 'transnational advocacy networks in defence of migrants' rights (see Law 2002; Piper 2003). These groups are imagining and creating new territorial affiliations and networks that cut across both symbolic and territorial borders. Yet, even within civil society, there are borders between women of different classes and status. For instance middle class women's organizations that represent employers in destination countries often fail to support foreign domestic workers (see Lyons 2005; Wee and Sim 2005). There are also important boundaries between male migrants' networks and those of female migrants as exemplified by the often unsuccessful attempts that women make to join or link up with their male counterparts (Dannecker 2005). The latter example shows that neither ethnicity nor shared nationality offer any guarantee for solidarity and inclusion in destination countries. Stratified migration, therefore, results in stratified boundaries and borders.

Conclusion

In this chapter we have explored some aspects of how female migration in Asia challenges the notion of borders from both the perspective of destination and origin countries. We suggest that physical borders are continuously being reshaped in a postcolonial world, so that it is not only women who move across borders, but also borders that move around women. Most bordering activities are also usually considered in the context of destination countries, but we show some ways in which origin countries too are involved in drawing borders around who can migrate and who cannot. As a result, there is a decline in the strength of borders for some, while for others migration has been met by a system of increasingly securitized and militarized border re-enforcements. Moreover, the discussion of borders and bordering has to go beyond the physical crossing of state borders and must be supplemented by recognition of the constructed and dynamic nature of borders. More importantly, borders also constitute gendered identities. In other words, spatial mobilities and gendered political subjectivities are both shaped by border skirmishes. Some of these skirmishes have historical roots in postcolonial Asia while others are more recent. Finally, borders are seen to enclose territorial entities that are in some ways marked by homogeneity or uniqueness but our chapter shows that this, too, is usually untrue. Borders have proliferated within geographic boundaries, as class and gender shape the female body's migration within Asia.

References

Agrawal, A. (ed.)(2006), *Migrant Women and Work* (New Delhi: Sage).

Anderson, B. (2000), *Doing the Dirty Work* (London: Zed Press).

Arnold, D. and Hewison, K. (2005), 'Exploitation in Global Supply Chains: Burmese Workers in Mae-Sot', *Journal of Contemporary Asia* 5:3, 319-40.

Asis, M.M.B. (2008), 'Human Trafficking in East and South-East Asia: Searching for Structural Factors', in Cameron, S. and Newman, E. (eds.), *Trafficking in Humans:*

Social, Cultural and Political Dimensions (Tokyo: United Nations University Press), 181-205.

Asis, M.M.B. (2005), 'Recent Trends in International Migration in Asia and the Pacific', *Asia-Pacific Population Journal* 20:3, 15-38.

Ball, R. (2004), 'Divergent Development, Racialised Rights: Globalized Labour Markets and the Trade of Nurses: The Case of the Philippines', *Women's Studies International Forum* 27:2, 119-33.

Barber, P.G. (2000), 'Agency in Philippine Women's Labour Migration and Provisional Diaspora', *Women's Studies International Forum* 23:4, 399-411.

Beaverstock, J.V. (2002), 'Transnational Elites in Global Cities: British Expatriates in Singapore's Financial District', *Geoforum* 33:4, 525-38.

Benhabib, S. and Resnick, J. (eds.)(2009), *Citizenship, Gender and Borders* (New York: NYU Press).

Bigo, D. (2002), 'Security and Immigration: Toward a Critique of the Governmentality of Unease', *Alternatives* 27:1, 63-92.

Bowlby, S., Gregory, S. and McKie, L. (1997), '*Doing Home,* Patriarchy, Caring and Space', *Women's Studies International Forum* 20:3, 343-50.

Briones, L. (2006), *Beyond Agency and Rights: Capability, Migration and Livelihood in Filipina Experiences of Domestic Work in Paris and Hong Kong*, Unpublished PhD Thesis (Flinders: University of South Australia).

Cameron, S. and Newman, E. (eds.)(2008), *Trafficking in Humans: Social, Cultural and Political Dimensions* (Tokyo: United Nations University Press).

Carnoy, M. and Castells, M. (2001), 'Globalization, the Knowledge Society, and the Network State: Poulantzas at the Millennium', *Global Networks* 1:1, 1-18.

Carter, M. (1995), *Servants, Sirdars and Settlers: Indians in Mauritius* (Delhi: Oxford University Press).

Chin, C. (2003), 'Visible Bodies, Invisible Work: State Practices Toward Migrant Women Domestic Workers in Malaysia', *Asian and Pacific Migration Journal* 12:1-2, 49-74.

Cunningham, H. (2004), 'Nations Rebound? Crossing Borders in a Gated Globe', *Identities: Global Studies in Culture and Power* 11:3, 329-50.

Cunningham, H. and Heyman, J.M. (2004), 'Introduction: Mobilities and Enclosures at borders', *Identities: Global Studies in Culture and Power* 11:3, 298-302.

Dannecker, P. (2005), 'Transnational Migration and the Transformation of Gender Relations: The Case of Bangladeshi Labour Migrants', *Current Sociology* 53:4, 655-74.

Dauvergne, C. (2009), 'Globalizing Fragmentation: New Pressures on Women Caught in the Immigration Law-Citizenship Law Dichotomy', in Benhabib, S. and Resnik, J. (eds.), *Migrations and Mobilities: Citizenship, Borders, and Gender* (New York: New York University Press), 333-55.

Devasahayam, T., Yeoh, B. and Huang, S. (2004), 'South East Asian Women: Navigating Borders, Negotiating Scales', *Singapore Journal of Tropical Geography* 25:2, 135-40.

Dumont, J.-C., Martin, J.P. and Spielvogel, G. (2007), 'Women on the Move: The Neglected Gender Dimension of the Brain Drain', *IZA Discussion Paper* 2920 (Bonn: IZA).

Espiritu, Y.L. (2002), 'Filipino Navy Stewards and Filipina Health Care Professionals: Immigration, Work and Family Relations', *Asian and Pacific Migration Journal* 11, 47-67.

Grundy-Warr, C. and Wong, E.S.Y. (2002), 'Geographies of Displacement: The Karenni and the Shan across the Myanmar–Thailand Border', *Singapore Journal of Tropical Geography* 23:1, 93-122.

Grundy-Warr, C., King, R, and Risser, G. (1996), 'Cross-border migration, trafficking and the sex industry: Thailand and its neighbours', *Boundary and Security Bulletin* 4:1, 86-91.

Gulati, L. (1994), 'Women in International Migration', *Social Development Issues* 16:1, 75-97.

Heyzer, N., Lycklama à Nijeholt, G. and N. Weerakoon (eds.)(1994), *The Trade in Domestic Workers: Causes, Mechanisms and Consequences of International Migration*, volume 1 (New Jersey: Zed Books).

Huang, S., Yeoh, B.S.A. and Rahman, N.A. (eds.)(2005), *Asian Women as Transnational Domestic Workers* (Singapore: Marshall Cavendish).

Huang, S. and Yeoh, B.S.A. (2003), 'The Difference Gender Makes: State Policy and Contract Migrant Workers in Singapore', *Asian and Pacific Migration Journal* 12:1-2, 75-98.

Huysmans, J. (1995), 'Migrants as a Security Problem: Dangers of "Securitizing" Societal Issues', in Miles, R. and Thränhardt, D. (eds.), *Migration and European Integration: Dynamics of Inclusion and Exclusion* (London: Pinter), 53-72.

Ibrahim, M. (2005), 'The Securitization of Migration: A Racial Discourse', *International Migration* 43, 163-87.

International Labour Office (ILO) (2004), *Towards a Fair Deal for Migrant Workers in the Global Economy* (Geneva: ILO).

International Labour Office (ILO) (2003), *Preventing Discrimination, Exploitation and Abuse of Women Migrant Workers: An Information Guide – Booklet 1: Why the Focus on Women International Migrant Workers* (Geneva: ILO).

International Organization for Migration (IOM) (2005), *World Migration Report* (Geneva: IOM).

Khoo, S.-E., Graeme, H. and McDonald, P. (2008), 'Which Skilled Temporary Migrants Become Permanent Residents and Why', *International Migration Review* 42:1.

Kusakabe, K. and Mar Oo, Z. (2007), 'Relational Places of Ethnic Burman Women Migrants in the Borderland Town of Tachilek, Myanmar', *Singapore Journal of Tropical Geography* 28:3, 300-13.

Laungaramsri, P. (2006), 'Imagining Nation: Women's Rights and the Transnational Movement of Shan Women in Thailand and Burma', *Focaal: European Journal of Anthropology* 47, 48-61.

Law, L. (2002), 'Sites of Transnational Activism: Filipino Non-government Organisations in Hong Kong', in Yeoh, B.S.A., Teo, P. and Huang, S. (eds.), *Gender Politics in the Asia-Pacific* (London: Routledge), 205-22.

Lee, J.H. (2005), 'Human Trafficking in East Asia: Current Trends, Data Collection and Knowledge Gaps', *International Migration* 43:1-2, 165-202.

Lim L. and Oishi, N. (1996), 'International Labor Migration of Asian Women: Distinctive Characteristics and Policy Concerns', *Asian and Pacific Migration Journal* 5:1, 85-116.

Lyons, L. (2005), 'Transient Workers Count Too? The Intersection of Citizenship and Gender in Singapore's Civil Society', *Sojourn* 20:2, 208-48.

Manalansan IV, M.F. (2006), 'Queer Intersections: Sexuality and Gender in Migration Studies', *International Migration Review* 40:1, 224-49.

Maniam, K.S. (2003), *Between Lives* (Kuala Lumpur: Maya Press).

McGovern, L. (2003), 'Labor Export in the Context of Globalization: The Experience of Domestic Workers in Rome', *International Sociology* 18:3, 513-34.

Miles, R. and Thränhardt, D. (eds.)(1995), *Migration and European Integration: Dynamics of Inclusion and Exclusion* (London: Pinter).

Ministry of External Affairs (2001), *Report of the High Level Committee on the Indian Diaspora* (New Delhi: Government of India).

OECD (2002), *International Mobility of the Highly Skilled* (Paris: OECD).

Oishi, N. (2005), *Women in Motion: Globalization, State Policies, and Labor Migration in Asia* (Stanford: Stanford University Press).

Parreñas, R. (2001), *Servants of Globalization* (Palo Alto: University of Stanford Press).

Percot, M. (2006), 'Indian Nurses in the Gulf: From Job Opportunity to Life Strategy', in Agrawal, A. (ed.), *Migrant women and work* (New Delhi: Sage), 155-76.

Piper, N. (2008), 'Feminization of Migration in Asia and the Social Dimensions of Development', *Third World Quarterly* 29:7, 1287-303.

Piper, N. (ed.)(2007a), *New Perspectives on Gender and Migration: Livelihood, Rights and Entitlements* (London: Routledge).

Piper, N. (2007b), 'Political Participation and Empowerment of Foreign Workers – Gendered Advocacy and Migrant Labour Organising in Southeast and East Asia', in Piper, N. (ed.), *New Perspectives on Gender and Migration: Livelihood, Rights and Entitlements* (London: Routledge).

Piper, N. (2005), 'A Problem by a Different Name? A Review of Research on Trafficking in Southeast Asia and Oceania', *International Migration* 43:1-2, 203-33.

Piper, N. (2003), 'Bridging Gender, Migration and Governance: Theoretical Possibilities in the Asian Context', *Asian and Pacific Migration Journal* 12:1-2, 21-48.

Piper, N. (1999), 'Labor Migration, Trafficking and International Marriage: Female Cross-Border Movements into Japan', *Asian Journal of Women's Studies* 5:2, 69-99.

Piper, N. and Roces, M. (eds.)(2003), *Wife or Worker? Asians Marriage and Migration* (Boulder: Rowan & Littlefield).

Piper, N. and Yamanaka. K. (eds.)(2003), 'Gender, Migration Governance in Asia', *Asian and Pacific Migration Journal* 12:1-2, Special Guest-Edited Issue.

Piper, N. and Ball, R.E. (2001), 'Globalisation of Asian Migrant Labour: The Philippine-Japan Connection', *Journal of Contemporary Asia* 31:4, 533-54.

Raghuram, P. (2005), 'Global Maid Trade: Indian Domestic Workers in the Global Market', in Huang, S., Yeoh, B.S.A. and Rahman, N.A. (eds.), *Asian Women as Transnational Domestic Workers* (Singapore: Marshall Cavendish), 146-74.

Raghuram, P. (2004), 'Migration, Gender and the IT Sector: Intersecting debates', *Women's Studies International Forum* 27:2, 163-76.

Raghuram, P., Sahoo, A.K., Sanghe, D. and Maharaj, B. (2008), *Tracing Indian Diasporas: Contexts, Memories, Representations* (New Delhi: Sage).

Rose, N. (1999), *Powers of Freedom* (Cambridge: Cambridge University Press).

Rumford, C. (2006), 'Theorizing Borders', *European Journal of Social Theory* 9:2, 155-69.

Shamir, R. (2005), 'Without Borders? Notes on Globalization as a Mobility Regime', *Sociological Theory* 23:2, 197-217.

Siddiqui, T. (2001), *Transcending Boundaries: Labour Migration of Women from Bangladesh* (Dhaka: The University Press).

Tangseefa, D. (2006), 'Taking Flight in Condemned Grounds: Forcibly Displaced Karens and the Thai-Burmese In-Between Spaces', *Alternatives* 31, 405-29.

Truong, T.-D. (1996), 'Gender, International Migration, and Social Reproduction: Implications for Theory, Policy, Research and Networking', *Asian and Pacific Migration Journal* 5:1, 27-52.

United Nations (UN) (2006), *International Migration and Development: Report of the Secretary General, Sixtieth session, Agenda item 54:c Globalization and interdependence: international migration and development* (New York: UN).

United Nations (UN) (2004), *World Survey on the Role of Women in Development – Women and International Migration* (New York: United Nations).

Verité (2005), *Protecting Overseas Workers – Research Findings and Strategic Perspectives on Labor Protections for Foreign Contract Workers in Asia and the Middle East*, Research Paper (Amherst: Verité).

Walters, W. (2006) 'Border/control', *European Journal of Social Theory* 9, 187-203.

Wickramasekara, P. (2002), 'Asian Labour Migration: Issues and Concerns in the Era of Globalization', *International Migration Papers* 57 (Geneva: ILO).

Wilson, B. (2008), 'Meta-Mobilis: The Case for Polymorphous Existence in K.S. Maniam's *Between Lives*', in Raghuram, P., Sahoo, A.K., Sanghe, D. and Maharaj, B. (eds.), *Tracing Indian Diasporas: Contexts, Memories, Representations* (New Delhi: Sage).

Yamanaka, K. and Piper, N. (2003), 'An Introductory Overview', *Asian and Pacific Migration Journal* 12:2, 1-20.

Yea, S. (2006), 'Introduction', *Asian and Pacific Migration Journal* 15:4, Special Issue on Sex Trafficking in Asia and Australia, 441-8.

Yeoh, B.S.A., Teo, P. and Huang, S. (eds.)(2002), *Gender Politics in the Asia-Pacific Region* (London: Routledge).

Yeoh, B.S.A. and Willis, K. (2005), 'Singaporeans in China: Transnational Women Elites and the Negotiation of Gendered Identities', *Geoforum* 36:2, 211-22.

Western Sahara –
Territoriality, Border Conceptions
and Border Realities

Elisabeth Bäschlin and Mohamed Sidati

Introduction

Among nomadic populations, territories – not borders – are of vital importance to their daily life. And just as these territories, the nomads' living areas, are continually redefined along the lines of the balance of power between the different tribes, the border itself – both territorial and social – does not have a permanent meaning, but rather changes within time and space according to situations, interests and the balance of power. Thus the notion of a political border, of a permanent limit, is by essence foreign to the nomads' way of life. The history of Western Sahara in the past decades and the way in which the Sahrawi populations have adapted, used and experienced borders, according to the needs of the time, provide a telling example of this fact.

Pre-colonial period

In general, the nomadic way of life is characterized by great territorial mobility and a high degree of specialization in activities, as well as, for Moorish[1] nomads in particular, considerable social mobility. Traditionally, Moorish tribes were mostly camel, sheep and goat herders, continually looking for pastures for their cattle. Indeed the movements of these so-called 'cloud people' have been dictated by the rains that transform the arid regions of the Sahara into natural and ephemeral pastures for a few days or weeks.

---

[1]   Moorish means all the nomads in North Western Sahara, originally Berber clans, who have been converted to Islam in the seventh century, have assisted Arabic troupes to conquer Spain, and incurred Arabic language.

Figure 26.1 Western Sahara

Source: Copyright: Institute of Geography, University of Berne 2008; Cartography: A. Brodbeck.

Recessional agriculture practiced in the river basins after the rain, which allowed for barley being harvested three months later, provided considerable sources of complementary income. Moreover, hunting (ostriches, antelopes and so on) and gathering (seeds; edible leaves and berries) were also practiced in periods of want or when cereal stocks were insufficient, as was fishing in some of the tribes living on the coast.

The Moorish nomads exchanged their produce for the consumer goods they needed such as barley, durum, millet, rice, dates, oil, honey, henna, tobacco, peanuts, textiles and slaves on markets in the South – Timbuktu, Aoudaghost, Oulata or Atar – and North Sahara – Sidjilmassa, Marrakech or Tindouf –, as one of the main trans-Saharan routes went through their territory. 'Western Sahara was the home of an intense and well-organized commercial activity. The confederations monopolizing the great trade between Sub-Saharan Africa and the Maghreb and Europe were powerful. They controlled the main markets, the points of passage, and the trails' (Caratini 1989b, 7). Thanks to their camels, the Rgaybât nomads' realm of action was sizable. The various Moorish nomadic tribes travelled the Sahara region on great distances looking for pastures.

It was not only the geographical, but also the social mobility that allowed the Moorish to adapt to the conditions of the desert and use it as a living space. At first sight, the Moorish society was highly structured, composed of *warriors* (sword people) who held military power, *literati* (book people), whose social prestige was based on religious knowledge, tributaries, *haratin* (freed slaves), and slaves. The tributaries were forced to pay taxes to the warriors, and sometimes to groups of literati as well, while the literati at times paid tributes to the warriors. But all these dependencies could change with the balance of power in the field, and were thus continually transformation. The Western Sahara Moorish nomads' use of territory was chiefly determined by social structures, by one's belonging to a tribe and a fraction, and not primarily by territorial conceptions. While the notion of territory as private propriety was unknown to the nomads, 'collective priorities on pastoral resources' (Caratini 2003, 29) did exist, because, according to oral traditions, an ancestor, Ahmed ar-Rgaybi, had allegedly bought land in the Saghiet al-Hamra, a region in Western Sahara, from native populations (Caratini 1989a, 50-2).

In a saturated pastoral area, access to resources was not free, but acquired through negotiations or war, 'through a balance of power, based upon both the number and the military value of the men in the "tribe"', as Caratini says:

> This constantly questioned balance of power gave birth to access priorities, a mosaic of territories collectively owned by dominant groups, but that could be exploited by others, following reciprocal agreements or the payment of a tribute. The boundaries of these territories were never fixed, and the history of the Sahara could be declined in the form of a never-ending re-composition of groups and territories. (Caratini 2003, 29)

Hence the borders of nomad territories were continually both boundary and frontier, representing simultaneously a limitation, and the possibility of conquest and expansion. Nevertheless, the notion of belonging to a fixed territory was deeply rooted in these populations, each one knowing the limits of its roaming area. The roaming areas overlap, and thus cannot be strictly delimited. These borderlands were named *tessya* by the Sahrawi, which means 'line of contact'.[2]

---

2   *Tessya* has a positive connotation, in the sense of 'community' or even 'voluntary nation' [Willensnation]. This implies that beyond all former territorial conflicts and power relations, there is a common feeling considering all other Moorish nomads as 'cousins'.

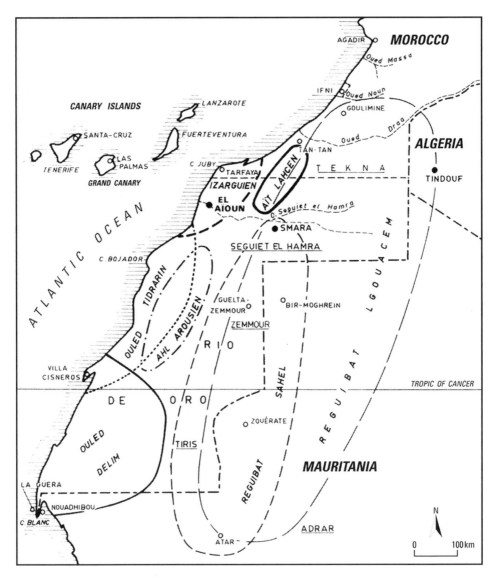

Figure 26.2 Tribal Travelling Areas
Source: Barbier 1982.

In the pre-Colonial period, the nomads' movements were not limited by national boundaries: they were the uncontested masters of their living area. The territories, in which they could move freely, belonged to them. The only – yet essential – limitations were the lack of resources as pasture and water and the territories of other groups of nomads in the immediate vicinity.

The colonial era: 1884–1975

The arrival of the first European colonists in the fifteenth century, first Portuguese, then Spanish, was initially restricted to the installation of a few coastal trading posts, and thus did not influence the Moorish nomads' movements or use of space. And even when the European powers, meeting at the Berlin Conference in 1884, agreed to portion Africa out amongst themselves and Western Sahara became a Spanish colony with fixed borders, as if drawn with a ruler though the landscape, very little actually changed on the ground level. The presence of Spain was still limited to the coastal trading posts, and the nomads continued to roam freely in the back country: for the Sahrawi, these borders thus remained virtual.

Around the beginning of the nineteenth century, France, a colonial power occupying all of West Africa, was starting to enter the Saharan area without respecting former territorial boundaries, and occupying the roaming areas that Sahrawi nomads had always considered as their own. Fearing for their living area, the nomads led by Cheikh Ma al-Ainin organized resistance to defend their territory. Conforming to their tradition, they sought exterior alliances with the Mauritanian sheikhs and the sultan of Morocco, without great success. Indeed after a few initial victories, the resistance was defeated. In 1912, the sultan of Morocco finally accepted to bow to the colonial authority: Morocco became a French protectorate. For a time, Ma al-Anin and the Moorish tribes continued to fight back on their own. They were defending a territory that had been their living area for centuries, and was at risk of being considerably diminished by the colonial borders contested by the nomads. In 1913, the French troops, chasing Sahrawi troops, entered Smara, the holy city of Western Sahara, and destroyed the library and hundreds of precious manuscripts belonging to Ma al-Anin. Hence the Sahara was now 'pacified'. But for many years after that, inland Western Sahara remained an unsafe region for Europeans, solely under the control of Sahrawi nomads.[3] Then it was colonial Spain that started occupying the inland and building garrisons. The two colonial powers concerted on the control of nomad tribes, in order to 'pacify' them and to break their capacity for resistance by forcing the settlement of their populations. The colonial borders hence began restricting the nomads' living area. At times, the nomads succeeded in using colonial borders to their advantage: during census, recruitment campaigns for colonial armed forces, tax collection or criminal proceedings against them for cattle theft, they crossed the border into another country to escape the authority of one or the other colonial power.[4] In the era of colonization, the segmented Sahrawi society 'led to the more or less voluntary repartition of tribes and fractions between 'French subjects' and 'Spanish subjects' (Caratini 2001, 28), depending on their roaming areas or their choice in hopes of foreseen advantages. It was in fact quite

---

3   See the travel journals of Michel Vieuchange from 1930.
4   According to witnesses, the nomads were sometimes quite surprised at the effect of this 'invisible' border that now went through their territory: to them, it seemed to have an almost magical influence, since beyond that limit, the Spanish or French army respectively no longer chased them down.

common for people to have several identity documents, and this has remained the case to this day.

Ultimately, the era of colonialism and the occupation by a foreign power contributed to the birth of an emerging Sahrawi national sentiment, as the feeling of belonging to a tribe gradually gave way to a feeling of national belonging. The birth of nationalism as a form of opposition to the colonial power also explains why the Sahrawi supported the liberation movements in Morocco and Algeria.

In January 1958, Spain changed the status of its colony and declared the Sahara a Spanish province. The colonial borders thus became Spanish national borders. That same year, a French-Spanish military pacification action called operation 'Hurricane' took place. Thousands of soldiers and hundreds of vehicles from both armies stormed the Saghiet al-Hamra, poisoning wells, destroying nomad tents and bombing their herds. The fierce fighting caused many deaths and forced countless Sahrawi families into exile in Mauritania and Southern Morocco, also inhabited by Sahrawi nomads. The exodus occurred without taking colonial borders into account, but was shaped by social links. Morocco, rather: that had recently gained independence, supported this colonial action, while Spain handed over the region of Tiznit and Tarfaya to Morocco in order to show its gratitude. The new colonial border now ran along the 10th parallel, just South of Tarfaya.

In May 1973, a Sahrawi assembly – young students and workers from Algeria and Mauritania, founded the *Front Polisario* (The Saghiet al-Hamra and Rio de Oro Liberation Front). Military actions against Spain, the colonial power, immediately ensued. In 1974, in the declaration of its second congress, the Polisario called for the independence of Western Sahara within the boundaries of colonial borders, in conformity with the principles of the Organization of African Unity.[5] For the Polisario and the Sahrawi, respecting inherited borders was meant to ensure international recognition and represented the basis of their claims according to international law.

On 12 October 1975, all the tribes and fractions that considered themselves Sahrawi joined the Polisario, while the vast majority of sheikhs within the *djemaâ* (council of elders) proclaimed 'National unity', the end of the tribal era and the birth of the Sahrawi people, thus joining Polisario and its claim for independence.

Makhzen and 'Grand Maroc' – the Moroccan view

During that time, in Morocco, other territorial conceptions of Western Sahara appeared. In 1956, the year of Morocco's independence, Al Fassi, the leader of the independence party Istiqlâl, launched the idea of a 'Greater Morocco': he claimed that

---

5   In its constitutive session in 1963, the OAU, aware of such borders-related issues, had adopted the principle of maintaining the borders inherited from colonialism in order to avoid territorial conflicts. Colonial borders could thus only be changed by referendum, on the basis of the peoples' right to self-determination.

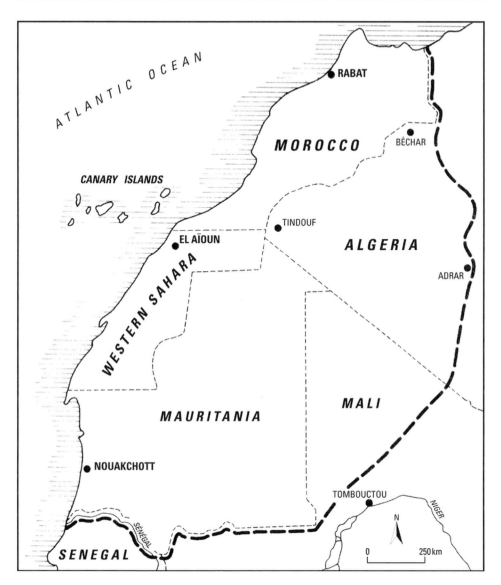

Figure 26.3 Territories Claimed by Greater Morocco
Source: Barbier 1982.

historically, Morocco had covered a territory stretching from the Mediterranean coast to the Senegal River, encompassing a sizable portion of Western Algeria and Mali as well as all of Mauritania.[6] He justified his claim on 'historical rights', based on the occasional allegiance of some Sahrawi tribal chiefs to the sultan of Morocco. This idea

6   *Al Alam* newspaper, 7 July 1956.

of Al Fassi proved a great mobilizing force, first within his party, as it enabled Istiqlâl to secure its political influence. Moreover, the idea of a Greater Morocco provided a convenient explanation to justify an expansionist policy, and was thus immediately adopted as official policy by King Mohamed V, and later on by Hassan II.

In the *Grand Maroc* concept, new borders were 'built' and claimed, different from those inherited from colonialism; running across the current national territories of Algeria, Mauritania and Mali. With such a discourse, Morocco sought to construct itself a history, that of a unified and influential ancient Moroccan kingdom. In reality, until colonization in 1912, Morocco's territory

> ... *was not a unified nation-state. Rather, it was a mosaic of tribes, many of whom were often no more than nominally ruled by the sultan's government, the Makhzen. The regions which were under the sultan's direct administration [and control] normally the plains and the towns, were known as the bilad el-makhzen, the 'government's land', while the regions beyond the sultan's control, usually regions of difficult access such as mountains of the Rif and the three Atlas ranges, were known as the bilad es-siba, the 'lands of dissidence'.* (Hodges 1983, 25)

With the 'Greater Morocco' strategy, the Moroccan government was demanding to be granted the status of a state 'dismembered' by colonialism, according to paragraph six of the UN resolution 1514 on Decolonization. The Moroccan power thus 'denounced the Spanish occupation of the Sahara as a violation of its territorial unity and of its national integrity' (Mohsen-Finan 1997, 24).

Morocco laid its claims on the Western Saharan territory on the basis of a Makhzenian conception of *bilad es-siba* who had to submit themselves to the sultan by an oath of allegiance, repeated annually. Ultimately, considering this reference to allegiance, Morocco did not base its claims on a set territory it would have once owned, but rather on the alleged social relations that the people living on those territories would once have maintained with the sultan, which, according to their discourse, made those territories Moroccan.

In order to bestow international legitimacy onto his territorial claims, King Hassan II asked the UN to submit the question of the ownership of Western Sahara to the International Court of Justice in The Hague in 1974. On 16 October 1975, the Court made its verdict known to the public:

> *The materials and information presented to the Court show the existence, at the time of Spanish colonisation, of legal ties of allegiance between the Sultan of Morocco and some of the tribes living in the territory of Western Sahara. ... On the other hand, the Court's conclusion is that the materials and information presented to it do not establish any tie of territorial sovereignty between the territory of Western Sahara and the Kingdom of Morocco or the Mauritanian entity. Thus the Court has not found legal ties of such a nature as might affect the application of resolution 1514 (XV) in the decolonisation of Western Sahara and, in particular, of the principle of self-determination*

through the free and genuine expression of the will of peoples of the Territory.
(Hodges 1982, 186)

In accordance with his 'right of arbitration', given to him by the Moroccan Makhzen system, as well as article 3 of the 1962 Moroccan Constitution, King Hassan II interpreted the International Court's verdict in his own way, focusing on the first part. In a statement released to the press on 16 October, he declared: 'The verdict of the International Court of Justice can only mean one thing, that what is now called Western Sahara is a part of the Moroccan territory, on which the king's sovereignty was exerted, and the population of this territory considered itself and was considered Moroccan'. This was obviously not the Sahrawi's interpretation, nor was it recognized by the international community.

In the Makhzenian ruler's view, the Sahrawi, inhabitants of Western Sahara, were thus to be considered 'unruly' and 'dissident', a part of the *bilad es-siba*. In this framework, the Green March, consisting of 350,000 people coming from Morocco to take back the 'Saharan provinces' in November 1975 can be placed within the Moroccan *Harka* tradition, a punitive expedition meant to punish dissidence. The symbol was used within Morocco to place the Saharan issue within 'the continuity of an ancestral mode of government, that became traditional' (Mohsen-Finan 2002, 43). Since the Green March, King Hassan II, now considered as 'unifier' of the land, has frequently called upon his 'Saharan subjects' or 'lost brothers' to 'rejoin the lenient and merciful homeland', promising 'forgiveness and leniency' if they mended their ways. Religious terminology was deliberately used to recall the Moroccan monarchy's religious legitimacy, adding a religious connotation to the Moroccan borders.

It is true that the principle of allegiance was part of the Moorish nomads' culture, but it was certainly not restricted to the sultan of Morocco: when a group or tribe was unable to impose the conquest or control of a pastoral area to another group, allegiance to the dominant tribe remained an acceptable alternative. These allegiances could vary considerably in duration and only affected the use of the land, but never its 'ownership'. The borders of a given territory thus remained unchanged.

For Morocco, contrary to OAU principles, the borders inherited from independence were thus not untouchable, but at the most a means to achieve, step by step, the realization of a 'Greater Morocco': today claiming Western Sahara – and, maybe, tomorrow Mauritania and the Tindouf region? Morocco has only recognized Mauritania in 1970, ten years after its independence. However, for strategic reasons, it agreed in 1975 on sharing the Spanish Sahara and on a joint occupation of the land with Mauritania.

Times of War: 1975 – 1991

On 14 November 1975, during General Franco's agony, a three-party agreement was secretly signed in Madrid between Spain, Morocco and Mauritania: Spain vowed to remove its troops from Western Sahara by 28 February 1976, thus handing the administration of the territory over to Morocco and Mauritania. With this agreement, the parties implicitly abolished the former borders and established a new 'national' border between Morocco and Mauritania, going from Dakhla in the North to Mijek in the South, but unrecognized by any international body.

In November and December 1975, both the Moroccan and the Mauritanian armies invaded the Saharan territory. The great majority of Sahrawi populations fled inland and regrouped around Oum Dreyga, Guelta Zemmour and Tifariti, where they were bombarded with napalm and phosphor by the Moroccan air force in February and March 1976. The border then – for once – became a saviour, as the panicked Sahrawi populations took the narrow passage of the common border with Algeria to seek refuge there.

On 27 February 1976, in retaliation to the three-party agreement and the invasion of Moroccan and Mauritanian troops, the Sahrawi sheikhs assembly declared the creation and independence of the SADR, the Saharan Arab Democratic Republic. In the Tindouf region, where the Algerian government had granted them a part of the Algerian national territory, the Sahrawi and the Polisario, its liberation movement, set up a state in exile. From there, they continued to fight the occupying armies.

The Sahrawi army's tactics were speed and mobility. It functioned in the way of the traditional *ghazi*, with attacks by small mobile groups in all-terrain vehicles. Indeed in the first years of the war, Sahrawi fighters succeeded several times in interrupting the conveyor belts in the Bou Crâa mine and the Zouérat (Mauritania) railway line. In June 1976 they attacked the city of Nouakchott, where their leader El Ouali died, and entered cities in Southern Morocco: for example in Tan Tan in December 1978, where they managed to free Sahrawi prisoners and helped hundreds of others to escape to camps. In August 1979, they attacked the important Moroccan military base of Lebouirate. In the course of these attacks in Mauritania and Southern Morocco, the Sahrawi fighters operated on their traditional roaming area as a whole, without concern for colonial or current borders. As the Sahrawi fighters had perfect knowledge of the terrain, as well as an undying determination, at the beginning of the 1980s, the military situation on the ground had become disastrous for the Moroccan army: while they occupied the cities of El Ayoun, Smara, Bojador and Dakhla, more than 80 per cent of the Western Saharan territory was controlled by Polisario!

Between 1980 and 1987, Morocco finally succeeded in reversing the balance of power on the ground by building a 'wall' (see Figure 26.4), with the technical help of American and French experts and financed by Saudi Arabia. The 'wall' is actually a three meter-high and two meter-wide embankment, reinforced with masonry and fitted with a sophisticated radar system with Westinghouse detectors (Rössel 1991, 200-2). Protected by vast fields of landmines, it was first built to protect the 'useful Sahara', the capital El Ayoun and the Bou Crâa phosphate mine, and then constantly enlarged until 1987. This wall in effect created a new and impermeable border currently separating Western Sahara in two different parts: a zone under Moroccan control (two thirds of the surface), which the Sahrawi called the 'occupied zone', but considered by Morocco as 'freed areas by integration to the homeland'; and a zone under the control of Polisario (one third of the surface), called the 'free zone' by the Sahrawis.

During the war years, Morocco many times threatened to attack the camps and chase the Sahrawi on Algerian soil, but up to now, it has respected its neighbour's borders.

Figure 26.4 'The Wall'

Source: RADDblog 2009 – available at <http://raddblog.wordpress.com/2009/11/09/20th-anniversary-of-the-fall-of-berlin-wall-walls-still-standing-or-built-since-nov989/>.

Refugee camps and the SADR

As of the arrival of refugees in Tindouf in the winter of 1975/76, Polisario set up the infrastructure of the future SADR state, provisionally on Algerian territory but with the intention of transferring it to independent Sahara in the future. Indeed the Sahrawi created schools, health centres, women and child protection centres, regional hospitals and a national hospital, ministries, radio and television stations. To facilitate an efficient management of the camps, they decided to group people by place of origin, so as to keep the pre-existing social structures among family members and neighbours. The four *wilayate* (districts) in the camps were named after the four most important cities in Western Sahara – El Ayoun, Smara, Dakhla and Aousserd – while the six or seven *dayrate* (communes) in each of the *wilaya* were named after settlements on the territory.

Nowadays, on the road from the Algerian airport of Tindouf and Rabouni – the SADR and refugee camps administrative centre – the first Algerian checkpoint is followed by a second Sahrawi one, as if to show that the area south of the city of Tindouf has been handed over to the Sahrawis and is under Polisario control. Within the area, around the various camps, the Sahrawis move freely. And the access to the city of Tindouf, though it does require a permit, is also very easy for Sahrawis. For foreign visitors however, the necessary Algerian entry visa for visiting the camps is not automatically valid for the rest of Algeria: they can therefore not visit Tindouf or other regions in Algeria. Likewise, the Sahrawis need to get clearance to enter the Algerian territory, which is delivered in cases of necessity. The area of the Sahrawi camps and exiled SADR state is thus surrounded by an imagined political border. However, the Algerian border towards the Western Saharan territory has almost entirely been put 'out of use', first for the armed forces during the war, and since 1991 increasingly for civilians as well.

Within the framework of the Polisario's project for society, which calls for an egalitarian society without class, race or gender discrimination, in which all individuals have equal rights and opportunities, several traditional constraints and social inequalities have declined. In August 1976, at its third congress, the Polisario abolished slavery and the tributary system, and proclaimed social equality. Hence all children, boys and girls, are schooled as of the age of six. The feeling of belonging to the Sahrawi nation, rooted in a common history of struggles, in shared experiences and in the principles of an equal rights society, has increasingly replaced the tribal system as the basis of social cohesion.

Although Sahrawi women had always had a strong position in the nomad family, their position has been further strengthened by the conflict. Between 1975 and 1991, during the war, the men were all either fighters or in the diplomatic service abroad. It was the women who organized and managed the camps and everyday life, thus expanding their field of activity beyond what it had traditionally been restricted to. Nomad women had always ruled over the tent, but are now also in charge of public areas. As heads of committees, schools, administrations and health centres, they have learned to speak in public. Indeed, in today's SADR parliament, 16 out of the 51 MPs are women.

Another factor encouraging tribal diversity is the young couples' matrilocality that developed over the past 30 years in the camps. Within this traditionally patrilineal and patrilocal Sahrawi society, the young women now set themselves up around their mothers' tents or houses after marriage, since their husbands are so often away. This means that the children, although of paternal lineage, in fact grow up in their mothers' family and tribe, and not in the tribe that gave them their identity through paternal ascendance (Dedenis 2006, 32).

For international organizations and various NGOs, the Sahrawi camps are a humanitarian management area on Algerian soil, not a Sahrawi state. Thus all NGO donations and interventions are carried out in agreement with the Algerian Red Crescent (CRA), considered responsible for humanitarian aid on Algerian soil, although Algeria has given Polisario and the SADR total autonomy for the organization and management of the camps. This autonomy becomes self-evident at the Algerian and Sahrawi checkpoints on the road between Tindouf and Rabouni, where the administration, government, presidency and various ministries of the SADR are located. The Sahrawi state thus exerts its power on the population and organization of the camps on Algerian territory on the one hand, and on the zones liberated in the framework of the ceasefire on the other. The Sahrawi parliament currently convenes regularly at its new offices in Tifariti on Western Saharan territory. The SADR government is in exile in Rabouni, waiting to be able to exert power on the whole of the former Spanish colony's territory, but all official declarations are made from Bir Lehlou in Western Sahara.

Identity and alterity

While nationalism was unknown to nomadic traditions, the sentiment of belonging to tribes stemming from a common culture and acting within a common area nevertheless existed. The struggle for self-determination and independence, fought as of the 1960s first against the colonists and then against the new occupant – Morocco – acted as a wake-up call for nationalist sentiments and a Sahrawi identity, beyond that of the tribe. The common history of struggle and the shared experience of living in exile since 1975 have given birth to a national sentiment.

But beyond the political option, the Sahrawi's belief in their alterity came from factors that clearly separated the nomadic Sahrawi culture from its sedentary Moroccan counterpart: the *hassanya* language, nomadic tradition, religious practice, social structures, the place of women, the clothing – the *melhfa* for women and the *drâa* for men – and last but not least, the influence of the language and the culture of the former colonial rulers, France for Morocco and Spain for the Sahrawis. Spanish is the first foreign language taught in camps and remains a *lingua franca* in various domains within the state and society. The struggle against Moroccan occupation and Sahrawi nationalism have stressed and reinforced the importance of these cultural differences. The experiences shared daily in the refugee camps – the changes on the social level, the mixing of ancient tribes and tribal diversity, the participation in political and social life – have strengthened the feeling of differentiation with Moroccan culture. The Sahrawi thus form a *tessya* community (a community of choice, option or partisanship) that corresponds with their nomadic tradition, consisting of a kind of mutual allegiance, which one would in modern terms call a 'voluntary nation' [Willensnation]! Indeed 'being Sahrawi', first an ethnic and cultural concept, has become a national identity.

Actually Sahrawi tribes had always been 'both diverse and similar, forming quite a homogenous whole, with an identity of their own and several common features' (Barbier 1982, 367). But it was only with colonization, and then increasingly with Moroccan occupation, war and a common struggle that the awareness of being part of a common destiny and the common desire for independence arose. The overwhelming majority of the Sahrawi people refused Morocco's occupation and, rather than submit to it, preferred exile. The Moroccan occupation hence 'allowed them to become aware of their identity and to deeply realize their unity' (Barbier 1982, 367). The struggle and the experience of life in exile are hence a fundamental component of the Sahrawi collective conscience, and continue to strengthen and confirm the population's determination to fight for independence. The camps' relative isolation within their host country has allowed them, according to Caratini (2001), to develop according to their own norms and values and to preserve their specificity, while simultaneously building and strengthening borders toward the outside, even toward the friendly population in the Algerian territories.

The Moroccan authorities' conception of alterity, as far as the Western Saharan population is concerned, is ambiguous. Since the beginning, Morocco has defended the idea that the inhabitants of Western Sahara were all Moroccan. It has consequently negated the fundamental cultural differences between sedentary Moroccans and nomadic Sahrawi and proclaimed a common identity. But when the UNHCR in 1992 started to identify voters in view of the referendum on the future of Western Sahara and Morocco tried to register more than 200,000 Moroccan citizens[7] as voters, the Moroccan ministry of the interior prepared them for identification by teaching them words in *hassanya*, how to wear the *melhfa* and the *drâa* correctly, and how to make tea in the Sahrawi way. The operation was not a great success, as very few of these additional voters were actually admitted to the electoral lists by the UN officials. But implicitly, Morocco had thus admitted that there were true cultural differences between Moroccans and Sahrawi.

Since the Sahrawis, from the very beginning, have sought international support, the Polisario had favoured contacts with Europe in particular, but also with African Union and Latin America. The compulsory schooling of all children for nine years could only be implemented with the loyal support of friendly allies. The children could be schooled in the camps for primary school, but for secondary school and higher education they had to go to Algeria, Libya or Cuba, all of which welcomed numerous Sahrawi children. Many girls and boys thus escaped the camps to study abroad, transgressing many national, cultural and social borders. Indeed in that sense, they experienced 'multiple exiles' (Abjean 2003). After the exile of the entire population to the Tindouf camps, children exiled again to secondary school in Algeria, and, sometimes after lengthy studies abroad, the return to camp society often felt like a third 'exile', especially for those returning from Cuba, a society

---

7   Alexandre Gschwind, a Swiss radio journalist, used to call them 'Sahrawis by acclamation' ['Jubelsahraouis'].

so different from that of the Sahrawi nomads. Nevertheless, living together in boarding houses in camps, in Algeria, Libya or Cuba contributed to the creation of solidarity among them and a common sentiment of being Sahrawi.

Several European countries, from East to West and North to South, have granted scholarships or studying grants to young Sahrawi men and women to allow them to get a university education. Many young people have encountered diverse cultures: indeed there are Sahrawi who speak not only Spanish, French, English and German, but also Dutch, Swedish, Russian, Ukrainian, Hungarian and Polish.

Moreover, every year more than ten thousand children between the ages of eight and eleven spend the hottest summer months on holiday with families in Europe: a few thousands in Spain, a few hundreds in Italy, and small groups in other European countries and the United States. Most Sahrawi children have thus had trans-cultural experiences. In addition, these holidays have given rise to 'solidarity tourism', as many families – particularly from Spain – wish to visit 'their' child. Indeed every year, around Christmas and Easter, several charter flights bring hundreds of European visitors to the refugee camps.

Current situation

Since the ceasefire, the borders with Mauritania and, in particular, the frontiers with Tindouf have become permeable to the inhabitants of the camps. Travel is nowadays essentially limited by financial factors. Those who can afford it shop in Tindouf. And for the merchants in the camps, Mauritania has become the preferred destination to replenish their stock.

The Algerian border with Western Sahara is open, which allows Sahrawi to move freely between the camps and the free zone. Today, some Sahrawi families have started keeping cattle and living with their livestock in the free zones as nomads again, notwithstanding the risk of accidents with landmines, which do sometimes happen. They are visited by family members, especially the elderly, who wish to spend the summer months at the *badya*, fleeing the scorching heat of the Tindouf *hammada*, or for holidays or health stays.

As many Sahrawi – or their parents – used to have a Spanish passport, citizens of Western Sahara have easier access to a certificate of residence in Spain or even a passport. An increasing number of them – especially young people – while waiting for a solution to the conflict, are therefore seeking employment in Spain so as to be able to bring financial support to their family in the camps.

The most hermetically closed border is the 'wall' across the Sahara, built by the Moroccans. For several years, contacts between Sahrawi family members separated by the war were almost non-existent. Since 1991, some of them have been able to call one another from abroad or to meet in Mauritania or the Canaries. In the framework of the 'trust measures' in preparation for a future referendum, the HCR set up a free telephone line for the population in 2003, between the camps in Tindouf and the occupied zones. Thus the families – parents and children, husbands and wives – separated since 1975, were at last able to chat and exchange news as often as they wished. Moreover in March 2004, the first mutual visit took place under the patronage of the UNHCR: an HCR plane transported twenty people on either side of the wall for a five-day visit to their relatives on the other side. These visits had been planned to occur on a weekly basis, but have been interrupted several times for weeks and months because of Moroccan vetoes. The number of weekly beneficiaries is small, and thousands of people are on waiting lists. Nevertheless, it remains the only way of crossing the separation wall for the time being.[8]

At the moment, there is no end in sight to the conflict: the Moroccan and Sahrawi territorial conceptions remain diametrically opposed. Both parties have settled in a situation of 'neither war nor peace'. This situation mostly benefits Morocco, as every passing day is one day closer to a *de facto* reality in the occupied territories where Morocco can establish itself increasingly as the administrative power and consolidate the integration of the territory to the Moroccan state. The only clouds in Morocco's sky are the demonstrations by the Sahrawi population living under occupation, demanding a referendum and independence, which have been occurring daily since 2006 and are severely repressed by the Moroccan authorities.

The Polisario continues to claim the independence of Western Sahara within the borders of the former Spanish colony from 1976, when the Spanish troops left. The Sahrawis and the Polisario are aware of the fact that in a modern world, states can only be formed within borders that are recognized and guaranteed by the international community. They have therefore accepted that the region of Tarfaya and Tan Tan in southern Morocco, although inhabited mostly by Sahrawi populations, was handed over to Morocco in 1958.

For young Sahrawi in refugee camps, Western Sahara is increasingly becoming an 'imagined' and mythical territory, as it remains unseen. The young generation is 'desperately attached' to it (Caratini 2003, 12). The territory is becoming essential to the constitution of these peoples' identity. The touching tales of young Sahrawi who have spent a few summer days in Tifariti, in the free zones, on their own country's soil, provide a vivid testimony of this: 'To feel at home and no longer to be in exile, it is extraordinarily moving!'

The Sahrawi in Tindouf are asking to be allowed to live on a territory in which they feel at home, a 'homeland' where they can develop roots. The feeling of living in exile – in a 'non place' – is very strong among the Sahrawi population, including the younger generations: the homeland is on the other side of an un-crossable border, the 'wall'. This is why young people are now calling increasingly loudly for the Tindouf camps to be moved to the 'free zone' so as to, at least, 'live on the Saharan territory!'.

---

8   Another option would be to reintegrate Morocco, which very few Sahrawi refugees have done, notwithstanding financial promises from Morocco and the difficulty and deprivation of life in the refugee camps.

References

Abjean, A. (2003), 'Histoires d'exils: Les jeunes Sahraouis', in Abjean, A. and Julien, Z. *Sahraouis: Exils -- Identité* (Paris: Collection L'Ouest Saharien, Hors série no. 3, L'Harmattan), 19-128.

Barbier, M. (1982), *Le conflit du Sahara occidental* (Paris: L'Harmattan).

Bäschlin, E. (2004), 'Democratic Institution Building in the Context of a Liberation War: The Example of Western Sahara und the POLISARIO Front', in Barlow, M. and Wastl-Walter, D. (eds.), *New Challenges in Local and Regional Administration* (Aldershot: Ashgate), 137-53.

Caratini, S. (2003), *La république des sables* (Paris: L'Harmattan).

Caratini, S. (1989a), *Les Rgaybât (1610-1934), tome 1: Des chameliers à la conquête d'un territoire* (Paris: L'Harmattan).

Caratini, S. (1989b), *Les Rgaybât (1610-1934), tome 2: Territoire et société* (Paris: L'Harmattan).

Dedenis, J. (2006), 'La territorialité de l'espace des camps de réfugiées sahraouis en Algérie', in Territoires d'exil: les camps des réfugiés, *Bulletin de l'Association de géographes français* 83:1, 22-34.

Hodges, T.Y (1982), *Historical Dictionary of Western Sahara* (Metuchen NJ and London: The Scarecrow Press Inc.).

Hodges, T. (1983), *The Roots of the Desert War* (Westport, Connecticut: Lawrence Hill and Company).

Mohsen-Finan, K. (1997), *Sahara occidental. Les enjeux d'un conflit régional* (Paris: CNRS Histoire).

Rössel, K. (1991), *Wind, Sand und (Mercedes-)Sterne. Westsahara: Der vergessene Kampf für die Freiheit* (Bad Honnef: Horlemann).

Saad, Z. (Sidati M.) (1987), *Les chemins Sahraouis de l'espérance* (Paris: L'Harmattan).

Schiffers, H. (1973), 'Die Nomaden', in Schiffers, H. (ed.), *Die Sahara und ihre Randgebiete*, volume III (Munich: Weltforum Verlag), 29-65.

Scholz, F. (ed.)(1991), *Nomaden, mobile Tierhaltung* (Berlin: Das arabische Buch).

Thiriet, M. (1997), *L'intégration de l'Ex-Sahara espagnol au Maroc*, Maitrise de Géographie, option géopolitique, Université de Nancy II (unpublished).

Vermeeren, P. (2002), *Histoire du Maroc depuis l'indépendence* (Paris: Répères/La Découverte and Syros).

Vieuchange, J. (ed.)(1932), *Smara - Carnets de route de Michel Vieuchange* (Paris: Librairie Plon).

Villemont, R. (1999), 'Les Sahraouis et l'enfermement', in Bernault, F. (ed.), *Enfermement, prison et châtiments en Afrique du XIXe siècle à nos jours* (Paris: Kathala Editions), 387-410.

Wastl-Walter, D. and Staeheli, L.A. (2004), 'Territory, Territoriality, and Boundaries', in Staeheli, L.A., Kofman, E. and Peake, L.P. (eds.), *Mapping Women, Making Politics* (New York and Abingdon: Routledge), 141-52.

PART VII
CREATING
NEIGHBOURHOODS

Different Neighbours:
Interaction and Cooperation at
Finland's Western and
Eastern Borders

Heikki Eskelinen

Introduction

Finland shares a land border with three countries (Sweden, Norway and Russia) and a sea border with Estonia (as also with Sweden and Russia). In both political and scholarly debates, the country's eastern border with Russia receives by far the most attention. This is due to its longstanding role in definitions of the Finnish national identity, and since 1995 as part of the European Union's external border. The Finnish-Swedish border, for its part, represents a contrasting case. There is no geopolitical tension, and it was open to various forms of border spanning activities already before these countries joined the European Union.

The present chapter surveys and compares the eastern and western borders of Finland as arenas of cross-border interaction and cooperation at a local and regional level. The investigation is informed by the conceptual framework which Brunet-Jailly (2005) has suggested for the interdisciplinary analysis of borders and borderlands. According to this, the evolution of an economically, politically and culturally integrated borderland region presupposes that the following four factors (or *analytical lenses* as Brunet-Jailly calls them) enhance and complement each other: First, local cross-border culture; second, policy activities of multiple levels of government; third, local cross-border political clout; and fourth, market forces and trade flows.

In the following section, a brief introduction to the formation of Finland and its borders is presented. Then, cross-border interaction and cooperation at the Finnish-Swedish and the Finnish-Russian borders are discussed in general, after which, the contrast between the eastern and western borders is analyzed by focussing on two local cases. Finally, experiences from and prospects for widening and deepening interaction and cooperation are evaluated. It is argued that the Finnish-Swedish border regime is stable and clearly makes further cross-border integration possible, but potential for major advancements in the future remains limited. In contrast, in the Finnish-Russian case, there are untapped resources for increasing integration and cooperation, but the border regime has been characterized by uncertainties, and this seems to be the case also in the future. In general, progress towards an integrated borderland is conditioned by Russia's future role in Europe, and in a global context.

A brief history of the Finnish borders[1]

The first border on the current Finnish terrain was created in the fourteenth century when Sweden and Novgorod delineated their areas of dominance in the European north. Yet these structures were not territorial states, and their borders were rather outposts for controlling, protecting and taxing of important trade routes. In the following centuries, first the Swedish Empire extended its limits eastwards until the eighteenth century when the rise of the Russian Empire pushed the border westwards to areas settled by Finnish population. The Swedish era came to the end in 1809 when Finland was annexed to the Russian Empire, and the current Finnish-Swedish land border (then the Russian-Swedish one) was drawn through the region of the Tornedalian culture in the north, even if the linguistic border went further south on the Swedish side. Later, especially since the late nineteenth century, this border has developed into a culturally divisive and delineating one through the processes of Swedification and Finlandization, which have represented what Mann (1993) calls the infrastructural power of states. Notwithstanding this differentiation, the border has been most of the time administratively and functionally permeable.

In the Swedish era, Finland was not a separate administrative unit. In the Russian Empire, Finland gained the status of a Grand Duchy, with its own laws, religious organizations and administrative structures, including a customs border towards Russia. Yet this border did not follow a clear ethnic division. Towards the end of the nineteenth century, the eastern border was increasingly defined in terms of an autonomous nation state in the context of the Finnish nation-building process. This created preconditions for the country's independence which was realized in the aftermath of the October Revolution in Russia in 1917. Three years later, the Tartu Peace Treaty was signed, and a strictly guarded military border was erected between the Soviet Russia and Finland. In the west, the League of Nations solved the only significant border dispute, which existed between Finland and Sweden. In 1921, it declared that the Åland Islands archipelago, between the

---

1   This historical outline of the Finnish borders is based on Liikanen et al. (2007, 22-25), and Eskelinen and Jukarainen (2000). For the seminal analysis of the formation of the Finnish-Russian border see Paasi (1996).

Finnish mainland and Stockholm, is an autonomous, monolingual (Swedish), and demilitarized region of Finland.

Since these early years of Finland's independence, the eastern and western borders of Finland have developed in very different ways. With the abovementioned exception of the Åland Islands, the political and administrative position of the Swedish border has not been questioned in fact; the peaceful conditions have existed even longer, from 1809 onwards. The same applies to the Finnish-Norwegian border in the high north.

In contrast, the eastern border was practically closed in the Soviet era from the point of view of individual actors. The political confrontation in the 1920s and 1930s ended up in the two wars, Winter War November 1939 – March 1940 and Continuation War June 1941 – September 1944. As a result approximately 10 per cent of the Finnish territory was annexed to the Soviet Union, and the border was transferred to its current position. The population of the ceded territory (more than 400,000 people) was resettled in other parts of Finland. Under post-war geopolitical conditions, the Soviet Union could largely impose the new political regime on Finland, which was established by the Treaty of Friendship, Cooperation and Mutual Assistance in 1948. This treaty formed the political and institutional basis of the relations of the two countries, including cross-border exchanges, until the disintegration of the Soviet Union.

The disintegration of the Soviet Union triggered a major upheaval of the Finnish-Russian border regime, even if the regulation of border crossings such as the practices of border guarding and required documents remained about the same. The fundamental change was normalization in the sense that interaction between individuals, firms, administrative units and other interested partners was generally allowed. In addition, crossing points were opened and other important infrastructures were built for facilitating connections. The new regime was regulated by the treaties which Finland and Russia signed in 1992 on neighbourhood relations, trade, and so-called near-region cooperation. The last-mentioned treaty implied that also the Russian Federation accepted cross-border cooperation, and committed to support it at a local and regional level.[2] Thus, a regionalization process was initiated across the border in the early 1990s, largely from scratch.

Another major change of the Finnish borders resulting directly from the disintegration of the Soviet Union was that Estonia regained its independence in 1991. Since then, Finland's southern sea border has been transformed from the border to the Soviet Union to an internal border of the European Union (EU). Finland's membership in the European Union in 1995, for its part, meant that the geopolitical role of the country's eastern border was redefined. Finland has since then participated in the formulation of EU policies towards Russia, and EU policy

---

2   According to the treaty, 'the signatories … ensure that regional and local authorities have the necessary means for cooperation as set out in this treaty', see <http://www.finlex.fi/fi/sopimukset/sopteksti/1992/19920062/19990062_2>.

instruments such as programmes for promoting cross-border cooperation have been taken into use also in this border region.

Figure 27.1 describes the current Finnish borders, and serves as the point of reference to the location of regions, cities and cooperation areas referred to in the text.

Figure 27.1 The Western and Eastern Borders of Finland

Source: Cartography: Karelian Institute.

Cooperation and interaction: main lines and experiences

Finland and Sweden: How to boost cooperation at an open border?

Since the 1950s, cross-border cooperation has been actively promoted across the Finnish-Swedish border as an integral part of cooperation between the Nordic countries, which has more recently been extended to the neighbouring areas, especially to the Baltic and Barents Sea Regions. Links at the civil society level as well as market processes have given support to this activity. For instance, the Nordic connection has been enhanced by the fact that Swedish is the second official language in Finland, and there is a large Finnish-speaking minority in Sweden.[3] Economically, Sweden is one of Finland's largest trading partners and Finnish-Swedish company mergers have been a distinctive feature in business life.

Nordic cooperation is initiated and conducted by means of two organizations, the Nordic Council and the Nordic Council of Ministers. The former one, responsible for inter-parliamentary cooperation, was established already in 1952, and the latter one, responsible for intergovernmental cooperation, in 1971. Their missions and tasks have been formulated in the way that cooperation is possible even if the Nordic countries do not form a geopolitically unified grouping, and they have pursued country-specific approaches in relation to European integration. In general, inter-Nordic cooperation has developed in a distinctive way, conditioned by the joint historical legacy and specific circumstances. Even if it is not transnational, and relies on consensus-based decisions, its concrete achievements have been important in some fields. For instance, passport-free areas and common labour markets were established already in the 1950s. Against this background, it is understandable that the membership of Finland and Sweden in the EU was not a fundamental upheaval for their mutual cross-border interaction and cooperation.

For promoting inter-Nordic cross-border cooperation, the Nordic Council has provided funding to organizations, whose governing bodies include representatives of local and regional organizations, and which are co-funded by the respective states. It is noteworthy that these organizations differ from each other in terms of their institutional form, activities and aims, that is, there is no single Nordic model in this field. According to Perkman (2003), Nordic cross-border cooperation organizations form a distinctive group of their own in the European context. Typically, they represent high intensity of cooperation, and they involve large areas.

There are four cross-border cooperation areas at the Finnish-Swedish border. Skärgården and Kvarken comprise only Finnish and Swedish regions; whereas Mittnorden and North Calotte include also Norwegian regions – and North Calotte cooperation has been more recently extended to include a part of Northwestern

---

3   The role of the Swedish language in Finland derives from the common history of these countries, whereas the Finnish-speaking minority in Sweden is mainly due to mass migration in the 1960s and early 1970s.

Russia (see Figure 27.1). Three out of these four regions cover sea border areas and archipelagos, and the only land border region, North Calotte, is characterized by harsh climate, its settlement pattern is scattered, and its location peripheral in respect to national centres. In addition, northernmost areas have traditionally been based on the exploitation of natural resources, and thus competed with their neighbours in international markets. These factors have been effective obstacles to the development of cross-border functional regions, and have undermined the joint dynamics of border regions (see Wiberg 1999).

Even if the membership of Finland and Sweden in the EU was no break with the past in Nordic cross-border cooperation, it had a number of implications for its context and practices. Some were problematic for the patterns of interaction which prevailed at that time; for instance, the abolition of intra-EU duty free sales weakened ferry business, which had grown into an important economic activity between Finland and Sweden. Largely due to this anticipated change in the border regime, the autonomous territory of Åland Islands negotiated a separate membership treaty with the EU. However, the overall impacts of the membership were positive in regional and local cross-border cooperation. In particular, regional cooperation organizations were given access to new resources, and in the conditions of the radically transformed East/West setting in Europe, cross-border cooperation was widened to the external border areas of the Nordic countries in the Baltic Sea Region, and in the Barents Region. The concrete impact is especially visible in border areas where there is potential for deepening local cooperation from the removal of barriers to actively constructing cross-border communities (Löfgren 2008). This is illustrated in the later part of this chapter which focuses on the Finnish town of Tornio and the Swedish town of Haparanda which are seen as the flagship case of the Finnish-Swedish cross-border cooperation at a local level.

Finland-Russia: differentiated paths of regional development

The border region of Finland and Russia is a textbook example of how changes in the border regimes are reflected in regional development. In conditions of a relatively open border before 1917, south-eastern Finland was tightly linked to St. Petersburg, which, at the time, was a European metropolis. When the border was closed, this connection ceased to exist, and Finnish border regions were not any more relatively developed bridgeheads to Russia but rather remote peripheries with respect to Western Europe. In the aftermath of World War II, they were locked in this role even more tightly. Firstly, the transfer of the border resulted in a situation where Vyborg, the then second-largest city of Finland, became part of the Soviet Union, and key infrastructure links were cut off. Secondly, even if economic and other interaction between these two countries grew in altered geopolitical conditions, it was with a few exceptions organized in a way that excluded cross-border links benefiting from geographical proximity. On the Soviet side, respectively, the role of St. Petersburg (Leningrad) in the international and regional division of labour underwent a complete upheaval when this capital of the Russian

Empire and its gateway to Europe was turned into a focal area of the Soviet Union's military-industrial complex. The administratively separate unit surrounding it, the Leningrad Region, specialized in activities that served the metropolis. The other regions (Karelian Republic and Murmansk Region) bordering Finland were developed into resource-based production areas (Eskelinen and Fritsch 2006). The key industry of the former one was forest-based industry, and that of the latter one mining.

Against the background outlined above, it is understandable that the disintegration of the Soviet Union raised high expectations on emerging cross-border links in the same way as in many other regions along the East-West divide in Europe, although the Finnish-Russian case can be regarded as a kind of extreme case among these regions (see Christiansen and Joenniemi 1999). Due to the closure of 70 years, socio-economic and cultural disparities had grown to the extent that geographical neighbours were functionally very distant from each other.

In the first stage after the opening up of the border, local links were spontaneous. Many Finnish individuals and representatives of firms, administrative bodies and civil society organizations went to see their neighbours, and also Russian visits to Finland started to grow. The regulatory framework of this activity was not created until somewhat later when Finland and Russia signed the new treaties (see above). In the then prevailing turbulent conditions, Finland launched a specific assistance programme, which was later developed so that it could serve as seed money for larger international assistance and cooperation projects. During the first years of this new border regime, trade links between Finland and Russia reached their nadir when the bilateral system was removed, contributing to a major depression in Finland.

The period since the early 1990s can be divided into two main stages, with different patterns of cross-border interaction (for a detailed analysis see Liikanen et al. 2007). Firstly, Russia experienced a deep political, economic and wider societal crisis, and close integration and partnership with the West were emphasized in its development strategies. The 1997 PCA (Partnership and Cooperation Agreement) represents this approach, according to which Russia promoted, or at least did not put obstacles to, the development of cross-border links in various fields of life. At that time, the introduction of the EU's cross-border programmes was also facilitated by the devolution of decision-making powers from the federal level to regions, and the overall *Europeanization process* was probably constrained primarily by the unwillingness of foreign actors to commit themselves to Russian initiatives and projects in politically and economically risky circumstances.

Since then, the transformation of Russia and its relations with the West have taken a different route. Instead of Europeanization, Russia has redefined its geopolitical strategy towards a more inward-looking and sovereignty-oriented approach. As part of its policy, it has developed a more uniform border regime, which does not encourage increasing cross-border interaction on such borders as with Finland, which is from the Russian point of view relatively well-functioning. This approach, which Sergei Prozorov (2006) encapsulates as the notion 'limits to integration', is also reflected in concrete decisions. This includes, for instance, a domestic ownership of the sectors which are seen as strategically important, the strengthening of the centralized power, and a reserved attitude towards cooperation with the EU. Until the global economic downturn in 2008, Russia's strong economic growth provided resources for this geopolitical and geo-economic strategy, from the point of which the eastern enlargement of the EU in 2004 was an epochal change. For cross-border cooperation, a particularly important decision was the refusal of the Russian Federation to join the European Neighbourhood Policy (ENP) as an ordinary neighbour. Notwithstanding this opting-out from the ENP, a solution has been found so that cross-border cooperation programmes utilizing the ENP's funding instrument can be continued also on the Finnish-Russian border in the period of 2007-2013.[4]

Parallel to official cooperation at different levels, various connections and flows across the Finnish-Russian border have intensified since Soviet times. In 1991, the number of border-crossings was 1.3 million; in 2008 the respective number was 7.7 million (Rajavartiolaitos 2009). The share of Russians has grown clearly, and accounts currently for two-thirds. The majority of both Russian and Finnish visitors make very short trips, and they utilize border-related differences in the way which is typical for asymmetrical border regions. However, also tourism has grown considerably, and Russian visits are of increasing economic importance in eastern Finland. In addition to short-term visits, migration from Russia to Finland has grown considerably. Although the numbers are small in an international comparison, the net flow of Russians has compensated for a part of eastern Finland's population loss to other parts of Finland. Work-related migration has been growing, and also thousands of Russians work in Finland in seasonal activities (Alanen 2009).

Russia has rapidly returned to be among the key trading partners of Finland; its share of the exports is currently more than 10 per cent (Ollus and Simola 2006). However, the respective share in eastern border regions is lower than the national average, that is, local firms have been slow to turn towards Russian markets. The reason for this seemingly paradoxical neighbourhood effect is due to the peripheral legacy of the region. The leading industrial sector (chemical and mechanical wood-processing) is focussing on other markets, border-related barriers are relatively more important to small local firms, and there are no major cities that would provide urbanization economies and attract investments of Russian-oriented businesses. Given these conditions, the opening up of the border has not transformed the overall development trends in eastern Finland. In terms of regional development theories, this supports the argument of the importance of path dependency. However, it is worth emphasizing that in eastern Finland there are also economic activities that clearly benefit from, or are dependent on, the border (Eskelinen 2008). In addition to the above-mentioned tourism, informal economy, commuting and migration, the growth of the Russian connection has been of particular importance for the Finnish eastern border regions in two specific fields: forest-based industries and

---

4   After long negotiations, the financing agreements for the period until 2013 were signed on 18 November 2009, see <http://europa.eu/rapid/pressReleasesAction.do?reference=IP/09/1727&format=HTML&aged=0&language=EN&guiLanguage=en>.

transit traffic. Their development is closely linked to Russian geo-economic and geopolitical strategies.[5]

In the Soviet Union, the Karelian Republic (see Figure 27.1) specialized in the so-called forest complex (forestry, wood-processing including pulp and paper, and related engineering industries). In the beginning of the 1990s, the opening up of the border rapidly became a key driving power in transforming the production structure of the Karelian Republic. Under market economy conditions, the Republic's industrial products lost their competitiveness in less accessible domestic markets, and overall deindustrialization was especially drastic in the years of political and economic transition. At the same time, the export of round wood and semi-processed goods for Finnish companies grew, and the Karelian Republic largely turned into a raw material exporting region (Druzhinin 2001). This process is an illustrative example of how an opening up of a closed border can trigger new trajectories of regional economic change that result in a lock-in situation from which it is very difficult to deviate. Seen from the point of view of eastern Finland, the import of round wood from neighbouring Russian regions grew into the most important single cross-border economic connection, and it became a decisive element in the growth of forest-based industries. The other side of the coin is that the access to this additional resource base has not provided incentives for transforming the traditional non-diversified production structure of Finland's eastern border region.

In St. Petersburg, the adaptation to market economy conditions was very difficult in the first years of the Russian transition. More recently, the metropolis and the surrounding separate administrative Leningrad region have undergone a remarkable recovery and growth. This functional region, the population base of which is larger than that of Finland as a whole, is turning into a key route of Russia's foreign trade. In this transformation, market-driven development processes are reinforced by investments, which are motivated by the geopolitically and geo-economically strategic position of the city (Zimin 2008). Also from the point of view of Finnish border regions, St. Petersburg plays a key role. Firstly, an important share of Finland's economic connections (trade and investments) with Russia is actually with this metropolitan region. Secondly, the rapid economic growth in St. Petersburg since the late 1990s has had a visible impact on neighbouring Finnish border regions; especially due to the fact that approximately 20 to 25 per cent of Russia's total imports have been transported through south-eastern Finland. This huge flow of goods has been of major local importance in harbour towns and in some communities along the routes, but it has also led to congestion and long queues, and formed an everyday problem to local citizens.

These cross-border flows, round wood trade and transit traffic, have emerged as critical issues in Finnish-Russian relations, and they have received attention even at EU-Russian level. Following its sovereignty-oriented geopolitical strategy, Russia

---

5   The present account does not deal with the complex case of the Murmansk Region in the High North. Its links with Finland have remained small due to its industrial base (mining, fisheries and military activities) and low accessibility.

aims at increasing domestic processing of raw materials, and has made a decision to raise export duties on timber. This has been in recent years the single most debated issue in Finnish-Russian relations. Even if the implementation of export duties has been delayed as a result of complex negotiation process, it has already contributed to mill closures in eastern Finland, and it is improbable that round wood trade will continue on a large scale after the global recession. With regard to transit traffic, border-related tensions deal with technical standards, transport quotas and competition, and border formalities (see Pursiainen 2007). For years, they grew in line with the growth of traffic volumes, but have received less attention more recently when the global economic crisis has resulted in a decrease of imports of consumer goods to Russia.

The above findings illustrate how, firstly, the opening up of a border may lead to highly differentiated impacts in different types of regions, and secondly, how the prevailing geopolitical context can be reflected in cross-border market processes either as a positive factor or as a constraint. Obviously, this context also plays an important role with respect to cross-border cooperation programmes at different spatial levels on the Finnish-Russian border. In the early years of programme-based policies, the key challenge and target was to link Interreg and TACIS programmes, which were quite separate lines in EU policy. The most important achievement of this work was the establishment of Euregio Karelia in 2000 between the Karelian Republic and three Finnish regional councils (see Cronberg 2003; Figure 27.1). This was a concrete indication that the neighbouring regions were able to create a joint strategy. The continuation of this cooperation has turned out to be possible also in changing geopolitical conditions. Regional actors have been able to utilize links that were created through market-based interaction and programme-based cooperation, focusing on practical cross-border issues, for instance, in promoting small and medium-sized businesses and tourism. Currently, the Russian partner has an equal role in this work, and the EU, co-funding the programmes, seems to accept this pragmatic cooperation in the shadow of geopolitical tensions (see ENPI 2007).

Two cases of local cooperation: Tornio/Haparanda and Imatra/Svetogorsk

Irrespective of the indisputable dissimilarities of the eastern and western borders of Finland, they share certain characteristics which bear influence on cross-border integration and regionalization potential. Both land border regions are rural, without major urban centres (assuming that St. Petersburg at the distance of approximately 150 kilometres from the border is not seen as a border city). In fact, there is at both borders only one potential cross-border urban community: Tornio/Haparanda on the Finnish-Swedish border and Imatra/Svetogorsk on the Finnish-Russian border. These two border towns can be seen as contrasting cases for promoting cross-border cooperation in highly different conditions.

The paired town of Tornio/Haparanda can be seen as an example of a border town (city) as defined by Buursink (2001): its development derives from a border-crossing point, or it has been established as a counterpart to a settlement on the other side of the boundary. The town of Haparanda was established on the Swedish side of the border river after Sweden had lost Tornio to Russia (Grand Duchy of Finland) in the beginning of the nineteenth century. The current population of Tornio is about 22,000, and that of Haparanda 10,000. Imatra and Svetogorsk on the Finnish-Russian border represent a somewhat different history. After World War II, the new border split the industrialized river valley of Vuoksi into two parts, and a few years later adjacent industrial communities were organized into Imatra in Finland, and Svetogorsk in Russia, that is, their birth does not derive from the existence of a border, although the Finnish-Russian border has since World War II played a crucial role in their development. The current population of Imatra is 29,000 and that of Svetogorsk 15,000 (Eskelinen and Kotilainen 2005).

The border between Tornio and Haparanda is open, and the number of annual crossings is more than ten million. This means that a major share of the local population crosses the border several times a week in their daily activities. This is due to the fact that Tornio and Haparanda share public and private service infrastructure – even the golf course cuts across the national border. However, albeit the border being functionally open, it still serves as an important marker of identity for local citizens living on both sides (Jukarainen 2003). Also local media is clearly organized in terms of language groups.

Cooperation between Tornio and Haparanda has a long history. These two towns, for instance, organized some infrastructural facilities jointly already in the 1970s. The most important cross-border cooperation organization, Provincia Bothniensis, was established in 1987. This body, governed by local politicians, prepares and coordinates joint activities, and represents the towns in their external relations. In addition, the decision-making bodies of the towns organize regular joint meetings. On a regional level, the activities of the Tornio/Haparanda cooperation are linked to the Bothnian Arc Association, which aims at promoting the competitiveness of the coastal zone surrounding the Gulf of Bothnia in the northernmost part of the Baltic Sea (Löfgren 2008; Lundén and Zalamans 2001).

Although intensive cooperation between Tornio and Haparanda was initiated long before Finland and Sweden became EU members, the membership has become its important driver. The two towns have been able to implement new projects by utilizing EU programmes, and they have also improved links with other paired border towns. The flagship project is entitled *På Gränsen/Rajalla* (literally meaning 'at the border'), which aims at building a joint centre for the two cities, and at putting the place on the maps of Europe. Its construction started in 2003, and was given a boost in 2006 when IKEA opened its department store in the area.

As already mentioned, Imatra and Svetogorsk are much younger towns.[6] Until the 1970s, they were completely separated from each other. The first contacts between them were created when the Svetogorsk pulp and paper combine was

---

6   The description of the case is largely based on Eskelinen and Kotilainen (2005).

modernized by Finnish firms as a major construction project in the context of bilateral trade between Finland and the Soviet Union. Although this project was a strictly controlled undertaking in the enclave and did not represent cross-border cooperation in the sense that this concept is currently used, it was necessary to open a temporary crossing point, and regular contacts between the municipalities were created. The crossing point was used with special permits and arrangements even after the construction project was finished in the 1980s. Actual cooperation at a local level was initiated in the early 1990s, and a specific agreement for this promotion was signed in 1992. Yet it was not until 2002 that Imatra and Svetogorsk agreed on a joint strategy, which focused on improving their competitive positions by means of joint activities, including the establishment of an industrial park. The strategy was formulated under the heading of *twin city* for emphasizing the similarities of this case with other paired border towns in Europe.

In practice, cooperation between Imatra and Svetogorsk has been characterized by asymmetries. The town of Imatra has implemented several projects in Svetogorsk that have aimed at upgrading technical infrastructure and environment, and developing social and health services. For daily interaction and cooperation, a key precondition was that the crossing point for international traffic could be finally opened in 2002. This project, as most other cooperation projects, has been based on EU funding. In 2008, more than one million persons crossed the Imatra/Svetogorsk border (Rajavartiolaitos 2009, 70).

Many studies on urban communities sharing a state border support the view that cooperation strategies and citizens' views are two different things (see Buursink 2001). Although people are encouraged to cross the border and construct a cross-border community in daily life, many people do not do so. This is clearly visible in the case of Imatra and Svetogorsk. According to a survey in 2007, no less than 80 per cent of the inhabitants in Imatra, and 48 per cent in Svetogorsk did not see to live in a twin city. In Imatra, only every third inhabitant could mention at least one form of cooperation, and also in Svetogorsk this share was less than 50 per cent. Overall, knowledge on twin city cooperation and attitudes towards it were in correlation with whether a respondent had visited the neighbouring town and whether he/she had friends or acquaintances there. From this point of view, it is especially noteworthy that approximately one third of those living in Imatra had never visited Svetogorsk, and only 11 per cent reported to visit the Russian town at least once a month. In Svetogorsk, the setting was different in the sense that even if the share of non-visitors was almost as high (30 per cent), a relatively larger share of local citizens crossed the border frequently, mostly for shopping (Kaisto and Nartova 2008).

As already mentioned in the Introduction, a process of cross-border integration requires simultaneous transformations at different levels in various fields of societal activities: in addition to economic interaction across the border, this entails policy activities that take place at different governmental levels and are within the specific political clout and culture of adjacent communities. When comparing Tornio/Haparanda and Imatra/Svetogorsk in these respects, it is clear that they are at strikingly different stages of this process.

In the former case, the border is not a barrier to interaction and cooperation in the classical sense, but it is still an important factor in the identity-building on both sides (Jukarainen 2003). Thus it is not at all self-evident that even if cooperation between these border towns covers many fields of human activity, they would evolve into a truly bi-national place. In contrast, the border does separate Imatra and Svetogorsk, and is an important barrier to contacts between them. Irrespective of this, these urban municipalities have initiated cooperation, and attempted to adapt it to local realities. The main purpose is comparable to that of Tornio/Haparanda, that is, cross-border interaction is seen as a potential local development strategy. However, the possibilities of turning it into practice are to a major degree conditioned by the future development of the geopolitical context and border regime.

Discussion and conclusions

This chapter derives from a comparative setting: The Finnish-Russian and the Finnish-Swedish border represent two different regimes and transformation processes. Their differences concern all the four lenses which are according to Brunet-Jailly (2005) important for the formation of an integrated borderland.

The upheaval in the European geopolitical scene from the late 1980s onwards led to profound transformation processes in regions along the East-West border from the Arctic Sea to the Mediterranean. Actors in these border regions have responded to the opening up of the closed border in various ways, for instance, by creating contacts with their neighbours on the other side, establishing business activities and launching cooperation projects. These different types of border-spanning activities have followed their own dynamics, and to a major degree evolved quite independently of one another. An important conditioning factor has been the changing geopolitical framework, especially due to the EU enlargements of 1995 and 2004/2007. In this setting, the Russian Federation represents a specific case due to its earlier position as a Great Power, its size, and its emerging strategic ambitions after the crisis period in the 1990s. In fact, Russia's recent strategic initiatives can be seen to bear certain resemblance to those of the EU: on one hand, the external border is largely defined in terms of security, and, on the other hand, internal administrative structures and development strategies are streamlined to the extent possible in the difficult process of Russia's reconstitution. In this strategic framework, the relative stabilization of political and economic conditions in Russia since the late 1990s has not contributed to cross-border integration and regionalization in the way as it was expected by many observers in the 1990s. Rather, its relations with the EU have become characterized by uncertainties and tensions. As part of this setting, the EU cooperation and assistance regime has been questioned and challenged by Russia, one of the most visible cases being its refusal to be covered by the European Neighbourhood Policy.

However, the findings on the development of cross-border contacts at a regional and local level between Finland and Russia open a different perspective into the above outlined transformation process. Market-based processes have grown, many actors have actively built contacts and even launched joint strategies such as the Imatra/Svetogorsk cooperation and Euregio Karelia, and official cooperation programmes have been run in their own niche irrespective of geopolitical changes. Due to differences in local conditions and historical legacies, the resulting patterns of border-spanning interaction and cooperation have become locally and regionally differentiated, and the potential for their further development is far from being fully utilized. In more general terms, it can be asked whether and to what extent local and regional actors such as municipalities and companies could have a say in the future formation of the border regime in a way that could facilitate a gradual integration of border regions.

At Finland's western border, the agenda of cooperation looks quite different: The geopolitical frame is problem-free, daily contacts are intensive in land border areas in the north, and the institutional support in terms of tight policy networks is available. However, actors still identify themselves with the two respective nations, and thus in practice the aim of constructing an integrated borderland remains limited to the strengthening of functional cross-border links so that inhabitants of both communities can benefit from them.

References

Alanen, A. (2009), 'Suomessa jo 50 000 venäjänkielistä', *Tieto & Trendit* 6, 38-41.

Brunet-Jailly, E. (2005), 'Theorizing Borders: An Interdisciplinary Perspective', *Geopolitics* 10:4, 633-49.

Buursink, J. (2001), 'The Binational Reality of Border-Crossing Cities', *GeoJournal* 54:1, 7-19.

Christiansen, T. and Joenniemi, P. (1999), 'Politics on the Edge: On the Restructuring of Borders in the North of Europe', in Eskelinen, H., Liikanen, I. and Oksa, J. (eds.), *Curtains of Iron and Gold. Reconstructing Borders and Scales of Interaction* (Aldershot: Ashgate), 89-115.

Cronberg, T. (2003), 'Euregio Karelia: In Search of a Relevant Space for Action', in Hedegaard, L. and Lindström, B. (eds.), *The NEBI Yearbook 2003* (Berlin: Springer), 223-40.

Druzhinin, P. (2001), '"Dutch Disease" of Karelia: Challenges of the Wood-Processing Industry in the Border Area', in Hytönen, M. (ed.), 'Social Sustainability of Forestry in Northern Europe: Research and Education', *TemaNord* 2001:575, 151-60.

ENPI (2007), *Karelia ENPI CBC Programme Document 2007-2013*, available at <http://www.kareliaenpi.eu/index.php/en.programme/programme-document>, accessed 16 November 2007.

Eskelinen, H. (2008), 'Market-Driven Processes in an Altered Geopolitical Context: Evolving Patterns of Cross-Border Interaction in the Finnish-Russian Case', *paper presented at the BRIT IX Conference* 12-15 January 2008 (Victoria BC, Canada and Bellingham WA, United States).

Eskelinen, H. and Fritsch, M. (2006), 'The Reconfiguration of Eastern Finland as an Interface Periphery', in Eskelinen, H. and Hirvonen, T. (eds.), *Positioning Finland in a European Space* (Helsinki: Edita).

Eskelinen, H. and Jukarainen, P. (2000), 'New Crossings at Different Borders: Finland', *Journal of Borderland Studies* 15:1, 255-79.

Eskelinen, H. and Kotilainen, J. (2005), 'A Vision of a Twin City: Exploring the Only Case of Adajacent Urban Settlements at the Finnish-Russian Border', *Journal of Borderland Studies* 20:2, 31-46.

Jukarainen, P. (2003), 'Definitely Not yet the End of Nations: Northern Borderland Youth in Defence of National Identity', *Young: Nordic Journal of Youth Research* 11:3, 217-34.

Kaisto, V. and Nartova, N. (2008), *Imatra-Svetogorsk-kaksoiskaupunki. Asennebarometri 2007* (Lappeenranta: Etelä-Karjala-instituutti, Lappeenrannan teknillinen yliopisto).

Liikanen, I., Zimin, D., Ruusuvuori, J. and Eskelinen, H. (2007), 'Karelia - a cross-border region? The EU and cross-border region-building on the Finnish-Russian border', *Publications of the Karelian Institute, University of Joensuu* 146.

Löfgren, O. (2008), 'Regionauts: the Transformation of Cross-Border Regions in Scandinavia', *European Urban and Regional Studies* 15:3, 195-209.

Lundén, T. and Zalamans, D. (2001), 'Local Co-Operation, Ethnic Diversity and State Territoriality – The Case of Haparanda and Tornio on the Sweden-Finland Border', *GeoJournal* 54:1, 33-42.

Mann, M. (1993), 'Nation-states in Europe and other Continents: Diversifying, Developing, Not Dying', *Daedalus* 122:3, 115-40.

Ollus, S.-E. and Simola, H. (2006), 'Russia in the Finnish Economy', *Sitra Reports* 66 (Helsinki: Sitra).

Paasi, A. (1996), *Territories, Boundaries and Consciousness: The Changing Geographies of The Finnish-Russian Border* (Chichester: John Wiley).

Perkman, M. (2003), 'Cross-border Regions in Europe. Significance and Drivers of Regional Cross-border Co-operation', *European Urban and Regional Studies* 10:2, 153-71.

Prozorov, S. (2006), *Understanding Conflict between Russia and the EU: The Limits of Integration* (Basingstoke: Palgrave Macmillan).

Pursiainen, C. (2007), *Russia Between Integration and Protectionism: International Road Transport, Ports, and the Forestry Sector* (Stockholm: Nordregio).

Rajavartiolaitos (2009), *Rajavartiolaitoksen toimintakertomus 2008*, available at <www.raja.fi>, accessed 16 November 2009.

Wiberg, U. (1999), 'The Barents Region in European Spatial Planning', in Hedegaard, L. and Lindström, B. (eds.), *The NEBI Yearbook 1999* (Berlin: Springer), 229-38.

Zimin, D. (2008), 'Geopolitics of Russian Border Regime', in Okuda, H. and Kortelainen, J. (eds.), *Russian Border Regions from the Perspective of Two Neighbours* (Hokkai- Gakuen University, Sapporo: Center for Development Policy Studies).

Borders and Neighbourhoods in the Carpatho-Pannonian Area[1]

Károly Kocsis and Monika Mária Váradi

Introduction

The Carpatho-Pannonian Area (C–PA) is located in the southeastern corner of Central Europe, surrounded by the Carpathians, the Alps and the Dinaric ranges. At present, there are eight nation states in the area: Hungary, Austria, Slovakia, Ukraine, Romania, Serbia, Croatia and Slovenia. The area under examination (approximately 300,000 square kilometres) is the largest multicultural macroregion in Europe – since the ethnic cleansings in the north (on Czech, Polish and Ukrainian territories) between 1944 and 1950, and in the south (in the Balkans) between 1991 and 1999. The ethnic borders and settlements in this area were stabilized during the eighteenth and nineteenth century, and the present-day borders of the states were fixed during the twentieth century. However, the borders of the nation states, mainly formed after World War I, are seldom identical with the ethnic borders, a fact that has had a basically negative impact on the twentieth century relations between neighbouring nations. The interethnic neighbourhood relations both across the border and within the state borders have been affected and defined by a number of factors; social and economic regime changes, the consequences of the EU accession, the new eastern borders of the EU, the transformation of the roles and characteristics of national borders, and the renewed ethnic rivalry and discourse in which the large Hungarian and Roma minorities have played a prominent role.

1   This chapter is based on research carried out within the scope of the project *SeFoNe* (Searching for Neighbours), financed by the European Union's Sixth Framework Programme for Research (see <http://www.sefone.soton.ac.uk>) and the project *Ethnic geography and cartography of the countries in the Carpatho-Pannonian area* (contract: K77973), financed by the Hungarian Scientific Research Fund (OTKA).

The historical roots of interethnic neighbourhood relationships

The C–PA was an undivided political unit between 900 and 1918, except for the period of the Turkish occupation of Hungary during the sixteenth and seventeenth century. It officially formed the territory of the Hungarian Kingdom, which was one of the most stable states in Europe during those thousand years. After World War I, the Treaty of Trianon (Versailles 1920) required two thirds of Hungary's territory to be annexed to the newly established neighbouring states of Czechoslovakia, Romania, the Kingdom of Serbs, Croats and Slovenes, and Austria. The treaty referred to peoples' right to self-determination, but not the principle of plebiscite. The new state borders were drawn at the expense of the Hungarians, and were seldom adjusted to the ethnic and linguistic borders. As a consequence, there were more than 3.3 million Hungarians whose residences were annexed to neighbouring states (Lőkkös 2000). The designation of the new borders was not intended to be along ethnic lines; rather it was meant to serve other purposes: to divide Hungary along geopolitical, military-strategic and economic lines, to satisfy the territorial claims of the Little Entente nations (the 'Czechoslovaks', Romanians and Serbs). As a result, a large number of Hungarian residents living in the border zones found themselves in a politically subordinate minority position, and their presence has imposed a serious burden on the internal and foreign affairs of those countries since 1920, also invoking the danger of Hungarian irredentism. The 'Hungarian question' created in 1920 still casts a shadow over the interethnic and interstate neighbourhood relations; the extent of the difficulties in a given neighbouring state corresponds to the size of its Hungarian minority.

The new borders shocked Hungary, and between 1918 and 1938, its foreign policy was characterized by open and unconditional efforts for a territorial revision. The aims of neighbouring Czechoslovakia, Romania and Yugoslavia were to prevent Hungarian irredentism, and to maintain an anti-Hungarian alliance and the Little Entente. During World War II, the Axis powers (Germany and Italy) decided to reannex the territories with a Hungarian ethnic majority from Czechoslovakia, Romania and Yugoslavia to Hungary. Although the state borders were more in accordance with ethnic reality between 1938 and 1945, they poisoned the relationship of the Slovaks, the Romanians and the Serbs to Hungarians, which manifested itself between 1944 and 1948 in massacres, expulsions and deportations of people belonging to the Hungarian minority.

After World War II, the Paris Peace Treaty (1947) restored the pre-1938 borders in the C–PA, except that Czechoslovakia handed Transcarpathia (with its Ukrainian majority) over to the Soviet Union (Soviet-Ukraine). The peoples of the C–PA were divided by several 'iron curtains' along the Austrian–Hungarian, Hungarian–Yugoslavian, Romanian–Yugoslavian and Soviet borders during the communist period (1949 to 1989), which were also characterized by an opposition between either East and West, or the Soviet Union and Yugoslavia. While the borders had been relatively easy to cross until 1945, the number of border-crossing points and opportunities for residents of neighbouring states to meet were now reduced to a minimum. This prevented the Hungarians living on different sides of the borders from maintaining relationships. The situation began to return to normal from the 1960s on; at first, between the allied socialist countries (Hungary, Czechoslovakia, Romania and later Yugoslavia) with the institution of the 'local border traffic' that facilitated border crossing and allowed for repeated crossing along a 15 to 20 kilometre stretch of border zone. Despite this, the state borders of the socialist period, with their very low permeability, functioned as separating devices rather than enabling neighbouring people to meet. Coupled with this low permeability was Hungary's socialist educational policy of not informing students about the existence of Hungarian minorities beyond the borders. These two factors caused the state borders to become cultural and mental borders dividing Hungarians during these decades. By the 1980s, most average Hungarian citizens called the ethnic Hungarians living beyond the borders 'Romanian', 'Czech', 'Soviet' or 'Yugoslav', based on their citizenship. The people belonging to the borderland Hungarian minorities thus began to feel like 'no man's people', hovering between the Hungarians in Hungary who excluded them and the neighbouring nations (Fox 2007). A similar phenomenon may be observed in Europe among the Germans of Alsace (since 1648), the Catalans of Roussillon in France (since 1659) and the Austro-Germans of South Tyrolia in Italy (since 1919). The existence of such borderland minorities that have an uncertain ethnic self-identification, are multilingual, have multiple ties, and often play a mediatory role has become a worldwide phenomenon (Anzaldúa 1987; Alvarez 1995).

The political-economic regime change taking place in the former socialist countries after 1989, the demolition of the 'iron curtains', the sudden increase in freedom of movement, the collapse of the Soviet Union and the federal states of Yugoslavia, and Czechoslovakia, and the rearrangement of federal systems (the Warsaw Pact, Comecon – NATO, EU) resulted in a definite improvement and a conspicuous rapprochement in the relationship between Hungary and some of its neighbours, Austria, Croatia, Slovenia and Ukraine. The various relationships (depending on the governments) between Hungary and Slovakia and Romania, however, are still negatively influenced by the unspoken fear of Hungarian irredentism and the rebirth of the 'Hungarian problem'. At the same time, the shift in the characteristics of state borders from a rigid separation of nations to a more 'ethereal' image – especially in the case of the countries in the same federative systems (the NATO and the EU) – created the feeling of an 'ethnic and national reunion' between Hungarians and Hungarians. This process of strengthening relationships between Hungarians across state borders was also supported by a law accepted by the Hungarian Parliament in 2001 and 2003 (Act on Hungarians Living in Neighbouring Countries, LXII. 2001, amendments 2003, see <http://www.kum.hu>). The neighbouring countries (for example Romania, Slovakia, Croatia and Serbia) had already accepted similar protectionist laws and regulations to help their ethnic kin living abroad during the previous decade (Halász 2004).

During the two decades following these regime changes, the majority of the C–PA has become part of the European Union: Austria in 1995, Hungary, Slovakia and Slovenia in 2004, and Romania in 2007. Although customs and border control became more lenient and then disappeared, and borders became gradually more permeable, the historically rooted differences in the economic development of these countries have not disappeared. There are still differences between development and incomes in the West and the East and the stream of intellectual and material goods and services is still asymmetrical in the C–PA; only the degree of the disproportion has diminished along certain border sections. The rearrangement of Europe's geopolitical map through the 'Eastern enlargement' of the EU also bears the marks of empire building and colonialism on the part of the old 'Western' member states; one can see the disparity between the developed, rich, dominant West and the less developed, poor, subordinate East in the politics of enlargement (Böröcz 2001), a kind of *orientalist discourse*, which curiously enough also flourishes in the everyday political discourses of the C–PA countries (both members and prospective members of the EU). Those who come from the east or southeast (even if they are Hungarians living on the other side of the Trianon borders) are regarded as dangerous strangers and rivals or 'poor relatives' (Feischmidt 2004). For the former socialist countries, EU accession also implied the promise of sharing its wealth and prosperity, and this made them rivals. This rivalry among other things, means that their reshaped ethnic and national identities 'are influenced by desire and shame as well as their consequences: feeling hurt and defiant' (Kovács 2002b, 15). Besides the historically-rooted conflicts and fears, the constraints of adjustment and integration to the West and competition have also played a role in the massive survival of essentialist discourses about identity and ethnicity in the region (Kovács 2002b).

The general features of present-day neighbourhood relationships in the Carpatho–Pannonian Area

Apart from Ukraine, which is very large, there are seven small- or medium-sized countries sharing the area under examination (Table 28.1). Croatia, Hungary, Slovakia, Slovenia and Romania are members of NATO; while Ukraine is negotiating to become a member; except for Croatia and Ukraine, the countries mentioned above as well as Austria are members of the European Union. Serbia and Ukraine are not included in the above-mentioned military and political-economic organizations: their Schengen borders with the EU are the last serious impediments to free neighbourhood relations. Most countries in the area have signed basic treaties in which they mutually recognize each other's borders.

The countries of the C–PA are connected via Hungary: of its 2,243 kilometre state border only 53.7 per cent also represents an ethnic border, along which the majority ethnic groups of the neighbouring countries are in direct contact with each other (Table 28.2). Along other border sections that make up more than 1,000 kilometres, the borders fixed in 1920 and 1947 separate Hungarians from Hungarians (Figure 28.1). More than half of the 2.5 million ethnic Hungarians in the neighbouring states live close to the border of their motherland. This situation produces explicit or implicit fears of Hungarian irredentism and territorial revision in Romania, Slovakia and Serbia, the countries which had the largest share of historical Hungary's territory and are home to the most populous Hungarian communities in states neighbouring Hungary (Tables 28.1 and 28.3). The so-called 'Hungarian question' is still a burden on the neighbourly relations of these three countries with both Hungary and the local Hungarian minority.

Table 28.1 Basic Data of the Countries of the Carpatho-Pannonian Area (2009)

Country	Territory (km²)		Population	GDP per capita (USD)	
	total	belonged to Hungary before 1920		nominal	PPP
Austria	83,859	3,967	8,372,000	45,090	38,896
Croatia	56,542	1,937	4,435,000	13,913	17,876
Hungary	93,030	93,030	10,013,000	12,386	18,548
Romania	238,391	102,724	21,466,000	7,503	11,755
Serbia	77,474	22,266	7,334,000	5,742	10,540
Slovakia	49,035	49,035	5,463,000	16,315	21,374
Slovenia	20,253	938	2,055,000	24,583	28,524
Ukraine	603,700	12,772	45,963,000	2,538	6,461

Note: GDP (gross domestic product), PPP (purchasing power parity).
Source: GDP data: International Monetary Fund.

Table 28.2 Ethnic Stability of the Studied State Borders in the Carpatho-Pannonian Area (2008)

Border section	State border total		Out of this			
	km	%	Ethnic boundary*		Non-ethnic boundary**	
Hungary – Austria	356	100.0	356	100.0	0	0
Hungary – Slovakia	681	100.0	95	14.0	586	86.0
Hungary – Ukraine	137	100.0	7	5.1	130	94.9
Hungary – Romania	448	100.0	244	54.5	204	45.5
Hungary – Serbia	174	100.0	106	60.9	68	39.1
Hungary – Croatia	345	100.0	345	100.0	0	0
Hungary – Slovenia	102	100.0	52	51.0	50	49.0

Notes:
* The state border is an ethnic-lingual boundary (e.g. in case of Hungary – Romania: on the Hungarian side live ethnic Hungarians, on the Romanian side mostly ethnic Romanians).
** The state border is not an ethnic-lingual boundary. On both sides of the border live predominantly ethnic Hungarians.
Source: © K. Kocsis and M.M. Váradi.

Table 28.3 Ethnic Reciprocity in the Countries of the Carpatho-Pannonian Area (around 2001)

Minority	Absolute number	Minority	Absolute number	Reciprocity ratio
Hungarians in Romania	1,431,807	Romanians in Hungary	7,996	179.0 : 1
Hungarians in Slovakia	520,528	Slovaks in Hungary	17,693	29.4 : 1
Hungarians in Serbia	293,299	Serbs in Hungary	3,816	76.9 : 1
Hungarians in Ukraine	156,600	Ukrainians in Hungary	6,168	25.4 : 1
Hungarians in Croatia	16,595	Croats in Hungary	15,620	1.1 : 1
Hungarians in Slovenia	6,243	Slovenes in Hungary	3,040	2.1 : 1
Hungarians in Burgenland (A)	6,641	Germans in West-Hungary	2,831	2.3 : 1

Source: © K. Kocsis and M.M. Váradi.

Except for the Austrian–Hungarian and Croatian–Hungarian border sections, the everyday neighbourhood relations of the different ethnic groups does basically not take place along frontier zones but in the ethnic contact zones 20 to 50 kilometres away from the state borders in Slovakia, Ukraine, Romania and Serbia – especially in urban areas. The ethnic relations between autochthon communities are unproblematic on the level of individuals. Tensions occur in territories where there are both many Hungarians and many of majority nationals (for example Serbs, Romanians and Slovaks) who were settled there by their states and were not used to ethnic tolerance and/or coexistence.

The mediatory language in neighbourhood relations has basically been the state language since the mid-twentieth century: that is, almost all minority communities were compelled to learn the state language. The members of the politically dominant (majority) nationalities have mostly become monolingual, and even if they form a demographic minority, they rarely learn the language of the politically subordinate ethnic group (mostly Hungarians). The bilingualism that characterized for centuries the ethnic and linguistic contact zones in the historical Hungary, which is the present-day C–PA, has disappeared. Interethnic neighbourhood relations are free from tensions until minorities demand collective rights and the right to self-

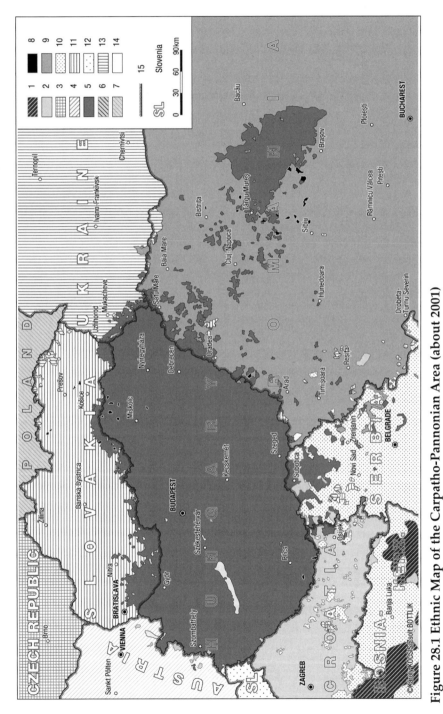

Figure 28.1 Ethnic Map of the Carpatho-Pannonian Area (about 2001)

1= Bosnians, 2= Croats, 3= Czechs, 4= Germans, German speaking Austrians, 5= Hungarians, 6= Montenegrins, 7= Poles, 8= Roma, 9= Romanians, 10= Serbs, 11= Slovaks, 12= Slovenes, 13= Ukrainians, 14= others, 15= State border.

Source: © K. Kocsis and Zs. Bottlik.

determination with their ethnic and territorial implications. Because of underlying tensions and distrust coupled with the populous Hungarian communities' desire to preserve their ethnic identity, they maintain parallel (cultural-educational and political) institutional systems in (the frontier zones of) Romania, Slovakia, Serbia and Ukraine. It is partly due to this that the relationship of ethnic Hungarians and members of other ethnic groups in these regions/areas can be regarded as living next to one another rather than living together.

The neighbourhood relations of the communities organized on the basis of nationality are of course related to the states' frontier zones, and are basically defined by the economic development of the given country as well as the supply and demand of the work force, workplaces, goods and services. Migration and commuting to work across borders are largely affected by the differences in per capita GDP (Table 28.1). The work force usually moves towards the countries providing higher income, but there are border zones where the dynamically developing area of the 'poorer' country attracts the unemployed workforce from the underdeveloped, peripheral border zones of the 'wealthier' state (for example many Hungarians from the border zones find jobs in Oradea or Arad in Romania). Recent statistical data about people crossing the different Hungarian border sections (with very different goals) show that the intensity of the traffic has been increasing along the internal borders of the EU, while stagnating or decreasing along the Schengen (Ukrainian and Serbian) border sections. About 24 million people crossed the Hungarian border from the neighbouring states (including the transit traffic) in 2007, while 16.7 million people left Hungary. It is the Hungarian–Austrian and the Hungarian–Slovakian border sections that have the most intense traffic, mostly because of people commuting to work.

A particular type of neighbourhood relations is construed by the Euroregions, a form of cross-border cooperation encouraged by the European Council. These regions, which include two or more countries, do not have political power; the cooperation means that local governments, small- and medium-sized businesses and local economic organizations are offered an opportunity to build networks and communicate. The Euroregions may help not only to bridge the differences present since the borders were established between Hungary and its neighbouring states (1920, 1947), but also lead to the economic and cultural reunion of the Hungarian communities divided by state borders. This development might also contribute to the political stabilization of the given area. The first Euroregion in the C–PA (formed in 1993) was the very large Carpathian Euroregion on the common frontier zone of Hungary, Slovakia, Ukraine, Romania and Poland. Between 1997 and 2004, Carpathian was followed by the establishment of fourteen further Euroregions, mostly initiated by the local Hungarian self-governments along the Slovakian–Hungarian border section.

Good neighbourly relations: the Austrian–Hungarian borderland

Austria and Hungary are good neighbours. The relationship between these countries is basically defined by the memories of the Austro–Hungarian Monarchy, a period characterized by peace and growth. Common Hungarian speech calls the Austrians 'brothers-in-law', which characterizes this exceptionally strong neighbourhood – almost family – relationship. Every time a conflict casts a shadow on the relationship between the two states, maintaining good neighbourly relations is regarded as a priority and a value to preserve even in the arena of interstate politics, for example today, when river pollution by Austrian companies or their investment plans raising reasonable concerns about the environment lead to conflicts in the border areas.

There is a major symbolic event related to the Austrian–Hungarian border: On 27 July 1989 the barbed wire fence was cut through by the foreign ministers of the two countries, and this act symbolically opened the way to masses of people wanting to leave East Germany and go to the West and later to the reunion of the two Germanys and Europe. This border section is markedly different from others: Events happened earlier here than at other borders; this was where the 'East' met the 'West', the EU met the countries outside the EU, and Schengen countries met those outside Schengen; and it was also here that the EU began to support joint development projects and regional cross-border cooperation. And, not independently, many researchers of various disciplines have been interested in this border section (see for example Baumgartner et al. 2002; Horváth and Müllner 1992; Kovács 2002a; Nárai and Rechnitzer 1999; Seger and Beluszky 1993; Wastl-Walter and Váradi 2004).

The tearing down of the Iron Curtain that had divided Europe for decades was followed by euphoria, anticipation and then a silent sobering along the Austrian–Hungarian border section. The expectations were related to the revival of neighbourhood relations, economic development and attaining higher living standards on the Hungarian side of the border. These expectations, however, have only been partially fulfilled – and several factors have contributed to this.

As the Austrian–Hungarian border constitutes an ethnic-linguistic border, there were no national injuries and ethno-political conflicts tied to it. This fact resulted in the disappearance of people knowing the other language (except for a few minority 'islands'); the memories referring to one another were thus broken, and the memory communities dissolved. If these connections had been remembered, they could have formed the basis of the everyday neighbourhood relations between the people living along the borders (Wastl-Walter et al. 2002).

As research has shown, the border was 'natural' for the Austrians; they had nothing to do with it and it did not affect their identity. On the Hungarian side, however, the people who lived in strictly closed border zones (both internal and external) had to cope with marginalization and double isolation; they could only minimize the significance of the Iron Curtain and try to perceive the border and their lives along the border as normal and self-evident (Horváth and Müllner 1992; Wastl-Walter et al. 2002). For those living on the Hungarian side, the opening of the border meant the end of their double isolation.

After the tearing down of the Iron Curtain, it became clear that the Austrians were not interested in the full opening of the border on either a local or provincial/ national level (Baumgartner et al. 2002; Váradi 1999; Wastl-Walter et al. 1993). During the 1990s, several settlements protested against the establishment or enlargement of border crossing points, and since the first negotiations about joining the EU they have voiced their fears of their 'Eastern' neighbours flooding the Austrian labour market. Later, in 2007, when the Schengen zone was enlarged, many were afraid that the peacefulness and security of borderland Austrian villages would be disturbed and ruined by criminals. It is not difficult to discover a version of *orientalist discourse* in the reasons brought up against the full opening of the border: what stands behind it, is, however, the fear that the unequal distribution of the economy and incomes, that is, wealth and poverty, would be overturned, putting Austrians at a disadvantage (Böröcz 2002).

The asymmetric stream of people and goods came about very early, and is still effective. While capital is generally directed towards Hungary (and other countries of the former socialist block), the labour force and the profit of investments are directed outwards (Böröcz 2001; Kovács 2002b).

When referring to the Austrian–Hungarian border zone, many emphasize that it did not separate two peripheral regions that were dropping behind, but regions that could synergize (Rechnitzer 1999). In this regard, three facts are worth mentioning. Firstly, the West-Transdanubian region is one of the most developed areas of Hungary, which attracts Western, including Austrian capital; secondly, Burgenland (the Eastern border area of Austria) gained access to significant (EU) resources after Austria's accession to the European Union; and thirdly, joint development projects were started in this border zone during the 1990s. If we examine the different border zones using the dimensions of development/ underdevelopment and center/periphery, we find that the Austrian–Hungarian border zone is indeed not a poor area dropping behind, but we must also see that the capital and development resources have usually dynamized the economies of the centers or sometimes smaller settlements with good transportation potential. However, the deeply rooted structural problems of the rural areas along the border (like the weakness of the economy and the city centers, the lack of job opportunities, or the unfavorable demographic structures caused by outmigration) could not be solved, so their isolation and peripheral situation have not greatly changed. EU and bi- or tri-regional cooperation has aimed at reducing developmental differences and advancing the areas on the eastern side of the border. Our observation is that this cooperation has been characterized by a peculiar asymmetry: Austria has been interested in them because it has been thus able to acquire EU financial aid, while the Hungarian (or Slovak) side has been motivated by the constraint of adjusting to the EU member state (and the EU itself) and meeting its requirements, as well as the competing for the available resources (Kovács and Váradi 1996).

From the border of 'fear and control', the Austrian–Hungarian border has become a 'disappearing' border throughout the last almost 20 years. The movement of people and goods is free but not fully unrestricted and symmetrical. Many people who live in settlements close to the border have permanent or occasional jobs in Austrian enterprises and on farms, partly illegally, even though the Austrian government restricts and wants to legalize the employment of foreigners. Austrians still travel to Hungarian towns seeking cheaper services, but they do not flood the shops any more, as prices have evened up on both sides. Thus shopping has become two-directional. Farmers from Burgenland have appeared as renters although they are often owners in disguise in the Hungarian land market of the border zone, where local agrarian producers have become disadvantaged when competing with them.

Despite the two-directional movement of people, capital and goods, stereotypical images about one another have not disappeared, Hungarians are often seen as slightly lazy, careless people who even tend to steal and who want to live as well as their hard-working neighbours, while the Austrians are thought to be envious and haughty people who exploit others and employ different measures at home than they do in Hungary (see Hardi 1999; about the German–German border zones Armbruster and Meinhof 2002; Jeggle 1994). These well known, deeply rooted and lasting *clichés* are based on looking down on the poorer and more backwards neighbour on the one hand, and on the frustration stemming from the constraint to adjust and catch up on the other. If we apply Simmel's (1909) bridge-and-door metaphor to the Austrian–Hungarian border (which is now an internal border of the EU), we can say that the movement is free across the bridge, but the doors are not fully open yet – they selectively let through or exclude goods and people.

Neighbourhood relations burdened with serious historical conflicts: the Hungarian–Romanian and the Hungarian–Slovakian borderlands

The Hungarian–Romanian borderland

The Romanian principalities Wallachia and Moldova (or the united Romanian state, Romania since 1862) have been Hungary's neighbours since their establishment. After World War I, Romanian diplomacy was remarkably successful. It managed to push the Hungarian–Romanian border 200 to 400 kilometres to the West, as far as the middle of historical Hungary, and annexed almost 103,000 square kilometres (43 per cent of the territory of the present-day Romania) to their country (Table 28.1). At present, 1.4 million ethnic Hungarians live in this area which includes Transylvania, an area equally important for Hungarians and Romanians, especially in the so-called *Székelyföld* (Szeklerland) and in the Hungarian-Romanian border area. The ethnic reciprocity between the two states is thus extremely asymmetric, as there are only 8,000 Romanians living in Hungary. It is partly because of the dismembering of the Hungarian state and ethnic territory and the reannexation of Northern Transylvania to Hungary between 1940 and 1944 that this border zone became the venue of grave conflicts between 1919 and 1945. The Romanians' continuous fears of Hungarian revenge and irredentism led to the development of the *Carol-Line*, a chain of smaller fortresses along the Hungarian border during the 1930s. Since 1948, the two countries have belonged to the same military and economic federative systems (the Warsaw Pact, Comecon, and today NATO and EU), which has alleviated and kept in check the deeply-rooted tensions between the two neighbouring states. As a result, Hungary and Romania signed in 1996 an agreement on mutual understanding, friendship and cooperation.

The southern section of the 448-kilometre state border is mostly an ethnic border separating Hungarians and Romanians, but the northern section (north of Oradea) separates areas with a Hungarian ethnic majority on both sides (Kocsis and Kocsis and Hodosi 2001). While there are dynamically developing cities and county towns with good traffic conditions on the Romanian side (Arad, Oradea, Satu Mare), there are economically declining rural areas that have lost their above-mentioned centers on the Hungarian side. In order to break up the Hungarian ethnic space and to prevent a possible future border revision, hundreds of thousands of Romanians have been settled along the border areas since the 1920s, but especially during the decades of socialist urbanization (Kocsis 1999). As a result, formerly Hungarian cities became cities with a Romanian majority, for example Arad in 1940 and Oradea and Satu Mare in 1973. This kind of state-directed colonization increased the tensions between the Hungarian autochthonous population, living predominantly in cities, and the less tolerant settlers who spoke only Romanian and who were usually moved from distant villages into new housing estates in the above-mentioned towns of the border area. The separation has been strengthened by historical and linguistic factors as well as by religious factors: Hungarians are mostly Calvinists or Roman Catholics, while Romanians are Orthodox Christians (or Greek Catholics). Thus, it is not surprising that Hungarians and Romanians remain relatively separated by operating parallel institutional structures in these areas. In other words, they live side by side rather than coexist (Blomqvist 2006). There are still tensions below the surface in the Romanian–Hungarian relationship, but their existence often counts as a taboo topic. Everyday interethnic relations, primarily in the workplace, are unproblematic. However, problems arise when Hungarians put forward collective or political demands. This is not tolerated by the Romanian community, which feels such action hurts its 'supremacy'. In these instances, then, a political unity/solidarity is formed along ethnic boundaries.

The relations extending across the borders are excellent: a telling example is the formation of the three Euroregions operating here (Carpathians 1993, Danube – Körös / Criş – Maros / Mureş – Tisza 1997, Hajdú–Bihar – Bihor 2003). These are characterized by complex economic, cultural, touristic and infrastructural cooperation, shaped mostly by the Hungarians living on both sides of the border. For the last decade, especially since Romania joined the EU on 1 January 2007, the relationship between cities in Romania (for example Arad, Oradea and Satu Mare) and their former districts on the Hungarian side of the border has been restored. At present, it is usual for Romanian citizens to buy cheap real estate on the Hungarian side and make use of the country's more developed services, while increasingly more people from the rural Hungarian side arrive in the dynamically developing Romanian border towns to seek employment.

The Hungarian–Slovakian borderland

Slovakia is one of the youngest states of the world: An independent country between 1939 and 1945, it became a separate and independent state according to international law in 1993. Previously, between 1919 and 1939 and between 1945 and 1993, it existed within the framework of Czechoslovakia (as *Slovensko*). Before 1919, for more than a thousand years, the territory of the present-day Slovakia had been part of Hungary, in that there were no borders separating the two ethnic groups. After Czechoslovakia was established following World War I, the Treaty of Trianon (1920) marked the border between Hungary and Czechoslovakia 10 to 50 kilometres south of the Hungarian–Slovak linguistic border mostly along the rivers Danube and Ipoly. Based on economic, military strategic and transport-geographic considerations, this demarcation satisfied the moderate Czech demands. As a result, more than 1,070,000 (or 880,000 excluding Transcarpathia) Hungarians found themselves inside the borders of Czechoslovakia (Slovakia). Since then, as some of them fled, were deported or *Slovakized*, their number was reduced to 520,000 in Slovakia, which significantly exceeds the number of Slovaks living in Hungary (18,000). This asymmetry is mirrored by the fact that the present-day Slovak-Hungarian border is 681 kilometres long, and is not an ethnic border; rather it separates Hungarians living on both sides. In 1938, at the time of the First Vienna Award, the Slovak–Hungarian border was drawn close to the ethnic border (Rónai 1989). After World War II, the Paris Peace Treaty (1947) essentially restored the borders defined by the Treaty of Trianon, and the northern Hungarian ethnic territory was reannexed to Czechoslovakia. Soon after, hundreds of thousands of Slovaks were settled there, and tens of thousands of Hungarians were deported (Kocsis 1999).

The relations between Czechoslovakia (and Slovakia) and Hungary were extremely tense between 1919 and 1948, because of the 'Hungarian question' – especially between 1945 and 1948, when Hungarians in Slovakia were deprived of their rights, and one sixth of them were deported. Even though the two countries belong to the same military and economic federations and Hungary recognized Slovakia's territorial integrity in a basic treaty between the two states in 1995, the Slovaks, like the Romanians, are still distrustful of the Hungarian minority and Hungary because of their constant fears of Hungarian irredentism.

Since the two states joined the EU in 2004 and the 'Schengen zone' in 2007, the Hungarian–Slovakian border has also become quite 'ethereal', which has opened the way towards the economic and cultural reunion of Hungarians living on both sides, and thus significantly contributed to the stabilization of the region. This increasingly tight 'Hungarian-Hungarian' connection had previously been indicated by the fact that nine of the fourteen Euroregions established in the C–PA between 1997 and 2004 were formed along the Slovak–Hungarian border. The Slovakian–Hungarian border crossing points are used by daily commuters and shopping tourists (because of the differences in prices and currencies), which also reflects the neighbourly relations of the two – economically similarly developed – states. Most people commute from the Western section of the border zone, that is, the southern Slovakian area, which is ethnically Hungarian, and was not really developed during the socialist era, to the Hungarian industrial centers on the other side (for example Győr, Komárom and Esztergom). Those who want to maintain their relationship with Hungary because of their ethnic and family ties also frequent the crossing points. Although both the Hungarian and the Slovak populations maintain parallel institutional structures in order to strengthen their own ethnic identities, it is possible to talk about an increasingly close coexistence between the two ethnic groups, especially in the towns along the linguistic border. Since most of the religious Hungarians and Slovaks are Roman Catholics, the ethnic separation here is not reinforced by religious differences, as is the case in Romania, Serbia and Ukraine.

A people surrounded by invisible borders: the Roma minority and their neighbours

One of the best-known scattered ethnic minorities of the world is the Roma (Gypsy) community whose global number is estimated at seven million. The majority, an estimated 5.3 million, live in the post-communist countries of Europe. The earliest records of the presence of Roma in the C–PA originate in the fourteenth century. According to the first 'Roma census' of the Hungarian Ministry of Internal Affairs, their number was 275,000 in 1893. During the communist era, between 1950 and 1990 there was a genuine demographic explosion among the region's Roma population; their estimated number grew from 542,000 to 1,951,000 and their proportion changed from 2.2 per cent to 6.5 per cent (Kocsis and Bottlik 2004). According to census data from about 2001, only one quarter of the population of Roma origin in the C–PA declared they were ethnically Roma (579,000 or 2 per cent).

The regional concentration of the Roma is high (over 8 to 10 per cent) in eastern Slovakia, northeastern Hungary, the middle Tisza Region and Romania (in the borderlands and in the Transylvanian Basin). Roma concentration is also considerable in some other areas of the region, for example the southern part of Hungarian Transdanubia, the Serbian Banat, as well as the cities of Belgrade, Budapest and Bratislava.

The census data based on self-assessment in fact do not authentically indicate the number of Roma people, or those who are considered as Roma in Hungary. Behind this distortion several factors can be pointed out, such as Roma people's effort to be assimilated and integrated into the majority society as well as a sort of 'hiding' strategy of the Roma, aiming to become invisible, a strategy which has been shaped by centuries of coexistence.

The Roma who live in multi-ethnic areas and settlements adopt and speak the majority language, identify themselves as Hungarians, Slovaks, Romanians, for example, in the census, and usually follow the locally dominant religion.

The ever-present physical and symbolic borders between the Roma and the majority population have become markedly stronger during the past years. Opportunities for the region's Roma population to find a livelihood have been undermined twice in a century, which has also determined the patterns of their living together with the majority society. Up to the middle of the twentieth century, the livelihood of the various Roma groups in the rural areas depended on the peasantry, as they produced tools needed in farming and provided services by taking odd jobs. This created a kind of patron-client relationship between peasants and the Roma on a local level. Socialist modernization led to radical changes in the structures of subsistence and living together, partly by extending compulsory schooling, and partly by its need of masses of untrained workers for its extensive industrialization projects. This meant that most Roma men, and a few women, became industrial or agricultural workers during the socialist era, although they were usually unqualified workers on the lowest levels of the division of labour. However, they worked together with those belonging to the majority, and they were all wage labourers, even though they went on pursuing certain traditional activities like trading, sometimes walking a tightrope between legality and illegality. With the regime change, the assimilation and integration strategies that had begun during the socialist era proved to be quite fragile and collapsed dramatically. Masses of Roma lost their jobs and have been living in exclusion ever since, fallen into the vicious circle of unemployment, lack of education, poverty and dependence on distribution systems for more than two decades (Gagyi 1996; Kertesi 2005; Ladányi and Szelényi 2002).

The selective migration processes initiated in the socialist era were first supported by the state, as in the case of liquidating Roma colonies, but then mainly accompanied by economic and social changes. These processes have increased in strength since the regime change, which has caused a number of villages and city districts to become poor Roma ghettos (Havas 1999; Virág 2010). It is very difficult to leave these ghettos for several reasons: Those who live in them lack models from either the majority or their own group. People living day by day have neither perspectives nor plans. In addition, in homogeneous poor communities the network of relations called 'strong ties' (Granovetter 1973) is indispensable for survival, restraining and sanctioning the individual ambitions of the community's members, while at the same time providing support and protection for them (Durst 2008; Ladányi and Szelényi 2004). Further, at some places, the ghetto settlements are even surrounded by strong walls from the outside, and the majority is not at all interested in pulling them down. The interventions from public funds that are meant to help usually also end in failure, and, despite their original intentions, only contribute to reinforcing the borders.

Although the majority of the Roma live in exclusion, the group as a whole cannot be regarded as a homogeneous mass. They have different languages, cultures, traditions and traditional livelihoods (Prónai 2006; Szuhay 1999), but they are also differentiated by their present livelihood strategies. Modes of earning an income also differentiate Roma groups, because these modes are dependent on the history of any given Roma group and its wider social environment. In fact, many have found a living through crossing borders. Certain Roma families and groups have been able to use the permeability of borders to their advantage, giving evidence of their mobility. Some of them get (mainly illegal) jobs abroad, in line with the given majority environment. For example, Hungarian-speaking Roma (from neighbouring countries) go to Hungary, while the Romanian-speaking Roma prefer southern Europe, but Hungarian Roma living in Transcarpathia also go to Russia to take seasonal agricultural jobs. Others cross the borders to trade in various goods, money, or even consumer goods cleared from Western households. Street musicians and beggars, who often frighten the public in the countries concerned, are usually exploited by criminals, who, by organizing and controlling these Roma, also receive an income.

Local reports recant that, whenever Roma families manage to gain wealth as a result of cross-border jobs and trading and express this, for example by building alpine-type houses in the middle of a village among majority-group homes and not among Roma, the given majority groups are deeply startled. The majority group then try to prevent the crossing of social and symbolic borders that might follow the spatial border crossing ensuing from material growth, because they want to maintain the traditionally asymmetric relationship that defines the rules of communication between majority and minority communities (Bíró and Bodó 2003; Fosztó 2003; Oláh 1996b; Pozsony 2003).

What seems to be a process of differentiation for the majority environment is a world divided by culture, language, traditional professions and material and social positions, in which certain Roma groups are strictly separated from each other. The members of these groups want to maintain the internal social and symbolic borders, perhaps making it even more difficult to cross these Roma borders than the border separating the Roma from the majority society. This applies to the diverse Roma groups both regionally and locally. The local Roma elite disdains redundant the poor Roma living in the ghettoized streets, avoids contact with them, and adjusts to the patterns of the majority society in its lifestyle and strategies of finding a livelihood or studying. This, however, does not mean that the majority society treats them differently than those living in the poorer parts (Bíró and Bodó 2003; Fosztó 2003; Oláh 1996a, Pozsony 2003).

We can observe the operation of the so-called tribal stigma (Goffmann 1990; Fosztó 2003) in the majority's discourse on the Roma and its relations to them. Individuals, always treated as the members of a given group, are not given the opportunity to construct and show a personal identity that differs from the image construed about the group. The Roma are associated with almost exclusively negative (or at the least exotic) attributes, which even the Roma who aspire to integrate into the majority society and step out of their stigmatized position adopt and use against those living in poverty, whom they find 'too Roma'. Given this situation, it is difficult, if not impossible, to construct a positive Roma identity.

Conclusions

The C–PA has undergone radical and rapid changes for almost two decades, which have included the transformation of the physical and mental borders. A geopolitical system collapsed and old/new nation states were formed and became stronger or weaker. The transition to a market economy as well as the development of more or less democratic political systems brought about new structures to which millions of people had to adjust, while also giving up (and changing) their seemingly secure living strategies in this multiethnic space.

Borders thought to be permanent have disappeared or become ethereal, thus allowing the unimaginable to occur: the free movement of people, goods and services. In the meantime, the borders of the new dominant geopolitical system (the EU) have been pushed to the East and the prevailing external borders have been strengthened, which have resulted in constant competition and the constraint to adjust in the area. Many inhabitants also remark that feeling 'not being suitable and equal' or being left out have caused frustrations.

The fact that borders separating nation states have become permeable and ethereal does not (and cannot) mean that they simply disappear. On the contrary, several factors maintain the border: the asymmetric flow of goods, services and persons; a long-lasting inequality between wealthier and poorer areas; and deeply rooted injuries and mistrust stemming from the critical formative period of nation states in the twentieth century. The massive symbolic and mental structures arising from these circumstances constantly reproduce borders.

In Europe's largest multicultural macroregion (which can still be regarded as that, despite the 'successes' of the peaceful or violent assimilation politics of the past one and a half centuries) the inflexibility or permeability of ethnic borders and the everyday practices of living together are often shaped by the current relationship between states as well as the interplay of national/nationalist discourses. This is due to historically rooted, still unresolved offences and mutual real or imaginary injuries. Even though the living together of majority and minority groups seem to be peaceful and harmonic, it can only be maintained, if the minority communities do not question the political *status quo* and the balance of power that are in force in the country and/or locally.

However, there is a minority against which the competing minority groups uniformly define themselves as the majority: the Roma, most of whom have to cope with deepening social exclusion. The ever-present physical and symbolic borders between the Roma and the majority have become stronger; only a few have managed to cross them, and at costs that remain hidden to the majority.

The neighbourhood relations of the diverse ethnic groups in the region can generally be described as living next to one another rather than coexistence.

BORDERS AND NEIGHBOURHOODS IN THE CARPATHO-PANNONIAN AREA

References

Alvarez, R.R. (1995), 'The Mexican–US Border: The Making of an Anthropology of the Borderlands', *Annual Review of Anthropology* 24, 447-70.
Anzaldúa, G. (1987), *Borderlands / La Frontera: The New Mestiza* (San Francisco, Spinster: Aunt Lute Press).
Armbruster, H. and Meinhof, U.H.(2002), 'Working Identities: Key Narratives in a Former Border Region in Germany', in Meinhof, U.H. (ed.), *Living (with) Borders* (Aldershot: Ashgate), 15-32.
Baumgartner, G., Kovács, É. and Vári, A. (2002), *Távoli szomszédok – Entfernte Nachbarn. Jánossomorja és/und Andau 1990–2000* (Budapest: Teleki László Alapítvány).
Bíró, A.Z. and Bodó, J. (2003), '"Hát ezek kezdtek sokan lenni..." Magyarok és cigányok Korondon', in Bakó, B. (ed.), *Lokális világok. Együttélés a Kárpát-medencében* (Budapest: MTA Társadalomkutató Központ), 65-82.
Blomqvist, A. (2006), 'One City – Two Images – Two Communities: The Case of the Romanian Hungarian City of Satu Mare / Szatmárnémeti', *Eurolimes* (Oradea) 2, 37-44.
Böröcz, J. (2002), 'A határ: társadalmi tény', *Replika* 47-48, 133-42.
Böröcz, J. (2001), 'Bevezető, Birodalom, kolonialitás és az EU "keleti bővítése"', *Replika* 45-46, 23-44.
Durst, J. (2008), 'Bárók, patrónusok versus komák – eltérő fejlődési utak aprófalvakban', in Váradi, M.M. (ed.), *Kistelepülések lépéskényszerben* (Budapest: Új Mandátum), 232-267.
Feischmidt, M. (2004), 'A határ és a román stigma', in Kovács, N., Osvát, A. and Szarka, L. (eds.), *Tér és terep. Tanulmányok az etnicitás és az identitás kérdésköréből III* (Budapest: Akadémiai Kiadó), 43-58.
Fosztó, L. (2003), 'Szorongás és megbélyegzés: a cigány–magyar kapcsolatok gazdasági, demográfiai és szociokulturális dimenziói', in Bakó, B. (ed.), *Lokális világok. Együttélés a Kárpát-medencében* (Budapest: MTA Társadalomkutató Központ), 65-82.
Fox, J.E. (2007), 'From National Inclusion to Economic Exclusion: Ethnic Hungarian Labour Migration to Hungary', *Nations and Nationalism* 13:1, 77-96.
Gagyi, J. (1996), *Egy más mellett élés. A magyar–román, magyar–cigány kapcsolatokról*, KAM–Regionális és Antropológiai Kutatások Központja (Csíkszereda: Pro-Print Könyvkiadó).
Goffmann, E. (1963), *Stigma. Notes on Magagement of Spoiled Identity*, reprinted 1990 (London: Penguin Books).
Granovetter, M. (1973), 'The Strength of Weak Ties', *American Journal of Sociology* 78, 1360-80.
Halász, I., Majtényi, B. and Szarka, L. (eds.)(2004), *Ami összeköt? Státustörvények közel és távol* (Budapest: Gondolat).
Hardi, T. (1999), 'A határ és az ember, Az osztrák–magyar határ mentén élők képe a határról és a "másik oldalról"', in Nárai, M. and Rechnitzer, J. (eds.), *Elválaszt*

és összeköt a határ. Társadalmi–gazdasági változások az osztrák–magyar határ menti térségben (Pécs–Győr: MTA Regionális Kutatások Központja), 159-90.

Havas, G. (1999), 'A kistelepülések és a romák', in Glatz, F. (ed.), A cigányok Magyarországon (Budapest: Magyar Tudományos Akadémia), 163-203.

Horváth, T. and Müllner, E. (1992), '"...die Grenze ist für uns ganz normal.", Ausgewählte Ergebnisse eines grenzüberschreitenden Forschungsprojekts', in Horváth, T. and Müllner, E. (eds.)(1992), Hart an der Grenze. Burgenland und Westungarn (Wien: Verlag für Gesellschaftskritik), 163-74.

Jeggle, U. (1994), 'Határ és identitás', Regio 2, 3-18.

Kertesi, G. (2005), A társadalom peremén. Romák a munkaerőpiacon és az iskolában (Budapest: Osiris).

Kocsis, K. (1999), 'Die ethnische Struktur in den Grenzräumen der karpatho pannonischen Region', in Schultz, H. (ed.), Bevölkerungstransfer und Systemwandel. Ostmitteleuropäische Grenzen nach dem Zweiten Weltkrieg (Berlin: Verlag Arno Spitz), 69-104.

Kocsis, K. and Kocsis-Hodosi, E. (2001), Ethnic Geography of the Hungarian Minorities in the Carpathian Basin, Simon Publications (Florida, USA: Safety Bay).

Kocsis, K. and Bottlik, Z. (2004), 'Die Romafrage in der Karpato–Pannonischen Region', Europa Regional 12:3, 132-40.

Kovács, É. (2002a), 'Határmítoszok és helyi identitásnarratívák az osztrák–magyar határ mentén', Replika 47-48, 143-56.

Kovács, É. (2002b), 'Identitás és etnicitás Kelet-Közép-Európában', in Fedinec, CS. (ed.), Társadalmi önismeret és nemzeti önazonosság Közép-Európában (Budapest: Teleki László Alapítvány), 7-24.

Kovács, K. and Váradi, M. (1996), 'Karöltve – A regionális együttműködés esélyei a Bécs–Győr–Pozsony háromszögben', Műhely 3, 60-7.

Ladányi, J. and Szelényi, I. (2004), A kirekesztettség változó formái (Budapest: Napvilág).

Ladányi, J. and Szelényi, I. (2002), 'Cigányok és szegények Magyarországon, Romániában és Bulgáriában', Szociológiai Szemle 4, 71-94.

Lőkkös, J. (2000), Trianon számokban (Budapest: Püski).

Michalkó, G. (2004), A bevásárlóturizmus (Székesfehérvár: Kodolányi János Főiskola).

Nárai, M. and Rechnitzer, J. (eds.)(1999), Elválaszt és összeköt a határ. Társadalmi–gazdasági változások az osztrák–magyar határ menti térségben (Pécs–Győr: MTA Regionális Kutatások Központja).

Oláh, S. (1996a), 'Szimbolikus elhatárolódás egy település cigány lakói között', in Gagyi, J. (ed.), Egy más mellett élés. A magyar–román, magyar–cigány kapcsolatokról (Csíkszereda: KAM–Regionális és Antropológiai Kutatások Központja, Pro-Print), 207-24.

Oláh, S. (1996b), 'Gazdasági kapcsolatok cigányok és magyarok között', in Gagyi, J. (ed.), Egy más mellett élés. A magyar–román, magyar–cigány kapcsolatokról (Csíkszereda: KAM–Regionális és Antropológiai Kutatások Központja, Pro-Print Könyvkiadó), 225-46.

Pozsony, L. (2003), 'Magyarok, románok és cigányok a háromszéki Zabolán', in Bakó, B. (ed.), *Lokális világok. Együttélés a Kárpát-medencében* (Budapest: MTA Társadalomkutató Központ), 65-82, 109-38.

Prónai, CS. (ed.)(2006), *Cigány világok Európában* (Budapest: Nyitott Könyvműhely Kiadó).

Prónai, CS. (ed.)(2005), *Lokális cigány közösségek Gömörben. Identitásváltozások marginalitásban* (Budapest: MTA Etnikai–nemzeti Kisebbségkutató Intézet).

Rechnitzer, J. (1999), 'Határmenti együttműködések Európában és Magyarországon', in Nárai, M. and Rechnitzer, J. (eds.), *Elválaszt és összeköt a határ. Társadalmi–gazdasági változások az osztrák–magyar határ menti térségben* (Pécs–Győr: MTA Regionális Kutatások Központja), 9-72.

Rónai, A. (1989), *Térképezett történelem* (Budapest: Magvető).

Seger, M. and Beluszky, P. (eds.)(1993), *Bruchlinie Eiserner Vorhang. Regionalentwicklung im österreichisch–ungarischen Grenzraum* (Wien: Böhlau).

Simmel, G. (1909), 'Brücke und Tür', *Der Tag. Moderne illustrierte Zeitung* 683, Morgenblatt 15 September 1909, available at <http://socio.ch/sim/bru09.htm>.

Szuhay, P. (1999), *A magyarországi cigányság kultúrája: etnikus kultúra vagy a szegénység kultúrája* (Budapest: Panoráma).

Váradi, M.M. (1999), 'Pinkamindszent (Allerheiligen). Verlustgeschichte einer Grenzgemeinde. Ein alternativer Forschungsbericht', in Haslinger, P. (ed.), *Grenze im Kopf* (Frankfurt am Main: Peter Lang), 141-56.

Virág, T. (2010), *Kirekesztve. Falusi gettók az ország peremén* (Budapest: Akadémia Kiadó).

Wastl-Walter, D., Kocsis, K. and Váradi, M. (1993), 'Leben im Dorf an der Grenze', in Seger, M. and Beluszky, P. (eds.), *Bruchlinie Eiserner Vorhang. Regionalentwicklung im österreichisch–ungarischen Grenzraum* (Wien: Böhlau), 225-64.

Wastl-Walter, D., Váradi, M.M. and Veider, F. (2002), 'Bordering Silence: Border Narratives from the Austro–Hungarian Border', in Meinhof, U.H. (ed.), *Living (with) Borders* (Aldershot: Ashgate), 75-94.

Wastl-Walter, D. and Váradi, M.M. (2004), 'Ruptures in the Austro–Hungarian Border Region', in Pavlakovich-Kochi, V., Morehouse, B.J. and Wast-Walter, D. (eds.), *Challenged Borderlands. Transcending Political and Cultural Boundaries* (Aldershot: Ashgate), 175-92.

Transcending the National Space: The Institutionalization of Cross-Border Territory in the Lower Danube Euroregion

Gabriel Popescu

Introduction

European integration has significantly altered the traditional links between social relations and political territoriality. We are witnessing a reterritorialization of European social life where social relations are partially uncoupled from nation-state territories and stretch beyond state borders, even as the latter continue to remain key territorial units for the organization of space. At the cross-border level, the renegotiation of the relationships between Westphalian territoriality and social life has found its foremost expression in cross-border region building. Cross-border regions spanning two or more national borderlands (also known as Euroregions) have been the preferred vehicles to institutionalize cross-border cooperation in Europe. They are means of territorially organizing and formalizing previously unstructured cross-border regional and local spatial interaction. This is achieved by building multilevel networks of institutions that stretch across state borders and exert governance prerogatives over cross-border territories. The end goal is to overcome the traditionally divisive role of nation-state borders in order to allow the integration of border regions with shared interests (Perkmann and Sum 2002).

After the early 1990s, the process of the European Union (EU) enlargement has provided the context in which these political-territorial dynamics have been projected well beyond the EU borders proper. In the neighbouring spaces, cross-border cooperation has been often seen as a forerunner to broader EU integration (Yoder 2003). It is in this context that borderlands situated outside the EU space were introduced to cross-border cooperation practices and discourses. Subsequently, successive rounds of EU enlargement have expanded the EU supranational umbrella to incorporate these borderlands and brought the EU external borders to new borderlands. Such developments have further impacted the cross-border cooperation environment in these regions.

The Romanian-Ukrainian-Moldovan borderlands achieved complete cross-border institutionalization coverage by 2002. The four Euroregions currently straddling these borderlands were initially located outside the EU space. After the 2007 EU expansion to include Romania, the EU external borders cut across the Romanian-Ukrainian-Moldovan neighborhood. The Lower Danube Euroregion (LDE) is the first to be established exclusively between Romania, Ukraine and Moldova in 1998, and it is representative of the nature of the issues facing cross-border cooperation along the EU's eastern borders. The Euroregion is located in the southernmost sector of the tri-national borderlands and it includes the low-lying territories surrounding the Danube River Delta on the northwest shores of the Black Sea (see Figure 29.1).

In this chapter, I am examining the impact of the institutionalization of the LDE territory on the dynamics of cross-border interaction in the Romanian-Ukrainian-Moldovan borderlands. Specifically, I am seeking to illustrate the nature of the space being created in the LDE and what this reveals about the reterritorialization of social relations at cross-border level? Moreover, how is the process of cross-border cooperation in the LDE advancing the integration of the three national borderlands in the context of their development at the interface of EU and non-EU space? Central to addressing these issues is the analysis of the cross-border cooperation dynamics along a series of dimensions of territorial change that show how patterns of social action are being modified by the institutionalization of cross-border cooperation processes in the LDE.

Cross-border cooperation in the LDE is actively shaped by the multiscalar interaction between supra-, sub-, trans- and national forces (Popescu 2006). Generally, top-down management characterizes the institutionalization of the LDE as a cross-border territory. National and supranational priorities often take precedence over local needs. Consequently, the Euroregion's impact as a space of reterritorialization falls short of initial expectations of integrating the Romanian, Ukrainian and Moldovan borderlands. However, it would be misleading to assume that the Euroregion failed to generate cross-border changes. The institutionalization of cross-border cooperation practices in the LDE engendered change across main aspects of social life ranging from territorial, to economic and cultural. These developments help us to understand the nature of the neighbourhood that is being created in the LDE.

In what follows, I will first introduce the multiscalar context in which the LDE operates. I continue with a discussion of the gradual institutionalization of cross-border cooperation processes in the LDE. Then, I will critically examine the impact of these processes on cross-border integration in the region using a series of dimensions of territorial change that emerge out of archival research, interview material and participant observation carried out in the area. I will conclude with an assessment of the role of the LDE as a space of cross-border integration across national and supranational borders.

Figure 29.1 The Lower Danube Euroregion

Source: Cartography: C. Scarlat, Center for Advanced Spatial Technologies at the University of Arkansas.

Contextual underpinnings

The EU position that regards the institutionalization of cross-border cooperation in Euroregions as a key strategy of its Cohesion policy, and as a way to help integrate divided borderlands and to provide political, economic and social stability is well known (Cristiansen and Jorgenson 2000). During the 1990s, the Lower Danube borderlands were of secondary concern for the EU cross-border cooperation agenda, as they were situated outside the EU's immediate neighbourhood. However, in the early 2000s, Romania's progress toward EU membership changed this situation and caused the EU to become actively involved in the region. By 2003, the EU developed the European Neighbourhood Policy (ENP) that had major implications for the LDE. The ENP is a comprehensive geopolitical and geo-economical strategy toward neighbours such as Ukraine and Moldova that the EU does not envisage integrating in the foreseeable future (Emerson 2004). It includes the European Neighbourhood and Partnership Instrument (ENPI), a sizable financial program with the capacity to disburse funds for transnational cooperation between EU

609

members and their non-EU neighbours worth over 10 billion Euros by 2013. At the cross-border level, the ENP aims to further the institutionalization of cross-border cooperation along the EU external borders as a mean of providing stability and to reduce economic disparities between EU and non-EU borderlands. Specifically, the ENPI has set aside over one billion Euros for supporting cross-border cooperation projects (ENPI 2007).

At the same time, the ENP also places a strong emphasis on border security in an attempt to insulate the EU members from what they perceive as potential instability and migration flows emerging from the neighbouring spaces (Apap and Tchorbadjiyska 2004). Funds totalling over one billion Euros have already been spent on strengthening border control capacities along Romania's eastern borders (Popa 2004) before the ENPI funds even reached these borderlands. In essence, the presence of the supranational EU borders in the LDE has increased the complexity of the cross-border cooperation environment. Contradictory EU policies regarding its neighbours actively shape the nature of the neighbourhood that is being created in the LDE. The ENP support for cross-border cooperation can generate increased investment of capital in borderlands that critically need it. Nonetheless, this does not necessarily translate into increased cross-border integration at the level of civil society. The securitization of borders increases the hurdles in obtaining EU travel visas for the non-EU citizens. This in turn adversely affects the intensity of cross-border interaction at the level of the civil society, which is affecting the core rationale of cross-border cooperation.

The positions of the Romanian, Ukrainian and Moldovan national governments regarding the institutionalization of cross-border cooperation in Euroregions has been influenced by the nature of their bilateral intergovernmental relations, as well as by their positions with respect to the European integration process. From 1990 to 1997, support for institutionalized cross-border cooperation was not a priority on these governments' agenda. Having parts of their national territory institutionally linked to other territories in neighbouring countries was not a perspective that many leaders in Romania, Ukraine and Moldova contemplated. At the same time, during this period the border regime between these three countries experienced a period of unprecedented liberalization that lead to burgeoning interpersonal cross-border contacts. For example, Romanian and Moldovan citizens did not need a passport to cross their common border (Prohnitski 2002).

A series of issues marked the relationships between these three governments, creating mutual mistrust and preventing them for capitalizing on the growing grassroots cross-border linkages. Ukraine and Moldova emerged as independent states in 1991 after the dismantling of the Soviet Union. These governments' main concern was statehood consolidation, which included the recognition of their borders by neighbouring states and the maintenance of their territorial integrity in the face of separatist movements (Kuzio 1998). Romania was emerging from a painful communist dictatorship that shattered the civil society and the economy. Its leaders sought European integration while at the same time trying to cope with the new geopolitical circumstances created by the emergence of Ukraine and Moldova. The newly created Ukrainian and Moldovan borderlands were territories that belonged to Romania between the two world wars, and where a large population of Romanian descent lives.[1] A widely expected union between Romania and Moldova failed to materialize, as the Moldovan government chose to follow an independent path (King 2000). This situation presented the Romanian government with two broad options: to pursue territorial demands against the two countries or to find ways to move beyond this historical legacy. Romanian leaders opted for the latter, understanding that territorial claims against their neighbours would undermine the country's chances for European integration. However, the Romanian government maintained an interest in the Romanian ethnics living in the neighbouring borderlands that will later lead to support for the institutionalization of cross-border cooperation in the LDE.

Intergovernmental relations throughout the 1990s and the 2000s have been dominated by pragmatic cooperation punctuated by up and down periods. Romania and Moldova maintained a privileged relationship, strengthening their cultural and economic ties. Nonetheless the intensity of this relationship declined after 2001 (Skvortova 2006), when the Communist party came to power in Moldova and accused the Romanian government of expansionist policies in Moldova. At their turn, the Romanian-Ukrainian bilateral relations are soured by several issues such as the delineation of the maritime boundary in the Black Sea in an area where oil has been recently discovered, and the building of a canal by Ukraine in the Danube Delta that both countries share. At times, these intergovernmental disputes have a chilling effect on cross-border cooperation in the LDE (Popescu 2006).

After 1997, the national governments reversed course and become actively involved in the institutionalization of cross-border cooperation across their common borderlands. National leaders come to understand the benefits institutionalized cross-border cooperation could bring to these borderlands, and even further to their bilateral relations and to their relationship with the EU (Prohnitski 2002). Under these circumstances, the Euroregions have been seen as frameworks where cross-border cooperation can be used to address contentious issues emerging from the borderlands and to prove these governments' readiness for European integration.

The 1997 Romanian-Ukrainian bilateral treaty provided the backdrop for the institutionalization of cross-border cooperation in the region. The treaty specifically stipulated the creation of Euroregions in order to support ethnic minorities inhabiting the borderlands and to implement policies aimed at borderlands. In the aftermath of the treaty, Romanian, Ukrainian, and Moldovan presidents met in Izmail, a border town on the Ukrainian side of the Danube Delta, to launch comprehensive trilateral Romanian-Ukrainian-Moldovan cooperation that sanctioned the creation of the tripartite Lower Danube Euroregion (Ilies 2004).

From the perspective of the borderlands the establishment of the LDE makes sense if we consider the model of older Euroregions in the EU space (Deica

---

1   Moldova has a population of about four million (including the separatist region of Transnistria) of which approximately 70 per cent are of Romanian descent. The population of Romanian descent in Ukraine at the 2001 Ukrainian census is 409,000, divided between Romanians (151,000) and Moldovans (258,000).

and Alexandrescu 1995). There are strong arguments supporting cross-border integration in the Lower Danube borderlands. First, a shared Romanian ethnic basis that can constitute the mainstay of cross-border cooperation is present in all three national borderlands. Second, there is a sense of shared history in the LDE space, since the Lower Danube borderlands functioned as a whole territory during the Ottoman rule, and more recently between the two world wars when the region was ruled by Romania. Third, the lower Danube space has a significant economic potential that can be cooperatively exploited in order to further development in the borderlands. The Danube River, one of the main European waterways, and the Danube Delta's enormous environmental and economic potential are two economic assets that can be used as major cross-border integration axes in the LDE. The territorial entanglement generated by border manipulation in the 1940s when the current borders came into being, and the subsequent strict border regime during the Soviet era, prevented this potential to be fully exploited. Fourth, the presence of industrial and port cities in the LDE such as Galati, Braila, and Tulcea in Romania, and Odessa, Izmail and Reni in Ukraine, together with the existence of price and wage differentials between the three national borderlands, can assure a sustainable base for cross-border integration. Fifth, the peripheral geographical position these borderlands occupy vis-à-vis core areas in their nation-states can be overcome through cross-border integration in the LDE.

However, the arguments supporting cross-border integration in the LDE can work against it as well. Ukrainian officials may not necessarily perceive as favourable the existence of a shared Romanian ethnic basis in the LDE. Instead, some Ukrainian officials may be uneasy of an ethnically Romanian-dominated LDE that they interpret as a potential threat to Ukraine's territorial integrity. Furthermore, there are other significant ethnic minorities in the LDE, particularly in the Ukrainian and Moldovan borderlands, that may not wish for an ethnically Romanian-dominated Euroregion. Thus, both of these categories of actors may have reasons to oppose deeper cross-border integration.

At the same time, the sense of shared history in the Lower Danube space may not be perceived in the same way by all borderland inhabitants. Its power to generate a common identity should not be taken for granted. The Romanian ethnic background of part of the Ukrainian borderland inhabitants, as well as of many Moldovans, is mediated by their half century of life outside the borders of the Romanian state and does not automatically translate into a Romanian identity similar to the one Romanians in Romania hold. Moreover, the region experienced considerable population changes during the past fifty years, and many of the current inhabitants are not natives of the Lower Danube space.

The economic potential of the Lower Danube space can deter cross-border integration as well. The existence of the shared Danube River and the Danube Delta, together with industrial and port cities, and with the predominantly agricultural character of the region means that there are numerous similarities among the three national borderlands. The history of communist economics that all LDE borderlands share accentuates these similarities, limiting cross-border complementarities. In the circumstances of contemporary global capitalism, borderlands can choose engage in competition for various resources instead of cooperatively exploiting the existing ones.

Lastly, the peripheral position Lower Danube borderlands occupy vis-à-vis their national core areas does not automatically translate at the local level to a desire for cross-border integration. The national framework of organization of social life continues to captivate people's imagination to such an extent that it may obscure envisioning the possibility of organizing social life in other territorial frameworks such as the LDE, in spite of the borderlands' lasting peripheral status.

The development of the LDE does not fit neatly into any prescribed scenarios. A combination of elements that work in favour of, as well as against, deepening cross-border integration can be identified in the LDE. The broader context in which the Euroregion operates is responsible for the outcome of the combination of these elements and for the prevalence at times of one or another course of cross-border institutionalization.

Institutionalizing cross-border territory between Romania, Ukraine and Moldova

The making of the LDE was carried out in several stages during 1997 and 1998. The initiative came from the Romanian government and presidency on the premise of improving interstate relations between Romania and Ukraine. The 1997 Izmail declaration on trilateral cooperation included the consent of the national governments for the establishment of the LDE. Subsequently, in February 1998 at Izmail, a meeting took place under the supervision of the Council of Europe where a Statement supporting cross-border cooperation between the Romanian, Moldovan, and Ukrainian local and regional authorities was adopted (Ghiorghi 2003). On 14 August 1998, the representatives of the three borderlands involved met in the border town of Galati, Romania to adopt an Agreement formally establishing the LDE. At the same time, the bylaws outlining the Euroregion's legal status were approved, and its institutional structure was determined (Acord 1998).

The LDE did not acquire an autonomous legal status. The bylaws specified that the LDE as an entity is not a subject of law; rather its constitutive parts have their own independent legal status, and only they have the authority to engage in legal matters. At the same time, the bylaws do not bind the parts beyond national legislation, thus in the process of cross-border cooperation national laws take precedence over the bylaws of the LDE. Consequently, the LDE emerged as a quasi-governmental institution, devoid of executive, legislative, and judicial powers, thus having a quasi-legal status.

The bylaws also established the LDE's formal position vis-à-vis the multi-scalar system of political-territorial institutions, by stating that the Euroregion 'is not intended to replace the existing local administration or to create a new one' (Statut 1998). Also, the Euroregion is not intended to be a supranational organization, but to constitute a framework to facilitate inter-regional cooperation between its members. These attributes seem to point toward the LDE's status as a transnational institution. Furthermore, the bylaws mention that the 'LDE does not act against the interest of the states', and that 'the national governments have the right to obtain information regarding the activities of their local authorities that are LDE members' (Statut 1998). However, the LDE's bodies have the right to engage in cooperation with other international organizations.

A succinct description of the goals of the Euroregion as specified in its constitutive documents offers an insightful perspective on the nature of expectations from the institutionalization of cross-border cooperation between the three countries involved. First, the LDE is imagined as a framework that enables cross-border cooperation between its members along several fields, such as economics, science, culture, environment, and others. Second, the Euroregion is intended to allow its members to identify fields of common interest and to create cross-border cooperation projects to help develop cooperation in these fields. Third, the LDE's members intended to facilitate cross-border contacts between economic institutions, NGOs, and individual experts. Fourth, the Euroregion is expected to facilitate cooperation between its members and other international organizations (Statut 1998).

A more detailed description of the LDE's goals is found on the Odessa's Regional Administration website (<http://www.odessa.gov.ua>). Here, in addition to borderland regional development objectives, a series of social and cultural objectives are also mentioned. For example, the document specifies 'forming the single cultural area near the Danube', and the necessity of 'improving the capability of local authorities' (<http://www.odessa.gov.ua>). The same document offers further insights regarding the goals of the Euroregion. The LDE is considered 'a special mechanism of international relations' and 'the channel on which the negative energy of border tension, international misunderstandings, and economic contradictions could have been transformed into the new co-operation mechanisms' (<http://www.odessa.gov.ua>).

Acquiring the Territorial Shape

The territory of the LDE resulted from combining the territories of several borderland territorial-administrative units from Romania, Ukraine, and Moldova (see Figure 29.1). Currently these include Tulcea, Galati, and Braila counties (judete) from Romania, Cahul and Cantemir districts (raioane) from Moldova, and the Odessa Region (oblast) from Ukraine. The LDE has an approximate territory of 53,300 square kilometres and a population of roughly four million people (Ilies 2004).[2]

The use of existing national territorial-administrative units as the territorial base for the LDE was taken for granted at the time of its establishment. This seemed a logical choice that allowed the use of the existing sub-national administrative

---

2   The LDE is larger than Moldova both in land area and population.

apparatus, instead of creating a new one. At the time, lower rank territorial-administrative units in the three countries, such as cities and villages, were not considered as having enough governance clout to become meaningful cross-border actors. Additionally, the central governments favored this territorial make-up of the LDE as they felt more comfortable having their sub-national level administration managing cross-border cooperation.

The territorial structure of the LDE displays an apparent territorial mismatch between the proportions of the participating national borderlands. This situation has a considerable impact on the overall functioning of the Euroregion, making integrated planning strategies difficult. The Odessa Region has a total of 33,300 square kilometres which is equivalent to the size of Belgium. Its share of the LDE amounts to roughly 63 percent of the land area. At the opposite end are the Moldovan districts that amount to less than five percent of the territory of the LDE.

There can be identified two distinct areas of the LDE (Ilies 2004). First, there is the area centred on the lower Danube River, on the meeting point of the Romanian, Ukrainian, and Moldovan borders, that extends eastward until the Dniester River. This area includes all Romanian and Moldovan LDE territories and the southern part of the Odessa Region (see Figure 29.1). This is the sector where most of the cross-border cooperation in the LDE takes place. At the same time, this is the area that belonged to Romania between the two world wars. Today it displays a remarkable ethnic diversity with over 100 ethnic minorities recorded. The second area centers on the northern part of the Odessa Region. This sector runs north of the city of Odessa and is bordered by the Dniester River in the west. As there are no Moldovan LDE member districts in this area, institutionalized cross-border cooperation in this sector is non-existent.

However, the proportions of each of the three national borderlands forming the LDE from the territory of the country to which they belong show a much more balanced picture, with all three national borderlands accounting for five to seven percent of their respective national territories. The same observation applies regarding the proportion of the population of the each LDE national borderland to the total population of the country it belongs to. This situation raises important questions regarding the criteria used to establish the LDE: has this been done with the needs of the LDE in mind, or according to the needs/interests of the nation-states?

The selection of the specific borderland territorial-administrative units to form the Euroregion also points towards an opaque process shaped to a considerable extent by domestic and international geopolitical considerations. For example, in the case of Moldova the districts participating in the Euroregion cluster around the Moldovan, Romanian, and Ukrainian border meeting point covering mostly the Moldovan-Romanian borderlands (see Figure 29.1). The eastern borderlands of Moldova adjacent to the Odessa Region are formed by the self-proclaimed Transnistrian Republic over which the Moldovan government has not had effective control since the early 1990s. Membership of the eastern Moldovan borderlands in the LDE has never been raised. In the south, the districts of the Gagauz ethnic Autonomous Territorial Unit of Gagauzia and Taraclia (populated in majority by the

Bulgarian minority) do not participate in institutionalized cross-border cooperation although their neighboring the Odessa Region would seem to recommend them for LDE membership (Cimpoaca 2001).

The Governance Apparatus and its Financial Support

The formal administrative structures that make up the governance apparatus of the LDE were created at the time of the establishment of the Euroregion. Other type of structures, such as various departments in the national governments and EU-related institutions, participate in the governance of the LDE only marginally. Certain local NGO's and Chambers of Commerce are occasionally involved in various cross-border cooperation actions in partnership with the formal administrative structures of the Euroregion, or they may offer specialized consulting to various LDE bodies.

The administrative apparatus of the LDE consists of a number of employees from the staff of the borderland territorial-administrative units of the three states involved. The main decision making body of the LDE is the Council of the Euroregion that adopts decisions by consensus. By default, the Council's members are the heads of the regional administrations of the five territorial units involved in the LDE. The Council has a President and two Vice-Presidents elected by rotation for a period of two years (Statut 1998). These are unpaid positions.

The Coordination Center is the second institution in the formal administrative structure of the LDE, and it is directly subordinated to the Council. Its membership is selected by the Council for a two year period and is composed of one chief and two coordinators who work for the President and the Vice-Presidents. In many ways this is the most important institution of the Euroregion. The Coordination Center functions as a 'secretariat' of the Euroregion, managing most of the cross-border cooperation activity. However, a stable Coordination Center with its own staff and office space has not been implemented so far. The headquarters of the Center reside in the district/county that is home to the then-president. As a result, the LDE does not have an independent office.

The Specialized Commissions constitute the third administrative body of the LDE. They draft cross-border cooperation projects, design programs, and compile reports that are then submitted to the Council for approval. Currently, there are seven commissions covering a broad range of issues ranging from regional development and economy, to transportation, the environment, interethnic relations and law enforcement. They are staffed by various members from the local administrations who have additional administrative duties non-related to cross-border cooperation as well.

The financial means for the operation of the LDE are derived from all members equally. The Euroregion has a budget of its own, but it does not have an independent bank account. The fact that the LDE does not have an independent legal status prevents it from having a common bank account. The funds each member allocates are kept separately in a special account. The funds obtained for the implementation of projects from international organizations are also kept in a special account that can be used only by the member mentioned in the program that received funding. Typically, the member holding the Presidency assures financing for the Council's meetings and the functioning of the Coordination Center. These funds came from the budgets of the local administrations of the LDE members. There are no independent taxes to contribute to the LDE's budget.

The dimensions of cross-border change

The mere establishment of the LDE across national borders does not automatically translate into integrated borderlands. The territorial delineation and the emergence of institutional structures that the establishment of the LDE involved was the first phase in the process of building cross-border territories. For this process to have substance, first national borders have to significantly loosen their barrier function so that social relations can develop unrestricted across the LDE space, and second, these social relations have to acquire substantial density across the LDE space so that the Euroregion can be meaningful enough as a framework for social life to instill a sense of shared interests. This is the next phase in the process of integrating the LDE space. The examination of the decade long cross-border cooperation processes suggests five main dimensions along which the LDE space is changing.

The Territorial Dimension

The establishment of the LDE raised unprecedented territorial challenges for the Romanian, Ukrainian and Moldovan leaders. They had to make an effort of political-territorial imagination to manage them. Membership in the LDE suggests a certain measure of outward orientation in the scope of the participating national borderlands. Assembling cross-border territories would have been unthinkable in the not so distant past, given the strict border regime between the Soviet Union and Romania on the one hand, and the border-induced territorial sovereignty logic of the national states in which claims of exclusive rights over the national territory gravitate inward toward the centre/capital. From a territorial perspective, the LDE is a new territory that by its very (cross-border) nature is situated beyond the exclusive reach of any single sovereign control (Popescu 2008).

Another significant territorial dynamic in the LDE is illustrated by the spatial pattern of cross-border cooperation that displays little resemblance to the Euroregion's formal borders. The most intense cross-border exchanges involve territories immediately adjacent to the national borders where shared interests predominate. This suggests that national administrations do not exclusively determine the shape of the Lower Danube neighbourhood. Rather, we are witnessing how local social processes mold the LDE's territorial shape according to their interests. This is an instance of active production of a territory from the bottom-up in contrast to the top-down institutionalization of the LDE. While in the short run territorial adjustments in the structure of the LDE are not foreseeable, the existence of an institutionalized territorial framework for cross-border cooperation that is actively shaped by local social processes keeps open the potential for deeper integration in the long run.

Other territorial developments support the idea that national governments perceive the LDE as little more than a tool they can use in international politics for addressing contentious issues. For the most part, the three national governments attempted to minimize potential loss of territorial sovereignty in the Lower Danube borderlands. The establishment of the LDE's territorial structure to include domestic territorial administrative units without any territorial adjustments suggests that territorial politics trumped concerns regarding the LDE's territorial functionality. Altering the shape of the existing domestic territorial-administrative units would have meant the creation of new domestic borders incongruent with the territorial-administrative grid of the nation-state, and would have required additional efforts for central governments to manage. During the 1990s, the Romanian, Ukrainian, and Moldovan governments were not ready to accept such challenges.

The Euroregion also serves national governments and the EU pursuit of territorial strategies at the European scale. For the EU, the LDE can be used as springboard toward the former Soviet space in the context of the ENP. For the Ukrainian and Moldovan governments, the LDE is part of their strategy of territorial integration into the EU. After 2007, the LDE constitutes a territorial interface between these two countries and the EU. While formally the EU stops at Romania's eastern borders, LDE represents an informal territorial overlapping between Ukraine and Moldova and the EU space. It is important to point out that by working this way, cross-border integration between Romania, Ukraine, and Moldova signifies the continuation of the territoriality principle as a mode of organization of social relations. An alternative would be a cross-border reterritorialization imagined more as a set of spatial social relations emerging from routine activities of social actors unconfined by the LDE's borders. The LDE as a medium for cross-border reterritorialization rests on solid territorial norms, but social action in the LDE space can follow more independent paths.

The Legal Dimension

European (that is the Additional Protocol to the Madrid Convention) as well as national legislation regulating cross-border cooperation that Romania, Ukraine and Moldova adopted since the late 1990s established a legal basis for institutionalized cross-border cooperation and empowered the LDE authorities in the legal field. Such regulation covering local interaction at the cross-border level is unprecedented in the Lower Danube space, and departs from the traditional model of international relations between nation-states. There are already signs that local communities are taking advantage of the newly created legal framework. One such example is the possibility for municipalities to contribute local funds to projects implemented in the neighbouring national borderlands. Thus, although at a disadvantage when compared to national and European regulatory power, the LDE's legal framework shows the potential to sustain more active cross-border integration.

Cross-border integration in the LDE is seriously handicapped by the lack of an autonomous legal status for the Euroregion, by the mismatch of legislation between its national components, as well as by the poor implementation of newly adopted legislation pertaining to the right of local authorities to engage in cooperation across national borders. These shortcomings of the LDE's legal framework restrict opportunities for local authorities to engage in cross-border projects of a larger scope. The legislative structure the LDE has been endowed with in its bylaws is not sufficient to sustain intensive cross-border integration in the Euroregion. The fact that the LDE's constitutive parts have their own independent legal status while the Euroregion as a whole lacks such status inhibits the LDE from functioning as a coherent space. The existence of the LDE as a quasi-legal entity exposes it to the dominance of the national governments and the EU since their laws take primacy over the LDE's bylaws. Nonetheless, Romania's EU membership has generated further developments along the legal dimension. Recently, the local leaders have decided to overhaul the LDE's bylaws to allow an independent legal status under private law for the Euroregion (Domniteanu 2007).

The Institutional and Governance Dimension

Given the fact that there were no previous institutions to straddle national borders in the region, the establishment of the LDE constitutes a new institutional framework of territorial organization beyond the scope of traditional national institutions. A significant outcome of the process of the LDE's institutionalization is the emergence of an interpersonal network of local elites that appears fairly integrated at the cross-border level. The existence of such network is a necessary condition for unifying the LDE's space. Yet, this is not a sufficient condition. For the LDE to function as an integrated space, interpersonal networks have to sink in at the level of ordinary inhabitants far beyond the ad hoc networks involving cross-border smuggling.

The over reliance on interpersonal relations in the governance process is a way of substituting for the lack of formal institutional power. While this is a phenomenon often hailed by many theorists of multi-level governance, the LDE experience also points out that over reliance on interpersonal relations generate less consistency in the process of cross-border integration. The LDE top officials are beholden primarily to their national electorate. As the LDE top leaders can change following national elections, the intensity of cross-border cooperation experiences ups and downs as well.

The LDE's institutional structure is far from being adequate for the goals the Euroregion is expected to accomplish. The LDE's institutions display a reduced degree of cross-border integration, as each national territory has its own set of institutions that mirror each other across the border. Although these institutions do work together across borders, their logic remains national in essence. In addition, the geographical location of the LDE's institutions carefully reflects a national logic of territorial organization. There is no LDE institution with oversight over the entire LDE territory. However, this situation is about to change. The recent legal overhaul mentioned earlier includes the creation of a permanent LDE headquarter in Galati, Romania.

The LDE displays a multilevel structure of governance as far as the involvement of institutions situated at other spatial scales than the local administration is concerned. However, active and constant interaction among these multi-scalar governance structures is feeble. Among governance actors involved in the LDE, national government structures play a key role. The absence of the EU supranational territorial coverage at the time of the LDE's institutionalization influenced its governance structure. National governments assumed several functions that the supranational institutions traditionally assume in the EU space, while other functions typically carried out by these institutions were neglected in the LDE. The fact that the Moldovan president participated in a LDE Council meeting is one extreme example of national level actors involved in the LDE's governance (Interlic 2004). Generally, national government structures are not directly involved in the governance of the LDE. Rather, their clout results from their preeminent power position in a system dominated by nation-states. While local institutions are typically involved in the daily governance of the LDE, they need the assistance of national-level institutions to be effective in managing significant cross-border projects. Institutions situated at supranational and transnational scales such as the EU and AEBR have played less important roles in the LDE governance so far. However, the implementation of the ENP is currently changing this situation.

The Economic Dimension

The necessity for an economically integrated lower Danube space is genuine, and the opportunities such integration can offer for the civil society are real. There is a broad convergence of interests on the part of national governments, supranational institutions, and local leaders in the LDE's capacity to promote economic development in the region. The majority of cross-border cooperation projects funded so far are economic in nature. Apparently, the economic dimension of the LDE is one of the most non-contentious cross-border cooperation issues among Romania, Ukraine, and Moldova, as the interview data attest. It appears paradoxical then, that this is one of the fields where the least progress has been made.

Currently, progress in economic cross-border integration is modest. The LDE administration pursues several strategies with a certain degree of success, such as organizing economic fairs, building cross-border business databases, and others aimed to bring into contact potential cross-border business partners. As well, more sustained cross-border economic activity clusters between main cities close to the border, such as Galati and Reni and Galati and Cahul; and Izmail and Tulcea. At the level of local civil society, the small cross-border trade constitutes the main form of cross-border economic activity. We can also add smuggling activities here, since such operations display a considerable degree of cross-border integration (Candea et al. 2003).

There are high expectations that the implementation of the ENP will invigorate cross-border economic integration in the region. Indeed, the Romanian borderlands already witness increased levels of foreign investment, and the ENP is bringing certain investments into Moldovan and Ukrainian borderlands. EU-related investment in the LDE as a whole is expected to increase considerably and may prove beneficial for the LDE in the long term. Yet it is too early to assess the economic effects the ENP will have on cross-border integration in the LDE since these effects are contingent on the type of border regime the EU establishes. There may be more foreign investment in the LDE, but this will not automatically mean an integrated LDE economy.

While the reduced degree of complementarity in the economic structure of national borderlands and their generally low level of development are serious impediments for cross-border economic integration, the most important obstacle is the reluctance of central governments to change the way they imagine their national territory and to enact special economic regulation for border regions to stimulate economic actors to cooperate across borders. The building of much needed transportation infrastructure, such as bridges and ferry terminals, as well as increasing the number of permanent border checkpoints, reflects the logic of domestic geopolitics in which national geo-economic arguments prevail over the needs of borderland inhabitants. Bridge connections over the Danube River, i.e. between Tulcea and Izmail, can boost economic cross-border integration in the LDE. However, given the peripheral status of the LDE such costly projects figure very low on the list of central governments' infrastructure priorities, despite the tangible benefits for the local civil society.

The Cultural Dimension

It is often agreed by local and national leaders that most progress toward cross-border integration in the LDE has taken place in the cultural realm. Certainly this is accurate if we consider that before 1990, cross-border cultural contacts at the local level were non-existent. The functioning of the LDE does impact the ways local inhabitants think of each other across borders. Increased informal and formal cross-border contacts among borderland inhabitants contribute to mutual understanding and help to dispel various myths and stereotypes about each other.

Generally, local inhabitants have a pragmatic attitude toward each other across borders, and they do not oppose cross-border integration. Moreover, support for cross-border integration in the LDE does not break along ethnic lines. Most local leaders interviewed in Ukraine were not ethnic Romanians, and they declared that they are keenly aware of the benefits cross-border integration can bring to their region. This demonstrates the desirability of an integrated LDE space among local inhabitants irrespective of their ethnic identity.

However, the LDE is far from becoming a culturally integrated space. Indifference toward the other side of the border is what characterizes the attitude of many LDE citizens today. The markers of difference still outweigh the markers of common identity in the LDE. The LDE's symbols, such as its flag and its name, as well as its history and its image reflected in local leaders' discourses, evoke modest shared feelings when compared with the well established national symbols. The crossing of national borders continues to be a complex ritual that 'reminds' citizens where they 'belong'. As long as crossing the national borders means that local inhabitants have to produce a passport or other forms of national identification, the attitude of indifference toward the other side will likely continue. While the free passage through national borders is not a panacea to the formation of shared identities, as the example of EU Euroregions demonstrates (Paasi and Prokkola 2008), in the LDE's case the physicality of national borders is an additional burden in the process of building common social spaces.

National borders remain the most important marker of identity in the LDE space, and they are markers of difference as far as cross-border integration is concerned. National governments continue to be involved in cultural politics in their borderlands. The Romanian government attempts to use the LDE framework to achieve objectives it cannot accomplish through intergovernmental negotiations, such as increased cultural rights for the Romanian/Moldovan minority in Ukraine. The Ukrainian government at its turn attempts to nationalize this borderland, especially given its distinct multicultural and less Ukrainian character. The Moldovan government walks a fine line in its southern borderlands between competing Gagauz, Bulgarian and Moldovan identities. It is this national cultural politics that can explain the lack of common television and radio stations covering the LDE space despite local attempts to establish them.

Conclusions

During the 1990s, cross-border cooperation discourses and practices were introduced to the Romanian-Ukrainian-Moldovan borderlands in the context of the process of European integration. The institutionalization of the LDE across the borders of Romania, Ukraine, and Moldova represents an attempt to integrate national borderlands beyond the national space. This process leads to the emergence of novel forms of territorial configurations in which many actors have a stake but no one exclusively controls them. Under these circumstances, the development of the LDE is shaped by a series of interests situated primarily at supra-, sub-, and national scales that often have contradictory aims. EU policies seek to project stability and development to its neighbours while reinforcing the border regime with these neighbouring spaces. National policies aim to create frameworks to address inter-governmental issues. Local actors demand exceptions from national regulation to empower them to engage in partnerships across borders. Private and transnational interests also play a role in the development of the LDE.

The intersection of these interests generates a complex cross-border cooperation environment that drives the integration of the national borderlands in the LDE. Such dynamics are best illustrated by identifying and analyzing several cross-border cooperation dimensions that capture the nature of the transformations the LDE is undertaking. These dimensions show that the creation of cross-border integrated spaces is an ambiguous process that contains simultaneously cross-border cooperation progresses and setbacks. Consequently, the assessment of the LDE as a space of integration across national and supranational borders is contingent on the metrics applied. If we are considering LDE's achievements in relation to what is needed to build integrated territories, then these achievements appear modest. If we are considering LDE's achievements in relation to both former and current regional cross-border cooperation contexts, then these achievements appear unprecedented. In the end, the primary significance of institutionalized cross-border cooperation in the LDE resides in increasing the scope and the level of cross-border interactions, and in creating a cross-border territorial and institutional framework that presents a significant potential for further integration of social life in the Romanian, Ukrainian and Moldovan borderlands.

Acknowledgements

I would like to acknowledge the assistance of Cristina Scarlat, Center for Advanced Spatial Technologies at the University of Arkansas, for her contribution of cartography to this chapter. Many thanks are also due to Darren Purcell for his comments on an earlier draft of this chapter.

References

Acord cu Privire la Constituirea Euroregiunii Dunarea de Jos (1998), *Acord cu Privire la Constituirea Euroregiunii Dunarea de Jos* (Galati), unpublished.

Apap, J. and Tchorbadjiyska, A. (2004), 'What about the Neighbours? The Impact of Schengen along the EU's External Borders', *Centre for European Policy Studies Working Document* 210, available at <http://shop.ceps.be/BookDetail.php?item_id=1171>.

Candea, S., Ozon, S., Kazangi, Z. and Calucareanu, V. (2003), *The Final Frontier* (The Romanian Center for Investigative Journalism), available at <http://www.crji.org/arhiva/e_031202.htm>.

Christiansen, T. and Jorgenson, K.E. (2000), 'Transnational governance "above" and "below" the State: The changing nature of borders in the new Europe', *Regional and Federal Studies* 10:2, 62-77.

Cimpoaca, G. (2001), 'Regiunea Autonoma Gagauzia doreste sa devina membru al Euroregiunii', *Viata Libera* 19 December 2001.

Deica, P. and Alexandrescu, V. (1995), 'Transfrontiers in Europe. The Carpathian Euroregion', *Revue Roumaine de Géographie* 39, 3-11.

Domniteanu, A. (2007), *Festivitate de predare a presedentiei in euroregiunea 'Dunarea de Jos'*, available at <http://www.cjgalati.ro/index.php?option=content&task=view&id=775&Itemid=2>.

Emerson, M. (2004), 'European Neighbourhood Policy – Strategy or Placebo?', *Centre for European Policy Studies Working Document* 215, available at <http://classes.maxwell.syr.edu/psc490/other%20material/CEPS%20paper%20on%20ENP.pdf>.

European Commission (2006), *European Neighbourhood and Partnership Instrument (EPNI) – Cross-Border Cooperation Strategy Paper 2007-2013*, available at <http://ec.europa.eu/world/enp/pdf/country/enpi_cross-border_cooperation_strategy_paper_en.pdf>.

Ghiorghi, I. (2003), *Raport Privind Activitatea Euroregiunii 'Dunarea de Jos'* (Galati), unpublished.

Ilies, A. (2004), *Romania. Euroregiuni* (Oradea: Editura Universitatii din Oradea).

Interlic (2004), 'Vladimir Voronin: "Statul Nostru Sustine Intru Totul Activitatea Euroregiunilor"', *Interlic* 22 March 2004.

King, C. (2000), *The Moldovans: Romania, Russia, and the Politics of Culture* (Standford: Hoover Institution Press).

Kuzio, T. (1998), *Ukraine: State and Nation Building* (London: Routledge).

Lower Danube Euroregion (1998), *Statutul Euroregiunii 'Dunarea de Jos'* (Galati), unpublished.

Negut, S. (1998), 'Les Euroregions', *Revue Roumaine de Géographie* 42, 75-85.

Paasi, A. and Prokkola, E.-K. (2008), 'Territorial dynamics, cross-border work and everyday life in the Finnish-Swedish border area', *Space & Polity* 12:1, 13-29.

Perkmann, M. and Sum, N.L. (2002), 'Globalization, Regionalization, and Cross Border Regions: Scales, Discourses and Governance', in Perkmann, M. and Sum, N.-L. (eds.), *Globalization, Regionalization, and Cross-Border Regions* (London: Palgrave), 3-24.

Popa, R. (2004), 'Securizarea Frontierelor – ori 800 milioane, ori 1 miliard de euro', *Adevarul* 1 October 2004.

Popescu, G. (2006), 'Geopolitics of Scale and Cross-border Cooperation in Eastern Europe: The Case of the Romanian-Ukrainian-Moldovan Borderlands', in Scott, J. (ed.), *EU Enlargement, Region Building and Shifting Borders of Inclusion and Exclusion* (Aldershot: Ashgate), 35-51.

Popescu, G. (2008), 'The conflicting logics of cross-border reterritorialization: geopolitics of Euroregions in Eastern Europe', *Political Geography* 27:4, 418-38.

Prohnitski, V. (2002), 'Moldova-Ukraine-Romania: a regional portrayal of economy and trade', *South-East Europe Review for Labour and Social Affairs* 5:2, 35-47.

Skvortova, A. (2006), 'The Impact of EU Enlargement on Moldovan-Romanian Relations', in Scott J. (ed.), *EU Enlargement, Region Building and Shifting Borders of Inclusion and Exclusion* (Aldershot: Ashgate), 133-48.

Yoder, J. (2003), 'Bridging the European Union and Eastern Europe: Cross-Border cooperation and the Euroregions', *Regional and Federal Studies* 13:3, 90-106.

PART VIII
NATURE AND
ENVIRONMENT

Natural Resources and Transnational Governance

Juliet J. Fall

Introduction

In September 2003, the fifth World Parks Congress titled *Benefits beyond Boundaries* was held in Durban, South Africa, in a huge conference centre close to the ocean. Dozens of parallel sessions were filled with over three thousand people from around the world. They each represented international organizations, United Nations agencies, non-governmental organizations and universities. They met to set out international nature conservation policy for the following ten years. Despite being the result at the end of a long series of preparatory sessions, for an individual on the ground it seemed an extraordinary place and an extraordinary moment: A huge group of professional people with apparently less than two weeks to define and write out what should be happening in national parks, nature reserves and other areas designated for nature conservation, all around the world. Responding to the main theme and reflecting the location of the hosting country, former President Nelson Mandela made the opening speech calling for international transboundary initiatives that would link parks in several countries to be vehicles of peace and development. The room was abuzz.

As the title *Benefits beyond Boundaries* reflected, international political boundaries were overwhelmingly presented as something negative: as international obstacles to be overcome through new partnerships between states, but also through links between different areas within countries, as well as between conservationists, the private sector and local communities. The idea was to use nature, boundless nature, to unite people. At the same time, ironically, and despite the talk about having to move beyond boundaries, the meeting was held in a vast conference centre surrounded by barbed wire, high fences and tight security patrols. Meanwhile, in a further twist of irony, maps of the town of Durban were handed out to us showing blacked-out *no-go areas*: Areas of the city considered too dangerous for foreign delegates. This chapter explores some of the themes emerging in current research around themes of boundless nature and bounded political spaces and people. It explores how natural resources and transnational governance are global phenomena with uneven geographies, constructed in particular places by particular people and with effects in distant places. This chapter will review some of the key themes and scholarship on nature, politics, boundaries and the re-grounding of the nation-state. The aim throughout is not to be comprehensive but rather to give some idea of current debates.

Putting nature in its place(s)

The idea is widespread that the natural world and the political world are fundamentally divided along different lines and within different non-congruent entities. In some arenas, natural divisions (between ecosystems, biomes or continents) are presented as *more real* and more concrete than *artificial* political boundaries such as states; while in other contexts, on the contrary, political boundaries are presented as concrete and problematic while nature is presented as effectively boundless. I will start by examining the idea that nature contains de facto divisions. In this section, I will then move on to explore how this idea has been challenged and critiqued, while indicating its continued ubiquity in natural resource management.

In 1975, Miklos Udvardy, a Hungarian natural scientist, suggested that the Earth could be divided into eight bio-geographical realms. These were seen to be coherent natural spatial entities, different from the unnatural political divisions of the world. This was used to determine rationally what realms suffered from insufficient protection. This powerful idea was used by The World Conservation Union (IUCN) to 'classify continent or sub-continent-sized terrestrial areas according to unifying features of geography, fauna and flora' (Worboys and Winkler 2006, 18). More recent classifications such as the European Union's *bioregions*, The World Wide Fund for Nature's (WWF) *Global 200 hotspots*, or Conservation International's *biodiversity hotspots* are also designed similarly, at different scales.

The latter two international conservation organizations divide the world into places they consider needing urgent attention. WWF, for instance, seeks to target the loss of biodiversity strategically, extending Udvardy's classifications to oceans and freshwater systems. This has led to the listing of 867 *ecoregions*, or areas of what WWF calls outstanding biodiversity and representative communities, 'with boundaries that approximate the original extent of natural communities priori to major land-use change' (Olson 2001 in Worboys and Winkler 2006, 34). Conservation International, meanwhile, identifies its own 34 regions worldwide within which, it claims, 75 per cent of the world's most threatened species still live, within an area that covers just 2.3 per cent of the Earth's surface (Worboys and Winkler 2006, 37). Called *biodiversity hotspots*, these places are destined for priority focus, with success defined as extinctions avoided.

The fact that none of these classifications are the same, and that none identify the same so-called *natural boundaries*, indicates that these are social constructions, rather than natural divisions. As such, they reflect the particular world-view of these organizations, and are far from apolitical. The terms used are instructive: When Conservation International states that hotspots require *priority focus* this isn't just an organizational strategy, but rather a claim made on behalf of the world's population as a whole (Katz 1998).

There is of course a long history of scholarship on natural boundaries, critiquing the use of natural features such as rivers, mountains and other topographical features as the basis for the political boundaries of states or sub-state jurisdictions. Political geographers, in particular, have addressed this issue at length (Ancel 1938; Bodénès 1990; Brunet 1967; Foucher 1991; Gay 1995; Hubert 1993; Minghi 1963; Pounds 1951, 1954; Prescott 1978; Raffestin 1980, 1991; Ratzel 1897; Velasco-Graciet 1998), yet they are rarely referred to in conservation literature on natural divisions (Fall 2005). While I am not suggesting that all proponents of hotspots or bioregions imply that these are entirely neutral, there is a strong tendency within conservation literature to consider them apolitical or politically neutral. This has important consequences for assigning responsibility for conserving natural resources, as I will argue in the next section.

Geographical inquiry has traditionally taken as given the separation between nature and culture, and studied the influence of one on the other in both directions. Despite a rich history of engaging with nature and the environment, the social sciences have often failed to interrogate nature in itself (Bakker and Bridge 2006). Literature stemming broadly from so-called science studies (Haraway 1991; Latour 1991, 1997) has however provided the impetus and theoretical grounding for a rescripting of the divide between nature and culture (or society). In parallel to this, the emergence of social constructivism within the social sciences in the 1980s led to attention being given explicitly to the *social* dimensions of nature (Cronon 1983). Nature, in this line of thinking, was no longer simply natural, but rather intrinsically social since taking it *in itself*, non-social and unchanging, was taken to lead to the perpetuation of power and inequality in the wider world.

In a series of works by geographers (Braun 2002; Braun and Castree 1998; Castree 2005; Castree and Braun 2001; Demeritt 2001) an agenda emerged exploring the politicized construction of social natures (for recent reviews see Bakker and Bridge 2006; Castree and MacMillan 2004; Walker 2005). Diverse appeals to relations, actors, materiality and material encounters led geographers to explore and spatialize concepts such as hybridity, exploring the physicality and co-presence of the non-human, both animate and non-animate, within conventional human worlds (Fall 2005; Whatmore 2002; Zierhofer 2002; for a review see Braun 2005). In this line of thinking, suggesting that nature contains unproblematic material boundaries is impossible and counterproductive: Such divisions can only be thought of as constructions, as lines drawn politically, following a particular project. This does not mean that nature is only considered to be discourse: On the contrary, recent (re)engagements with the materiality of nature have led to a material engagement with nature as something that is always already unpredictable, vital, and always shot through with multiple, transversal, non-linear relations (Clark 2000). These turbulent global natures, stretching across the globe in complex uneven ways, are assemblages made socially through networks of relations that remain inextricably vital and material. In arguing that global natures are always specific assemblages 'whose intricate geographies form tangled webs of different length, density and duration, and whose consequences are experienced differently in different places' (Braun 2006, 644), Braun dismisses all temptation of returning to the notion of nature as singular and universal. *Global nature*, in this context, is therefore an effect not a condition, and uneven rather than uniform, the consequence of specific connections and encounters that work across and through difference (Braun 2006).

Placing global nature?

Despite the innovative ways of thinking about nature within recent scholarship mentioned above, the prevalent Western practices follow the modern binary of nature and culture, seen as opposite ends of a spectrum or dichotomy. Nature has therefore often been assigned to particular *natural places* (Fall 2002), seen as removed from the places of society or urban life. Many so-called protected areas, such as national parks and nature reserve, have been designated in the past 140 years. These have been defined internationally as areas 'of land and/or sea especially dedicated to the protection and maintenance of biological diversity, and of natural and associated cultural resources, and managed through legal or other effective means' (IUCN 1994). They are a huge global success story: with over 106,926 protected areas in the world, covering an area of 19,617,833.60 square kilometres or 11.59 per cent of the surface of the Earth (UNEP-WCMC 2007). Yet this quantitative success is not unproblematic. It is almost as if these are considered the only places where nature is located, or at least where nature exists in a purer form. There remains a problematic distinction between the protected and the unprotected, as the preservation of certain places legitimates and mystifies the continued or even heightened destructive use of all that is outside the protected area's boundaries.

The World Conservation Union (IUCN), responsible worldwide for classifying categories of protected areas states that: 'The world's protected areas are the greatest legacy we can leave to future generations' (IUCN 2007). Not, for example, an intact environment in general, or clean water, or a stable climate. Protected areas are usually designed on the ground following a mixture of both biophysical criteria such as levels of high endemism or biodiversity, and socio-economic and political criteria such as low population density, political opportunism or aesthetic value. Because protected areas have been so successful in capturing the idea of nature, and seeming to reflect and embody it, the temptation to use these as privileged geographical objects to move *beyond (political) boundaries* has been immense. Yet rather than being a simple act of defining an area for conserving specific biodiversity, putting nature in one place, and society in another, designating a protected area is a profoundly political process, set within an inevitable web of power relations that is renegotiated or forcefully modified with all boundary changes.

In the next section, I explore how transboundary protected areas have been imbued with particular power to transcend political boundaries. At the same time, I will mention recent scholarship that indicates how difficult this has been in practice.

Transnational governance: transboundary protected areas

A wealth of articles has appeared on the subject of transboundary natural resource management in protected areas in the past 15 years, largely produced by international conservation organizations or non-specialist journals such as *National Geographic*. Protected areas in locations spanning international political boundaries have existed around the world since the 1950s, yet *transboundary protected areas* as such only became a global fashionable cause around the beginning of the 1990s (Fall 2005). This followed increased understanding about what constituted a critical mass or area in ecosystem health and therefore what was necessary for the maintenance of biodiversity. The importance of migration corridors, for example, was better understood in the light of emerging evidence of climate change and the crucial role of population size in sustaining genetic diversity became clearer as bio-molecular studies threw more light on genomes. In an increasingly competitive world of organizations vying for limited funding, transboundary planning became a leading paradigm for a multitude of actors. These new players recruited into the world of conservation and the promotion of peace and cooperation included international development agencies, United Nations agencies, transnational corporations and the tourism industry.

Building on this growing trend, the World Parks Congress held in South Africa in September 2003 was a key moment in the anchoring of this issue at a global level. Transboundary issues were one clearly visible theme, reflecting the fact that since 1990, the total number of transboundary protected areas doubled and many others were set to launch within the following few years. However, while this sounds impressive, it also reflects the fact that there existed no definition of what these might be, and contexts on the ground ranged from simple twinning agreements between two park authorities in neighbouring countries to more official and integrated management strategies. These spaces have often been called *Peace Parks* although the extent to which they foster or build upon existing peace is varied, and often unclear – or overblown.

> *Many places in the world where clusters of protected areas already exist are along international boundaries. ... But nature does not recognize political boundaries. In many cases, ecosystems have been severed by arbitrarily drawn political boundaries, while species continue to migrate across those borders as they always have, oblivious to customs regulations.* (Zbicz 1999, 15)

In this quote, Zbicz draws heavily on the widespread image of nature as primitive, untouched, existing as a form of timeless Eden before being brutalized by human divisions. According to the social nature approach, this is not a pertinent distinction as all boundaries are intrinsically social. Such an idea of pure nature is problematic because it fails to recognize human interactions with nature over space and time, as well as nature as the result of an intrinsically political and societal construction. Yet this idea that international political borders sever nature is particularly pervasive.

The bulk of the critique of transboundary protected areas has come from Southern Africa and, to a lesser extent, South America and Europe (Duffy 2005, 2006, 2007; Fall 2005; Katerere et al. 2001; Ramuntsindela 2007; Wolmer 2003). These have focussed on issues of neoliberalism and the privatization of conservation and of the state, rescaling and globalization, changes in the role of the state in transnational governance, border identities and the difficulties of reconciling different cultural constructions of nature in border areas. Critiques have noted how, rather than requiring less state control of border zones, the creation of transboundary protected areas in developing countries paradoxically reinforces control and raises significant issues for the management or control of globalizing forces in weakly administered regions of the developing world (Duffy 2006). These transboundary projects, rather than simply being about conserving species, represent a 'kind of regulated globalization which aims to gain control over unmanaged and unregulated wild places sited around international borders' (Duffy 2006, 3). In fact, Duffy argues that in the contexts of Southern Africa and South America rather than requiring states to relinquish power in some sort of transnational space, such areas 'often assist in extending state power over areas that had been previously beyond the reach of law enforcement and other government agencies' (Duffy 2006, 4). They therefore conceal not a freeing of nature but rather a will to control, in which 'the previously dominant role of the state is supplemented and displaced by supranational bodies, non-governmental organizations and local community groups' (Duffy 2006, 10). In other words, it implies placing a particular marginal geographical space under the control of sub-state and supra-state bodies. These changes in governance trends and the corresponding simultaneous *rescaling* in governance practices upward to the supranational and downward to the local have been noted in a number of other arenas, such as transboundary water management (Norman and Bakker 2005).

Because transboundary protected areas captured the imagination of both conservation bodies and states, the web of support for transboundary work extends on an international level to a number of different players. Research and management guidance, including the publication of many guidelines and case studies, have been sponsored by organizations as diverse as the Biodiversity Support Program, the International Tropical Timber Organization, Conservation International, the German development agency Invent, in addition to the usual global players such as The World Conservation Union (IUCN), the United Nations Educational, Scientific and Cultural Organization (UNESCO), as well as non-governmental organizations such as Conservation International, The World Wide Fund for Nature (WWF), EUROPARC and the Peace Parks Foundation. This diversity of partners, although the sign of an increase in interest also inevitably reflects a variety of different or conflicting perspectives and priorities. The International Tropical Timber Organization (ITTO) and the Peace Parks Foundation, for example, could be considered the organizational arms of commercial firms' intent on exploitation, via management plans, of the resources within these sites. The two examples in the next paragraph illustrate the paradoxes and contradictions these networks of diverse players can provoke.

During the 2003 World Parks Congress, a presentation by the Peace Parks Foundation of an aesthetically pleasing succession of images of wild Africa consisted wholly of animals trampling an Earth devoid of humans. Red sunsets and charismatic megafauna set the scene, branding the landscape as a product, accompanied by a soppy song in English. This was a landscape for Western and white consumers, not for local people. This was made all the more mordant by the fact that the Peace Parks Foundation, founded by Anton Rupert, a very wealthy South African tobacco magnate, had multiple business ventures in these areas, including in tourism (Wolmer 2003, 269). Another example illustrates the links between big business and conservation. A couple of years after the World Parks Congress conference, a very glossy coffee-table book titled *Transboundary Conservation: A New Vision for Protected Areas* (Mittermeier 2005) entirely funded by CEMEX, a global mining corporation, was produced by people linked to the Global Transboundary Protected Areas Network. This was published in collaboration with three non-governmental organizations, including Conservation International, an extremely wealthy and influential global non-governmental organization. In stark contrast to the declared policies of all these organizations in involving local populations, and as enshrined in international recommendations drafted during the previous World Parks Congress, the photos in this glossy book showed no people whatsoever, only charismatic fauna and fauna. In these two examples, it is *wild nature*, devoid of populations and presented as edenic and pure, that is constructed in sharp contrast to international political boundaries. But these are also spaces of boundlessness for global capital; spaces for the transnational circulation of investments, within which certain particular categories of people such as wealthy foreign tourists and investors are allowed to transcend political divisions.

This new balance of power between conservation and private interests is played out in concrete ways, beyond the simple financing of publications illustrated above. Encouraging partnerships between governments, the private sector and civil society in sustainable development and natural resource management was one of the major and most controversial themes of the World Summit on Sustainable Development held in Johannesburg in South Africa in 2002. This global recommendation is that public/private networks provide goods and services should operate in what were once the preserve of state controlled public sectors. This idea of public/private partnerships has a long established history in other areas of international environmental policy, such as forestry. It has therefore been argued that these ventures are more about opening up spaces for capital to make a profit from the conservation industry than they are about effective conservation policies.

Wolmer (2003), for instance, has written that one tension inherent in the governance of transboundary protected areas is the curious intersection of ecological and scientific discourses with discourses of global governance that emphasize the extension of neoliberal economic management. He notes that, in Africa, these are sold as the African dream-ticket combination of economic growth and environmental conservation and as a means of restoring investor confidence in the continent. With massive funds necessary for large-scale ecoregional planning initiatives, large conservation organizations are becoming increasingly business-like, developing funding strategies in conjunction with multilateral development banks and building corporate linkages. These funding structures as well as the managerial tools these large-scale and top-down initiatives inevitably privilege international actors, such as transnational conservation organizations, at the expense of grassroots or even national conservation organizations. Thus the private sector and international financial institutions have found common cause with global environmental organizations, with donor-recipient governments forced to adapt. This new melting of conservation and commercial goals throws up certain problems: Conservation and business do not necessarily pull in the same direction and when they do it can be to the detriment of stakeholders other than investors, particularly local communities.

The examples above suggest different answers about what nature is, whom it is for, and who benefits from its protection. Transboundary initiatives, well-funded by international conservation organizations and transnational corporations, promote a global idea of nature as something to be managed and defined globally. Yet these rely on an understanding of nature defined by the most powerful actors in each context, leading to a weakening of the nation-state as the most pertinent scale for environmental management. However, at the same time, research in Europe has shown that rather than weaken the state as a scale of identity politics, and create shared boundless understanding centred on nature, such projects paradoxically reinscribe the scale of the nation-state (Fall 2005). Nature, in these cases, is used as a further means of *othering* neighbours, of reinscribing differences presented as irreconcilable.

Embodying global natures?

In many transboundary spaces, a host of opposing and conflicting dominant stories coexist within administrations and organizations involved, created discursively along the way by individuals as part of the dynamic process of negotiating personal and collective identities. These are often tales – or myths – of animals crossing the border and getting shot, being poached or stolen, or are about mismanagement and bad policy choices, often associating the neighbouring country's policies with retrograde, unscientific practices. Dynamic relations between integration and distinction permeate such spaces. Individuals and groups such as park rangers and scientists construct nature, and speak about plants, animals or landscapes as somehow imbued with diverse national characteristics, irreconcilably different.

In the Alpi Marittime (Italy) / Mercantour (France) transboundary protected area, a story was told repeatedly about the lammergeyers – a type of vulture – being progressively reintroduced in the mountains. One bird was released each year, in alternate countries (Fall 2005). The birds were given either a French or an Italian name, depending on the country where they were released. French managers repeatedly noted that even the French birds inevitably went to live in Italy. Although this was always told tongue-in-cheek, the recurrence of the tale indicated its symbolic strength. The different versions hinted either at the nature-knows-no-boundaries myth (the birds ignore political designations) or else, more tellingly, as boundaries-reflect-fundamentally-different-natural-conditions (boundaries are natural). For the French managers, this implied that the neighbours had in practice stolen the French birds; for the Italians this meant that the birds preferred to live in Italy because of essential differences, because nature was more natural there. Birds, bears and beetles were not the only animals used as icons of difference. In the same area, the wolf was returning, moving into France from parks on the Italian side. Again, this iconic animal served to highlight differences in the way nature was constructed. Again, the animals were symbolically attributed a nationality: 'It's difficult when there are prickly subjects such as the wolf that we have in the parks, because this isn't an easy subject and so is really quite polemical. And in addition the wolves came from Italy, so it's not easy' (Interview in fall 2005 with a member of a French administration).

Thus not only were the wolves a problem in themselves, but they were additionally problematic because they were associated with *the other side*: This comment referred to the difficulty in convincing French shepherds that the wolves were natural and were not part of a *foreign* invasion. The usual accusation heard in offhand comments and debated in the local press was that ecologists had covertly released the wolves, threatening the local practice of keeping sheep in unguarded flocks on the high pastures. The idea that the wolves had been reintroduced, like the lammergeyers, was pervasive among shepherds and local politicians eager for their votes. One local mayor referred to the threat the wolf posed to the 'indigenous fauna' [*faune indigène*],[1] a populist appeal to biophysical imagery serving political ends. The wolves, not only unnatural but also foreign, were presented as having no place in the French mountains. This tale served to denaturalize them, making them legitimate targets for destruction in an area were hunting was prohibited. In this case, there was a clear recognition by one manager that while actual conditions differed, representations of nature were culturally-contingent and based on collective myths:

> On the Italian side they don't have the same problem at all in as far as they have many less flocks [of sheep] and also they have in their culture a cult of the wolf, Remus and Romulus, so it's the female wolf who raised Remus

---

1   Comment noted during the expert seminar in Entracque (Italy) and Menton (France) entitled 'Un parc européen pour le 21ème siècle [Un parco europeo per il 21° secolo]', on 14-15 October 1999.

and Romulus, it's a different culture, we have Little Red Riding Hood, it's not exactly the same! (Interview in fall 2005 with a member of a French administration)

On the ground, individuals struggled with the various notions, tempted by images of science-based boundlessness and yet distracted by the difficulties of implementing common policies. The performances of the animals were presented as self-evident, sufficient arguments for upholding a specific myth of boundless nature. After all, the argument went, how could you contest something that exists in the flesh? This intrinsic corporeality of animals as figures of embodied otherness gained further performative value when, in a different administration, animal nicknames were applied systematically to individuals they were trying to work with across the border. One German protected area manager was for example referred to as *le Blaireau* [the badger], a highly abusive term when used in this way in French, allegedly because of his pet dachshund (*Dachs* in German means badger) but more simply as a plain insult. Even if animal names are 'often harmlessly applied to individuals and typically invoked in jest' (Anderson 2000, 310), quite creatively in this case, the 'essential animality on which such superficial allusions rely reveal the potential for more significant boundary efforts. ... Discourses about animality have regularly found their way into institutional life and collective efforts at exclusion, the interrogation of which clarifies [how] they relate to European racist formations' (Anderson 2000, 310). The essential otherness of the other was reinforced by referring to innate bestiality, placing people as doubly *Other*: Beyond the bounds of humanity and beyond the (naturalized) political boundary.

In the following section, I will explore another example of this process of negation of the political in matters of nature around the issue of mobile and invasive species. Discourses of mobility, invasion and identity are further projected on to plants and animals, rehearsing in different ways issues of identity, boundaries and nature.

Transgressing political boundaries: mobile natures

In a context of accelerated world travel and increased global trade, the policing of living matter and the focus on good and bad circulations across national boundaries are part and parcel of globalization. This raises another aspect of transnational governance of natural resources: the increase in attention given within the conservation community to non-native species. Terms such as invasive, exotic, non-native, non-indigenous and alien are used to describe a *global swarming* of plants and animals, a term creatively coined with reference to climate change (Wittenberg 2005). These are seen as out-of-place and out-of-control species, far beyond their native habitats. This global problem is increasingly framed as a problem of security: the survival of native species versus the swarming success of new arrivals, of uninvited guests. These tales of swarming, invading, foreign, and out-of-control natures, with concurrent stories of a global homogenization of biodiversity that reduces local diversity and distinctiveness – the McDonaldization of nature (Wittenberg 2005) – is another arena where discourses of boundless nature and bounded states are rehearsed.

Governments have expressed their concern about this within the Convention on Biological Diversity (CBD), which calls on the Parties to 'prevent the introduction of, control or eradicate those alien species which threaten ecosystems, habitats or species' (CBD, Article 8h). A number of factors mean that people are both intentionally and inadvertently introducing so-called alien species that may become invasive: increasing globalization of the economy; people directly designing the kinds of ecosystems they find productive or congenial, for instance when they emigrate, incorporating species from other parts of the world; growing travel and trade coupled with weakening customs and quarantine controls. This can reduce biodiversity by crowding out a particular habitat since the new arrivals do not encounter natural predators or are able to colonize particular ecological niches crowding out other species.

The image of global swarming conjures up an idea of an out-of-place vital nature that continuously challenges political boundaries, and echoes Cresswell's (1996) notion of people and things being constructed as *out of place* through a variety of rhetorical processes. These global natures challenge the old European medieval idea of nature, viewed as a single entity in which each creature had its own place reflecting the divine and perfect order (Macnaghten and Urry 2000). Instead, species moving around the world in an uncontrolled manner challenge attempts to fix and assign nature to particular places, such as protected areas. This 'grunting, lowing, neighing, crowing, chirping, snarling, buzzing, self-replicating and world-altering avalanche' (Crosby 1986, 194) has been written about predominantly by authors focussing on former European colonies (Clark 2002; Crosby 1986; O'Brien 2006). This dynamism and boundary-defying characteristics 'suggest that nature has come in from the margins and may well be wreaking its cosmopolitan revenge upon human agents. Such humans are not the only species to move rapidly, indeterminately, chaotically and "naturally" from place to place' (Clark quoted in Macnaghten and Urry 2000, 9).

In this context, animals and even plants are scripted as dynamic, crossing boundaries, setting forth outside the spaces set aside for them, and beyond the spaces they were thought to belong to. *Global Black Lists* and *Watch lists* of plants, animals, fungi and invertebrates are produced by international bodies such as The World Conservation Union (IUCN) within the Invasive Species Specialist Group, or the Global Invasive Species Programme of the Convention on Biological Diversity, selecting what are seen as the worst offenders across the entire globe. At national levels, government bodies and concerned groups of scientists are also busy producing lists of species, each stemming from rehearsed fears of the rapid ecological collapse of local native species as new arrivals take over. In Switzerland, for example, the Swiss Commission for Wild Plant Conservation lists some of the following plants as the worst offenders: Canadian Pondweed, Himalayan Balsam, Japanese Honeysuckle, Himalayan Knotweed, Japanese Knotweed, Sakhalin Knotweed, Armenian Blackberry, South African Ragwort, Canadian Goldenrod,

Indian Pokeweed, Caucasian Stonecrop, Oxford Ragwort or even Chinese Windmill Palm.

How can a plant suddenly become *foreign*? Categories such as wild, native or alien, for instance, transport values beyond the intent of any individual or group of speakers, using the well-rehearsed *foreigner-as-threat* language that finds its way into conservation discussions, mainly by playing on feelings of insecurity. There is a naming convention in biology that serves to distinguish one particular species from another, but these common names are different from Latin names that have codified conventions for species and sub-species. Reading lists of common names of invasive species, it is impossible not to be struck by how out-of-place many of them are presented as being. They read like lists of people, like histories of human migration, as much as of plants – things that are usually seen to be static, not on the move. These names and assigned nationalities indicate that they have crossed international political boundaries, and are considered to be on the wrong side.

The underlying assumptions redraw and reinforce what is defined as natural and what isn't by simultaneously making different species appear more or less part of nature: Plants and animals are assigned native ranges and nationalities; plants are implicitly assigned a political and quasi-military plan of invasion; and nations need securing and protecting. One author has suggested that 'the "invasion" metaphor … is the most popular means of suggesting the potential for catastrophic damage resulting from the uncontrolled influx of exotics, and evokes a sense of insecurity that helps motivate action from an otherwise distracted public' (O'Brien 2006, 69).

While the antagonism against exotics need not be xenophobic and can be justified as a means of preserving the diversity of ecological systems from the homogenizing forces of globalization (O'Brien 2006, 73), it is important to understand that the science underpinning it is in itself contested, or at least more complicated than simple tales of swarming imply. Change is inextricably bound up with the dynamics of nature. Given the fact of past climate change and evolutionary responses to it by migration, as well as genome changes through mutation and natural selection, the whole idea of *native* species and invasion is absurd on a biological level. Yet many still fall into this trap. In a context of climate change, many biologists are arguing that the whole idea of invasive species should be abandoned. Many species will not be able to make the rapid adjustment that is needed if they are to survive changes in their ecosystem as conditions change. Given this, if a species migrates, then it may increase its chances of survival.

In this example, questions of biology are subtly shifted into other explicitly political arenas, subtly re-grounding the nation state as a natural, rational and therefore depoliticized geographical entity.

Conclusions

This chapter has meandered through the wide and exciting literature dealing with transboundary issues, boundaries, and the naturalization of politics. Key themes and debates about the changing role of borders and the rescaling of the state have been briefly evoked in parallel and in dialogue with the literature on transboundary protected areas and mobile, boundary-crossing species. Throughout, I have sought to illustrate how global natures and natural resources are made and performed in a variety of arenas and are not just things that require management. The issue therefore is not that political boundaries are a hindrance to rational scientific management, or that political boundaries are anti-nature or unnatural. Instead, by reintroducing the political into every step of the analysis, I have attempted to work beyond apparent binaries of nature versus society or culture – nature versus political boundaries – to suggest future fertile paths for research.

References

Ancel, J. (1938), *Géographie des Frontières* (Paris: Gallimard).

Anderson, K. (2001), 'The nature of race', in Castree, N. and Braun, B. (eds.), *Social Nature: theory, practice, and politics* (Oxford: Blackwell), 64-83.

Bakker, K. and Bridge, G. (2006), 'Material worlds? Resource geographies and the "matter of nature"', *Progress in Human Geography* 30:1, 5-27.

Bodénès, S. (1990), *Théorie limologique et identités frontalières: le cas franco-genevois*, PhD thesis (Genève: Université de Genève).

Braun, B. (2006), 'Environmental issues: global natures in the space of assemblage', *Progress in Human Geography* 30:5, 644-54.

Braun, B. (2005), 'Writing geographies of hope', *Antipode* 37:4, 834-41.

Braun, B. (2002), *The Intemperate Rainforest: Nature, Culture and Power on Canada's West Coast* (Minneapolis: University of Minnesota Press).

Braun, B. and Castree, N. (1998), *Remaking Reality: Nature at the Millenium* (London: Routledge).

Brunet, R. (1967), *Les phénomènes de discontinuités en géographie* (Paris: CNRS).

Castree, N. (2005), *Nature* (London and New York: Routledge).

Castree, N. (2001), 'Socializing nature: theory, practice and politics', in Castree, N. and Braun, B. (eds.), *Social Nature: Theory, Practice, and Politics* (Oxford: Blackwell), 1-21.

Castree, N. and MacMillan, T. (2004), 'Old news: representation and academic novelty', *Environment and Planning* 36:3, 469-80.

Castree, N. and Braun, B. (eds.)(2001), *Social Nature: Theory, Practice, and Politics* (Oxford: Blackwell).

Clark, N. (2000), 'Botanizing on the asphalt? The complex life of cosmopolitan bodies', *Body & Society* 6:12, 12-33.

Coates, P. (2007), *American Perceptions of Immigrant and Invasive Species: Strangers on the Land* (Berkeley: University of California Press).

Cresswell, T. (1996), *In Place/Out of Place: Geography, Ideology and Transgression* (Minneapolis: University of Minnesota Press).

Cronon, W. (1995), *Uncommon Ground: Rethinking the Human Place in Nature* (New York: Norton).

Crosby, A. (1986), *Ecological Imperialism* (Cambridge: Cambridge University Press).

Demeritt, D. (2001), 'Being Constructive about Nature', in Castree, N. and Braun, B. (eds.), *Social Nature: Theory, Practice, and Politics* (Oxford: Blackwell), 22-40.

Duffy, R. (2007), *Peace Parks*, unpublished.

Duffy, R. (2006), 'Global governance and environmental management: The politics of transfrontier conservation areas in Southern Africa', *Political Geography* 25:1, 89-112.

Duffy, R. (2005), 'The politics of global environmental governance: The powers and limitations of transfrontier conservation areas in Central America', *Review of International Studies* 31:1, 307-23.

Fall, J.J. (2005), *Drawing the Line: Nature, Hybridity, and Politics in Transboundary Spaces* (Aldershot: Ashgate).

Fall, J.J. (2002), 'Divide and rule: constructing human boundaries in "boundless nature"', *GeoJournal* 58:4, 243-51.

Foucher, M. (1991), *Fronts et Frontières: Un Tour du Monde Géopolitique* (Paris: Fayard).

Gay, J.-C. (1995), *Les Discontinuités spatiales* (Paris: Economica).

Haraway, D. (1991), *Simians, Cyborgs, and Women: The Reinvention of Nature* (London: Free Association Books).

Holdgate, M. (1999), *The Green Web* (London: Earthscan).

Hubert, J.-P. (1993), *La Discontinuité critique: Essai sur les principes a priori de la géographie humaine* (Paris: Publications de la Sorbonne).

IUCN (2007), *IUCN Protected Areas Programme* (Gland: World Commission on Protected Areas).

IUCN (1994), *Guidelines for Protected Area Management Categories* (Gland: IUCN).

Katerere, Y., Hill, R. and Moyo, S. (2001), 'A Critique of Transboundary Natural Resource Management in Southern Africa', *IUCN-ROSA Series on Transboundary Natural Resource Management* 1 (Southern Africa: IUCN).

Katz, C. (1998), 'Whose Nature, Whose Culture? Private Productions of Space and the 'Preservation' of Nature', in Braun, B. and Castree, N. (eds.), *Remaking Reality: Nature at the Millenium* (London: Routledge), 46-63.

Latour, B. (1997), *Nous n'avons jamais été modernes: Essai d'anthropologie symétrique* (Paris: La Découverte).

Macnaghten, P. and Urry, J. (2000), 'Bodies of nature: Introduction', *Body & Society* 6:1, 1-11.

Minghi, J.V. (1963), 'Boundary studies in political geography', *Annals of the Association of American Geographers* 53:3, 407-28.

Mittermeier, R.A., Kormos, C.F., Mittermeier, C.G., Gil, P.R., Sandwith, T. and Besançon, C. (eds.)(2005), *Transboundary conservation: a new vision for Protected Areas* (Mexico: CEMEX).

Norman, E. and Bakker, K. (2005), 'Drivers and Barriers of Cooperation in Transboundary Water Governance: A Case Study of Western Canada and the United States', *Report to the Walter and Duncan Gordon Foundation* (Toronto: The Walter and Duncan Gordon Foundation).

O'Brien, W. (2006), 'Exotic invasions, nativism, and ecological restoration: on the persistence of a contentious debate', *Ethics, Place and Environment* 9:1, 63-77.

Pounds, N.J.G. (1954), 'France and "les limites naturelles" from the Seventeenth to the Twentieth Centuries', *Annals of the Association of American Geographers* 44:1, 51-62.

Pounds, N.J.G. (1951), 'The origin of the idea of natural frontiers in France', *Annals of the Association of American Geographers* 41:2, 146-57.

Prescott, J.R.V. (1978), *Boundaries and Frontiers* (London: Croom Helm).

Raffestin, C. (1991), *Géopolitique et histoire* (Lausanne: Payot).

Raffestin, C. (1980), *Pour une géographie du pouvoir* (Paris: Litec).

Ramutsindela, M. (2007), *Transfrontier Conservation in Africa: At the Confluence of Capital, Politics and Nature* (Wallingford and Cambridge: CABI Publishing).

Ratzel, F. (1897, translated 1988), *Politische Geographie* (Paris: Economica).

UNEP-WCMC (2007), *World Database on Protected Areas* (United Nations Environmental Programme and World Conservation Monitoring Centre), available at <http://www.unep-wcmc.org/wdpa/>, accessed 2 May 2007.

Velasco-Graciet, H. (1998), *La frontière, le territoire et le lieu: Norme et transgression dans les Pyrénées occidentales*, PhD Thesis (Pau: Université de Pau et des Pays de l'Adour).

Walker, P.A. (2005), 'Political ecology: where is the ecology?', *Progress in Human Geography* 29:1, 73-82.

Whatmore, S. (2002), *Hybrid Geographies: Natures Cultures Spaces* (London: Sage Publications).

Wittenberg, R. (ed.)(2005), 'An Inventory of alien species and their threat to biodiversity and economy in Switzerland', *CABI Bioscience Switzerland Centre report* (Switzerland: CABI).

Wolmer, W. (2003), 'Transboundary conservation: The politics of ecological integrity in the Great Limpopo Transfrontier Park', *Journal of Southern African Studies* 29:1, 261-78.

Worboys, G. and Winkler, C. (2006), 'Natural Heritage', in Lockwood, M., Worboys, G.L. and Kothari, A. (eds.), *Managing Protected Areas: A Global Guide* (London: Earthscan).

Zbicz, D.C. (1999), *Transboundary Cooperation in Conservation: A Global Survey of Factors Influencing Cooperation between Internationally Adjoining Protected Areas* (Durham: Duke University).

Zierhofer, W. (2002), *Gesellschaft: Transformation eines Problems* (Oldenburg: BIS).

One Decade of Transfrontier Conservation Areas in Southern Africa

Sanette L.A. Ferreira

Introduction

In the past ten years of the post-colonial era, the establishment of so-called Transfrontier Conservation Areas (TFCAs)[1] has become an imaginative new strategy which, in principle, can play a very important role in the survival of wildlife in Southern Africa (Myers et al. 2000). These TFCAs can be seen as being part of a series of Transboundary Natural Resource Management (TBNRM) initiatives that attempt to facilitate or improve the management of natural resources across boundaries to the benefit of all parties in the area concerned (Griffin 2003). These areas give effect to the stated objectives of the Southern African Development Community (SADC) which aim for synergistic initiatives for economic, social and conservation benefits over the subcontinent (Kessler 2007). It is evident from the international literature that TFCAs also play a significant role in the mutual strengthening of the tourism industries of neighbouring countries (Chadwick 1996; de Villiers 1999; Ghimire 1997; Mabudafhasi 2008; Shonge 2006; Timothy 2001). They are indeed a key factor in increasing tourism in the entire Southern African region. This initiative is supposed to boost tourism, protect biodiversity, uplift communities and promote harmony in Southern Africa. Significantly, it provides a platform to address the individual parks' most serious threats to wildlife, for example illegal poaching and the loss and fragmentation of habitats (Cumming 1987; Holt-Biddle 1998; Kessler 2007).

However, while there is widespread excitement about and support for the establishment of these cross-border conservation areas, there are factors that constrain and undermine the realization of this *African dream* (Ferreira 2003). Direct land use conflicts over protected areas and their resources are the norm in many

---

1   Note that the words transborder, transboundary and transfrontier will be used interchangeably in the chapter.

parts of South Africa, and with poverty endemic in many of the country's rural areas, illegal encroachment on as well as hunting and harvesting in protected areas, are often part of the survival strategies of the poor (Ferreira 2004, 2006).

In this section on Nature and Environment, the author of Chapter 31 introduces the concept of Transfrontier Conservation Areas (TFCAs); describes the sub-continental contexts for TFCAs; demonstrates the link between conservation and tourism; provides a current status report on the establishment of TFCAs; and, before making some concluding remarks, discusses three critical issues that constrain the *African Dream* of a vast network of protected areas for conservation, travel and recreation.

Conceptual background of Transfrontier Conservation Areas (TFCAs)

A world system of protected areas is the dream of the Man And the Biosphere Programme (MAB) – an ongoing international effort to expand the extent and reinforce the relevance of the conservation of biological diversity, including genetic resources (Batisse 1997; Fall 2003, 2005). In 1996 the World Bank suggested an important conceptual shift away from the idea that transfrontier cooperation in the field of wildlife management should be restricted only to protected conservation areas such as national parks. They recommended greater emphasis on multiple land use[2] practices, especially by local communities, by introducing the concept of a TFCA (World Bank 1996). A TFCA has been defined by Sandwith et al. (2001, 3) as an

> area of land and/or sea that straddles one or more boundaries between states, sub-national units such as provinces or regions, autonomous areas and/ or areas beyond the limits of national sovereignty or jurisdiction, whose constituent parts are especially dedicated to the protection and maintenance of biological diversity, and of natural and associated cultural resources, and managed cooperatively through legal or other effective means.

TFCAs can be seen as building blocks in the world system of protected areas. TFCAs normally include core areas (transfrontier parks and/or other protected areas with a very high conservation status), surrounding buffer/support/transition zones (multiple use zones with different forms of land use and conservation status) and wildlife corridors connecting core areas (enabling the migration of wildlife and tourists).

---

2   Multiple land use encompasses varying mosaics of land use which incorporate private land, communal land, forest reserves and wildlife management areas including, where appropriate, the consumptive use of wildlife (Hanks 2000).

The development of TFCAs, commonly known as *Peace Parks*,[3] is one of the boldest cross-border initiatives currently unfolding in Southern Africa. The TFCA concept entails the creation of environments that allow for a balance between the improvement in the livelihoods of local populations and the sustainable use and protection of their regions' biodiversity (Kessler 2007). These interconnected, unfenced parks preserve and nurture whole bioregions rather than just ecosystems (Harmon 2006; Zbicz 2001).

The International Union for Conservation of Nature (ICUN) has been promoting the establishment of transfrontier conservation areas because of the many benefits purported to be associated with them (Hamilton et al. 1996). However, if TFCA initiatives are not done properly, they have the power to create new tensions and reinforce pre-existing divisions among interested parties, to the detriment of international peace and resource management.

In Southern Africa, governmental wildlife departments, Non-Governmental Organizations (NGOs) and donors began to plan international, cross-border parks and protected areas in the mid 1990s. The energy driving this initiative is vested in a non-profit NGO called the Peace Parks Foundation (PPF). This organization, founded on 1 February 1997, is the champion responsible for facilitating the establishment of TFCAs (Smith and de Klerk 2007). Although the concept of TFCAs is a timely one that makes sense to a large group of scientists, economists and conservationists, the parlous agricultural and economic situation of the sub-continent presents serious challenges to the SADC in creating an enabling environment to realize the *African Dream*. The next section sheds light on this state of affairs.

The sub-continental context for Transfrontier Conservation Areas

The Southern Africa Development Community (SADC) region is home to some of Africa's most valued faunal and floral species and wildlife sanctuaries and it also has a number of World Heritage Sites. The extremely high dependence of the region's economy on its varied natural resources and their availability is strongly influenced by human and climatic factors. Recent droughts and floods, and the prospect of accelerated global warming, reinforce the need for the SADC to consider options for a more sustainable management and sharing of the region's natural resources. According to Preston-Whyte and Watson (2005) the Peace Parks initiative that is striving to integrate conservation areas in close proximity to one another across national boundaries will substantially enhance the chance of biota adapting to climate change. But the regional economy tellingly faces many obstacles

---

3   These areas are also referred to as *transfrontier parks, binational parks, trinational parks* and *super parks*.

to such development (Table 31.1). As pressure on natural resources increases in the region due to human population growth, there is growing concern about the sustainability of transboundary resource use.

Table 31.1 Selected Basic Indicators for SADC – 2005

	Area Sq km ('000)	Population ('000)	GDP/ Capita US$	Imports US$ (million)	Exports US$ (million)
Angola	1247	15,116.0	1985.0	5,831.8	13,475.0
Botswana	582	1,711.0	4958.2	4,778.5	3,530.1
DR Congo	2,345	59,554.0	87.7	1,580.0	1,440.0
Lesotho	30	2,333.8	341.4	1,120.0	568.0
Madagascar	587	16,900.0	282.1	1,310.0	2,133.0
Malawi	118	11,938.0	258.1	926.0	484.0
Mauritius	2	1,233.0	5075.0	2,760.0	1,990.0
Mozambique	799	18,961.5	341.0	2,035.0	1,504.0
Namibia	824	2,001.0	2939.1	2,107.0	1,829.0
South Africa	1,219	46,586.6	5056.0	57,600.0	56,500.0
Swaziland	17	1,105.0	1629.0	1,470.0	1,780.0
Tanzania	945	35,300.0	319.0	2,430.0	1,452.0
Zambia	753	10,987.5	401.1	2,013.0	1,457.0
Zimbabwe	391	11,892.0	229.0	2,600.0	1,900.0

Source: Bank of Namibia (2006) and SADC (2008a).

Many resources are shared across international borders in the region, such as drinking water, and especially fish and wildlife populations because of their migrating behaviour. Every country of the SADC region listed in Table 31.1, with the exception of the two islands states (Madagascar and Mauritius), shares a major river basin with at least one neighbouring country (Shonge 2006). The SADC region is continually plagued by undesirable levels of chronic vulnerability of HIV/AIDS and food insecurity (SADC 2008a; USAID 2008). The sub-continent produces too little food, and food production per capita is declining by an annual average of at least one per cent (SADC 2008b). On average, over 40 per cent of the SADC population continue to live in abject poverty (SADC 2008b).

In the drier areas where rain-fed agriculture is practically impossible, either for cultivation of arable lands or for commercial livestock production, TFCAs have the potential to generate at least some income from tourism and contribute to a more sustainable system of land use (Hanks 2003). Whether mega-mergers of conservation areas can be successfully achieved where people are starving, is doubtful. According to John Hanks, Director of Transfrontier Conservation Initiatives in South Africa, national parks in Africa need sustained support of massive amounts of money for their survival (Bonthuys 2003). The conservation, efforts of 14 African countries are being drastically impeded by a shortage of funds. Certain conservation areas in Zambia and Angola exist only in name.

SADC countries boast a large wildlife population. It has been estimated that there are at least 300,000 elephants in the region and this number could reach 500,000 by 2020 (Soto 2007). In the Greater Limpopo Transfrontier Area alone, there are 147 mammal species, 507 species of birds, 114 of reptiles, 49 of fish, 34 of amphibians, and 336 of trees (Mulrooney 2008). The super park is home to several endangered animals such as rhinoceroses (both black and white), wild dogs, Juliana's golden moles, eptesicus bats, roan antelopes, sable antelopes and tsessebes (GLTP 2003). Wildlife-based tourism is by far the most important use of wildlife resources in the SADC region and has the potential to significantly contribute to poverty alleviation.

However, in most rural areas of the SADC region, bush meat consumption by humans remains the major and traditional source of animal protein (Bakarr et al. 2001). If we consider wildlife in its broader understanding as the combination of wild animals and wild plants, this offers an important and diverse range of consumable and commercial products which are indispensable to rural livelihoods in the region. These products include wild fruits, mushrooms, honey, fish and building materials. Viewed idealistically, the development of TFCAs will accelerate the harmonization of natural resources management policies and strategies, as well as promote the sustainable and compatible use of natural resources that straddle international boundaries in the SADC region.

Transfrontier conservation areas which form an important part of the resource base of the subcontinent contribute to the perception that Southern Africa as a whole is a single tourist destination (de Villiers 1994; Ferreira 2003; Pinnock 1996). New life is being breathed into the imaginative initiative that aims to see parts of Southern Africa turned into large networks of parklands spanning land on both sides of national boundaries. A prime driving force is the 2010 Soccer World Cup. The South African government sees the transfrontier parks as an ideal way of sharing the event's tourism and marketing benefits with the rest of the Southern African region. The ministers responsible for tourism and environmental affairs in the southernmost SADC countries (South Africa, Angola, Botswana, Lesotho, Mozambique, Namibia, Swaziland, Zambia and Zimbabwe) support the idea of a *univisa* to make it easier for tourists to travel between the various countries

(Marshall 2008). In the first week of May 2008, Southern African countries pooled their tourism expertise to promote the region as *Boundless Southern Africa.*[4]

Unfortunately, two weeks later a *xenophobic outburst* in South Africa shocked the international community. Very poor South Africans rallied against immigrants from neighbouring states (some of them refugees from Zimbabwe) (Pucci 2008; van Vuuren 2008). More than 60 immigrants were killed, reminding SADC leaders that the ministerial level vision of regional integration makes less sense at grass-roots level where peasants compete for scarce resources and job opportunities. Regrettably, the critical state of the subcontinent's economies clouds and constrains the prospects of a boundless Southern Africa and bedevils the process of TFCA establishment. Southern African conservation areas appear to be maturing faster as a discourse than as material practice, but even the discourse has its complex and contradictory currents. This dialogue manifests in the varied views about and the contested relationships between conservation and tourism development.

Conservation, tourism development and TFCAs

The conservation of natural resources and the provision of opportunities for tourism and recreation are often considered to be contradictory reasons for establishing transfrontier parks. Yet, the national parks movement seeks both to conserve nature and make it pay for itself (McNeely 1993) – a convincing argument for environmental conservation by many cash-strapped Third World governments (Telfer and Sharpley 2008). Wildlife is likely to be envisaged in terms of the potential income it can generate through safaris and game watching. This is sound economic justification for the retention and development of these activities. In addition, many of the sites chosen for parks are places of unique scenic beauty, providing spectacular settings for wildlife observation (McNeely 1993). From this perspective, sustainability is conceived as sustainable development and involves sustaining the environment for production (the creation of national parks) and consumption (for the enrichment and enjoyment of tourists) purposes. A report by the World Travel and Tourism Council (WTTC) states that tourism in Sub-Saharan Africa generated 73.6 billion U.S. dollars in 2005 (Cromberge 2005).

However, tourism has been criticized for perpetuating external dependency and reinforcing regional and international inequality. These processes are repeated at the local scale and they resonate among the debates on the role of nature-based tourism in rural development (Goodwin et al. 1998; Telfer and Sharpley 2008). Nevertheless, conservation and tourism development are undoubtedly vitally important in Southern Africa. Similarly, transborder approaches to policymaking and management enhance both conservation and tourism development.

---

4   Nine Southern African countries have chosen to support the *Boundless Southern African* brand as a means of showcasing the Transfrontier Conservation Areas during the 2010 Soccer World Cup in terms of tourism.

Apart from the greater efficiency provided by such cooperation and the increased conservation opportunities inherent in larger park units, such cooperation almost always improves the opportunities to manage according to nature's units – populations and ecosystems – rather than according to boundaries determined by political expediency (MacNeil et al. 1991). The wide-ranging discussion of *boundaries* as elements to be overcome institutionally, internationally and physically at the Fifth World Parks Congress in 2003, illustrates the momentum and the support for transfrontier initiatives (Fall 2005). These areas also promise increased tourist revenues since visitors would be free to benefit from the enhanced transnational space that the parks provide (Duffy 2001).

West European and North American scholars have for decades been promoting tourism as the salvation for Africa's economic woes, poverty and underdevelopment (Telfer and Sharpley 2008). The conservation of the continent's natural heritage (wildlife) is central to this advocacy. In fact, 'tourists are willing to pay an additional 100 U.S. dollars per day in order to protect elephants' (Bonner 1993, 219). The primary goal of a system of protected areas is to conserve biodiversity, but the economic contribution of such a system must not be underplayed. Biodiversity is undeniably a tourism product that gives South Africa a competitive edge globally (South Africa 2001). According to the *African Competitive Report* (Schwab and Sachs 1998) and the *South African Tourism Growth Strategy* (SAT 2007), Southern Africa's competitive advantage is almost entirely resource-based. The remaining wilderness of Africa may be its only hope for overcoming its poverty and competing in the global economy. Notwithstanding all the worthy efforts of the many who care about the environment, conservation must be made to pay for itself and be seen doing so. Otherwise, Africa's heritage will be destroyed and the cornerstone of its tourism potential will disappear.

The fusion of conservation and tourism development as mutually interdependent issues using protected areas and heritage sites as beacons in the formation of tourist routes, is clearly one of the methods by which wealth can be spread and conservation of what is precious can take place simultaneously (Ferreira 2004; Hanks 2003). This has positive implications for conservation through increased visitor numbers and awareness. But, more significantly, it integrates the value of heritage resources into the economies of the communities living in the vicinity of the resources, thus gaining the support of the inhabitants for conservation efforts. One of the most important goals in the establishment of a TFCA is that local communities will benefit from increased nature-based tourism to the area. In fact, community participation and the sharing of benefits have become a condition for funding by donor agencies (Ramutsindela 2004). The success of any wildlife park or conservation area is largely dependent on the communities' support and involvement.

The author of this chapter acknowledges the positive long-term effects of peaceful co-existence and friendly neighbourliness as well as all the positive ecological reasons why TFCAs could be the conservation dream of the twenty-first century. But, the risks attached to the dismantling of borders cannot be ignored. The development and the implementation of transfrontier parks will require a slow

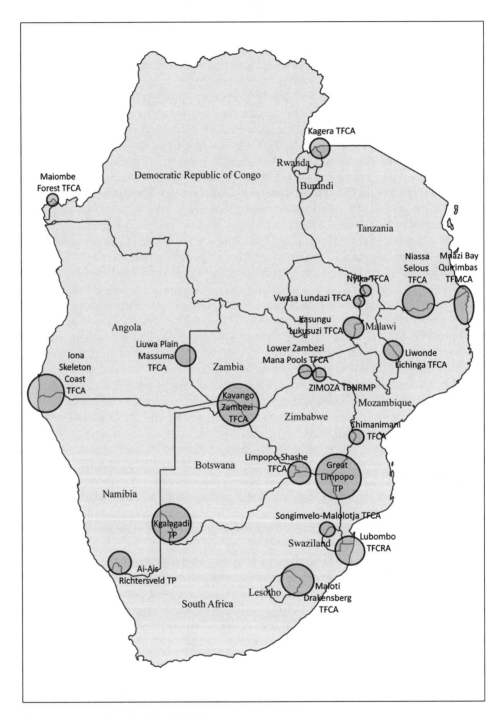

Figure 31.1 TFCAs in the SADC
Source: Peace Park Foundation 2008.

step-by-step approach. The role and actions of the Peace Parks Foundation (PPF 2002, 2004) – lobbying for political will, sourcing and management of donor funds, project planning and the implementation of the four pillars (signing of international agreements, training of wildlife managers, training of tourism managers and ensure accessibility to TFCAs) among others – place them in a unique position regarding conservation in Southern Africa (Smith and de Klerk 2007).

Current status of the TFCAs

In 1997 six TFCAs at the borders of South Africa were identified. In 2002, the SADC's ministers of environmental affairs and tourism commissioned a feasibility study which later reported 22 potential TFCA sites covering approximately 48 per cent of the total area formally protected by the continental SADC member states. These sites enjoy the support of the authorities in the region.

There are now 20 TFCAs at different stages of development (Figure 31.1 and Table 31.2), three having been established by treaties and six with Memoranda of Understanding (MoU) signed to facilitate their establishment. The other eleven are awaiting consultations to establish them as TFCAs. The continued increase in the number of TFCAs is a clear indication of the interest, buy-in and social acceptance – at least in a conceptual sense – of TFCAs as spaces for rural development.

The first transfrontier park launched in Southern Africa was the Kalagadi Transfrontier Park in 2000, which united the Gemsbok National Park in Botswana with the Kalahari Gemsbok National Park in South Africa. This union presented few problems, as only an unfenced dry riverbed separated the two parks and no people have to be resettled outside this area. The merging of the other transfrontier parks is markedly more complex and ambitious. The fact that only three transfrontier parks (Kgalagadi, Ai-Ais/Richterveld and The Great Limpopo) have been achieved so far, after a decade of intensive and dedicated championing by the PPF, is a clear indication of how complicated these mergers across boundaries in the SADC are.

The next section focuses on some critical issues to be resolved before the vast network of TFCAs can be accomplished. The Greater Limpopo Transfrontier Park (formerly known as the Gaza-Kruger-Gonarezhou Transfrontier Park) exemplifies how complex the fulfilment of this dream can be.

Table 31.2 Existing and Potential TFCAs within SADC Region

Name of TFCA (in alphabetical order)	Countries Involved	Status
1. Ai-Ais/Richtersveld Transfrontier Park	Namibia and South Africa	Treaty signed 1 August 2003
2. Chimanimani TFCA	Mozambique and Zimbabwe	MoU signed
3. Great Limpopo Transfrontier Park	Mozambique, South Africa and Zimbabwe	Treaty signed 9 December 2002
4. Iona-Skeleton Coast TFCA	Angola and Namibia	MoU signed 1 August 2003
5. Kagera TFCA	Rwanda / Tanzania	Conceptual phase
6. Kavango/Zambezi TFCA	Angola, Botswana, Namibia, Zambia and Zimbabwe	MoU developed, to be signed during 2006
7. Kgalagadi Transfrontier Park	Botswana and South Africa	Treaty signed May 2000
8. Limpopo/Shashe TFCA	Botswana, South Africa and Zimbabwe	MoU signed 13 June 2006
9. Lower Zambezi/Mana Pools TFCA	Zambia and Zimbabwe	Conceptual phase
10. Lubombo Transfrontier Conservation and Resource Area	Mozambique, South Africa and Swaziland	Trilateral Protocol signed 22 June 2000
11.Maiombe Forest TFCA	Angola / Congo Republic / Democratic Republic of Congo	Conceptual phase
12. Malawi/Zambia TFCA (combination of Nyika and Kasungu/Lukusuzi TFCAs)	Malawi and Zambia	MOU signed 13 August 2004
13. Maloti/Drakensberg Transfrontier Conservation and Development Area	Lesotho and South Africa	MOU signed 11 June 2001
14. Mnazi Bay /Quirimbas Transfrontier Marine Conservation Area	Mozambique and Tanzania	Conceptual phase
15. Mussuma/Liuwa Plain TFCA	Angola/ Namibia	Conceptual phase
16. Niassa /Selous TFCA	Mozambique and Tanzania	Conceptual phase
17. Nyika TFCA	Malawi / Zambia	Conceptual phase
18. Songimvelo/Malolotja TFCA	South Africa / Swaziland	Conceptual phase
19. Vwaza/Lundazi TFCA	Malawi / Zambia	Conceptual phase
20. ZIMOZA TFCA	Mozambique, Zambia and Zimbabwe	Conceptual phase

Source: Peace Park Foundation (2008).

Critical issues in TFCAs: the Greater Limpopo Transfrontier Conservation Area as a case study

For Mozambique, South Africa and Zimbabwe, the TFCA concept has evolved over a long period, dating back to 1938, when a Portuguese ecologist, Gomes de Sousa proposed that the Mozambican colonial administration negotiate with the neighbouring states to establish transfrontier parks. However, it was only after the Mozambique Peace Accord of 1992 that the Council of Ministers of Mozambique recommended that the feasibility of establishing some pilot TFCAs to be investigated. The Global Environmental Facility (GEF), through the World Bank, provided funds for the feasibility studies which examined the ecological, social, economic and political viability of the initiative. These studies were finalized in 1996 with a recommendation that the Gaza-Kruger-Gonarezhou be established.

The Greater Limpopo Transfrontier Park (GLTP), measuring 35,000 square kilometres, forms the core of a broader Greater Limpopo Transfrontier Conservation Area (GLTCA) (Figure 31.2). The GLTP includes the area currently known as Limpopo Park in Mozambique, the Kruger National Park, including the Makuleke region of that Park in South Africa and Zimbabwe's Gonarezhou National Park, as well as a Sengwe corridor of land which links Gonarezhou with the Kruger National Park. The larger region around the GLTP core comprises areas having different forms of conservation status. The area made up by the GLTCA, including the GLTP, comes to some 99,800 square kilometres (Braak 2000).

Although there are other factors (such as the effects of civil war, lack of conservation capacity, lack of infrastructure and tourism superstructure, smuggling, poaching, illegal immigration and trade in narcotics) constraining the realization of the Greater Limpopo Transfrontier Park, the discussion in this section focuses on three crucial issues, namely the position of communities in Limpopo National Park; the political and economic instability in Zimbabwe; and the uncompleted land restitution process (land claims) in the Kruger National Park.

Position of the communities in Limpopo National Park (LNP)

The GLTCA was initially intended to be a *multiple use area*, particularly with regard to its Mozambique parts where the aim was to help impoverished communities in communal land areas. Communal areas enclosed in the TFCA plan in Mozambique were even larger than the Coutanda 16 Wildlife Utilization Area, Zinave National Park and Bahine National Park combined (Ferreira 2004). Like other TFCAs, donor countries and park planners hoped that by using participatory approaches, local people would have a real stake in protecting wildlife (Duffy 1997). But what has come out of it was the creation of another game park (Wels and Draper 2002). Approximately thirty thousand Mozambicans live in the area targeted for the mega-park. The people who reside in the park can be divided in two groups. First, the approximately 6,500 people who live in the Shingwedzi catchment area,

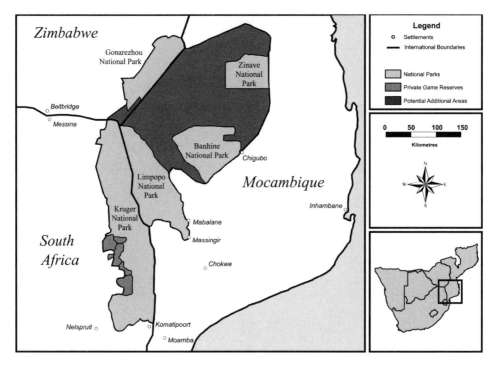

Figure 31.2 Greater Limpopo Transfrontier Park
Source: Peace Park Foundation 2008.

more or less in the middle of the park (Figure 31.3), will be affected directly by the development.

Second, a group of approximately 22,000 people living in the buffer zone (or support zone) along the Limpopo River will be affected minimally. These people will not have to leave their land and will continue with their livelihoods. Resettlement for those in the Singwedzi area is voluntary, but the government is encouraging them to move out of the park through incentives such as the provision of certain services and other *livelihood* opportunities (van Wyk 2004). The German Development Bank (KfW) will contribute six million Euros for assistance in this resettlement process. According to the park's director, Gilberto Vincente, 'there will be no forced removals à la the apartheid thinking in the early days of Kruger. This time we need to get it right. If we don't, they will return in no time at all and try to reclaim their land' (cited in Edwart-Smith 2005, 28). By May 2008, the relocation of people from the Shingwedzi area was uncompleted. States and conservation organizations are reluctant to grant sole control of landscapes, wildlife or forests to local villages or other local political entities in the LNP. Instead, the language of participatory conservation development schemes conceals the will of states and international agencies to take control and govern remote areas (Dzingiri 2004). Regarding the GLTP, the notion of bounded spaces immobilizes peasants

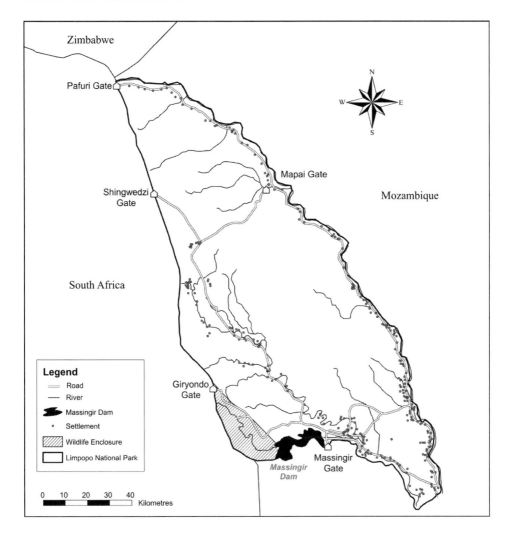

Figure 31.3 Limpopo National Park

Source: Peace Park Foundation 2008.

and denies them a future. As Spenceley (2003, 112) noted, 'ownership of land provides the strongest and most stable position for the rural poor to work from'. In Mozambique, the subsistence farming families in Manesa and Makandezulu are growing, and they are lamenting the situation that their children will have no place to live in the future.

Political and economic instability in Zimbabwe

Ecologically, the south-eastern part of Zimbabwe – the Gonarezhou National Park – is a basalt plain with a relatively low degree of biodiversity, but in a spatial and strategic sense this park is a very important *capstone* or link in the Southern African system of parks (Ferreira 2004). Gonarezhou Game Reserve was declared a national park in 1975 and subsequently the local Shangaan people were forced to resettle outside the park's boundaries – an act that has caused major discontent in the area ever since. Smouldering resentment among those previously evicted has recently led to the invasion of parts of Gonarezhou. This so-called *moving back* process has occurred in a stepwise fashion in a number of separate phases. By November 2000, sections of Gonarezhou were being occupied, cleared and set alight by residents of neighbouring villages (Sharman 2001). The situation deteriorated as the Agricultural and Rural Extension Department (Agritex) began demarcating and pegging out 520 plots for allocation within the park. Since November 2002, Josiah Hungwe, Governor of Masvingo Province, who had already been responsible for the invasion of privately owned wildlife conservancies, has been encouraging families of the previously evicted Shangaans, as well as opportunistic *war veterans* to take over 5,000 ha within Gonarezhou, north and south of the Runde River (Zwecker 2002). The invasion of Gonarezhou is just another occurrence in a line of crises in Zimbabwe's wildlife landscapes since the *fast-track* resettlement programme started to affect key conservation areas.

Although Gonarezhou's importance as a link in the proposed system of parks is vital, there are serious doubts whether this role can be realized, because of current conditions in Zimbabwe in general and their local manifestations in Gonarezhou Park. Since 2002 Zimbabwe has been facing severe socio-economic challenges. These have been compounded by hostile external and domestic environments, arising from the opposition to the government's ill-conceived and contentiously managed Land and Agrarian Reform Programme. Sanctions imposed on Zimbabwe have seen important sources of foreign exchange – donor funding for development projects, banks' lines of credit, and foreign direct and portfolio investment – dry up. This, coupled to a worsening export performance, has heightened failure to adequately provide fuel, electricity, food, medicine, spare parts, capital and equipment.

What is really sad about the current situation of Zimbabwe is that until the late 1990s, this country was a leader regarding issues of natural resource use in Africa's rural areas. It pioneered the concept of community involvement in the management of wildlife resources, a practice widely copied elsewhere on the continent. Under the transfrontier park and TFCA initiatives too, local community participation is through the promotion of Community-Based Natural Resource Management (CBNRM) in interstitial areas – a philosophy which Zimbabwe has long promoted through their Communal Areas Management Programme For Indigenous Resources (CAMPFIRE) (Manjengwa 2007; Ramutsindela 2004). Unfortunately, the political instability and its link with the social and economic crises of the country (2002 to 2008) have destroyed the proud heritage of the Zimbabwean conservation tradition. In Gonarezhou National Park, militants backed by Zimbabwe's ZANU-

PF have seized land (Ferreira 2004). The Mugabe regime initiated the chaotic land grab in Zimbabwe (Sokwanele 2005), with the result that the Gonarezhou National Park is now (2008) unfit to be included in the GLTP. What used to be a strictly controlled eco-zone of outstanding beauty, is now a ravaged piece of land with all its fences torn down and thousands of indigenous trees felled, leaving bare and empty plains where mixed woodlands once stood. The settlers have penetrated more than ten kilometres into Gonarezhou from what used to be the western boundary of the park. It is in this vast swathe of land that the greatest destruction of fauna and flora has occurred and apart from the cattle and the goats the only wildlife noticed in May 2008 was a herd of about 30 elephants (Rodrigues 2008).

The two fundamental requirements for the successful integration of Gonarezhou into the GLTP are positive attitudes and perceptions among its cross-border partners and the support and cooperation of the local population (Marshall 2003). Both requirements point to the crucial role the Zimbabwe government must play. The chaotic months following the March 2008 national elections in Zimbabwe, have reinforced the PPF's decision not to proceed with plans for a transfrontier park in this area until law and order has been restored in Zimbabwe under new political dispensation which is serious about tourism, employment and wildlife conservation.

Land claims in the Kruger National Park (KNP)

Since the end of apartheid and the introduction of a new political dispensation in South Africa in 1994, land reform has become a focal part of the country's new constitution. The main goal of land reform in South Africa is to give back land to those who were disadvantaged by being removed from land during the era of white dominance. In South Africa, land reform is nothing new, especially concerning conservation areas. The impact of land claims on conservation areas depends on two factors, namely effective nature conservation policy and the strength of central conservation authorities (Ahas 1999). According to South African law, restituted land with a certain conservation status has to remain in conservation as changes in land use practice are not allowed (South Africa 2003).

The Makuleke community lodged the first successful land claim in the KNP in 1995 (de Villiers 1999; Kepe 2003). They were compensated for their forced relocation in 1998 by the creation of a contractual park, and the land now owned by the Makuleke is managed by an agreement between the community and the National Parks Board (Reid et al. 2004).

The KNP is one of two profitable national parks in the South African parks system. Presently, communities are claiming large swathes of the northern KNP, including the headquarters at Skukuza and prime tourist attractions such as Letaba and Pretoriuskop. In February 2005, the *Mail & Guardian* broke the story that about one quarter of KNP was under claim – a revelation that shocked conservationists and transfrontier park developers (Mail and Guardian 2005). Two years later, Groenewald and Macleod (2007) reported that about 40 land claims lodged on parts of the KNP covering almost 50 per cent of the two-million-hectare park are on the table of the Limpopo Land Claims Commission. The commission is under great pressure to resolve the issue before the March 2008 deadline for settlement of all land claims. In October 2007, the commission was working on the settlement deal for the Makahane-Marithenga claim in the north of the park (Groenewald and Macleod 2007). The claim covered 89,773 hectares in the Punda Maria region and the settlement package negotiated included the stipulation that the area on the periphery of the KNP can be rezoned or demarcated. Claimed land falling within the demarcated area can be owned in full title without any developmental restrictions, but it remains part of the KNP. Conservationists expressed concern about the damage the land claims could inflict on the crown jewel of the country's tourism industry. One of their gravest concerns is that unscrupulous developers with an eye on creating luxury ecotourism or private estates could raise unrealizable expectations among poor communities. Another concern is the potentially negative effects of increased infrastructure for tourism on the ecology of the park.

Land claims in the KNP have to be resolved urgently, the better option being to keep the KNP intact, maintained its legal status as a national park, and for the government to compensate land claimants. Estimates of the cost of compensation range from less than 9 million to 4 billion U.S. dollars, depending on whether compensation is calculated with a similar formula as paid for agricultural land south of the park or prices charged for private tourism development on its western borders (Groenewald and Macleod 2007; The Citizen 2007). Eventually, it is all about affordability and the prioritization by the South African government of its socio-economic obligations.

Conclusions

In Southern Africa, Transfrontier Conservation Areas (TFCAs) provide an opportunity for achieving some of the primary aims of the Southern African Development Community (SADC), namely the promotion of self-sustaining development on the basis of collective self-reliance and the interdependence of member states, the achievement of sustainable utilization of natural resources, and the effective protection of the environment. However, in the case of the Greater Limpopo Transfrontier Park (GLTP) its success appears to depend to a considerable extent on the resolution of prevailing problems in the Zimbabwean part of the park, the successful relocation of communities living in the Singwedzi region of the Limpopo National Park (Mozambique) and the urgent settling of the land claims in the Kruger National Park. Generally speaking, it is likely that the GLTP will be a signal test case for the final part of the Nepad's vision, that is 'the promotion of regional co-operation for peace and socio-economic development between countries' (The Citizen 1999).

Despite some reservations, most conservationists agree that transfrontier conservation areas are Southern Africa's best hope of protecting its fragile environment and stimulating its tourism industry in such a way that it encourages fruitful collaboration among its neighbours without sacrificing the needs of rural communities. The value-added synergies of *going transboundary* have to outweigh the significant transaction costs, and participants in the process need to share a sense of interdependence (Griffin 2003). The key challenge is to develop policies, legislation and institutional structures that recognize wildlife as a viable land use option and allow community-based management and beneficiation of the wildlife resources.

It was only in the mid 1990s that the superimposition of colonial boundaries in Africa was challenged by the SADC vision of opening borders for conservation and tourism purposes. The regional identity of the SADC encapsulated by its new tourism brand – *Boundless Southern Africa* – may have some tourism-marketing significance but the xenophobic violence, which erupted in May 2008, has made it clear that the sharing of resources has proved to be an emotive and complicated issue, especially among the poorest of the poor citizens of South Africa (Pucci 2008). There are dire risks in sharing a natural resource base with neighbours. These risks must be identified, evaluated and properly managed as they cannot be simply ignored in a wave of euphoria over peace park awards.

Ultimately, conservation is about people. 'If you don't have sustainable development around the parks then people will have no interest in them and the parks will not survive' (Goodwin 1998: 29). For wildlife resources to be sustainable for the next 100 years, it will have to begin with the examination of the stereotypes and prejudices about *good* conservationists and *good* conservation practices. Despite the potential problems associated with natural areas – which are shared by two or more countries or other resource-owning jurisdictions – it is important to realize that in a world of complex interdependencies, states and other actors have two choices: cooperation or destruction.

References

Ahas, R. (1999), 'Impact of Land Reform on the Nature Conservation System in Estonia', *Discussion Paper* (Helsinki: University of Tartu).

Bakarr, M.I., da Fonseca, G.A.B., Mittermeier, R., Rylands, A.B. and Walker-Painemilla, K. (2001), 'Hunting and Bush Meat Utilization in the African Rain Forest: Perspectives Towards Blueprint for Conservation Action', *Advances in Applied Biodiversity Science* 2.

Batisse, M. (1997), 'Biosphere Reserves: A Challenge for Biodiversity Conservation and Regional Development', *Environment* 39:5, 10-15.

Bonner, R. (1993), *At the Hand of Man: Perils and Hope for Africa's Wildlife* (New York: Vintage Books).

Bonthuys, J. (2003), 'Parke van Papier – Geldknyp Verswelg Bewaringsgebiede in Africa', *Die Burger* 15 March 2003, 15.

Braak, L. (2000), *Conceptual Plan for the Establishment of the Proposed Gaza-Kruger-Gonarezhou Transfrontier Park* (Pretoria: SANparks).

Chadwick, D.H. (1996), 'A Place for Parks in the New South Africa', *National Geographic Magazine* 190, 2-27.

Cromberge, P. (2005), *Rural Communities Benefit from Game Parks – Increasing Drive to Integrate Conservation and Upliftment*, available at <http://www.peaceparks.org/new/news>, accessed 15 May 2008.

Cumming, D. (1987), 'Zimbabwe and the Conservation of the Black Rhino', *The Zimbabwe Science News* 21, 59-62.

de Villiers, B. (1999), *Peace Parks – The Way Ahead: International Experience and Indicators for Southern Africa* (Pretoria: Human Sciences Research Council).

de Villiers, N.N. (1994), *The Open Africa Initiative* (Claremont: OAI).

Dzingiri, V. (2004), *Disenfranchisement at Large Transfrontier Zones, Conservation and Local Livelihoods* (Harare: ICUN).

Duffy, R. (2001), 'Peace Parks: The Paradox of Globalisation', *Geopolitics* 6, 1-26.

Duffy, R. (1997), 'The Environmental Challenge to the Nation-State: Superparks and National Parks in Zimbabwe', *Journal of Southern African Studies* 23, 441-51.

Edwart-Smith, C. (2005), 'Greater Limpopo Transfrontier Park: Hope after all the Hype', *Drive Out* 10, 25-33.

Fall, J.J. (2005), *Drawing the Line: Nature, Hybridity and Politics in Transboundary Spaces* (Burlington: Ashgate).

Fall, J.J. (2003), 'Planning Protected Areas Across Boundaries: New Paradigms and Old Ghosts', *Journal of Sustainable Forestry* 17:1-2, 81-102.

Ferreira, S.L.A. (2006), 'Communities and Transfrontier Parks in Southern African Development Community: The Case of Limpopo National Park Mozambique', *South African Geographical Journal* 88:2, 166-76.

Ferreira, S.L.A. (2004), 'Problems Associated with Tourism Development in Southern Africa: The Case of Transfrontier Conservation Areas', *GeoJournal* 60, 301-10.

Ferreira, S.L.A. (2003), 'Sustainable Tourism in Post-colonial Southern Africa', *African Insight* 33, 36-42.

Ghimire, K.B. (1997), 'Emerging Mass Tourism in the South: Reflections on the Social Opportunities and Costs of National and Regional Tourism in Developing Countries', *UNRISD Discussion Paper* 85 (Geneva: United Nations).

Great Limpopo Transfrontier Park (GLTP) (2003), *About: Wildlife in the Area*, available at <http://www.greatlimpopopark.com>, accessed 18 November 2003.

Goodwin, H., Kent, I., Parker, K. and Walope, M. (1998), *Tourism, Conservation and Sustainable Development* (London: International Institute for Environment and Development).

Griffin, J.D. (2003), 'Dreams or Solid Means to Achieve Real Benefits for Real People', *Journal of Sustainable Forestry* 17:1-2, 229-30.

Groenewald, Y. and Macleod, F. (2007), 'Kruger Threatened by Land Claim', *Mail & Guardian online* 19 October 2007, available at <http://www.mg.co.za/article/2007-10-19-kruger-threatened-by-land-claim>, accessed 23 May 2008.

Hamilton, L.S., Mackay, J.C., Worboys, G.L., Jones, R.A. and Mason, G.B. (1996), *Transborder Protected Areas Cooperation* (Canberra: Australian Alps Liasion Committee and IUCN).

Hanks, J. (2003), 'Transfrontier Conservation Areas (TFCAs) in Southern Africa: Their Role in Conserving Biodiversity, Socioeconomic Development and Promoting a Culture of Peace', *Journal of Sustainable Forestry* 17:1-2, 127-48.

Hanks, J. (2000), 'Transfrontier Conservation Areas: Their Role in Socio-economic Development, Conserving Biodiversity and Promoting a Culture of Peace', *Paper read at the Transboundary Protected Areas Conference* (New Haven: Yale School of Forestry and Environmental Studies).

Harmon, D. (ed.)(2006), *People, Places, and Parks: Proceedings of the 2005 George Wright Society Conference on Parks, Protected Areas, and Cultural Sites* (Hancock: The George Wright Society).

Holt-Biddle, D. (1998), 'The Painted Wolf of Africa: Zimbabwe-wildlife, Conservation and Environment', *Africa and Wildlife* 6:3, 110.

Kepe, T., Wynberg, R. and Ellis, W. (2003), 'Land reform and biodiversity conservation in South Africa: Complementory or in conflict?', *Occasional Paper* 25.

Kessler, C. (2007), *Transfrontier Conservation Areas (TFCAS) – SADC's Choice to Promote Biodiversity Conservation and Economic Development* (Frankfurt: KfW-Development Bank).

Mabudafhasi, B. (2008), 'Wild Game Plan – Boundless Southern Africa', *Sunday Tribune* 11 May 2008.

MacNeil, J., Winsemius, P., and Yakushij, T. (1991), *Beyond Interdependence: The Meshing of the World's Economy and the Earth's Ecology* (Oxford: Oxford University Press).

Mail and Guardian (2005), 'Land Claim Could Kill Kruger', *Mail and Guardian* 24 February 2005, 18.

Manjengwa, J.M. (2007), 'Linking Environment and Development, Easier Said than Done: Learning from the Zimbawean Experience', *Development Southern Africa* 24:2, 225-39.

Marshall, L. (2008), *Transfrontier game reserves to share out 2010 benefits*, available at <http://www.ppf.org.za/news.php?pid=15&mid=748>, accessed 17 March 2008.

Marshall, L. (2003), 'Poaching Across Border Mars Idealistic Vision of New Transfrontier Park', *The Sunday Independent* 26 January 2003, 6.

McNeely, J.A. (1993), *Parks for Life: Report of the IVth World Congress on National Parks and protected Areas* (Gland: IUCN).

Mulrooney, B. (2008), 'A Century of Memories', *South African Country Life* 134, 38-44.

Myers, N., Mittermeier, R.A., Mittermeier, C.G., da Fonesca, G.A.B. and Jent, J. (2000), 'Biodiversity Hotspots for Conservation Priorities', *Nature* 403, 853-8.

Peace Parks Foundation (PPF) (2008), *Annual Review* (Stellenbosch: Peace Parks Foundation).

Peace Parks Foundation (PPF) (2004), *Conceptual Plan for the Establishment of the Proposed Gaza-Kruger Gonarezhou Transfrontier Park* (Stellenbosch: Peace Parks Foundation).

Peace Parks Foundation (PPF) (2002), *Annual Review* (Stellenbosch: Peace Parks Foundation).

Pinnock, D. (1996), 'Superparks: The Impossible Dream?', *Getaway* 8, 88-97.

Preston-Whyte, R.A. and Watson, H.K (2005), 'Nature, Tourism and Climatic Change in Southern Africa', in Hall, C.M. and Higham, J.E.S. (eds.), *Tourism Recreation and Climate Change* (Clevedon: Channel View Publications).

Pucci, R. (2008), 'South Africa: Xenophobic Attacks', *Info USA Magazine*, available at <http://www.infousamagazine.com >, accessed 19 May 2008.

Ramutsindela, M. (2004), *Parks and People in Postcolonial Societies. Experiences in Southern Africa* (Dordrecht: Kluwer Academic Publisher).

Reid, H., Fig, D., Magome, H. and Leader-Williams, N. (2004). 'Co-Management of Contractual National Parks in South Africa: Lessons from Australia', *Conservation and Society* 2:2, 377-409.

Reid, H. and Turner, S. (2004), The Richtersveld and Makuleke Contractual Parks in South Africa: 'Win-Win for Communities and Conservation?', *Rights, Resources & Rural Development: Community-Based Natural Resource Management in Southern Africa* 16, 223-34.

Rodrigues, J. (2008), *Oh Zimbabwe! Part Two*, available at <http://www.tirzahsworld. blogspot.com>, accessed 30 May 2008.

Sandwith, T., Shine C., Hamilton, L. and Sheppard, D. (2001), *Transboundary Protected Areas for Peace and Cooperation* (London: Gland and Cambridge).

Sharman, J. (2001), 'Invasions Threaten Peace Park', *Weekly Mail and Guardian* 1 November 2001, 17.

Schwab, K. and Sachs, J.D. (1998), *The Africa Competitive Report 1998* (Cambridge: The World Economic Forum and the Harvard Institute for International Development).

Shonge, L.B. (2006), *The Implications of Transfrontier Conservation Areas (TFCAs): A Comparative Policy Analysis Study of Sustainable Development in South Africa Between the Greater Limpopo Transfrontier Conservation Area and the Lubombo Transfrontier Area*, MA Thesis (Pretoria: University of Pretoria).

Smith, N. and de Klerk, H. (2007), 'Geo-information Pyramids for Up-to-date and Flexible Conservation Plans: A Case Study for Transfrontier Conservation Areas', *South African Journal of Science* 103:11, 442-8.

Sokwanele (2005), 'Zimbabwe: Transfrontier Park and World Heritage Site under threat Sokwanele', *Sokwanele - Zvakwana - Enough is Enough* 1 August 2005, available at <http://www.sokwanele.com/articles/sokwanele/transfrontierpark andworldheritagesiteunderthreat_1august2005.html>, accessed 18 May 2008.

Soto, B. (2007), *Mozambique SADC Wildlife: SADC Approves Regional Elephant Management Plan*, available at <http://www.apanews.net/apa.php?page=afric>, accessed 22 May 2008.

South Africa (2003), *National Environmental Management: Protected Areas Act 57 of 2003 as amended by National Environmental Management: Protected Areas Amendment Act 31 of 2004* (Pretoria: Department of Environmental Affairs and Tourism).

South Africa (2001), *A Bioregional Approach to South Africa's Protected Areas* (Pretoria: Department of Environmental Affairs and Tourism).

South African Tourism (SAT) (2007), *Tourism Growth Strategy*, third edition (Johannesburg: South African Tourism).

Southern African Development Community (SADC) (2008a), *Social and Economic Indicators*, available at <http://www.sadc.int/summit/sadc_info/socio_economic.php>, accessed 12 May 2008.

Southern African Development Community SADC (2008b), *SADC Declaration on Poverty Eradication and Sustainable Development on 20 April 2008*, available at <http://www.fews.net/south>, accessed 19 May 2008.

Spenceley, A. (2003), *Tourism, Local Livelihoods and the Private Sector in South Africa: Case Studies on the growing role of the private sector in natural resource management*, Research Paper 8 (Sussex: Institute of Development Studies).

Telfer, D.J. and Sharpley, R. (2008), *Tourism and Development in the Developing World* (London: Routledge).

The Citizen (2007), 'Land Claims on Half of Kruger National Park: 40 Lodge only Four Sorted out', *The Citizen (South Africa)* 19 September 2007, 7.

The Citizen (1999), 'SADC to Formulate an Environmental Policy', *The Citizen (Johannesburg)* 10 October 1999, 6.

Timothy, D. (2001), *Tourism and Political Boundaries* (London: Routledge).

USAID (2008), *Southern Africa food security outlook - October 2007 to March 2008*, available at <http://www.fews.net/south>, accessed 19 May 2008.

van Vuuren, M.E. (2008), 'Vermoë om Massa Geweld te Keer Helfte Minder', *Rapport* 25 May 2008, 4.

van Wyk, A.W. (2004), *Personal communication* 5 February 2004.

Wels, H. and Draper, M. (2002), 'Modern Myths and Primitivist Powerplay: Community Development in Transfrontier Conservation Areas in South Africa', *paper presented to the International Association for the Study of Common Property Meetings* 17-21 June 2002.

World Bank (1996), 'Mozambique: Transfrontier Conservation Areas Pilot and Institutional Strengthening Project', *World Bank Report* 15534-MOZ (Washington: The World Bank).

Zbicz, D. (2001), *List of Transfrontier Protected Area Complexes* (Geneva: ICUN/WCPA).

Zwecker, W. (2002), 'Zimbabwe Wolk oor Oorgrensparke - Beleggers Skrikkerig vir Afrika Droom', *Beeld* 10 December 2002, 8.

The Delimitation of
Maritime Boundaries:
An Incomplete Mosaic

Clive Schofield

Introduction

Recent decades have witnessed a tremendous extension of coastal state claims to maritime jurisdiction offshore. Where once coastal state claims were restricted to a relatively narrow band of waters, generally out to three nautical miles (nm) from the coast, now claims of 200nm breadth are commonplace and in numerous cases may extend even further offshore.[1] Accordingly, there has been a significant proliferation in overlapping claims to maritime jurisdiction and potential maritime boundaries. The stakes have also been raised as valuable marine resources within these claimed maritime spaces, which are of increasing significance to coastal states, are at issue.

The majority of these 'new' potential maritime boundaries have yet to be delimited, in large part because of the relatively recent nature of these more expansive maritime claims. Broad and often ambiguously defined claims of relatively recent vintage, allied to the limited guidance provided by the relevant law of the sea rules relating to delimitation has led to numerous overlapping claims and maritime boundary disputes. This chapter examines a number of the complex and contentious issues that have emerged in the ongoing process of the delimitation of maritime boundaries and thus the completion of the 'mosaic' of maritime boundaries worldwide. The fundamental purpose and value of maritime boundary delimitation is outlined at the outset. The importance of maritime delimitation to coastal states is underpinned by the enormous extension of the spatial extent of national maritime claims and thus the important marine resources that they encompass. The chapter then provides an assessment of the state-of-play

---

1   It is recognized that, technically, the correct abbreviation for a nautical mile is 'M', with the 'nm' referring to nanometres. However, 'nm' is widely used by many authorities (for example the UN Office of Ocean Affairs and the Law of the Sea) and appears to cause less confusion than 'M', which is often taken to be an abbreviation for metres.

in terms of the maritime political map of the world, reviews the key principles and methods of maritime boundary delimitation and explores the principle causes of maritime boundary disputes. Two key issues for contemporary research on maritime boundary delimitation are then examined, namely baselines issues, especially the vulnerability of 'normal' low-water line baselines to the impacts of climate change induced sea level rise and contentious disputes related to islands, both in terms of sovereignty over such features and in respect of their role in maritime boundary delimitation. Some concluding thoughts are then offered.

The Purpose and Value of Maritime Boundary Delimitation

Fundamentally, the delimitation of maritime boundaries provides clarity and certainty to all maritime states and users and helps to minimize the risk of friction and conflict by eliminating a source of bi-lateral and multilateral dispute. This can, arguably, remove barriers to cooperation, thus enhancing the potential for the sustainable management and governance of the oceans. This, in turn, has the potential to lead to the conservation of marine resources and the environment as well as enhanced maritime and economic security for both coastal and user states.

Conversely, lack of delimitation can often lead to the persistence of extensive overlapping claims to maritime jurisdiction and this situation tends to exacerbate management problems. While a distinction can be drawn between merely undelimited maritime boundaries and active maritime boundary disputes, the existence of broad areas of competing claims to the same maritime space is problematic. Where overlapping maritime claims exist, the resultant uncertainty over jurisdiction may complicate ocean resource management. With regard to living resources, the oceans remain an important source of living resources, with fisheries representing a major industry and playing a key food security role for many coastal states (despite increasing rates of stock depletion). The sustainable management of, for example, fish stocks, can be severely hampered through, at the least, uncoordinated policies and, at the more severe end of the spectrum, potentially destructive and unsustainable competition for access to the resources in question. Such activities can lead to confrontation between rival fishing fleets and such friction can lead to the involvement of the armed forces of the coastal states concerned with the attendant potential for incidents, clashes and ultimately escalation towards conflict. In short, rival maritime claims can act as a major irritant in bilateral, and indeed multilateral, relations.

Offshore areas are also an increasingly important source of non-living resources such as hydrocarbons. This is especially significant in the context of dwindling near and on-shore reserves, growing populations and generally therefore resource demands, and improved technology increasingly allowing economically viable exploration and exploitation of offshore oil and gas resources in more hostile conditions including deeper waters further offshore. In this context it is important to note that the presence of overlapping claims generally tends to prevent access to any hydrocarbon resources that may be present in the disputed area. International oil and gas companies tend to be extremely reluctant to invest the enormous sums necessary to conduct offshore exploration, let alone exploitation, operations in the absence of fiscal and legal certainty and continuity. Seabed energy resources located in disputed areas, which could potentially have a crucial role to play in the economic well-being, energy security and political stability of the coastal states involved, therefore tend to remain untapped in the absence of maritime boundary delimitation or, alternatively, agreement on joint development. While discussion of marine resources tends to be framed in terms of access to fish and oil, it should be noted that these are not the only resources that the oceans have to offer. A range of other biological and mineral resources exist which are increasingly being exploited. Of particular note here is the growing interest and use of marine genetic resources and the collection and utilization of minerals such as phosphorites, evaporates, polymetallic sulphides, and non-traditional seabed hydrocarbons such as gas hydrates (Schofield and Arsana 2009, 51-4). While the exploitation of some of these 'new' marine resources such as hydrates does not appear to be viable yet, efforts to develop others, such as sulphides are being actively pursued In many cases, however, the actual presence of ocean resources is not really the critical issue. Instead the vital factor is the *perception* on the part of the governments concerned that valuable resources and thus the state's vital economic interests are at stake.

Furthermore, the jurisdictional uncertainty inherent in areas of overlapping claims has the potential to undermine maritime security as, where jurisdiction is contested, it follows that coastal state rights with regard to surveillance and enforcement will remain similarly uncertain. Additionally, such a scenario tends to place rival naval vessels in close proximity to one another providing the potential for incidents and even confrontation between them as each side exerts its enforcement rights in what they regard as rightfully 'their' maritime space (Schofield 2005).

The above is not to suggest that the delimitation of maritime boundaries is some kind of panacea which will necessarily engender transboundary maritime cooperation among neighbouring states. Indeed, it can be argued that arbitrary, invisible political boundaries do not readily fit the continuous, fluid ocean environment. Many marine living resources similarly pay scant regard to maritime boundaries and it is also the case that many marine activities are transboundary and transnational in character. Nonetheless, the delimitation of maritime boundaries does provide a clear jurisdictional framework for cooperation. Importantly, even if spatially bounded national maritime spaces are not necessarily the ideal or only way to achieve sustainable oceans management and governance, they are one way to achieve these ends and, crucially, represent the approach overwhelmingly favoured by states.

Overall, it can be argued that the delimitation of maritime boundaries provides clarity and certainty to all maritime states and users, helps to minimize the risk of friction and conflict by eliminating a source of bi- and multilateral dispute and removes barriers to cooperation, thus enhancing the potential for cooperative maritime enforcement and enhanced maritime security. Maritime boundary delimitation therefore assists in providing a stable maritime regime, which helps to assure the freedom of navigation that is essential to the functioning of the global economy as over 80 per cent of global trade by volume is transported by sea

(UNCTAD 2008, 8). Additionally, and no less importantly, maritime delimitation can also help to facilitate the sustainable management and preservation of important ocean resources, assist in protecting the marine environment and enhance global oceans governance.

An Incomplete Mosaic

The United Nations Convention on the Law of the Sea (LOSC) of 1982 (United Nations 1983) provides the generally accepted legal framework governing maritime jurisdictional claims and the delimitation of maritime boundaries between national maritime zones. LOSC has gained widespread international recognition and at the time of writing 161 states had become parties to it (United Nations 2010). A key achievement of LOSC was agreement on spatial limits to national claims to maritime jurisdiction. Consequently, maritime claims are predominantly defined as extending to a set distance from baselines along the coast (see below). In accordance with the terms of LOSC, the breadth of a coastal state's territorial sea is not to exceed 12nm from baselines along the coast (LOSC, Articles 3 and 4). Previously, the issue of the appropriate breadth of the territorial sea had been a particularly contentious one so the LOSC definition of a 12nm territorial sea limit represented significant progress. In accordance with the provisions of LOSC, a coastal state's contiguous zone may not extend beyond 24nm from the baselines from which the breadth of the territorial sea is measured (LOSC, Article 33(2)). As most states claim a 12nm breadth territorial sea the contiguous zone, if claimed, generally extends from the 12nm to 24nm limits as measured from baselines along the coast. LOSC also introduced the concept of the exclusive economic zone (EEZ) which 'shall not extend beyond 200 nautical miles from the baselines from which the breadth of the territorial sea is measured' (LOSC, Article 57). As noted above, most coastal states claim a 12nm territorial sea, meaning that the actual breadth of the EEZ is usually 188nm seaward of territorial sea limits. Claims to contiguous zone and EEZ rights therefore overlap – wholly so for the contiguous zone, partially for the EEZ. Accordingly, the key factors required for the definition of the outer limits of each of the international zones of maritime jurisdiction is an understanding of the location of the baseline, coupled with a geodetically robust (that is, precise) means of calculating the relevant distance measurements of 12nm, 24nm and 200nm.

The definition of the outer limits of the continental shelf is a more complex task, specifically where areas of 'extended' or 'outer' continental shelf seawards of the 200 nautical mile limit are under consideration (LOSC, Article 76). This is because extended continental shelf entitlements are not determined solely by reference to a distance formula. Where the continental margin extends beyond 200nm from a state's baselines, the coastal state may be able to assert rights over that part of the continental shelf beyond the 200nm limit that forms part of its natural prolongation. However, in order to fulfil the complex series of criteria laid down in Article 76 and prepare a submission on extended continental shelf rights to the relevant

United Nations technical body, the Commission on the Limits of the Continental Shelf (CLCS), a coastal state is therefore required to gather information related to the morphology of its continental margin and its geological characteristics as well as bathymetric information relating to water depth. Additionally, distance measurements are necessary in order to determine, for example, the location of 200nm and 350nm limit lines (Schofield and Arsana 2009, 31-35).

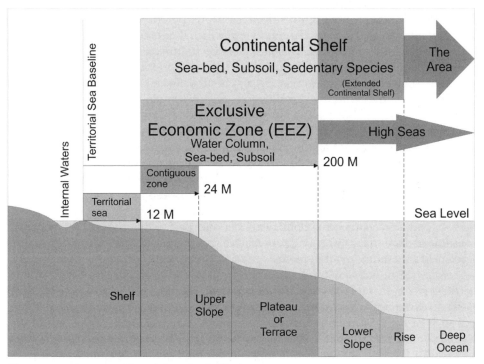

Figure 32.1 Zones of Maritime Jurisdiction
Source: adapted from Geoscience Australia 2010.

A key consequence of this enormous extension of maritime claims seawards has been the creation of a multitude of 'new' potential maritime political boundaries. Wherever a coastal state's claims to maritime space abut or overlap either an opposite coastal state's maritime area or an adjacent coastal state's maritime area, a potential maritime boundary situation will exist. As a consequence of the advance of national maritime claims offshore, coastal states 400nm or more distant from one another suddenly found themselves to be maritime neighbours with potentially overlapping maritime claims to jurisdiction. Indeed, in the case of extended continental shelf claims coastal states whose nearest land territories are located in excess of 700nm distant from one another may have a potential maritime boundary between them.

Reaching a clear understanding of the number of potential maritime boundaries worldwide can, however, be challenging as certain assumptions need to be made. For example, if maritime boundaries composed of multiple distinct segments are treated as one boundary (for example treating the potential delimitations between Canada and the United States as one maritime boundary), a figure of 366 can be reached. However, if each individual boundary segment is counted as a maritime boundary (Canada and the United States on this basis contributing four to the total), the figure rises dramatically to 434 maritime boundaries (Pratt 2008; Prescott and Schofield 2005, 244). These figures do not include potential maritime boundaries beyond 200nm from the coast, the number of which that may be required is difficult to predict given that many coastal states have yet to finalize the outer limits of their extended continental shelf areas.

While significant progress has clearly been achieved in the delimitation of maritime boundaries with many contentious disputes having been resolved, the task is a daunting one and is currently far from completion (Charney and Alexander 1993 and 1998; Charney and Smith 2002; Colson and Smith 2005; Colson and Smith 2011). Given the relatively recent nature of the maritime claims in question, many of which have only been advanced since the 1970s onwards, it is unsurprising that the maritime political map of the world, in sharp contrast to the terrestrial political map, is far short of completion (Grundy-Warr and Schofield 2005). It is also worth noting that many of the maritime boundary agreements that have been reached among coastal states are only partial in character – relating to either only part of the length of the potential maritime or dealing with only one zone, such as continental shelf. Additionally, many agreements are interim, not in force or relating to the same boundary. Furthermore, numerous additional 'new' maritime boundaries and extensive areas of overlapping claims have been created as a consequence of recently articulated coastal state assertions in respect of areas of so-called 'outer' or 'extended' continental shelf located seawards of the 200nm limit. Overall, it is safe to state that fewer than half of the potential maritime boundaries around the world have been even partially delimited (Pratt 2008). The incomplete nature of the maritime boundary delimitation picture has excited, and continues to attract, considerable research attention.

The Delimitation of Maritime Boundaries

Principles and methods of maritime boundary delimitation

The provisions of LOSC governing the delimitation of maritime boundaries provide limited guidance as to how such undelimited boundaries may be defined. In relation to the delimitation of the territorial sea, Article 15 of LOSC does offer a clear preference for the use of an equidistance or median line. This does not apply, however, if the states concerned agree to the contrary or there exists an 'historic title or other special circumstances' in the area to be delimited which justify a departure from the equidistance line. Under the 1958 Conventions, delimitation of the continental shelf was also to be effected by the use of median lines unless, similarly, an agreement to the contrary or 'special circumstances' existed that justified an alternative approach. However, under LOSC there was a distinct shift away from equidistance as a preferred method of maritime delimitation. Articles 74 and 83 of LOSC, dealing with delimitation of the continental shelf and EEZ respectively, merely provide, in identical general terms, that agreements should be reached on the basis of international law in order to achieve 'an equitable solution'. No preferred method of delimitation is indicated and thus the LOSC's 'rules' on delimitation, such as they are, can be viewed as ambiguous and open to conflicting interpretation and thus dispute. Indeed, as the Arbitral Tribunal in the Eritrea-Yemen Arbitration stated in reference to the drafting of Article 83, this was 'a last minute endeavour … to get agreement on a very controversial matter', and therefore, 'consciously designed to decide as little as possible' (Eritrea-Yemen Arbitration, Second Phase, para. 116).

In order to achieve delimitation of the continental shelf and/or EEZ in accordance with LOSC, therefore, a theoretically limitless list of potentially relevant circumstances needs to be taken into consideration in the delimitation equation in order to reach the goal of an equitable result. Nonetheless, it has become abundantly clear from the practice of coastal states, allied to the rulings of international courts and tribunals that geography, and particularly coastal geography, has a critical role in the delimitation of maritime boundaries. Aspects of coastal geography that have proved especially influential include the configuration of the coasts under consideration, the relative coastal length and the potential impact of outstanding geographical features, notably islands (see below) (Prescott and Schofield 2005, 221-2).

The salient role of coastal geography in maritime boundary delimitation is linked to the widespread use of equidistant lines. While, as noted, there has been a shift away from equidistance as a preferred method of delimitation over time in the law of the sea, not least because in certain circumstances the application of strict equidistance can lead to clearly inequitable results, equidistance has nonetheless proved extremely popular as a basis for maritime boundary delimitation in practice. The construction of equidistance lines offer considerable advantages – if there is agreement on the baselines to be used (see below), there is only one strict equidistance line and this provides the appeal of mathematical certainty and objectivity as well as affording coastal states with the not inconsiderable attraction of jurisdiction over those maritime areas closest to them. Equidistance lines can also be flexibly applied and may be simplified, adjusted or modified to take specific geographical circumstances into account (Carleton and Schofield 2002, 7-31; Legault and Hankey 1993; Prescott and Schofield 2005, 236). In practice the equidistance method has proved more popular than any alternative method by far and most agreed maritime boundaries are based on some form of equidistance (Legault and Hankey 1993, 205). Consequently, equidistance lines are often constructed at least as a means of assessing a maritime boundary situation or as the starting point for discussions in the context of maritime boundary negotiations. Such lines have also frequently been adopted as the basis for the final delimitation line. Furthermore, it is the case that in recent cases the International Court of Justice's (ICJ) approach has been to construct an equidistance line as a provisional delimitation line in the first instance. Indeed, in its most recent judgment in the Black Sea Case between Romania and Ukraine, the Court was explicit in stating that '[i]n keeping with its settled jurisprudence on maritime delimitation', a provisional delimitation line should be established consisting of an equidistance line 'unless there are compelling reasons that make this unfeasible in the particular case' (ICJ 2009, 116-8). Once a provisional, equidistance based boundary line has been constructed, the ICJ's practice has then been to determine whether there exist any reasons to modify the provisional equidistance line in order to achieve an equitable result (Prescott and Schofield 2005, 240-1).

Overlapping claims and maritime boundary disputes

Perhaps inevitably, just as many 'new' maritime boundaries have been created, there has likewise been a proliferation in overlapping claims to maritime jurisdiction and maritime boundary disputes. The exact scope of such overlapping claims areas is, however, often difficult to distinguish. This is frequently because many maritime claims are ill-defined, simply consisting of broad distance-based claims, for instance to a 200nm EEZ. Only relatively rarely do coastal states provide unilateral definitions as to the precise extent of their maritime jurisdictional claims. A degree of what might be characterized as educated guess work is therefore necessary in the analysis of coastal state claims to maritime jurisdiction.

Whilst in the past maritime boundary delimitation, confined in scope to such a relatively narrow band of inshore waters this is clearly no longer the case. Not only are the maritime zones subject to delimitation themselves far broader but offshore activities have become considerably more diverse and offshore resources appreciably more important to the economic well-being of coastal states. In addition to the considerably greater spatial scope of the maritime areas to be delimited, therefore, these developments have served to enhance the complexity of maritime boundary delimitation negotiations whilst simultaneously significantly raising the stakes. A key factor driving competing maritime claims and boundary disputes is therefore the desire on the part of coastal states to gain access to marine resources, whether living or non-living.

Additionally, as alluded to above, competing interpretations of the relevant law of the sea provisions on maritime boundary delimitation may lead to overlapping claims. Political, strategic and long-standing historical claims may also make reaching agreement with neighbouring states, or even entering into negotiations with them problematic. For example, the United Kingdom remains keen to preserve its claims to the Chagos Archipelago (contested by Mauritius) primarily because of the strategically advantageous position of the islands in the Indian Ocean and presence of a major UK/US base on Diego Garcia. Regarding historical claims, the Philippines' claim to territorial sea jurisdiction from its baselines to its so-called

'Treaty Limits' established in accordance with treaties between the United States and Spain in 1898 and 1900 and between the United States and Great Britain in 1930 have greatly complicated potential maritime boundary negotiations between the Philippines and its neighbours, not least because the maritime claims of these neighbouring states extend into the 'box' defined by the Philippines Treaty Limits.

Where sovereignty over territory that includes a coast is under dispute, it necessarily follows that a maritime dispute also exists in relation to the maritime claims associated with the disputed coastline. A number of sovereignty disputes over islands have led to broad areas of overlapping maritime claims. Additionally, the role of islands in maritime boundary delimitation can be a key factor (see below). A further notable and enduring cause of maritime boundary disputes is excessive baseline claims. These issues are considered below.

Dividing the Land from the Sea

Baselines and basepoints

The interface between the land and sea for maritime jurisdictional purposes is termed a coastal state's baselines. Baselines are of fundamental importance to a coastal state's claims to maritime jurisdiction as they provide the starting point for measuring its claimed maritime zones. The establishment of the location of baselines is therefore a necessary precursor to defining maritime jurisdiction limits. Additionally, baselines also represent the outer limit of a state's internal waters. Furthermore, baselines are often crucial to the delimitation of maritime boundaries. This is the case because baselines have a direct bearing on the construction of an accurate equidistance or median line and such lines, as noted above, are often highly relevant to the delimitation of maritime boundaries.

An important consideration here is to distinguish between a coastal state's baselines and controlling, or critical, basepoints along that baseline. By no means all of a coastal state's baseline necessarily contributes either to the envelope of arcs making up the outer limit of a claimed maritime zone or in the construction of a strict equidistance line. This dependence on a limited number of critical basepoints may influence coastal state policy and actions in terms of the maintenance of baselines and preservation of key basepoints. From a technical perspective it is therefore vital to acquire a sound understanding of the baselines and basepoints. Once baselines and basepoints have been properly defined it is relatively straightforward to generate the various maritime zone limits and boundaries required in a geodetically robust and technically sound manner using modern computer software.

Determining the location of baselines and basepoints is not, however, necessarily a straightforward task, not least because there exist multiple different types of baseline that may be claimed for different types of coastal circumstances (Carleton and Schofield 2001, 26-47). Under usual circumstances, in accordance with Article 5 of LOSC, the coastal state will possess 'normal' baselines, which coincide with 'the low-water line along the coast as marked on large-scale charts officially recognized by the coastal state'. Normal baselines represent the predominant type of baseline worldwide and, in effect, represent a state's 'default' baselines. It is worth noting in this context that as coastlines are themselves dynamic, so normal baselines can change significantly over time or 'ambulates' '(Reed 2000, 185) and this necessarily has an impact on the generation of the outer limits of claims to maritime jurisdiction (Prescott and Schofield 2005, 100-1). This is not a new issue by any means but is an especially problematic issue in an era of significant predicted global sea level rise. The linkage between ambulatory normal low-water baselines and the limits of maritime zones of jurisdiction necessarily dictates that as normal baselines recede as a consequence of sea level rise, so too the maritime zones measured from such baselines will also retreat leading to erosion in the scope of the coastal state's maritime claims. In this context it is important to acknowledge that even relatively slight changes in sea level vertically can result in significant shifts in the location of the low water line horizontally, notably where the coastline in question is gently shelving. Sea level rise also has the potential to threaten insular status and this, in turn, may have a knock-on impact in respect of potential maritime jurisdictional claims that can be made from the insular feature concerned. Indeed, it has been suggested that a number of low-lying island states ultimately face the dire prospect of total inundation of their territory (Patel 2006, 734). The potential for the loss of the entirety of the territory constituting an island state raises further complex and serious legal questions marks over the preservation of national maritime claims (Schofield 2009).

While, as noted above, a broad consensus exists concerning the breadth of maritime zones, where such zones are claimed from can be problematic as LOSC also provides for a variety of baselines other than normal baselines to be constructed along the coast, namely straight baselines (LOSC, Article 7), river closing lines (Article 9), bay closing lines (Article 10), lines related to ports and roadsteads (Articles 11 and 12) and in respect of archipelagic states (Article 47). A number of these provisions, especially regarding straight baselines, have been liberally or flexibly interpreted and applied giving rise to allegations that states have made excessive baseline claims (see Prescott and Schofield 2005, 139-66; Roach and Smith 1996, 57-161). Such arguably excessive baselines claims have the potential to impact on the construction of, particularly, theoretical equidistance lines between opposing coastlines and thus give rise to maritime boundary disputes.

Issues Involving Islands

The importance of islands

Islands are the focus of numerous maritime boundary disputes. Such disputes tend to fall into two broad categories: those relating to sovereignty over islands themselves, their land territories and their related maritime space; and those concerned with the role of particular insular features in the delimitation of maritime boundaries.

As illustrated in Figure 32.2, sovereignty disputes over islands occur globally (Prescott and Schofield 2005, 265-84). Many such sovereignty disputes over islands appear to be over the possession of a handful of remote, barren, small and often uninhabited islands, rocks, low-tide elevations and reefs. Nonetheless, such features have the capacity to prompt fierce diplomatic exchanges between states, sour bilateral relations and even act as the trigger for military confrontation. The question of the treatment of islands in maritime boundary delimitation is similarly vital to coastal states around the world and examples of this type of dispute are numerous.

These factors are clearly closely interrelated, and the potential role of islands in delimitation and the generation of claims to maritime jurisdiction can itself be a key factor influencing any dispute over sovereignty. The geopolitical dimensions of disputes over islands also cannot be ignored in this context. States are inextricably linked to their territory and any potential loss of claimed territory, however slight, can be construed as a threat to a state's sovereignty, security and integrity. In consequence, such disputes frequently provide fertile ground for nationalistic rhetoric and flag-waving. Furthermore, disputes should be seen in their overall context, including the history of relations between the parties. The territory at stake may well be insignificant, but the dispute may often represent a useful pressure point and, in reality, merely represents a symptom of an already strained or traditionally antagonistic relationship. The disputes between Greece and Turkey over Aegean and island sovereignty disputes between Japan and her neighbours where there is a long history of mutual animosity and unresolved grievances provide good examples of this type of issue (Prescott and Schofield 2005, 249-50).

Crucially, Paragraph 2 of Article 121 of LOSC provides that islands, in an identical fashion to mainland coasts, are capable of generating a full suite of maritime zones:

> ... the territorial sea, the contiguous zone, the exclusive economic zone and the continental shelf of an island are determined in accordance with the provisions of this convention applicable to other land territory.

In the context of extended claims to maritime jurisdiction, therefore, even small islands potentially have huge maritime zone generative capacity with significant resource/security implications. Critically, if an island had no maritime neighbours within 400nm, it could generate 125,664 square nautical miles (431,014 square kilometres) of territorial sea, EEZ and continental shelf rights. In contrast, if deemed a mere 'rock' incapable of generating EEZ and continental shelf rights (see below), a territorial sea of 452 square nautical miles (1,550 square kilometres) could be claimed. This goes a long way to explaining both the significance attached to islands in the recent past and the allied rise in the number of international disputes involving islands.

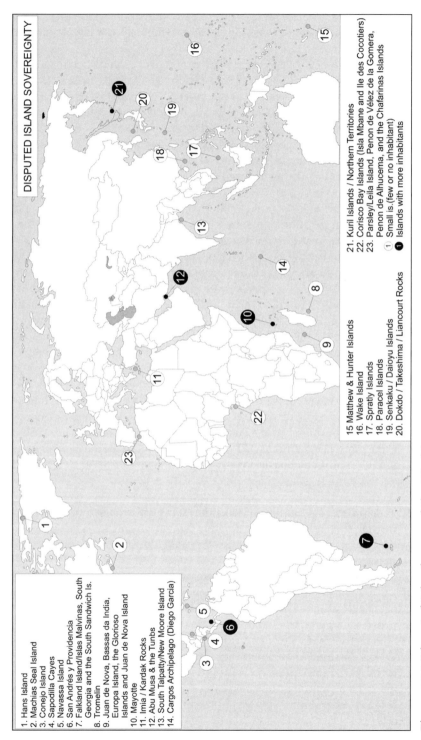

Figure 32.2 Disputed Islands around the World

Source: adapted from Pratt 2006.

DISPUTED ISLAND SOVEREIGNTY

1. Hans Island
2. Machias Seal Island
3. Conejo Island
4. Sapodilla Cayes
5. Navassa Island
6. San Andrés y Providencia
7. Falkland Island/Islas Malvinas, South Georgia and the South Sandwich Is.
8. Tromelin
9. Juan de Nova, Bassas da India, Europa Island, the Glorioso Islands and Juan de Nova Island
10. Mayotte
11. Imia / Kardak Rocks
12. Abu Musa & the Tunbs
13. South Talpatty/New Moore Island
14. Cargos Archipelago (Diego Garcia)

15. Matthew & Hunter Islands
16. Wake Island
17. Spratly Islands
18. Paracel Islands
19. Senkaku / Daioyu Islands
20. Dokdo / Takeshima / Liancourt Rocks

21. Kuril Islands / Northern Territories
22. Corisco Bay Islands (Isla Mbane and Ile des Cocotiers)
23. Parsley/Leila Island, Penon de Vélez de la Gomera, Penon de Alhucema, and the Chafarinas Islands

① Small is. (few or no inhabitant)
● Islands with more inhabitants

Quite apart from the maritime zones, and thus marine resources, associated with the possession of islands, control over certain islands can be considered especially attractive to states as a consequence of their strategic location. The proximity of the contested Spratly Islands in the South China Sea to a strategic waterway of global significance, providing the key maritime link between the Indian Ocean and East Asia carrying, for instance, the vast majority of China, Korea and Japan's imported energy supplies, is an oft-cited example of this factor.

An allied consideration is that sovereignty disputes over islands and the waters associated with them, as well as disputes over the role certain islands should have in maritime boundary delimitation often give rise to overlapping maritime claims. This leads to considerable uncertainties over the extent of coastal state jurisdiction, which in turn has implications for maritime security. Disputes over islands and a lack of agreed maritime boundaries result in a complex mosaic of overlapping jurisdictional and sovereignty claims, undermining maritime security enforcement efforts. This can be viewed as an urgent concern in a post-9/11 world that has elevated maritime security to an issue of leading importance, especially in light of the global economy's dependence on sea borne trade.

Islands and rocks

The question of the definition of islands and their treatment in the context of the delimitation of maritime boundaries is a complex and crucially important one to coastal states. Although the question of the definition of islands has provoked fierce debate over the years, particularly during the drafting of LOSC, the four requirements for a feature to legally qualify as an island under LOSC Article 121(1) are relatively uncontroversial (Prescott and Schofield 2005, 58-61). These insular criteria are that an island must be 'naturally formed', be an 'area of land', be 'surrounded by water' and, critically, must be 'above water at high tide'.

However, one of the key issues under debate prior to and during the drafting of LOSC related to island size and habitability. Several proposals were made, including Hodgson's notable one based on island size, which were designed to restrain the capacity of small, isolated features, even if permanently above water at high tide, from generating expansive maritime claims (Hodgson 1973). Ultimately, no size criteria for defining islands were included in LOSC. However, concerns over size and habitability were included in the form of Article 121(3) of LOSC states that 'Rocks which cannot sustain human habitation or economic life of their own shall have no exclusive economic zone or continental shelf'.

Rocks therefore represent a disadvantaged sub-category of island whose zone-generative capacity, and thus value to a potential claimant, is significantly reduced. This provision provokes questions not only as to what constitutes a 'rock' but also presents a twofold interpretational problem, as LOSC provides no definition as when a feature 'cannot sustain human habitation' or what constitutes the 'economic life' of a particular feature. While considerable academic ink has been spilt on these issues (for example, Charney 1999; Elferink 1998; Kwaitkowska

677

and Soons 1990; Prescott and Schofield 2005, 61-75; van Dyke et al. 1988; van Dyke and Brooks 1983), it is abundantly clear that no consensus has been reached on this issue. Indeed, it seems clear that Article 121(3) was drafted in a deliberately ambiguous manner in order to appease opposing positions in the drafting of LOSC (Prescott and Schofield 2005, 58).

What is clear, however, is that the problem of dealing with islands in the delimitation of maritime boundaries remains. This represents a developing area in terms of the practice of states and thus in research terms. In particular, considerable advances have been made in terms of innovative approaches to addressing island problems in delimitation, for example by affording islands reduced weight in the construction of equidistance lines or partially or wholly enclaving them (Carleton and Schofield 2002, 13-20).

Conclusions

The maritime political map (or mosaic) of the world remains profoundly incomplete with many maritime boundaries yet to be delimited. Large areas of overlapping maritime claims exist, as do serious bi- and multilateral maritime boundary disputes, which continue to generate considerable contemporary research. Issues associated with baselines, especially normal baselines in the context of sea level rise, as well as excessive claims to straight baselines remain problematic. A key cause of overlapping maritime claims and maritime boundary disputes between states are disputes over or related to islands, as exemplified by the enduring dispute over the Spratly Islands (see for example, Emmers 2005; Schofield and Storey 2009; Valencia et al. 1997).

In the face of enduring disputes over maritime space, alternatives to maritime delimitation are increasingly being explored, both by states, and in contemporary research on maritime boundaries. Such cooperative mechanisms providing for shared rather than unilateral management of maritime space, notably through maritime joint development zones, are in keeping with LOSC, which provides at Articles 74(3) and 83(3) (dealing with the delimitation of the continental shelf and EEZ) that: 'provisional arrangements of a practical nature' are encouraged pending agreement on the delimitation of the EEZ or continental shelf. The fundamental advantage of such approaches is that, when negotiations reach deadlock, joint development provides an alternative option, enabling the parties to sidestep a seemingly intractable maritime dispute and proceed with functional cooperation aimed at the development or management of the resources or environment in the disputed area. In light of its potential benefits, maritime joint development has been backed by enthusiastic advocates in the academic literature (see for example, Jagota 1993; Lagoni, 1984; Miyoshi, 1999; Ong 1995; Richardson 1988).

The alternate view is that it seems inappropriate to promote joint development simply on the basis that the parties to a dispute over overlapping maritime claims have proved unable to resolve their differences. It can also be argued that if joint zones are based on the limits of such overlapping claims areas, as tends to be the case, then this serves to encourage and reward extreme unilateral maritime claims. Furthermore, the practical task of establishing and maintaining such potentially dauntingly complex arrangements should not be underestimated as this requires considerable political commitment from all parties as they do represent a significant challenge to state sovereignty (Stormont and Townsend-Gault 1995). Nevertheless, it is clear that emerging state practice provides support for joint development arrangements, especially where negotiations have reached deadlock, and that such arrangements are consistent with international law, including the LOSC.

Acknowledgements

Dr Schofield is the recipient of an Australian Research Council QEII Fellowship (DP0666273) and Future Fellowship (FT100100990). The author is indebted to I Made Andi Arsana of ANCORS and the Department of Geodesy and Geomatics, Gadjah Mada University, Indonesia, for preparing the figures accompanying this chapter.

References

Carleton, C.M. and Schofield, C.H. (2002), 'Developments in the Technical Determination of Maritime Space: Delimitation, Dispute Resolution, Geographical Information Systems and the Role of the Technical Expert', *Maritime Briefing* 3:4 (Durham: International Boundaries Research Unit).

Carleton, C.M. and Schofield, C.H. (2001), 'Developments in the Technical Determination of Maritime Space: Charts, Datums, Baselines, Maritime Zones and Limits', *Maritime Briefing* 3:3 (Durham: International Boundaries Research Unit).

Charney, J.I. (1999), 'Rocks that Cannot Sustain Human Habitation', *American Journal of International Law* 93:4, 863-78.

Charney, J.I. and Alexander, L.M. (eds.)(1998), *International Maritime Boundaries*, Vol. III (Dordrecht: Martinus Nijhoff).

Charney, J.I. and Alexander, L.M. (eds.)(1993), *International Maritime Boundaries*, Vols. I and II (Dordrecht: Martinus Nijhoff).

Charney, J.I. and Smith, R.W. (eds.)(2002), *International Maritime Boundaries*, Vol. IV (Dordrecht: Martinus Nijhoff).

Colson, D.A. and Smith, R.W. (eds.)(2005), *International Maritime Boundaries*, Vol. V (Leiden: Martinus Nijhoff).

Colson, D.A. and Smith, R.W. (eds.)(2011), *International Maritime Boundaries*, Vol. VI (Leiden: Martinus Nijhoff).

Elferink, A.O. (1998), 'Clarifying Article 121 (3) of the Law of the Sea Convention: The Limits Set by the Nature of International Legal Processes', *Boundary and Security Bulletin* 6:2, 58-68.

Emmers, R. (2005), 'Maritime Disputes in the South China Sea: Strategic and Diplomatic Status Quo', *Institute for Defense and Strategic Studies Working Paper* 87 (Singapore: Institute for Defense and Strategic Studies).

Eritrea-Yemen (1999), *Arbitration between Eritrea and Yemen, Award of the Arbitral Tribunal in the Second Stage of the Proceedings (Maritime Delimitation)*, Award of 17 December 1999, available at <http://www.pca-cpa.org/showpage.asp?pag_id=1160>.

Grundy-Warr, C.E.R. and Schofield, C.H. (2005), 'Reflections on the Relevance of Classic Approaches and Contemporary Priorities in Boundary Studies', *Geopolitics* 10:4, 650-62.

Hodgson, R.D. (1973), *Islands: Normal and Special Circumstances* (Washington D.C.: US Department of State: Bureau of Intelligence and Research, Research Study).

International Court of Justice (ICJ) (2009), *Case Concerning Maritime Delimitation in the Black Sea* (Romania v. Ukraine), Judgment of 3 February 2009, available at <http://www.icj-cij.org/docket/files/132/14987.pdf>, accessed 10 December 2009.

Jagota, S.P. (1993), 'Maritime Boundary and Joint Development Zones: Emerging Trends', *Ocean Yearbook* 10, 110-31.

Kwaitkowska, B. and Soons, A.H.A. (1990), 'Entitlement to Maritime Areas of Rocks Which Cannot Sustain Human Habitation or Economic Life of their Own', *Netherlands Yearbook of International Law* XXI (1990), 139-81.

Lagoni, K. (1984), 'Interim Measures Pending Maritime Delimitation Agreements', *American Journal of International Law* 78, 345-68.

Legault, L. and Hankey, B. (1993), 'Method, Oppositeness and Adjacency, and Proportionality in Maritime Boundary Delimitation', in Charney, J.I. and Alexander, L.M. (eds.), *International Maritime Boundaries*, Vols. I and II (Dordrecht: Martinus Nijhoff), 203-42.

Miyoshi, M. (1999), 'The Joint Development of Offshore Oil and Gas in Relation to Maritime Boundary Delimitation', *Maritime Briefing* 2:5 (Durham: International Boundaries Research Unit).

Ong, D. (1995), 'Southeast Asian State Practice on the Joint Development of Offshore Oil and Gas Deposits', in Blake et al. (eds.), *The Peaceful Management of Transboundary Resources* (London: Graham and Trotman), 77-96.

Patel, S.S. (2006), 'A Sinking Feeling', *Nature* 44, 6 April 2006, 734.

Pratt, M.A. (2008), *International Boundaries Research Unit, University of Durham* (Personal communication).

Prescott, J.R.V. and Schofield, C.H. (2005), *The Maritime Political Boundaries of the World* (Leiden and Boston: Martinus Nijhoff Publishers).

Reed, M.W. (2000), *Shore and Sea boundaries: the development of international maritime boundary principles through United States practice* (Washington DC: US Department of Commerce).

Richardson, E.L. (1988), 'Jan Mayen in Perspective', *American Journal of International Law* 82, 443-58.

Roach, J.A. and Smith, R.W. (1996), *United States Responses to Excessive Maritime Claims* (The Hague: Martinus Nijhoff Publishers).

Schofield, C.H. (2009) 'Shifting Limits?: Sea Level Rise and Options to Secure Maritime Jurisdictional Claims', *Carbon and Climate Law Review* 4, 405-16.

Schofield, C.H. (2005), 'Cooperative Mechanisms and Maritime Security in Areas of Overlapping Claims to Maritime Jurisdiction', in Cozens, P. and Mossop, J. (eds.), *Capacity Building for Maritime Security Cooperation in the Asia-Pacific* (Wellington: Centre for Strategic Studies, New Zealand), 99-115.

Schofield, C.H. and Arsana, A. (2009), 'Beyond the Limits?: Outer Continental Shelf Opportunities and Obligations in East and Southeast Asia', *Contemporary Southeast Asia* 31:1: 28-63.

Schofield, C.H. and Storey, I. (2009), *The South China Sea Dispute: Increasing Stakes, Rising Tensions*, Occasional Paper (Washington D.C.: The Jamestown Foundation, October).

Stormont, W.G. and Townsend-Gault, I. (1995), 'Offshore Petroleum Joint Development Arrangements: Functional Instrument? Compromise? Obligation?', in Blake, G.H., Sien, C.L., Grundy-Warr, C.E.R., Pratt, M.A. and Schofield, C.H. (eds.), *The Peaceful Management of Transboundary Resources* (London: Graham and Trotman).

United Nations (1983), 'The Law of the Sea', *UN Document* UN/Doc.A/CONF.62/122 (New York: United Nations).

United Nations Conference on Trade and Development (UNCTAD) (2008), *Review of Maritime Transport 2008* (Geneva: UNCTAD).

United Nations, Division for Ocean Affairs and the Law of the Sea, Office of Legal Affairs (2010) 'Status of the United Nations Convention on the Law of the Sea, of the Agreement Relating to the Implementation of Part XI of the Convention and of the Agreement for the Implementation of the Convention Relating to the Conservation and Management of Straddling Fish Stocks and Highly Migratory Fish Stocks', (United Nations, Division for Ocean Affairs and the Law of the Sea, Office of Legal Affairs, New York, updated to 30 November 2010), available at <http://www.un.org/Depts/los/convention_agreements/convention_overview_convention.htm>.

Valencia, M.J., van Dyke, J.M. and Ludwig, N.A. (1997), *Sharing the Resources of the South China Sea* (The Hague: Martinus Nijhoff).

Van Dyke, J.M. and Brooks, R.A. (1983), 'Uninhabited Islands: Their Impact on the Ownership of the Oceans' Resources', *Ocean Development International Law Journal* 12, 265-84.

van Dyke, J.M., Morgan, J. and Gurish, J. (1988), 'The Exclusive Economic Zone of the Northwestern Hawaiian Islands: When do Uninhabited Islands Generate an EEZ?', *San Diego Law Review* 25:3, 425-94.

Names Index

Places Index